THE CANADIAN NORTHERN RAILWAY

Canadian Northern Railway train at Dauphin, Manitoba. (PAC)

THE CANADIAN NORTHERN RAILWAY

Pioneer Road of the Northern Prairies
1895-1918

T. D. REGEHR

MACMILLAN OF CANADA
MACLEAN-HUNTER PRESS

Canadian Cataloguing in Publication Data

Regehr, T. D., 1937–
The Canadian Northern Railway

Bibliography: p.
Includes index.

ISBN 0-7705-1285-2

1. Canadian Northern Railway Company — History.
I. Title.

HE2810.C18R43   385'.065'71   C76-017052-5

*This book has been published
with the help of a grant from the
Social Science Research Council of Canada,
using funds provided by the Canada Council.*

Printed in Canada for
The Macmillan Company of Canada Limited
70 Bond Street, Toronto
M5B 1X3

CONTENTS

ABBREVIATIONS

APL	Provincial Library of Alberta, Edmonton
CAR	*Canadian Annual Review*
CNR	Canadian National Railways
CNRHQ	Canadian National Railways, Headquarters Library, Montreal
CR & MW	*Canadian Railway and Marine World*
CRC	*Canadian Railway Cases*, published by the *Canadian Law Book*
DOT	Department of Transport, Canada
MG	Public Archives of Canada designation of "Manuscript Group"
MHS	Minnesota Historical Society, St. Paul, Minnesota
PABC	Provincial Archives of British Columbia, Victoria
PAC	Public Archives of Canada, Ottawa
PAM	Public Archives of Manitoba, Winnipeg
PANS	Public Archives of Nova Scotia, Halifax
PAO	Ontario Department of Public Records and Archives, Toronto
PAQ	Archives du Québec, Quebec City
PAS	Saskatchewan Archives Board, Regina and Saskatoon
QUA	Queen's University Archives, Kingston, Ontario
RG	Public Archives of Canada designation of "Record Group"
UAA	University of Alberta Archives, Edmonton
UTA	University of Toronto Archives, Toronto
VanA.	Vancouver Archives

Arbitration   Proceedings, Board of Arbitration, Canadian Northern Railway, *Transcript of Hearings*

Statutory History   *A Statutory History of the Steam and Electric Railways of Canada 1836–1937*, compiled by Robert Dorman, Department of Transport, Canada

Synoptical Histories   *Tabulated and Synoptical Histories of Canadian National Railways* prepared by the Bureau of Economics, Canadian National Railways

MAPS

TABLES

Appendixes

INTRODUCTION

SOME OF THE HAPPIEST PEOPLE in Canada on Christmas Day in 1896 lived in Dauphin, Manitoba. After years of petitions, demands, and even threats, they had finally got what they wanted most —a railway track and a train. In comparison with many other railways Dauphin's seemed very small; little more than a plaything. The track was only 101 miles long; there were only three locomotives, two first-class coaches, one baggage car, fifty boxcars, two conductor's cabooses, and a crew of fourteen.[1] For the people of Dauphin, however, the railway was a dream come true. They gathered in large numbers at 12:30 p.m. on 26 December to see conductor "Dad" Risteen and engineer Walker stoke up a shiny Engine No. 3 to take the first twenty-seven passengers from Dauphin to Portage la Prairie. The sweetest music in northwestern Manitoba that Christmas was said to be wheel music interspersed with the staccato of the train whistle on the lonely prairie and bush land. It was an invitation to all to come to "the region destined to be one of the most desirable in Manitoba".[2] In the ensuing months and years the settlers and immigrants came, in unprecedented numbers and from many lands, to enjoy the bounties of the northern plains and the services of the new railway.

The first permanent residents had only arrived in Dauphin on 7 October 1896. The railway company had chosen a vacant site on the bank of the Vermilion River as its townsite. Once this choice was known and the necessary surveys had been completed, the older towns of Lake Dauphin and Garthmore near by lost not only their citizens, but most of their buildings as well. Stores, hotels, banks, churches, and other buildings in the vicinity were put on wheels, never ceasing to do

1 *Canadian Northern Railway Arbitration, 1918*, mimeographed, 392–407, hereafter cited as *Arbitration*.

2 *Manitoba Free Press*, 17 and 28 Dec. 1896.

business while on the move to the stubble field which became a settlement of 400 inhabitants within two months. New buildings and new
businesses grew like mushrooms in apparent determination to make up
for time lost since 1889 when new wagon roads and promises of a railway had brought in the first settlers.

The people of Dauphin welcomed their new railway, the Lake
Manitoba Railway and Canal Company, as their salvation. Many of
the new line's early inadequacies were accepted with good-natured
humour. It was widely known, for example, that two of the railway's
three locomotives were retired American steamers that required constant tinkering and caulking. One locomotive was needed on the construction train, thus often leaving a single locomotive and crew to
handle a twice-weekly passenger train and a rather irregular freight
service. No one therefore doubted the statement on the company's
first time-table that "Train No. 4 will not leave until No. 3 has arrived."[3] Even this kind of service, however, was a great improvement
on what had been available before.

What the railway lacked in initial capital and facilities it made up
for in enthusiasm, optimism, and resourcefulness. Within two years
these characteristics enabled it to become the more pretentious Canadian Northern Railway. What it had done for Dauphin in 1896 it did
in the ensuing twenty-one years for 550 other towns and villages that
before were nothing but prairie. Its trackage grew from the original
101 miles to 9,433.4 miles, on which 735 locomotives and 32,401 railway cars of various descriptions were operated by a staff of 23,500.[4]
This is the story of that railway, and of its place in the economic
development of Canada.

No comprehensive history of the Canadian Northern Railway is
available at present. When it is mentioned in other railway and transportation studies the references are almost invariably critical and
hostile.[5] One of Canada's earliest and most influential railway his-

3 *Arbitration*, 401–2.
4 *Ibid.*, 392–3.
5 O. D. Skelton, *The Railway Builders*, Chronicles of Canada Series, vol. 32 (Toronto and Glasgow: Brook and Co., 1916); O. D. Skelton, *The Life and Letters of Sir Wilfrid Laurier* (New York: Century, 1922);

G. P. de T. Glazebrook, *A History of Transportation in Canada* (Toronto: Ryerson, 1938); G. R. Stevens, *Canadian National Railways*, II, *Towards the Inevitable, 1896–1922* (Toronto: Clarke, Irwin, 1962), here-after referred to as Stevens.

torians has referred to railway financing as "the most corrupting single factor in Canadian politics since Confederation times".[6] Popularly, the railway is known only as the project of two rather unsavoury promoters. When they got into trouble the Canadian government had to nationalize their railway and make it a part of the Canadian National Railways.

The Canadian Northern was not always regarded thus. In 1896 one reporter found the track "a marvel of what first class contractors can accomplish in a short time". Others praised the smoothness of the roadbed, the stability and beauty of its buildings, and the integrity of the contractor-promoters "who gave better value than they were called upon to do". Residents of the Dauphin area referred to it as "the Farmers' Friend". Bankers said they had never had better customers than promoters William Mackenzie and Donald Mann of the Canadian Northern, and politicians were "very much delighted when they found what had happened". Those who knew the railway, or were associated with it in its early years, expected historians to deal favourably with it. "If the story of the rise and fall of the Canadian Northern is ever written by some man who can by no possibility be called an interested partisan, his findings, on the unquestionable facts, can only be that the creators of the enterprise deserve more of their country than it is now possible for both of them to receive."[7]

This great divergence of opinion between some contemporary views of the railway and its image in our railway histories indicates the need for a new study. The necessary source materials to support such a study became available when the Canadian National Railways transferred the records of its predecessor companies to the Public Archives of Canada. This is the first attempt at a major study of the Canadian Northern Railway based on the company's own records, supplemented and modified by various relevant political papers, government publications, and newspaper references. The story is told within the context of Canada's rapid economic development and expansion during the Laurier era, with particular reference to the needs and demands of Canadians who used the railways.

Canadians at the turn of the century were very optimistic about the

6 Skelton, *Laurier*, 419.
7 D. B. Hanna, *Trains of Recollections* (Toronto: Macmillan, 1924), hereafter referred to as Hanna.

future of their country. They demanded three basic services from their railways. The main or trunk lines were to be laid out in a way which would facilitate interprovincial trade and provide export traffic for Canadian maritime ports. Branch and colonization lines were expected to bring rail services to within ten miles of every accessible community in Canada. At the same time Canadians insisted that freight rates must be sufficiently low to leave the farmers and other shippers a profit from their operations after they had paid transportation costs. Any railway that could provide these basic services and still earn a profit was assured of success; failure to provide such services invariably left railways in trouble. Various expedients were used, particularly by the Canadian Northern Railway, to meet public demands and ensure the railway's early success. Later serious problems, many well beyond the control of the promoters, made it impossible to meet the requirements of the country. The primary emphasis in this study will be on the needs and demands of the country and the manner in which the Canadian Northern Railway succeeded or failed in meeting these needs and demands.

In the writing of this study I have benefited greatly from the comments, suggestions, and criticisms of many friends and colleagues. Foremost among these is Dr. Lewis G. Thomas of the University of Alberta, under whose supervision I began my study of the Canadian Northern Railway in a doctoral thesis. His encouragement, interest, and comments were invaluable.

Archivists from coast to coast have responded willingly to my many requests for materials and information. The courteous and intelligent service which has long characterized Canadian archival institutions is invaluable to historical scholarship. The staff at the Baker Library, Harvard University, allowed me to read relevant portions of the Henry Villard Papers, while the extensive records of the Northern Pacific Railroad were made available to me at the Minnesota Historical Society.

Dr. Ivo Lambi of the University of Saskatchewan and Dr. Lewis G. Thomas of the University of Alberta have read all or portions of the final manuscript and have made many helpful suggestions. Errors of fact or interpretation that remain are, of course, the sole responsibility of the author.

The final manuscript has been typed by or under the supervision of our very capable departmental assistant, Mrs. Margaret MacVean. Her excellent work is very much appreciated.

My wife Sylvia deserves a particular word of thanks. There were times when she must have wondered whether she had married me or the railway. With gratitude and appreciation I dedicate this book to her.

CHAPTER ONE

IN THE LAND OF THE CPR 1881-1888

THE CANADIAN PRAIRIES have peculiar problems resulting from the geographic isolation of the region. The Canadian Shield, a 1,000-mile barrier of rock and bush, separates the prairies from the Canadian industrial and financial heartland of the St. Lawrence lowlands. In addition, the Rocky Mountains to the west, an inhospitable climate and landscape to the north, and an equally effective political barrier to the south, all combine to make isolation the outstanding geographic feature of the prairie region.

This isolation has made transportation a matter of utmost importance in the history of the Canadian North-West. Transportation facilities and costs largely determined the outcome of the struggle between rival fur-trading interests in the eighteenth and early nineteenth centuries. After 1870 the availability or lack of transportation facilities largely determined the pace and location of prairie settlement and the economic activities which the settlers could profitably undertake. The railway and the steam-engine were as important to prairie settlers as the rivers and lakes and the canoe or the York boat had been to the fur traders. Unless the settler had access to nearby rail facilities at a reasonable cost he simply could not continue successful farming operations. Railways, according to one eminent historian, "were the key to full membership in the society of the economically privileged".[1] Canadian prairie settlement followed the railways and for many years remained dependent on them.

The first railway built in western Canada was the Pembina line, which ran from Winnipeg south to the Minnesota border. It was part of the larger Canadian Pacific Railway which was being constructed

[1] J. Lorne McDougall, *Canadian Pacific* (Montreal: McGill University Press, 1968), 11.

in a piecemeal fashion by the federal government in the 1870s. The Pembina line was built to meet the requirements of a national policy which called for the development and settlement of the prairies and the tying together of the widely separated regions of the nation into a new political and economic entity.

When the Macdonald government signed its contract with the second CPR syndicate in 1880, the Pembina branch was turned over to the new company; but the objectives of Canadian railway policy remained unchanged. It was the railway that determined the nature of economic development on the Canadian prairies, and in the 1880s and 1890s the Canadian Pacific Railway was western Canada's only rail contact with the outside world. It was the most important and powerful influence in western Canada during the decades of its monopoly.

This importance and power was recognized by both the railway's officials and its users. George Stephen, the CPR's first president, believed that what was good for his company must also be good for the area it served. "A fair and unbiased consideration," he informed Prime Minister Macdonald, "must result in the conviction that the interests of the country and the company are identical, and every advantage or privilege granted to the latter are necessary for the due protection of the joint interests."[2]

Farmers and shippers in the West, however, believed that the company's advantages and privileges were ruinous. They were inclined to blame the company for their many problems and difficulties. In a fit of desperation in 1883 the influential Manitoba and North West Farmers' Protective Union denounced the railway, its monopoly and its high freight rates, in the most scathing terms. "The burdens laid on the people of Manitoba," the farmers alleged, "are so great that agricultural operations cannot be made to yield a fair profit; that immigration before the removal of these burdens will benefit neither the province nor the immigrants to settle in the province till full redress of the grievances complained of by this convention shall have been attained."[3]

2 PAC, Macdonald Papers, CCLXVIII, 121862, George Stephen to John A. Macdonald, 23 Jan. 1881.
3 Resolution of the Manitoba and North West Farmers' Protective Union, 1883, as quoted in Alexander Begg, *A History of the North West*, III (Toronto: Hunter Rose and Co., 1895), 89.

The desperation of the farmers and the arrogance of the railway president are both evidence of the great power and influence of the CPR in western Canada in the 1880s. They are also an indication of the need for changes—changes which came in the late 1890s when a western provincial government sponsored construction of a new railway in accordance with its own economic and political predilections. Many years later the superintendent of this provincially supported railway referred to his company as "the West's own product, designed to meet the West's own needs".[4] The needs and problems of the West during the time the CPR controlled all Canadian transcontinental freight traffic form the historical background of the Lake Manitoba Railway and Canal Company, which built its first line to Dauphin in 1896, and of its successor company, the Canadian Northern Railway.

The Canadian Pacific Railway, considered from a simple business point of view, was built in advance of immediate operational requirements and along an unnatural route. When it was incorporated in 1881 there was simply not enough traffic available on the prairies to justify the project in conventional business terms. It was the government of Canada which was most eager to have the railway built, and was willing to offer very substantial assistance to any financial syndicate willing to undertake the project. Settlement was expected to follow the railway and eventually to provide the traffic needed for profitable operations. Until then the railway had to be built and operated on faith and government assistance. It was built, moreover, along a route which no sane businessman would have selected under normal circumstances. The natural route from the St. Lawrence lowlands to the Canadian prairies lay to the south of the Great Lakes. The Canadian Pacific Railway, however, was built along the north shore of Lake Superior through a thousand miles of all-Canadian wilderness that was not expected to contribute much traffic to the railway. Political considerations prompted Macdonald to insist on the northern route, which CPR president George Stephen referred to as "great folly".[5] Only very sub-

---

4 Hanna, 237.
5 PAC, Macdonald Papers, CCLXVIII, 121954, Stephen to Macdonald, 12 Sept. 1882. The opposition to the all-Canadian route by syndicate member J. J. Hill and the circum-

stances of his resignation strongly suggest that the syndicate had very grave doubts about the route, even after the contract was signed. UAA, William Pearce, *Memoirs*, 14–19; PAC, Macdonald Papers, CCLXVIII, 121837,

stantial government incentives eventually persuaded Stephen and his associates to build, well in advance of immediate economic requirements, along an extraordinarily expensive and unnatural route.

Construction, however, marked only the first phase of the CPR's struggle. The syndicate also had to find ways and means of operating the expensive new line without incurring ruinous deficits. When the CPR project was discussed in Parliament in 1881, Opposition members had argued that if the line were built, it would never carry enough traffic to pay for even its axle grease.[6] The government, however, was under no obligation to provide further assistance to meet early operational deficits, although the very nature and location of the national road increased operational costs even more sharply than they had increased construction costs.

The only way the CPR could possibly meet its operational costs was if all the traffic originating on or going to the prairies was assigned to it at fairly high rates. The CPR could not afford to see any western Canadian traffic go to American rivals, particularly since these rivals did not have the operational disadvantages of a long, unproductive section of line.[7]

The syndicate insisted, and Macdonald agreed, that the Canadian railway must secure all the western-Canadian traffic and be protected from American competition. The charter provided such protection: it gave to the CPR all the government-built railway mileage on the prairies, including western Canada's only connection with any American railroads. In addition, a clause was inserted in the contract which forbade the construction, for twenty years, of any railway lines within fifteen miles of Latitude 49. Thus the CPR had a complete monopoly on all western traffic and could charge whatever it thought necessary to meet its operational costs. The only limitation was that the government could interfere if company profits on investment exceeded 10 per

---

Stephen to Macdonald, 18 Oct. 1880; Hill to Angus, July 1880, as quoted in J. G. Pyle, *The Life of James J. Hill*, I (New York: Century, 1920), 314–15; G. P. de T. Glazebrook, *Transportation in Canada* (Toronto: Ryerson, 1938).

6 Arthur S. Morton and Chester Martin, *History of Prairie Settlement and Dominion Lands Policy* (Toronto: Macmillan, 1938), 397.
7 PAC, Macdonald Papers, CCLXVIII, 121836–8, Stephen to Macdonald, 18 Oct. 1880.

cent—a highly unlikely situation in the early years of the company's operations.

The normal procedure adopted by railway companies in setting rates is to estimate both the expenses of operating the system and the amount of traffic to be carried. Once these figures are known, it is a relatively easy matter to set a rate that will yield at least a moderate return on investment. In the case of the CPR in the 1880s, it was known that costs, especially on the Lake Superior section, would be high. Traffic volume, at least during the early years of the company's operations, would be very small. Rates, therefore, had to be set at a high level if the company was to meet all expenses and, perhaps, to return a modest profit.

The first CPR rates were published in January 1883, and were to become effective on 1 July in the same year. These rates were designed to meet the needs of the company, and were certainly not exorbitant from their point of view. Unfortunately they made no allowance for the economic realities facing prairie farmers. The rates on wheat were particularly important and farmers were appalled when they learned that it would cost them 36¢ to ship one hundred pounds of wheat from Winnipeg to Thunder Bay. From Moose Jaw the proposed rate was 51¢ per hundredweight or 30.6¢ per bushel. To this an additional 15¢ per bushel had to be added for shipping from Thunder Bay to the seaboard.[8] At a time when the price received by the western farmer for some of his frost-damaged wheat reached lows of 40¢ per bushel these rates seemed entirely prohibitive.

The issuing of the CPR's freight tariff coincided with and hastened the collapse of a huge land-sales and speculative boom which gripped the prairies in 1881–2 and left a legacy of bitterness and frustration. The railway had failed to do what had been expected of it. An apprehensive Conservative informed the Prime Minister that "times could not be much worse than they are."[9] He feared that receipts for the damaged wheat crop would not cover expenditures on it. Macdonald blithely dismissed the problem as a creation of "a ring of land sharks

8 PAC, Van Horne Letterbook, No. 1, 211–12, W. C. Van Horne to E. B. Osler, Managing Director, Canada and West Land Co., 27 Jan. 1883.

9 PAC, Macdonald Papers, CCLXVIII, 77427, J. C. Aikins to Macdonald, 30 Nov. 1883.

and homestead jumpers."[10] For several Manitoba Conservative MPs, however, the matter was so serious that they promised, during the 1887 election campaign, to introduce a motion of non-confidence in their own party's railway policy. Macdonald, confident of sufficient eastern support to defeat such a motion, raised no objections.[11] Even the general manager of the CPR admitted that the rail rates would leave scarcely anything for the farmers. He ordered a 33.33-per-cent rate reduction for frost-damaged grain but he failed to allay public fear that farming on the prairies under prevailing conditions would prove very difficult, if not impossible.

The situation was further aggravated by the action of western millers and elevator operators. CPR officials believed that "the reputation of Manitoba flour, as well as Manitoba wheat, should be put above all the rest of the world and kept there, as it can and should be." In an effort to build this reputation, the CPR refused permission to build elevators or other grain-handling facilities alongside its tracks unless they had complete cleaning equipment and storage facilities which would keep damaged or inferior wheat in separate bins. This stipulation, it was alleged, made elevator services too costly for farmers with frost-damaged wheat. It also concentrated the elevator and grain-handling services in the hands of a few wealthy eastern capitalists—most notably William Ogilvie. The farmers wanted flat grain warehouses which would handle their damaged grain cheaply. The general manager of the CPR, William C. Van Horne, refused to accept any grain from warehouses, insisting that "it is only by prohibition of the flat warehouses that we can secure the elevators."[12]

Van Horne's arguments were probably sound, but Ogilvie seriously abused his monopoly in the grain-handling business. In 1883 farmers charged that Ogilvie's agents were treating all wheat, including some harvested two years earlier, as frost-damaged. Dockage was excessive

10 PAC, Lorne Papers, I, 296–8, Macdonald to Lorne, 2 Dec. 1882.
11 PAC, Macdonald Papers, CCLXII, 119215, Scarth to Macdonald, 2 Feb. 1887, and Macdonald to Scarth, 6 Feb. 1887.
12 PAC, Van Horne Letterbook, No. 4, 10–26, Van Horne to the editor

of the *Manitoba Free Press*, 24 Dec. 1883. The grain warehouses were cheaply built structures which had no cleaning facilities and usually only one large storage bin. Good wheat was mixed with bad, thus making it impossible to obtain wheat of superior quality.

and weights were challenged. Even CPR president Stephen became exasperated and wrote, "W. W. O. [William Ogilvie] is an awful fool both in speech and action."[13] Speaking of the agents, Van Horne admitted that "samples of wheat which have been sent down with a statement of the prices paid, indicate that they frequently take advantage of their opportunities to buy on unreasonable margins."[14] The result was that the CPR, already unpopular because of its own monopoly, was also blamed for the Ogilvie elevator monopoly because it refused to accept grain from the flat grain warehouses.

To the farmers of Manitoba the situation seemed desperate. A strong farmers' union was organized which quickly became vociferous in its demands for immediate relief. Premier Norquay of Manitoba was convinced that the agitation would result in a request for secession from Confederation. A threatened Fenian attack from the United States added to the concern of the local government. Many western farmers simply left, voting non-confidence with their feet. Norquay complained that "men who have broken up large sections of land are actually mortgaging their farms and raising what money they can get therefrom and from the sale of their other effects and pulling up stakes and leaving, as they say they cannot farm to advantage owing to the excessive freight rates."[15] According to one Conservative newspaper, "the trails from Manitoba to the states were worn bare and brown by the wagon wheels of departing settlers."[16]

The farmers believed that relief could come only from American railway competition, but this development the CPR charter specifically forbade. At first there was some doubt as to whether the restrictions of the monopoly clause applied only to federal legislation. The Manitoba government, at the urging of the dissident farmers, decided to pass provincial railway charters authorizing local companies to build from Winnipeg to the international boundary. The federal government promptly disallowed the Manitoba legislation. Macdonald did not question the right of the provinces to pass the legislation. He merely

13 PAC, Macdonald Papers, CCLXVIII, 122028, Stephen to Macdonald, 6 Dec. 1883.
14 PAC, Van Horne Letterbook, No. 4, 181, Van Horne to J. M. Egan, 6 Jan. 1884.

15 PAC, Macdonald Papers, CXIX, 48489–92, Norquay to Macdonald, 8 Jan. 1884.
16 O. D. Skelton, *The Life and Letters of Sir Wilfrid Laurier* (New York: Century, 1922), 45.

contended that the legislation was not in the national interest and that it should therefore be disallowed. The economic problems were thus transformed into a constitutional and political struggle over provincial rights.

Macdonald and the CPR were prepared to do whatever was necessary to maintain the monopoly. They could argue very cogently that the monopoly was not used to charge exorbitant rates. In fact the railway was having a great deal of difficulty in meeting its operating costs. Yet the rates were so high that many western farmers simply found it impossible to continue farming.

As the hardships and frustrations of the 1880s multiplied, the Manitoba government of Premier Norquay became increasingly aggressive. Norquay was nominally a Conservative, but tended to place provincial and regional interests above party loyalties. At first he sought a friendly accommodation with Macdonald and made numerous pilgrimages to Ottawa to seek better terms. Growing impatience and hostility in Manitoba, the repeated disallowance of provincial railway legislation, and the failure to obtain major concessions in Ottawa forced the Premier to become more aggressive. In 1887 he launched a new and daring policy. Another charter to build a railway from Winnipeg to Emerson on the international boundary was passed by the legislature. It was similar to many others that had been granted by the provincial government and disallowed by the federal government. In the case of the new company, the Red River Valley Railway, the Premier announced that the provincial government would take over the project as a public work and complete it if Ottawa again resorted to disallowance. The CPR immediately responded by threatening to remove its divisional headquarters from Winnipeg to Fort William, but this threat simply reinforced Manitoba's determination.[17]

The expected federal disallowance came in July 1887, and the province promptly took over the project and continued with construction. To pay for the construction, the Manitoba government, with only very limited financial resources of its own, decided to float a new issue of government bonds. The London financial house of Morton, Rose and Company was contacted and it indicated interest in these bonds. When

17 T. D. Regehr, "The National Policy and Manitoba Railway Legisla-tion, 1879–1888", unpublished MA thesis, Carleton University, 1963.

Macdonald heard of the plan, he wrote directly to John Rose, a personal friend and senior partner of Morton, Rose and Company, warning him not to underwrite the Manitoba bonds. He made it very clear that he was prepared to use federal powers to break the new Red River Valley Railway and, if necessary, the Manitoba government with it.[18] It was even rumoured that Macdonald had asked for imperial troops to stop the construction forcibly. Canadian militiamen were allegedly too sympathetic to the Manitoba cause and therefore unreliable for this task.[19]

As a result of Macdonald's activities, Premier Norquay was unable to find a buyer for his provincial bonds, and construction on the Red River Valley Railway was halted for lack of funds. The fate of "Norquay's shinplasters" allowed Macdonald to hope that the Premier had "come nearly to the length of his tether, I think, and he and his government will be very submissive."[20] When the City of Winnipeg indicated its intention to help financially, Manitoba confidants of Macdonald instituted a series of lawsuits and injunctions designed to prevent the city from spending tax money in this manner.[21]

Premier Norquay had openly defied the authority of the federal government. Macdonald was determined to use any means, fair or foul, to destroy the Premier and his railway. He found an opportunity in another railway transaction, quite unrelated to the Red River Valley Railway, and he used it unscrupulously.

This opportunity came in connection with a complex financing arrangement for a proposed railway to Hudson Bay. Throughout the 1880s many people believed that a railway to the Bay, utilizing one of the region's oldest trade routes, could provide the desired competition without violating the CPR's monopoly clause. Charters for railways to the Bay were granted as early as 1881, although nothing could be done without substantial government assistance. The original charters

18 PAC, Stephen Papers, 191, Macdonald to Stephen, 2 July 1887; Macdonald Papers, DXXVII, 197–8, Macdonald to Rose, 25 June 1887.
19 PAC, Macdonald Papers, CCLXXIV, 130341–7, Tupper to Macdonald, 23 Aug. 1887, and Macdonald to Tupper, 24 Aug. 1887; R. G. W. Herbert to Tupper, 24 Aug. 1887; and Colonial Secretary Holland to Governor General Lansdowne, 24 Aug. 1887.
20 PAC, Stephen Papers, 210, Macdonald to Stephen, 6 Oct. 1887.
21 PAC, Macdonald Papers, CCLXIV, 120010–11, Schultz to Macdonald, 25 Oct. 1887; Stephen Papers, 216–17, Macdonald to Stephen, 15 Oct. 1887.

provided a federal land subsidy, and in 1886 a federal transportation contract was negotiated that guaranteed the railway a fixed payment of $80,000 annually for the carriage of mail and other federal transports.

The Manitoba government decided that it too should assist the proposed railway. Unfortunately, it had neither public lands nor funds to grant subsidies. The railway's greatest need, however, was immediate capital to finance construction. The federal land subsidy was not particularly helpful, since the lands would be transferred to the railway only after construction was completed. Government officials, promoters, and contractors had to find ways and means of converting the land subsidy into immediate cash. A complex arrangement was worked out. The contractors, Herbert Holt and Donald Mann, agreed to finance immediate construction costs for the first forty miles if they were promised payment in full when they completed their work. They wanted payment in negotiable securities, not in land. The provincial government agreed to issue government bonds to pay the contractors. The promoters, in turn, agreed to mortgage all federal lands that they earned to the provincial government as security for the government bonds. Thus, the federal government was to transfer title to the lands to the promoters as soon as construction was completed. The promoters would then mortgage the lands to the provincial government, and the government in turn would issue bonds with which the contractors would be paid.[22]

The contractors completed the first forty miles late in 1887. As soon as the completion of this stage was reported to him, promoter Hugh Sutherland asked for a federal inspection and for the transfer of the land grant. He also asked the provincial government to prepare the promised government bond issue. To assure himself that all was in order the provincial attorney general, A. A. C. LaRivière, travelled to Ottawa and met with Prime Minister Macdonald and other officials. Evidently he was assured at this meeting that all was in order and that the lands were being transferred to the railway company. LaRivière sent a cablegram from Ottawa to Premier Norquay stating that the

22 H. A. Fleming, *Canada's Arctic Outlet: A History of the Hudson Bay Railway* (Berkeley and Los Angeles: University of California Press, 1957), 26–7, hereafter referred to as Fleming.

matter had been arranged and that the provincial bonds could be issued.[23] Norquay then issued the bonds and gave them to promoter Hugh Sutherland, who promptly turned them over to the contractors.

At this point difficulties arose. The federal Department of Railways and Canals reported that the line was not properly built and the lands could not be transferred. When the defects were corrected, department officials argued that the railway must build fifty, not forty, miles before any lands could be transferred. The result was that the federal government refused to transfer the lands to the railway, which was therefore unable to mortgage them to the provincial government. The provincial bonds, however, had been issued. These bonds now had no security whatsoever.

Macdonald emphatically denied that he had ever met with La-Rivière and agreed to transfer the lands: "I had to tell LaRivière that he must have dreamt this story."[24] LaRivière promptly produced both telegrams and memoranda, one of them in Macdonald's own hand, which proved that they in fact met. The memoranda, however, related to another railway matter and LaRivière could not prove that any agreement about the Hudson Bay Railway lands had been reached at the same meeting.[25] Conservatives could offer only a lame excuse for Macdonald's emphatic denial of any meeting with LaRivière. "I have said to all and sundry," wrote one federal member, "Sir John's memory may have failed him as to having no interview with Mr. LaRivière in Mr. Pope's office, and if it has he will be the first to admit it, but that is no proof of any promise as to the HBR."[26]

Macdonald would admit nothing, and Manitoba Conservatives were left the choice of accepting the word of the Attorney General or of the Prime Minister. The provincial caucus accepted LaRivière's and Norquay's explanations about the bonds and the agreement regarding the land transfer, but when Macdonald intimated that he was willing to settle the disallowance problem if Norquay and LaRivière resigned, they could not hold the caucus. Both men resigned on the last day of

23 PAC, Macdonald Papers, CLXXXVI, 77505–6, Aikins to Macdonald, 12 Nov. 1887.
24 *Ibid.*, DXXVII, 327, Macdonald to Aikins, 12 Dec. 1887.
25 *Ibid.*, CCCXXVIII, 148458, Memo-

randum in Macdonald's handwriting on stationery of the Minister of Railways and Canals, given to LaRivière to send to his government.
26 *Ibid.*, 148463, Scarth to Macdonald, 16 Jan. 1888.

1887, and Dr. D. H. Harrison, a "John A. man", became premier.

It quickly became obvious that Macdonald had succeeded in defeating not only Norquay, but also the provincial Conservative party. Although initially he had had strong bipartisan support as a "Manitoba First" man in 1878, Premier Norquay's moderate response to federal disallowance until 1887 had cost him a great deal of political support. The provincial Liberals under the leadership of Thomas Greenway had slowly but steadily gained support in the 1880s on a provincial-rights platform. In the provincial election of 1887 the Liberals fell just short of victory. They were willing to support Norquay's defiant attitude after that election, but they eagerly challenged the Harrison government in the ministerial by-elections following the resignations of Norquay and LaRivière. Harrison quickly realized that any apologies for federal actions and policies would ruin his government. He consequently made a rather confused attempt to outdo the Liberals in their criticism of John A. Macdonald and his policies. It was too late. Harrison lost two of the three ministerial by-elections, and with them control of the Assembly. He resigned both as premier and as party leader less than a month after taking over these positions. Macdonald accused him of "making an awful mess".[27]

Harrison explained that he "thought it best to resign before the mudslinging began and save as much of the party as possible."[28] A federal MP was even more specific. He said Harrison resigned "to avoid a discussion on the floor of the House on the question of the disagreement between you and LaRivière".[29] Local Conservatives no longer trusted Macdonald and they re-elected John Norquay as their leader when Harrison resigned. This move infuriated Macdonald, who had already written on one occasion, "I should much prefer myself that Greenway was at the head of affairs instead of Norquay who is really a nuisance."[30] The Prime Minister began to look seriously for ways and means of getting rid of Norquay, but in 1889 he was spared further trouble. The ex-Premier and re-elected party leader died suddenly of acute appendicitis at the age of forty-eight.

27 *Ibid.*, DXXVII, 408, Macdonald to Scarth, 1 Feb. 1888.
28 *Ibid.*, CCCXXVIII, 148471, Harrison to Macdonald, 17 Jan. 1888.

29 *Ibid.*, CCLXII, 119406–12, Scarth to Macdonald, 27 Jan. 1888.
30 PAC, Smith Papers, Macdonald to Smith, 17 June 1884.

Norquay, more than any other western leader, represented the moderate elements in prairie politics in the 1880s. He repeatedly sought to negotiate better terms in Ottawa, and was finally defeated because the disgruntled farmers thought he had not gone far enough in opposing federal and CPR policies. Macdonald, on the other hand, believed he had already gone much too far and would do nothing to help him.

Harrison's resignation opened the way for the Liberals to take office in Manitoba. They did so with a belligerent air of confidence. They were determined to break the CPR monopoly and the federal disallowance policy that kept that monopoly in force. Greenway promised to go to Ottawa once more to give Macdonald a last chance to settle the problem peacefully. If these final negotiations failed he would enter into direct discussions with American railroad interests and, if necessary, provide provincial police protection against federal and CPR intervention. His flamboyant but rather unstable Attorney General and Railway Commissioner, Joseph Martin, was preparing to swear in special local police in case of trouble.[31]

In Ottawa, both the CPR and the federal government were rapidly coming to the conclusion that the monopoly clause had lost its usefulness. Not only was the internal peace of Manitoba threatened, but the agitation and the expected results if and when American competition was brought into Manitoba frightened British investors and drove down the value of CPR securities. The company had hoped to float new securities to relieve a tight financial situation in 1887, but the threat of American competition in Manitoba made this impossible. Stephen complained bitterly to Macdonald, "CPR shares today 49½ against 75 last year. The shrinkage is more than Winnipeg is worth with all the people in it thrown in." Stephen realized that the monopoly had become a financial liability. In 1887 he began to urge the federal government to buy back clause fifteen of the charter.

The CPR made up its mind that it must face American competition. Stephen proposed two new measures which he believed would enable

31 Canada, *Orders in Council Nos. 514, 553, 577 of 1888 (Dormants). Memorandum, Supplementary Memorandum, and Final Memorandum* *respecting the visit of the delegation of the Manitoba Government in reference to the disallowance of Provincial Legislation.*

the company to do this. First, the federal government should guarantee the payment of interest on a new $15,000,000 land-grant bond issue which the CPR wanted to sell but in which the London market seemed to have no confidence. The money thus obtained would allow the company to bring its line into a state of competitive efficiency. His second, and probably much more important, suggestion was that the federal government should support the CPR in its attempts to gain control of the Minneapolis, St. Paul and Sault Ste. Marie Railway and the Duluth South Shore and Atlantic Railway. The "Soo line", as the first of these two lines became known, gave the CPR a second transcontinental connection; this one utilized the more economical international route south of the Great Lakes. With this control the CPR was in a strong position to meet its chief American competitors in their own territory. In a tight fight it could invade Northern Pacific territory. It could even temporarily abandon the more costly line north of Lake Superior and fight only in the south. Stephen, about to resign as president of the CPR, considered this, "if my last, my greatest service to the maintenance of the power and independence of the national highway".[32]

Macdonald finally agreed to cancel the monopoly clause, but not before Premier Greenway had been left to cool his heels in Ottawa for over a week. Only when the Premier left the capital to seek independent help from American financiers did Macdonald finally agree. He informed the Manitoba premier by letter that the federal government would no longer disallow provincial bills similar to the charter of the Red River Valley Railway. The CPR got the federal bond guarantee it needed, and permission to acquire the American lines south of the Great Lakes.

With the monopoly broken, Greenway returned to Winnipeg in triumph. He called a provincial election immediately and was returned with an overwhelming majority. Construction of the Red River Valley Railway was resumed, and negotiations were opened with American railroads for running rights and traffic connections on the new provincial road.

32 PAC, Macdonald Papers, CCLXXI, 123913, Stephen to Macdonald, 22 April 1888; 123835–7, Stephen to Macdonald, 15 Feb. 1888; CCLXX, 123661–2, 123567–3, 123721–2, Stephen to Macdonald, 20 Sept. 1887, 12 July 1887, and 19 Oct. 1887.

The Greenway government quickly discovered that Manitoban expectations regarding American competition were little more than wishful thinking. They had planned to open the Red River Valley Railway to all interested and competing American railway interests. No American road would accept such a proposal. The Northern Pacific, the most likely competitor, demanded exclusive control over the Red River Valley Railway and several other local roads before it would make any connection. There were even some fears that the provincial road might simply end at the boundary without any American connections.

Railroads in the American Northwest were experiencing serious financial difficulties in 1888. They lacked the means, and probably the interest, to start a fight with the strongly entrenched CPR for the sparse traffic of the Canadian prairies. Northern Pacific president Henry Villard was eventually persuaded to take over the Red River Valley Railway and four smaller Manitoba lines which were reorganized as the Northern Pacific and Manitoba Railway. Villard's reasons for doing this, however, gave little promise of major rate reductions in Manitoba.

The Northern Pacific entered Manitoba in 1888 for much the same reason that the CPR acquired the Soo line. Their purpose was not to cut rates but to maintain them at a high level. Just at that time the CPR was trying to capture some of the Pacific coast traffic of Puget Sound by cutting rates on Seattle traffic. The rival American roads had what in effect amounted to a rate-fixing agreement on the Pacific coast, but the CPR was not a party to this agreement. It was difficult for the American roads to reduce their Seattle rates to meet CPR competition because the Interstate Commerce Commission rulings prohibited discriminatory rates for any specific area in the United States. If the Seattle rates were reduced, the rates along the entire Northern Pacific line would have to be reduced proportionately. The CPR's Canadian traffic was not subject to the American regulations. Thus, the CPR could reduce its Seattle rates without making similar reductions in rates on Canadian traffic.

Henry Villard decided that the best way to bring the CPR to terms was to make a connection at Winnipeg and threaten to cut rates there. The CPR immediately saw the danger. It became much more amenable on the Pacific coast after the Northern Pacific entered Manitoba. A

Northern Pacific official later stated very candidly:

the Canadian Pacific management are like the rest of them, only
perhaps a little abler than the management of many roads on the American
side, because they have to do a great deal more work; they saw that
point at once, and we have had no trouble since that, and it has resulted
in the saving of a large sum to the Northern Pacific in the maintenance of
those rates. I was going to say that as the outcome of this understanding
there has been no disturbance of rates.[33]

Henceforth the Northern Pacific carried the Puget Sound business at
good rates while the CPR remained supreme in Manitoba.

The Puget Sound problem brought the Northern Pacific into Manitoba, but certainly not on the terms expected by the Premier and the
people of Manitoba. American competition had long been proclaimed
as the panacea for all the economic problems of the prairie farmers.
Drastic rate reductions and many new branch lines were expected.
John A. Macdonald had warned many years earlier that

the Americans would offer to carry freight for nothing, and aye to pay
shippers for sending freight that way. . . . They could afford for a series of
years with their enormous wealth, and with their enormous capital,
exceeding the revenue of many, many first-class Governments in Europe to
put their freights down to such a figure as would ruin our road.[34]

Manitobans believed that the time was at hand when Macdonald's
nightmare would become reality.

Premier Greenway learned very quickly that the Americans would
not act as foolishly as he and his fellow Manitobans had predicted. The
directors of the Northern Pacific, preoccupied with their road's serious
financial problems at home, were singularly unimpressed with the
prospective Manitoba business. They refused to enter into any mean-
ingful negotiations with the Manitoba premier. Only President Villard
was interested. He offered to organize a new company, the Northern
Pacific and Manitoba Railway Company, and arrange a running-rights

33 Harvard University, Baker Library, Villard Papers, Northern Pacific and Manitoba Railway Testimony File, Evidence of Thomas Oakes in North-ern Pacific Railroad Receivership Hearings, 14 June 1894.

34 Canada, *House of Commons Debates, 1881*, 493–4.

agreement between the Manitoba company and the American trans-continental company. This meant that the Manitoba company initially had only very tenuous connections with the Northern Pacific; certainly the American company was not committed to a rigorous rate war with the CPR. Villard did agree that rates on the new line would be about 15 per cent lower than those in force on the CPR. The provincial government was given the right to review Northern Pacific and Manitoba rate schedules before they became effective, and construction of some local branch lines was also promised. In return, however, Villard demanded exclusive rights on the Red River Valley Railway mileage. This agreement would shut out several other local railways which had hoped to build in northwestern Manitoba and to ship over the new line. Villard was more interested in control than in competition. He sought and obtained a weapon that might be used against the CPR if problems arose elsewhere. Greenway had to accept Villard's terms if the province was to gain anything for all its troubles in building the Red River Valley Railway.

When the terms of the government's agreement with the Northern Pacific and Manitoba Railway Company were announced, the Premier was faced with a major political crisis. Several members of his party, including R. P. Roblin, who later became a very successful Conservative premier of the province, broke their association with the Liberals to sit as Independents or Conservatives. The Premier had great difficulty in retaining any control over his own caucus. Bitter wrangling and denunciations resulted in a wild caucus meeting which began at 4 p.m. on 20 August and continued until 6 the next morning.[35] The politicians were unable or unwilling to understand that American railroads were far more interested in high rates and profits than in competition for competition's sake. They apparently believed their own foolish promises and now insisted that these be fulfilled. Unfortunately no American railroad would do so: the traffic of Manitoba was simply not worth a fight with the CPR. Greenway could do little more than argue that the disappointing agreement was the best that could be negotiated.

The CPR, seeing the frustration and disarray in government ranks,

35 PAC, Macdonald Papers, CXXXI, 54425–7, Schultz to Macdonald, 28 Aug. 1888.

was not averse to making further trouble. This led to one of the most colourful and controversial but rather pointless confrontations between the CPR and the Manitoba government. The CPR was confident that it could cope with the Americans, but it still hoped that they could be kept out. When the Northern Pacific and Manitoba Railway resumed construction on the frequently begun Red River Valley route, it had to cross CPR tracks in several places. One of these points of crossing was on a new branch line from Winnipeg to Portage la Prairie. The normal procedure when one railway wished to cross another was to obtain permission from the Railway Committee of the federal Cabinet. Hearings were held when necessary and permission was usually granted subject to proper safety precautions and compensation. Manitoba Railway Commissioner Martin feared that the federal Railway Committee would prove uncooperative in this case because of the animosities associated with the breaking of the monopoly clause. He decided that the intended crossing should be made without permission. Construction crews were instructed to put in the crossing secretly, under cover of darkness, during the night of 24 October 1888. They were promised protection by a force of specially sworn constables, recruited for the occasion by the Railway Commissioner, who also served as the province's Attorney General.

The next morning, when CPR superintendent William Whyte discovered the deed, he quickly mobilized the men in his Winnipeg shops and dispatched them by special train to the disputed spot on the outskirts of Winnipeg, which soon became known as "Fort Whyte". Greatly outnumbered, the untried special constables were uncertain about further action. A show of some resistance earned their leader a black eye from a vigorous CPR partisan. Considering discretion appropriate to the occasion, the special constables offered no further resistance as CPR crews tore out the offending diamond and carried it triumphantly back to Winnipeg as a trophy of war. A dead CPR engine was ditched in the path of the Northern Pacific and Manitoba line and a CPR train was parked at the disputed point of crossing.[36]

36 For detailed accounts of the happenings at Fort Whyte, see reports carried through the week by the *Manitoba Free Press*. A "dead engine" is one in which the boiler pipes above the fire box have burst or sprung leaks, thus allowing water to put out the fire.

Before long, an aroused citizenry with various more-or-less-lethal implements of battle arrived at the scene, inspiring new courage and bravado in the dejected special constables. The Attorney General also arrived with welcome news. It was illegal to obstruct passage on a road allowance. The Northern Pacific and Manitoba Railway would next attempt its crossing of the CPR line by building along a road allowance. Here it would be illegal for the CPR to ditch locomotives or park trains.

The CPR responded to this new tactic by running an engine slowly back and forth across the intended crossing point and loudly clanging its bell, but never stopping it and thus being guilty of obstruction. The driver was subjected to considerable verbal abuse, and he suffered physically from the heat of his locomotive because fear forced him to keep all doors and windows shut and locked. The contractors, meanwhile, built right up to the CPR track, and then carried materials across the track as the guarding engine moved back and forth, continuing to build on the other side without actually putting in the crossing. At nightfall, only the diamond had to be placed under the CPR rails and the crossing would be complete.

A providential change in the weather delayed further construction and maintained peace in Manitoba. The CPR, meanwhile, armed itself with a variety of legal injunctions against the rival road. It was becoming clear, however, that the disputed crossing would probably not be put in until spring; certainly it would serve no useful purpose any earlier. Since he had to wait anyway, Attorney General Martin announced that he would seek permission from the federal Railway Committee, but warned that in the spring the crossing would be put in no matter what the politicians in Ottawa might decide.

The Railway Committee, as expected, was inclined to make difficulties. Grave doubts were expressed about the competence of the local legislature to charter railways which made international connections. As a result, the question was referred to the Supreme Court of Canada for a ruling on the constitutional validity of the Manitoba charter.

It is difficult to envision what might have happened if the Supreme Court of Canada had found the Northern Pacific and Manitoba Railway charter *ultra vires* of the provincial legislature. A return to disallowance would have been disastrous; yet it seemed most unlikely that the federal government would have been willing to pass the very measure it had fought against bitterly for nearly eight years. Fortunately the Supreme Court saved the country further difficulty. On the basis of a legal technicality it avoided any reference to the constitutional question and restricted its findings entirely to the immediate problem of the railway crossing. On this question it declared that the Railway Committee had authority to permit the crossing of one railway by another. This had never been questioned, and Macdonald called the decision of the Court a "foolish answer . . . which settles nothing".[37] In fact this decision settled the question. It again put the onus of decision on the federal Cabinet committee. There was no longer a valid legal reason for the Cabinet to refuse permission, and in January 1889 the necessary authorization was given.

The Northern Pacific and Manitoba Railway continued its work in the spring, eventually crossing the CPR tracks in several places and building or acquiring a total of 301 miles of railway. Thus, the monopoly granted to the CPR in 1881 was effectively broken, but without giving substantial relief to the prairie wheat farmers. This monopoly had engendered a great deal of ill will, but had left the western railway problem unresolved. The Fort Whyte incident and the "misunderstanding" between Attorney General LaRivière and Prime Minister Macdonald were representative of the more unfortunate aspects of railway affairs in the land of the CPR before 1888.

The CPR had completed its main line and thus had opened the West. It had not, however, provided services at costs prairie farmers could afford, and most areas of the prairies were still too far away from CPR tracks to make farming feasible. As a result, the effective occupation and settlement of the Canadian prairies proceeded at a slow pace. It would continue to do so until freight rates were reduced and branch-line facilities were expanded. In the 1880s, however, the CPR regarded as utterly impossible these very two conditions that settlers and farmers regarded as absolutely essential.

37 PAC, Stephen Papers, 278–81, Macdonald to Stephen, 6 Jan. 1889.

CHAPTER TWO

A NORTHERN BEGINNING 1889-1896

PEOPLE ON THE CANADIAN PRAIRIES were not satisfied with the railway service provided by the Canadian Pacific Railway. In the 1880s they looked south to American competitors for help, but the Americans failed to live up to the advance billing given them by both the supporters and the opponents of the CPR monopoly. In the 1890s developments in the north offered new hope and confidence.

The early 1890s were disastrous for western railways. In the United States, the Northern Pacific went into receivership in 1893 and remained in financial difficulties for the rest of the decade. Its main rival, the Great Northern Railroad, was fully preoccupied with concerns south of the border. Except for a few probes into the mining districts of southern British Columbia, Canadians could expect little from it. Canadian Pacific stocks hit the lowest level in the company's history in 1895. That the existence of the Canadian road was no longer in serious jeopardy was due to the company's high rates and the fact that it ceased altogether to build any new branch lines. Other locally chartered lines on the prairies showed no progress whatsoever, and from 1893 to 1896 not a mile of new track was laid in western Canada. Rates remained at the 1888 levels until 1897 and the problems of the farmers remained unresolved. They operated on very small profit margins and those more than ten miles from the nearest railway delivery point could ship their products only at a high cost and with great exertion.

Political attention in Manitoba was temporarily diverted from the railways in the 1890s when the provincial government passed highly controversial school legislation that destroyed the financial basis for the Catholic separate schools of the province. The Greenway government had come to power on a provincial rights issue. It received strong

RAILWAYS OF WESTERN CANADA IN 1896

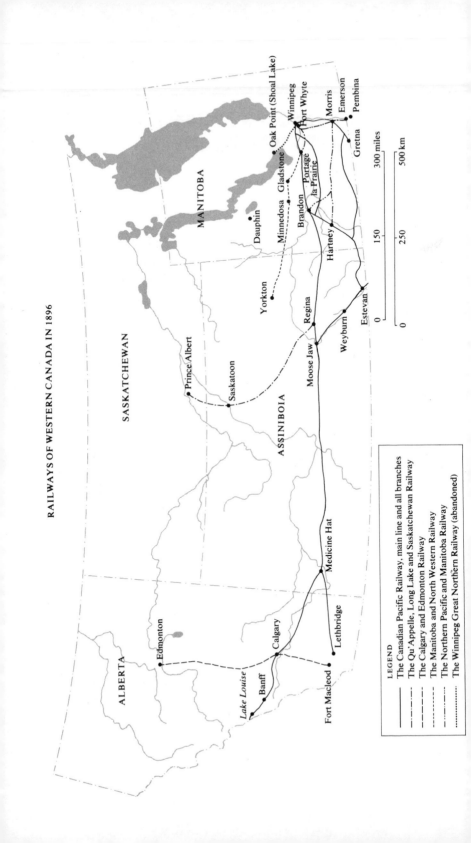

LEGEND
——— The Canadian Pacific Railway, main line and all branches
—·—·— The Qu'Appelle, Long Lake and Saskatchewan Railway
— — — The Calgary and Edmonton Railway
---------- The Manitoba and North Western Railway
—··—··— The Northern Pacific and Manitoba Railway
················· The Winnipeg Great Northern Railway (abandoned)

ALBERTA
SASKATCHEWAN
ASSINIBOIA
MANITOBA

Edmonton
Lake Louise
Banff
Calgary
Lethbridge
Fort Macleod
Medicine Hat
Prince Albert
Saskatoon
Yorkton
Dauphin
Moose Jaw
Regina
Weyburn
Estevan
Hartney
Brandon
Minnedosa
Gladstone
Portage la Prairie
Oak Point (Shoal Lake)
Winnipeg
Fort Whyte
Morris
Gretna
Emerson
Pembina

0   150   300 miles
0   250   500 km

electoral endorsement when it successfully broke the CPR monopoly and the federal policy of disallowance of provincial railway legislation. The subsequent record of the government, however, proved very disappointing. There was, first of all, disillusionment and frustration when the Northern Pacific and Manitoba Railway legislation was announced. In addition, Greenway soon proved himself a weak and inexperienced administrator who quickly fell under the influence of a strong lieutenant-governor.[1] Greenway's political competence and morality were undermined and Lieutenant-Governor Schultz began to report various pieces of malicious gossip to John A. Macdonald in Ottawa. On one occasion the Prime Minister was informed that

Greenway, who is the father of twelve, seems to have yielded, while suffering from a mild attack of La Grippe at the Clarendon, to the pitiful sympathy of a pretty housemaid and when better of La Grippe, so rumour says, used to take her to a House of Meeting (a second class hotel in Market Square) kept by a widower. The visits are said to have become noticed and the boys on one occasion opened a middle door and in some way got possession of the clothes of both and after detaining the pair for some time, gave up the clothes on payment of a round sum.[2]

Schultz behaved as Macdonald believed a lieutenant-governor should behave. He used all means at his disposal to ensure that federal policies were carried out, including those to which his Premier was publicly opposed. Schultz furnished both Ottawa and the CPR with information and suggestions on ways and means to thwart the policies of his government. It was a sad and tawdry state of affairs, but Macdonald was so pleased with the way Schultz was managing Greenway that he expressed the hope that nothing would be done to defeat the local Liberal government.[3]

Greenway and his colleagues were fortunate to find another issue

1 PAC, Macdonald Papers, CXXXI, 54535–7, Schultz to Macdonald, 6 Oct. 1888; CCLXIV, 120084–6, Schultz to Macdonald, 16 Oct. 1888; PAC, Stephen Papers, 243–4, Macdonald to Stephen, 7 July 1888.

2 PAC, Macdonald Papers, CCLXIV, 120213, Schultz to Macdonald, 4 Feb. 1890.

3 PAC, Stephen Papers, 243–4, Macdonald to Stephen, 7 July 1888; PAC, Macdonald Papers, CXXXI, 54425–7, Schultz to Macdonald, 28 Aug. 1888.

on which they could pose as champions of provincial rights against threatened federal intervention. For six years the issue of tax support for separate schools dominated Manitoba politics. On the strength of this issue, the Liberals earned two more terms in office. Once the school question was settled, however, the railway issue was likely to reoccupy the centre of political life in the province. Ambitious members of the government realized that something must be done to bring in railway competition—or at least its principal benefits of lower rates and more branch lines.

Premier Greenway never really gave up hope of persuading the Americans to build a truly competitive rail connection between Winnipeg and Duluth. He spent many fruitless hours negotiating in New York, Chicago, St. Paul, and Duluth, but the Americans refused to build unless they were offered very substantial government assistance.[4] The province's treasury was virtually empty, and public lands in Manitoba were still controlled by the federal government. Greenway could offer neither cash nor land subsidies. Rate concessions or monopoly provisions were clearly impossible, since the whole purpose was to see rates reduced and competition established.

In 1895 a younger member of Greenway's Cabinet decided to initiate a different and daring new railway policy. He had allegedly entered the Cabinet in an unusual manner. In 1891, during a minor disagreement with the Premier, the mercurial Attorney General, Joseph Martin, had talked a little too freely of resignation. On returning to Winnipeg after a weekend in Portage la Prairie, he found the bright and ambitious young member from Brandon North, Clifford Sifton, busily at work in the Attorney General's office. A placid and staid premier had accepted as a resignation what Martin had intended merely as a protest.[5]

Sifton recognized the need for new railway initiatives. His own constituency of Brandon North urgently needed branch lines, but the CPR refused to build, arguing that "it was a very bad time to propose to the shareholders any new branch lines in the North West in view of the bad showing the existing branch lines have made and the present

4 PAM, Greenway Papers, Folios 10883, 10369, 8000, 10986, 11125, 11164, and 11247.

5 Hanna, 127–8.

unsatisfactory state of affairs generally."[6] This was hardly encouraging news for constituents who could not get their produce to market. Sifton's brother-in-law, T. A. Burrows, further reinforced the Attorney General's awareness of the railway problem. Burrows was a government contractor and timber agent in the Dauphin area. He had held contracts on the two wagon roads which were built into the fertile but isolated country west of Lake Manitoba in 1889 and 1891, and was an enthusiastic promoter of settlement on the northern prairies.

Settlement possibilities in the north had long been recognized. In fact, early geographic surveys had consistently indicated that the northern parklands were preferable to the dryer southern areas. The famous Canadian surveyor J. B. Tyrrell had declared publicly that if he were choosing a farm he would go to the Dauphin country.[7] Captain John Palliser, head of a British geographical expedition that explored the Canadian prairies in 1857–60, spoke of the northern parklands as the "fertile belt", and the southern regions as merely an extension of the great American desert. Heads of Canadian geographical expeditions, while not as emphatic as Palliser, also considered the northern areas superior to the more arid south.

The CPR nevertheless decided to build across the south. It feared American incursions into Canadian territory and wanted to cut them off. Old surveys and reports were disregarded and a southern location was sought. Originally the CPR wanted to build through the Crow's Nest Pass, but the Canadian government was afraid that this route would bring the line too close to the American border and thus make it vulnerable in the event of war. Consequently the CPR directors chose the Kicking Horse and Rogers passes as the most southerly route acceptable to the government.[8]

This decision effectively halted agricultural developments on the northern prairies. Without adequate transportation facilities it was impossible to farm there. Farm machinery agents refused to advance credit to farmers in the north. Law enforcement was sufficiently lax to

6 PAM, Greenway Papers, Folio 10336, W. C. Van Horne to Charles Castle, 2 April 1897; PAC, Sifton Papers, xxxv, 23324–5, Van Horne to Sifton, 8 April 1897.

7 Hanna, 124.

8 PAC, Shaughnessy Letterbook, No. 51, 785, memorandum by Shaughnessy to Oliver Mowat, 14 April 1897; PAC, Van Horne Letterbook, No. 52, 118, Van Horne to J. D. Edgar, 2 Oct. 1896.

provide a judgement-proof haven for broken speculators and adventurers trying "to keep themselves going or to get themselves going for a second time".[9]

Burrows and Sifton recognized the settlement potential of the northern plains and parklands. They also knew that there would be no settlement until adequate rail service was extended northward. Two major lines into the north, one from Calgary to Strathcona and the other from Regina to Prince Albert, were built between 1888 and 1891. They brought in some new settlers, but showed only very modest returns for their owners. Other independent railways with northern ambitions were so encumbered that they could do nothing. The need for inexpensive rail service in the north was nevertheless very obvious.

Governments seeking to encourage new railway construction faced a twofold problem. Financial backing had to be found for the needed railways. At the same time safeguards were needed to ensure that rates would be low and that contractors and promoters would provide service commensurate with the assistance granted them. The history of the Calgary and Edmonton line and the Qu'Appelle, Long Lake and Saskatchewan Railway from Regina to Prince Albert clearly revealed these problems.

Federal assistance in the form of land grants and transportation contracts enabled several promoters not directly associated with the CPR to build the two lines. Once built, both lines were leased to the CPR after the promoters had helped themselves to lucrative construction and promotional profits. Huge sums had been raised through the sale of bonds, some of which were backed by the federal government, leaving the railways with heavy interest charges. In order to pay this interest, freight rates on the new lines had to be high.[10]

The plan initiated by Clifford Sifton in 1895 differed somewhat from

9 *Arbitration,* 402–4.

10 R. A. Christenson, "The Calgary and Edmonton Railway and the *Edmonton Bulletin*", unpublished MA thesis, University of Alberta, 1967, 83–4. The *Edmonton Bulletin* alleged that the Calgary and Edmonton Railway issued $5,474,513 worth of bonds and had a total of $13,738,513 available for financing. The estimated cost of building the railway was, according to the *Bulletin*, $3,743,652. These figures are misleading in several important respects, but the fact remains that the bonded indebtedness, and consequently the railway's fixed charges, were very high. These expenses led directly to high freight rates.

that adopted by the federal government to assist the Edmonton and Prince Albert lines. Instead of offering land or money to prospective railway companies, Sifton suggested that the local government underwrite or guarantee the payment of interest and principal on construction bonds issued by new railway companies. This meant simply that the government committed itself to pay interest and principal on specific bonds in case the railway itself was unable to meet these obligations. The guarantee made the bonds a fairly safe investment. They would sell much more easily and, more important, at significantly lower rates of interest. Careful safeguards had to be incorporated into any agreement to ensure that all monies raised through bond sales were actually used for legitimate construction expenses. The simplest way to do this was to make the province a trustee for funds raised. The funds would be turned over to the railway company only on presentation of vouchers or other certification that the appropriate amount had actually been spent on construction.

The details of the new provincial plan took considerable time to develop. The Northern Pacific Railroad was the first to be invited to participate, but it declined because of financial difficulties. Sifton had considerably less faith in the Americans than Greenway did, and for a time there was some tension between the two men.[11] Sifton represented the constituency of Brandon North where new branch lines were the most urgent requirement. He was therefore willing to offer provincial guarantees to local companies who promised to build the needed branches. Greenway, on the other hand, represented Mountain constituency in southern Manitoba where both the CPR and the Northern Pacific had already built branch lines. Greenway wanted a competitive through line to Duluth, which, it was hoped, would bring about a reduction in freight rates.

Neither the Northern Pacific, nor the Great Northern, nor the Canadian Pacific showed much interest in the provincial bond guarantee plan. Neither Sifton's branch lines nor Greenway's competitive line to Duluth appealed to them. Sifton had to look elsewhere for railway promoters willing to build the desired lines. Eventually he found a temporarily unemployed railway contractor who saw some merit in

11 PAM, Greenway Papers, Folio 10551, Sifton to Greenway, 20 July 1897.

the new Manitoba proposals. He was Donald Mann, a tough but respected railway builder.

Mann entered into negotiations with the Manitoba government in 1895. He was soon joined by another former railway contractor, William Mackenzie. Together these two obtained provincial assistance to build a local line from Portage la Prairie to Dauphin, Manitoba. Their agreement with the province marks the beginning of one of Canada's most unusual and notorious business enterprises.

The personalities and early careers of the two promoters must be related in some detail if the nature of the 1895 agreement is to be understood fully.[12] The history of the railway, of the early experiences of its promoters, and of the various other business ventures in which Mackenzie and Mann became involved, are often interrelated. It is clear, for example, that the business insights and experiences Mackenzie and Mann gained prior to 1895 influenced their decision to accept the Manitoba government's railway assistance plan.

Both William Mackenzie and Donald Mann were Protestant Ontario pioneers. The Protestant work ethic and the challenge of developing and utilizing a continental treasure-house of natural resources provided both the purpose and the methods of their undertakings. The satisfaction of building something permanent and worth while was of far greater importance to them than the mere accumulation of wealth.[13]

12 The information on the early lives of Donald Mann and William Mackenzie is very incomplete. Neither man left any extensive collection of private papers. The most complete source of information is the recollections of Mann, Hanna, and Lash, as given in the evidence before the Canadian Northern Railway arbitration proceedings in 1918. The published recollections of D. B. Hanna and Martin Nordegg, as well as several unpublished memoirs, provide further detail, although it is not always easy to distinguish fact from fiction. Biographical dictionaries, newspaper reports, and other secondary sources provide additional information. In reply to an inquiry from the author, Sir William Mackenzie's grandson, A. G. S. Griffin of Toronto, wrote, "I am virtually certain there is nothing extant. Some years ago I thought myself of doing a biography of my grandfather; but it seemed impossible to do more than report anything second hand." The business records of the contracting firm of Mackenzie, Mann and Co. Ltd. were taken over by the firm's chief creditor, the Canadian Bank of Commerce, shortly after Sir William Mackenzie's death. The Bank has categorically and repeatedly refused the author access to any of these records, despite assurances that nothing from those records would be published without prior permission of the Bank.

13 *Canadian Railway and Marine World*, Jan. 1924, 31.

William Mackenzie, the older of the two men, was born at Kirkfield, Ontario, in 1849. He first tried his hand at school-teaching, but the classroom was evidently not the place for him. He allegedly lacked a sense of humour and exhibited a strong tendency to bully those who crossed his path. These characteristics were certainly not unknown in the Ontario school system at that time, but Mackenzie soon left the school to open a small lumber business. The business did not prosper and Mackenzie was compelled to supplement his earnings by cutting and preparing ties for the railway that was just then opening up the area north of Toronto. This work led naturally to contracting work for the railway, and in 1872 Mackenzie obtained a small contract on the Victoria Railway between Lindsay and Haliburton.

A rather typical piece of Mackenzie-and-Mann folklore eventually came to be connected with that first contract. The contract required Mackenzie to post a $5,000 performance bond. He did not have the necessary money or credit to post the bond, and therefore stood in danger of losing his contract. The situation was saved in what became typical Mackenzie financing. Mackenzie's wife, the former Margaret Merry, was a Catholic who had been educated in a Montreal convent. The Mother Superior of that convent was somehow persuaded to loan the $5,000 to the devout Presbyterian husband of her former pupil. Thus financed, Mackenzie completed his contract on time and promptly repaid the borrowed money.[14] This marked the beginning of a financial career in the course of which Mackenzie and his associate eventually borrowed over $300,000,000 from Canadian, American, and British investors.

From the Victoria Railway Mackenzie moved to the Credit Valley Railway and later to other local Ontario railways. As a contractor he was exemplary in meeting his deadlines and other commitments, a rather unusual trait among contractors of the time. He got things done promptly and on schedule, and thus came to the notice of the larger contracting outfits of Herbert Holt and James Ross. Both contractors obtained large construction contracts on the CPR main line, and in 1884 Mackenzie followed them west.

For a time he evidently became the object of curious and even con-

14 Martin Nordegg, *The Possibilities of Canada Are Truly Great: Memoirs,* *1906–1924,* ed., T. D. Regehr (Toronto: Macmillan, 1971), 128–9.

temptuous comment in the West. He could not afford new teams and outfits. Instead he brought his horses, harnesses, and supplies from Ontario. These consisted mainly of stock obtained from local Ontario farmers at bargain prices, and the odd-looking equipage became known as the "Farmer's Outfit".[15]

While in the mountains the Presbyterian contractor earned a further distinction. He was allegedly the first man to bring a piano into that portion of the Rockies. A piano in a railway construction camp was indeed an oddity, as was Mackenzie's penchant for gathering his crew around the piano on Sunday evenings to sing "Mr. Sankey's hymns".[16] Mackenzie's clear tenor voice was always in evidence on such occasions. During the week the entire team worked in the best traditions of the Protestant ethic, intent on saving their souls by hard work. Despite a latter-day reputation for sharp dealing, both Mackenzie and Mann apparently had an unusual degree of religious feeling and devotion. Mackenzie served for many years as an elder of St. Andrew's Presbyterian Church in Toronto, and when Mann was asked for a comment after Mackenzie's death in 1923 he urged all his friends to pray for the departed entrepreneur. Both partners, according to Mann, had always believed in the power of prayer.[17]

It was while working in the Rocky Mountains that William Mackenzie first met his future business partner, Donald Mann. Mann had been born at Acton, Ontario, in 1853. His family had come to Canada from Inverness-shire ten years earlier, moving up through the bush to Acton at a time when the railway ended at Toronto.[18] Railways became a passion with the Mann family, and three Mann brothers became railway contractors.

In early life Donald Mann thought of a calling in the ministry and briefly attended a Methodist divinity school. He remained, despite his rough construction-camp manners and language, a rather sensitive and mystical person. He greatly enjoyed long, lonely treks into the wilderness and became, in later life, a spiritualist. But the cloth was not for him in the 1870s and he took up the darker pursuits of the blacksmith's shop. The opportunities and the free life of the lumber camps and

15 Hanna, 117.
16 Ibid.

17 Canadian Railway and Marine World, Jan. 1924, 31.
18 CNRHQ, C. J. Quantie interview.

later of the railway construction gangs drew his attention and enthusiasm. Here men were developing Canada's vast natural resources, and Donald Mann found his life's work in their company.

Mann remained, throughout his business career, a frontiersman. His bluff manner, curt but incisive habits of speech, and refusal to adopt the conventions of high society where these did not suit his purpose made him unique among Canadian businessmen. His friends loved to tell the story of Donald Mann's encounter with a pompous German army officer in Hong Kong, where Mann had once undertaken some railway construction work. Mann had apparently offended the German in some manner and was challenged to a duel. He had very little experience in such aristocratic diversions, but recalled that the challenged party normally had the right to choose the weapons to be used. This fact was confirmed by the challenger, whereupon Mann announced, "Very well, I am more familiar with axes than with any other weapon. We will fight with axes."[19] That ended the matter, but it is clear that neither Mann nor some of his later associates were always gentlemen.

An alleged incident at Donald Mann's funeral in 1934 illustrates the true roots of the man and his family. A large floral arrangement in the shape of an anchor, representing the anchor of faith, had been sent to the funeral. Lady Mann, mistaking it for another and perhaps more appropriate item, inquired indignantly and indiscreetly, "Who sent that damned pick?"[20]

One of Mann's closest associates described him as "the most conservative of men" who "weighed with deliberance anything that was of importance".[21] In Canadian politics at that time this attitude apparently made him a staunch Liberal, while his more daring and ambitious partner became a very strong supporter of the Conservative party. For lobbying purposes this became a most useful division of labour. On the railway a similar division of labour evolved. Mackenzie handled most of the financing, while Mann became the mastermind in construc-

19 W. H. Lyon, "The Canadian Northern: A Railroad with no stock on the market, which may soon become Canada's Third Transcontinental Line", *Moody's Magazine*, March 1909.

20 As told to the author by Norman Robertson, former Undersecretary of State for External Affairs.
21 *Canadian Railway and Marine World*, Dec. 1934, 523.

tion. He had a blacksmith's inventiveness and an ability to accomplish things with materials immediately at hand.

Mann arrived in western Canada in the late 1870s. He first came to the attention of the public on Christmas Day in 1879 when the first railway locomotive was brought into Winnipeg under his supervision. The Pembina Railway along the east side of the Red River had been completed as far as St. Boniface in 1878. A locomotive was needed for construction work on the west side before the railway bridge across the Red River could be completed. Mann used temporary tracks laid on the ice of the river to bring the needed locomotive across.[22]

Mann was among the first contractors to obtain work on the new transcontinental Canadian Pacific Railway after that company signed its famous contract with the federal government in 1881. He remained with the CPR until the main line was completed in 1885, earning an estimated $100,000 from his contracts with that company.[23] In the process, like several other politicians, contractors, and promoters associated with the building of the CPR, he saw and came to believe in the promised land of "the last, best west". He also met the man who later became his partner in the railway ventures which opened the parklands to agricultural settlement.

The first meeting between William Mackenzie and Donald Mann has been described in considerable detail by several of their associates. Two shipments of mules for the two contractors were turned, by mistake, into the same pen at the railhead. Attempts by the contractors to sort them out led to hot words, but a mutual contractor friend introduced the two and devised a scheme whereby the mules might be satisfactorily divided between the two disputants. The two would take turns in choosing one mule at a time, in much the same manner as later entrepreneurs would draft hockey players.

The peace plan was accepted, but Mann later reported with great pleasure that he had definitely been able to outwit Mackenzie in the draft. Mann's foreman had known the former owner of the mules. He also knew that some rather unimpressive roan mules were in fact superior animals. Mann and his foreman decided that if they chose one of the more impressive greys in their first round Mackenzie was unlikely to choose the roans. Only in subsequent rounds did Mann pick up the roans.[24] Victory in such a battle of wits certainly pleased Mann, while Mackenzie apparently came to the conclusion that the sharp, black-bearded, and cigar-chewing contractor might make a very useful partner. Both men lived by their wits, and respected others who did likewise.

A partnership between the two did not materialize immediately. After the CPR main line was completed late in 1885, Mackenzie obtained a further contract to build snowsheds for the CPR in the Rockies. Mann joined Herbert Holt, another CPR contractor and one of Canada's most successful businessmen, in a contract to build twenty-five miles of the Manitoba and North Western Railway. This railway, operating under several successive names, was owned by the Allan interests of Montreal. It was a rather curious remnant of the lingering ambitions of the man who had promoted the first Canadian Pacific Railway project which had ended in scandal in 1873. Part of the difficulty then had been Allan's heavy involvement with American interests, but the experience of 1873 had taught Sir Hugh Allan little about economic nationalism. Throughout the 1880s he continued to hope the government would assist him in building from the American border in Manitoba to Prince Albert and Edmonton. Some government aid did become available in 1885 and contracts were let for new construction. After he had built the first one hundred miles, however, all available government aid was exhausted and the Allans refused to sink more of their own money into a railway that produced nothing except deficits.[25]

Holt and Mann had none of their own money in the Manitoba and North Western Railway. They were simply the contractors who built a part of it. Sparse traffic and steep grades produced little revenue but high operational costs. Yet Mann saw something in the parklands, and later returned to them with a railway project of his own. A railway with low operating costs, devoting itself to the promotion of settlement in the rich area, might well succeed where the Allans had failed.

The Manitoba and North Western mileage was built in 1886. When that work was completed, Holt and Mann obtained a contract to build the first forty miles on the troubled Hudson Bay Railway. That con-

24 Hanna, 117–20.
25 PAM, Greenway Papers, Folio 560,   Confidential Memo re Manitoba and North Western Railway.

tract, while potentially lucrative, ultimately left the two contractors with unsecured provincial bonds after the 1887 "misunderstanding" between Manitoba Attorney General LaRivière and Prime Minister Macdonald. In this way Mann became familiar with and gained an unwanted interest in one of the railways serving the area north of the CPR main line.

Following the Hudson Bay Railway imbroglio, Mann obtained contracts from the CPR for the construction of two sections on a "short line" that company was building to the Maritimes across the state of Maine. He discovered that William Mackenzie had the contracts for the two sections adjacent to his own on the Maine short line. The two former CPR contractors found it in their interest to pool their resources and work the four sections together. "We had four sections; Sir William had two and I had two, and after the contracts were awarded we amalgamated."[26] It was the beginning of a momentous entrepreneurial partnership.

Construction of the Maine short line in 1888, however, turned out to be a less than successful beginning for the partnership. Where the contractors had expected soil that could be easily graded, they found hardpan along the proposed road bed. They stood to lose a lot of money, but appealed to the CPR. Eventually a compromise was reached which, Mann said, "let us out even, we did not lose anything or gain anything out of that contract".[27]

The Maine line was barely completed when Mackenzie and Mann, together with their contractor friends, Herbert Holt and James Ross, obtained further and more profitable work in western Canada. Two railways running northward from the CPR main line showed particular promise. These were the Qu'Appelle, Long Lake and Saskatchewan Railway, which ran from Regina to Saskatoon and Prince Albert, and the Calgary and Edmonton Railway, which connected those two centres. Both these railways were promoted by interests not directly connected with the CPR, but after they were built, both were leased to that company. Both carried federal charters and were entitled to land grants of 6,400 acres per mile. In addition, in 1886 the federal government added an $80,000-a-year transportation contract for the carriage of federal mail and other shipments. If the actual value of transportation services provided by the railway companies fell short of $80,000, portions of their land grants could be held back. The chief advantage of this contract was that the railway had an assured income even if it carried very little traffic. That assured income could be used to pay interest at the rate of 4 per cent on $2,000,000 worth of construction bonds. In fact, most of the construction costs for the two new railways were met in this way and also by the issue of land-grant bonds.

The financing of the Qu'Appelle, Long Lake and Saskatchewan Railway and of the Calgary and Edmonton Railway was an important lesson in high finance for the contractors. Equity investment was kept at a minimum, while government- and land-backed bonds provided funds for construction. Even a man of modest means might become a railway magnate on such terms. Equally important for Mackenzie and Mann was the fact that they saw for themselves, and worked on, the fertile lands of the northern prairies. They became convinced that the region must be developed before long. When that happened, well-planned railways would almost certainly prove profitable.

After the completion of the Calgary and Edmonton Railway, however, economic problems in western Canada increased. Money for new railways could not be raised, construction came to a halt, and contractors who had spent nearly two decades building western railways dispersed to find new opportunities for work and profit elsewhere. Donald Mann sought further work in railway construction, but he had to go abroad to find it. His first foreign contract was with the government of Chile, where he undertook a rather difficult railway project. He hoped to make a quick $100,000 profit, but political instability and adverse ground conditions made the project much more expensive than had been originally anticipated. Mann, who was associated with James Ross on this contract, later claimed, "it took me seven years to make the $100,000 instead of four months."[28] Attempts to get railway contracts as far afield as Manchuria also proved much less remunerative than had been anticipated, and by 1894 Mann was back in western Canada searching for new opportunities.

William Mackenzie returned to his native Kirkfield, Ontario, in 1891. He had plans for settling down to the life of a gentleman farmer,

28 *Ibid.*

having earned enough as a contractor to become comfortably established. He also cherished ambitions of public service in the Canadian House of Commons. In 1891 he sought the Conservative nomination for the constituency of Victoria North in Ontario. His rival for the nomination was Sam Hughes, a personal friend and the editor of the Lindsay newspaper.[29] Hughes won the nomination and later the election, but this initial reverse did not completely dash Mackenzie's political ambitions.

Throughout the 1890s there were rumours that William Mackenzie would again seek the Conservative nomination. The next election, however, was still some years away, and Mackenzie continued his interests in business and financial matters. In 1892 a unique financial opportunity in Toronto was presented to him. Three of the Toronto horse-drawn tramway systems were on the verge of bankruptcy. Funds for necessary modernization and consolidation could not be raised by the owners, and the municipal authorities were becoming increasingly concerned about the rapidly deteriorating situation. Electricity was then just making its first major impact on the transportation industry, and promotionally minded entrepreneurs began to think of electricity as the answer to the tramway problem.

Mackenzie became interested in the situation and, together with several associates, began negotiations with the municipal authorities and the owners of the horse-drawn tramways. The objective was to take over, consolidate, modernize, and expand the existing tramway systems of Toronto. The biggest difficulty for Mackenzie and his associates was that they too lacked the kind of money required to carry out the project.

The existing tramways were valued at $1,453,788. Modernization and electrification were expected to cost at least $1,000,000. Nevertheless, negotiations continued, and eventually three concurrent arrangements were worked out. They closely resembled the kind of arrangements Mackenzie later made to finance his steam railways, and they are indicative of his methods.

29 Correspondence between Sam Hughes and C. E. L. Porteous provides considerable information on the political rivalries between Hughes and Mackenzie. See particularly Porteous Papers, IV, Hughes to Porteous, 8 Dec. 1896.

First, the owners of the existing tramways agreed to sell for only $475,000 in cash. The remaining amount, consisting mainly of the liabilities of the old companies, was to be paid out of a percentage of gross receipts. Second, a new tramway company, the Toronto Street Railway, was to be organized, with a capitalization of $1,000,000. Stock to the value of $100,000 was to be subscribed immediately and 10 per cent paid with the subscription. Third, the municipal authorities agreed to guarantee interest payments on $2,000,000 worth of new debenture bonds. Returns from the sale of these bonds were to be used to pay for immediate construction and modernization costs and to satisfy the $475,000 purchase obligation.

The most notable feature of the transaction was that Mackenzie and his associates paid only $10,000 to meet the 10 per cent call on $100,000 worth of capital stock, but they gained control of a new company with an authorized capitalization of $1,000,000 and a municipal guarantee for a $2,000,000 bond issue. William Mackenzie then obtained a contract to construct and modernize the system. Actual construction costs were paid out of the proceeds of the bond issue, but instead of taking any contractor's commission or any profit in cash, Mackenzie was given fully-paid-up capital stock of the Toronto Street Railway and thus became its major shareholder.[30]

The key to the arrangement was the municipal guarantee of interest on the construction bonds. Only such a guarantee was likely to assure investors that these bonds deserved attention. The matter evidently took some hard bargaining in Toronto. Sam Hughes later claimed that it was his influence in Toronto that carried the day for Mackenzie and his associates. "When the question of the Ry. was before Toronto Council where tens of thousands were wasted by both competing companies, I spent four days in Toronto, at my own expense, and without the outlay of one dollar brought about a change in the Committee of three and in the Council of five or six, in favour of William's Company. He knows nothing of it."[31]

The reasons for Hughes's intervention are quite clear, and he openly

30 Carl A. S. Hall, "Electrical Utilities in Ontario under Private Ownership, 1890–1914", unpublished PHD thesis, University of Toronto, 1968,

63–5; Stevens, 23–4.
31 PAC, Porteous Papers, IV, Hughes to Porteous, 8 Dec. 1896.

admitted them. His object was "to get William interested in such great undertakings as would make membership for North Victoria too small for him, and give me a clear course, unopposed by him."[32] Hughes was ever prone to exaggeration. The letter, moreover, was a request for financial assistance from Mackenzie's business agent. There was good reason, therefore, for Hughes to emphasize and exaggerate past but unknown services. He probably did contribute, but in only a minor way, to the successful outcome of the municipal negotiations.

There were also very persistent rumours and charges that Mackenzie and his associates had resorted to unethical activities in order to get the contract. Public officials had allegedly been bribed, or at least had received large loans and advances from the prospective promoters on unusually easy terms. Many of these allegations of dubious actions were subsequently confirmed, although no successful legal action to nullify the contract resulted.[33] The entire affair certainly stained the reputation of Mackenzie and his associates. The fact remains, however, that Mackenzie also had a good record of completed contracts. The municipal government was eager to see the project operational, and William Mackenzie and his associates seemed likely persons to do this. Mackenzie was a sharp negotiator, given to activities often regarded as ethically dubious, but he was also a person who got things done.

The electrification and consolidation of the Toronto tramways proved a great success, and Mackenzie became president of the re-organized Toronto Street Railway. James Ross and CPR President William C. Van Horne joined Mackenzie in the venture. Puritanical Lord's Day legislation, ecology-conscious municipal planners, and demanding accident victims periodically threatened the profits of the Toronto Street Railway, but it soon proved a successful and profitable undertaking.

With this success to their credit, Mackenzie and his associates began to think of other electrical and urban street railway schemes and of electrical generating and transmission companies. In Sao Paulo, Brazil, they became interested in extensive power developments which were ultimately consolidated as the Brazilian Traction, Light, Heat and

32 Ibid.
33 H. V. Nelles and Chris Armstrong, paper presented at the Annual Meeting of the Canadian Historical Association, June 1973.

Power Company. In Montreal, Winnipeg, and Saint John, as well as in Birmingham (England), Jamaica, Cuba, and various South American cities, members of the same group of entrepreneurs became involved in electric traction companies. In all these ventures a sound basis for profitable operations was soon established. Thus, by 1895 Mackenzie was an active and successful businessman with a promising future.

Neither Mackenzie nor his erstwhile partner, Donald Mann, ever forgot the Canadian prairies and the prospects of settlement there. Sooner or later the fertile northern parklands they had learned to know while they were building railways had to be developed. When that happened there would be a great need for more railways, especially in the areas north of the CPR main line. Aggressive entrepreneurs looking for new challenges might well find these in western Canadian railway projects.

Numerous local "paper" railways were projected into the northern districts in the decades after the CPR main line was completed, but in the early 1890s none was in a very strong position. The Allans had given up on their proposed line to Prince Albert, but Prince Albert had not given up hope of getting an eastern rail connection. T. O. Davis, the Liberal MP for Prince Albert, took the initiative in promoting a new line from Portage la Prairie to Prince Albert. The Lake Manitoba Railway and Canal Company was incorporated for this purpose. The original plan was to build a railway to Lake Manitoba and utilize water communications on Lake Manitoba and the Saskatchewan River to reach Prince Albert. A 6,400-acre-per-mile land subsidy was obtained for the railway portion, but Davis and his associates lacked the funds to begin construction.[34]

In 1892 Davis intimated to Mann, who had returned briefly to Manitoba after his frustrations in Chile, that the charter of the Lake Manitoba Railway and Canal Company might be sold. Mann was interested. He needed new construction work, and was convinced that the northern railway could prove profitable. He paid $1,000 for an option and began looking for capital. The 1893 financial panic made this impossible and Mann dropped the option. Within a year, however,

34 *Arbitration*, 404.

he obtained a second option, this time for $2,000. He was convinced the scheme was viable, if only the necessary capital could be raised at reasonable cost. Finally, in 1895, he decided to purchase the charter, paying $38,000 in cash for it.[35]

The Manitoba government's plan to guarantee payment of interest and principal for railway bonds provided Mann with an answer to his financial problem. While his railway would not really be a main-line competitor for the CPR, it would extend rail service to an important area in which several Manitoba politicians had an interest. Negotiations were therefore begun with the provincial government. The proposed line would begin either at Portage la Prairie or at Gladstone, depending on whether the Manitoba and North Western agreed to a reasonable running-rights arrangement for its line from Portage to Gladstone. At Portage connections could be made with both the Canadian Pacific and the Northern Pacific railways.[36]

Negotiations were sufficiently advanced in 1895 for Mann to be confident he would get the provincial bond guarantee. In addition, there was, of course, the 6,400-acre-per-mile federal land subsidy. Both the guaranteed bonds and the land grant, however, had to be earned; they would become available to the promoter only after the line, or at least significant portions of it, was completed. Extensive interim financing was needed. Bank officials were highly dubious about the project. They advised Mann that the sums required could be made available only if he associated himself with one or more of his former contracting associates.

Mann approached Herbert Holt, James Ross, and William Mackenzie. Only William Mackenzie responded favourably, and he was enthusiastic. Mackenzie's success with the Toronto Street Railway evidently impressed officials of the Canadian Bank of Commerce, who agreed to provide the needed loans to get construction on the Lake Manitoba Railway and Canal Company started.[37] The loan was to be repaid from the proceeds of the provincially guaranteed construction bonds.

35 Hanna, 126–7.
36 PAC, Sifton Papers, 1895, III. All these details are discussed at great length in numerous letters between Walter Barwick, Manitoba Legal Counsel, and Clifford Sifton.
37 Hanna, 130; PAC, Porteous Papers, XXI, Letterbook, 1898–9, Porteous to Ross, 24 July 1899.

Before coming to a final agreement with the Manitoba government, however, another possibility of obtaining further federal assistance was explored. The bond-guarantee land fiasco on the Hudson Bay Railway had left contractors Mann and Holt in effective control of that ill-fated enterprise. They had no intention of rehabilitating the line and extending it to the Bay. The original route between Lakes Winnipeg and Manitoba was certainly the most direct, but there was very little local traffic in that area. The Lake Manitoba Railway and Canal Company line, on the other hand, was to be built west of Lake Manitoba through partially developed areas which might produce considerable local traffic. It did run in a northwesterly direction, however, and might thus be promoted as the first section of a new line to the Bay. It would certainly be longer, but it would also be easier to build and in a position to earn more revenue from local traffic.

The federal government had already voted a land subsidy and a transportation contract for the Hudson Bay Railway. Mackenzie and Mann, controlling both the Lake Manitoba Railway and Canal Company and the Hudson Bay Railway, began to work on a plan whereby the provincial and federal government assistance available for the two projects might be combined, and earned by a single line. They were particularly interested in applying the provisions of the federal transportation contract of the Hudson Bay Railway to the Lake Manitoba Railway and Canal Company. The transportation contract guaranteed annual federal payments of $80,000 for the transport of mail and supplies, and could be converted into a guarantee for the payment of interest on a large bond issue.

Unfortunately the transportation contract became effective only when the railway was built to the Saskatchewan River, and Mackenzie and Mann had no intention of building their Lake Manitoba Railway any farther than half that distance. They were building to Prince Albert, not northward to the Bay. They therefore began negotiations in Ottawa to ensure that half the transportation contract would become payable when the railway was built half-way to the Saskatchewan River. In addition, they wanted provisions whereby the contract would become payable if the railway were built along an alternate route.

After considerable lobbying in Ottawa, in which Sam Hughes again claimed to be the decisive force in favour of William Mackenzie and

Donald Mann, the federal government agreed to pass legislation under which the Hudson Bay Railway's construction contract could be applied against one of three alternative routes if the Hudson Bay Railway indicated it did not intend to build along its authorized route. One of the alternative routes happened to coincide exactly with the proposed route of the Lake Manitoba Railway and Canal Company. The federal government also agreed that half the transportation contract would become payable when the railway was completed half-way to the Saskatchewan River.[38] One of the reasons the federal government was willing to grant such generous terms in 1895 was undoubtedly the imminence of a federal election. Battered by the Manitoba schools question, the Conservatives needed a popular issue in Manitoba. The promise of new construction on the Hudson Bay Railway by a reliable contracting firm was expected to help the Tory cause.

Once the federal negotiations were finalized, Mann formally took possession of the Lake Manitoba Railway and Canal Company and negotiations were completed with the provincial government. The province agreed to guarantee the payment of both interest and principal, up to $8,000 per mile, on construction bonds to be issued for the first 125 miles of the railway. In return, the government insisted that the rates be kept low, and that no rates be implemented without prior approval by the provincial Cabinet. It was this provision that worried other businessmen, but Mackenzie and Mann agreed, provided they got a fair division of rates from the roads which would receive their traffic at their eastern terminus of Gladstone. They were confident that the contingent liability assumed by the provincial government would prevent it from demanding unreasonably low rates. If the railway failed to earn enough to pay its fixed charges the government would have to make the payments. This would be both politically and economically disastrous for the local government. Mackenzie and Mann were confident that Manitoba had committed itself not only to the construction of 125 miles of railway, but also to the long-term success of the new railway.[39]

38 *Arbitration*, 2674–5; PAC, Porteous Papers, IV, Sam Hughes to Porteous, 8 Dec. 1896; for further details of the negotiations see Porteous Papers, XXIV, 211, 224–5, and XXV, 476–81, Porteous to Mackenzie, 18 and 23 July 1895, and 14 March and 13 April 1896.
39 PAC, Sifton Papers, III, 1130–2, 1137–40, Walter Barwick to Sifton, 3 and 7 March and 22 April 1896.

Construction of the Lake Manitoba Railway and Canal Company was begun under very favourable financial arrangements. The line got a provincial guarantee of $8,000 per mile and a federal land grant of 6,400 acres of land "fairly fit for settlement" for every mile built. In addition, the company would be entitled to a regular income of $40,000 per year, under the federal transportation contract, when the line was built half-way to the Saskatchewan River. This money could be pledged or designated for payment of interest on a further $1,000,000 bond issue. There was also the possibility that, with limited tinkering and repairs on the original forty miles of the Hudson Bay Railway the promoters could still earn the lands that the federal government had refused to transfer in 1887. It was estimated that construction on the new line would cost $11,000 per mile. The financial arrangements, therefore, left something for equipment, terminal facilities, and even operational deficits, in the early years.[40]

Perhaps the most serious difficulty encountered by Mackenzie and Mann was the negotiation of running-rights agreements with other lines that would take their local traffic at reasonable rates to destinations they did not serve. Portage la Prairie offered connections with both the CPR and the Northern Pacific and Manitoba Railway. The CPR, eager to control all western-Canadian transcontinental traffic but not interested in potentially unprofitable branch lines, was willing to make suitable arrangements. The area between Portage la Prairie and Gladstone, Manitoba, however, was served by the Manitoba and North Western Railway which had ambitions to serve the northern prairies. Neither the Manitoba government nor Mackenzie and Mann saw any reason to parallel Manitoba and North Western mileage, but that railway's directors were most reluctant to do anything to assist an aggressive new line in the area. A good running-rights arrangement, whereby the Lake Manitoba Railway and Canal Company would use Manitoba and North Western track from Gladstone to Portage la Prairie, was difficult to negotiate.

40 The average investment per mile of railway in Canada in 1895 stood at $55,000. It must be noted, however, that construction costs on the prairies were lower than in other parts of Canada. The Lake Manitoba Railway and Canal Company, moreover, would build to branch-line rather than main-line standards. The $55,000 also represented some watered stock.

Clifford Sifton took a direct interest in these negotiations. Only the threat of direct provincial assistance for a parallel line from Gladstone to Portage la Prairie finally brought the Allans to terms. With this agreement, the initiative for railway development on the northern prairies passed from the Manitoba and North Western to the Lake Manitoba Railway and Canal Company.

For a time the negotiations with the Allans went very badly. Mackenzie and Mann disagreed between themselves, and Manitoba counsel Walter Barwick complained of "a good deal of want of reason". At this critical juncture Mackenzie and Mann sought the counsel of Zebulon A. Lash, KC. Lash was a Newfoundlander who had done well in Ontario. He was called to the bar in Ontario in 1868, and became Deputy Minister of Justice in Ottawa in 1872. He particularly impressed Edward Blake, the brilliant but somewhat erratic Liberal Minister of Justice. Blake left federal politics in 1876 and shortly thereafter Lash joined him in a Toronto legal practice. He quickly became a recognized authority on commercial law, and by all accounts was a man of uncommon ability. He took particular interest in legal matters that involved original work where no precedent was available. The negotiations with the Manitoba and North Western certainly involved a good deal of difficult and original work. Lash soon demonstrated a tough flexibility that secured the major objectives sought by Mackenzie and Mann but offered sufficient concessions to sugar-coat the bitter pill he was administering to the Allans.[41] It was the beginning of a long and fruitful business relationship between lawyer and promoters.

In the years after 1895 Mackenzie and Mann accomplished many new and unusual feats. The legal talents of Zebulon A. Lash were an indispensable ingredient of their success. He guided them safely past many unknown and dangerous legal shoals. The extensive legal papers of the Canadian Northern Railway are a model of clarity and order, although many agreements were far more precise in stating the claims and rights of Mackenzie and Mann than those of the other parties. A fellow officer of the Canadian Northern was unstinting in his praise of

41 PAC, Sifton Papers, III, extensive correspondence between Barwick and Sifton in 1896.

Lash. "So exquisite was his appreciation of word values, that although others might embody an intention in a series of paragraphs apparently beyond criticism, his mastery of precision and shade was such that he could clothe it in language which had the exactitude of a multiplication table and the clarity of a mirror."[42] In 1902 Lash joined Mackenzie and Mann as their chief solicitor and continued in that capacity until the line was nationalized. He then became Senior Counsel of the Canadian National Railways. Like the railway promoters he served, Lash had an excellent knowledge of the natural resources of Canada and an unbounded faith in the future of the country.[43]

During the negotiations Mackenzie and Mann also became well acquainted with, and soon lured to their project, a man who was described as "the principal asset of the Manitoba and North Western". He was an unusually capable accountant and superintendent by the name of David Blythe Hanna. Hanna was a Scotsman who had come to Canada in 1882 and had held junior positions with several Canadian and American railways before joining the Allans. He had done an excellent job in a difficult situation with the Manitoba and North Western. To supplement his earnings in those difficult years he often undertook odd jobs in the evenings, among them the auditing of the books of the Winnipeg Electric Railway Company in which Donald Mann and associates held controlling interests. Hanna was one of the first to see that the future of the northern prairies lay with the Lake Manitoba Railway and Canal Company, not with the moribund Manitoba and North Western. A few months after the Lake Manitoba Railway and Canal Company opened for business he joined the new venture as superintendent. He quickly became as important in the operational side of the venture as Lash was in the legal department. He served the Canadian Northern for many years as its third vice-president and even in its darkest hour was always proud to refer to himself as "Exhibit A of that Company". He became president of the Canadian Northern Railway when the government nationalized it.[44] The abilities of Hanna and Lash, and of the other principal employees of the Canadian Northern, made possible the company's success in the early 1900s.

42 Hanna, 172.
43 *Canadian National Railways*

Magazine, Feb. 1920, 19.
44 Hanna, 132–3; *Arbitration*, 391.

Running rights on the Manitoba and North Western enabled the Lake Manitoba Railway and Canal Company to take its traffic as far as Portage la Prairie. There contact could be made with both the Canadian Pacific and the Northern Pacific systems. Most of the early Lake Manitoba traffic went east on CPR trains. That company did not regard the local prairie lines as competitors, but rather as valuable feeder lines for its own main line. They developed traffic in areas where the CPR was not yet willing to build its own lines. The new lines also imported most of their construction equipment and supplies from the east over the CPR. As the only Canadian through line to eastern Canada, the CPR could control the general railway situation in western Canada, at least for a number of years. The existence of small independent local companies helped to silence criticism of its monopoly position without doing it any serious damage. Moreover, to crush these small independent companies would be politically disastrous. It would both encourage hostile measures and greatly increase pressure on the CPR to build into areas where that company still had very little interest. The CPR found it in its interest to deal leniently, even generously, with the newcomers. Hanna later admitted that in the early years "we were treated with fair consideration. We never had much, if any complaint to make of the CPR in the early days in that regard [division of rates]."[45]

There was also a good personal relationship between some of the senior officers of the CPR and Mackenzie and Mann, the former CPR contractors. In fact, the relationship was so friendly that there were persistent rumours that Mackenzie and Mann were really working for the CPR and would lease or sell their railway to that company as soon as they completed construction.[46] By posing as independent operators, it was alleged, Mackenzie and Mann obtained more government assistance than would have been available for a project directly identified with the CPR.

It was known that Van Horne and Mackenzie were partners or associates in the Toronto Street Railway and in several foreign traction companies. Van Horne was pleased to send his son Benny on a Lake Manitoba Railway and Canal Company survey so that the youngster

45 *Arbitration*, 455, 658–9, 665.
46 PAC, Hays Papers, I, 3–9, Hays to Wilson, 14 April 1902; PAC, Sifton Papers, III, 1137–40, Barwick to Sifton, 22 April 1896.

might gain practical survey experience on a pioneer line.[47] Van Horne and other senior CPR officials also provided Mackenzie and Mann with technical advice on such matters as motive power, rolling stock, rate policies, and other operational matters.[48] In later years Hanna enjoyed telling stories of how his officials were inclined simply to "borrow" CPR rolling stock in the Winnipeg yards without asking anyone's permission. CPR officials were prepared to overlook such irregularities in the early years.[49]

The early financial arrangements made by Mackenzie and Mann further increased fears that they were working in collusion with the CPR. At an organizational meeting, on 29 January 1896, $200,000 of the authorized $800,000 capital stock was subscribed and a call of 10 per cent or $20,000, was paid and deposited in the Canadian Bank of Commerce.[50] With the exception of qualifying shares for five directors, all the shares were subscribed by Mackenzie and Mann. The five, C. E. L. Porteous, James Gunn, J. M. Smith, Frederic Nicholls, and A. J. Sinclair were promptly elected as directors. Mackenzie and Mann became neither directors nor officers of the company. The Canadian Railway Act, in an effort to prevent contractors from exercising undue influence on decisions of railway directors in the letting of construction contracts, disqualified contractors from election to the board of a railway company with which they held contracts. Mackenzie and Mann intended to become the main contractors for their new railway; thus they could not become directors and officers. This difficulty was circumvented in 1902 when Mackenzie and Mann became incorporated as Mackenzie, Mann and Co. Ltd. Thereafter it was the construction company itself which held Canadian Northern contracts, and Mackenzie and Mann themselves were released for election as directors and officers of their railway.[51]

The newly elected directors met on 20 February 1896 to approve a construction contract with Mackenzie and Mann. Under the terms of this contract the contractors were to receive, in payment for their

---

47 PAC, H. W. D. Armstrong, unpublished autobiography, 197.
48 The Porteous Papers contain some interesting letters in which CPR officials offer advice on operational matters to their newest competitors.

49 Hanna, 143.
50 PAC, CNR Records, MCCLXV, 1–4, Meeting of Provisional Directors of the Lake Manitoba Railway and Canal Company, 29 Jan. 1896.
51 Arbitration, 2498–9.

services, both the railway's transportation contract with the federal government and the federal land subsidy. Actual construction expenses were to be met from the sale of provincially guaranteed bonds. The railway's shareholders, of course, approved of the contract without dissent since all the shares were owned or controlled by the contractors.[52]

The Manitoba government was not pleased with this arrangement. Under this contract the railway would be separated from its principal assets—the transportation contract, the land subsidy, and the guaranteed bonds. If Mackenzie and Mann followed the example of other unscrupulous railway contractors, they would build a cheap road, pocket healthy construction profits, and simply abandon, lease, or sell the railway itself. The government therefore refused to assent to this scheme, insisting that Mackenzie and Mann must become more directly and personally committed not only to the construction but to the successful operation of the railway.

The construction contract approved by the directors on 20 February and signed on 9 April was therefore cancelled on 7 May and a new contract, acceptable to the Manitoba government, was approved. The difference between the two contracts was that under the new arrangement the land grant would remain the property of the railway, although bonds against the security of this grant could be issued and used to pay construction costs. Instead of getting the lands, the contractors would now be entitled to receive, fully paid up, the entire capital stock of the railway.[53] Thus they were to receive the proceeds from the sale of government-guaranteed and/or land-grant bonds for actual construction expenditures upon the presentation of proper receipts or vouchers, and the transportation contract and the entire capital stock of the company in lieu of contractors' fees, commissions, and profits.

The Lake Manitoba Railway and Canal Company had an authorized capitalization of $800,000. This did not mean that the railway or its securities were actually worth $800,000, or that Mackenzie and Mann

---

52 PAC, CNR Records, MCCLXV, 11–18, Meeting of Directors, 20 Feb. 1896, and of Shareholders of the Lake Manitoba Railway and Canal Company, 7 April 1897.
53 Ibid., 20–5, Meetings of Directors of the Lake Manitoba Railway and Canal Company, 12 and 18 May 1896.

earned a real profit of $800,000 when they built the first 125 miles of their railway. Common stock was only worth something if the company that issued it realized profits on its operations, and hence paid dividends. The par or face value of capital stock meant very little in terms of real value on the market. Shares in an unprofitable company might carry a par value in the millions of dollars and yet be totally worthless and unmarketable. Companies issued common stock as an act of hope for the future and a wishful prediction of future earning power. The holders of such stock, in addition to having a say in the operations of the company, enjoyed only one right: that of sharing in future earnings and profits of the company. Ownership of capital stock did not mean and was not taken to mean that the owners had actually made investments equal to the par value of the stock, or that they would necessarily realize that amount on future sales of the stock.

In taking the common stock of the Lake Manitoba Railway and Canal Company as their only reward for contracting services rendered, Mackenzie and Mann committed themselves to the future of the company. Under the terms of the contract of 7 May 1896 both the promoters and the Manitoba government were convinced that the other was committed not only to immediate construction but also to profitable operation of the railway. Only profitable operations would ensure that interest on the guaranteed bonds would be paid without resort to the provincial treasury, and only profitable operations would allow the promoters to realize any financial gain from their association with the railway.

It is very doubtful whether the common stock of the Lake Manitoba Railway and Canal Company, or later of the Canadian Northern Railway, had any real market value at the time it was issued to Mackenzie and Mann, although they have been severely criticized by later historians for not selling more shares. What is quite clear is the fact that Mackenzie and Mann took the common shares as their reward for services rendered to the railway. The true value of that reward lay in the future earning power of the railway, not in the meaningless "par value" of the stock issued.

The immediate construction costs on the Lake Manitoba Railway and Canal Company were financed directly by Mackenzie and Mann. They had confidence in the railway when other promoters and bankers did not. The credit and substantial cash advances that Mackenzie and Mann received from the Canadian Bank of Commerce were granted only after the two promoters had pledged as security their own credit, and with it their sizable assets. In 1896 the Bank had much more confidence in Mackenzie's Toronto assets than in the western branch line he was building. It was Mackenzie and Mann, imbued with the spirit of the prairie frontier, who saw what could be done in the West. The Bank, at least in 1896, had no thought of tying western Canada to the metropolitan influences of Toronto. It was merely providing a financial service for one of its best customers who had decided to venture into a highly dubious undertaking but whose credit the bankers believed to be strong enough to justify the advances.

As the guaranteed bonds of the Lake Manitoba Railway and Canal Company were earned, they went as collateral to the Canadian Bank of Commerce. When the bonds were eventually sold in London, the proceeds from their sale were used to repay bank advances.[54] On a number of occasions in the early years the bankers worried that the bonds would not sell, and they relied heavily on the contractors' personal credit—although in time they feared that even that might prove insufficient as Mackenzie and Mann's western interests and expenses increased. Z. A. Lash later claimed that Mackenzie and Mann had to finance initial construction costs entirely "on their own credit with the securities which they received from the first, namely the bonds, and when these bonds were sold the advances which they got through them were repaid as far as the money went. Whatever came from those securities there certainly were no commission profits."[55] By pledging their personal credit and offering their skills as railway contractors, Mackenzie and Mann made possible the financing and construction of a new prairie branch line in which they and the Manitoba government, unlike many bankers and businessmen, had real confidence.

Actual construction of the line from Gladstone to Dauphin was begun early in 1896, long before all the details of construction contracts and government guarantees were settled. The first construction contract, with its generous terms, was apparently drawn up with a view to

54 PAC, Hays Papers, I, 15–16, Hays to Wilson, 18 Sept. 1902. 55 *Arbitration*, 2502–4.

obtaining large cash advances from the Bank. If construction had been delayed until all negotiations were completed, an entire year would have been lost.[56] When the Manitoba government objected to the original contract the bankers refused further advances.[57] The new arrangement, which would give Mackenzie and Mann the railway's common stock as their reward, did not impress officials of the Canadian Bank of Commerce. Only the new contract and additional securities pledged by Mackenzie and Mann loosened the purse-strings and enabled the contractors to complete the first 100 miles of track before the winter freeze-up of 1896.

In 1896 the significance of this new line was not yet entirely clear. It was the first branch-line construction in western Canada in nearly five years. The renewed activity was certainly encouraging, particularly to the people living alongside the new line. There were still fears that the new line might go the way of the Qu'Appelle, Long Lake and Saskatchewan and the Calgary and Edmonton railways or, worse still, of the Manitoba and North Western. The provincial government was confident, however, that it had ensured that the two promoters would also operate the line, and that they were committed to rather vaguely defined but potentially very important rate reductions. The government itself could have the last word on rates. Here at last was the promise of more branch lines and lower rates, the two things prairie farmers had demanded of the CPR, with no results, for many years.[58]

The northern prairies were at last getting the transportation services essential for their settlement and development. Mackenzie and Mann had found the region that would respond most favourably to their promotional genius. In 1896 Mackenzie's friend Sam Hughes led an expedition which reported enthusiastically that no less than 90 per cent of the lands adjacent to the new railway were suitable for agriculture and would be settled once the railway provided the necessary transportation facilities.[59] The railway was offering transportation services that would open a new region for settlement and development. That settlement and development, in turn, would provide the traffic needed by the railway. If Sam Hughes was right, the development of a new

56 PAC, Porteous Papers, XXV, 335, Porteous to Mackenzie, 19 Nov. 1896.
57 PAC, Sifton Papers, V, 2655,

Greenway to Sifton, 21 April 1896.
58 Arbitration, 398–402.
59 Ibid., 2675.

region and the success of the new railway were both assured. In 1896 the band of believers was still very small: Sam Hughes, Clifford Sifton, Z. A. Lash, D. B. Hanna, and, of course, William Mackenzie and Donald Mann. The band was destined to grow, however, and by 1904 the entire country enthusiastically endorsed not only more branch lines but two more transcontinental railway systems.

CHAPTER THREE

UNCONNECTED PROJECTIONS OF STEEL 1896–1898

BOTH THE TOWN OF DAUPHIN and its railway were new in 1896. The surrounding area, however, was "pretty well built up". The northern prairies were well suited for agriculture and awaited only the arrival of the railway. The Lake Manitoba Railway and Canal Company showed profitable operations from the beginning, although neither the promoters nor their political benefactors had expected this early success.[1] It allowed Mackenzie and Mann to improve and expand their railway at a rapid rate after 1896. Yet they also found time to pursue

1 *Arbitration*, 403–8. The Canadian Northern Railway accounts were kept in accordance with accepted accounting principles of that time. Reporters and business historians have demonstrated repeatedly that these accounting procedures were flexible and accounts were often adjusted in order to produce favourable annual statements. The most important concern of the Canadian Northern accountants and promoters was certainly to show high initial profits and, thereafter, steadily increasing net earnings. There was always much preoccupation with the ratio of total revenues to operating costs. In the interests of a good annual statement, Canadian Northern accountants sometimes "deferred" some maintenance and other incidental costs from a poor year to the next and hopefully more profitable year of operations. Revenues from rentals of equipment and trackage rights might also be shifted forward during pros-

perous times. The Canadian Northern Railway, like other North American railways, kept no depreciation accounts for tracks and right of way, and the depreciation accounts for equipment and buildings were kept at minimum figures. As a result, the Canadian Northern accountants were able, to some extent, to level out the peaks and valleys in the railway's financial affairs and to show fairly steady operating ratios. The figures nevertheless provided information which the Department of Railways and Canals and other accountants regarded as generally reliable. There were no glaring misrepresentations, except possibly the well-known but dubious accounting for depreciation. Discounts on the sale of securities and operational deficits on incomplete lines that were operated for the convenience of local shippers before construction was completed were always charged to construction or capital account, not to operations.

other railway schemes, one in the south and the other in the far north. Only when these failed did they become irrevocably committed to the Canadian Northern Railway.

The first 125 miles of the Lake Manitoba Railway and Canal Company were built under adverse weather conditions. The spring of 1896 was unusually wet in northwestern Manitoba, and as late as 23 June Mann was still complaining that "the slews [sic] are full of water and . . . the grading is going on slowly."[2] One of his surveyors later wrote, "the country for miles [was] covered with water through which we waded knee deep all day and [it was] difficult to find a dry space large enough to pitch camp."[3] Nevertheless, four and half months later, construction was sufficiently advanced to allow the railway to accept its first commercial shipment—one hundred head of cattle sent by Mr. Glen Campbell from Ochre River to Winnipeg.[4] Construction deadlines were met. To accomplish this, local subcontractors reportedly "used their womenfolk to help them and these women I saw for the first and only time carrying earth, sand or gravel in baskets on their heads to make the railway embankment."[5] The railway was ready to begin regularly scheduled service between Dauphin and Gladstone in January 1897.

In the construction camps Donald Mann and Roderick Mackenzie, the eldest son of William Mackenzie, quickly established relatively amicable relations with their construction workers. They were certainly authoritarian and arbitrary at times; troublemakers were fired or heavily fined without hesitation, and law enforcement agencies were called in when serious trouble arose. But despite a rigorous discipline, Rod Mackenzie allegedly "could get anything out of the men". Two early incidents reflect the strict yet sympathetic attitude the promoters extended to their employees.

On the first contract, Swedes, Italians, and Irishmen constituted the work force. Weather conditions were adverse, working conditions were deplorable, and the Italians decided to strike for higher wages. To enforce their demands they laid ties and other obstacles on the track,

2 PAC, Porteous Papers, XXV, 134, Porteous to Mackenzie, 23 June 1896.
3 PAC, H. W. D. Armstrong, unpublished autobiography, 191–7.
4 Manitoba Free Press, 4 Nov. 1896, 8.
5 Armstrong, unpublished autobiography.

UNCONNECTED PROJECTIONS OF STEEL, 1898-1902

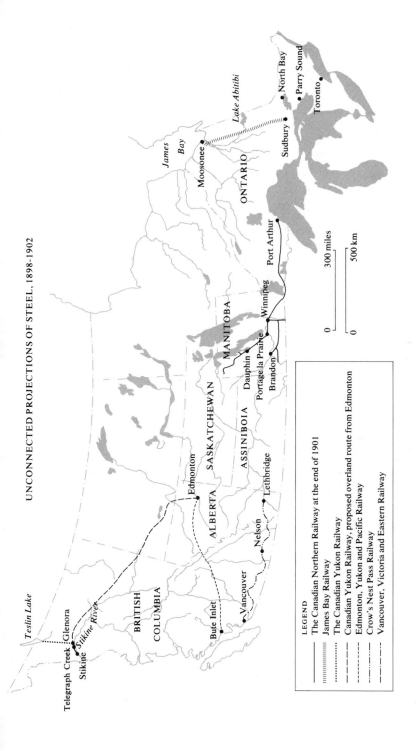

LEGEND
——— The Canadian Northern Railway at the end of 1901
——— James Bay Railway
||||||| The Canadian Yukon Railway
----- Canadian Yukon Railway, proposed overland route from Edmonton
– – – Edmonton, Yukon and Pacific Railway
—·—· Crow's Nest Pass Railway
—··— Vancouver, Victoria and Eastern Railway

Teslin Lake

Telegraph Creek   Glenora
Stikine   Stikine River

BRITISH
COLUMBIA

Bute Inlet

Vancouver

Nelson

Lethbridge

Edmonton

ALBERTA

SASKATCHEWAN

ASSINIBOIA

MANITOBA

Dauphin
Portage la Prairie
Brandon

Winnipeg

Port Arthur

Moosonee

James Bay

ONTARIO

Lake Abitibi

Sudbury

North Bay

Parry Sound

Toronto

0   300 miles
0   500 km

greatly infuriating the management, which sent the Irish and Swedish workers to round up the dissident Italians. Outnumbered and intimidated, the Italians gave way, and the lone police constable from Gladstone was called to take the dissident leaders into town. Lacking handcuffs or ropes to tie the men up, the constable used two-inch cables which the railway company used as stay ropes on its decker cars. The men were taken into Gladstone and fined. Discipline had been re-established and construction proceeded on schedule.

Such arbitrary treatment, however, was often tempered by a sympathetic and humanitarian concern for unfortunate employees. On the same Gladstone to Dauphin line where the Italian difficulty arose, a fireman by the name of George Messenger was seriously injured when he fell under an engine. Roderick Mackenzie immediately began to take up a collection for Messenger, promising to put up twice any amount that might be collected from the men. Five hundred dollars was collected and Mackenzie put in $1,000. Messenger recovered from his injury and eventually returned to his job on the railway.

Mackenzie and Mann had come from humble backgrounds themselves. Practical experience had given them an understanding of the working man which few other promoters could match.[6] Incentives such as special bonuses or holidays were often given to the men when an important line was completed or after some new construction record was set. A disciplined *esprit de corps* was soon established, and many of the Canadian Northern employees became intensely loyal to the company and its management. Even at the time of Mackenzie's death in 1923 a Toronto union leader said of him, "I found him [Mackenzie] very sympathetic and I don't think that there was any other man with the same interests as sympathetic to labour as he was."[7]

Mackenzie, Mann and Co. Ltd. served as the railway's main contractor, but usually did only the tracklaying. Much of the heaviest construction work, particularly in later years, was contracted out. Tracklayers, by the nature of their work, had more contact with the outside world and often enjoyed more of the amenities of civilization than their compatriots who worked in isolated advance camps clearing bush, grubbing stumps, making heavy rock cuts, or moving dirt and

6 CNRHQ, Osborne Scott and George Bemister interviews.

7 *Canadian Railway and Marine World*, Jan. 1924, 31.

rock onto the embankments or into fills on the future railway. American, Swedish, and Irish workers tended to constitute the main groups in the tracklaying gangs. Poorly paid immigrants from southern and eastern Europe were most frequently to be found in the heavier construction work. The Galician women, carrying earth-filled baskets on their heads to build the railway embankments, were one unfortunate example. Similarly, in 1898, a Doukhobor subcontractor seriously exploited his kinsfolk while working on the Gilbert Plains extension. Allegedly he mixed some inferior coarse-ground grain with dried grass and fed his men bread baked from this vile mixture; and he provided drinking water taken directly from the contaminated swamps near by. The men were then required to do extremely heavy work on the swampy ground because the subcontractor failed to provide enough horses. It is clear that in heavy construction work, whether it was done by Mackenzie, Mann and Co. Ltd. or by subcontractors, workers often laboured very hard for low wages, under highly unsatisfactory conditions.[8]

To Mackenzie and Mann, however, the immigrant was far more important as a prospective settler than as a cheap labourer, although special efforts were sometimes made to find railway work for local settlers who needed funds to start farming. The Barr colonists at Lloydminster, for example, were given some work of this kind. On occasion Mackenzie and Mann, or their railway's officers, acted as intermediaries between the new immigrants and hostile Anglo-Saxon settlers. They agreed with Clifford Sifton that "a stalwart peasant in a sheepskin coat, born on the soil, whose forefathers have been farmers for ten generations, with a stout wife and a half-dozen children, is good quality."[9] They wanted that peasant settled and prospering on his own homestead, shipping his freight over their railway lines. His services as a cheap construction labourer were of secondary importance.

The standard of construction on the new Lake Manitoba Railway in 1896 was not very high, although all work met and sometimes exceeded specifications. Rails weighing only fifty-six pounds per yard were used. The apron on the roadbed was narrow and poorly ballasted.

8 CNRHQ, Osborne Scott and George Bemister interviews.

9 J. W. Dafoe, *Clifford Sifton in Relation to His Times* (Toronto: Macmillan, 1931), 142; Hanna, 137–9.

It was built to the standards normally required for branch or local service lines. As such it could handle the traffic immediately available and passed federal inspection shortly before Christmas without difficulty. The rolling stock was also less than fully adequate. Only a minimum of new stock was purchased, the remainder coming from wealthier roads willing to sell old or obsolete equipment.[10] Additional rolling stock was purchased only as the traffic increased and proceeds from bond sales made more money available.

The redeeming feature of the operation was that the new railway provided comparatively inexpensive local service which had not been available earlier, or had been offered only at prohibitively high rates. Cheapness, not speed, was the essence of the early service on the road, and this was appreciated in an area where high freight rates had been the subject of chronic complaints. Low financing costs (thanks to the government guarantee), low construction costs, favourable rate agreements with other roads, and various operational economies made low rates possible. These soon earned the new railway a reputation as "the farmers' friend".[11]

Operations on the Mackenzie and Mann lines during the early years were always something of an adventure. Old engines could die almost anywhere as rusted boiler pipes sprang unexpected leaks and extinguished the fire. Traffic was of the utmost importance and was obtained wherever and whenever it presented itself. The Lake Manitoba Railway had as many unscheduled stops as it had scheduled ones. Superintendent Hanna later wrote, "Over most of the route, where settlement was beginning, we put down and took up passengers and way freight to suit our patrons' pleasure."[12]

Management was not averse to generating its own traffic, especially if it would also help the farmers. This led to a variety of economic ventures not directly associated with the railway. The first instance of this kind of initiative was the selling of seed grain to farmers in the Dauphin area. Hanna was responsible, and later described the venture.

These settlers had gone in years before unable to get seed of a proper kind to carry on their business; I at my own expense in the spring of 1897 pur-

10 *Arbitration*, 407, 1696–1723. 12 Hanna, 134–5, 208–9.
11 Stevens, 26, 32.

chased 3,000 bushels of seed wheat, had it properly cleaned, put in sacks, and shipped to Dauphin. It was not a philanthropic act, because I collected from the farmers the price of that wheat. But that gave them for the first time an opportunity of growing grain from the best kind of seed. Now what we have done there has been repeated in so many other enterprises that it would take a whole day to tell the whole story in that respect.[13]

These activities were generally undertaken where farmers simply lacked certain commodities, or where local merchants, often associated with the CPR, were charging unreasonably high prices. The first objective was always to create or capture freight traffic, but in the process the railway became the farmers' friend and ally against middlemen and monopolists, notably the elevator and grain interests that had become closely associated with the CPR. That company had tended to ally itself with these middlemen, its best customers; when Mackenzie and Mann arrived they broke the local monopolies these men often enjoyed. Actions such as Hanna's purchase and resale of seed grain generally led to sharply reduced prices and earned the new road a good deal of hostility from established businesses. The settlers, of course, were impressed and pleased when reductions in retail prices accompanied the arrival of a Mackenzie and Mann road. For the railway it was a most effective way to build up traffic, good will, and political support.

To earn a profit despite the low rates, it was necessary to take great care to ensure that non-essential expenses were kept to a minimum. On one occasion a Lake Manitoba Railway train hit a cow and broke its legs. The indignant owner demanded immediate compensation, and the superintendent, who was on board, managed to settle at a reasonable price. Then he turned the matter over to his brakeman, who had once been a butcher. While the train waited and the passengers looked on, the cow was properly butchered and the meat was later sold to one of the railway's construction contractors. A potential loss had thus been turned into a small profit.[14]

Careful and imaginative management allowed the railway to earn $70,119.28 during its first year of operations. After paying all operating costs and fixed charges, a net profit of $5,560.98 remained. Neither

13 *Arbitration*, 404.   14 Hanna, 145.

the promoters nor the Manitoba government had expected the railway to earn enough in the first years of operation even to meet all its fixed charges. The government had in fact indicated a willingness to meet interest payments on the guaranteed bonds for four years without imposing any penalty on the railway.[15] This assistance was not necessary, and the railway continued to operate profitably until wartime disasters overtook it. All profits were immediately turned back into further development and improvement of the line.

The success of the first year of operations was impressive, and Mackenzie and Mann had little difficulty in persuading the Manitoba government to offer further guarantees so the line could be extended northward and westward. The mileage as far as Sifton Junction, sixteen miles north of Dauphin, was completed and opened for service in 1897. An additional twenty-one miles, to Winnipegosis on the shores of the lake of the same name, were also completed in 1897.

Dauphin was something of a cross-roads for Mackenzie and Mann. They could revive the old Lake Manitoba Railway and Canal scheme of a northern "water stretches" policy, in which transport by water on the northern lakes and rivers would merely be supplemented by essential rail connections. This plan was rejected at an early date, however, and the mileage to Winnipegosis was built to earn the land subsidy and to serve that settlement and capture its traffic. There were no plans to place steamships on the lakes.[16]

Mackenzie and Mann hoped to build northward eventually, in order to earn the full transportation contract and the appropriate land-grant subsidy of the Hudson Bay Railway. Local traffic north of Dauphin, however, was sparse, and there were delays. Traffic, particularly in the fertile Gilbert Plains area, tended to pull the railway westward towards Prince Albert, the acknowledged objective of the Lake Manitoba Railway and Canal Company charter. A westward extension from Dauphin into the Gilbert Plains district was clearly the most promising and logical course of action in 1897. Mackenzie and Mann had exhausted

15 During the negotiations Mackenzie asked the government to pay interest without penalty for a maximum of fifteen years. "It is, of course, perfectly plain," he allegedly said, "that the Company will not be able to pay its interest for several years." PAC, Sifton Papers, III, 1127, Barwick to Sifton, 3 March 1896.

16 *Arbitration*, 408–12.

TABLE I

Operating Statistics of the Lake Manitoba Railway and Canal Company

Year ending	Mileage operated*	Gross earnings	Operating costs	Net earnings	Fixed charges	Surplus
		($)	($)	($)	($)	($)
31/12/1897	101	70,119.28	39,059.30	31,060.98	26,500.00	5,560.98
31/12/1898	161	106,698.72	54,594.40	52,104.32	40,000.00	12,104.32
31/12/1899	290	161,534.63	81,870.06	79,664.57	67,034.83	12,629.74

*Includes operating results of the Manitoba and South Eastern Railway.

Source: Arbitration, evidence presented by D. B. Hanna.

their credit with the bank, however. The guaranteed bonds earned in 1896 and 1897 had to be sold, and the indebtedness to the bank reduced, before major new construction could be undertaken.[17] This task took up much of William Mackenzie's time in 1897 and 1898.

At the same time the two promoters became involved in several projects far removed from their railway in northwestern Manitoba. The first of these was a projected line through southern British Columbia to serve the mining developments in the Kootenays.

When the CPR built its transcontinental railway it abandoned the more northerly route through the Yellowhead Pass recommended by Sir Sandford Fleming. It did so in order to prevent incursions by American roads into southern areas. This strategy had not been altogether successful, even with the help of the monopoly clause. Manitoba successfully brought the Northern Pacific into the province and at Vancouver both that company and the Great Northern threatened the position of the CPR. When the mining developments of southern British Columbia opened the Kootenay region in the early 1890s, J. J. Hill began to push Great Northern branch lines into these southern British Columbia communities. The CPR, the federal government, the British Columbia government, and the city of Vancouver were all eager to prevent such a diversion of Canadian traffic to American railways and American ports. Construction of a government-assisted line through the Crow's Nest Pass was the logical course of action.

Several alternatives were considered. One of the most frequently mentioned, especially in the monopoly-conscious West, was the incorporation of a new company which would obtain substantial government subsidies, build the line, and either operate it itself or lease it, under favourable government-approved terms, to the CPR. Mackenzie and Mann eagerly sought to secure the line with the prospective government assistance for themselves or for a partnership in which they would be associated with Senator George Cox and with others who later promoted the Grand Trunk Pacific Railway project.[18]

The CPR was not altogether opposed to the idea of having an inde-

17 PAC, Porteous Papers, IV, Mackenzie to Porteous, 7 Nov. 1896; Hays Papers, I, 15–16, Hays to Wilson, 18 Sept. 1902; Sifton Papers, XVII, 10719–21, T. O. Davis to Sifton, 2 April 1897.
18 PAC, Porteous Papers, XIX, 232–3, Porteous to Ross, 20 March 1897.

pendent company build the Crow's Nest Pass Railway, provided the traffic from this railway would find its way onto the CPR main line at Medicine Hat. The federal government, however, was unwilling to offer substantial subsidies unless firm freight-rate concessions to the Lakehead were promised. An independent company with a line from Lethbridge to Nelson could not promise such reductions unless the CPR rates east of Lethbridge were also reduced. The only way to get rate concessions that would be effective to the Lakehead was to get a definite commitment from the CPR itself. This could best be done by giving the entire project to the CPR, and a suitable agreement with that company was eventually signed.

The Crow's Nest Pass Agreement was the federal response to the danger that the resources and traffic of the Kootenays might be lost to Canada. It was by no means the only response. When the terms were announced there was a great deal of criticism in British Columbia because the agreement did nothing to connect the Kootenay region with the coastal cities of the province. To meet this requirement the provincial government sponsored a measure of its own. Under the terms of a provincial Loan Act, $2,500,000 was to be made available to subsidize several railway projects, including one from Vancouver and Victoria to the Kootenays. The main contender for the subsidy to build from the Pacific coast eastward was the Vancouver, Victoria and Eastern Railway. Local Vancouver and Victoria businessmen incorporated this road, but Mackenzie and Mann took a keen interest in it from the beginning. A tentative agreement between the provincial government, the local promoters, and Mackenzie and Mann for the construction of the new railway was signed on 15 June 1898. It was agreed that in return for building the road Mackenzie and Mann were to receive a majority of the capital stock. The provincial government offered a subsidy of $4,000 per mile on the understanding that construction was conditional on the granting of further federal aid.[19]

The federal government refused to grant the needed assistance in

19 Patricia Roy, "Railways, Politicians, and the Development of Vancouver as a Metropolitan Centre, 1886–1929", unpublished MA thesis, University of Toronto, 1963; PAC, CNR Legal File 1007–20–1, W. S. Deacon to W. H. Moore, 28 Feb. 1902; PAC, Laurier Papers, LXVII, 21079, G. L. Milne to Laurier, 28 Feb. 1898.

1898. The provincial administration with whom the agreement had been signed was defeated several weeks later. The new premier, Charles Semlin, decided to invalidate all inactive railway legislation passed by his predecessor. Semlin argued that the failure to secure federal aid nullified the provincial agreement with the Vancouver, Victoria and Eastern Railway, and all work on the railway was stopped shortly after he became premier.

Mackenzie and Mann hoped to gain control of both the Crow's Nest Pass Railway and the Vancouver, Victoria and Eastern Railway, and to negotiate generous subsidy agreements for both roads. These two projects were interrelated parts of a larger scheme to build an alternative main line across southern British Columbia. The federal government, however, was reluctant to assist the scheme because no firm rate reductions on east-west trade could be obtained from Mackenzie and Mann, since they had no eastern connections. Equally important was the fact that the Laurier government had decided to review the entire railway policy when it came into office,[20] and it was reluctant to deal with Mackenzie and Mann until this review was complete. The Crow's Nest Pass Agreement was an *ad hoc* measure designed to meet an immediate problem. Mackenzie and Mann would have to wait until the government had completed its review of the railway situation and had formulated a new national railway policy.

Mackenzie and Mann were disappointed when the federal government failed to support their southern British Columbia schemes. At one point their financial agent was convinced "that Mr. Mackenzie and Mr. Mann are to get the Crow's Nest contract. The government have brought their proposal down to the House and the Canadian Pacific and Mr. Mackenzie and Mr. Mann have some sort of an understanding."[21] The proposals introduced in the House, however, had nothing for Mackenzie and Mann. Porteous blamed the CPR and called the agreement "the turn down of the Crow's Nest". He said Mann urged him "to keep away from Van Horne".[22] Certainly the federal government's decision to give the Crow's Nest Pass subsidy directly to the

20 PAC, Laurier Papers, LXXXI, 22032–3, Sifton to Laurier, 26 March 1898.

21 PAC, Porteous Papers, XXVI, 102, Porteous to Ross, 15 June 1897.
22 *Ibid.*, 119, Porteous to Mackenzie, 29 June 1897.

CPR ended Mackenzie and Mann's prospects of playing a major role in the railway development of southern British Columbia. They allowed control of the Vancouver, Victoria and Eastern to fall into the hands of J. J. Hill of the Great Northern Railway while they sought quick success in another unusual scheme, this time in the far north.

In September of 1897 gold was discovered in the remote wilds of the Yukon Territory. Large numbers of miners, prospectors, and speculators rushed into the area. This avalanche created two immediate problems for the Canadian government. First, there was the difficulty of effectively maintaining law and order in the area. Second, and equally important, was the government's concern over control of the trade and commerce of the area. Both these concerns were urgent because of the presence of numerous and often unruly Americans who might seek to establish an American-style provisional government. The boundary between British and American territory was only vaguely defined, thus permitting some pretence of legality should the Americans decide to establish their own government. The main access routes into the Yukon Territory, moreover, were from the Pacific, where American territorial claims might be used to cut off Canadian contact with the goldfields. While the goldfields themselves were certainly in Canadian territory, a breakdown of law and order or the disruption of Canadian commercial connections might easily lead to situations not dissimilar from those which had developed several decades earlier in the Oregon country or in the Mexican possessions. American immigrants there had established their own governments without reference to the niceties of international laws or agreements, and in due course all these territories were added as states of the Union.

To counteract the threat of unilateral American action the Canadian government immediately began negotiations to define the boundary. They also sent two divisions of the experienced North West Mounted Police into the area and passed a series of measures to regulate the gold-mining activities, particularly claim disputes, in the area. In addition, the Canadian government offered to assist in the construction of an all-Canadian trade and supply route to the Yukon.

Two main Canadian supply routes to the Yukon seemed feasible. The first was from Vancouver by steamer to some Canadian debarkation point. From there, overland transportation would be required as far as the head of inland navigation on Teslin Lake. Steamers could then move the goods across Teslin Lake and on to the goldfields. A second and much more expensive alternative was to build an overland rail route from Edmonton.

The Canadian government chose the first alternative. The details of the government's plan to secure the Yukon trade for Canada were worked out late in 1897 and in early 1898.[23] Sifton, the minister responsible for the administration of the Yukon, took a leading part in the formulation of government policy, although the legislation was later introduced in Parliament by A. G. Blair, the Minister of Railways and Canals. In January 1898 the government's proposals were made public. They provided for steamboat navigation to the head of navigation on the Stikeen River, either at Glenora or at Telegraph Creek, and for the immediate construction of a wagon road, and within a year a railway, from one of these points to Galbraith's post on Teslin Lake. From here there was uninterrupted navigation to Dawson. The proposed wagon road and railway were to be about 130 miles in length. Since events were moving very rapidly in the goldfields, speed was of the utmost importance. The wagon road was to be completed in six weeks, and the railway was to be built and in operation within seven months. The deadline for completing the railway was 1 September 1898. A suitable railway charter for this new Canadian Yukon Railway had already been obtained, with both Mackenzie and Mann and the CPR taking an interest, although the CPR later turned the project over entirely to Mackenzie and Mann.

A contract was immediately let, without tender. The successful contractors were William Mackenzie and Donald Mann who, by their assurances and past performance, convinced the government that they could do the work within the short time allowed. Blair later stated they were the only contractors known to the government who could be relied upon to work at that pace. The contract provided a 25,000-acre-per-mile land-grant subsidy as well as a measure of government control over rates to be charged on the line. The contractors paid a $250,000 deposit as evidence of good faith and immediately began

23 PAC, Sifton Papers, CCIII, 940, Sifton to Mackenzie, 18 Dec. 1897.

work on the wagon road. The contract was then referred to Parliament for ratification.

In Parliament serious opposition developed to the entire scheme. It was argued that Canada could not be assured of unimpeded shipping to Glenora, the southern terminus of the wagon road and railway. The whole scheme would be entirely futile if shipping to Glenora were obstructed by the Americans. Some members, including Frank Oliver from Edmonton, apparently with the support of the CPR, were convinced that the only true all-Canadian route via Edmonton should be used.[24] Others found the terms of the contract far too generous to the contractors. They denounced the large land grant as "acres of goldfields" and regretted that, after refusing for five years to make land grants to new railways, the federal government had now taken such a retrograde step. It was also argued that the contract had been written by solicitor Lash in such a way that Mackenzie and Mann were not committed to operate the railway after it was built. They might, therefore, build it for the sake of the subsidy and, if operations proved unprofitable, leave it to the government to run. The tricks and schemes of railway promoters who had construction profits rather than the welfare of their railway in mind were recounted with considerable venom.

The criticisms of the contract cut across party lines. Some of its most outspoken and persistent opponents were eastern Liberals whose own constituencies were well supplied with railways and who had learned to denounce all governmental aid to new railways during their long years as Members of the Opposition in Parliament when the Conservatives were promoting western railway schemes. The Conservatives clearly sensed the division in Liberal ranks and in public opinion, and decided to make the most of it. Liberal party discipline was sufficiently strong to carry the measure in the House of Commons, but the Conservatives enjoyed a strong majority in the Senate, reflecting their long tenure of office prior to 1896 when only Conservatives had been appointed to the upper chamber. The Conservatives decided to use their

24 PAC, Porteous Papers, XX, 5–6, 12, Porteous to James Ross, 17 Feb. and 8 March 1898; PAC, Sifton Papers, XL, 26644–5, Isaac Campbell to Sifton, 18 Feb. 1898.

Senate majority and on 30 March 1898 the government bill was defeated in the Senate by a vote of 52 to 14.[25] For a time there were suggestions that the government might call an election on the issue of Senate "reform". The Liberals, however, were too divided to make the Yukon Railway bill an election matter. "The Council," according to Porteous, "stood equally divided for and against, the decision remaining with Laurier, who funked."[26]

The division within the Liberal ranks on this issue is of considerable interest, since the entire history of the Canadian Northern Railway was in large part the product of continuing divisions in Laurier's Cabinet. With the exception of the proponents of the Edmonton route, western politicians were inclined to support the scheme. Sifton was the bill's most outspoken supporter. The opposition came primarily from Ontario and Quebec. Charles Fitzpatrick of Quebec took a leading part in opposing the measure in Cabinet, thereby increasing and accentuating the enmity between himself and Clifford Sifton. The remnants of the Ontario Clear Grits were inclined to see evil and corruption in all railway subsidies. This scheme, furthermore, offered nothing in the way of patronage or other political advantages to Ontario and Quebec.[27]

The Maritime members seemed generally willing to accept the scheme, although with some reservations. The position of the Minister of Railways and Canals, A. G. Blair from Saint John, is of particular interest in this case and in later Canadian Northern ventures. Porteous accused Blair of "treachery", and of being instrumental in defeating the scheme.[28] The tone of Blair's correspondence, however, suggests support for the measure throughout. "I am satisfied," he wrote to Sifton, "we would do ourselves a very great deal of credit if we take

25 Canada, *House of Commons Debates, 1898*, 217; Journals of the Senate, 1898, 102–3, and Appendix No. 5, being reports of a Special Committee on Opening Up Direct Communication Between the Railway Systems of Canada and the Navigable Waters of the Yukon; PAC, Laurier Papers, LXIX, 21457–60, Charles Fitzpatrick to Laurier, 12 March 1898.

26 PAC, Porteous Papers, XX, 133–4, Porteous to Ross, 27 May 1898.
27 PAC, Sifton Papers, XL, 26644–6, Isaac Campbell to Sifton, 18 Feb. 1898; PAC, Porteous Papers, XX, 133, Porteous to Ross, 27 May 1898; PAC, Laurier Papers, LXIX, 21457–60, Charles Fitzpatrick to Laurier, 12 March 1898.
28 PAC, Porteous Papers, XX, 50–1, Porteous to Ross, 1 April 1898.

this thing [wagon road into the Yukon] up vigorously."[29] A careful reading of Blair's introduction of the bill in the Commons hardly justifies the charge of treachery, although the occasion certainly lacked brilliance. It has been asserted, however, that Blair had unscrupulous and avaricious friends in New Brunswick and Montreal, and that various railway schemes prospered or suffered accordingly. These friends are not directly identified in the secondary sources in which the charges are made. Newspaper accounts of the day, however, indicate they were Mackenzie and Mann, William Pugsley of Saint John, and J. N. Greenshields and David Russell of Montreal and Saint John. In 1897 the latter three already had interests in several western railways and might, therefore, have favoured the Edmonton route.[30] In fact the Railways and Canals department drew maps to show that the Yukon Railway might eventually become a part of a larger overland railway from Edmonton. There is no firm evidence or even strong circumstantial evidence that Blair, with or without the urging of his friends, turned against the Yukon scheme.

In the House of Commons the Yukon Railway bill was passed on a straight party vote. Liberal divisions in this case are only important in that they prevented a direct appeal to the electorate on the issue. After the Senate defeat, Sifton immediately began negotiations for an alternative contract with Mackenzie and Mann, but this never passed the Liberal caucus. Porteous summed up the situation when he wrote, "Sifton is determined to drive the contract through in some shape but the rank and file of the party are unmistakably lukewarm."[31]

British Columbia, which had most to fear from the Edmonton route, decided to sponsor a bill of its own for the construction of a railway to the Yukon. The British Columbia government also looked to Mackenzie and Mann, but the victory of Charles Semlin in the 1898 elections and the refusal of the federal government to offer any assistance ruined the provincial scheme.

The defeat of the Yukon Railway scheme was felt very keenly by Mackenzie and Mann: they had committed themselves heavily to it. The $250,000 deposit seriously strained their private resources. In

29 PAC, Sifton Papers, XII, 7535–6, Blair to Sifton, 24 July 1898.
30 Skelton, Laurier, 190–1.

31 PAC, Porteous Papers, XX, 50–1, Porteous to Ross, 1 April 1898.

addition, they had done extensive work on the wagon road before the bill was defeated in the Senate. The defeat of the government bill cast considerable doubt on their ability to collect for expenditures already incurred. The Canadian Bank of Commerce, which had advanced the contractors the necessary funds, became increasingly apprehensive about granting any further credits or advances for any and all Mackenzie and Mann projects. It was years, in fact, before the contractors obtained full compensation from the government. The deposit was returned four years later, but other claims were not settled until 1920.[32]

Mackenzie evidently thought the defeat extremely serious. Porteous described its effects on the contractor: "His face was ghastly, a grey-greenish colour pulled out of shape, with the veins standing out like knotted string. He complained of pains in the head. I could see he had lost his grip. They tell me he looked worse in Ottawa."[33] The railway schemes in southern British Columbia and the Yukon had undermined the promoter's financial stability and had cast serious doubts on his political influence in Ottawa. In 1897 and 1898 he seemed unable to achieve any of his objectives in the capital.

In the end the Yukon Railway defeat was not as disastrous as Mackenzie had feared. He might have suffered much more if the bill had passed and the railway in the far north had been completed, since traffic to the Yukon soon dropped sharply. Moreover, the affair had at least one positive result. The defeat left the contractors with a large unsatisfied claim against the government at a time when the politicians were eager to forget the whole thing. This provided valuable political leverage of the kind Mackenzie and Mann could use most adroitly.

The defeat in Ottawa and a few months later in British Columbia apparently persuaded Mackenzie and Mann that the scheme was indeed faulty and that the Edmonton route had become more promising. Thus, in August 1898, they purchased control of an Edmonton-based railway, the Edmonton District Railway Company.[34] Both William Pugsley and A. G. Blair had early associations with this railway, which carried

32 PAC, Meighen Papers, Series 2, File 247, 32954–33016. Contract, Orders in Council, and Court Statements and evidence regarding claims by Mackenzie and Mann in connection with their Yukon contract, 1901–21.

33 PAC, Porteous Papers, xx, 50–1, Porteous to Ross, 1 April 1898.
34 PAC, CNR Records, MCCXI, Meetings of Shareholders and Directors of the Edmonton, Yukon and Pacific Railway, 25 Aug. 1898.

charter rights to build northward. These rights were greatly expanded and the name of the railway changed to the Edmonton, Yukon and Pacific Railway in 1899. Mackenzie and Mann then had charter rights to build from Edmonton to the Yukon and also from Edmonton through the Yellowhead Pass to a southern or central British Columbia coastal port. In 1902 the British Columbia government, now led by Premier Dunsmuir, approved a provincial subsidy agreement under which the Edmonton, Yukon and Pacific was to build to Bute Inlet. Again construction was dependent on additional federal aid, which was not forthcoming. As a result very little was done. Mackenzie and Mann had, however, obtained charter rights and were in an excellent position to negotiate if and when a railway to the Pacific coast or to the Yukon should ever be demanded.

Mackenzie and Mann's 1897 and 1898 interests in the far west and north were matched by similar seemingly disconnected projects in Ontario. As early as 1895 the two men, together with other Toronto promoters, sought incorporation for a railway from Parry Sound to James Bay. In 1897 the James Bay Railway Company charter was amended to empower the promoters also to build from Parry Sound to Toronto, and in 1898 the Ontario government was persuaded to grant the promoters a $4,000-per-mile cash subsidy to build the section from Parry Sound to Sudbury, a distance of about ninety miles. The following year this subsidy was extended and $2,000 per mile in cash and 5,000 acres per mile in land were provided for that part of the line from Sudbury to Lake Abitibi, a distance of 175 miles. None of this, however, led to any new construction before 1902. The difficulty again was the failure of the promoters to obtain expected additional federal assistance.

At the same time that Mackenzie and Mann were seeking aid for the railway to James Bay, they also began negotiations for provincial and federal assistance on another Ontario railway: the Ontario and Rainy River Railway in western Ontario. This railway was chartered in 1886 to build through the fertile Rainy River and Fort Frances areas which still lacked rail facilities. Between Fort Frances and Port Arthur it passed through areas with promising mineral and timber resources. Its early promoters, like so many others, were unable to obtain sufficient funds to begin construction. In May 1897, however, the Ontario and Rainy River Railway signed a construction contract with Mackenzie and Mann. Twelve days later they formally took over complete control of the railway, which had moderate subsidies from both provincial and federal governments.[35] The former owners allegedly sold their interest at a fairly high price. Construction was begun immediately, but negotiations for further government assistance were also continued.[36]

In 1897 and 1898 Mackenzie and Mann were obviously charter- or perhaps contract-hungry. It is doubtful whether they themselves knew how all these various projects might be operated or combined in any sensible fashion. They did, however, take one major step in integrating several of their lines when they gained control of a local charter in southeastern Manitoba in 1898. This was the Manitoba and South Eastern Railway which had charter rights to build from Winnipeg southeasterly towards Lake of the Woods. This railway, like many others, had been incorporated by interests not directly associated with Mackenzie and Mann. It carried a 6,400-acre-per-mile land grant, but the original promoters were unable to find the necessary capital to begin construction. In 1897 the charter was about to lapse unless a new time extension could be negotiated. The government was unwilling to grant the extension without definite assurances of early construction.[37] The Manitoba and South Eastern, therefore, negotiated a construction contract with Mackenzie and Mann, and the contract was signed on 11 February 1898. The time extension was granted, the subsidy protected, and three months later Mackenzie and Mann received the company's capital stock in return for their construction services.[38] The first forty-five miles were completed the same year and operated on the same basis as the Lake Manitoba Railway and Canal Company. D. B. Hanna was again responsible for involving the railway in several traffic-producing subsidiary ventures.

35 PAC, CNR Records, MCCCXXXVI, 36–8, Meetings of Directors of the Ontario and Rainy River Railway, 15 and 27 May 1897.
36 PAC, Laurier Papers, 23442–5, 23651–3, D. F. Burk to Laurier, 19 May 1898, and A. T. Wood and James Sutherland to Richard Cartwright, 25 May 1898.
37 PAC, Sifton Papers, CCXCI, 150–2, Sifton to Greenway, 20 July 1897.
38 PAC, CNR Records, CMV, 88–9, 91–2, Meetings of Directors of the Manitoba and South Eastern Railway, 11 Feb. and 26 May 1898.

I organized a cordwood company, which was a logical thing to do, for the benefit of the railway itself. I put men in the bush, arranged with the Dominion Government to get permits to cut, and at various times we had as many as 40,000 cords of wood cut and piled on the track waiting to move it to Winnipeg. The point I make about this is that we made business for the road, we made money for the lumberjacks, who moved up and down day after day, when we ran that little service and the result of it was that I earned enough out of operating all these things to pay the interest charges of the forty-five miles for two years.[39]

The little cordwood train running along the Manitoba and South Eastern, affectionately known as the "muskeg special", helped the railway through its early years. The competition it provided in cordwood and other commodities brought strenuous complaints from some Winnipeg merchants who were annoyed at Mackenzie and Mann's aggressiveness.[40] Yet it created extra traffic and Winnipeg price reductions which were popular with the public. The Manitoba and South Eastern Railway, like Mackenzie and Mann's other early projects, was a pioneer road which succeeded in identifying its policies with the interests and needs of local farmers and settlers. In time it might also become a connecting link between the Lake Manitoba Railway and Canal Company's line in northwestern Manitoba and the Ontario and Rainy River Railway which Mackenzie and Mann were building in western Ontario. In 1898, however, the gaps in that line were still much greater than the constructed mileage.

The years 1897 and 1898 were a time of frantic but rather unrewarding activity for Mackenzie and Mann. The 125-mile Lake Manitoba Railway and Canal Company mileage did surprisingly well, and forty-five miles of the Manitoba and South Eastern were built and were at least breaking even. In southern British Columbia the promoters met only disappointment, while in the Yukon disappointment had been compounded by unrewarding financial expenditures and political humiliation. Both Ontario projects were at a virtual standstill, and even in Manitoba the situation was not unclouded.

39 *Arbitration*, 404–5.

40 PAC, Sifton Papers, LXVI, 57798, Burrows to Sifton, 24 June 1900.

In 1897 the Northern Pacific suffered one of its recurrent but rather mild attacks of "Canadianitis" and began negotiations with the Greenway government for the construction of the long-awaited competitive railway to Duluth. Premier Greenway welcomed the American proposals enthusiastically. He immediately notified Mackenzie and Mann that under the circumstances provincial aid would be devoted to the construction of this line and that they should expect no further assistance from his government, at least not in the immediate future. Clifford Sifton, now a member of the federal government, was sceptical about the American offer and irritated at Greenway's treatment of Mackenzie and Mann. They were the only railway promoters who had actually accomplished something worth while in Manitoba in the 1890s. For a time relations between Greenway and Sifton became strained.[41]

The Northern Pacific negotiations in 1897 proceeded in much the same way as had earlier negotiations between the provincial government and that company. No agreement was reached. The American company lacked both the interest and the money to engage the CPR in a serious competitive battle. When the negotiations failed, Mackenzie and Mann suggested a provincial bond guarantee for the Manitoba and South Eastern Railway, which happened to run in the general direction of Duluth, as a suitable alternative plan that might get the premier out of the difficulty created by the failure of the Northern Pacific scheme. There were even rumours that Mackenzie and Mann, still generally regarded as contractors rather than promoters, were building on speculation and expected to sell their constructed mileage to the Northern Pacific or perhaps to the Canadian Pacific.

It was difficult to perceive any master plan in all the various railway schemes Mackenzie and Mann promoted in 1897 and 1898. They behaved like contractors in search of work, or like promoters in search of a major project, rather than like men already committed to a particular course of action.

The first clear indication that the two ex-contractors had found their purpose came in December 1898 when the Lake Manitoba Railway and Canal Company and the Winnipeg Great Northern Railway and

41 PAC, Porteous Papers, CCXCI, 162–3 and 150–2, Sifton to R. L. Richardson, 31 July 1897, and Sifton to Greenway, 20 July 1897.

Steamship Company (the Hudson Bay Railway under its latest title)[42] were amalgamated to form the Canadian Northern Railway Company. A new federal charter with rights to build extensive new mileage was obtained in July 1899 and, significantly, amalgamation with or sale to the CPR was expressly forbidden. The Manitoba and South Eastern Railway was amalgamated with the Canadian Northern as soon as the federal charter was passed in Ottawa, and Mackenzie and Mann began to make serious plans to connect the two Manitoba sections and to extend them eastward to the Lakehead. The years of uncertainty were over. A major new railway system serving the needs of the northern prairies was being created in the West. D B. Hanna described the process as it must have appeared to an observer in the 1890s.

It was very like what movie fans frequently see when they are about to observe some event which has recently taken place in a distant part of the world. The feature is heralded by the appearance of what looks like several sticks thrown into the air—all, seemingly, without direction or intention, but presently falling into an ordered announcement which he who sits may read. That is how the Canadian Northern transcontinental system took shape. From a series of disconnected and apparently unconnectable projections of steel, hanging in suspense, a continuous track was formed, trains ran on it, and all the organs of a great commerce began to function.[43]

42 The corporate history of the Hudson Bay Railway began in 1880 with the incorporation of the Nelson Valley Railway and Transportation Company and the Hudson's Bay Railway and Steamship Company. These two companies were amalgamated in 1883 under the name of the Hudson's Bay Railway and Steamship Company. Four years later the name was changed to the Winnipeg and Hudson Bay Railway and in 1894, following a reorganization of the company's affairs, it was renamed the Winnipeg and Great Northern Railway Company. Amalgamation with the Lake Manitoba Railway and Canal Company to form the Canadian Northern Railway followed in 1899. The mileage up to The Pas was built by Mackenzie and Mann. The remaining mileage was completed by the federal government under the arrangement discussed in Chapter VIII below.

43 Hanna, 174.

CHAPTER FOUR

THE MANITOBA BRANCH LINES 1898–1901

N 1898 Mackenzie and Mann operated 161 miles of railway consisting of two rather short and separated local lines. After 1898 the two promoters concentrated on expansion and integration of their various railway projects in Manitoba and western Ontario. The two Manitoba sections were connected. Government guarantees were obtained, lines were extended northward and westward, and charter rights were acquired and financial arrangements made to build eastward to Port Arthur. By 1901 the promoters' intention to build a through line from the prairies to Port Arthur had become clear. Then, by a stroke of good fortune, they were able to acquire the entire Northern Pacific and Manitoba Railway system and gain strong government support for the immediate completion of the main line to Port Arthur. The acquisition of the Northern Pacific's Manitoba branch lines "changed the Canadian Northern from a boy into a man".[1] By 1901 the Canadian Northern had 512 miles in operation and an additional 700 under construction and ready to be added to the system the following year.[2] A major new railway system, capable of competing with the CPR, was being created in the West.

At the northwestern end of the system, Mackenzie and Mann moved first in a northerly direction, mainly because extensions to the north carried a federal land grant and brought the railway closer to the Saskatchewan River and the federal transportation contract. After the Northern Pacific flurry in 1897, the provincial government again indicated its willingness to assist Mackenzie and Mann. In 1898 a new bond guarantee agreement was signed, facilitating construction north-

1 *Arbitration*, 2532–4.   2 *Ibid.*, 412, 425–6.

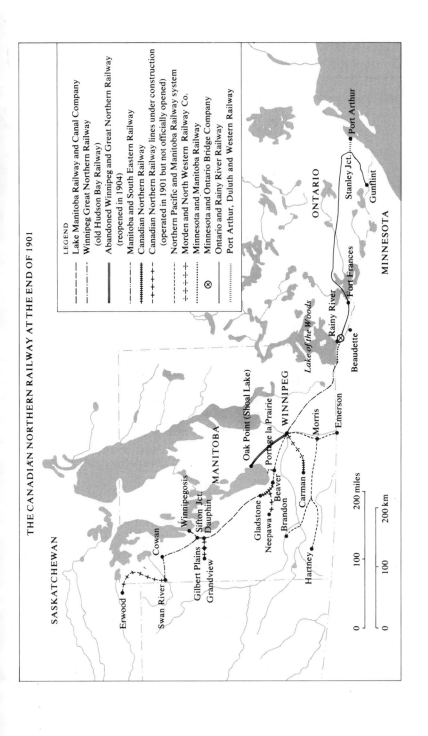

THE CANADIAN NORTHERN RAILWAY AT THE END OF 1901

LEGEND

- - - - - Lake Manitoba Railway and Canal Company
- · - · - Winnipeg Great Northern Railway
(old Hudson Bay Railway)
━━━━━ Abandoned Winnipeg and Great Northern Railway
(reopened in 1904)
- · · - · · Manitoba and South Eastern Railway
+++++++ Canadian Northern Railway
+ + + + + Canadian Northern Railway lines under construction
(operated in 1901 but not officially opened)
- - - - Northern Pacific and Manitoba Railway system
÷ ÷ ÷ ÷ ÷ Morden and North Western Railway Co.
·········· Minnesota and Manitoba Railway
⊗ Minnesota and Ontario Bridge Company
················· Ontario and Rainy River Railway
Port Arthur, Duluth and Western Railway

SASKATCHEWAN

MANITOBA

ONTARIO

MINNESOTA

Erwood

Swan River

Cowan

Winnipegosis

Sifton Jct.

Gilbert Plains

Grandview

Dauphin

Oak Point (Shoal Lake)

Gladstone

Neepawa

Beaver

Brandon

Carman

Hartney

Portage la Prairie

WINNIPEG

Morris

Emerson

Lake of the Woods

Rainy River

Beaudette

Fort Frances

Stanley Jct.

Gunflint

Port Arthur

0   100   200 miles

0   100   200 km

ward to the Saskatchewan River. The first fifty-two miles, from Sifton Junction to Cowan, were completed and opened for operations late in 1898. An additional thirty-two miles, to Swan River, were completed in 1899, while in 1900 this line was extended an additional ninety miles to Erwood, just outside the then northwest corner of the province of Manitoba. Here, of course, all prospects of further Manitoba aid for the northern line stopped. The Manitoba government was willing, however, to grant additional assistance for a line running westward from Dauphin through the fertile and partially settled Gilbert Plains area. A provincial bond guarantee for a twenty-five-mile extension to Grandview, Manitoba, was approved. Construction was begun immediately and the new mileage was opened in 1902.[3]

While building these extensions in the North-West, Mackenzie and Mann also moved closer to connecting their northern lines with those in southeastern Manitoba. Running-rights arrangements with the Manitoba and North Western Railway to Portage la Prairie and from Portage la Prairie to Winnipeg with either the Northern Pacific or the Canadian Pacific gave them the needed connections. The running-rights arrangement with the Manitoba and North Western Railway certainly worked out very satisfactorily for Mackenzie and Mann. The Manitoba and North Western, however, continued to lose money, and in 1900 the Montreal shipping magnates who owned the line decided to get rid of this financially encumbered and unprofitable railway on the prairies. They had been moving for some years towards a friendly accommodation with the CPR. On 1 May 1900 the Manitoba and North Western was leased to the CPR for 999 years. This made Mackenzie and Mann entirely dependent on CPR connections at Gladstone, a situation they had always sought to avoid. They quickly made arrangements with the Northern Pacific to construct a common line that would bridge the gap between Gladstone and Portage la Prairie. With government help each company agreed to build half the required thirty-eight miles of track, the two systems to meet at Beaver, Manitoba, in 1901.[4] The Canadian Northern thus regained the choice of sending

3 PAC, CNR Records, MMCCCXXV, 202, 207, *Tabulated and Synoptical Histories of Canadian National Railways,* hereafter referred to as *Synoptical Histories.*

4 *Arbitration,* 426.

traffic east over either the Northern Pacific or the Canadian Pacific systems. Later the same year Mackenzie and Mann acquired the Northern Pacific's entire Manitoba system, and with it the connection between Beaver, Portage la Prairie, and Winnipeg.

These developments in northwestern and central Manitoba were impressive, but between 1898 and 1901 they were largely overshadowed by developments in southeastern Manitoba and western Ontario. The charter of the Manitoba and South Eastern Railway provided the right to build to the far southeastern corner of the province. In 1898 the provincial government provided a $8,000-per-mile bond guarantee for this line—this in addition to a 6,400-acre-per-mile federal land subsidy to which the line was also entitled. There was never any doubt, however, that despite Hanna's valiant efforts in the cordwood business, this southeastern line was only worth while if it became a link in a new rail line from the prairies to the Great Lakes. Beginning in 1897, Mackenzie and Mann assembled a series of charters which gave them the power to build a new line to the Canadian Lakehead at Port Arthur.

In 1897 they acquired the Ontario and Rainy River Railway Company under the terms of a construction contract.[5] Then, in 1899, Mackenzie and Mann privately purchased the charter of the Minnesota and Manitoba Railway from its parent company, the Minnesota and Manitoba Lumber Company.[6] This purchase was the result of a fortuitous circumstance. The lumber company was interested in the railway charter only because it needed a reliable carrier for its products and was willing to make favourable arrangements with anyone who would build the railway. Mackenzie and Mann needed the Minnesota charter to bridge the forty-five-mile gap between Rainy River, the western terminus of the Ontario and Rainy River Railway, and the eastern terminus of the Manitoba and South Eastern Railway. The lumber company, moreover, was willing to offer an attractive transportation contract to anyone who would relieve them of the necessity to build and operate the railway. The lumber carried under this con-

5 PAC, CNR Records, MCCCXXXVI, 36–8,   May 1897.
Meetings of Directors of the Ontario   6 Stevens, 30.
and Rainy River Railway, 15 and 27

tract provided a considerable volume of local traffic. Thus Mackenzie and Mann became committed to an international line running south of Lake of the Woods to Port Arthur.

A separate company, the Minnesota and Ontario Bridge Company, was incorporated under Minnesota law in the same year. This company was authorized to build a steel railway bridge across Rainy River, from Baudette, Minnesota, to Rainy River, Ontario, thus connecting the Ontario and Rainy River Railway with the Minnesota and Manitoba Railway. Once the Minnesota and Manitoba Railway and the Minnesota and Ontario Bridge were constructed, they were assigned to the Canadian Northern Railway under a long-term lease.[7]

A fourth company, whose charter Mackenzie and Mann used to reach Port Arthur, was acquired in 1900. The charter of the Ontario and Rainy River Railway empowered it to build directly from Port Arthur. In 1890, however, it had signed a running-rights agreement with the Port Arthur, Duluth and Western Railway[8] which, as its name indicated, hoped to build from Port Arthur to Duluth. The first eighty-six miles, from Port Arthur to Gunflint, Minnesota, were built in 1893. The first nineteen miles of this road, from Port Arthur to Stanley Junction, paralleled the proposed route of the Ontario and Rainy River Railway. The management of the Ontario and Rainy River Railway therefore negotiated a running-rights arrangement, although they were unable to build any mileage of their own until Mackenzie and Mann took them over in 1897.

The Port Arthur, Duluth and Western Railway proved entirely unsuccessful and was accurately dubbed the Poverty, Anguish, Distress and Wretchedness Railway. In 1900 the High Court of Justice for Ontario ordered it to be sold at a bankruptcy sale. Mackenzie and Mann purchased it.[9] They hoped to use the first nineteen miles for their western traffic, and believed the remaining mileage might prove useful if the Mesabi iron ore range was found to extend that far north. They had no intention of building from Duluth to Port Arthur.

7 PAC, CNR Records, MCDXXXVI, 128–9, Special General Meeting of Shareholders of the Canadian Northern Railway, 17 Dec. 1901.

8 PAC, CNR Records, MCCCXXXVI, 15–27, Meeting of Directors of the Ontario and Rainy River Railway, 6 Oct. 1890.

9 *Arbitration*, 2510–12; PAC, CNR Records, MCCCXXXVI, 55–62, Meeting of Shareholders of the Ontario and Rainy River Railway, 27 April 1900.

Thus Mackenzie and Mann acquired the legislative authority to build from Winnipeg to Port Arthur. There was, of course, a vast difference between assembling such a railway on paper and actually getting it built. Mackenzie and Mann certainly did not have the financial resources to complete construction without substantial government assistance. The real test of their ability as promoters would be whether they could persuade the various governments and financiers to support them in their endeavours. Construction of their Manitoba lines had been and was still financed mainly through provincial government bond guarantees and the promise of federal land subsidies and transportation contracts. No such assistance was immediately available for the Minnesota and Ontario projects. It was clear, however, that the extension to Port Arthur would greatly strengthen the position of the Canadian Northern Railway. It could then become the long-awaited competitor of the CPR.

Mackenzie and Mann cheerfully began their search for funds. On 24 April 1900 they subscribed $500,000 of the capital stock of the Ontario and Rainy River Railway and paid a call of 10 per cent.[10] The sale of capital stock, however, was not the way Mackenzie and Mann raised large sums of money. They simply paid enough for their own stock to get started and to finance the search for larger funds. Too many ambitious railway projects had brought shareholders nothing but worry and frustration, and the market for equity in another such venture was highly discouraging. Mackenzie and Mann could probably have obtained very little from the sale of capital stock in the early years, even if they had been willing to sell it. Widely dispersed ownership would also seriously restrict the promoters' freedom of action. Their undisputed control stood them in good stead in several instances in which concessions and quick negotiations were essential. Mackenzie and Mann invariably served as their own contractors and took payment for the construction and promotional services by issuing the capital stock of their railways to themselves, fully paid up.[11]

In the late 1890s the search for financial support for the line to Port Arthur began. Among the first to contribute was the troubled

10 PAC, CNR Records, MCCCXXXVI, 43–5, Meeting of Directors of the Ontario and Rainy River Railway, 24 April 1900.

11 *Arbitration*, 105, 195–6, 2549–50.

town of Port Arthur. Grass was not yet growing in its streets, as a vengeful Van Horne had promised when he made Fort William the CPR centre, but the fate of the Port Arthur, Duluth and Western Railway and of other Port Arthur business ventures seemed to herald the fulfilment of Van Horne's curse. To redeem earlier niggardliness the town had already granted the Port Arthur, Duluth and Western Railway a $25,000 cash subsidy. Mackenzie and Mann, with their new promises, persuaded the town to double that subsidy. If the through line to Winnipeg were built, the future of Port Arthur would be assured.[12]

While Mackenzie and Mann appreciated such assistance, it was hardly enough to build a terminal, much less to finance a railway. The two promoters were looking for much larger amounts when they approached the government of Ontario. Several of the original Port Arthur, Duluth and Western promoters were local businessmen who recognized the need for a new railway, and who also enjoyed considerable political influence. The spokesman of the group was James Conmee, Liberal Member of the Legislative Assembly. The Rainy River country desperately needed a railway, and many in the area had long suspected that legislators in faraway Toronto had forgotten about western Ontario. An election was approaching and the time was appropriate for a faltering Liberal government to demonstrate greater concern for the area. A cash subsidy of $3,000 per mile for a line from Stanley Junction to Rainy River was therefore voted by the provincial government in 1898. This was increased to $4,000 per mile in 1899.[13]

While negotiating successfully in Toronto, Mackenzie and Mann did not forget the federal government in Ottawa. The Laurier government had declared itself opposed to further land grants to railways, partly for the excellent reason that it was becoming increasingly difficult to find suitable land. Instead, it carefully reviewed its entire railway policy, finally deciding to modify only slightly a cautious cash subsidy

---

12 PAC, CNR Records, MMMCXXI, Miscellaneous Documents, Agreement between Port Arthur and the Ontario and Rainy River Railway, 30 April 1900; Pierre Berton, *The National Dream, the Great Railway,* *1871–1881* (Toronto: McClelland and Stewart, 1969), 229–39.

13 Ontario, *61 Vict., Cap. 22* and *62 Vict., Cap. 23; Manitoba Free Press,* 31 Dec. 1901, and 2 and 4 Jan. 1902.

program initiated by the Conservatives shortly before the 1896 election. Under this program, any railway specifically declared to be in the general interest of Canada was eligible for a cash subsidy of $3,200 per mile for construction costing up to $15,000 per mile, and half of any additional construction costs, up to a maximum subsidy of $6,400 per mile. On 29 July 1898 Mackenzie received private assurances from the Prime Minister that this subsidy would be made available to the Ontario and Rainy River Railway.[14] This was later confirmed by appropriate legislation that declared the road to be in the general interest of Canada. Thus, cash subsidies totalling $10,400 per mile were available to the Ontario and Rainy River Railway from the two levels of government.

Early estimates of construction costs for the line to Port Arthur varied a great deal. The Department of Railways and Canals, probably the most neutral and accurate source, estimated it would cost $28,000 per mile. Some Members of Parliament, critical of the entire affair, stated that only $12,000 per mile was needed.[15] Regardless of which estimate was accepted, however, there were still not enough funds to build the road from subsidies alone. To raise more funds Mackenzie and Mann decided to bring out a bond issue, up to $20,000 per mile, for the entire line between Port Arthur and Rainy River. It was felt that this bond issue would be more attractive if the Ontario and Rainy River project were seen as an integral part of the larger Canadian Northern Railway system to which the Manitoba government was already heavily committed. Thus, on 3 May 1900, two days before the construction bonds were brought out, the Ontario and Rainy River Railway was amalgamated with the Canadian Northern Railway.[16]

Construction was begun before most of these bonds were sold, and often before they were even issued. The Canadian Bank of Commerce advanced substantial sums to Mackenzie and Mann personally. When the bonds were issued they were often deposited as collateral with the bank for further cash advances. Ultimately, the bonds were to be sold

14 PAC, Laurier Papers, LXXX, 24682, Laurier to Mackenzie, 29 July 1898.
15 Canada, *House of Commons Debates, 1901*, 5040–3.
16 PAC, CNR Records, MCCCXXXVI, 64–5, and MCDXXXVI, 50–61, 75–81, Meeting of Shareholders of the Ontario and Rainy River Railway and the Canadian Northern Railway, 3 May 1900, and of the Directors of the Canadian Northern Railway, 5 May 1900.

in London, England, and the proceeds used to repay the bank advances. This procedure worked fairly well for the provincially guaranteed bonds of the Manitoba lines. The same could not be said for the bonds issued by the Minnesota and Ontario lines. These bonds were guaranteed by no government, and despite an attractive 4.5-per-cent interest rate, did not sell well in London.[17] Railway bonds whose only security was the railway itself did not have a good reputation in financial markets at the turn of the century. By late 1900 the Canadian Bank of Commerce became worried about the value of the collateral against which it had advanced cash and credit. There was a growing danger that all cash and credit would be exhausted long before the railway to Port Arthur was completed. An incomplete railway would earn very little revenue, but interest had to be paid on all money already invested. The difficulty in selling the unguaranteed bonds nearly brought the system to disaster.[18] Fortunately, help arrived in 1901; it relieved the two promoters of serious financial difficulties for several years.

The help came from Mackenzie and Mann's first and most important benefactor, the provincial government of Manitoba. The primary objectives of that government's railway policy were the construction of new branch lines, and the establishment of a competitive rail service to the Lakehead that would provide stiff rate competition for the CPR. The long-awaited link to the Lakehead was finally in sight. Yet if Mackenzie and Mann ran out of money before completing construction, the venture might well collapse. Only the CPR would then be in a position to pick up the pieces.

Mackenzie and Mann sought more government help. At the same time the Northern Pacific Railroad approached the Manitoba government and asked to be relieved of its obligations under the Northern Pacific and Manitoba Railway agreement. The parent Northern Pacific

17 PAC, CNR Records, MCDXXXVI, 88–94, Meetings of Directors of the Canadian Northern Railway, 20 Sept. and 5 Oct. 1900. The Company hoped to sell the unguaranteed 4.5-per-cent bonds at 85 per cent of par value, but in 1900 the market was so weak that most of these unguaranteed bonds were simply pledged as collateral with the Canadian Bank of Commerce, which agreed to provide some short-term loans. The guaranteed 4-per-cent bonds were subsequently sold at 94 per cent of par value.

18 PAC, Sifton Papers, 384–5, CCCXXXIII, 191–2, Sifton to Willison, 16 May 1899, and Sifton to Macmillan, 22 June 1899.

Railroad had taken over the Manitoba line from President Henry Villard's privately organized syndicate in 1891, but operations on the Canadian lines had never been profitable. A total of 351 miles had been built, the main lines being the north-south line from Winnipeg to Emerson on the International Boundary, and western extensions from Winnipeg to Portage la Prairie and from Morris to Hartney and Brandon.

During the troubled years when the parent American company was in receivership, the president of the Northern Pacific and Manitoba Railway operated that company virtually in his own private interests. President James McNaught, a former Northern Pacific solicitor, made himself useful to several of the receivers and encountered little interference in Manitoba. Most of the financial books of the Manitoba company were subsequently reported lost or misplaced, but evidence presented at later court hearings and investigations suggested a bizarre state of affairs. President McNaught was reportedly in the habit of periodically phoning his treasurer and asking how much money was in the company's account. He would then make a withdrawal for that exact amount. No reports were presented indicating how this money was spent. When challenged by the Northern Pacific's comptroller, McNaught claimed the money had been used for sensitive political purposes, specifically to bribe Manitoba politicians. It was not at all clear to the comptroller why these politicians needed to be bribed. The Northern Pacific was quite popular in Manitoba since it was considered a competitor of the CPR. Thus, the Northern Pacific comptroller came to the conclusion that McNaught had simply used the money himself. Only the threat of a countersuit and the airing of various allegedly unpleasant matters persuaded the Northern Pacific to refrain from court action to recover these amounts from McNaught.[19]

With management of this calibre it was hardly surprising that the Northern Pacific and Manitoba Railway lost money. During the ten years that it was directly affiliated with the Northern Pacific, the Northern Pacific and Manitoba Railway had operating deficits totalling

19 MSHS, Northern Pacific Railroad Company Records, Northern Pacific and Manitoba Miscellaneous Correspondence File, John Scott to Henry C. Rouse, 7 June 1895; Secretary's Correspondence File No. 70, John Scott to Edward D. Adams, 10 Nov. 1896.

TABLE II

Operating Statistics of the Northern Pacific and Manitoba Railway

Year ending	Mileage operated*	Gross earnings	Operating expenses	Net earnings
		($)	($)	($)
31/12/1896	265.12	271,559.75	268,662.54	2,937.21
31/12/1897	265.12	246,627.59	324,162.38	−77,534.79
31/12/1898	265.12	315,876.97	323,528.87	−7,651.90
31/12/1899	311.61	378,724.23	398,577.59	−19,852.36
31/12/1900	316.17	391,947.40	577,525.61	−185,578.21
31/12/1901	320.51	258,042.07	300,724.86	−42,682.79

*Includes mileage of subsidiary companies owned and operated by the Northern Pacific and Manitoba Railway.

Source: The Public Archives of Canada, R.G. 46.

$766,276.70. In addition to these operating deficits the parent company had to meet interest payments of more than $300,000 annually on the Manitoba company's $6,010,000 bond issue. In its worst operating year the Northern Pacific and Manitoba Railway earned a mere 68¢ in revenue for every dollar spent in operating expenses and, taking bond interest payments into account, lost nearly $500,000.[20]

In 1897 President McNaught devised a fantastic program of expansion which he hoped would make his company profitable. The lines in Manitoba were to be expanded, and the Manitoba and South Eastern line was to be acquired and extended to Duluth. Connections with other American roads were to bring the system as far as Sault Ste. Marie, where connections were to be made with a moribund trans-Quebec railway scheme. There were huge gaps in the scheme and it never advanced further than some preliminary negotiations with the Manitoba government, although McNaught and several associates had sufficient confidence in it to acquire an interest in the Great Northern Railway of Canada and several other smaller Quebec railway charters.[21]

20 Canada, Appendices to the Annual Reports of the Department of Railways and Canals, 1891–1902. Published as Sessional Papers.
21 MSHS, Northern Pacific Railroad Company Records, President's Correspondence Subject File No. 167, James Fisher to President Winter, 12 April 1897, and James Fisher to C. S. Mellon, 25 April 1898.

Senior officers of the Northern Pacific were dubious. Sporadic negotiations with the Manitoba government continued through 1900. Premier Greenway desperately wanted an agreement with the American company, but he insisted on substantial rate reductions in return for any assistance granted. Clifford Sifton, then federal Minister of the Interior, allegedly put considerable pressure on the Manitoba premier to negotiate with Mackenzie and Mann rather than with the Northern Pacific, and in 1900 negotiations with the American company were terminated. The Northern Pacific officials were informed by their chief Manitoba negotiator, "Sifton is the minister representing Manitoba and the Northwest in the federal cabinet and Sir William Van Horne's special friend in that cabinet. Sifton is also a special friend—some people suggest more than a friend—of Mackenzie and Mann, and he was the author of their Dauphin scheme and their late lamented Teslin Lake Scheme."[22] A few weeks later the same writer stated, "I have received sufficient information to convince me that these gentlemen [Mackenzie and Mann] are operating in the interests of the Canadian Pacific."[23]

These communications convinced Northern Pacific President Mellon that both the Manitoba provincial government and the Canadian federal government were hostile to the Northern Pacific. In one of his letters he complained, "It seems to me the people of Manitoba are going to be obliged to work out the railway problem themselves. It is hopeless for a corporation like ours to compete successfully with the Canadian Pacific, subsidized as it is by the Government; and discriminated against in what we have tried to accomplish in the Province."[24] The subsidies Mellon complained of were those granted to Mackenzie and Mann. He seriously misread the Manitoba situation and the intentions of Mackenzie and Mann, considering them merely a front for the CPR. The Northern Pacific's basic difficulties in Manitoba did not arise from an unduly favourable attitude on the part of the government to either the Canadian Pacific or the Canadian Northern. They were due entirely to Mellon's refusal to promise substantial

22 *Ibid.*, President's Correspondence File No. 310 D–1, Fisher to Mellon, 3 March 1899.
23 *Ibid.*, Mellon to Fisher, 27 March 1899.

24 *Ibid.*, President's Correspondence File No. 310A, Mellon to Graham, 25 Jan. 1900, and Mellon to Fisher, 2 Sept. 1899; *Arbitration*, 2530.

reductions on the grain rates to the Lakehead, which the Manitoba government wanted and Mackenzie and Mann were willing to promise.

The initiative in Manitoba really passed to Mackenzie and Mann and their Canadian Northern Railway when the negotiations between the Northern Pacific and the Manitoba government for a through line to Duluth, begun in 1897, collapsed. Thereafter, the Northern Pacific began to look for opportunities to sell. Neither the Manitoba politicians nor the senior officers of the Northern Pacific seriously considered James McNaught's wild scheme of a Quebec connection.

The CPR indicated an immediate interest in their American rival's Manitoba properties and a tentative agreement was quickly worked out between the two companies. The 1889 Northern Pacific and Manitoba agreement with the provincial government, however, forbade any rate agreement with or sale of the assisted American line to the CPR. The provincial aid had been granted solely and specifically in order to obtain railway competition. Thus, the Northern Pacific had to approach the provincial government and seek special legislative authorization setting aside the most important part of their 1889 contract before any sale to the CPR could be finalized.

The request for such enabling legislation was rejected by the Manitoba government, whereupon the Northern Pacific asked the provincial government to lease or buy the unprofitable lines.[25] The provincial government of the new Conservative premier, R. P. Roblin, found itself in a serious quandary. The Northern Pacific, brought in by the Liberals in 1888-9, had failed to provide the desired competition and now wanted to get out of the province altogether. The Canadian Northern, begun with aid from the Greenway government, was having serious financial difficulties and might fail if further assistance was not provided. The CPR seemed determined to make the most of the situation and was seeking to restore its undisputed control over the prairies. Its new president, Thomas Shaughnessy, was inviting himself to Winnipeg to negotiate for the acquisition of the Northern Pacific and perhaps the Canadian Northern lines.

Politically it was almost unthinkable in Manitoba that Shaughnessy should succeed, even though he was willing to promise substantial rate

25 *Arbitration*, 2530-2.

reductions. The Liberal government's defeat in 1899 was generally attributed to the failure of their railway policy.[26] The Conservatives, led first briefly by Hugh John Macdonald and later by Roblin, were elected on a railway policy which favoured far greater government assistance and possible government ownership of railways, which would provide the required services and competition. Macdonald, however, lacked the political skill and adroitness of his famous father. In 1900 he was persuaded to resign the premiership and in the federal election of that year he unsuccessfully challenged Clifford Sifton. Rodmond Roblin, a farmer, grain merchant, and railway promoter, who had begun political life as a Liberal, succeeded Macdonald. He had a deep "grass roots" understanding of the railway problem in Manitoba and was not the man to preside over the re-establishment of a CPR monopoly. The Tuppers and other old Conservatives might complain that Roblin was not "true"—indeed, he made no secret of his opposition to the CPR and its federal supporters—but he was a true Manitoban on the railway question. Macdonald, like Greenway before him, was inclined to favour a competitive American line to Duluth. Roblin soon became convinced that the projects of Mackenzie and Mann were far more promising.

The Northern Pacific would have been willing to sell to the Canadian Northern, with whom it already had some traffic exchanges and running rights, but alas, the Canadian Northern already had too many projects in hand that it seemed unable to finance. Shaughnessy tried very hard to get the Northern Pacific lines. He offered the province "a bonus of $550,000 to go into the consolidated revenue, and reductions of rates amounting to between five and six millions of dollars to the farmers and consumers of the country within five years."[27] He got nothing but frustration for his efforts. His offer of substantial rate reductions simply convinced the Manitobans that the rates were unnecessarily high, and would remain too high until effective competition was established. Shaughnessy's proposals could be considered only as a last resort. It never seemed to occur to the politicians that railway companies might be more interested in maximizing profits than in

26 PAC, Sifton Papers, CCXCI, 426–9, Sifton to Laurier, 10 Dec. 1899.
27 Canada, *House of Commons* *Debates, 1901*, 5012; PAC, Pamphlet No. 2648, *Memorandum, Railway Policy of Manitoba.*

competing with one another simply for the sake of competition.

In the initial discussions with Shaughnessy the Manitobans demanded significant additional concessions. These Shaughnessy was unable to grant. He had come fresh from a directors' meeting with specific proposals. Any significant changes had to be referred back to the directors in Montreal, several of whom doubted the wisdom of making any concessions to the hostile Manitoba government. Shaughnessy, therefore, found himself handicapped in the fast-moving Manitoba negotiations.[28]

Shaughnessy's proposals might have carried the day had it not been for the presence of Canadian Northern officials, for whom the CPR president developed an intense dislike. Mackenzie and Mann knew how to use the political unpopularity of the CPR to their own advantage. They presented a feasible and politically very attractive alternative scheme which promised the desired competition. The 350 miles of railway built and operated so unprofitably by the Northern Pacific would fit beautifully into their own developing system. Their two lines in opposite corners of the province would then be connected, and the southern Manitoba lines would become very valuable feeder lines to their main line from Winnipeg to Port Arthur. There was no reason, they argued, why they could not operate these southern lines profitably since they generated more local traffic than their own northern lines. With a strong branch line and feeder network in Manitoba, the line to Port Arthur would become the long-awaited competitor for the CPR. Mackenzie and Mann ridiculed Shaughnessy's proffered rate reductions, promising even better terms if the Manitoba government would help them. In their negotiations they had complete freedom. No obstreperous or doubting directors and shareholders restricted their action. This freedom and flexibility in negotiations was later credited with the success of the Northern Pacific branch-lines transaction.

Mackenzie and Mann wanted two things from the government in 1901. They needed a government guarantee for the construction bonds on the mileage from Winnipeg to Port Arthur, since their unguaranteed bonds were not selling in London. In addition, they wanted the provincial government to help them acquire the Northern Pacific lines.

28 *Arbitration*, 2549–50.

The Manitoba government wanted a competitive through line to the Lakehead which from the beginning was committed to significant rate reductions.

The Manitoba politicians had to listen to what Mackenzie and Mann had to offer, and the more they listened the better it sounded. While Shaughnessy and the CPR were left to cool their heels, knowing that Mackenzie and Mann could and would underbid them, the Manitoba government arranged a package deal with the Canadian Northern Railway. The main points of the agreement were that the Manitoba government would lease the Northern Pacific and Manitoba lines from the parent Northern Pacific Railroad at a 4-per-cent rate of interest on an assessed value of $7,000,000, with an option to purchase at that price. This lease and option would then be reassigned to the Canadian Northern Railway. In addition, the Manitoba government agreed to help the Canadian Northern by guaranteeing new construction bonds, up to $20,000 per mile, on the entire Ontario section, and $8,000 per mile on the Minnesota section. This new guaranteed bond issue was to replace the Canadian Northern's earlier unguaranteed 4.5-per-cent bond issue. The new interest rate on the guaranteed bonds was reduced to 4 per cent.[29]

It was certainly somewhat unusual for a provincial government to guarantee bonds on railway mileage in another province and even in another country. In the case of the Minnesota and Manitoba Railway, a special stratagem had to be adopted. Legally the Manitoba government could not become the mortgagor of the Minnesota mileage since it could not take possession of foreign lines in case of a default. The Minnesota and Manitoba Railway issued its own unguaranteed bonds, but these were then immediately deposited as security with the provincial government. Using these bonds as collateral, the provincial government issued its own bonds and gave these to Mackenzie and Mann.[30]

In return for its assistance in solving the Canadian Northern's financial difficulties through bond guarantees, and for securing for it the

29 MSHS, Northern Pacific Railroad Company Records, President's Correspondence File No. 310D, Leasing of Northern Pacific and Manitoba Railway Lines; PAC, CNR Records, MCDXXVI, 107–27, Meeting of Directors of the Canadian Northern Railway, 11 Feb., 20 Sept., 21 Oct., and 7 Dec. 1901, and Meetings of Shareholders, 20 Sept. 1901.
30 *Arbitration*, 697–721.

lease of the Northern Pacific and Manitoba Railway, the Manitoba government expected rigorous railway competition. Lest there be any misunderstanding, and to prevent any tricks by the promoters, the Manitoba government specifically defined what the competitive rates should be. The rate on wheat moving from Winnipeg to the Lakehead was to be set at 10¢ per hundredweight—down 4¢ from the Crow's Nest Pass rates—when the new railway became fully operational.[31] Similar reductions of between 15 and 25 per cent were to apply on a variety of other commodities. It was further agreed that the government would have final control over the rates charged on the assisted lines. No rate schedules could be implemented without prior government authorization.

Mackenzie and Mann were rather hesitant about committing themselves unequivocally to a fixed rate, notably to the fixed 10¢ grain rate. This might prove disastrous if costs rose; but rates remained fixed by law. They were told that the fixed 10¢ rate was a political necessity, but received private assurances that it was not the intention of the government to force the railway into an unprofitable position. If it turned out that the rates were too low and operations became unprofitable, the government would be forced either to permit rate increases or to pay the railway's fixed charges. Mackenzie and Mann were told that the 10¢ rate need not become effective until the line to Port Arthur was fully operational. They finally agreed to the fixed rates, believing the unwillingness of the government to pay interest and principal on its guarantees would permit upward rate revisions if costs should rise significantly. They were satisfied that under the 1901 conditions they could operate profitably at the 10¢ rate. They were convinced that the government guarantees had committed the government to the success of the railway. The railway, in turn, had delivered into the hands of the provincial government all control over its rates to the Lakehead, and with it an effective instrument with which the government could pursue its own railway policy. Manitoba had at last gained the power to

31 The agreement required that the 10c rate should come into effect on 1 July 1903. By that time, it was expected the traffic would be sufficiently large. It is clear that the government did not wish to force the railway into an unprofitable operating position.

pursue sectional railway policies and the means to fight unpopular national railway policies.[32]

The successful conclusion of the negotiations in Manitoba did not bring the agreements into force immediately. Both the Northern Pacific and Manitoba Railway and the Canadian Northern Railway held federal charters and therefore needed enabling legislation from the federal government to complete the bargain. The Liberals in Manitoba, with Sifton's encouragement, took a strong stand against the contracts negotiated by their political opponents. They hoped that Sifton and the Liberal government in Ottawa would use their authority to refuse the enabling legislation, or possibly even to disallow the Manitoba bills on the grounds that control of rates on interprovincial traffic was a federal matter and beyond the powers of the provincial government. The federal Minister of Railways and Canals publicly denounced the bills and Sifton was also known to be very critical of them. "My own private impression," he wrote, "is that an Act to confirm this agreement would not have a ghost of a chance of getting through."[33]

This gave the Manitoba Liberals their cue, and they launched a vigorous fight against the bills in the Legislative Assembly. Sifton, however, had written before Mackenzie and Mann had explained to him the merits of the agreement they had made with his political opponents. "You may rest assured," Mann, the Liberal in the Mackenzie and Mann promotional team, wrote to Sifton, "that our Company will not use their power to the disadvantage of your political friends in the West or elsewhere."[34] This, it turned out, was not an empty promise, and the provincial Conservatives became very critical of Mackenzie and Mann's failure to allow political patronage on their road.[35] D. B. Hanna, the railway's general manager, issued a general directive forbidding employees to participate actively in provincial or federal poli-

32 Manitoba, *Sessional Papers, No. 9, 1902, Report of the Department of the Railway Commissioner for the year ending 31 Dec. 1901*; *The Winnipeg Tribune*, 7 March 1901, reporting on Premier Roblin's speech, 31 Dec. 1901; PAC, Hays Papers, 109–11, Hays to Wilson, 27 March 1903.

33 PAC, Sifton Papers, CCXLII, 36, and XCV, 75097–9; Sifton to Magurn, 26 Feb. 1901, and Campbell to Sifton, 13 March 1901.

34 *Ibid.*, XIV, 82297 Mann to Sifton, 25 June 1901.

35 UTA, Walker Papers, Plummer to Walker, 4 Oct. 1902.

tics. He made it clear that all attempts by friends of the government to influence appointments would be rebuffed, and later boasted that "the few attempts that were made . . . failed ignominiously."[36]

Sifton also wrote his letter from Ottawa before he had sampled public opinion in the West on the matter. Once the terms of the agreement were explained to him and he became aware of local sentiments, he came to a very different conclusion. He, along with many other Liberals who had long considered themselves the defenders and champions of provincial rights, strongly disliked federal interference in provincial affairs. They became convinced that federal obstruction of the Canadian Northern contracts would be politically disastrous. "I would be inclined to think," Sifton noted laconically, "that the most effective way of making them all [Manitobans] think that this is a good contract, would be for the parliament of Canada to refuse to pass it."[37]

While the conventions of political warfare had to be maintained, Sifton discovered that Roblin and his followers shared many of his ideas, while the local Liberals were often a disappointment. Roblin's connections with the old guard of the Conservative party were always less than harmonious, and to a large extent the policies and activities of the Manitoba Conservatives complemented those of the federal Liberals. Federal Conservatives after 1896 complained that the Liberals had simply "stolen their clothes" (that is, the National Policy). The reverse could be said of the situation in Manitoba. Sifton, at any rate, came to the conclusion that the federal government should not interfere. If Mackenzie and Mann were successful, no one could doubt that substantial advantages would accrue to Manitoba. Sifton was still sceptical of their chances of success, but felt that Liberal interests would be adequately safeguarded if the federal government passed the enabling legislation but ensured that, should the arrangement end disastrously, all the blame would attach to the provincial Tories.[38] If Mackenzie and Mann succeeded, the federal government might, of course, claim considerable credit, since it had passed the enabling legislation.

36 Hanna, 254; CNRHQ, C. D. Prosser interview.
37 Canada, *House of Commons Debates, 1901*, 4995.
38 PAC, Sifton Papers, CCXCII, 109–10, Sifton to Magurn, 12 Mar. 1901.

Sifton's reversal of policy left the Manitoba Liberals, who had committed themselves to vigorous opposition, in a completely untenable position. Many never forgave Sifton, and in the next provincial election there were widespread rumours that Sifton, who stayed out of the province, was hoping for a Conservative victory.[39]

Early in May 1901 Sifton moved behind the scenes in Ottawa to ensure the passage of the enabling legislation. He advised Laurier, "I also wish you would quietly see that the Manitoba railway bills are pushed along. I have gone over the whole matter carefully in my mind and am satisfied that it is in every way the best policy that they should pass. I think you should speak to Blair and Davies, *particularly the former.*"[40] Only a few weeks earlier Sifton had suggested that the Manitoba lieutenant-governor, a Liberal appointee, should refuse to assent to the bills.[41]

Once Sifton got to work there was little doubt that the enabling legislation would pass. Blair was silenced and did not participate in the debate. In fact only three men attacked the measure with any vigour in Parliament. These were R. L. Richardson, editor of the *Winnipeg Tribune*, a former Liberal who had quarrelled with Sifton and whose newspaper was reportedly under the influence of the CPR; John Charlton, a long-time Liberal member for Norfolk who saw little need for government assistance to railways anywhere; and Henri Bourassa, a man who hated Manitoba sectionalism in language, religion, and economics as much as he loved Quebec nationalism. Bourassa was undoubtedly the most effective and telling of these critics.

The major criticisms of the bills were related to the clauses concerning control of freight rates from Manitoba to Port Arthur by the provincial government. This control, it was feared, could be used to implement railway policies which would only look to the welfare of one section of the country and ignore national considerations. It was

---

39 *Ibid.*, CXXVIII, 110236–8, and CXL, 111898, Burrows to Sifton, 21 July 1903, and Dafoe to Sifton, 24 June 1903.

40 PAC, Laurier Papers, CXCVI, 55862–3, Sifton to Laurier, 1 May 1901. The last phrase is underlined in the original letter. The unsettled Canadian Yukon Railway account with Mackenzie and Mann received prominent mention in this letter.

41 PAC, Sifton Papers, CCXLII, 333, Sifton to Macmillan, 12 March 1901.

a direct attempt by the provincial government to reduce or shift a part of the burden of railway rates from Manitoba to other areas of Canada. It undermined the whole concept of a national rate structure set in accordance with national railway rate policies and controlled by the federal Railway Committee of the Privy Council.

The CPR had long assured all petitioners that railway rates were as low as possible and could not be reduced unilaterally in one region without corresponding increases elsewhere. Continuing complaints from Manitoba and the North-West Territories had led to the appointment of a federal commission to investigate the matter in 1894–5. The commissioners quickly dismissed complaints that western rates should be the same as those charged in the east. "Your commissioners," they wrote, "are of the opinion that no fair comparisons of rates can be made between railways traversing a sparsely settled country in the west, having very light local traffic, with railways passing through a comparatively old and thickly settled country, with large and numerous populous centers."[42] When compared with rates in adjacent American states the ton-mile rates on the CPR were actually lower than those on the American transcontinentals, although the CPR mileage, and therefore the total cost to the Canadian farmers, was considerably larger. The fact that the grain traffic entailed the hauling of about 75 per cent of the cars empty one way and that it was practically confined to a short season of the year confirmed the commissioners in their conclusion that the rates in Manitoba and the North-West Territories were neither exorbitant nor excessive. Many of the western complaints, according to the commissioners, "have arisen from a misunderstanding of the tariffs."[43]

It seemed unlikely that the federal government would change the national railway rate structure after receiving this report. When Manitoba decided in 1901 to force unilateral reductions on western rates, other areas had good reason to worry that their rates might be increased. Henri Bourassa, already much aggrieved over Manitoba policies in regard to Catholic schools and the use of the French language, recognized what Manitoba was trying to do and warned, "Whatever the language is, the meaning is clear, that you put in the hands of a

42 *Report of the Railway Rates Commission, 7 May 1895* (Ottawa: Queen's Printer, 1895), 3.
43 *Ibid.*, 15.

provincial government a power that may be used at any time against the general interests of Canada."[44]

It was clear that Manitoba was determined, and had now discovered a means of obtaining lower freight rates. The provincial government was not particularly concerned if this meant higher rates elsewhere. Manitoba had always regarded railway policies and rate structures as unduly burdensome to the West. They were concerned with little more than lightening this burden. The hope of all who supported the bills was that immigration to the prairies had increased the volume of traffic to the extent that the railways could get along on the reduced rates. Opponents of the bills, however, expressed fears that the Canadian Northern would seek to recoup losses on the Manitoba traffic by exorbitant rates in the Rainy River-Fort Frances area and in the North-West Territories. The CPR, which would be compelled to match the Canadian Northern rates to retain a share of the Manitoba traffic, might similarly recoup its losses on other traffic.

During the debate on the enabling or confirming legislation, a second kind of criticism was also voiced. It reflected the suspicions of rural areas already well supplied with railways. John Charlton, in a speech on 1 May 1901, expressed this suspicion of big business in general and of the railways in particular, using tactics that were to plague Mackenzie and Mann continually, but against which they were unable to offer effective defences.

I believe the bargain was run through with hot and indecent haste, and what the influences were, of course, it is not for me to say. I read a story once that occurs to my mind now, of the celebrated Abraham Lincoln, in connection with the trial of a man accused of stealing hams in Illinois. The man accused was seen on a moonlit night to make three trips to the smokehouse, and come away each time with a load of hams. He was arrested, arraigned and tried. And although the crime was proven beyond peradventure, the jury brought in a verdict of "not guilty" and the lawyer for the prosecution inquired from the lawyer for the defence how he could account for that verdict. He said, "I know Sir Matthew Hale has said that if anything could possibly exceed the foreknowledge of God, it would be the verdict of a jury, but even on that supposition, I am

44 Canada, *House of Commons Debates, 1901*, 4455–6, 4493, 4506.

unable to account for the verdict." "Well," said the lawyer for the defence,
"My friend, there are some features about the administration of justice
in this country of a character so high and so far beyond the comprehension
of men from the east like you, that you fail to take in the situation
but the truth about this case is, that every man on the jury had one of
those hams."

Now, I would not for a moment charge; I would not for a moment
venture to insinuate that such influence was brought to bear upon the
legislature of Manitoba, and I would not think of asserting that anything
beyond pure ordinary dunderheaded stupidity actuated them in the
passage of this Bill.[45]

This was followed by a lengthy diatribe on the varied and grievous
sins of American railroad promoters. The implications, of course, were
clear, although very difficult to deal with. There were no specific
charges and in this case few of the members who voted on the measure
followed Charlton's lead. Many undoubtedly realized that political corruption was not an adequate explanation for the strong support the
bills enjoyed in the West. The drastic rate reductions and the definite
promise of competition with the CPR were the fulfilment of railway
policies pursued by Manitoba politicians for nearly two decades. Clifford Sifton said this was the fulfilment of railway policies consistently
pursued by three successive Manitoba premiers.[46] Two of these were
Conservative, one Liberal. Frank Oliver, another western Liberal de-
fending the policies of the Manitoba Conservatives, pointed out that
the province stood to gain more from the proposed rate reductions than
from the amount of the interest on all Canadian Northern bonds.[47]
Mackenzie and Mann, however, assured all who would listen that they
could operate their railway profitably at the lower rates. As long as
prairie politicians could believe this they were virtually unanimous in
their support of the Canadian Northern bills. A. A. C. LaRivière, the
former Manitoba attorney general and now a federal Conservative
MP, summed up this feeling: "The majority of hon. members on both
sides of the House, coming from the West, are in favour of the legislation, throwing away all their party ideas and uniting together to secure

45 Ibid., 4695–6.   47 Ibid., 4493.
46 Ibid., 4983–6.

the passage of this legislation which is considered to be beneficial in the best interests of the West."[48]

There were very serious doubts in Ottawa about the constitutional validity of provincial regulation of interprovincial and even international traffic. The federal government was just in the process of establishing a federal Board of Railway Commissioners which would replace the old Railway Committee of the Privy Council. One of the major functions of this Board was to be the regulation of rates on all railways to be assisted by the federal government. The rulings of the federal Board might conceivably conflict with the rate policies imposed on the Canadian Northern by the Manitoba government. In 1901, however, the federal government took the position that the maximum rates approved by the proposed Board of Railway Commissioners should never be exceeded, but that there could be no compulsion on any railway to charge the maximum rates. Private arrangements between the railways and a province to reduce rates below maximums authorized by the Board of Railway Commissioners were acceptable, provided these rates did not prove discriminatory. Premier Roblin made the same point very effectively when he told Opposition leader Greenway, "My hon. friend does not propose to take that position that because the railway charges $4.00 from here to Crystal City it is prohibited from carrying my hon. friend on a pass if it chooses."[49]

The Manitoba rate reductions did not, as many had feared, lead to higher rates elsewhere, but proportionately the West paid lower rates after 1901. The balance of rates between East and West was adjusted. In a sense such an adjustment might be considered discriminatory or, as westeners believed, it simply removed, in part, the discrimination against western traffic which had existed since the introduction of the National Policy. Premier Roblin of Manitoba mistakenly believed that, as a result of the Canadian Northern agreement, the subject of oppressive and discriminatory freight rates "is no longer, and will never be again, a live or debatable issue in this Province."[50]

The takeover of the Northern Pacific lines and the securing of provincial bond guarantees on the line to Port Arthur established the

48 *Ibid.*, 5032.
49 *Ibid.*, 5016.
50 Manitoba, *Sessional Papers, No. 9,*

1902, Report of the Department of Railway Commissioner for the year ending 31 Dec. 1901.

Canadian Northern Railway as a major railway system in Canada. In the West it was the second-largest and most popular system, and it already had a larger mileage, if not yet a larger debt, than the eastern Intercolonial Railway. The railway's solicitor aptly summed up the importance of the agreements when he said that they changed the Canadian Northern Railway from a boy into a man.[51]

51 *Arbitration*, 2532–3.

CHAPTER FIVE

TRANSCONTINENTAL RIVALRIES 1902-1903

THE MANITOBA AGREEMENTS solved the Canadian Northern Railway's immediate financial problems. It could now complete the line to Port Arthur and consolidate its position in Manitoba. Within a year, however, a new challenge had to be faced. In 1902 the Grand Trunk Railway of Canada formulated a plan whereby it would extend its system into the prairies and, if possible, take over the Mackenzie and Mann mileage. Mackenzie and Mann, however, were firmly convinced that western settlement and development would soon make their Canadian Northern Railway a very profitable venture and they had no intentions of selling out. With no immediate financial problems and with good prospects for the future, they were determined to resist all attempts by the Grand Trunk to take over the Canadian Northern. A desperate fight for survival followed. "Driven by the laws of self preservation",[1] as Mackenzie later put it, the Canadian Northern fought off the Grand Trunk challenge, and then rushed its own plans for major extensions into Grand Trunk and Canadian Pacific-controlled areas in eastern Canada, thus avoiding being bottled up in the West without any connections with the commercial centres of eastern Canada.

The immediate result of the 1901 agreements was an easing of the financial problem. In 1900 Mackenzie and Mann transferred to the railway various assets they had earned, including the land grant which they had earned under various construction contracts. In return for 4,000,000 acres of land, they took $4,000,000 of Canadian Northern capital stock. The railway then mortgaged the lands under a special land-grant bond issue and pledged these bonds with the Canadian

1 PAC, Borden Papers, File OC 153, 10454, William Mackenzie to Robert Borden, 4 Jan. 1913.

Bank of Commerce for desperately needed cash advances.[2] In this way the large construction crews on the difficult Ontario and Rainy River mileage were kept at work. The failure of the unguaranteed Ontario division bonds, however, made the Bank very reluctant to advance additional credits.[3]

Construction of the Ontario section was fraught with very serious engineering and construction problems. Much of the proposed route crossed muskeg, which could devour enormous amounts of fill and pile budging. One fifteen-mile section required no less than 13,900 feet of pile budging and trestle-work.[4] The numerous streams greatly increased the number of bridges and trestles that had to be built, and the isthmus of Rainy Lake had to be crossed by means of a long and expensive causeway. The latter was reportedly the longest of its kind in North America at the time. This was the most ambitious Canadian railway project since the building of the CPR main line, and Mackenzie and Mann extended their resources to the limit before help finally came from the Manitoba government.[5] In the end, only the promise of federal and provincial cash subsidies to be earned once the line was built, and the fact that the line could earn nothing until completed, persuaded the Bank to advance the funds that were needed.

Once the Manitoba guarantee was assured, Mackenzie hurried to London to arrange for the sale of the bonds. In London he had the good fortune to meet R. M. Horne-Payne, who was intimately acquainted with the London money markets and shared the railway promoter's optimism about the future development of western Canada. Confined to a wheelchair by a serious spinal disorder, Horne-Payne was testy and cantankerous. Other financiers often found him very difficult, but he had an almost uncanny ability to sum up a situation and determine precisely how many securities could be placed in particular places. He greatly impressed other Canadian Northern officials by his ability to determine how much a district would subscribe just by driving through it.[6] He was the founder and president of the British Empire Trust Com-

2 PAC, White Papers, File 24, 6691–8, Memorandum by Z. A. Lash for W. T. White outlining the relations between the contractors, Mackenzie, Mann and Co. Ltd., and the Canadian Northern Railway; *Arbitration*, 49.

3 PAC, Hays Papers, I, 15–16, Hays to Wilson, 18 Sept. 1902.
4 *Manitoba Free Press*, 31 Dec. 1901.
5 *Arbitration*, 2519–20.
6 Hanna, 245.

RIVAL TRANSCONTINENTAL RAILWAY SCHEMES, 1903-1904

LEGEND

Grand Trunk-Grand Trunk Pacific-National Transcontinental System

Canadian Northern Railway System

Canadian Government Railways

Approximate Route of the Projected Trans-Canada Railway

pany which, together with the National Trust Company of Canada, became the trustee for most Canadian Northern bonds and debenture stock. Perhaps a part of the success in marketing the 1901 Manitoba-guaranteed bonds was that these were the first securities handled by Horne-Payne, who was subsequently appointed London director of the Canadian Northern Railway. Most of the 1901 bonds were placed with Messrs. Sperling & Co. in London at 94 per cent of par value.[7] Horne-Payne was a partner in Sperling & Co. at the time.

Sale of the bonds enabled the Canadian Northern to repay the money borrowed from the Canadian Bank of Commerce. New credits were then arranged with both the Commerce and, in the British Isles, the Bank of Scotland. In 1902 the Commerce agreed to grant Mackenzie and Mann credits of up to $3,000,000.[8] A rapid construction program could thus be pursued without major financial disruptions. Agreement by the Manitoba government to increase its guarantee on the already constructed Manitoba lines from $8,000 to $10,000 per mile, thus allowing various improvements, further eased the financial situation,[9] as did the provincial government's willingness to grant guarantees for various new branch lines. Mackenzie and Mann also spent considerable amounts of their own money in the venture. Their various traction and electrical development projects were very profitable, and in 1902 the Canadian Bank of Commerce estimated that they had about $1,000,000 of their own money in the Canadian Northern.[10]

The funds were thus available to complete the line to Port Arthur. A serious attempt was made to get the line ready to take out the 1901 wheat crop, but adverse weather conditions and seemingly bottomless muskeg made this impossible. Nevertheless, on New Year's Eve, 1901, trains were able to leave Port Arthur and Winnipeg simultaneously. They arrived the following day at Winnipeg and Port Arthur respectively. Some temporary trackage had to be used at one point and the trains had to wait several hours while the last rails were spiked down. The waiting officials organized a $75 wager on the length of the last rail which would connect the system. The bet was won by Clifford

7 PAC, CNR Legal Series, File 6–3; and Vol. 2194, Miscellaneous Documents.
8 UTA, Walker Papers, Walker to Plummer, 15 Sept. 1902.
9 PAC, CNR Records, MMMCXXV,

Memorandum of Bond Issues of the Canadian Northern Railway Company and Predecessors, 15 Nov. 1903.
10 UTA, Walker Papers, Walker to Plummer, 15 Sept. 1902.

Sifton's brother-in-law, T. A. Burrows, who was also a Manitoba Liberal MLA and the Canadian Northern land agent at Dauphin, and would in the future be Lieutenant-Governor of Manitoba. Roderick Mackenzie, the eldest son of William Mackenzie, was in charge of the construction crews and refused to participate in any celebrations until the last spike was safely driven by his father and Donald Mann at Commissioner Inlet, twelve miles east of Fort Frances. A ceremonial last spike "of gleaming silver" was also driven the same day at Atikokan by E. J. Davis, Ontario Commissioner of Crown Lands, and James Conmee, the local MLA and one of the early promoters of the Ontario and Rainy River Railway. Then, to celebrate the great occasion properly, Mackenzie and Mann gave a present of $2 to each workingman on the line, $5 to every gang foreman, and $25 to every foreman, in addition to their regular salaries. Settlers along the right of way brought out their families to see the first train, gaily decorated, make the trip from Port Arthur to Winnipeg.[11]

The previous evening the city of Port Arthur had given an elaborate and enthusiastic banquet in honour of the new railway and its promoters. The *Manitoba Free Press* described the scene.

The banqueting hall was decorated in a unique and beautiful way.
Besides potted plants, evergreens, flags, buntings and the usual decorations
one end of the hall was taken up with an almost life-size painting of
a train of passenger cars. The cars were all enscribed with the CNR and
the engine number was 1902. On one end of the hall was a big motto with
portraits of Messrs. Mackenzie and Mann, with "energy, enterprise,
ability" below. Some of the other mottos were "Port Arthur, the Silver
Gateway of the Golden West". . . . A unique feature of the decorations was
a model CNR railway over two hundred feet long. The stations along
the line and the telegraph lines are reproductions of each section and a
final model of the proposed new terminal station was also pictured.[12]

Speeches, political and practical, were the order of the day. Amid cheers for the King, the new road, Messrs. Mackenzie and Mann, the Ontario and Manitoba governments, and the Bank of Commerce,

11 *Manitoba Free Press*, 10 Aug.   12 *Ibid.*, 31 Dec. 1901.
1901, 31 Dec. 1901, 2 Jan. 1902.

Donald Mann, perhaps carried away by the spirit of the occasion, expressed the hope that within seven years they would be able to celebrate the driving of the last spike in the second Canadian transcontinental railway. A moonstruck eastern reporter had, somewhat earlier, predicted an even greater, although rather impractical, future for the Canadian Northern.

There will be railroad connections from Edmonton to Dawson City, and through Alaska across Behring straits to Asia, connecting with the Great Russian Railway, nearly completed, and about 5,000 miles long. This will give all rail connection with the New and Old World points. In less time probably than fifteen years we will hear the call, "All aboard at Winnipeg for an all rail ride for Paris, France."

This enthusiast had to admit, "We do not think that the promoters of the Great Northern [sic—talking of Mackenzie and Mann throughout the article] have entertained a thought of so extensive a connection with their road, but it is a well known fact that often enterprises extend far beyond the most sanguine expectations."[13] Perhaps it was fortunate that Mackenzie and Mann, rather than reporter "A.P.C.", were building the new railway.

The prospect of building from coast to coast in 1902 was only a vague and ill-defined hope. Mackenzie and Mann's immediate ambition was to extend their lines westward as far as Edmonton and Prince Albert. The promoters were encouraged, however, when Premier Dunsmuir of British Columbia reopened negotiations whereby assistance would be given for an extension from Edmonton to the Pacific coast. At the same time Premier Ross of Ontario suggested hopefully that the two promoters would soon come to Toronto to seek financial aid to extend their line eastward to the St. Lawrence River.[14]

Mackenzie and Mann were not really interested in immediate transcontinental expansion. Mann called the 1902 arrangements to build to the Pacific coast "crazy".[15] The basic decision ultimately to expand the Canadian Northern to the Atlantic and Pacific was apparently made in 1900, but this was strictly a long-term plan. "I always maintained,"

13 *Ibid.*, 16 Jan. 1901.   15 *Arbitration*, 2681.
14 *Ibid.*, 23 and 26 Nov. 1901.

Mann said later, "that we should not build east or west until we had about five thousand miles in operation in the prairies, which would feed the lines east and west; and my judgement was that that was sufficient to make the road pay."[16] This carefully planned transcontinental expansion program was completely upset, however, when the Grand Trunk Railway decided to expand its system to the Pacific coast.

The Grand Trunk had hitherto been cautious and indifferent about westward expansion. In 1880 it declined all government invitations and permitted the big project of that year to go to the Canadian Pacific Railway. In 1895, however, a new management assumed control of Canada's largest railway. Charles Rivers Wilson, a distinguished British diplomat and civil servant, who had been a member of the international commission for the liquidation of Egypt's debts, was elected president. Personal charm, integrity, and courage, rather than a practical knowledge of railways, characterized the new president. To compensate for his lack of practical railway knowledge, Wilson appointed an American, Charles Melville Hays of the Wabash, St. Louis and Pacific Railroad, as his general manager. Wilson remained at the Grand Trunk headquarters at Dashwood House, London, while Hays, resident in Canada, looked after all the local affairs of the company.

Both Wilson and Hays were convinced the Grand Trunk must build to the prairies if and when the settlement policies of the Laurier government bore fruit. In 1902 they thought the opportune time had come. A few months after Mackenzie and Mann opened their new road to Port Arthur, Wilson and Hays began serious discussions about Grand Trunk expansion. Both men assumed that transcontinental expansion by the Grand Trunk would force Mackenzie and Mann out of the field, although they differed on the ways and means of dealing with the Canadian Northern promoters.[17]

Wilson became acquainted with Mackenzie when the latter was in London in March 1902 to market his government-guaranteed bonds. Mackenzie called on the Grand Trunk president with proposals for a traffic exchange agreement between his company and the eastern railway. Mackenzie evidently made a good impression on Wilson, who

16 *Ibid.*, 2510–12, 2683–4.
17 PAC, Hays Papers, I, 1, 14–24, Wilson to Hays, 20 March, 27 Aug. and 1 Oct. 1902, and Hays to Wilson, 18 and 22 Sept. 1902.

wrote to his general manager, "From what I have heard of these people [Mackenzie and Mann], the work they have already done and the work they are likely to do in the future, I believe they may be valuable allies, and I shall be glad to know whether you share this opinion, and if so whether you think that we can allow it to make some practical development."[18]

Hays was unwilling to co-operate with Mackenzie and Mann. He, too, saw that the Canadian Northern lines might be useful and complementary to his company's transcontinental ambitions, but urged that "a policy of aggression and extension" be adopted by the Grand Trunk. "My own preference," he wrote, "would be the acquisition of a controlling interest in the Canadian Northern line either by purchase of a majority of the stock by the Grand Trunk Railway, or by the formation of a syndicate which should do so in the interests of this company." He assured Wilson that Mackenzie and Mann, if pressed, were likely to agree.

The firm named [Mackenzie, Mann and Co.] are not building the road for purposes of operation, but for the subsidies involved and for the profit they can make at a subsequent disposal of their lines to other parties. If this view is correct, the line will doubtless be built on a basis that affords the greatest profit and with much less regard to economy and advantage in subsequent operations than would be the case were we directing the construction ourselves.

The matter, as it appeared to Hays, required quick and aggressive action.[19]

The view that Mackenzie and Mann were nothing more than opportunistic contractors who would sell when they could do so at a profit was widespread in the business community in 1902. To some extent the Canadian Northern promoters were quite willing to allow such rumours to spread. Prospects of a future lease or sale to either the CPR or the Grand Trunk invariably increased the confidence of investors in London. The earlier experiences of the Qu'Appelle, Long Lake and Saskatchewan Railway and of the Calgary and Edmonton Railway,

18 *Ibid.*, 1, Wilson to Hays, 20 March 1902.

19 *Ibid.*, 3–9, Hays to Wilson, 14 April 1902.

which Mackenzie and Mann knew well, clearly indicated that bond sales could be expedited by rumours of an arrangement with one of the larger and stronger railway systems. Mackenzie never said his railway had any arrangement with the CPR or the Grand Trunk, but he was remarkably slow and vague in denying such a connection during the time his bonds were on sale. Hays, therefore, had some reason to write, "undoubtedly M. & M. are giving that impression [that the Grand Trunk was interested] in connection with their own enterprise."[20]

Wilson had serious doubts about the aggressive policy proposed by Hays. When he had met Mackenzie in the early months of 1902 the Canadian Northern promoter had given no indication that he wished to sell; on the contrary, he had given every indication that he intended to operate and expand the Canadian Northern Railway.[21] The guaranteed bonds sold very well, and the year ending 30 June 1902 showed operations which were "a very delightful surprise" to Canadian Northern officials. Gross receipts that year totalled $1,400,973.43. After all operating costs, fixed charges, and rentals were paid, a profit of $79,992.83 remained.[22]

Wilson urged Hays to seek a friendly accommodation with the Canadian Northern. Hays, on the other hand, had gained his railway experience in the rough world of United States railroading during the age of the robber barons. It was his intention to force Mackenzie and Mann out of the field. If they were unwilling to accept his terms he was quite prepared to parallel their lines and engage in a fight to the finish. In order to sell his ideas of an aggressive expansion policy Hays travelled to London to discuss the matter with a rather sceptical group of Grand Trunk shareholders. Neither Wilson nor the shareholders were prepared to commit the Grand Trunk to Hays's policy, but he was given permission to investigate the matter further and to prepare an application for federal assistance for a new line to the Pacific. He was told specifically, however, that he must not commit the Grand Trunk directly to such a project.[23]

When he returned to Canada, Hays proceeded with his own plan.

20 *Ibid.*, 15–16, Hays to Wilson, 18 Sept. 1902.
21 *Ibid.*, 1, 9–11, Wilson to Hays, 20 March, 26 April, and 18 June 1902.
22 *Arbitration*, 427–30.

23 PAC, Hays Papers, I, 9–11, 15–16, 23–4, Wilson to Hays, 26 April 1902, and Hays to Wilson, 28 May 1902, Hays to Wilson, 18 Sept. 1902, and Wilson to Hays, 1 Oct. 1902.

He approached George Cox, president of the Bank of Commerce—Mackenzie and Mann's principal creditor. Cox, a prominent Liberal, was invited to become the president of the proposed new line to the Pacific. He was also asked to use his influence with the Bank to put pressure on Mackenzie and Mann, which would compel them to sell at Hays's price.[24] Officials of the Bank were quite prepared to urge Mackenzie and Mann to sell, and at one point persuaded Mann, and certainly Lash, that a sale to the stronger Grand Trunk was inevitable.[25] The Bank was unable, however, to put sufficient pressure on Mackenzie.

Despite a $3,000,000 credit Mackenzie and Mann were not dependent on the Bank after the successful 1902 bond sales. Cox regretfully reported to Hays that the Bank had "no hold of any kind upon them".[26] The Canadian Bank of Commerce officials thought Mackenzie and Mann should sell their capital stock of $25,000,000 par value and estimated that $12,500,000 or $15,000,000 might be a fair purchase price.[27] Hays was not prepared to pay nearly that much, while Mackenzie was "feeling in all directions for some way of turning the matter into lines more acceptable to him: he hates the idea of losing control."[28] The best that Hays could get from Mackenzie was a statement that he thought the capital stock was worth at least par, but that it was not for sale. Instead, Mackenzie and Mann suggested an arrangement between the two roads whereby they would control the western portion while the Grand Trunk maintained its influence in the east. A traffic interchange between the two would create a transcontinental system capable of meeting CPR competition.[29]

Prime Minister Laurier invited the rival companies to a meeting at which the differences were to be resolved, but it ended disastrously. Wilson, while impressed with Mackenzie's wit and ability, still regarded the Canadian Northern Railway as a backwoods line. He contemptuously dismissed the arrangement suggested by Mackenzie and Mann

24 *Ibid.*, 14–16, Wilson to Hays, 27 Aug. 1902, and Hays to Wilson, 18 Sept. 1902.
25 UTA, Walker Papers, Plummer to Walker, 4 Oct. 1902.
26 PAC, Hays Papers, 15–16, Hays to Wilson, 18 Sept. 1902.

27 UTA, Walker Papers, Plummer to Walker, 4 Oct. 1902.
28 *Ibid.*, Plummer to Walker, 27 Sept. 1902.
29 PAC, Hays Papers, 15–16, 109–11, Hays to Wilson, 18 Sept. 1902, and 27 March 1903.

as a proposed partnership between two very unequal railways. The general manager of the Canadian Bank of Commerce reported despairingly of the meeting, and described "Sir Rivers Wilson acting in a most tactless manner and showing a complete ignorance of the political situation as well as that of the railroads in the North West."[30]

This meeting made it clear that the Canadian Northern was not for sale on terms acceptable to Hays. Some officials of the Canadian Bank of Commerce, moreover, were at last becoming convinced that western railways, particularly the Canadian Northern, might be profitable after all. B. E. Walker, general manager of the Bank, began to fear the Bank might lose Mackenzie and Mann as customers if it continued to exert pressure on them to sell. When rumours began to spread that Mackenzie and Mann were in trouble with their bank, Walker issued highly reassuring statements, making it clear that the Canadian Bank of Commerce would continue and increase its support of Mackenzie and Mann and their Canadian Northern Railway.[31]

Charles Melville Hays was convinced, none the less, that the rival Canadian Northern line could be starved into submission. He knew that Canadian Northern construction depended on government bond guarantees, and he believed he could persuade at least the federal government not to grant Canadian Northern guarantees until Mackenzie and Mann accepted his terms. He urged that a Grand Trunk subsidiary be organized and chartered to build a railway "on practically the same route as that contemplated by Messrs. Mackenzie and Mann".[32] This company should then apply for federal aid. "The mo-

30 UTA, Walker Papers, Walker to Robert Stewart, 30 April 1903.
31 Statement by B. E. Walker, general manager of the Canadian Bank of Commerce to Toronto shareholders' meeting, 18 Nov. 1902, as reported in CAR, 1902. For the Bank of Commerce this announcement marked a turning point. B. E. Walker, later president of the Canadian Bank of Commerce, became a strong believer in Mackenzie and Mann's vision of western Canada and its future, as a result of an inspection trip he made in September of 1902. That trip, and Walker's public endorsement of Mackenzie and Mann a few months later, marks the beginning of the Canadian Bank of Commerce's strong commitment to western development. Prior to that date the Bank had granted Mackenzie and Mann credit because they were wealthy and were willing to pledge their personal credit; after 1902 because their western railway was regarded as a most promising venture. UTA, Walker Papers, Walker Diary and Journal, 1902.
32 PAC, Hays Papers, I, 15–16, 105–6, Hays to Wilson, 18 Sept. 1902 and 24 March 1903.

ment we should do this," he wrote confidently, "the importance of Messrs. Mackenzie and Mann as a factor in the situation would at once cease and the subsidies, concessions, etc., that they would otherwise obtain would be given to the new company. Messrs. Mackenzie and Mann would also be placed in a position where they would come to us to open negotiations for the sale of their line to the Grand Trunk Railway which they are unwilling to do now except at an unreasonable price."[33] Hays reportedly had already received private assurances from the Prime Minister that his company would, in fact, be given preferential treatment if no arrangement with Mackenzie and Mann could be made.[34]

This was railroading in the American tradition, and Hays was convinced that the Grand Trunk would win in an all-out fight with the Canadian Northern. Wilson and his fellow Grand Trunk directors were sceptical. They certainly would have preferred an amicable arrangement with Mackenzie and Mann, but they finally authorized the preparation of a memorial to the Prime Minister of Canada in which aid for a Pacific extension would be requested. Hays was again told, however, that he must not commit the Grand Trunk directly to the project.[35] The memorial was prepared by Hays, George Cox, and William Wainwright, another ex-American railroader recruited by Hays for this project.[36]

Mackenzie and Mann fully realized the dangerous position in which they were placed by the Grand Trunk petition. The situation was made worse by the fact that they did not get on very well with the Prime Minister, who personally preferred the cultured and urbane Grand Trunk president to the backwoods promoters of a pioneer prairie road. They were not, however, without political friends and influence. Their branch lines and the rate reductions to which they had committed themselves were very popular in western Canada. They received strong assurances from prairie Members of Parliament that their interests would be protected. Clifford Sifton and Frank Oliver were quite explicit in their assurances of a federal bond guarantee for proposed Canadian

33 *Ibid.*, 31–6, Hays to Wilson, 22 Oct. 1902.
34 UTA, Walker Papers, Plummer to Walker, 4 Oct. 1902.
35 PAC, Hays Papers, I, 23–4, 36,

Wilson to Hays, 1 and 24 Oct. 1902.
36 PAC, Laurier Papers, CCXLIII, 67887–9, George Cox, C. M. Hays, William Wainwright to Laurier, 2 Nov. 1902.

Northern extensions from Grandview to Edmonton and from Erwood to Prince Albert. Few westerners were opposed to the Grand Trunk scheme as such, but they were determined that the advantages gained in the 1901 agreement with the Canadian Northern must not be lost. That agreement was the basis of the western railway's political strength in the struggle with the Grand Trunk. It was also one of the principal reasons why Hays, who regarded the agreement as a "troublesome and hurtful thing", refused to make any really generous purchase offers to Mackenzie and Mann. Hays made it very clear that he would have nothing to do with the kind of government rate regulation that Mackenzie and Mann had accepted. Western politicians, on the other hand, were determined to retain these regulatory powers. If government controls over rates were to be retained, the Canadian Northern had to be saved. Consequently, Mackenzie and Mann got sufficiently strong assurances from Sifton that they believed the government was committed to a $13,000-per-mile bond guarantee for the 620-mile Edmonton line.[37] The appropriate federal guarantee was voted by Parliament in July 1903. Hays had failed in his attempt to starve the Canadian Northern into submission. With both federal and Manitoba governments behind them Mackenzie and Mann could defy further Grand Trunk attacks. Hays ruefully informed Wilson that Mackenzie was "as cocky as ever".[38]

While the federal guarantees for the Canadian Northern's Edmonton line made their way through Parliament, Hays encountered serious difficulties in having his proposals accepted. In their original memorial the Grand Trunk officials had asked for a cash subsidy of $6,400 per mile, a 5,000-acre-per-mile land-grant subsidy, a generous transportation contract, full tax exemptions for twenty years, and duty-free importation of all construction materials and rolling stock. In return, a new railway, enjoying a traffic interchange but no direct financial backing from the Grand Trunk, would be built from North Bay to the Pacific coast. Nothing was said about rates to be charged on the new railway.

It is doubtful whether even Hays expected that these proposals

37 PAC, Hays Papers, I, 99–101, Hays to A. W. S., 6 March 1903; UTA, Walker Papers, Plummer to Walker, 4 Oct. 1902.

38 Ibid., 159–62, Hays to Wilson, 19 June 1903.

would be accepted. Certainly no government aware of the political and economic conditions of the time could have accepted them. Laurier had no alternative but to reject the request,[39] but he expressed his own strong desire that Hays submit new proposals, and he hoped that a satisfactory agreement would eventually be reached. Hays immediately prepared a new proposal which was submitted to the government in February 1903. It called for either a $16,400-per-mile cash and/or land subsidy, or a $15,000-per-mile bond guarantee, the guaranteed bonds to rank after a proposed $10,000-per-mile first-mortgage bond issue.[40]

The federal government was not entirely satisfied. It wanted a direct and full endorsement of the project from the Grand Trunk. Safeguards and specific undertakings that traffic from the assisted lines would be routed through Canadian maritime ports rather than to the much closer Grand Trunk Atlantic terminus at Portland, Maine, were demanded. The Maritimes demanded traffic interchanges and extensions of the Intercolonial Railway, while Members from Ontario and Quebec began to talk of a new transcontinental development road across the northern clay belt. Railways Minister A. G. Blair wanted the railway to be subject to fairly rigid rate controls under the proposed Board of Railway Commissioners, while others demanded a very substantial $1,000,000 deposit which would be forfeited if the railway failed to live up to all its commitments. Still others demanded that Canadian contractors and workers be given preference when construction work began.

Hays was not afraid of government bargaining, but he soon found himself seriously handicapped. Mackenzie and Mann were always on hand, eagerly promising whatever the government wanted if it would give them the contract.[41] It was almost impossible for Hays to bargain with the government when these rivals were in town, and the Canadian Northern promoters soon became a tremendous burden to the Grand Trunk Pacific officials. The rate issue, which Hays described as "a very serious blemish on the value of the property", could not be ignored by the politicians, and Hays lamented that the government "are continu-

---

39 PAC, Hays Papers, I, 37–9, 47–8, Hays to Wilson, 24 Oct. and 18 Nov. 1902.
40 PAC, Laurier Papers, 70057–9,

Hays to Laurier, 9 Nov. 1903.
41 PAC, Hays Papers, I, 231–3, 455–7, Hays to Wilson, 20 July 1903, and 2 Feb. 1904.

ally confronted with the precedents already established by their aid to the Canadian Northern."[42] Federal aid for the Edmonton line included provisions for the regulation of rates by the Board of Railway Commissioners, to which Mackenzie and Mann had consented without difficulty.

By the end of 1903 it was clear that Mackenzie and Mann were far stronger and more determined than Hays had anticipated. Wilson became convinced that it would be better to allow the entire Grand Trunk Pacific project to fall through than to compete with Mackenzie and Mann, "who will swallow any conditions he [Laurier] may impose on them."[43] There is no doubt that the Grand Trunk Pacific scheme would have failed, had it not been for repeated assurances by the Prime Minister, who was determined to see the Grand Trunk on the Pacific coast. Eventually a contract was drawn up, but it was accepted by Hays only after Laurier pledged his personal support for ameliorative amendments at a later date.[44]

Laurier was determined to deal with the Grand Trunk. He got on well with Wilson and also thought the new transcontinental Grand Trunk system would benefit the Liberal party politically in much the same way as association with the CPR had benefited the Conservative party. His determination to deal with the Grand Trunk eventually placed great strain on several Cabinet ministers and nearly destroyed Cabinet unity. The ministers were sharply divided on the issue, but none was particularly enthusiastic about the Grand Trunk proposals. Clifford Sifton, the spokesman of the West in the Cabinet, made it clear that he would not support any scheme which forced the Canadian Northern out of the field, unless similar or better concessions were obtained from the new company. He wanted the two roads to work together, the one operating the western section and the other the eastern portion of a new transcontinental system. Failing such an arrangement, the Canadian Northern should continue to receive federal support to continue its building program.

Sifton's attitude towards the Grand Trunk itself was rather ambivalent. He was suspicious and sometimes openly hostile. At times he

42 *Ibid.*, 91–2, Hays to Wilson, 21 Feb. 1903.
43 *Ibid.*, 460–2, Wilson to Hays, 3 Feb. 1904.
44 *Ibid.*, 487, Hays to Wilson, 13 Feb. 1904.

urged Laurier to break off all negotiations with the Grand Trunk, and to build a railway link between Winnipeg and Sudbury by government commission and allow both the Grand Trunk and the Canadian Northern to use this trackage. At other times he seemed prepared to leave the construction of this necessary link to the Grand Trunk, provided that the railway would negotiate a perpetual traffic contract with the Canadian Northern which would "ensure the Grand Trunk getting all the business of the Canadian Northern from the West, and would ensure the Canadian Northern getting all the business of the Grand Trunk from the East."[45] The consistent element in Sifton's policy was that the Canadian Northern should continue to serve the West. He considered the building of two new transcontinental lines to be excessive, but as a westerner he was unable to prevent it. It was politically inexpedient to advocate the construction of only one railway system in the rail-hungry West when there was a possibility of having two. Neither Sifton nor his western supporters would exchange the Canadian Northern for the Grand Trunk Pacific, but many westerners would be very happy to have both.

Further and more determined opposition to the Grand Trunk proposals came from the Minister of Railways and Canals. Andrew G. Blair became the chief spokesman of a policy of government ownership of railways, and he received considerable support from some prairie Members, but concerted opposition from Sifton. These men felt that if the government was required to supply most of the money for the Grand Trunk Pacific, or at least underwrite most of the risks, it might as well build the road itself and reap all the benefits of public ownership. It was never clear, however, whether these anticipated benefits were to be primarily financial or political.

Almost immediately after the first Grand Trunk proposals were

45 PAC, Sifton Papers, CCXCII, 264–9, Sifton to Laurier, 20 March 1903. After formally breaking his associations with the Laurier government, Sifton said of Hays, "I have never known so coldblooded a raider of the treasury as the man who is in charge." *Ibid.*, CXCIX, 158133, Sifton to Dafoe, 9 Jan. 1912. Of the Grand Trunk Pacific he wrote, "So far as I am able to judge the GTP never keeps its word. If it does, I have never known the case." *Ibid.*, 158133–7, Sifton to Dafoe, 21 Nov. 1912. PAC, Laurier Papers, CCCVI, 82781–2, Sifton to Laurier, 21 Feb. 1904. PAC, Sifton Papers, CCXCII, 264–9, Memorandum respecting the Grand Trunk Pacific Railway, by Sifton, 20 March 1903.

received, Blair drafted a lengthy memorandum on the railway question. He offered a strong defence of the policy of government ownership and held up the record of the Intercolonial Railway as an illustration of the merits of such a policy. "The main object to be attained in railway administration is the highest efficiency at the lowest cost. The Intercolonial has come closer to that point than any other railway in Canada, and if other than high State considerations had influenced its location it would now be enjoying a most successful career."[46] Blair then went on to recommend that the Intercolonial Railway be extended to Georgian Bay by a government purchase of J. R. Booth's Canada Atlantic Railway, which was for sale. At Georgian Bay ports he expected traffic interchanges and agreements between the Canadian Northern and the Intercolonial, which would then carry all the traffic originating on the Canadian Northern and Canada Atlantic lines. Thus the Intercolonial would become profitable, an important consideration for the Minister, who represented Saint John, New Brunswick. The arrangement would, of course, give the Canadian Northern the advantage of a strong eastern connection.

Blair's scheme would bring the Intercolonial into Ontario and thus silence much criticism which, the Minister argued, had arisen only "because no considerable section of the people [of Ontario] has any direct friendly interest in the railway."[47] Of corruption, political-influence peddling, and waste on the Intercolonial, Blair professed complete ignorance, although he claimed to have investigated the matter thoroughly.

This memorandum is a remarkable document since it so blithely and blatantly ignored or denied one of the most widely held political beliefs of the period—that the Intercolonial was poorly run and patronage-ridden. It reflected Blair's firm belief in public ownership of railways, but his colleagues never took his arguments seriously. Stories were circulated that a man writing this kind of memorandum must be in the pay of the Intercolonial and possibly of the Canadian Northern as well.

---

46 *Confidential Memorandum of the Minister of Railways and Canals upon certain railway questions,* 8. A copy of this memorandum is available in both the Laurier Papers and the Borden Papers. Printed copy in author's possession.
47 *Ibid.,* 9.

Laurier disagreed sharply with Blair on the subject of public owner-ship and operation of railways. He was prepared to pass legislation regulating the activities and policies of the railways, and if necessary even to build needed new lines, but he had no confidence in the government's ability to operate railways successfully. He wrote,

The government's operation of railways in this country has not been successful, and, I very much fear, cannot be made successful, except under different conditions which have not yet arisen. There is at present a supreme consideration, superior to all others, against the acquisition by the government of Canadian railways; those railways would have to compete with railways managed by keen and ambitious men whose chief preoccupation is to take traffic away from their rivals, and are always planning and thinking over that object. For the government to own the railway of this country and to have to enter into competition with American railways would mean one thing, and that, disaster, which would certainly follow in the end.[48]

Obviously Laurier and his Minister of Railways and Canals did not view the subject in the same light, and when he received the Grand Trunk proposals, Laurier had a difficult decision to make. If he en-trusted the negotiations to the Minister of Railways and Canals—who should have conducted them but who was in basic disagreement with the whole proposition—a successful arrangement with the Grand Trunk seemed remote. Laurier was enthusiastic about the railway's western plans and wanted the negotiations carried to a successful conclusion. He therefore decided to carry the negotiations himself, arguing that the matter was of such importance that it merited his personal atten-tion. Blair was deliberately bypassed and kept in ignorance of the details and progress of the negotiations. When Blair discovered what was happening, he resigned. Blair's lengthy memorandum and his let-ter of resignation fully document the wide ideological rift between the two men which led to the Minister's resignation.[49] The Laurier govern-

48 PAC, Laurier Papers, CCCLIII, 94248–9, Laurier to Lighthall, 2 Feb. 1905.
49 *Ibid.*, CCLXXII, 74954–62 and 74963–9, Blair to Laurier, 10 and 13 July 1904; PAC, Brewin Papers, Blair to Rev. Frank H. Brewin, 3 Aug. 1903. There have been persistent suggestions, particularly by O. D. Skelton, that Laurier feared that Blair might be

ment had decided against government ownership and operation of the new railways that Canada needed.

Further political opposition to the Grand Trunk scheme developed in Ontario and Quebec. As soon as it became clear that the government would definitely grant assistance to one or more new transcontinental railways, the Ontario and Quebec members began to suggest very substantial enlargements of the original Grand Trunk proposal of a new railway from North Bay or Sudbury to the Pacific coast. Each began to voice the claims of his own section. Old Liberal objections to all government aid to railways gave way to demands for aid to new railways in every province. The project, as outlined, was of relatively little value to the people living east of North Bay, but it could cost them a great deal. Quebec Members in particular, already alarmed by Sifton's vigorous immigration program, which was upsetting the racial and ethnic balance between French and English in western Canada, began to see excellent settlement and pioneering opportunities in their own underdeveloped northern areas. With access by rail, French settlement could be promoted in these parts. Laurier shared the Quebec Members' enthusiasm, and it soon became apparent that eastern politicians would support the new Grand Trunk Pacific project only if it were substantially enlarged.

The Maritimers, never backward in recognizing the political benefits of a new railway, soon began to see merit in extending the proposed railway not only across the northern clay belt of Ontario and Quebec, but all the way to the Atlantic coast. Otherwise, many argued, the unfortunate location and operational inefficiency of the Intercolonial would still compel many shippers to send their winter traffic to American ports. They were particularly concerned that the Grand Trunk Pacific traffic would go to Portland unless a better rail connection

corruptly influenced, but at the time of Blair's resignation Laurier specifically reassured the Governor General that he had no definite evidence of any corrupt actions by Blair. PAC, Minto Papers, II, 20–1, Memo of a meeting of Lord Minto with Laurier, 20 Oct. 1902. After his resignation Blair was appointed the first chairman of the Board of Railway Commissioners, while his friend and close political associate, William Pugsley, later received the appointment as federal Minister of Public Works. The scope for corrupt dealing in these two posts was as great as, if not greater than, it was in the Railways and Canals portfolio.

with Quebec City and Montreal were obtained. Extension of the new railway to the Atlantic by a shorter and more direct route seemed the logical solution. Since the opening of new territories was to be one of the contributions of the new railway, arguments about the benefits of opening new territory in New Brunswick soon flourished.

As a result, the original proposals of the Grand Trunk rapidly grew larger and larger, and Hays had some bitter comments after one of the hearings of the Standing Committee on Railways, Canals and Telephone Lines. Members obviously appeared far more interested in increased local rail facilities than in the viability of the entire project. Hays and other Grand Trunk officials saw little value in a line to Quebec City, much less in one to the Atlantic. Hays, despite strong assurances to the contrary before the Standing Committee, was convinced that Portland should and would remain the most economical Atlantic port for the Grand Trunk and Grand Trunk Pacific. He had no sympathy for any form of Canadian economic nationalism that might force the traffic of his road into other than the most economical channels. He was realistic enough to recognize, however, that promises must be made that traffic originating on subsidized lines would be shipped through Canadian ports. He made the necessary promises, but steadfastly fought all suggestions that the Grand Trunk be fined or penalized in any way if it failed to send its traffic to Canadian ports. He reassured Wilson that his promises to the Standing Committee really meant nothing: "In the absence of any penalty for any breach of the provisions we may safely assume that those natural conditions which govern the movement of traffic will apply, notwithstanding anything to the contrary and that it will move via the shortest and most direct routes in future as it always has in the past."[50] Laurier and the members of the Standing Committee on Railways, Canals and Telephone Lines were foolish enough to take Hays at his word and did not prescribe any penalties that would apply in the event that the traffic of the Grand Trunk Pacific went to Portland.

The new demands, and the unwillingness of the Grand Trunk to build the additional mileage, led to a complete new plan. This plan

50 PAC, Hays Papers, I, 117–46, 232–3, Memo on the Proceedings of the Select Standing Committee on Railways, Canals and Telephone Lines, held on 7 May 1903, and Hays to Wilson, 20 July 1903.

was first enunciated by Postmaster General William Mulock of Ontario. Mulock suggested that the entire scheme be split into two parts. The line from Winnipeg to Quebec City or, if necessary, to Moncton should be built by government commission. He recommended that it be operated by the Intercolonial but serve as a common carrier for all railways engaged in east-west trade. Mulock further recommended that federal aid be granted to the Grand Trunk Pacific to build the more profitable section from Winnipeg west, but that at the same time federal aid to the Canadian Northern be continued.[51]

Laurier was prepared to support most of these recommendations, but he was unhappy about bringing the Intercolonial into the scheme to operate the mileage from Winnipeg to Quebec City or Moncton. He agreed that the eastern section should be built, and that no private company was likely to build it. He was not prepared, however, to see such a line operated by the government. Instead, he suggested that after the Winnipeg to Quebec or Moncton line was built by government commission, it be turned over to the Grand Trunk Pacific for operational purposes. The Grand Trunk would be required to pay a fixed annual rental and to grant running rights to other western roads, notably the Canadian Northern, which needed eastern connections.[52]

Politically this scheme was a compromise designed to give as much as possible to all factions within the Cabinet. Laurier was sick during the final negotiations and provided little effective leadership. He made certain that the project would be a political success simply by giving every region the railways it wanted, but the scheme lacked the careful planning necessary to ensure that the various parts were fully integrated.[53] Blair was the only Cabinet member to resign, and his resignation was virtually inevitable in view of the strong repugnance Laurier felt towards Blair's suggestions of government ownership and operation of railways.

Unfortunately, Laurier was a far better politician than businessman. From a business point of view the Liberal railway policy can be described only as a disaster. There were, first of all, no effective safe-

51 PAC, Laurier Papers, CCLII, 70245–52, W. Mulock to Laurier, 14 Feb. 1903.
52 PAC, Laurier Papers, CCLXXII, 74974–7, Laurier to Blair, 14 July
1903; PAC, Hays Papers, I, 155–8, Wilson to Laurier, 11 June 1903.
53 PAC, Hays Papers, I, 206, Wilson to Hays, 8 July 1903.

guards to ensure that the traffic of the new system would find its way to Canadian Atlantic ports, and in fact most Grand Trunk and Grand Trunk Pacific traffic going to the Atlantic coast went to Portland, Maine, until the entire Grand Trunk Railway system was nationalized. The Liberal policy merely saddled the Grand Trunk Pacific with responsibility for the operation of the long stretch of line from Winnipeg to Moncton—a section in which it had very little interest because there were few significant connections between the old Grand Trunk system and this new line across the northern clay belt. The matter was later made even worse when the Laurier government provided assistance for the construction of a Lake Superior cut-off, which effectively short-circuited the rest of the National Transcontinental.

By turning operations of the National Transcontinental over to the Grand Trunk Pacific, the Laurier government brought about another very unfortunate result. It thereby ensured that the Canadian Northern would have nothing to do with the scheme, and would soon begin construction of its own line north of Lake Superior. Only a neutral or friendly connection with the east could serve the Canadian Northern's purposes. Most of the Canadian Northern freight shipments originated on the prairies and were eastbound. This was particularly true of the bulky grain traffic. For the railway to operate efficiently, a substantial volume of westbound traffic was needed. As long as the Grand Trunk, on which a large volume of westbound traffic originated, was an eastern company only, mutually beneficial traffic exchanges were possible. Once the Grand Trunk built westward the Canadian Northern, in Mackenzie's words, "would be entirely deprived of all sources of westbound traffic and limited to that freight originating on the Lake and river ports during the season of navigation."[54] If the Grand Trunk Pacific operated the National Transcontinental line east of Winnipeg, it would almost certainly try to route as much westbound traffic as possible to its own prairie lines. The National Transcontinental, moreover, could accept eastbound shipments from the Canadian Northern only at Winnipeg, not at the Canadian Northern's eastern terminus at Port Arthur. With the two companies engaged in vigorous competition on the prairies, it was impossible for the Canadian North-

54 PAC, Borden Papers, File OC 153, 10454, Mackenzie to Borden, 4 Jan. 1913.

ern to be dependent on the Grand Trunk Pacific-operated National Transcontinental for its eastern connections. That the Prime Minister would seriously suggest that the Canadian Northern should use the Grand Trunk-operated National Trancontinental reveals his utter naïveté in railway matters,[55] rather than Canadian Northern intransigence.

The choice facing the Canadian Northern was either to sell out to the Grand Trunk Pacific or to build its own eastern system, including the expensive section north of Lake Superior where one line could still handle all the business. Certainly three lines were not needed in 1903. The proposals made by Railways Minister Blair and by Clifford Sifton would have accommodated the Canadian Northern's needs. Even Mulock's original proposal that the National Transcontinental be operated by the Intercolonial would have made a third line north of Lake Superior unnecessary.

Opposition leader Robert Borden suggested yet another scheme. He urged the government to nationalize and double-track the CPR's line north of Lake Superior, operate it through a neutral government commission, and open it to all companies engaged in transcontinental traffic.[56] All these proposals failed, however, because the Prime Minister was personally opposed to government-operated railway schemes and was determined to assist the Grand Trunk Pacific in its plans to build to the Pacific.

The government measures left the Canadian Northern in a difficult position which made expansion into eastern Canada almost inevitable. "We were in the West," Mann later recalled, "and we were bottled up; anything we had to send or get from the east had to go over our rival's railway."[57] Once the government policy was announced, how-

---

55 Blair very forcefully pointed out the absurdities of the scheme in the Cabinet before his resignation. When he resigned, Laurier informed him that he must no longer discuss these matters because "the deliberations of the Council, upon all matters which engage their attention, are strictly private and confidential." PAC, Laurier Papers, CCLXXII, 74963–77, Blair to Laurier, 13 July 1903, and Laurier to Blair, 14 July 1903.

56 PAC, *The National Transcontinental Railway Project: Speeches delivered by Mr. R. L. Børden, KC, MP, in 1903 and 1904, with Introduction,* pamphlet; Henry Borden, ed., *Robert Laird Borden: His Memoirs,* I (Toronto: McClelland and Stewart, 1969), 47.

57 *Arbitration,* 2683–6.

ever, Canadian railway men tried to give it the best possible interpretation. Ever hopeful of further government subsidies and guarantees, they began to make highly optimistic statements about the traffic potential of western Canada. The possibilities of the West suddenly became limitless to the railway presidents who wanted federal aid for further construction, or sought to avoid federal compulsion to cooperate with their rivals. Van Horne was one of the first to strike the brave new note of optimism. In a famous New York speech he said Canada urgently needed more railways. "We would hail with delight a parallel route from Atlantic to Pacific to help us develop the country. There is enough of it up there for us all."[58]

William Mackenzie was not far behind when he wrote in 1903,

Your directors wish to refute the suggestion which has been made in some quarters, that the Company has, or will have, serious competition to contend with. There is no fear of anything of the kind occurring. If all the contemplated and proposed railway schemes in Canada should be carried out, they will only tend to increase the Company's traffic by opening up the country and facilitating emigration.[59]

Even the Northern Pacific was affected, and it submitted an ambitious but rather vague scheme to build a new 2,500-mile railway system in western Canada. This proposal, apparently born of an internal power struggle in the management of the Northern Pacific, died an early death. The Canadian and Manitoba governments failed to respond as generously as the Americans had hoped they would.[60]

The negotiations and complaints of the railway magnates when dealing privately with the politicians or with their rivals strongly suggest that their optimism was not as great as their public pronouncements indicated. While Mackenzie simply exuded confidence in his 1903 annual report, he later admitted to Robert Borden,

The outlook was, to say the least, most discouraging. The Government of the day gave enormous assistance to one railway to invade the Western

58 *Manitoba Free Press*, 13 Nov. 1902.
59 *First Annual Report, Canadian Northern Railway, 1903*.

60 *Manitoba Free Press*, 1 March 1902; PAC, Sifton Papers, 16212–13, Mann to Sifton, 25 Feb. 1903.

field, and neglected to give corresponding assistance to the company, which by the Government's action was forced to build in the Eastern field, although the latter enterprise was more costly and as much in the public interest.[61]

The Manitoba bond guarantees of 1901 and the federal guarantees for the Edmonton and Prince Albert lines enabled Mackenzie and Mann to survive the first major Grand Trunk assault. The long-term interests of the Canadian Northern, however, were not assured. The company had to establish its own eastern connections if it expected to become more than a western feeder line of its transcontinental rivals.

61 PAC, Borden Papers, File OC 153, 10454, Mackenzie to Borden, 4 Jan. 1913.

CHAPTER SIX

A BEGINNING
IN THE EAST
1903-1904

MACKENZIE AND MANN were not ready to push a rapid transcontinental construction program in 1903. Their first priority was to develop the prairie system to the point where it could originate sufficient traffic to make transcontinental connections operationally feasible. They felt, nevertheless, that the federal railway policy made transcontinental expansion inevitable and that eastern connections had to be secured as they became available.

Attempts to secure eastern connections in 1903 were greatly facilitated by the fact that the National Transcontinental–Grand Trunk proposals made several other major promotional ventures in Ontario and Quebec untenable. A number of eastern railways, some with a good deal of completed construction, became available at precisely the time when Mackenzie and Mann began their search for transcontinental connections. It was therefore possible for them to gain control of a series of financially troubled lines in Quebec, to seek important railway connections and charter rights in Ontario, and to create a profitable local system in Nova Scotia.

Initially Mackenzie and Mann hoped to use a joint water-and-land route from Port Arthur to Montreal and Quebec City. In order to do this they acquired an interest in several Great Lakes shipping ventures[1] and began serious negotiations with several eastern railway promoters and owners who were known to be willing to sell their properties.

The most desirable eastern railway that Mackenzie and Mann tried to acquire was the Canada Atlantic Railway. It was owned by Ottawa

1 PAC, Laurier Papers, CVIII, 137228–31, Confidential Memorandum, Unofficial and for Discussion Only,   Andrew T. Thompson, Solicitor, to Laurier, 2 June 1904.

lumber baron J. R. Booth and had a completed line from Depot Harbour on Georgian Bay to Coteau Junction near Montreal. It was the easiest and most natural link between the Canadian Northern lines on the prairies and any connections with the St. Lawrence lowlands that Mackenzie and Mann might acquire.

Serious negotiations with J. R. Booth were already under way when the Grand Trunk formally announced its plans to build to the Pacific,[2] although Mackenzie and Mann became much more enthusiastic about the line when those plans were revealed. General Manager Hays of the Grand Trunk was certainly aware of the strategic importance of the Canada Atlantic in any Canadian Northern plans for eastward expansion and he began to think of acquiring the Booth property in order to forestall Mackenzie and Mann. The Canada Atlantic did not really fit into the Grand Trunk Pacific plans, but Hays recommended in June 1902 that the Grand Trunk try to get it for ten million dollars.[3]

Mackenzie and Mann had great difficulty in arranging the financing necessary to purchase the Booth line. Booth wanted cash. Mackenzie and Mann had very little cash and offered securities instead. Booth would accept these only if they were backed by a federal guarantee, and this stipulation brought the Canadian Northern promoters to the Prime Minister's doorstep.[4] Their scheme was to buy the capital stock of the Canada Atlantic with federally guaranteed Canadian Northern securities issued especially for that purpose. Their request for the necessary federal guarantees came in the midst of the negotiations between the federal government and the Grand Trunk for assistance to build the Grand Trunk Pacific. Laurier was understandably reluctant to do anything until the larger negotiations of the Grand Trunk Pacific were completed. Booth, seeing the intense rivalry between the Canadian Northern and the Grand Trunk, was quite happy to pit them against one another in their attempts to acquire his railway.

Negotiations between Mackenzie and Mann and Laurier on the matter proceeded very slowly, but by June 1904 Mackenzie felt that the federal government was at least unofficially committed to giving

2 PAC, Hays Papers, I, 11, Wilson to Hays, 18 June 1902.
3 Ibid., 13, Hays to Wilson, 27 June 1902.

4 PAC, Laurier Papers, CVIII, 137228–31, Confidential Memorandum, Unofficial and for Discussion Only, Andrew T. Thompson to Laurier, 2 June 1904.

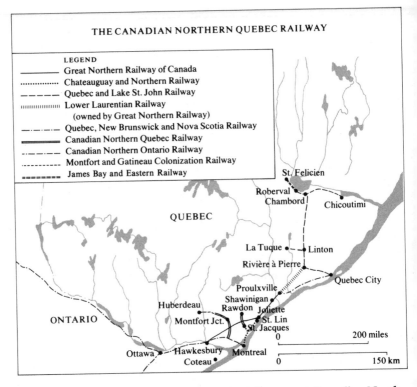

THE CANADIAN NORTHERN QUEBEC RAILWAY

LEGEND
——————— Great Northern Railway of Canada
.... Chateauguay and Northern Railway
— — — — Quebec and Lake St. John Railway
ııııııııııı Lower Laurentian Railway
 (owned by Great Northern Railway)
—··—··—·· Quebec, New Brunswick and Nova Scotia Railway
══════ Canadian Northern Quebec Railway
—·—·—·— Canadian Northern Ontario Railway
- - - - - - - Montfort and Gatineau Colonization Railway
════════ James Bay and Eastern Railway

him a guarantee on $14,000,000 worth of 3-per-cent Canadian Northern bonds which would be used to purchase the Canada Atlantic.[5] Unfortunately for Mackenzie, the federal Cabinet was divided on the issue and Laurier himself was distinctly unenthusiastic.

Hays of the Grand Trunk kept a watchful eye on these proceedings. When negotiations between Mackenzie and Mann, J. R. Booth, and the federal government approached a successful conclusion, Hays urged his superiors in London to make a counter offer. Laurier, in an apparent breach of confidence, informed Hays that the Cabinet had not yet reached a firm and binding decision and was in fact divided on the issue.[6] Some wanted the Canada Atlantic to go to the Canadian Northern, others wanted it to go to the Grand Trunk, and still others wanted the government to buy it and turn it over to the Intercolonial. This information from Laurier enabled Hays to act at just the right time. In June 1904 he urged the Grand Trunk to offer $12,000,000.

5 PAC, Hays Papers, 621–5, Hays to Wilson, 21 June 1904.

6 Ibid., 611–12, Hays to Wilson, 17 June 1904.

This was $2,000,000 more than he had recommended in 1902 but still $2,000,000 less than the amount of securities Mackenzie and Mann hoped to have available.[7]

Hays argued that the Canada Atlantic would be useful to the Grand Trunk in several ways. First, it would give the Grand Trunk a railway connection with Ottawa, and therefore greater political influence in the capital. Second, it would prevent the line from falling into the hands of Mackenzie and Mann. Third, it would effectively stop the threat of an Intercolonial extension to Georgian Bay. Fourth, and apparently most important to Hays, a portion of the line could be used to divert traffic from Canadian to more direct and therefore more economical American channels by "deflecting Chicago and Boston traffic via Coteau Junction and St. Albans, at a considerable saving in distance as against handling it as at present via Montreal and St. John."[8] Hays, however, cautioned his London superiors that "it would not be politic at this time to make any reference thereto."[9]

Hays got authorization from London to offer up to $12,000,000 in 3-per-cent Grand Trunk guaranteed bonds.[10] Booth, seeing that the time was opportune, decided also to get rid of his Georgian Bay port facilities and lake vessels at a good price.[11] A secret agreement was worked out between Hays and Booth for a total purchase price of $16,000,000.[12] Booth and Hays then approached the federal government for the necessary enabling legislation. There were several very stormy Cabinet sessions, and Mackenzie and Mann did all they could to persuade the federal government not to authorize the transaction, but in the end Laurier agreed to Hays's request and the transaction was finalized in September 1904, shortly before the federal election.

Mackenzie and Mann and their friends were furious. They had suffered a very serious reverse, and there was talk of a complete estrangement between them and the Laurier government. It was claimed that the Canadian Northern refused to make contributions to the Liberal election campaign, and during the election various

7 *Ibid.*, 621–8, Wilson to Hays, 24 June 1904, and Hays to Wilson, 21 June 1904.
8 *Ibid.*, 621–5, Hays to Wilson, 21 June 1904.
9 *Ibid.*, 698, Hays to Wilson, 23 Sept. 1904.
10 *Ibid.*, 627–8, Wilson to Hays, 24 June 1904.
11 *Ibid.*, 621–5, Hays to Wilson, 21 June 1904.
12 *Synoptical Histories*, 31.

stories of railway cabals against the government gained considerable prominence. Hays was convinced that "with the possibility of their obtaining the Canada Atlantic removed, the Canadian Northern could not be very much of a factor as far as eastern Canada is concerned."[13] Their advance eastward had certainly been stalled, but only temporarily. They immediately laid plans to enlarge substantially the James Bay Railway's charter and then sought both provincial and federal assistance to build what soon became the Canadian Northern Ontario Railway.

The proposed purchase of the Canada Atlantic Railway was undoubtedly the most important aspect of the Canadian Northern's eastern strategy. That strategy, however, also included the acquisition and subsequent reorganization of several moribund Quebec railways.

Railway promotion in Quebec in the late nineteenth century was often a unique and curious mixture of French-Canadian nationalism and Anglo-American entrepreneurial avarice. Colonization and settlement programs for French Canadians in northern Quebec were regarded by many politicians and priests as patriotic and religious obligations. Government-subsidized colonization railways, often built by private entrepreneurs who were primarily interested in construction profits or the development of specific forest or hydro-electric resources, became fashionable. Most of these colonization roads rarely turned a profit unless they could obtain connections and some through traffic from more westerly roads in search of Canadian eastern connections.

One of the most ambitious and foolhardy Quebec colonization railway schemes was the Trans-Canada Railway. Its promoters projected a line from Quebec City to Moosonee on James Bay, to Norway House on the Saskatchewan River, to Lesser Slave Lake, and finally to Port Simpson or Essington on the northern British Columbia coast.[14] Incorporated in 1895, the Trans-Canada Railway certainly excited a number of Canadian railway engineers and builders. Sir Sandford

13 PAC, Hays Papers, 697–700, Hays to Wilson, 23 Sept. 1904.
14 According to some Trans-Canada Railway enthusiasts there were at least 108,000 acres of arable land around James Bay alone. J. G. Scott, *Paper on the Trans-Canada Railway read* *before the Literary and Historical Society of Quebec by J. G. Scott, General Manager of the Quebec and Lake St. John Railway and the Great Northern Railway of Canada* (Quebec: Chronicle Printing, 1903), 13.

Fleming, Canada's most respected surveyor and railway engineer, strongly endorsed the scheme, and CPR President Van Horne was quoted as saying, "The Trans-Canada road has started with better prospects than the Canadian Pacific once had."[15] Mackenzie and Mann gained control of the James Bay Railway in the same year that the Trans-Canada Railway was incorporated, and for a time they hoped their railway would serve as the Trans-Canada Railway's link with southern Ontario. The Trans-Canada Railway, however, never got beyond a few preliminary surveys and an impressive religious ceremony marking the beginning and also, as it happened, the end of construction.[16] Announcement of the Grand Trunk Pacific–National Transcontinental Railway proposals in 1902 extinguished the last flicker of hope for the Trans-Canada Railway.

The Trans-Canada Railway was never more than a paper scheme. Several of its promoters, however, also acquired interests in a second, more southerly, trans-Quebec railway. This was the Great Northern Railway of Canada, which had ambitions of building from Quebec City via the St. Maurice Valley to Hawkesbury on the Ottawa River. Its history was chequered and confused, but twenty miles of line were built in the 1890s and running rights or amalgamations arranged with a few smaller colonization railways. It was this railway that James McNaught, president of the Northern Pacific and Manitoba Railway, selected as a likely eastern connection for the Northern Pacific.[17] McNaught, together with H. H. Melville of Boston, acquired controlling interest in 1895 and began negotiations for running rights over the Intercolonial Railway in the east and the Canadian Atlantic Railway and the Duluth, Mesabi and Northern Railway[18] in the west. Assistance from the Manitoba government in the construction of a Northern Pacific and Manitoba extension to Duluth was a further and essential part of McNaught's moonstruck scheme.

15 *Ibid.*, 17.
16 *Ibid.*, 2.
17 MSHS, Northern Pacific Railroad Company Records, President's Correspondence, File No. 167, Fisher to Winter, 29 April 1897, and 12 April 1897, and E. A. Adams to C. S. Mellon, 28 Nov. 1898.

18 The Minute Books of the Great Northern Railway of Canada provide a great deal of detail on the rather complex arrangements which gave Melville and McNaught effective control of that railway. Those details are not directly relevant to the main theme of this study.

The collapse of Northern Pacific negotiations with the Manitoba government in 1897, and McNaught's forced departure from the Northern Pacific and Manitoba presidency, ended all prospects of a Quebec connection for the Northern Pacific. Melville and McNaught, however, were too deeply involved in the Great Northern Railway of Canada and its affiliates—the Lower Laurentian Railway, the Chateauguay and Northern Railway, and the Montfort and Gatineau Colonization Railway Company—to abandom them in 1897. Instead, they forged ahead with construction of the main Quebec City to Hawkesbury line of the Great Northern Railway of Canada,[19] hopeful that some western road in search of eastern connections would buy the line, leaving them with a sizable promoter's profit.

Prospects for such a happy development brightened in 1902 when Dr. W. Seward Webb, one-time chairman of the board of directors of the Rutland Road and president of the St. Lawrence and Adirondack Railway, became interested in both the Canada Atlantic and the Great Northern railways. Dr. Webb obtained a firm option to purchase the Canada Atlantic and had a new company, the Great Northern of Canada Consolidated, incorporated in the state of New Jersey with an authorized capitalization of $10,000,000.[20] It was widely believed that Dr. Webb was acting on behalf of the New York Central Railway, which was allegedly planning a major expansion into Canada.[21]

Dr. Webb dropped his Canadian options in 1902, and when the details of the Grand Trunk's transcontinental plans were revealed, it became clear to the owners of both the Canada Atlantic and the Great Northern railways that the most likely purchasers of their lines were the Grand Trunk or the Canadian Northern railways. Melville and McNaught, like J. R. Booth, contacted both railways. The Great Northern Railway of Canada, however, was a far less attractive property than the Canada Atlantic. Its 140-mile trackage carried a bonded indebtedness of $4,162,000 and had issued capital stock with a par

19 CNRHQ, Notes compiled on the Great Northern Construction Company Minute Book, beginning 3 March 1898. The Meeting of Directors of the Great Northern Construction Company, 4 Nov. 1898, was particularly important.

20 *Railway Gazette*, 9 May 1902, 354.
21 *Synoptical Histories*, 28–36; PAC, Hays Papers, I, 13, Hays to Wilson, 27 June 1902. A lengthy write-up on the reorganization of the Great Northern Railway of Canada appeared in the *Boston News Bureau*, July 1904.

value of $7,550,000. In addition, $500,000 worth of bonds had been issued for the bridge across the Ottawa River, and $173,000 in postal and terminal bonds was also outstanding. Finally, the railway owed substantial sums to its contractors.[22] Considering these heavy obligations, totalling over $88,000 per mile of track, it was not surprising that the railway found itself in a continuous state of crisis. As the financial difficulties increased, aggressive and often seriously misleading bond-selling campaigns were organized until the railway was considered a serious danger to the general reputation of Canada.[23]

Mackenzie and Mann were certainly not eager to take over the massive debt burden of the Great Northern, but together with the Canada Atlantic Railway, the trans-Quebec line did offer some attractions. It could provide the Canadian Northern with needed eastern connections and might even be presented as an alternative scheme in the event that the Grand Trunk Pacific–National Transcontinental negotiations with the federal government failed. Any acquisition agreement made by Mackenzie and Mann would, of course, exact everything possible from Melville and McNaught, and from governments interested in seeing the lines completed and efficiently operated. Mackenzie and Mann were certainly not in a position to assume major reponsibilities and obligations in Quebec until the Canada Atlantic negotiations and the Grand Trunk Pacific–National Transcontinental plans were settled one way or another. What they needed was some measure of control without binding commitments.[24]

Serious negotiations between Mackenzie and Mann on the one hand and Melville and McNaught on the other were begun in January 1903. A "Basis of Understanding" was signed on 22 January 1903. It provided for the formation of a holding company to which Melville and McNaught were to transfer their holdings in the Great Northern Railway and the Chateauguay and Northern Railway. The holding com-

22 PAC, CNR Records, MCCXXXI, undated memorandum kept together with other official documents relating to the Great Northern Railway of Canada; *Synoptical Histories*, 193–4.
23 PAC, CNR Legal Series, Deposit No. 62, *Prospectus of the Great Northern Railway of Canada* (Quebec: Morning Chronicle, 1896). *Ibid.*, CNR

Legal Series, File 1014–20–3, Horne-Payne to Lash, 23 April 1906.
24 PAC, Hays Papers, 81, Wilson to Hays, 3 Feb. 1903; PAC, Laurier Papers, CVIII, 137228–31, Confidential Memorandum, Unofficial and for Discussion Only, Andrew T. Thompson to Laurier, 2 June 1904.

pany was to have an authorized capitalization of $8,000,000. A total of $6,150,000 was to be issued, fully paid up, to Melville and Mc-Naught in return for all their Great Northern and Chateauguay and Northern stock. Melville and McNaught were then to transfer half of the $6,150,000 to Mackenzie, Mann and Co. Ltd. in return for a cash payment of only $300,000, and even of that amount only $100,000 was to go directly to Melville and McNaught. The balance was to be used to look after immediate and urgent requirements of the Great Northern Railway of Canada.[25]

A number of things happened before this Basis of Understanding was incorporated into a formal agreement in December 1903. Melville and McNaught opened negotiations with the Grand Trunk Railway in an attempt to get more generous terms. The transfer of $3,075,000 of capital stock in the proposed company to Mackenzie and Mann in return for only $300,000 cash, of which they would get a mere $100,000, seemed less than equitable to the beleaguered American. Hays initially indicated some interest, but eventually declined to become involved. He was convinced that the Quebec lines were of no use to his company, and would probably prove worse than useless to Mackenzie and Mann if they failed to get the Canadian Atlantic Railway.[26]

Almost immediately after signing the Basis of Understanding Melville and McNaught transferred to the Great Northern Railway of Canada one of their local Quebec properties. They had purchased the assets and properties of the Montfort and Gatineau Colonization Railway for $300,000 at a bankruptcy sale on 3 October 1902.[27] The Montfort and Gatineau Colonization Railway, which had been incorporated in 1890, was authorized to build local lines and to open up new territories in the area immediately to the north of Lachute, Que-

25 PAC, CNR Legal Series, Deposit 62, Basis of Understanding arrived at between Mackenzie, Mann and Company and McNaught and Melville re the Great Northern Railway of Canada and the Chateauguay and Northern Railway, 22 Jan. 1903.
26 It is clear that Melville and McNaught tried very hard to persuade Hays to make a better offer for the Great Northern than that made by Mackenzie and Mann; their last effort came just before the final agreement was signed in Dec. 1903. PAC, Hays Papers, 81, 336, Wilson to Hays, 3 Feb. 1903, Hays to Wilson, 4 Feb. 1903, Wilson to Hays, 4 Feb. 1904, and "F.W.M." to Hays, 10 Dec. 1903.
27 *Synoptical Histories*, 194–5; PAC, CNR Legal Series, Deposit 62, Basis of Understanding, 1.

TABLE III

Operating Statistics of the Great Northern Railway of Canada

Year	Mileage operated	Gross earnings	Operating costs	Net earnings
		($)	($)	($)
1896	28	7,247.51	6,514.06	733.45
1897	28	6,198.47	6,184.05	14.42
1898	28	6,023.67	6,299.10	−275.43
1899	28	5,068.34	7,762.10	−2,693.76

Source: The Public Archives of Canada, R.G. 46. The Great Northern Railway had issued almost $5,000,000 worth of bonds, on which the annual interest amounted to nearly $250,000.

bec. Thirty-three miles of track, terminating at Huberdeau, Quebec, had been completed. It was thought this line might become a feeder line to the Great Northern Railway, and perhaps a link in a new transcontinental line.

The Montfort and Gatineau Colonization Railway was sold to the Great Northern Railway of Canada on 10 February 1903. Melville and McNaught simply took Great Northern stock as payment for their Montfort and Gatineau stock. Henceforth, the local railway was owned outright by the Great Northern Railway of Canada.

A second Melville and McNaught property was handled differently. The two Americans had taken a strong interest in the Chateauguay and Northern Railway because it promised to provide them with a running-rights arrangement into downtown Montreal. It got into serious financial difficulties with its contractors in 1903. The promoters had hoped to pay the contractors with subsidy money that would be earned when the railway was completed. Unfortunately, both the railway company and its contractors ran out of money and credit before the construction was completed and the subsidy earned.

Mackenzie and Mann were well aware of the strategic importance of a Montreal connection. In 1903, while negotiating for the Great Northern, they agreed to advance funds to the Chateauguay and Northern contractors to ensure completion of that line. Mann explained the situation to Laurier: "As the Contractor found himself short of funds

TABLE IV

Operating Statistics of the
Montfort and Gatineau Colonization Railway Company

Year	Mileage operated	Gross earnings	Operating costs	Net earnings
		($)	($)	($)
1896	21	2,817.08	7,184.08	−4,367.00
1897	21	3,320.76	7,830.88	−4,510.12
1898	33	4,991.26	5,960.98	−969.72
1899	33	10,594.73	13,825.21	−3,230.48
1900	33	15,472.05	16,402.62	−930.57
1901	33	21,172.67	22,559.19	−1,386.52
1902	33	20,826.78	22,884.35	−2,057.57

Source: The Public Archives of Canada, R.G. 46. The Montfort and Gatineau Colonization Railway Company had a bonded indebtedness of $147,000 in 1896 and $231,000 in 1902 when it was purchased and merged with the Great Northern Railway of Canada.

before the line was completed and the subsidies earned, we had to step in and save the situation."[28] The needed funds were advanced to H. H. Melville, who paid the contractors, Hanson Brothers of Ottawa and Montreal. When they completed their work, Hanson Brothers accepted stock of the Chateauguay and Northern as partial payment for their services, apparently holding the stock on behalf of their principal creditors, Mackenzie and Mann. Shortly after Hanson Brothers obtained majority control of the Chateauguay and Northern Railway it was leased for 999 years to the Great Northern Railway.[29] Later, Hanson Brothers transferred the stock to the Mackenzie and Mann interests as repayment for the loans and advances they had received.[30]

The smaller local lines were certainly useful as local feeder lines and sometimes they provided vital connections for the Great Northern. The Great Northern, however, was clearly the focus of the interests of Mackenzie and Mann in Quebec. In June 1903 the railway was threatened with collapse and Mackenzie and Mann advanced the $300,000 to

28 PAC, Laurier Papers, CCCXXIX, 88336–8, Mann to Laurier, 25 July 1904.

29 PAC, CNR Records, MCXCVIII, Stock Transfer Book of the Chateauguay and Northern Railway.
30 *Synoptical Histories*, 192.

meet a bond interest payment.[31] Their investment, however, was still very small. It was fairly clear to them that the Quebec projects were probably not worth the amounts they already owed. A major reorganization and substantial new government assistance were needed.

Fortunately for Mackenzie and Mann, the Great Northern Railway and its affiliates served an area in which the Prime Minister was particularly interested. St. Lin, the Prime Minister's birthplace, was within a few miles of the Great Northern main line. Laurier always took a very strong personal interest in the railway developments of Quebec, particularly those immediately to the north of Montreal. Almost everything that happened on those railways, from an unsatisfied claim for a broken wine bottle to the appointment of local station agents to new government subsidies, was of interest to the Prime Minister.[32] Mackenzie and Mann, who were having their difficulties with Laurier over the Grand Trunk Pacific negotiations, were determined to exact as much aid as possible from the federal government before rescuing the moribund Quebec lines.

On 1 July 1903, six months before a final agreement with Melville and McNaught was signed, the Great Northern Railway of Canada defaulted on an important bond interest payment.[33] The railway's shareholders, bondholders, and creditors, as well as the politicians, stood in danger of losing a great deal if formal bankruptcy proceedings were instituted. The only hope any of these individuals had of recouping something from their investment was to have the railway reorganized, completed, and provided with traffic arrangements with other, larger, systems. Mackenzie and Mann indicated that they might be willing to save the railway and connect it with their western system, but only if more government help were made available. In the meantime, all new construction was halted and the railway went deeper into debt with every passing day, as operations ground to a halt but fixed charges continued to mount. Working through J. P. Mallarkey, the

31 PAC, CNR Legal Series, Deposit 62, Supplementary Agreement of 27 June 1903, between Mackenzie, Mann and Company Limited and Melville and McNaught.
32 The extensive correspondence between the Prime Minister and J. P. Mallarkey, president of the Chateauguay and Northern Railway is particularly revealing in this respect.
33 PAC, Laurier Papers, CCCXXIX, 88336–8, Mann to Laurier, 25 July 1904. A series of legal documents in the CNR Records, MMMCXXXI, provides further details.

aptly named contractor, promoter, and president of the Chateauguay and Northern Railway, negotiations for more federal help were begun. After the 1903 default, construction moved no faster than the munificence of the impatient and irritated Prime Minister permitted. Laurier wanted the railways. Mackenzie and Mann made sure he paid the price.[34] A comparatively small investment had given the western promoters effective control of the Great Northern, which the Prime Minister was unwilling to abandon to a deserved bankruptcy.

The negotiations with Melville and McNaught were brought to a successful conclusion on 17 December 1903. In accordance with the earlier Basis of Understanding, the Northern Consolidated Holding Company was incorporated and its capital stock divided between Melville and McNaught and Mackenzie and Mann. Provision was also made whereby Mackenzie and Mann could acquire an additional 12,500 hundred-dollar shares of the Northern Consolidated Holding Company from Melville and McNaught for a further cash payment of $250,000. Melville and McNaught also agreed to make particular efforts to buy out the remaining outstanding stock of the Great Northern Railway. Capital stock of $1,076,900 from a total issue of $4,550,000, and $488,634 debenture stock from a total issue of $3,000,000 were still "in the hands of the public". Much of it was held by the old Quebec City interests who were rapidly losing interest in western extensions and were concentrating on various projects looking eastward.[35] All the outstanding stock acquired by Melville and McNaught was then to be turned over at cost to Mackenzie, Mann and Co. Ltd.[36]

While exerting as much pressure as possible on the federal government to obtain needed subsidies, Mackenzie and Mann also began negotiations with the bondholders of the Great Northern Railway and its affiliated lines. A special bondholders' committee had been established when the railway defaulted on interest payments in July of 1903.

34 PAC, Laurier Papers, CCCXXIX, 88336–8, 88341, 88557–8, 89103–4, 89105, and 89107, Mann to Laurier, 25 and 28 July 1904, J. P. Mallarkey to Laurier, 29 July 1904, Laurier to Mackenzie, 17 and 18 Aug. and 7 Sept. 1904.

35 PAC, CNR Legal Series, Deposit 62, series of agreements dated 22 Jan., 18 Feb., 25 April, 27 June, n.d., 7 Dec. and 17 Dec. 1903.

36 PAC, CNR Legal Series, Deposit 62, Memorandum re The Holding Company.

It was in the interests of the bondholders, as well as of Mackenzie and Mann, to arrange some sort of financial reorganization. Lengthy and complicated negotiations were undertaken and federal co-operation was again needed. No permanent arrangement was reached until 1905,[37] when Mackenzie and Mann felt reasonably confident of federal support for a transcontinental Canadian Northern Railway system.

The results of the Quebec arrangements made by Mackenzie and Mann in 1903 were startling. For the very modest investment of $300,000 and some smaller amounts advanced to local contractors, they had gained effective control of a new railway route across Quebec. The Quebec railways were admittedly in serious financial trouble, but if the federal government demonstrated a willingness to support their transcontinental schemes, Mackenzie and Mann were willing to re-organize the troubled Quebec lines into a useful railway system.

Mackenzie and Mann really stood to lose very little if their entire eastern strategy collapsed. Alternate connections at Duluth with American lines could provide the eastern connections their prairie system needed. Such an arrangement was in fact favoured by the Canadian Bank of Commerce, and at one time both Donald Mann and Roderick Mackenzie were apparently favourably disposed to American connections.[38] It was William Mackenzie who had a burning desire to create a Canadian transcontinental railway system, and he used control of the Quebec railways to exert strong pressure on the federal government. The fact that the proposed Canadian Northern transcontinental would rescue the troubled Quebec lines and channel all its traffic through Canadian Maritime ports made it very attractive in eastern Canada. This attraction grew as it became more and more obvious that Portland, Maine, would remain the Grand Trunk's eastern terminus.

---

37 PAC, CNR Records, MCCXXXI and MMMCXXXI. The Indenture of Mortgage securing Guaranteed Bonds, Great Northern Railway of Canada to The Central Trust Company of New York and the Canadian Northern Railway Company, 1 April 1905, and the later Indenture of Mortgage dated 6 Oct. 1906 between the Canadian Northern Quebec Railway, the Canadian Northern Railway, the British Empire Trust Company, and the National Trust Company provide very considerable detail on the early bond issues of the Great Northern Railway and its affiliates. The last-mentioned mortgage agreement covers over 100 pages and was designed to cover all exigencies.

38 UTA, Walker Papers, Plummer to Walker, 4 Oct. 1902.

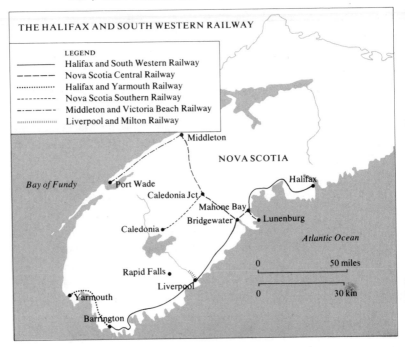

THE HALIFAX AND SOUTH WESTERN RAILWAY

LEGEND
——————— Halifax and South Western Railway
— — — — Nova Scotia Central Railway
················· Halifax and Yarmouth Railway
— — — — — Nova Scotia Southern Railway
—··—··— Middleton and Victoria Beach Railway
ıııııııııııııı Liverpool and Milton Railway

Middleton

NOVA SCOTIA

Bay of Fundy   Port Wade   Halifax
Caledonia Jct.
Mahone Bay
Bridgewater   Lunenburg
Caledonia

Atlantic Ocean

Rapid Falls
Liverpool

Yarmouth

Barrington

0   50 miles

0   30 km

As a result, the Canadian government eventually agreed to support the eastern Canadian schemes of Mackenzie and Mann, and by 1906 the two promoters were prepared to make a more forthright move than that made in 1903. From 1903 until 1906, however, the Quebec affairs remained uncertain. Failure to obtain the Canada Atlantic Railway in 1904 certainly contributed to that uncertainty, but it was the attitude of the Laurier government that concerned the two promoters most.

In an attempt to strengthen their political position in the Province of Quebec, Mackenzie and Mann became involved in a bizarre and notorious newspaper affair during the 1904 federal election campaign. The affair centred on the purchase of the newspaper *La Presse* in October 1904.

From the time the Grand Trunk proposals first came to the attention of the public, there were members and supporters of the Opposition Conservative party who hoped to attract all those dissatisfied with the railway policies of the Laurier government. Hugh Graham, the then moderately wealthy proprietor of the *Montreal Star* and one of the Conservatives' chief organizers and schemers in Montreal, became particularly enthusiastic about a rather wild scheme which would attract dissatisfied Liberals. As early as May 1903 he wrote to Opposition leader Robert Borden, "From now on you will see the biggest circus ever seen in Canada. . . . Watch the big ones tremble; watch them crawl. It will be good fun for you and some of us who have had trials and snubs and insults. The ammunition will come now. . . . The curtain is dropping on a scandalous regime, and I will, I hope, be on hand to cheer." Graham ended his letter with the endearing postscript, "Tear this in shreds and throw it out of the window."[39]

Graham had the highest hopes for Andrew Blair and expected the disgruntled Minister to campaign publicly against the Laurier policy if the Conservatives came up with a more acceptable alternative.[40] Railway officials and promoters unhappy with the government policy were to supply most of the funds required for the campaign. Graham was convinced that "we can change public opinion if we act together."[41] To do so, Graham proposed that several important newspapers, including *La Presse* of Montreal, be purchased. The editorial policies of these papers were to become highly critical of the government and serious scandals involving leading Liberal Cabinet ministers were to be published. Clifford Sifton, Joseph-Raymond Prefontaine, and Charles Fitzpatrick were to be the main targets.

Graham expected the government to call an election in the fall of 1903. Once the election was called and the scandals were published, Liberal candidates in Quebec were to be offered $10,000 each to withdraw from the contest "in disgust", thus ensuring the election of Conservatives. In any new Conservative administration Blair, or someone acceptable to him, would be named railways minister.[42]

The details and ramifications of this bizarre plot have never been fully explored. The most widely accepted version is one written by a newspaperman, Edward Farrer, at the request of Sir Wilfrid Laurier shortly after the election of 1904. Later historians have generally accepted the Farrer report as reliable.[43] According to Farrer, the power

39 PAC, Borden Papers, Additional, 192867–8, 192884–5.
40 *Ibid.*, 192886–7, "Arpents" to Borden, 13 May 1903.
41 *Ibid.*, 192875, undated and unsigned letter.
42 *Ibid.*, 192886–7, "Arpents" to Borden, 13 May 1903.

43 Skelton, *Laurier*, 209. Skelton writes that the Farrer report was "making clear the ramifications of the plot and illustrating Farrer's brilliant reportorial powers". Most later historians, when writing of the affair, have been content to follow Skelton's interpretation.

and the money behind the scheme were supplied mainly by Mackenzie and Mann of the Canadian Northern Railway, who allegedly wanted to unload all sorts of moribund railway projects on a willing government at grossly inflated prices and then abandon themselves to the pleasures of the rich. This is certainly a very surprising interpretation, in view of Mackenzie and Mann's clear refusal to sell their properties to the Grand Trunk, or even to negotiate seriously for such a sale. The reliability of Farrer's report must therefore be questioned.

Edward Farrer himself was a reporter of very dubious reputation. He is the subject of several odd incidents in Canadian history. He was certainly a capable and brilliant writer who became prominent, or notorious, in 1891 when, as an editor of the Toronto *Globe*, he visited Washington to discuss reciprocity with Secretary of State Blaine. It was widely assumed that he was acting on behalf of the Liberal party, which was then espousing the cause of Unrestricted Reciprocity. In the course of his discussions in Washington, Farrer wrote a pamphlet in which he tried to view Canadian-American trade relations as an American. The main point of the pamphlet was that closer economic relations might well lead to closer political relations and possibly to annexation. News of his secret meetings with the American Secretary of State was leaked to the press in an unexplained fashion, and parts of the pamphlet fell into Conservative hands. John A. Macdonald used it most effectively in the 1891 election campaign to destroy the Liberals. According to one historian, "Farrer and his like had presented themselves as Canadian guides to the realization of annexation."[44]

A Canadian governor general who knew Farrer well described him as "an able but dangerous personage, by no means fit to be in a confidential position in the PM's office".[45] He nevertheless proved very useful to the Liberals after their 1896 electoral victory. He had a smooth and convincing pen which could be used to refute rumours and allegations of Liberal scandals. When Clifford Sifton was repeatedly charged with favouritism, graft, and corruption, particularly in the running of the gold-recorder's office in the Yukon, Farrer proved invaluable. He wrote what Sifton wanted, but he had his price and was not backward

44 Donald Creighton, *John A. Macdonald: The Old Chieftain* (Toronto: Macmillan, 1955), 553–5.

45 PAC, Minto Papers, XII, 67, Lansdowne to Minto, 4 Feb. 1904.

in his demands. In March 1899 Sifton received a peremptory telegram from the reporter. "I am going to trouble you here and now, however, about another matter, namely the manifest obligation of the Government to give me who have lied so much for them in the newspapers a box of stationery."[46] When Sifton delayed, he received a more specific communication. "If that trunk of stationery is not sent to me at 174 Park Road, Toronto, very soon, I shall employ Sir Hibbert [Tupper] to properly ventilate the outrage."[47] The Yukon outrage was never ventilated, and one cannot help wondering whether this was achieved without stationery of a negotiable nature.

The same man who had looked after the Yukon outrage was asked by the Prime Minister to give the *La Presse* affair a decent burial. Farrer evidently wrote what Laurier wanted and presumably received an appropriate compensation. At the same time, however, he also tried to collect on some promises he claimed Robert Borden had made to him in connection with the writing of the report.[48] There can be little doubt that Farrer knew a good deal about the affair, since he was to some extent directly involved in it,[49] but the reliability of his later report is dubious. Farrer was, in fact, drawing a salary from the CPR and writing various pieces for that company throughout the period under consideration. The *La Presse* affair, and particularly Farrer's attempts to deny CPR involvement and to blame it all on Mackenzie and Mann, needs to be re-examined.

The main preoccupation of the Conservatives in 1903 and 1904 was to devise an alternative railway policy which would attract the support of all those opposed to the Grand Trunk Pacific–National Transcontinental scheme. Opposition leader Robert Borden carefully and methodically worked out what he considered to be the basic transportation requirements of the country. He believed the country needed more development and branch lines, freight-rate reductions, and transcontinental facilities that would bring Canadian traffic to Canadian

46 PAC, Sifton Papers, LXI, 43558–9, Farrer to Sifton, 23 March 1899.
47 *Ibid.*, 43564, Farrer to Sifton, April 1899.
48 PAC, Borden Papers, Additional, 192957, Borden to Blount, 24 Dec. 1904.

49 *Ibid.*, 192896–7, 192900, 193083, "Baker" (Graham) to Borden, 11 June and 30 June 1903 and a brief note on the financing of *La Presse* on the back of an envelope bearing a *Montreal Star* letterhead.

maritime ports. The country, in his view, certainly did not need a new line north of Lake Superior. Borden was prepared, if necessary, to have the government own and operate needed railways if private companies were unwilling to provide the services required. He criticized the government proposals for not meeting the real needs of the country.[50]

Borden consulted with Thomas Shaughnessy, president of the CPR, and then, in an apparent attempt to attract support from that company as well as from Andrew Blair and others, announced his alternative railway policy. The government, he suggested, should nationalize and if necessary double-track the CPR mileage north of Lake Superior and open it to all railways. The Intercolonial could be extended, either through the Canada Atlantic or by new construction, to connect with the nationalized mileage. Traffic interchanges between the Intercolonial and other western roads, not only the Canadian Northern, could be negotiated, and the Grand Trunk could build in the West without the necessity of building expensive new mileage north of Lake Superior.[51] Shaughnessy was willing to support the plan, and Blair, concerned about the routing of traffic through Canadian ports, saw much merit in it.

Hugh Graham made a number of contacts on behalf of the Conservatives in 1903 and was encouraged by the guarded responses of Blair, of CPR officials, and of several businessmen he visited in Boston and New York. Mackenzie and Mann were also contacted, but their immediate response was somewhat equivocal. The federal negotiations with Hays were not going well and the two promoters still hoped no workable agreement would be reached with the Grand Trunk. They might then get the big contract from the government. Their policy was not to fight the government but to seek federal assistance for their own transcontinental plans. In September 1903 they submitted a detailed request for aid, irrespective of the Grand Trunk Pacific scheme.[52]

Mackenzie and Mann also had reason to worry about the strong

50 Borden outlined these under nine separate headings in a careful speech he delivered on 18 Aug. 1903, PAC, *The National Transcontinental Railway Project, Speeches delivered by R. L. Borden, KC, MP in 1903 and 1904*, pamphlet.

51 Henry Borden, ed., *Robert Laird Borden: His Memoirs* (Toronto: McClelland and Stewart, 1969), 47.
52 PAC, Laurier Papers, CCLXXX, 76792–96, 76816–17, Mann to Laurier, 4 Sept. 1903 and Mackenzie to Laurier, 6 Sept. 1903.

influence of the CPR on the councils of the Conservative party. The Tories were as likely to sacrifice Canadian Northern interests to the CPR as the Liberals seemed willing to do to the Grand Trunk. With the acquisition of important railway holdings in Quebec, moreover, they had an instrument of influence with Laurier which would not be nearly as telling with Borden. Therefore, Mackenzie and Mann listened politely to the Conservative proposals in 1903 but remained in an uneasy and disgruntled alliance with the Liberals, who had agreed to provide guarantees for their new line to Edmonton and Prince Albert.

News of the Conservative attempts to gain Mackenzie and Mann's support reached Sifton, who wrote a worried note to the Prime Minister,[53] but was assured by Laurier, "I completely acquit Mackenzie and Mann of the charges which have been brought to me against them. They have acted loyally and they had not lifted a finger against our project."[54]

The "conspiracy" did not get very far in 1903. Laurier, who had intended to call the election in 1903, was forced to postpone it because of difficulties in settling various matters with the Grand Trunk after the initial agreement was signed in July. In addition, A. G. Blair, on whom Graham had counted very heavily, accepted the appointment of chairman of the Board of Railway Commissioners. He was thus, at least temporarily, removed from the temptations of the Conservatives. The entire conspiracy had amounted to very little and bore the marks of Hugh Graham's petty conspiratorial mind.

Only a curious and unexpected combination of circumstances made it possible to revive and modify the scheme in the summer and fall of 1904. Blair did not find his tenure as chairman of the Board of Railway Commissioners a pleasant one. The position was regarded as the greatest patronage plum that the government could give, but for Blair the fruit was bitter. The government seemed willing to give him the appointment to remove him from Conservative temptation, but they harassed their dissident ex-colleague wherever possible. Even the simplest requests from Blair met with governmental obstruction and lack of co-operation. There seemed interminable difficulties in finding office

53 *Ibid.*, CCLXXXII, 77108–9, Sifton to Laurier, 19 Sept. 1903.

54 PAC, Sifton Papers, CXLIV, 115567–9, Laurier to Sifton, 4 Oct. 1903.

space, furnishings, and staff for him. After only two months in office, Blair complained that the government was disregarding his recommendations and showing a marked lack of confidence in him and in his board.[55] His request for the government's confidence was denounced by Laurier as "dictatorial and lacking in courtesy and consideration which we should expect in such a communication".[56] It was obvious that Blair was not completely out of reach of further Conservative blandishments.

Several of Blair's New Brunswick and Montreal friends were also available for further schemes. Most notable of these were William Pugsley, a former New Brunswick attorney general; David Russell, a Saint John and Montreal railway promoter and owner of the Abbey Effervescent Salts Company; and Russell's lawyer friend, J. N. Greenshields. Blair, Pugsley, Russell, and Greenshields were all interested in the welfare of Saint John, and all had also worked together in the promotion of several prairie railways, the two most important being the Qu'Appelle, Long Lake and Saskatchewan and the Edmonton District railways.[57]

The 1904 plans were laid mainly by Hugh Graham and David Russell. Graham placed very considerable confidence in the CPR and carefully coached Robert Borden on how to "coddle" the senior officers of that company.[58] There are references to Graham urging Borden to tell influential businessmen, particularly Shaughnessy of the CPR, that the Conservative party was eager to obligate itself to them—for a consideration, of course.[59]

The plan began successfully when Russell gained control of two Saint John newspapers early in October and held a sumptuous banquet in a hotel he owned at Caledonia Springs. Blair and Pugsley were fêted and Pugsley was spoken of as the next Conservative railways minister.[60] This was followed on 17 October 1904 by the purchase of *La Presse*

---

55 PAC, Laurier Papers, 82253–4, Blair to Laurier, 11 Feb. 1904.

56 *Ibid.*, 82256, Laurier to Blair, 20 Feb. 1904.

57 *Arbitration*, 2552 and 2680–1; PAC, CNR Records, MCCXI.

58 PAC, Borden Papers, Additional, 192942–3, "Baker" to Borden, 15 July 1904.

59 *Ibid.*, 192880–1, Baker to Borden, 19 Aug. 1904.

60 CAR, 1904, 221–7. Borden was invited to the banquet but sent his regrets. Other prominent Conservatives from Montreal and Saint John were present.

of Montreal for $750,000 by a syndicate headed by Graham and Russell but allegedly backed by the CPR. Hugh Graham outlined the financing of the scheme as follows:

$100,000	Bank of N.S. GTR—McLeod told Pearson.
$200,000	Blair-Russell—Blair told Pugsley.
$200,000	Russell-Greensh.-Graham—Farrer told Pearson.
$200,000	M & M bonds—Farrer told Pearson.
$ 25,000	Russell to Harrison. R. Bank books in Halifax.[61]

Of the people mentioned in this short note, McLeod was the manager of the Bank of Nova Scotia. B. F. Pearson was a Nova Scotia engineer who had become interested in several Canadian and international railway and electrical development projects. He was also a director of the British Empire Trust Company, with which Mackenzie and Mann did business. Blair, Russell, Greenshields, and Pugsley are already familiar, as is Farrer, the author of the later report.

The exact conditions under which these various funds were pledged to the scheme is obscure. The only really tangible information available relates to the $100,000 Bank of Nova Scotia subscription. The Bank advanced this money on the security of a personal ninety-day note from David Russell, but only after it was co-signed by Hugh Graham and recommended by Conservative leader Robert Borden, a director of the Bank.[62] The bankers were told that after the election a new $1,000,000 bond issue, of which the CPR would subscribe $500,000, would provide the required financing, and that Russell would then redeem his $100,000 note, which fell due on 18 January 1905.[63]

On the day *La Presse* was purchased, Graham wrote Borden informing him of the transaction. Borden's response was cautious.

I cannot depart in any way from the pledges which I have made to the people, but subject to that consideration I am willing to endeavour to

61 PAC, Borden Papers, Additional, 193083, note on the back of a *Montreal Star* envelope.
62 *Ibid.*, 193094–5, W. P. Hunt (manager of the Bank of Nova Scotia, Montreal) to H. C. McLeod (general manager of the Bank of Nova Scotia, Toronto), 17 Oct. 1904.
63 *Ibid.*, Hunt to the general manager, Toronto, 18 Oct. 1904.

arrive at an understanding and confirm any preliminary arrangements approved by yourself and by Barker of Hamilton understands the situation most thoroughly [sic]. If you think well use my name to bring him to Montreal immediately.[64]

Borden later denied all knowledge of the affair. Barker distinguished himself as a rather bitter opponent of government aid to the Canadian Northern during the First World War and was generally regarded as an opponent of William Mackenzie.

On the day after *La Presse* was purchased, A. G. Blair resigned as chairman of the Board of Railway Commissioners, complaining of lack of government support and co-operation, and stating that he had been offered a more attractive position in private business. It was widely expected that he would campaign against the government in the election set for 3 November 1904.[65]

It is rather difficult to establish the exact sequence of events immediately after the purchase of *La Presse*. There were far too many people with very divergent interests involved, and the inevitable disagreements came very quickly. Apparently the purchase of *La Presse* itself produced a serious rift between Russell and the CPR, and the company then withdrew its support. The Bank of Nova Scotia manager felt the CPR withdrawal was due to the publicity Russell had given the purchase.[66] If it had become known that English Canadians were acquiring control of French Canada's largest newspaper, the government would have made political capital out of the issue.[67] A subsequent exchange of letters between Shaughnessy and Laurier, however, indicates a more basic disagreement. Writing after the election, Shaughnessy self-righteously claimed his company was in no way involved in the affair.[68] Laurier replied that he knew this, but then wrote, "I was told that it had been your intention to purchase *La Presse*, when Russell stepped in and got the control of it."[69] Russell had evidently gained

64 PAC, Borden Papers, Memoir Notes, I, 44–66.
65 CAR, 1904, 221–7.
66 PAC, Borden Papers, Additional, 193091, D. Waters (for McLeod) to Hunt, 16 Nov. 1904.

67 *Ibid.*, 193094–5, Hunt to general manager, Toronto, 18 Oct. 1904.
68 PAC, Laurier Papers, CCCLVII, 95149, Shaughnessy to Laurier, 25 Feb. 1905.
69 *Ibid.*, 95150, Laurier to Shaughnessy, 27 Feb. 1905.

control and wanted to use the paper in a way not entirely satisfactory to the CPR.

This led to a further disagreement among the conspirators. Russell was now unable to provide the long-term financial support which he had promised Blair and Pugsley, and on the basis of which the latter had joined the scheme.[70] Instead of joining the campaign against the government, Blair remained silent and took a position as director of the Toronto Roller Bearing Company in Toronto.[71] Pugsley, concerned about his own career, allegedly went to Laurier to present his version of the affair, while Russell got gloriously drunk.

The withdrawal of the CPR and the alienation of Blair and Pugsley ruined the scheme. There were persistent rumours that a wealthy New York syndicate, in search of Canadian railway contracts, was willing to support the scheme if appropriate assurances were obtained from Borden, or perhaps even from Laurier.[72] Russell, Greenshields, and Graham, in any event, appealed to Borden for help. Borden met them in Russell's private railway car at Fredericton Junction, only to tell them their help was no longer needed or desired.[73] If the conspirators could not work in harmony with the CPR, Borden obviously preferred to side with the railway company. Thus, before the scheme was a week old, it was destroyed by the divergent interests of the participants.

For Graham and Russell, however, the end had not yet come. They had invested a good deal of their own money, and the due date on the $100,000 Bank of Nova Scotia note was approaching. Russell did not have the necessary money, the bankers were determined to obtain payment on the due date, and Hugh Graham began to worry about ways and means of raising the necessary funds. Politically, the project was doubly dead. The conspirators had disagreed, and in the meantime the Laurier government had been re-elected with a substantial majority. Russell, Graham, and Greenshields no longer needed or wanted *La Presse*. The only people still interested in buying control of the paper were Mackenzie and Mann. They needed favourable publicity for their ventures in Quebec. There might be attacks against the

70 *Ibid.*, CCCXLVIII, 93071–3, Thomas Coté to Laurier, 30 Dec. 1904.
71 PAC, Borden Papers, Memoir Notes, I, 44–6.
72 CAR, 1904, 221–7.
73 PAC, Borden Papers, Additional, 193012–13, B. Macnab to Borden, 18 Sept. 1907.

acquiring by English entrepreneurs of the nationalistically inspired colonization railways. These attacks must be countered, and therefore control of *La Presse* might be most useful.

A series of negotiations involving Russell, Graham, Greenshields, Mackenzie, Mann, Sifton, and Laurier followed. It was clearly understood that if Mackenzie and Mann gained control of the paper it would give strong support to the Liberals.[74] For a time, Hugh Graham, the only real Conservative deeply involved, resisted this suggestion.[75] He acquiesced only as the due date on the Bank of Nova Scotia note drew nearer. On 1 January 1905, Sifton urged Laurier to expedite payment of important subsidies due Mackenzie and Mann, about which the Railway Department was making difficulties. In the same letter Sifton said he was sending Mann to Laurier to explain details whereby Mackenzie and Mann could take over David Russell's newspaper ventures.[76] By 14 January 1905 Graham was prepared to see *La Presse* sold to Mackenzie and Mann, but he suddenly began to worry that the railway magnates might not, after all, relieve him of his now burdensome obligation.[77]

The final arrangement was made only the day before the due date, but not, unfortunately, before Russell and Graham had an unpleasant disagreement.[78] On 18 January, apparently without any reward to Russell for all his troubles in the matter, *La Presse* passed into the control of what the bankers called "strong Liberal interests".[79] The bankers were very pleased to have their $100,000, which they received from men they described as "loaded to the muzzle . . . and ready to put up any part of $300,000".[80] On the same day Mackenzie and Mann wrote Laurier a brief note.

It is distinctly understood as a condition of procuring the consent of the holder of the majority of the stock of La Presse Company to sell to us

74 PAC, Laurier Papers, CCCXLIX, 93358, Arthur Dansereau to Laurier, 3 Jan. 1905.
75 *Ibid.*, CCCLI, 93723–4, unsigned letter (in code) evidently to Laurier.
76 *Ibid.*, CCCXLIX, 93314, Sifton to Laurier, 1 Jan. 1905.

77 *Ibid.*, CCCLI, 93720–1, Graham to Laurier, 14 Jan. 1905.
78 PAC, Borden Papers, Additional, 193087, Hunt to McLeod, 17 Jan. 1905.
79 *Ibid.*
80 *Ibid.*, 193086, Hunt to the general manager, Toronto, 18 Jan. 1905.

that the paper *La Presse* is not to be a Tory organ, that it is to be independent and that it is to give Sir Wilfrid Laurier a generous support.[81]

The role played by Mackenzie and Mann in these various manoeuvres requires some further comment. They certainly had an interest in the railway policies of the country, and in what was happening in Quebec. They were certainly not happy with Laurier's support of the Grand Trunk, but they were confident that they would get enough help from the Liberals to survive. The Conservative proposals were acceptable to them, but only marginally better than the policies of the Liberals. They hoped to come through the affair neither loved nor hated but still in a position to do business with whomever happened to occupy the Prime Minister's office. The Bank of Nova Scotia managers were certainly under the impression that Russell, Greenshields, and Graham based their hopes primarily on the CPR.[82] The Farrer report, on the other hand, suggests that these men were nothing more than Canadian Northern agents. It is true that Mackenzie and Mann had had some earlier associations with the Saint John and Montreal promoters in connection with the Edmonton, Yukon and Pacific Railway, but they had, in fact, disagreed on the policy to be followed in that situation.[83]

If Graham, Russell, and Greenshields were acting for Mackenzie and Mann, the objectives of the scheme as outlined by Farrer must be questioned. All the available evidence clearly indicates that Mackenzie, at least, had no intention of selling out. In Quebec the promoters most eager to sell were Melville and McNaught. Mackenzie and Mann's response to the Grand Trunk negotiations was to hasten their own transcontinental plans.[84] They certainly could have sold to the Grand Trunk if they had been so inclined. President Wilson, if not

81 PAC, Laurier Papers, CCCLI, 93729, William Mackenzie and Donald Mann to Laurier, 18 Jan. 1905. This note has actually been quoted by O. D. Skelton as proof that Mackenzie and Mann dominated the *La Presse* affair of October and November 1904. If it is proof of anything it is that Mackenzie and Mann did not, in fact, gain control of the paper until 1905, several months after the election.

82 PAC, Borden Papers, Additional, 193094–5, Hunt to general manager, 18 Oct. 1904.

83 *Arbitration*, 2680–1.

84 *Ibid.*, 2684.

General Manager Hays, was prepared to pay a very substantial sum for their property.[85]

The negotiations for the purchase of *La Presse* in January 1905 offer rather convincing proof that the two did not in fact control the paper in October and November 1904. On the basis of the information available, it seems clear that the 1904 *La Presse* affair was the product of Hugh Graham's conspiratorial mind and David Russell's rash and grasping temperament. Graham and Russell hoped to involve dissatisfied politicians and railway officials, and they looked primarily to the CPR. Mackenzie and Mann were participants, but they did not gain control of *La Presse* until January 1905. Their participation and their later purchase of the paper were certainly designed to increase their public and political influence in eastern Canada. The results of the 1904 election did not significantly alter these purposes. They looked after their own interests and never received enough from either political party in Canada firmly to support one and determinedly to oppose the other.

Mackenzie and Mann's Quebec affairs were a complex part of the promoters' attempt to develop their own transcontinental plans after 1903. Those plans, however, extended eastward beyond the province of Quebec. Beginning in 1901, Mackenzie and Mann also developed a relatively successful railway system in Nova Scotia. In that province, branch lines were urgently needed, particularly in the south. A number of small, locally sponsored companies had obtained charters to build, but petty disputes, rivalries, and conflicting ambitions prevented any of these local companies from achieving much, and the area continued to suffer from inadequate service. The separate and partially built local lines had to be connected and integrated, but substantial government assistance was needed for the construction and equipping of the new mileage. The provincial government was reluctant to grant any further assistance unless there were definite assurances that a coherent and integrated local railway system would be built.

A rail connection between Halifax and Yarmouth seemed particularly urgent, but the local railway with the best charter privileges, the Halifax and Yarmouth Railway, had fallen from political and financial

85 PAC, Hays Papers, 11–13, Wilson to Hays, 18 June 1902, and Hays to Wilson, 27 June 1903.

favour and wanted to sell out. A new arrangement was necessary, and in 1901 the Nova Scotia government announced the terms of a new provincial railway policy. It offered cash advances in the form of loans, up to $10,000 per mile, to anyone who would take over the Halifax and Yarmouth Railway—which already had fifty miles in operation between Yarmouth and Barrington Passage—and extend this line another 185 miles to Halifax. New charter rights were promised so that this could be done either through new construction or through the acquisition of any or all the moribund local lines along the way. Mackenzie and Mann were soon in Halifax to begin negotiations.[86]

It did not take long before a successful arrangement was worked out between the two promoters and Premier Murray. The arrangement provided the $10,000-per-mile loan and, in addition, a $3,500-per-mile cash subsidy. A new railway, under the name of the Halifax and South Western Railway, was to be incorporated. It would have power to build from Halifax to Yarmouth, and also to bring under its jurisdiction the troubled local roads. This agreement dashed any hopes these smaller ventures had of obtaining additional provincial aid, and most were very eager to sell. The construction of a railway from Yarmouth to Halifax was thus assured. At Halifax the new road was to connect and have a traffic interchange agreement with the Intercolonial Railway.[87]

Returning from Halifax, Mackenzie and Mann successfully negotiated with the federal government for the usual variable $3,200-to-$6,400 federal subsidy for the mileage between Halifax and Barrington Passage.[88] Some of the local and predecessor lines had already been declared in the public interest. In 1903 the appropriate subsidies were re-voted to the Halifax and South Western. Construction was begun immediately, and on 30 January 1905 the new line from Halifax to Yarmouth was officially opened for traffic.[89] In the early years the main

86 *Arbitration*, 2546–7.
87 Nova Scotia, *1 Edw. VII. Cap. 3*; PAC, CNR Records, MCCXXXII, 2–3, Meeting of Provisional Directors of the Halifax and South Western Railway, 4 Feb. 1902.
88 Canada, *3 Edw. VII. Cap. 57*; copies of these various federal agreements are included in a box of Miscellaneous Documents, PAC, CNR Records, MMMCXIX; see also PAC, Laurier Papers, CCXXXII, 64958–62, memorandum from Lash to Minister of Railways and Canals, 8 May 1902.
89 *Synoptical Histories*, 463.

items of traffic on this line were fish and lumber. One lumber company alone committed itself to shipping a minimum of 40,000 board feet of lumber annually.[90]

Other local and feeder lines in Nova Scotia were quickly brought under the Halifax and South Western umbrella. For each line built or purchased, the $13,500 provincial subsidy and loan was given. When additional financing was needed, bonds of the Halifax and South Western or of one of the constituent companies were issued. Payment of both interest and principal was guaranteed by the Canadian Northern Railway.[91]

Altogether, five local companies passed into the control of the Halifax and South Western Railway. The first of these was the Central Railway of Nova Scotia with a completed line from Lunenburg to Middleton, which was purchased on 1 July 1902 for $525,000. This was followed, on 11 April 1903, by the takeover of the Nova Scotia Southern Railway, which had no mileage constructed but under whose charter twenty-two miles between Caledonia and Caledonia Junction were built in 1903. The Halifax and Yarmouth Railway and the Middleton and Victoria Beach Railway were officially purchased on 15 May 1905 for $675,000 and $325,000 respectively. The former had fifty miles in operation, the latter none, but under its charter thirty-nine miles from Middleton to Port Wade were built in 1907. Finally, on 25 April 1907 the Liverpool and Milton Railway Company, with a short 4.63-mile line completed between Liverpool and Rapid Falls, was purchased for $71,550. In most cases the equity stock of these railways was purchased by Mackenzie, Mann and Co. Ltd. and then exchanged for stock in the Halifax and South Western Railway.[92]

The Halifax and South Western Railway was generally considered a part of the Canadian Northern system, mainly because its bonds had been guaranteed by the larger company. There were some plans to connect the Nova Scotia mileage with the rest of the system, either

90 A copy of this agreement is in PAC, CNR Records, MMMCXIX. It was approved by the directors on 16 Aug. 1904; PAC, CNR Records, MCCXXXII, 18.
91 Arbitration, 2546–7; for a discussion of the significance of these Canadian Northern Railway guarantees, see below, pp. 277–8.

92 The details of all these purchases are recorded in the Minute Book of the Halifax and South Western Railway, PAC, CNR Records, MCCXXXII; information is also available in Synoptical Histories, 460–5.

TABLE V

Operating Statistics of the Halifax and South Western Railway Company

Year	Mileage operated	Gross earnings	Operating costs	Net earnings	Net corporate profit or loss*
		($)	($)	($)	($)
1904	96	80,731.66	66,870.30	13,861.36	
1905	194	113,209.36	108,939.15	4,260.21	
1906	245	238,614.00	201,719.64	36,894.36	
1907	382	323,367.86	291,029.42	32,338.44	−19,588.44
1908	390	387,185.06	384,981.15	2,203.91	−15,579.48
1909	389	372,782.62	357,678.42	15,104.20	−3,360.22
1910	389	412,013.85	345,317.38	66,696.47	50,699.91
1911	401	435,810.45	397,060.33	38,750.12	22,569.15
1912	403	478,031.62	425,286.09	52,745.16	32,981.26
1913	401	531,338.62	528,217.46	3,121.16	−54,515.87
1914	404	561,052.79	527,636.96	33,415.83	−182,850.69

*Only fixed charges and rentals actually paid by the railway company were deducted from Net Earnings. These figures do not include any calculations for Fixed Charges paid by Mackenzie, Mann and Company Limited on behalf of the railway company, or the refinancing of fixed charges in some other way.

Source: The Public Archives of Canada, R.G. 46. The Halifax and South Western Railway paid interest on the bonds of the railways it took over only until these bonds could be exchanged for new bonds guaranteed by the Canadian Northern Railway. The interest on the new bonds was capitalized and later included in a new consolidated mortgage. Many of the bonds remained for some time in the hands of Mackenzie, Mann and Co. Ltd. and no interest was paid on bonds so held. That is why the fixed charges from 1908 to 1912 were so low.

by means of the Intercolonial or by the construction of the Quebec, New Brunswick and Nova Scotia Railway.[93] The integration of the Nova Scotia mileage into the larger system, however, depended on events and developments in Quebec and Ontario.

Mackenzie and Mann also gained control of a shorter line in Cape Breton Island which served the coal and steel industry there. This line, however, had no official connection with the Canadian Northern.[94] Both Nova Scotia railways were operated for many years as local service lines; the Halifax and South Western earned modest profits, while the Cape Breton mileage proved unprofitable.[95]

93 Arbitration, 2546–7.
94 Synoptical Histories, 501; Stevens, 298–9.

95 PAC, Laurier Papers, CCLXXVII, 100357–8, Mann to Laurier, 4 Aug. 1905.

The reorganization of local Nova Scotia railways, the involvement in Quebec railways, and the attempt to purchase the Canada Atlantic or to greatly expand the charter rights of the James Bay Railway laid the groundwork for a Mackenzie-and-Mann-promoted transcontinental railway system. In time, and with government help, the two promoters intended to build "in the true sense of the word, a great national highway".[96] Before doing so, however, they had to improve and strengthen their prairie system.

96 *Ibid.*, CDXV, 110803–10, Mann to Laurier, 1 June 1906.

CHAPTER SEVEN

SERVING THE PRAIRIE WEST THE MAIN LINES 1903-1906

THE IMMEDIATE SURVIVAL of the Canadian Northern Railway was assured in 1903 and 1904. The federal bond guarantee for the lines to Edmonton and Prince Albert and a strong position in Quebec after the acquisition of the Melville and McNaught interests were evidence that Mackenzie and Mann would not be forced into a hasty surrender to the Grand Trunk. There was no doubt, however, that a long and desperate struggle had only begun. The ultimate outcome of that struggle was still very much in doubt, and developments on the prairies were of the utmost importance.

The most important task confronting both new railway companies on the prairies after 1903 was the construction of main or trunk lines which would carry their through traffic and become a base from which local and feeder lines could be pushed into promising new farming areas. It quickly became clear that the two rivals would not adopt the same strategy on the prairies.

The Grand Trunk Pacific devoted most of its energy and funds to the speedy construction of a high-standard main line from Winnipeg to the Pacific coast. It was to be the shortest and most direct route, built as quickly as possible and to a standard which would make it "the best long railway ever to be built in North America".[1] Maximum grades of .5 per cent, minimum curvature, and rails weighing eighty-five pounds per yard were the standard throughout. First-class rolling stock was to be placed on the new line to handle the anticipated transcontinental traffic. Very little attention was paid to local needs

1 Stevens, 179.

THE CANADIAN NORTHERN RAILWAY'S MAIN LINES ON THE PRAIRIES

LEGEND
— The Canadian Northern main lines in 1902
– – – Main lines built under 1903 federal bond guarantees
–·–·– Qu'Appelle, Long Lake and Saskatchewan Railway
········· Southern main line completed in 1908 under federal guarantees
········· Hudson Bay Railway (built by Mackenzie, Mann and Co. Ltd.)
– – – Hudson Bay Railway (as proposed in 1906)

ALBERTA

SASKATCHEWAN

MANITOBA

ONTARIO

Edmonton
Strathcona
Lloydminster
North Battleford
Battleford
Prince Albert
Saskatoon
Warman
Humboldt
Melfort
Tisdale
Erwood
Hudson Bay Jct.
The Pas
Nelson

Kamsack
Grandview
Dauphin
Gladstone
Portage la Prairie
Brandon
Hartney
Hartney Jct.
Regina
Emerson
Morris
Winnipeg
Rainy River
Fort Frances
Port Arthur
Fort William

0   200 miles
0   200 km

and demands if these were thought to be at variance with the company's plans.[2]

Mackenzie and Mann tried to claim as much territory and to generate as much local traffic as possible, while keeping costs sufficiently low to ensure profitable operations from the beginning. They developed four main trunk lines in the North-West Territories and these became the basis for their effective occupation of the northern prairies and provided a good competitive position in the south. The Grand Trunk Pacific easily outdistanced the Canadian Northern in the construction of the main line to the Pacific, but its operations on the prairies were pretty effectively restricted to the fairly narrow corridor between the Canadian Northern system in the north and the CPR lines in the south.

The Canadian Northern prairie lines were built according to fairly well defined general principles. The first of these was to build as little mileage as possible through territory with poor development prospects. In his first report as president of the Canadian Northern Railway, William Mackenzie attributed the success of his railway to "the total absence of unproductive track. The railway throughout its length passes through some of the richest territory in Canada, which has hitherto, to a very large extent been without railway facilities."[3] Once the railways were built, the promoters participated in various traffic-generating ventures and did what they could to build up good will in an effort to secure the largest possible volume of traffic. This activity might delay completion of their transcontinental plans, but it ensured profitable operations from the beginning.[4]

A second principle guiding Canadian Northern policy-makers was

2 *Ibid.*, 223–6.
3 *First Annual Report, Canadian Northern Railway, 1903*, 2. Prior to 1902 and the incorporation of Mackenzie, Mann and Co. Ltd., of which William Mackenzie, Donald Mann, and Roderick Mackenzie were the shareholders, none of these men served on the Canadian Northern's board of directors. In 1902 Mackenzie became president and Mann vice-president of the Canadian Northern Railway. Their first annual report, therefore, does not report on the first year of operations but on the first year Mackenzie and Mann were formally at the head of the enterprise. Operational results for the earlier years were given by D. B. Hanna in the arbitration proceedings and are also available in the appendices of the Annual Reports of the Department of Railways and Canals.
4 Hanna, 231–5.

to build and equip lines according to the immediate traffic requirements of the area to be served, but to leave open the possibility, indeed the probability, of later improvements when traffic increased. If the expected traffic was light, a light construction standard was deemed sufficient. When the traffic improved, the line was improved to meet the new requirements. Each line in the system, in theory at least, grew with and at the same rate as the area it served. As a result, some of the main lines of the Canadian Northern eventually came to be very well built—the standard against which other railways were measured. Others were never improved. In sparsely settled areas the tracks were reported to jump with joy under the weight of every passing freight car. Construction of this kind made extensions possible into many areas of western Canada where there was insufficient traffic to justify a first-class CPR or GTPR road. Like the pioneers they served, who built inexpensive sod huts and log cabins before beginning work on more impressive frame houses, Mackenzie and Mann built inexpensive lines and made improvements when revenues increased. Their frugality enabled them to reduce initial operating costs and fixed charges to a minimum and thus ensure profitable operations from the beginning without recourse to high freight rates.

Low initial construction standards, however, were adopted only when they would not interfere with later improvements. Mackenzie and Mann were as impressed with grades, curvatures, ballasting, heavy steel, and permanent filling and bridging as was Charles Hays of the Grand Trunk Pacific. All their main-line mileage was located so that grades of more than .5 per cent, compensated for curvature, could be eliminated later at comparatively low cost. This meant that the resistance to forward motion, taking both grade and curvature into account, should not exceed the equivalent of a rise of twenty-six feet in a mile of track.[5] Superintendent Hanna had become very conscious of grades as a result of his experience on the Manitoba and North Western Railway. Grades of up to 3.1 per cent had contributed to that railway's unprofitable operating record and had increased the costs of the old Lake Manitoba Railway and Canal Company when it held trackage rights there. The steep 4.5-per-cent grades that the CPR had to contend

5 *Arbitration*, 118, 471.

with at Field, British Columbia, were known to increase that company's expenses greatly. A single locomotive at Field could generally take only three or four loaded cars up the grade. "Pushers" were needed, but these added to the operating costs. Construction of the famous spiral tunnels later reduced this grade to 2.2 per cent.

Canadian Northern surveyors were required to find routes which had good traffic potential, and could support trackage built cheaply but with the potential of being upgraded to more exacting standards. Mackenzie and Mann were fortunate in attracting unusually capable and dedicated surveyors and engineers who took great personal pride in the line they were laying out. Malcolm H. McLeod, chief engineer and surveyor of the Canadian Northern, was an exceptional man who frequently risked life and limb to secure the best possible location. His example inspired an *esprit de corps* from which the company benefited on numerous occasions, for the men often extended themselves well beyond the normal call of duty.[6] Donald Mann himself was very fond of tramping the fields and forests, always discovering new promises of future prosperity along projected Canadian Northern lines. For him and the senior members of his staff, the locating and building of new railways was not only a commercial proposition but a work of love to which they dedicated their lives.

Construction policies on the Canadian Northern were complemented by the manner in which Mackenzie and Mann acquired rolling stock for their railway. Again the primary objective was to keep operating costs as low as possible while the volume of traffic carried was small, thus ensuring profitable returns despite low rates. Only as much rolling stock was acquired as was needed for the available traffic. This policy drew serious criticism, particularly from prairie grain farmers, since the volume of grain traffic fluctuated greatly, and every fall, when the farmers were eager to get their wheat to market before the winter freeze-up, Canadian Northern rolling stock failed to meet immediate needs. Grain was often piled alongside prairie branch lines in the fall,

6 Hanna, 214–26, 2687. In 1902, Bank of Commerce officials, eager to see Mackenzie and Mann sell to the Grand Trunk Pacific, wrote rather pessimistically, "We are all anxious lest Mackenzie in his strong desire to be the head & front of a rival to the CPR will let his ambitions and his temper sway his judgement." UTA, Walker Papers, Plummer to Walker, 4 Oct. 1902.

awaiting boxcars which would take it east. Lack of sufficient boxcars during the busy harvest season was a major problem for many years, and the resulting piles of wheat awaiting shipment became known as grain blockades. Such blockades along Canadian Northern lines were frequently serious and irritated the farmers,[7] but at least the company escaped the criticism that it was saving its rolling stock for eastern traffic.

At the height of a grain blockade or any other rolling stock crisis, Canadian Northern officials frequently took to visiting the junkyards and repair shops of more affluent American railways to buy and press into service some of the dilapidated and decrepit rolling stock they found there.[8] On backward rural branch lines Canadian Northern engines died more often than the most tenacious feline, but wonders could be performed with caulking and tinkering. The old engines usually managed to get the traffic out somehow, and they were certainly not expensive to buy.

Canadian Northern boxcars were subject to a different hazard. In the early 1900s many of the larger railroads were switching from wood-framed to steel-framed cars. The old wooden cars could therefore be obtained very cheaply, and many soon bore the Canadian Northern insignia and became the curse of every major railway system. Trans-shipments of loaded cars to points of destination on other lines were common, but in any sudden stop the old wooden cars tended to get crushed between the new steel-framed cars of the more affluent railways. The road on which such an "accident" occurred was responsible for the loss, and thus a happy source of income for the Canadian Northern. To avoid crushing, wooden cars were often placed at the rear of a train, but this made shunting more complicated, and the lighter wooden cars, bouncing along at the tail end of a fast freight, jumped the tracks rather easily. Again this could mean nothing but a

7 PAC, CNR Legal Series, File 47–3, "Blockade of Spring, 1907"; *Manitoba Free Press*, 13 Nov. 1902, editorial entitled "The Question of the Day".
8 Mr. A. J. Hills, one of the officers of the Canadian Northern, stated in taped interviews with Dr. Lamb, the Dominion Archivist, and John C.

Andreassen, the Canadian National Railway Archivist, that he participated in transactions of this kind where any rolling stock that would pass perfunctory inspection was purchased and pressed into service. Typescript of interview in PAC.

good settlement for Mackenzie and Mann. Government regulations prevented "discrimination" against the cars of rival roads bound for destinations served only by another road.[9] Thus, old retired rolling stock often found new opportunities for service on the Canadian Northern Railway and generally proved a greater nuisance to its rivals than it did to the Canadian Northern.

Not all Canadian Northern rolling stock was of this calibre. On the busy main line the railway operated some of the most powerful locomotives and some of the best rolling stock available. Long grain trains made the line from Winnipeg to Port Arthur one of the busiest single-track lines in North America and became a model of modern railroading. The policy, simply stated, was to buy the kind of rolling stock required to meet the immediate situation. The best and most modern locomotive on the main line and the decrepit iron horse wheezing and puffing on an obscure branch line were both important parts of the Canadian Northern system.

Even the purchase of old, used rolling stock, however, failed to meet all the railway's requirements, although it certainly helped to keep operating costs down. After the Grand Trunk Pacific built into western Canada, Mackenzie and Mann's first concern was to expand into as many areas as possible before one of their competitors did so. The main emphasis was always on new construction, and in many cases the Canadian Northern long remained, and certainly looked like, a real pioneer road.

In building up their system Mackenzie and Mann had a third basic policy. That was to develop a strong network of branch and feeder lines on the prairies before building the long transcontinental connections that they believed would be needed sooner or later. Most of the traffic that was needed to make their railway profitable would either originate on, or be destined for, the prairies. Their priority was to build the main trunk lines on the prairies first, then to develop an extensive branch-line network around these trunk lines, and finally to build the transcontinental connections.

The first concern after 1903 was to extend the Manitoba system as far west as Prince Albert and Edmonton. The federal guarantee of

9 *Arbitration*, 1853, 2312.

$13,000 for what were in fact two northern trunk lines was of the utmost importance. Mackenzie and Mann owed it to their general popularity in western Canada—a popularity based on their willingness to reduce freight rates drastically. Since the new mileage passed through territory not yet well developed, Mackenzie refused an immediate rate reduction in the Territories comparable to the reductions already effected in Manitoba. He did promise some reductions, however, and agreed to government control over all rates to be charged on the assisted lines.[10]

Some construction on the new northern lines actually preceded any assurance from the federal government about the bond guarantee and probably encouraged western political determination regarding that guarantee. Mackenzie and Mann had long been acquainted with the serious railway problems and grievances of the city of Edmonton. In 1902 they built a short local line which, in effect, made that city Canadian Northern territory.

Edmonton had expected direct rail connections from the south and rapid development when the Calgary and Edmonton Railway was built. These expectations had been utterly frustrated in 1891 when the newly built railway established its northern terminus at Strathcona, on the south shore of the North Saskatchewan River, opposite Edmonton. Once built, the Calgary and Edmonton Railway was leased to the CPR, the original promoters being far more interested in construction contracts and the railway's land grant than in the successful operation of the road. The CPR steadfastly refused all demands by Edmontonians that the line be extended across the river. It was widely believed that the CPR's refusal was based on extensive real-estate interests that the company and its close friends held on the south side, and on its selfish determination to "boom" the rival site. The precedents for such action were numerous; prairie settlements touched by new railways inevitably had their development, and often their location, altered to suit the real-estate interests of the promoters and their friends. For ten years Edmontonians endured the frustration of living

10 PAC, Laurier Papers, CCXVIII, 61217–22, Frank Oliver, Walter Scott, James M. Douglas, to Laurier (1903?); PAC, CNR Legal Series, File 6-22A, "1903 3 per cent Debenture Stock", Mackenzie to Lash, 12 June 1903.

within sight of a railway which refused to extend its services to them and seemed determined to destroy their city for the sake of a rival site.

The discovery of gold in the Yukon in the mid-1890s gave Edmonton new hope for railway connections. Edmonton was the logical departure point on any overland route to the Yukon, and a group of Saint John speculators and civic officials obtained a charter which might serve such a purpose.[11] When the government decided against the overland route, the railway was reorganized, and Mackenzie and Mann acquired a minority interest in it. The name was changed from the Edmonton District Railway to the Edmonton, Yukon and Pacific Railway, and a contract was negotiated with the British Columbia government to build to the Pacific. The British Columbia plan quickly collapsed, whereupon Mackenzie and Mann gained full control of the railway and began negotiations with the city of Edmonton and the Hudson's Bay Company for the construction of a short spur line from Fort Edmonton to Strathcona.[12] A traffic interchange with the Calgary and Edmonton Railway was their immediate objective.

It was well known at the time that the owners of the Calgary and Edmonton Railway were hoping to sell, rather than continue their leasing arrangement with the CPR. Mackenzie and Mann desperately wanted to acquire the line, and to connect it with their proposed short Edmonton mileage and ultimately with the Manitoba system which was still 620 miles away. The CPR was determined to retain control of the increasingly profitable railway and to prevent any connections between it and Mackenzie and Mann's Edmonton line. A bitter contest between the rival systems developed. Mackenzie and Mann were unable to raise the capital or securities necessary to match CPR offers to purchase the Calgary and Edmonton Railway, but the CPR was compelled to pay an inflated price to retain control.[13]

With the CPR in control of the Calgary and Edmonton Railway, the proposed connection and traffic interchange of the Edmonton, Yukon

11 PAC, CNR Records, MCCXI, Edmonton, Yukon and Pacific Railway Minute Book, 1896–8, 1902, 1908. A majority of the Edmonton District Railway shares were initially held by George McAvity, trustee of the city of Saint John. The city's mayor was made an *ex officio* member of the board of directors.
12 *Arbitration*, 2681–2.
13 R. A. Christenson, "The Calgary and Edmonton Railway and the *Edmonton Bulletin*", 220–2.

and Pacific Railway became a matter of considerable controversy. Edmonton's Member of Parliament, Frank Oliver, was confident that an order could be obtained from the Railway Committee of the Privy Council which would compel the CPR to permit the connection and also to carry Edmonton traffic at non-discriminatory rates. Unfortunately, no unequivocal order to this effect was obtained before the new railway was built and ready to be put into operation. Canadian Northern officials said they had the required authority; the CPR claimed they did not, and decided to fight. Court injunctions, and eventually warrants for the arrest of Canadian Northern officials, were obtained by the CPR. Telegrams to Ottawa failed to clarify the situation, and on 6 October 1902 Canadian Northern workmen began laying track onto the Calgary and Edmonton railway right of way.

The CPR responded by running an idle engine on the intended points of juncture, thus halting further activity. Short of launching a direct physical attack on the CPR, Canadian Northern crews could do little except offer free passage to the aroused citizens of Edmonton, who crossed the river to lend whatever help they could. Some adventurous souls anticipated a minor civil war with the hated Strathconians and the CPR. The Canadian Northern manager, however, resorted to trickery rather than violence. Foiled in the initial attempt to make the connection, most of the Canadian Northern crews soon left the scene. At 5 p.m. only Manager J. W. Pace was to be seen. A CPR train from the south was scheduled to arrive at 5 p.m. To make way for it, and in the absence of any apparent threat, the guarding locomotive shunted north. The engine had scarcely left when a sharp whistle from Manager Pace brought the Canadian Northern crews scrambling from nearby bushes and ditches. Before the guarding engine could return, tracks were lifted, and within an hour the physical connection was completed. An obliging Department of Railways and Canals official, conveniently standing by, immediately made the required inspection and declared the connection completed and legal.[14] Edmontonians were jubilant, and the Canadian Northern appeared as nothing less than the saviour that had delivered the city from the malevolent power

14 Various issues of the *Edmonton Bulletin* in Oct. 1902 carried full details of this incident.

of the CPR. Edmonton finally had a rail connection with the outside world, and the promoters who had made it possible were firmly established in the city. The bills to provide federal bond guarantees for a Canadian Northern line from the east were already being drafted, and within six months strong western support ensured their passage.

Two weeks after the Strathcona incident the new railway, running from Edmonton over the low-level bridge along the Mill Creek valley to the junction with the Calgary and Edmonton Railway, was officially opened. A civic holiday was declared, and local dignitaries and citizens rode the new railway, less than two miles in length, in the bright sunshine of a splendid Edmonton autumn day. Speeches on the greatness of Edmonton and its unmatched future were the order of the day. The iniquities of the CPR, whose president had allegedly "declared with all the authority of the man who had the country in his pocket that a railway would never run into Edmonton",[15] were once more denounced, while the courage, wisdom, and enterprise of Frank Oliver and of Mackenzie and Mann were celebrated boisterously. Children were given free rides for most of the afternoon in an atmosphere of almost unbounded good will and optimism. The early inadequacies of the little Edmonton, Yukon and Pacific Railway seemed to concern no one. It operated almost entirely with second- and third-hand American railroad rolling stock and the approach to the low-level bridge was rather tenuous, but it met the needs of the day. It was a typical Mackenzie and Mann beginning, and many believed it would do for Edmonton and northern Alberta what a similarly unheroic system had already done for northern Manitoba.

The Edmonton celebrations were indicative of western attitudes toward the CPR and its aggressive new competitor. The federal bond guarantees of 1903 provided the means whereby the area of competition between the two could be substantially enlarged. It had been Mackenzie and Mann's original intention to make the more northerly route through Prince Albert and Battleford their main line to Edmonton. This plan was changed in 1901 when the Dauphin and Grandview to Edmonton line gained priority.[16] The new main line served a developing and prosperous area and also helped the Canadian Northern

15 *Edmonton Bulletin*, 24 Oct. 1902, and *Manitoba Free Press*, 21 Oct. 1902.
16 Stevens, 50.

to hold some of the more southerly areas that might otherwise have been lost to competitors. The political and economic influence of Prince Albert was nevertheless strong enough to ensure that both lines got federal assistance and, in deference to the Prince Albert MP, both lines were officially referred to as main lines. This was to provide some political ammunition for the importunate T. O. Davis, MP, who wearied Sifton with his many requests until the latter noted in exasperation, "I thought T. O. had asked for everything he has seen around this office, but apparently not."[17]

From the time the Port Arthur section was completed late in 1901 until the federal bond guarantees were passed in July 1903, Mackenzie and Mann had added very little new mileage to the Canadian Northern Railway. Manitoba bond guarantees assured continuing work on some branch lines in that province, while at the same time new track was laid in Nova Scotia and Quebec. The federal guarantees, however, brought a flurry of activity on the prairies. In 1903 many of the Manitoba branch lines were rushed to completion, and construction on both the Edmonton and Prince Albert lines was begun. Grading of the roadbed reached Kamsack and Melfort on the two lines before the winter freeze-up. Mackenzie and Mann spoke bravely of completing 500 miles in 1904. Track was laid on the roadbed that had been graded the previous year, and the grading of the southern line reached the South Saskatchewan River.[18] This achievement, however, fell somewhat short of the promoters' objectives for 1904. They blamed prosperity and a lack of sufficient manpower for the somewhat slower pace of construction.

Any disappointments were dissipated in 1905 when Mackenzie and Mann concentrated all their energies on the two federally assisted lines. Beginning in early spring, the work was pushed vigorously ahead. It proved to be a record year as construction crews completed track-laying from Kamsack to Edmonton and from Melfort to Prince Albert. No less than 546 miles of new track were laid, eclipsing the 500-mile mark William Van Horne had just failed to achieve in the CPR's drive across the prairies in 1882. A total of 606 miles of new track were

17 PAC, Sifton Papers, CXL, 112038, Sifton's note on a telegram from Davis to Sifton, Nov. 1903.

18 *Manitoba Free Press*, 1 and 24 Sept. 1903, 2 May and 17 Nov. 1904.

formally transferred from the construction department to the operating department in 1905 and the progress of the railway was rightly described as "phenomenal" and as an achievement that "demanded skill and energy and enterprise of no common order".[19]

Mackenzie, Mann and Co. Ltd. were the main contractors on both the Edmonton and the Prince Albert lines, receiving, as usual, capital stock for their services. Much of the construction work, however, had to be subcontracted. This arrangement was the focal point for the most persistent rumours and stories of sharp dealing and unscrupulous measuring and calculating of total work done. Mackenzie and Mann calculated with sharp pencils; nowhere were they sharper than when a subcontract was being negotiated or evaluated. They had not spent years on CPR contracts without learning the various tricks and devices of the trade. In dealing with their own subcontractors they had very meticulous standards and measures, and many a piece of work had to be improved or redone before the unfortunate subcontractor received any money. In all of the subcontracts in which Mackenzie and Mann were interested, they allegedly never once permitted an honest subcontractor to suffer losses as a result of unforeseen conditions, but there were no easy windfall profits in any of their contracts either. Many a dream of handsome profits was rudely dispelled when Canadian Northern engineers arrived to assess and measure the work done. Honest Canadian contracting firms, such as J. D. McArthur, or Welch, Foley & Co., made moderate but steady profits from their Canadian Northern contracts. Others complained that they made little more than enough to break even.[20]

On the mileage from Edmonton to Kamsack an American firm, S. P. H. Robinson of St. Louis, Missouri, submitted the lowest tender. Robinson evidently expected to build to a standard rather lower than that called for in the specifications. Bidding low, trimming specifications, and, if necessary, appealing for political support to obtain pay-

19 CAR, 1906, 658–9; *Fourth Annual Report, Canadian Northern Railway, 1906*; Stevens, 51.
20 See for example correspondence between Janet Tupper and Robert Borden in Sept. 1913, PAC, Borden Papers, File OCA 168, and difficulties in connection with contracts on Quebec railways as documented in rather extensive correspondence between Laurier, J. P. Mallarkey, and Mackenzie and Mann in the Laurier Papers in 1904. See also CR & MW, Dec. 1934, 523.

ment had paid off for him in the United States. Not so when he did work for Mackenzie and Mann. They found the work done by Robinson entirely unsatisfactory, and had no ear for the American's protests that building to the specifications would entail a considerable loss. The two promoters immediately cancelled the contract and sought a legal injunction restraining the contractor from proceeding with construction work.[21] They refused to pay more than Robinson's actual expenditures for materials and labour, and started proceedings for a breach of contract against the American who had plans to sue them. These suits were dropped only when a settlement was reached that paid the contractor his immediate costs. Mackenzie and Mann then undertook the work themselves. With considerable help from settlers along the way, particularly from eager Barr colonists at Lloydminster, they were able to speed the pace of construction considerably. For the settlers this was an opportunity to earn some desperately needed money, at the same time ensuring early construction of the railway and with it the means to send their crops to market.[22]

While the main line to Edmonton was being built the railway became involved in several disputes. The most important of these was its decision to bypass the old town of Battleford. The Canadian Northern crossed the North Saskatchewan River some eight miles upstream from the old territorial capital and established a new townsite on the north shore of the river. This decision marked the end of Battleford as a centre of major importance, and it was widely criticized as an attempt by the railway to "boom" a rival townsite where it allegedly had important land interests.[23] The reasons given by the railway related to technical and engineering difficulties. The problem was to build a bridge across the river without resort to heavy grades. The rapidly rising Eagle Hills and the shifting soil at the foot of those hills, as well as the increased costs of a bridge at Battleford proper, were the main considerations. It was estimated that to build according to one of two alternative plans at Battleford proper would increase costs by between $475,395 and $541,814. These alternative plans were care-

---

21 *Manitoba Free Press*, 17 Sept. 1904; *Arbitration*, 1935–6.
22 *Manitoba Free Press*, 1 Sept. 1903.
23 PAC, *Board of Railway Commis-*

sioners, Transcript of Evidence, VIII, 3495; PAC, Sifton Papers, CXL, 112007, 112035–36, T. O. Davis to Sifton, 18 Aug. and 16 Nov. 1903.

fully worked out, but Mackenzie and Mann refused to consider them unless they received a subsidy to meet the increased cost. Mann informed Sifton that a federal subsidy of $500,000 would get the main line into Battleford.[24] The federal government refused to grant a subsidy, and the town of Battleford was doomed, despite urgent appeals to the Cabinet and the newly created Board of Railway Commissioners. Canadian Northern cost estimates were challenged and land speculation was alleged but never proved in the hearings before the Board.[25] T. O. Davis, whose constituency included Battleford, suggested that a large land grant to the Canadian Northern on the south shore might achieve the same results as the requested subsidy,[26] but nothing ever came of his suggestion. Years later, during the arbitration proceedings, Canadian Northern officials again insisted that the higher construction cost, not land speculation, was the reason for bypassing Battleford.[27]

Developments after the Canadian Northern was built soon proved that the fears of Battleford residents were well founded. Their town quickly lost its commercial influence to the rival across the river, which also became a Canadian Northern divisional point. Battleford residents were particularly incensed when the Canadian Northern even stole the name of their town by naming the new site North Battleford. They appealed to Premier Scott of Saskatchewan, who tried to persuade Mackenzie to select a different name, but to no avail. Battleford, Mackenzie claimed, designated the entire region and not just one town: "We would not want to lose the advantage of calling the town North Battleford."[28]

The Canadian Northern Railway also bypassed the small but rapidly growing centre of Saskatoon, running some eight miles to the north through Warman, Saskatchewan. The reasons for this were apparently in part technical and in part strategic. Clarke's Crossing was generally considered the best place to cross the South Saskatchewan River, and the Canadian Northern simply followed well-established prairie trails and old survey routes in selecting that location for a crossing of the

24 PAC, Sifton Papers, CLXVI, 133935–6, Mann to Sifton, 22 March 1904.
25 PAC, Board of Railway Commissioners, Transcript of Evidence, VIII, 3495.

26 PAC, Sifton Papers, CXL, 112035–6, Davis to Sifton, 16 Nov. 1903.
27 Arbitration, 1522.
28 PAS, Scott Papers, Mackenzie to Scott, 5 March 1904.

South Saskatchewan. It was also thought that the soil near the North Saskatchewan River was better than it was further south. The poor sandy soil south of Saskatoon was to be avoided. It was also expected that the more northerly location would prevent rival companies from building into the rich farming areas north of Saskatoon between the North Saskatchewan and the South Saskatchewan rivers. Again there were charges of Canadian Northern real-estate speculation at Warman, especially when that site began to receive serious attention from various real-estate agents.[29] It soon became evident, however, that Saskatoon would prevail over its northern rival. Saskatoon already had rail connections from the south and the Grand Trunk Pacific was building to it from the east. For a time the Canadian Northern was certainly unpopular in Saskatoon, where the decision of the Grand Trunk Pacific was received with great enthusiasm. The initial advantages of the Grand Trunk Pacific were destroyed, however, when the Canadian Northern established itself in the city through the purchase of the Qu'Appelle, Long Lake and Saskatchewan Railway in 1906. The harsh tactics of the Grand Trunk Pacific, particularly its attempt to foist an unpopular taxi monopoly on the city, soon lost it much good will.[30]

Another, rather different, controversy arose near the Saskatchewan-Manitoba border. Canadian Northern surveyors had placed the proposed line across the southern portion of the Cote Indian reserve. Right of way for four and a half miles was required from the Indians. In addition, Canadian Northern officials recommended that a divisional station and townsite be established on the Indian lands. Negotiations were opened with the local Indian band and the federal department responsible for Indian affairs. Mackenzie, Mann and Co. Ltd. proposed the purchase of 574.46 acres of land on behalf of the Canadian Northern Railway. Assistant Indian Commissioner Carrothers felt that this was more land than was needed for right-of-way and townsite purposes. Consequently a second proposal was advanced. This time Mackenzie, Mann and Co. Ltd. asked to purchase 55.76 acres for the townsite if 30.06 acres for the station grounds were given free. They explained that in other cases where a townsite was opened by the railway company the station grounds were given free by the

29 *Narratives of Saskatoon, 1882–1927 by Men of the City* (Saskatoon: University Bookstore, 1927), 70–1.

30 Stevens, 200.

local authorities because the value of all lands in the vicinity was greatly enhanced by the coming of the railway and the establishment of a townsite.

The Indian band and the local Indian agent supported the proposed sale. Indeed, they presented a counterproposal offering to sell considerably more land to Mackenzie, Mann and Co. Ltd. However, Clifford Sifton, the Superintendent General of Indian Affairs, ruled that no town was to be established on any Indian reserve or within three miles of any reserve.

This federal ruling provoked very strong protests, particularly from the local Indian agent and from departmental officials in Ottawa. It was pointed out that the Indians desperately needed more money to get started in agriculture and that the establishment of a town nearby would allegedly enable Indians to buy the goods they needed at a reduction of 40 per cent.

Arguments that the railway and the town were essential for the settlement and agricultural development of the district eventually convinced Sifton that he should reverse his previous ruling. If the "national policy" to which he was committed was to succeed in the district under consideration, the railway and the townsite were needed. Consequently Mackenzie, Mann and Co. Ltd. were allowed to purchase 272 acres of Indian lands of the Cote Reserve for the Canadian Northern Railway. The purchase price was $10 per acre plus half of the proceeds over $5,000 that Mackenzie, Mann and Co. Ltd. might realize from subsequent sales of town lots. This agreement was finalized in March 1904, while construction crews were standing by at the reserve boundary where they had been halted in May 1903.

No town lots on the reserve were issued directly to Mackenzie, Mann and Co. Ltd., although they were the legal purchasers. Those lands needed by the Canadian Northern Railway for right of way or station grounds were patented directly to that company, while patents for the town lots were issued only after Mackenzie, Mann and Co. Ltd. had resold them and paid the Indians half of the proceeds over $5,000.[31]

31 PAC, Department of Indian Affairs, Black Series, File 81–1, Railways, Right of Way, Pelly Agency; John Tobias, *The Department of Indian* *Affairs' Management of the Land Resource of Cote Reserve, 1874–1930*, unpublished interim report, written in 1973 and made available by the author.

The townsite, which was named Kamsack, grew rapidly after 1904. Elevators and hardware, lumber, grocery, and drug stores were established, with Mackenzie, Mann and Co. Ltd. making the town lots available at reasonable prices to *bona fide* businessmen. In fact, they sold some of the town lots so cheaply that the Indians, who stood to gain 50 per cent of the later returns from sales, became somewhat disappointed at the lack of speculation.

The merits of a townsite in an Indian reserve long remained a matter of controversy. The beneficial effects for the Indians were certainly limited, while possible harmful results were obvious. At Kamsack, "national policy" had triumphed over concern as to whether the Indians could cope with the challenges of settlement and agricultural development to which the railway company, the Indian department, and the Minister were committed.

Completion of its two "main lines" across the prairies firmly established the Canadian Northern in the northern districts. There was, however, unfinished business in connection with the most northerly line. There were still many farmers and politicians who expected this line to provide western Canada with a rail connection to its own deep-sea port on Hudson Bay. Mackenzie and Mann certainly did not think highly of such a project,[32] but extensions further northward as far as the Saskatchewan River would earn attractive land grants and the transportation contract. Consequently, they arranged to build northward to The Pas in 1904, but there they stopped. Only very substantial additional government subsidies would induce them to build further. Once this condition was made clear, the matter became the subject of political dispute between federal and local politicians. A number of suggestions and counter-suggestions were made until Mackenzie finally offered to build if the government would accept one of three plans of assistance. The federal government, Mackenzie suggested, might give the railway a land subsidy of 6,400 acres per mile, but these lands must be subject to indemnity selection and fit for settlement. Alternatively, a $15,000-per-mile cash subsidy plus the 12,800-acre-per-mile land grant without indemnity selection could be given. The third suggestion was a $15,000-per-mile cash subsidy and a $15,000-per-mile bond

32 *Arbitration*, 2674–5.

guarantee with provisions for non-payment of interest by the company during the early years of operation.[33] Federal officials estimated that construction costs on the railway would amount to $20,000 per mile,[34] so Mackenzie's proposals would leave considerable sums to look after operational deficits. In one historian's view they amounted to "government construction, with the road being handed over as a gift to Mackenzie and Mann".[35]

Lack of Canadian Northern interest before 1907 and the exorbitant proposals finally advanced by Mackenzie left the Laurier government in an uncomfortable dilemma. No private railway company would build the Hudson Bay Railway on acceptable terms; yet the prairies seemed united in their demands for the railway. In 1905 the then recently selected Liberal leader in Saskatchewan threatened to resign immediately unless the federal government provided the needed assistance.[36] Many in the West urged the federal government to build the line as a government project, arguing that no railway with major east-west lines would give the new north-south route a fair chance since it would divert traffic from the lines to the east.[37] Laurier was personally opposed to government construction, believing the road needed "all the elasticity of operation which a company can and the Gov't. cannot have".[38] He would have preferred to see the Grand Trunk build to the Bay, but that company lacked both interest and charter rights in the area. Mackenzie seemed to be asking for more than the entire railway would cost, but Laurier reluctantly agreed that he was the only one who might possibly be persuaded to build. Unhappily he confided to a fellow Liberal, "I am certainly not in love myself with Mackenzie and Mann, but that is altogether beyond the question. The only thing in which I am interested is to have the railway built."[39]

It was left to Clifford Sifton, who, despite his resignation from the Cabinet in 1905, was still the master strategist of western Canadian

33 PAC, Laurier Papers, CDXLIII, 118351–2, Mackenzie to Laurier, 18 Jan. 1907.
34 Stevens, 433.
35 Fleming, 56.
36 PAC, Laurier Papers, CCCLXXXV, 102537–9, Scott to Laurier, 28 Oct. 1905.

37 PAC, Sifton Papers, CXCIII, 154612–15, J. W. Dafoe to Sifton, 16 Aug. 1910.
38 PAC, Laurier Papers, CDIX, 109057, Laurier to Cameron, 16 April 1906.
39 Ibid., 109053, Laurier to Cameron, 7 April 1906.

politics, to suggest a solution which eventually became the official government policy. In 1908, after years of indecision and delay, Sifton suggested in the House of Commons that the railway land-subsidy system be entirely liquidated. It had not been the policy of federal administrations to grant such subsidies since 1894, except in unusual situations, but now the railways were to be given only one more year in which to make good all claims and selections to which they might be entitled under pre-1894 legislation. After that the remaining odd-numbered sections on the prairies were to be thrown open to pre-emption, subject to only one exception. Three million acres were to be held back by the government and sold, with the proceeds going into a special fund to be used to finance construction of the Hudson Bay Railway. This meant, of course, that construction would be delayed until the special reserve fund was established and sufficient lands were sold to permit construction. Because of the inherent delays, Sifton's plan was not popular in the West and severely strained relations between Sifton and other western Liberals. The government nevertheless decided to adopt the plan without clearly specifying whether the funds thus accumulated would be used in direct government construction or in subsidization of private construction.[40]

Mackenzie and Mann were thus relieved of the responsibility of building 450 miles of railway for which they held charter rights but in which they had very little confidence. When the government finally decided to begin construction, however, the contractors who submitted the lowest tender for the first section were none other than Mackenzie and Mann.[41] In this case the Canadian Northern promoters obviously had more faith in construction contracts than in promotional exploits. As far as the Canadian Northern was concerned, its system went no farther than the Saskatchewan River at The Pas; but no traffic could be sent or received over any future road to the Bay without passing over and paying rates on Canadian Northern lines south of The Pas. The road to the Bay was not completed until 1929, long after the Canadian Northern ceased to be a private property, and its operations to date fully justify Mackenzie and Mann's scepticism about the project.

40 Fleming, 62–3.
41 Mackenzie and Mann built the bridge at The Pas. The railway proper was built by contractor J. D. McArthur. CR & MW, Oct. 1913, 470.

The Hudson Bay Railway was one of two major prairie railways in which the politicians seemed to take a much greater interest than the promoters. The other was a 200-mile extension to Regina from Brandon or Hartney, the most westerly points reached by the old Northern Pacific and Manitoba Railway. This line was to parallel the CPR, running approximately twenty to twenty-five miles south of that company's main line. Thanks to the Northern Pacific and Manitoba mileage, the Canadian Northern was able to compete with the CPR on almost equal terms in southern Manitoba. The proposed extension was to bring competition and better branch-line service to southern Saskatchewan. Its chief enthusiast was Saskatchewan Liberal leader Walter Scott.

The Manitoba government readily offered a $13,000-per-mile bond guarantee for the Manitoba portion of the proposed line. Mackenzie and Mann declared themselves willing to build in 1904 if the federal government would provide similar assistance for the mileage in the territories that would shortly be organized into the two new provinces of Saskatchewan and Alberta.[42] When Scott was selected as Liberal leader for the proposed province of Saskatchewan, he set federal aid for the Hudson Bay Railway and the Regina extensions as conditions that must be met before he would accept the position.[43] The federal Cabinet, as usual, found itself in disagreement over proposed railway legislation. Saskatchewan and Manitoba strongly supported Scott's demands, but Frank Oliver, who became Minister of the Interior when Sifton resigned, had doubts about the southern line. It might mean delays in the completion of the main line to Edmonton and distract Mackenzie and Mann from their true northern and Edmonton-centred mission. Oliver did not directly oppose the southern project, but he failed to give it his full support and generally acted in a way that delayed it.[44]

Eastern and Maritime Liberals were also becoming apprehensive. Large sums were voted regularly by the federal government to assist

---

42 PAC, Laurier Papers, CCCXXVIII, 87184, Mann to Minister of Railways and Canals, 23 June 1904.
43 Ibid., CCCLXXV, 99906a–9b, Walter Scott to Laurier, 2 July 1905.

44 Ibid., CCCLXXXIII, 102219–23 and CCCLXXXV, 102540–1, Oliver to Laurier, 17 Oct. 1905, and Laurier to Scott, 4 Nov. 1905; PAS, Scott Papers, 37861–5, Sifton to Scott, 25 Oct. 1905.

various prairie railways. The southern line, however, seemed quite unnecessary. This area already had adequate rail service. The new project was a direct invasion of Canadian Pacific territory at a time when the old road could easily handle the traffic of the area. Government assistance for the development of new territories was considered a very different thing from government assistance simply to promote railway competion for the various isolated centres on the prairies. As a result nothing tangible was done in 1904, and Scott had to be content with several soothing but noncommittal letters from Sir Wilfrid Laurier.[45]

In 1905 Scott, now Liberal leader in Saskatchewan, facing the province's first election, insisted that immediate steps be taken to ensure construction of the Regina and Hudson Bay railways. Scott claimed he had been promised as much when he took on the leadership, and he was strongly supported by Sifton. Laurier promised to do what he could but said he found the Cabinet difficult to handle. Discussions in the Cabinet were strained and inconclusive. They were indefinitely suspended when Frank Oliver left unexpectedly for Edmonton. Scott continued to hope for federal aid for the two railway projects and repeatedly threatened to resign the Liberal leadership unless the federal aid was granted. He was convinced that the CPR was supporting former Territorial Premier F. W. G. Haultain and the Conservatives, and that the influence of the Canadian Northern was needed in the south to ensure a Liberal victory.[46]

Late in October Scott set 9 November as the deadline on which he would resign unless federal aid was given. Laurier reassured him that he was doing all he could, and blamed Oliver's absence for the delays. Yet nothing at all was done, and on 9 November the provincial election writs were issued, with Walter Scott still the Liberal leader. Scott was only dissuaded from his determination to resign by a large campaign contribution arranged by Clifford Sifton.[47] With the help of this campaign money and an active and well-organized party machine that Sifton put at his disposal, Scott was able to defeat Haul-

45 PAC, Laurier Papers, CCCLXXXV, 102540–2, Laurier to Scott, 4 Nov. 1905.
46 Ibid., 102537–9, 102540–1, Scott to Laurier, 28 Oct. 1905, and Laurier to Scott, 4 Nov. 1905.
47 PAC, Graham Papers, LVIII, 32301–4, Scott to Sifton, 18 March 1911.

tain and his Conservatives. Scott nevertheless remained bitter. When Laurier congratulated him on his success, he replied tartly, "If you will take a glance at the map, you will see that we have lost the block of districts, Moosomin, Whitewood, Grenfell, Wolseley, and South Qu'Appelle, through which the proposed CNR southern extension would run. Had this railway been graded last fall according to the suggestions I made in July, we should not be mourning the loss of Moosomin, Grenfell, Wolseley, or Regina City. The majorities against us in these districts are respectively 36, 34, 25 and 19."[48]

It is difficult to see how Mackenzie and Mann could possibly have done much construction on the Regina line in 1905 unless there was a slowdown somewhere else. The failure to get federal assistance for this line and the Hudson Bay Railway in 1905 represented a greater failure for Scott than it did for Mackenzie and Mann. It amply demonstrates the claim later made by Canadian Northern officials that the prairie politicians always had much more work, sweetened by subsidies and guarantees, than even the ambitious Mackenzie and Mann could complete.[49] In any case, the 1905 failure in the south proved to be nothing more than a delay. In 1908 the federal government finally agreed to the bond guarantee Scott wanted, and the line was completed in the same year. It gave the Canadian Northern its southern trunk or main line in Saskatchewan; branch and feeder lines could be extended from it into a large territory hitherto controlled entirely by the CPR.

The value of this southern trunk line was greatly enhanced, and the Canadian Northern's Saskatchewan system more closely integrated, when Mackenzie and Mann purchased the Qu'Appelle, Long Lake and Saskatchewan Railway in 1906. This was Saskatchewan's major north-south line, connecting Prince Albert and Saskatoon with Regina. Since its construction in the late 1880s it had been leased to the CPR, but operations had not been profitable. Interest due on the railway's bonds had been met through the issue of special scrip or interest certificates.[50]

48 PAC, Laurier Papers, CCCXCIII, 104366–9, Scott to Laurier, 16 Dec. 1905.
49 These negotiations took place during the same year that Mackenzie and Mann set their construction record of 546 miles on the two northern lines.

Arbitration, 42, 422, 443.
50 PAC, CNR Records, MCCCLXIII–V, Qu'Appelle, Long Lake and Saskatchewan Railway and Steamboat Company Minute Books and Stock Certificate Book; MCCCLXVII, volume of documents and agreements.

TABLE VI

Operating Statistics of the Qu'Appelle, Long Lake and
Saskatchewan Railway

Year	Mileage operated	Gross earnings	Operating costs	Net earnings
		($)	($)	($)
1896	254	51,305.21	40,615.16	10,690.05
1897	254	60,744.85	48,535.72	12,209.13
1898	254	79,642.02	77,059.24	2,582.78
1899	254	88,740.81	90,675.05	−1,934.24
1900	254	100,702.68	115,479.24	−14,776.56
1901	254	132,089.97	124,843.95	7,246.02
1902	254	194,986.94	137,570.76	57,416.18
1903	254	378,800.03	336,689.39	42,110.64
1904	254	409,087.30	459,232.88	−50,145.58
1905	254	578,028.60	474,610.69	103,417.91
1906	254	718,482.64	502,395.83	216,086.81

Source: The Public Archives of Canada, R.G. 46.

The major shareholders in 1906 were the financial and land-development company of Osler, Hammond and Nanton, and Senator Donald MacInnis of New Brunswick. They were far more interested in the land grant than in the railway itself. As conditions on the prairies improved, they became eager to sell or give the railway, complete with all its assets and its $3,809,140 bonded indebtedness, to anyone who would take it, provided they could retain the lands earned for building the railway.[51]

The CPR, as lessee of the line, was accordingly informed that the owners would prefer to sell rather than continue the leasing arrangement. The CPR was given the first opportunity to purchase, although Mackenzie and Mann, as well as J. J. Hill, who was planning a Great Northern incursion into Canada, quickly learned of the availability of the line and indicated an interest in it. Premier Scott of Saskatchewan

51 *Ibid.*, MCCCLXVII, Qu'Appelle, Long Lake and Saskatchewan Railway, Miscellaneous Documents; *Arbitration*, 450–5, 2533–5; PAS, Scott Papers, 53628–30, Pugsley to Scott, 21 Dec. 1905, and Scott to Pugsley, 3 Jan. 1906.

favoured Hill's bid, believing this would further increase railway competition in Saskatchewan. He did not, however, oppose Canadian Northern attempts to get the line.[52]

When the owners saw the rivalry, they increased their price, asking also for a cash payment for the capital stock of the railway. The CPR refused the terms, thus giving Mackenzie and Mann their opportunity. They lost no time. Discussions with Qu'Appelle, Long Lake and Saskatchewan Railway officials began at 11 a.m. on 20 July 1906, and by 4 p.m. of the same day a purchase agreement had been negotiated and signed.[53] J. J. Hill never had a chance. Quick and decisive action turned the railway over to the Canadian Northern. It soon proved one of the system's most profitable lines. Mackenzie and Mann could act quickly since they controlled all the capital stock of the Canadian Northern. No shareholders or "doubting Thomases" had to be consulted. They knew the line well and saw that it would fit into and help tie together their Saskatchewan lines.[54] They snatched it away before any rivals were fully aware of what had happened. Later Canadian Northern officials said they got the line simply because the CPR lacked vision, but admitted, "it had to be done then and there and had it been known publicly other adverse interests would have intervened and stopped it. These interests did intervene but too late."[55]

With the railway, Mackenzie and Mann assumed responsibility for £307,601 in unpaid interest, and $235,880 in other outstanding obligations. The land grant remained in the hands of the original promoters, who were also to receive $201,000 for the common stock. Yet Canadian Northern officials believed the 254-mile line would "continue to grow rapidly in gross earnings and will more than earn its interest on the First Mortgage bonds." Its value as a feeder line to the Canadian Northern was fully recognized. The payment for the common stock consisted mostly of "various considerations and concessions". A cash payment of only $1 was made. Some outstanding claims of the railway, which the old directors had virtually written off, were subsequently collected in a strong Canadian Northern legal effort

---

52 PAS, Scott Papers, Pugsley to Scott, 21 July 1906.
53 *Arbitration*, 2533–5.
54 PAC, CNR Records, MCCCLXVII,

Confidential Memo re Qu'Appelle, Long Lake and Saskatchewan Railway by Hanna, 21 June 1906.
55 *Arbitration*, 450–1, 2550.

and "went a long way towards the cost of the stock to the Canadian Northern".[56]

Once Mackenzie and Mann had control of the capital stock, they negotiated a new agreement with the long-suffering bondholders. A new 4-per-cent bond issue to replace the old 6-per-cent bond-and-interest certificates, with the Canadian Northern Railway guaranteeing payment of both interest and principal, was proposed. The bondholders accepted the proposal and exchanged their old 6-per-cent bonds at 107 per cent of par value and the scrip at 30 per cent of par for the new guaranteed bonds.[57] This arrangement sharply reduced the fixed charges of the railway, which soon showed very profitable operations.

Even before the transaction with Mackenzie and Mann was completed, the former owners signed a Memorandum of Agreement to sell the entire Qu'Appelle, Long Lake and Saskatchewan Railway land grant to Montreal and Saint John adventurers and speculators J. N. Greenshields and David Russell. A total of 493,269.34 acres was sold for approximately $2 per acre. The former owners thus earned nearly $1,000,000 for their promotion of the Saskatchewan Railway.[58]

The existence of this Memorandum of Agreement undoubtedly increased the owners' eagerness to sell, and subsequent developments suggest there might have been collusion between them and Mackenzie and Mann. A bitter dispute between Greenshields and Russell and Mackenzie and Mann developed very quickly after the sale. Mackenzie and Mann had not been able to find sufficient lands fairly fit for settlement within the territories originally reserved to service the land grants of the Hudson Bay Railway, the Lake Manitoba Railway and Canal Company, and the Manitoba and South Eastern Railway. Some of the areas claimed by Mackenzie and Mann apparently seriously overlapped those reserved for selection by the Qu'Appelle, Long Lake and Saskatchewan. Mackenzie and Mann quickly persuaded the Min-

56 PAC, CNR Records, MCCCLXVII, Agreement of 17 July 1906 with bondholders of the Qu'Appelle, Long Lake and Saskatchewan Railway; *ibid.*, Confidential Memo by Hanna, 21 June 1906; *Synoptical Histories*, 675; *Arbitration*, 2533–5.

57 PAC, CNR Records, MCCCLXVII, Agreement of 17 July 1906, with bondholders of the Qu'Appelle, Long Lake and Saskatchewan Railway.

58 *Ibid.*, Memorandum of Agreement, 15 May 1906, between Pugsley, Osler and Hammond, and MacInnis, and James N. Greenshields and David Russell.

ister of the Interior to allow them to select their deficient lands in the area that Greenshields and Russell believed was reserved exclusively for Qu'Appelle, Long Lake and Saskatchewan Railway selections. Russell and Greenshields had invested nearly a million dollars in these lands, only to find Mackenzie and Mann making choice selections in areas they thought had been reserved for them. David Russell, whose private resources were never equal to those of Greenshields, was chagrined and became, in the words of the chairman of the Canadian Northern Board of Arbitration, "unbalanced . . . probably due to the treatment he received at that time".[59] Russell, it seems, was always looking for ways and means of getting rich quickly, but his business "friends" were invariably a disappointment to him. His career is strewn with broken dreams, followed by alcoholic excesses and liberal use of the effervescent salts from whose manufacture he derived much of his wealth.[60] He was a sheep that Mackenzie and Mann fleeced several times, but there is no evidence that he ever enjoyed great influence in the determination of their affairs.

For Mackenzie and Mann the acquisition of the Qu'Appelle, Long Lake and Saskatchewan Railway was certainly fortunate. They paid a relatively high price, but the new line quickly became the mainstay of their Saskatchewan operations in much the same way as the acquisition of the Northern Pacific and Manitoba lines five years earlier had established them in Manitoba.

There were, nevertheless, some serious problems connected with the acquisition of the Qu'Appelle, Long Lake and Saskatchewan Railway. Major construction work on the Edmonton and Prince Albert lines had placed great stress on the limited and often second-rate rolling stock the Canadian Northern had available. To some extent rolling-stock manufacturers were to blame since they fell seriously behind in deliveries, but it was also true that not enough had been ordered because of a tight financial situation. There would have been serious operating problems due to inadequate rolling stock on the Canadian

59 *Arbitration*, 2552; PAC, CNR Records, x̄ccxxx, Agreements re Qu'Appelle, Long Lake and Saskatchewan Railway and Steamboat Co.; Canada, Department of the Interior, File 505500, Canadian Northern Railway Land Grants; *ibid.*, File 158300, Qu'Appelle, Long Lake and Saskatchewan Lands.
60 PAC, Borden Papers, Additional, 192920–4, Brenton Macnab to Blount, 17 and 24 Sept. 1903.

Northern Railway even if the Qu'Appelle, Long Lake and Saskatchewan Railway had not been added to the system. The acquisition of it, coupled with one of the most severe winters ever experienced on the prairies, created monstrous problems.[61]

The Canadian Northern was scheduled to take over operation of the Qu'Appelle, Long Lake and Saskatchewan Railway on 15 December. Just prior to that date the CPR sent out a "clean-up train" which took virtually everything that could be moved, from coal and tools to the pencils and inkwells in the stations. The Canadian Northern sent up its first train with supplies on 15 December, but it ran into the first severe blizzard of the season. The temperature reportedly dipped to fifty-five degrees below zero and the entire train got stuck in blowing snow near McDowall, south of Prince Albert. It ran out of coal and completed the run fourteen or fifteen days later. The crew were forced to bring in the coal-burning locomotive on wood gathered alongside the track.[62] It was the beginning of an extremely difficult winter. In one place the drifts reportedly got so deep that one of the locomotives stuck in it was completely drifted over and hidden from view.

Since the CPR had taken out all its own unsold supplies, and the Canadian Northern was unable to bring in new ones quickly, settlers along the way soon faced serious food and fuel shortages. Urgent letters were despatched to the Prime Minister and bitter complaints were referred to the Board of Railway Commissioners.[63] "In an evil hour for Saskatchewan," one complainant wrote, "the CNR Co. bit off more than it can chew in a year."[64] The rolling stock that the Canadian Northern put on its new lines became the particular source of many a tall tale and not inconsiderable grumbling.[65] One of the accounts which reached the office of the Prime Minister was the following:

61 Details of the railway's problems are given in PAC, CNR Legal Series, File 47–3, "Blockade of Spring", 1907; Regina City Council Clerk to the Board of Railway Commissioners, 11 April 1904. One of the most graphic descriptions of the conditions during the winter of 1906–7 is provided in Wallace Stegner, *Wolf Willow: A History, A Story, and a Memory of the Last Plains Frontier* (New York: Viking, 1955).

62 CNRHQ, Osborne Scott Interview.
63 Laurier, as his correspondence reveals, became very concerned about the matter and brought to bear what pressure he could on the ambitious railway promoters in January and February 1907.
64 PAC, Laurier Papers, CDLXIV, 118452, Thomas O'Flynn to Laurier, 19 Jan. 1907.
65 PAS, special newspaper clippings file on railways, Regina.

Dead engines, the property of the CNR Co. strew the line from Regina to Prince Albert; dead of decrepitude, dead of overwork, engines worn out, leaky, rusty, caulked and tinkered in all their joints, and fit only for scrap iron, constitute the power which the CNR Co. have put on the line of railway which, if efficiently worked, can in point of profitable results compare favourably with any in Canada. Recently an engine died near Dundurn and another was sent to take it away, but, the second engine also died as it hove in sight of its dead brother. If things inanimate have eyes to see and hearts to feel, lo, how that second engine must have grieved while heaving its last breath at the thought of not being able to perform the work of mercy on which it had been dispatched, viz., to bring home a deceased brother either for recaulking and retinkering or for embalmment and burial; poor old engines, peace to their names, they died in harness, what a blessing in disguise it would be to the people of Saskatchewan if the owners of those old engines, following their example, would also die and make room for better people to handle the line, but I am afraid that no such luck is in sight just now.[66]

It took time to equip and integrate the new line into the larger system. The following summer the service was irregular and passengers often spent considerable time snaring gophers and partaking in other prairie pastimes while waiting for repairs or new motive power.[67] These were the growing pains of a very rapidly expanding railway system operating on a slim budget. The criticisms were usually less severe where the Canadian Northern line was the first into a district. Even bad service was better than none at all. Eventually the service, the rolling stock, and the condition of the roadbed improved as the traffic increased.

Despite the early inadequacies and accompanying difficulties, however, the acquisition of the Qu'Appelle, Long Lake and Saskatchewan Railway in 1906 marked the point at which the Canadian Northern Railway became an effective competitor of the CPR in Saskatchewan. Completion of the two northern lines, promise of federal aid for the

66 PAC, Laurier Papers, CDXLIV, 118450–2, Thomas O'Flynn to Laurier, 19 Jan. 1907.
67 The Saskatchewan Archives newspaper clippings files on railways con- tain interesting accounts of colonists' adventures on the Qu'Appelle, Long Lake and Saskatchewan Railway shortly after Mackenzie and Mann took it over.

southern line, and the acquisition of the Qu'Appelle, Long Lake and Saskatchewan Railway which linked all three, made 1906 the most important year in the Canadian Northern's development in Saskatchewan. The main outline of the Canadian Northern's prairie system was now complete. Many of the details, however, still had to be filled in.

CHAPTER EIGHT

SERVING THE PRAIRIE WEST THE BRANCH LINES 1906–1911

THE CANADIAN PRAIRIES were settled and developed principally during the years when Sir Wilfrid Laurier was Prime Minister. Clifford Sifton's aggressive and imaginative immigration policy brought large numbers of settlers from eastern Europe, the United States, and Great Britain to the prairie homesteads. They came with confidence and optimism, hoping to begin a new life in "The Last Best West",[1] which the Department of the Interior publicity described as the true land of milk and honey.[2] Many succeeded and prospered; others, often through no fault of their own, complained that they "would probably be better off if they had broken no land and attempted to market no wheat under the adverse conditions which they are now suffering from."[3] They had need of a railway branch line.

Many factors contributed to the success of prairie settlement in the 1900s. Sifton's administrative reforms and his massive advertising campaign made the federal Department of the Interior one of the most effective government agencies of the time. Government review and adjustment of the tariff removed some of the most serious western

1 This was the name of the most famous of the Department of the Interior's promotional pamphlets. Copy available in Saskatchewan Archives.
2 Terms such as these were specifically and repeatedly used in the promotional literature. See, for example, *Canada, the Land of Opportunity* (Ottawa, 1910); *Western Canada, Free Homes for all in the Great Province of*

Manitoba (Ottawa, 1892); *Canada, An Account of its Resources and Development* (Ottawa, 1904); *Canada, the Granary of the World* (Ottawa, 1903).
3 Judgment in the case of Mervin Board of Trade *v.* Canadian Northern Railway Company, Board of Railway Commissioners, File 11929.15, *Canadian Railway Cases*, XIV, 363–5.

complaints on that issue, and the construction of new railways opened many hitherto inaccessible areas. External factors also contributed to the new prosperity. The prolonged depression that had begun in 1873 finally ended. Gold discoveries in Africa and the Yukon increased and strengthened the currency of a world still slavishly looking to gold for financial stability. European industrialization opened large new markets, sharply increased world prices of Canadian foodstuffs, and provided Europeans with the means to pay for imports of Canadian cereals. Freight rates both on the railways at home and on Atlantic shipping fell sharply, thus allowing Canadian agricultural exports to compete in the European markets.

On the prairies, rainfall became more abundant as a wet cycle followed years in which drought and early frosts had seriously damaged or destroyed many prairie crops. Moreover, prairie farmers migrating from the United States to Canada had learned new techniques of cultivation which conserved moisture in the soil. Others brought with them a knowledge of irrigation techniques first successfully applied in the arid Mormon settlements in the heart of the great American desert. These techniques overcame many of the problems of inadequate rainfall. Equally important was the discovery of a new variety of wheat, which largely solved the problem of early frosts. The variety Marquis, developed by Charles D. Saunders in 1904, ripened from ten to fourteen days earlier than any known variety. This discovery "rolled back the Arctic a full two hundred miles".[4] It made extensive wheat farming on the northern prairies possible.

The times were good, and many of the homesteaders prospered. Unfortunately, some still faced a major obstacle. Lands near the established railways were often taken up early, and prospective settlers sought homesteads on more distant but rich and promising lands. It was the intention of the federal government to see all the arable prairie lands taken up in homesteads—not only those adjacent to the main lines of the railways. The hinterlands often responded to the exertions of the pioneers and produced abundant crops, but many farmers soon found that their efforts were in vain if no nearby railway was available to transport the crop. Branch lines, more branch lines, and still

4 Stevens, 50.

RAILWAY TERRITORIES ON THE PRAIRIES

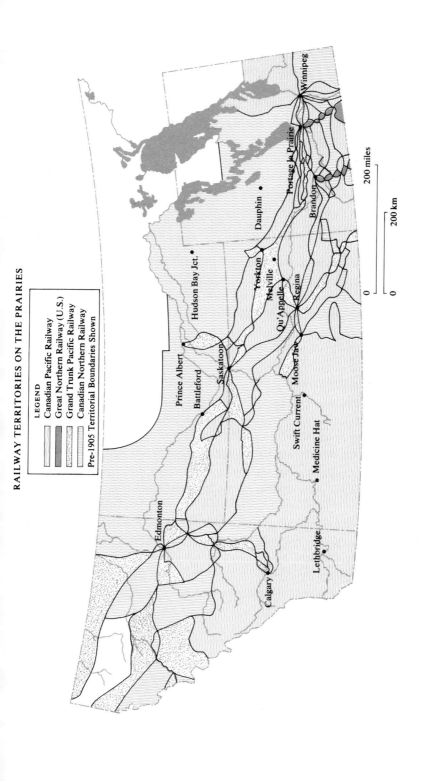

LEGEND
Canadian Pacific Railway
Great Northern Railway (U.S.)
Grand Trunk Pacific Railway
Canadian Northern Railway
Pre-1905 Territorial Boundaries Shown

Winnipeg

Portage la Prairie

Dauphin

Brandon

Hudson Bay Jct.

Yorkton

Melville

Qu'Appelle

Regina

Prince Albert

Battleford

Saskatoon

Moose Jaw

Swift Current

Medicine Hat

Edmonton

Lethbridge

Calgary

0   200 miles

0   200 km

more branch lines quickly became the most important economic and political issue of these prairie hinterlands. Often, at the time they took up a homestead, the settlers were promised a branch line within a year or two. When these promised railways failed to materialize, discontent, anger, and despair became widespread.

Prairie politicians were very keenly aware of the need for more railway branch lines. Their private papers are thick with petitions and complaints from dissatisfied farmers. The letter of a farmer in the Marriott district to Premier Scott of Saskatchewan is typical of the many letters received by the politicians.

I write to you on behalf of the farmers in this district, to bring before you the serious position of the farmers of this district. We began to settle in this part of the country in the spring of 1905. Some of us with very large outfits, and others with small ones for to make our home in this country with the expectation of having a railway within two years at a reasonable distance for to market our grain. With this point in view, we settled here, improved and broke up the land and invested all our money in this way. In the year 1906, we had to haul our wheat to Saskatoon, a distance of from 60 to 100 miles. This would take a team of horses from 5 to 8 days and a team of oxen from 8 to 10 days to make the round trip. We could only haul 70 bushels of wheat on a load. We got 40¢ to 50¢ per bushel for it at the elevator in Saskatoon. The cost of hauling one load was from $12 to $15, that is if the weather was favourable. After we deducted the working expenses from the amount we received for our grain, we found that we were farming at a loss. Still we were determined to try again trusting that we would not have to haul our grain so far next year. Sorry to say that we're even worse in 1907. This year we had the bright hope of having the Canadian Northern in through this district and we seeded all the land we have in crop, from 100 to 250 acres each and the outlook for a nearer market is not a bit better. Now the question is, what are we going to do? We are not going to farm here for a mere living. We must have the money we put into the land back again. We are not going to stand this treatment any longer. If we cannot get a railway into this district, we will have to call upon the Government for assistance because it was through them and their representatives that we came into this country. I would also like to call your attention to the fuel question which is getting serious too.

No wood can be got nearer than 40 miles, coal we have to haul from Saskatoon. We would earnestly ask you as a leader of the people to take this matter into consideration and let us have your advice by return as we are determined either to have a railway or we will pull out, and we don't mean to do the latter and say nothing.[5]

The petitions and complaints came from all parts of the province and stressed the same problems. A farmer from Hearts Hill in another part of the province wrote despairingly to the Premier, "We are in a desperate situation. The elevators pay 18–20 cents for a bushel of oats and it costs 20 cents to take the bushel 40 miles for to the elevator. Till latest next fall we must be helped anyhow by a better railroad connection or we have lost everything and have to suffer direct want with our families."[6]

Farmers in the settlement at Mervin, north of Battleford, organized themselves into a Board of Trade to take their complaints to the federal Board of Railway Commissioners. They stated categorically that they could not continue farming without better railway connections. A Canadian Northern branch line had been built as far as Edam, and plans had been filed and promises made to extend it northward another twelve miles to Mervin. The farmers had entered the district on the basis of these promises but now found themselves in desperate straits because of the railway's failure to build the additional twelve miles.

The Board of Railway Commissioners was very sympathetic. "So far as the necessities of the district are concerned, and the position the settlers find themselves in," they wrote in their judgement, "there is no doubt that the railway should be built, and built at once." Unfortunately the railway company lacked the money to build, and the Board had no authority to compel companies without money to build railways where they were needed.[7]

The railways were also sympathetic. Mackenzie and Mann were willing and eager to build branch lines on the prairies as quickly as pos-

5 PAC, Laurier Papers, DXX, 140918–29, Lachlan MacDonald to Scott.
6 PAS, Scott Papers, 53731–2, W. Kronsbien to Scott, 31 Dec. 1909,

20 May 1908.
7 Canadian Railway Cases, XIV, 363–5.

sible. When asked later if their railway would not be bankrupt if they had built according to the demands of western farmers, the Canadian Northern's chief engineer simply replied, "There is a necessity for them, and there is a necessity for a considerably greater mileage than they had got today." He was convinced that "in a good grain-producing territory the farmer thinks he is too far away to haul his grain if he has a greater distance than 6 miles to a haul; and lands that are close to a little station, that is within the 6 mile limit, are usually valued at $5 an acre more than land a greater distance away."[8]

Provincial politicians were equally well aware of the need, and determined to do all they could to get the required branch-line mileage. Premier Scott of Saskatchewan stated the situation forcefully when he wrote to the Prime Minister in 1905 urging federal aid for branch lines.

As it is now generally conceded that grain cannot be profitably marketed if it has to be hauled a greater distance than ten or twelve miles to a railway point, you can understand the very great disability under which the people in our new settlements are endeavouring to make homes for themselves and develop Western Canada. The result is widespread dissatisfaction. In fact in many of the larger and more progressive settlements, the conditions have become intolerable and there is a very grave danger indeed of an exodus unless the situation is relieved.[9]

Scott believed the responsibility for assisting in the construction of Saskatchewan railways rested with the federal government. Ottawa still controlled public lands on the prairies. Therefore, the settlement of those lands remained a federal responsibility, and with it the responsibility "to furnish reasonable transportation facilities to the thousands of settlers who are being placed on our vacant lands through the efforts of your various Immigration Agencies".[10] Even the federal Minister of Railways and Canals reported in 1902, "I went over portions of the Canadian Pacific, Northern Pacific, Canadian Northern and Great Northern, and found that while they had advanced very

8 *Arbitration*, 1589.
9 PAC, Laurier Papers, DXXIII, 141741–4, Scott to Laurier, 19 June

1908.
10 *Ibid.*

Sir William Mackenzie, 1849–1923. President of the Canadian Northern Railway, Mackenzie, Mann and Company Limited, and officer and director of numerous other companies. (PAC)

Sir Donald Mann, 1853–1934. First Vice-President of the Canadian Northern Railway, Vice-President of Mackenzie, Mann and Company Limited, director of numerous other companies. (PAC)

(*Above*) Laying railway tracks. (Western Development Museum)
(*Opposite*) Railway levelling on the prairie through the wheat fields,
*c.*1905. (PAC)

(*Above*) Canadian Northern Railway construction gang near Lumsden, Saskatchewan, *c*.1906. (PAC) (*Below*) Spring of 1899 at Swan River, Manitoba, end of steel. The Doukhobor men spent the first years in Canada as railway construction workers. (PAC) (*Opposite top*) Canadian Northern Pacific Railway construction at Lytton, British Columbia, *c*.1914. (PAC) (*Bottom*) The train that came from the United States bringing land seekers, mostly farmers. (PAC)

(*Opposite*) The first train into Edmonton, 20 October 1902. (PAC)
(*Above top*) Winter operations at Carlyle, Saskatchewan. (PAC)
(*Below*) The Canadian Northern Coal and Ore Dock at Port Arthur. (PAC)

(*Top*) Sir William Mackenzie driving the last spike on the transcontinental Canadian Northern Railway at Basque, British Columbia, on 23 January 1915. (PAC) (*Below*) Train carrying parliamentary and press party over the Canadian Northern Railways System from Quebec City to Vancouver, October 1915. (PAC)

rapidly they had been unable to keep up the remarkable progress of the country."[11]

Even in areas where rail service was already available there were complaints. A town or district served by only one railway invariably thought itself the victim of a railway monopoly. No matter how slight the available traffic, competition was considered an eminently fair demand. Overhead, fixed charges, and operational expenses on the railways, plus the need for a reasonable amount of traffic to meet these costs, were not understood or were deliberately ignored by the proponents of competition. A *Manitoba Free Press* editorial expressed the prevalent sentiment when it stated, "The vital importance to this portion of the Dominion of having all the transportation facilities that can possibly be secured is thus ever foremost in the public mind."[12]

Mackenzie and Mann were undoubtedly the most enthusiastic and successful builders of prairie branch lines. It was their intention to control and retain all the traffic north of their main line while at the same time making incursions into southern areas already served by the CPR. Their policy of building cheap lines in lightly settled areas often permitted profitable operations where the other roads with higher construction standards were unable to build. The local lines, even when not profitable in themselves, provided valuable long-haul traffic for the main lines and might therefore permit a net profit on the business thus generated.

All the prairie branch lines built by Mackenzie and Mann received direct or indirect government assistance of one kind or another. The specific financial and legal arrangements, however, varied somewhat from one line to the next. The original charters of the companies Mackenzie and Mann acquired to assemble their main line from Port Arthur to northwestern Manitoba contained provisions, sometimes coupled with government assistance, to build local service extensions. Thus the short branch to Winnipegosis, the extension from Hudson Bay Junction to The Pas, the original interlake route of the Hudson Bay Railway, and a deteriorating line from Stanley Junction to Gunflint were all built under charters used by Mackenzie and Mann for their main line.

11 *Manitoba Free Press*, 3 Nov. 1902, 1.

12 *Ibid.*, 25 Nov. 1902, 4.

In Manitoba both the main lines and the various branch lines received provincial bond guarantees in the early years. Originally, most of the Manitoba mileage that became the Canadian Northern's main line was thought of as providing nothing more than branch-line service. The amalgamations which created the Canadian Northern Railway, under the terms of the new federal charter, made further provincially assisted branch-line construction more difficult. Rather than seeking constant modifications and extensions of their federal charter rights, Mackenzie and Mann decided to resort to new provincially chartered companies to provide the legislative authorization for new branch lines. Thus, the Morden and North Western Railway Company was incorporated in 1901 with powers to build an extensive network of branch lines. The incorporation of the railway company was quickly followed by an agreement with the provincial government whereby local assistance was granted for the construction of some of the proposed mileage. Approximately seventy-two miles were built before the Morden and North Western Railway was amalgamated with the Canadian Northern Railway in 1903.

While the Morden and North Western was being amalgamated, a new local railway company with wide-ranging branch-line charter rights was incorporated. The new company, the Western Extension Railway, also collected provincial guarantees. Two hundred and twenty-three miles were built, mainly in westward extensions of Canadian Northern and leased Northern Pacific and Manitoba lines. The Western Extension Railway also lost its separate identity by amalgamating with the Canadian Northern Railway in 1903.[13]

Both the Morden and North Western Railway and the Western Extension Railway were subsidiaries of the Canadian Northern from the outset. The Manitoba government found it easier to grant guarantees to locally chartered companies which were then amalgamated with the federally chartered parent company. Both companies held charter rights to build branch lines in widely separated parts of the province. Most of these branch lines were extensions of existing lines or connecting links between older Canadian Northern lines. Some of the authorized mileage was built immediately, some only after the local

13 *Synoptical Histories*, 210.

company was amalgamated with the Canadian Northern, and some of the proposed extensions never advanced beyond the paper stage.

Whenever the need arose in Manitoba for government-assisted branch lines or extensions to existing local lines, a new company was incorporated. This company was granted the usual provincial guarantee and usually joined the Canadian Northern through amalgamation shortly thereafter. In 1904 it was the Northern Extension Railway, in 1906 the Winnipeg and Northern Railway Company, and in 1913 the Canadian Northern Manitoba Railway Company.[14] Often only a portion of the authorized mileage obtained provincial guarantees before the local company was amalgamated, and of course only the assisted lines were built.

The resulting Canadian Northern branch-line system in Manitoba was extensive, even if one takes into account only the lines that were actually built. North of their main line Mackenzie and Mann controlled almost all the branch lines. Although their main line from Winnipeg to Portage la Prairie, the old Northern Pacific and Manitoba line, ran to the south of the CPR line, they controlled as well most of the charter rights to build in the interlake and northern regions of the province, thanks to the charter of the old Hudson Bay Railway. The original forty miles of the latter railway, built to Shoal Lake and abandoned in 1887, were rehabilitated and extended northwestward to Gypsumville, with a northerly branch to Hodgson. Further, and much shorter, branch lines to the tourist resorts on the shores of Lake Winnipeg, and northward and westward from the main line west of Dauphin gave the Canadian Northern complete control over rail traffic from these northern areas.

In southern Manitoba the leased Northern Pacific and Manitoba Railway lines provided the basis for a profitable and competitive system. Very little had to be added except westward extensions and a few connecting links between the east-west lines. An east-west extension across southeastern Manitoba also allowed contact with the main line in the southeastern corner of the province, without the necessity of shipping southern traffic through Winnipeg. Basically, however, the mileage acquired from the Northern Pacific provided

14 *Ibid.*, 211–14.

Mackenzie and Mann with the branch lines needed to compete with the CPR in southern Manitoba.

The rather wide strip of land in western Manitoba, between the CPR main line and the Canadian Northern main line, proved the most seriously contested territory, and the scramble for control of it illustrates some of the most ludicrous aspects of western railway development. In the south the situation had been stabilized in a reasonably efficient way; not so in the central area of the province. The Grand Trunk Pacific built its main line through this area between the CPR main line and the old Manitoba and North Western Railway, which had been purchased by the CPR and was thereafter known as the Minnedosa line. Grand Trunk officials did not expect anyone to build immediately to the north of their main line. The Canadian Northern, however, obtained assistance from the Manitoba government and did just that. A local service line running as far west as Beulah, Manitoba, was built. The CPR then decided to build a branch line of its own between the new Canadian Northern branch line and the Grand Trunk Pacific main line. Mackenzie and Mann, not to be outdone, obtained further provincial assistance to build a branch line slightly to the north of the CPR's Minnedosa line. Yet this branch line was to be built sufficiently close to the Riding Mountains that further construction by rivals would be impractical. Thus, slightly to the east of Brandon, one could find no fewer than eight east-west lines in the space of only forty miles. No fewer than fourteen such lines crossed the Manitoba-Saskatchewan border, of which seven belonged to Mackenzie and Mann and six to the CPR; the fourteenth was the Grand Trunk Pacific main line.[15] Surely this was carrying government-assisted branch-line construction and railway competition to ridiculous lengths.

All these branch lines were certainly in great demand locally, and probably offered as much immediate traffic as some of the proposed branch lines in more sparsely settled areas farther west; but the potential for future development was limited. The chief victim in Manitoba, however, was the Grand Trunk Pacific, which did not participate in the scramble. Its main line was very closely crowded by its competitors, and it had no branch lines whatsoever in the province. Southern Manitoba divided its traffic between the CPR and the Canadian Northern, while the region north of the CPR's Minnedosa line was left entirely to the Canadian Northern.

Manitoba owed its extensive railway network to the provincial government's willingness to guarantee construction bonds of Canadian Northern lines and to provide small cash subsidies for local lines built by the CPR, which refused the provincial bond guarantees. The federal government followed Manitoba's example when it guaranteed the bonds for the Canadian Northern extensions into the North-West Territories. In 1905, when the Territories were organized into provinces, the Liberal premiers of both Saskatchewan and Alberta indicated that they expected Ottawa to continue its support of all railway construction. Ottawa retained control of public lands in the Prairie provinces and should therefore assume responsibility for railway construction. With budgetary surpluses, considerable optimism, and a determination to see the immigration and homestead policy succeed, the federal government did not immediately challenge this argument, particularly when the lines to be assisted were main or trunk lines designed to carry interprovincial traffic. By the end of 1906, however, federal assistance for most of the main lines had been provided. The clamour for more prairie railways nevertheless increased, with most of the proposed new lines being of the branch- or feeder-line variety. Financial, economic, and constitutional considerations began to weigh heavily in the mind of an increasingly reluctant Prime Minister. Eastern taxpayers would hardly support continuing federal aid for local lines which really were the responsibility of local governments.

The issue came sharply into focus in March 1908 when William Mackenzie presented the Prime Minister with three long memoranda. One of these requested federal aid for the construction of a Canadian Northern line across Ontario to connect the western and eastern railway systems controlled by Mackenzie and Mann. Another sought federal assistance for a Canadian Northern line to the Pacific. The third sought federal assistance for a number of larger Canadian Northern branch lines on the prairies.[16] The last memorandum was strongly endorsed by Premier Scott of Saskatchewan, who urged the federal government to "follow up its settlement policy with a systema-

---

15 These lines are shown most clearly in the *Department of the Interior's 1915 Atlas of Canada*, 45–6.

16 PAC, Laurier Papers, DVIII, 137215–16, 137221–7, and 137234–7, Mackenzie to Laurier, 6 March 1908.

tic, well planned, aggressive railway policy".[17] The urgent need for the new branch lines and the danger that settlers would abandon their homesteads if the railway were not built were stressed by the Premier. Laurier considered the Saskatchewan memorandum carefully, agreed to most items, but baulked at several.[18]

The time had come for the two new provinces to shoulder some of the responsibility for local railway development. Laurier agreed that the federal government had an obligation to assist in the construction of main or through lines which were clearly in the general interest of the country. Local lines, however, should be dealt with by the provincial governments. Manitoba had accepted that responsibility in 1896, and the premiers of Alberta and Saskatchewan were persuaded that they must do likewise. They urgently needed many more railways than the federal government would be likely to assist. The Manitoba plan was working well, and few in those optimistic days thought the guarantees would ever cost the province a penny. Elections were approaching in the two new provinces and both governments decided to espouse a railway policy designed to meet the need for railway branch lines. Provincial government guarantees for all worthy railroad projects were promised. There was to be a financial alliance[19] between the provincial governments and the railway companies that would solve the most urgent problem on the prairies in 1908.

The promise of government guarantees for branch-line construction was strongly endorsed by the electorate in both Alberta and Saskatchewan. In the 1909 sessions of the Legislative Assemblies in both Alberta and Saskatchewan important new railway legislation was passed. Local subsidiary or branch-line companies sponsored by the Canadian Northern Railway and the Grand Trunk Pacific were granted charters to build branch lines in various and often widely separated parts of the new provinces. Canadian Northern interests were to be served by the Saskatchewan and North Western Railway and the

17 PAC, Laurier Papers, DXXIII, 141742, Walter Scott to Laurier, 19 June 1908.
18 See notations in the margin of *ibid.*, DVIII, 137221–7, Memorandum

from Mackenzie to Laurier, 6 March 1908.
19 Scott referred to it specifically as an alliance. See PAS, Scott Papers, 54380–2, Scott to O. O. Winter, 12 June 1913.

Alberta Midland Railway.[20] The charters of these local companies were a curious compendium of local commercial and political pressures and aspirations. They look suspiciously like a list compiled after every government member had a chance to enumerate the railway requirements of his constituency.

At the same session, provincial bond-guarantee legislation to assist in the construction of many of the authorized branch lines was passed. Bonds up to $13,000 per mile, carrying a 4-per-cent interest rate, were to be guaranteed on lines defined somewhat more precisely than they were in the charters. In Saskatchewan the government offered guarantees on 525 miles of Saskatchewan and North Western mileage,[21] while in Alberta a similar guarantee for 805 miles was offered to Mackenzie and Mann.[22] Grand Trunk Pacific legislation in both provinces was somewhat less comprehensive, with about half as much mileage listed in the guarantees for that company. The legislation required that all the assisted roads be completed by 31 December 1911.[23]

Premier Scott in Saskatchewan discovered very quickly that while this legislation was popular in the districts directly affected, it failed to bring a railway to the doorstep of every farmer in the province. Many constituents consequently felt their region had been neglected, and they demanded equal treatment. The result was the incorporation of new Canadian Northern and Grand Trunk Pacific-sponsored branch-line companies in a special session held late in 1909. The politicians themselves, led by Attorney General William M. Martin, obtained a charter for the Saskatchewan Midland Railway on behalf of the Canadian Northern Railway.[24] Provincial guarantees for 390 miles of this new railway were immediately voted. Mackenzie and Mann thus obtained provincial guarantees for nearly 2,000 miles of branch lines on the prairies in 1909, and charter rights for many more. Additional guarantees were willingly voted by both provinces in the succeeding years. New local companies were incorporated after 1909 to meet new requirements. The Canadian Northern Saskatchewan,[25] the Canadian

---

20 Saskatchewan, *8–9 Edw. VII. Cap. 18*; Alberta, *9 Edw. VII. Cap. 45.*
21 Saskatchewan, *8–9 Edw. VII. Cap. 3.*
22 Alberta, *9 Edw. VII. Cap. 14.*

23 Alberta, *9 Edw. VII. Cap. 14*, Cl. 6.
24 Saskatchewan, *9 Edw. VII. Cap. 41*, Preamble.
25 Saskatchewan, *2 Geo. v. Caps. 11 and 43.*

Northern Alberta,[26] and the Canadian Northern Western railways[27] were thus brought into existence with extensive charter rights and new government guarantees for many of the authorized lines. One of these charters authorized the railway to build "also such other lines within the province as may be from time to time authorized by order of the Lt. Gov. in council",[28] while guarantees for "any extension of above designated by the Lt. Governor" were also authorized.[29] The titles of these branch lines were rarely an accurate indication of the location of the proposed new mileage. The Canadian Northern Western, for example, had authority to build in western Alberta. It also had authority to build to southeastern Alberta, to the Peace or Pine River passes, and north of the Saskatchewan River to the eastern boundary of Alberta.[30] Each of the local companies was authorized to build anywhere from six to sixteen larger new lines, many with local branches of their own. The legislation reflected the unbounded enthusiasm of the politicians for branch lines, more branch lines, and yet more branch lines, and their willingness to guarantee bonds as quickly—and often much more quickly—than the railways could be built.

In most respects the Alberta and Saskatchewan legislation closely followed the Manitoba bond-guarantee model. All monies from the sale of the guaranteed bonds had to be paid into a special trust account from which they could be transferred to the railway company only when certificates showing actual construction expenditures were submitted.

All interim financing had to be handled by the promoters. Organizational meetings of the Canadian Northern-sponsored Alberta Midland Railway and the Saskatchewan and North Western Railway were held on 22 April 1909. At each of these organizational meetings stock was subscribed, directors and officers were elected, construction contracts with Mackenzie, Mann and Co. Ltd. were approved, and the bond-guarantee agreements with the appropriate provincial governments were confirmed. Several by-laws were then passed, the last of which provided for the immediate amalgamation of the local company with

26 Canada, *9–10 Edw.* vii. *Cap. 6.*
27 Alberta, *1 Geo.* v. *Cap. 48.*
28 Saskatchewan, *2 Geo.* v. *Cap. 43.*
29 Saskatchewan, *2 Geo.* v. *Cap. 11.*
30 Alberta, *1 Geo.* v. *Cap. 48* and *2–3 Geo.* v. *Cap. 19.*

the parent Canadian Northern Railway.[31] A similar pattern was followed in the case of most of the companies later incorporated provincially. These companies were, from the outset, nothing more than local extensions of the larger systems and were amalgamated with those systems as soon as the available provincial aid had been collected.

The provincial legislation in Alberta and Saskatchewan did not provide the basis for the development of rational and well-integrated prairie networks. Every locality that had Liberal voters was presumed worthy of at least one railway, and probably of railway competition, and legislation to obtain this was passed. It was left to the railways themselves to decide which lines they should give priority to and which should remain unbuilt. The legislation provided the companies with the charters and guarantees they needed to follow whatever strategy they might choose.

The basic strategy was fairly simple. Mackenzie and Mann were determined to retain control in the north. They met with decisive action any attempts by rivals to invade northern territory. A Grand Trunk Pacific plan to build northward from Melville to Yorkton and possibly to Hudson Bay Junction was stopped by a northern line built by Mackenzie and Mann. This line was built from the Canadian Northern main line at precisely the point where the Grand Trunk Pacific branch line intended to cross. A parallel line would not be profitable, and the Grand Trunk Pacific branch built no farther than the Canadian Northern main line. A second Grand Trunk Pacific line northward to Prince Albert could not be stopped, but for many years it was the only rival line in operation north of the Canadian Northern main line between Gladstone and Edmonton. The Canadian Northern Railway was in fact *the* railway of the northern prairies.

Mackenzie and Mann fully intended to retain this control in the area west of Edmonton as well. In 1899 the Edmonton and Lesser

31 PAC, CNR Records, CCCX, 1–13, Minutes of Provisional Directors, Shareholders and Directors of the Alberta Midland Railway, all on 22 April 1909; *ibid.*, CMXXVII, Meetings of Provisional Directors, Shareholders and Directors of the Saskatchewan and North-Western Railway Company. For both these companies the provincial bond-guarantee legislation specifically stated that the guarantees would come into effect only after the amalgamation with the parent Canadian Northern Railway was agreed to.

Slave Lake Railway was incorporated with charter rights to build to Lesser Slave Lake and the Peace River. The Canadian Northern Western Railway later received similar charter rights and government bond guarantees. Construction of this line, however, was hampered by uncertainties about route selections for a planned line to the Pacific. Consequently, very little was done until the provincial government took a direct part in sponsoring a rival road, the Edmonton, Dunvegan and British Columbia Railway. A similar provincially supported railway scheme, the Alberta Great Waterways Railway, was offered to Mackenzie and Mann.[32] When they failed to react as enthusiastically as the Alberta government had expected, the politicians took the project in hand themselves, only to become embroiled in one of the province's most serious railway scandals of the period. Neither of these projects, however, seriously undermined Canadian Northern dominance in the north.

The strong position in the north did not preclude Canadian Northern incursions into southern areas. Two large areas were particularly inviting. In Saskatchewan and Alberta there was a wide gap between the Calgary-bound CPR and the later Edmonton-bound transcontinentals. The CPR had to bridge the South Saskatchewan River to get into the area, and thus seemed to be at a disadvantage. The Grand Trunk Pacific concentrated most of its initial efforts on construction of the main line to the Pacific. Mackenzie and Mann, after reaching Edmonton early in 1906, had the means and the interest to penetrate this area. They did so with a new government-assisted line from Saskatoon to Calgary[33]—the Goose Lake line as it was popularly known—and with a series of smaller branches designed to serve the entire region immediately to the north of the South Saskatchewan River. Some of this territory was very promising; some of it generated

---

32 UTA, Walker Papers, H. F. V. Jones to Walker, 9 April 1910. For a detailed discussion of the Alberta Great Waterways Railway, see L. G. Thomas, *The Liberal Party in Alberta, 1905–1921* (Toronto: University of Toronto Press, 1959), 58–94.

33 The government assistance for this line demonstrates the problems in defining federal and provincial respon-

sibilities. The Saskatchewan mileage received a federal guarantee in 1908, while the Alberta mileage was covered by a provincial guarantee provided in 1909. Political pressure from Scott apparently persuaded Laurier to grant the assistance for the line that was certainly needed in Saskatchewan, while the Alberta areas were less densely settled.

only very light traffic, but construction and operating economies permitted reasonable returns on most of the mileage in good years. The CPR eventually regained some of the territory by pushing its Minnedosa line westward to Saskatoon and ultimately to Edmonton. This CPR line, however, ran considerably closer to the Grand Trunk Pacific's main line than to Mackenzie and Mann's Goose Lake line, and was therefore much more damaging to Grand Trunk Pacific interests than to Canadian Northern interests.

The Goose Lake line served local agricultural needs and it also helped develop important coal-mining interests in and around Drumheller, Alberta. A part of the line also became a link in a Mackenzie and Mann road from Edmonton to Calgary. Plans to build from Edmonton to Calgary, Lethbridge, Medicine Hat, and Macleod were made at an early date. Initially, Mackenzie and Mann apparently planned to build west of the old Calgary and Edmonton Railway,[34] although charters and bond guarantees in 1909 and 1912 did not name any specific route. The Grand Trunk Pacific, in the meantime, built to the east of the Calgary and Edmonton line. In the end, however, Mackenzie and Mann opted for a line just to the east of the Grand Trunk Pacific line, connecting it with their Goose Lake line at Munson Junction. A westward extension from this line was also built to serve the Brazeau coal fields of the eastern Rockies at Nordegg. These lines left Mackenzie and Mann in a reasonably strong competitive position in the large triangle formed by Saskatoon, Edmonton, and Calgary.

A further area which looked inviting to Mackenzie and Mann was the nearly 100-mile-wide strip of territory south of the CPR main line in the extreme southern regions of Saskatchewan and Alberta. For many farmers in this area the CPR main line was too far away. South and southeast of Regina the CPR had a sound branch-line network, but the more westerly areas demanded further railway construction. Mackenzie and Mann had hopes of building a southern branch-line system from their southern line between Brandon and Regina. A line to the Souris coal fields at Bienfait was built, and westward extensions were planned for the entire southern region. This southern region was the driest part of the prairies. Settlement was sparse and the available

34 See map accompanying *Seventh Annual Report, Canadian Northern Railway*, 1909.

traffic small. Politicians regularly guaranteed bonds for the southern lines demanded by the farmers and politicians, but progress was slow. Mackenzie and Mann never got farther than about half-way across Saskatchewan with this southern branch-line system, which they hoped eventually to connect with their northern lines. In Alberta Mackenzie and Mann built no railways south of Calgary, despite extensive charter rights and provincial bond guarantees. Some surveys and token construction work to meet urgent political requirements were the extent of their work in that area.

As a result of all this branch-line construction the Canadian Northern Railway occupied a virtually unchallenged position in the north and was able to compete with the CPR in the central regions, but it remained weak in southern Saskatchewan and accomplished nothing in southern Alberta. The prairie network of main and branch lines quickly proved to be the most profitable and the strongest part of the Canadian Northern Railway system after 1914 when all of Mackenzie and Mann's scattered railway projects were brought under a single corporate entity.

The 1909 bond guarantees by the Alberta and Saskatchewan governments provided Mackenzie and Mann with the means to complete their prairie system. They also demonstrated the nature of the relationship between the railway company and successful prairie politicians; a relationship which at least one premier referred to as a partnership.[35] Basically this partnership was based on only two considerations. Bond guarantees were given in return for promises by the promoters to build needed branch lines. The evidence in the papers of prairie politicians and in the records of the Board of Railway Commissioners demonstrates conclusively that without rail facilities farming on the prairies was impossible.[36] Before the development of highways and the widespread use of the internal combustion engine, the railway was the only way bulky farm products could be taken to market. Perhaps if the cost of railway branch-line construction were taken into consideration the less promising areas should have been left unsettled. Many branch

35 PAS, Scott Papers, 54380–2, Scott to O. O. Winter, 12 June 1913.
36 See particularly submissions in the case of Mervin Board of Trade v. Canadian Northern Railway Company, File 11929–15, and Western Tolls Case, File No. 18755. Summaries of these cases are given in *Canadian Railway Cases*, XIV, 363–5, and XVII, 123–230.

TABLE VII
Construction of Canadian Northern Lines on the Prairies, 1897–1916*

Description	Mileage	Company
1897		
Gladstone to Dauphin	84.8	Lake Manitoba Railway and Canal Company
Dauphin to North Jct.	2.8	Lake Manitoba Railway and Canal Company
North Jct. to Sifton	13.1	Lake Manitoba Railway and Canal Company
Sifton Jct. to Winnipegosis	21.0	Lake Manitoba Railway and Canal Company
1898		
Marchand to Paddington Yard	41.0	Manitoba and South Eastern Railway
Paddington Yard to St. Boniface	4.8	Manitoba and South Eastern Railway
Sifton Jct. to Cowan	51.8	Winnipeg and Hudson Bay Railway
1899		
Cowan to Swan River	31.0	Winnipeg and Hudson Bay Railway
1900		
Sprague to South Boundary	12.6	Manitoba and South Eastern Railway
Sprague to Marchand	48.2	Manitoba and South Eastern Railway
Swan River to Bowsman	9.7	Canadian Northern Railway
Westgate to Erwood	22.6	Canadian Northern Railway
1901		
Beaver to Gladstone	17.8	Canadian Northern Railway
Carman Jct. to Sperling	30.0	Morden and North Western Railway
Sperling to Carman	13.6	Canadian Northern Railway
1902		
Muir to Hallboro	26.9	Canadian Northern Railway
Hallboro to Neepawa	6.8	Morden and North Western Railway
North Jct. to Grandview	26.7	Canadian Northern Railway

Description	Mileage	Company
1903		
Great Northern Jct. to Emerson Jct.	1.4	Canadian Northern Railway
Ridgeville to Great Northern Jct.	9.9	Canadian Northern Railway
Carman to Learys	19.6	Canadian Northern Railway
Neepawa to Birnie	15.1	Morden and North Western Railway
Birnie to McCreary Junction	21.7	Canadian Northern Railway
Rossburn Junction to Clanwilliam	20.2	Morden and North Western Railway
1904		
Mile 8.3 to Mile 10.0, Oak Point Sub.	1.7	Winnipeg and Hudson Bay Railway
Mile 10.0 to Mile 48.0 Oak Point Sub.	38.0	Winnipeg and Hudson Bay Railway
Mile 48.0 to Oak Point	2.6	Canadian Northern Railway
Grandview to Kamsack	71.4	Canadian Northern Railway
1905		
Learys to Somerset	15.6	Canadian Northern Railway
Portage la Prairie to Brandon Jct.	51.6	Western Extension Railway
Brandon Jct. to M. & B. Jct.	25.4	Western Extension Railway
Clanwilliam to Rossburn	58.5	Canadian Northern Railway
Brandon Jct. to Carberry Jct.	22.8	Canadian Northern Railway
Greenway to Adelpha	51.8	Western Extension Railway
Hartney to Virden	37.2	Canadian Northern Railway
Kamsack to Humboldt	146.4	Canadian Northern Railway
Erwood to Hudson Bay Jct.	8.5	Canadian Northern Railway
Humboldt to North Battleford	147.6	Canadian Northern Railway
Hudson Bay Jct. to Melfort	98.7	Canadian Northern Railway
1906		
Thunderhill Jct. to Interprov. Boundary	20.2	Western Extension Railway
Melfort to Cudworth Jct.	59.0	Canadian Northern Railway
Cudworth Jct. to Q.L.L. & S. Railway	2.9	Canadian Northern Railway
Union Jct. to St. Albert	5.0	Edmonton and Slave Lake Railway
1907		
St. Boniface to Clark St. Jct.	2.0	Canadian Northern Railway
St. James Jct. to Mile 5.3, Oak Point	5.3	Canadian Northern Railway
South Jct. to Ridgeville	61.1	Canadian Northern Railway
Oakland to Totogan	17.2	Northern Extension Railway
Battleford Jct. to Battleford	7.8	Canadian Northern Railway

Description	Mileage	Company
1908		
Cardinal to Notre Dame de Lourdes	2.6	Canadian Northern Railway
Rossburn to Russell	25.5	Canadian Northern Railway
Brandon to Kipling	128.2	Canadian Northern Railway
Kipling to Regina	91.7	Canadian Northern Railway
1909		
Paddington to Beach Jct.	1.5	Northern Extension Railway
Beach Jct. to Jct. Dundee Branch	2.7	Northern Extension Railway
Mile 2.7 to Mile 6.4 Bird's Hill Branch	3.7	Canadian Northern Railway
Benito to Pelly	15.4	Canadian Northern Railway
Saskatoon Jct. to Yorath	3.8	Canadian Northern Railway
Yorath to Zealandia	56.4	Canadian Northern Railway
Zealandia to Rosetown	11.5	Canadian Northern Railway
1910		
Ochre River to St. Rose	15.0	Canadian Northern Railway
Bowsman to Westgate	60.2	Canadian Northern Railway
Hudson Bay Jct. to The Pas	87.9	Canadian Northern Railway
Russell to Calder	40.9	Canadian Northern Railway
Dalmeny to Laird	27.8	Canadian Northern Railway
Rosetown to Kindersley	54.2	Canadian Northern Railway
Prince Albert to Shellbrook	28.6	Canadian Northern Railway
1911		
Oak Point to Gypsumville	96.1	Canadian Northern Railway
Oakland, Mile 15.4 to Mile 32.4	17.0	Northern Extension Railway
Hallboro to Beulah	75.5	Western Extension Railway
Maryfield to Carlyle	37.3	Canadian Northern Railway
Pelly to Preeceville	36.5	Canadian Northern Railway
Calder to Wroxton Jct.	7.6	Canadian Northern Railway
Wroxton to Rhein	15.0	Canadian Northern Railway
Rhein to Hampton	8.8	Canadian Northern Railway
Carlyle to Luxton	31.0	Canadian Northern Railway
Luxton to Radville	71.4	Canadian Northern Railway
Luxton to Bienfait	16.0	Saskatchewan and North Western Railway
Radville to Bengough Jct.	1.4	Canadian Northern Railway
Bengough Jct. to Mile 84.4	83.0	Saskatchewan and North Western Railway
Bengough Jct. to Ceylon	15.7	Canadian Northern Railway
Ceylon to Bengough	27.5	Canadian Northern Railway
North Battleford to Edam	38.0	Canadian Northern Railway

Description	Mileage	Company
Delisle to MacRorie	45.7	Saskatchewan Midland Railway
Shellbrook to Blaine Lake	35.7	Canadian Northern Railway
Shellbrook to Big River	57.5	Saskatchewan and North Western Railway
Kindersley to Alsask	44.0	Canadian Northern Railway
Munson Jct. to Drumheller	11.9	Alberta Midland Railway
Battle Jct. to Warden	55.8	Alberta Midland Railway
Warden to Munson Jct.	52.2	Alberta Midland Railway

1912

St. Boniface Terminals cut-off	.6	Canadian Northern Railway
Grosse Isle to Mile 31.0	31.0	Canadian Northern Branch Lines Co.
Hampton to Ross Jct.	13.6	Canadian Northern Railway

1913

Mile 5.3 to Mile 8.3, Oak Point Sub.	3.0	Canadian Northern Railway
Oakland, Mile 32.4 to Mile 44.2	11.8	Northern Extension Railway
Mile 84.4 to Moose Jaw	3.3	Saskatchewan and North Western Railway
Moose Jaw to Riverhurst Jct.	.7	Saskatchewan and North Western Railway
Gravelbourg Jct. to Gravelbourg	79.0	Saskatchewan Midland Railway
MacRorie to Jct. Elrose Sub.	4.5	Saskatchewan and North Western Railway
Jct. Elrose Sub. to Elrose	49.8	Canadian Northern Railway
Blaine Lake to Denholm	52.2	Canadian Northern Railway
Alsask to Hanna	92.3	Canadian Northern Railway
Hanna to Munson Jct.	40.5	Canadian Northern Railway

1914

Mile 6.4 to Grand Beach	50.7	Winnipeg and Northern Railway
Inwood, Mile 31 to Mile 74.5	43.5	Canadian Northern Branch Lines Co.
Mile 74.5 to Hodgson	6.4	Canadian Northern Railway
Steep Rock Jct. to Steep Rock	12.1	Canadian Northern Manitoba Railway
Adelphe to Deloraine	28.0	Canadian Northern Railway
Edam to Turtleford	17.2	Canadian Northern Railway
Drumheller to Calgary	83.2	Alberta Midland Railway

Description	Mileage	Company
Warden to Brazeau	166.8	Canadian Northern Western Railway
Peace River Jct. to Sanguedo	32.1	Canadian Northern Western Railway
1915		
Canora to Sturgis Jct.	21.4	Canadian Northern Branch Lines Co.
Wroxton to Yorkton	26.6	Canadian Northern Saskatchewan Railway
Yorkton to Willowbrook	15.5	Canadian Northern Saskatchewan Railway
Bienfait to Estevan	8.4	Canadian Northern Railway
Laird to Carlton	8.0	Canadian Northern Railway
Jct. Elrose Sub. to Dunblaine	9.1	Saskatchewan and North Western Railway
Elrose to Eston	34.6	Canadian Northern Railway
Melfort to St. Brieux	22.0	Saskatchewan Midland Railway
St. Albert to Peace River Jct.	26.0	Canadian Northern Alberta Railway
Peace River Jct. to Mile 68.4	37.4	Canadian Northern Alberta Railway
Obed to Old Snaring Jct.	56.0	Canadian Northern Alberta Railway
1916		
Grand Marais to Victoria Beach	14.1	Winnipeg and Northern Railway
1917		

No new Canadian Northern Railway mileage opened on the prairies.

Note: All mileages listed here are given according to the date on which they were officially opened. In many cases new mileage was operated by the railway before all the final inspections had been made and the official opening took place. The mileages in this table differ from those in Table I because Table I refers to mileage operated by the railway company while this table refers to mileage officially opened. Much of the mileage was only officially opened at the end of the construction season, often not until early in the new year, although it had been operating during the preceding year. The Board of Railway Commissioners was well aware of the practice and, in effect, ignored its own rules in order to allow incomplete lines to take out traffic, particularly the fall wheat crop, from territory adjoining the railway. Special rates, usually higher, were charged for traffic carried on mileage not yet officially opened, and at times there was a surprising time lag between the time when operations were begun and the time when the line was officially opened. Operations on the line between Bowsman to Westgate, for example, began in 1900, but the line was not officially opened until 1910.

lines were certainly built before the available traffic was very heavy, but there was always the hope that the railway itself would encourage settlement and generate new traffic. In many areas it did just that, but branch lines were always something of a speculation. Only future development could provide the traffic necessary to make them profitable.[37]

No politician of the time was willing to admit that prospects in any part of his constituency were so poor that a branch line should not be built. Branch lines could make or break a politician, and for many years they were responsible for the strong political influence of Mackenzie and Mann. Freight rates had been drastically reduced through the initiative of a partnership between the Canadian Northern Railway and the Manitoba government. Thereafter, the greatest favour Mackenzie and Mann could bestow on a political friend was to promise new branch lines. In 1900, for example, T. O. Davis became concerned about the need for progress on the railway to Prince Albert prior to the federal election. He told Sifton that grading on the roadbed should begin immediately. "If they could only let a contract of such grading at or about Melfort everything would be OK."[38]

Davis had a reasonably safe constituency, and a statement by Mackenzie and Mann of their intention to build to Prince Albert was sufficient to ensure his re-election. T. A. Burrows, the Liberal MLA for Dauphin, found himself in a much more difficult position in 1899. Relations between Mackenzie and Mann and the Greenway government were not particularly amicable and the provincial Liberals were in very serious political trouble. Burrows was very pessimistic about his own prospects. He could see only one way of averting defeat. "There is 15 miles of the Gilbert Plains Railway ready to lay the steel on," he informed Clifford Sifton, his influential brother-in-law, "and if we could only get Mackenzie to lay the rails at once it might be the means of saving my election."[39] Two weeks later a construction train laden with rails made its way to the prepared roadbed in the endangered constituency.[40] As a result, Burrows won personal re-

37 Hanna, 142–5.
38 PAC, Sifton Papers, LXXIX, 59985, Davis to Sifton, 21 Aug. 1900.
39 *Ibid.*, LVII, 40507, T. A. Burrows to Sifton, 23 Nov. 1899.
40 *Ibid.*, CDLXII, 45128, D. B. Hanna to Sifton, 10 Dec. 1899.

election by a comfortable majority of 425 votes, while elsewhere in the province the Liberals were decisively defeated.[41] The local member and the government that got the settlers the railways they needed had found the key to political success in the early 1900s.

There were certainly other ways in which Mackenzie and Mann might assist their political friends. Employees could be, and on occasion were, instructed on how to vote, although such instructions were not always followed. Nor did these instructions consistently favour one political party. In Saskatchewan and Alberta, Mackenzie and Mann were prepared to support the Liberals, but in Manitoba the provincial Conservatives were the Canadian Northern's best friends. This inconsistency, however, did not preclude assistance for Clifford Sifton and his Liberal friends in federal elections.

In most cases Mackenzie and Mann cared little for partisan political labels. Mackenzie and his son Roderick were Conservatives. The elder Mackenzie had sought the Conservative nomination in an Ontario constituency in 1891, while his son seriously considered the offer of a Conservative nomination in Dauphin in 1903.[42] Donald Mann, on the other hand, was a member of the Liberal party and eventually became a confidant and political emissary of Sir Wilfrid Laurier. Z. A. Lash was also well known as a Liberal, at least until 1911, when the threat of reciprocity with the United States induced him to lead the attack against the government's proposals. It would be erroneous, however, to take even these party associations of the promoters very seriously. Mackenzie and Mann simply helped and supported those politicians who helped and supported them. They were certainly not committed to unequivocal support of the major political parties. Indeed, their associations with the politicians were rarely motivated on either side by a desire to promote specific political principles. The associations were matters of expediency and could be ended whenever either side found that the arrangement was no longer useful. Sifton understood this relationship perfectly when he wrote to Burrows,

As to the extent to which the Railway Company will support you in Dauphin, it is quite impossible for me to say. I told you plainly when here

41 *Ibid.*, LVII, 40527–28, Burrows to Sifton, 20 Dec. 1899.

42 *Ibid.*, CXXXVIII, 110267–70, Burrows to Sifton, 9 Dec. 1903.

that all I could say was that I thought they would be friendly, but that their support would be of a modified character, as no railway company in their present condition in Canada wants to get out openly and take an active part in a political campaign. This is all I know about their attitude in my own riding, and I do not know any more in yours.[43]

The political influence of Mackenzie and Mann was often attributed to corrupt deals, large campaign contributions, and the use of patronage on the Canadian Northern Railway. The evidence gathered in Toronto in connection with the Toronto Street Railway contract supports many of the charges made. Similar charges relating to the Canadian Northern Railway were often made but are much more difficult to document. Certainly the minute-books and legal files of the company and the private papers of politicians do not provide such evidence. Other documentary evidence has not yet come to the attention of researchers. The available evidence does not prove innocence in regard to political bribery and corruption. It does demonstrate, however, that the political support and legislative concessions given Mackenzie and Mann could be and were strongly defended and justified on the grounds that the Canadian Northern provided vital rail services at reasonable cost. Each concession, subsidy, or bond guarantee certainly provided benefits for the promoters, but it also provided very substantial benefits to western farmers and shippers and would, therefore, prove attractive to these people and to their elected representatives.

Mackenzie and Mann certainly made campaign contributions to political friends, but these donations, in so far as they can be documented today, were rarely very large, and most frequently they were made by one of the partners personally to an individual candidate.[44] Party organizers and politicians frequently complained about the lack of generosity of the two promoters, but sizable campaign funds were rarely advanced by the Canadian Northern Railway. Political favour-

43 *Ibid.*, CCLIII, 960, Sifton to Burrows, 12 Dec. 1903.
44 A copy of the transcripts of proceedings under the Public Inquiries Act re charges made by John Sedgewick Cowper, sixth Member for the city of Vancouver, is available in the British Columbia Public Archives, Premiers' series; it clearly indicates how political contributions were handled.

ites were sometimes able to use inside information to good advantage, but such handouts rarely cost the promoters anything. The rumours of large contributions to political party slush funds have not yet been proven to be more than rumours.

The use of patronage on the Canadian Northern was similarly limited. Certainly some friends and relatives of influential politicians received appointments, but Mackenzie and Mann made sure these appointees earned what they were paid. Burrows' experiences with the promoters is fairly typical; he had to produce to remain on the staff.[45] Very little deadwood was allowed to accumulate. Either the so-called political appointees were, as was usually the case, very good value for their money, or they were sent packing. This determination of the railway not to allow patronage which would undermine both efficiency and morale was unequivocally announced in 1901.[46] It was perhaps the only way Mackenzie and Mann could accommodate both old Liberal friends such as Sifton and new Conservative friends such as Robert Rogers and Rodmond Roblin.

The Manitoba Conservatives did not take the 1901 announcement seriously. After providing the Canadian Northern with truly massive assistance in 1901 they expected a place for political favourites on the railway staff. Most of the requests met with firm refusals. For a time relations between Mackenzie and Mann and the Manitoba Conservatives became seriously strained,[47] but in the end Roblin and Rogers decided the railway deserved their continued support, even if it failed to accommodate their demands for patronage. Mackenzie and Mann were engaged in a highly competitive business and could not afford inefficient or incompetent employees. Nor could they afford to grant too many favours to one of their political suitors lest they offend the other. The services bestowed on prairie constituencies by their railway were their principal claims to political favours, and the branch-line guarantees were the most explicit expression of the true nature of the alliance between promoters and politicians.

The 1909 guarantees confirmed the Canadian Northern's political

45 PAC, Sifton Papers, LXXVI, 57738–9, Burrows to Sifton, 23 Jan. 1900.
46 *Manitoba Free Press*, 17 June 1901; Hanna, 254–6; CNRHQ,

O. D. Prosser interview.
47 UTA, Walker Papers, Plummer to Walker, 4 Oct. 1902.

position on the prairies and greatly strengthened its financial standing in London. The sale of various guaranteed bonds had been something of a mixed success until 1909. The necessary bonds had always been sold, but sometimes only after considerable worry and scrambling. Some of the first Manitoba guaranteed bonds had been sold in London to Speyer Brothers,[48] and others had been pledged as collateral with the Canadian Bank of Commerce. Speyers, however, declined to take the 3-per-cent Dominion guaranteed bonds in 1903.[49] This turn of events forced Mackenzie to scramble for short-term loans as best he could, to keep construction crews at work on the Edmonton line until a purchaser could be found. Mackenzie, Mann and Co. Ltd. was granted large credits by the Canadian Bank of Commerce and by the National Trust Company,[50] while loans to the Canadian Northern Railway were obtained from British firms that accepted guaranteed bonds as collateral but also required personal guarantees from Mackenzie. The Bank of Scotland provided a loan of £125,000, taking £250,000 in guaranteed bonds as collateral, while the British Linen Company Bank advanced £225,000 under similar conditions.[51] Short-term funds were thus provided, but the situation remained tense until March 1904 when the Canadian Bank of Commerce purchased £1,923,287 of the 3-per-cent Dominion guaranteed debenture stock outright at 90 per cent of par value.[52] Later the same year the prestigious New York financial firm of J. Pierpoint Morgan and Company purchased $5,000,000 of the Manitoba guaranteed Canadian Northern debentures.[53] This sale was made only after a careful inspection of the entire line had been made by an agent of J. P. Morgan. The inspection was reportedly "so favourable that it was likely Mr. Morgan would purchase the entire bond issue of the company."[54]

48 PAC, CNR Records, MCDXXXVI, 85–6, Meeting of Directors of the Canadian Northern Railway, 14 Aug. 1900; PAC, CNR Legal Series, File 6–3.
49 UTA, Walker Papers, H. V. F. Jones to Walker, 20 Nov. 1909. PAC, CNR Legal Series, File 6–15.
50 QUA, Flavelle Papers, W. E. Rundle to Flavelle, 4 Sept. 1917.
51 PAC, CNR Records, MCDXXXVII, 47–8, 3–4, Meetings of Directors of the Canadian Northern Railway, 12

Aug. 1903, and 22 Feb. 1904.
52 PAC, CNR Records, MCDXXXVII, 13–14, 30 March 1904; PAC, CNR Legal Series, Files 6–15, 6–22A, 6–22B, and 6–22C.
53 PAC, CNR Records, MCDXXXVII, Meeting of Directors of the Canadian Northern Railway, 3 Jan. 1905.
54 Manitoba Free Press, 29 Dec. 1904, 3; PAC, CNR Legal Series, File 6–10.

The international money markets weakened very considerably after 1906. Morgan did not purchase additional securities, as had been expected in 1905, and even in London Mackenzie and Horne-Payne found it very difficult to market any securities that did not carry strong government guarantees. Mackenzie was again required to pledge his credit for several large loans in London. This slump, coupled with the fact that Mackenzie would have substantially larger bond issues to sell if and when the Alberta and Saskatchewan governments passed guarantee legislation, necessitated a broadening of Canadian Northern contacts and associations with financial houses in London when the climate of opinion there improved in 1909. That climate, moreover, turned out to have improved to such a degree that Mackenzie soon had all the credit he needed in London, and since interest rates in London were somewhat more favourable than they were in New York, no attempts were made to renew contacts with J. P. Morgan.

It was the Canadian Bank of Commerce which initially suggested that Mackenzie and Horne-Payne seek to broaden their financial connections in London. The bankers suggested that Mackenzie establish relations with the rising and ambitious firm of Lazard Brothers, and also improve the railway's somewhat strained relations with Speyers.[55] Sir Robert Kindersley of Lazard Brothers was invited to visit Canada and inspect the Canadian Northern Railway's assets, facilities, and prospects.[56] He came in 1909 and was so impressed with what he saw that he made an immediate attempt to get as much of Mackenzie's business as possible.

A major tussle between the Canadian Bank of Commerce and the Bank of Scotland on the one hand, and Speyers and Lazard Brothers on the other, developed when Horne-Payne and Mackenzie agreed to place large issues of provincially guaranteed bonds with Lazard Brothers without consulting or offering any participation to their old financial friends. Mackenzie and Horne-Payne had acted on advice from their bankers who suggested that other financiers might be associated with them in a strengthened financial alliance. Kindersley,

55 UTA, Walker Papers, Oct. 1909 file, telegram from Canadian Bank of Commerce Head Office to London Office, 12 June 1909.

56 Ibid., H. V. F. Jones to Walker, 7 March 1910; also extract from Head Office letter, 15 Oct. 1908.

however, tried very hard to get control of all the Canadian Northern business. He specifically wanted a commitment that he would be given first refusal on all future Canadian Northern issues. For a time the situation threatened to disrupt relations between Mackenzie and the Bank of Commerce. Mann was asked by the Bank to use his influence with Mackenzie and he agreed to do so.

Fortunately a compromise was found. Lazards agreed to list the Canadian Bank of Commerce as an associate in the transaction. Forty thousand copies of their prospectus, which had already been printed, were destroyed and new ones were issued. The net result was that Speyers, Lazard Brothers, the Bank of Scotland, the Canadian Bank of Commerce, and Lloyd's Bank, which was brought in at the suggestion of the Bank of Commerce, participated in the underwriting and financing of Mackenzie and Mann's rapidly expanding railway ventures.[57]

German and French capital was also used in the construction of one of the Alberta branch lines. The charter of the Canadian Northern Western Railway authorized the company to build, among other things, a line to the Brazeau coal fields, which Mackenzie and Mann were developing in partnership with German capitalists. It was considered something of a courtesy that European financiers were also invited to share in the financing of the $6,000,000 railway to the coal mines. Continental investors proved most enthusiastic; their most frequent complaint was that they had not been given a sufficiently large share in the proposed debenture issue, since a portion had been held for Lazard Brothers.[58]

The financial position was obviously most encouraging, and Mackenzie began to think of quickly raising all the money needed for the branch lines and then clearing the market for other issues to finance new construction that would take the Canadian Northern to the Pacific and Atlantic coasts. He expected to float sufficient bonds to finance construction and to provide between one and two million dollars for

57 *Ibid.*, London Office to Head Office, 8 and 10 June, 1909, together with extracts from a number of other letters between the London and Toronto offices of the Canadian Bank of Commerce; PAC, CNR Records,

xccxiv, Secretary's Black Book, copies of the various agreements made.
58 Martin Nordegg, *The Possibilities of Canada Are Truly Great: Memoirs, 1906–1924*, ed. T. D. Regehr (Toronto: Macmillan, 1971), 122–49.

the first and possibly unprofitable years of operation on the trans-continental mileage.[59]

The relative ease with which large sums of money could be raised in 1909 and 1910 also made it easy for Mackenzie and Mann to abandon one of their early construction policies. The provincial governments demanded, and Mackenzie and Mann readily agreed, that the proposed branch lines should be built to a standard at least equal to that of the main line between Winnipeg and Edmonton. Mackenzie and Mann had in fact already begun a major improvement program on the main line and expected that the discarded lighter track from the main line could be used on the branch lines. This measure would provide for a reasonably good standard. No one wanted a mediocre second-rate line when a first-class line was obtainable. It could also be argued that it would actually be more economical to adopt higher standards at the outset than to build to a low standard, and improve the line later. Under the old plan, of course, such improvements were made only if local development justified them. Under the new plan there would be high interest charges regardless of the availability or lack of local traffic. The new construction policy was therefore more risky, but Mackenzie and Mann were optimistic and had plenty of money.[60]

The two promoters had also developed a strong craving for respectability. They were no longer struggling pioneers operating on a shoestring, but wealthy railway promoters. In Toronto William Mackenzie began construction of his massive and impressive new residence of Benvenuto. He followed the traditions of other successful businessmen on the continent, although the financial problems of his former partner, Henry Pellatt, led him to draw his plans somewhat more cautiously than Pellatt had drawn those of Casa Loma, that monument to entrepreneurial hubris.[61] Mackenzie also considered that his financial standing was sufficiently improved to warrant drawing up a lengthy new will. His family was rapidly climbing the Toronto ladder of social success, and one of his daughters married a viscount, the son of Ferdi-

59 UTA, Walker Papers, H. V. F. Jones to Walker, 20 Nov. 1909 and 7 March 1910.

60 A specific clause to this effect is included in the bond-guarantee legislation in both Alberta and Saskatchewan. *Arbitration*, 1713.

nand de Lesseps, promoter of the Suez Canal. The two Canadian railway promoters were moving up in the world, and henceforth their railway must also look more respectable. As long as rapid settlement of the prairies continued and business conditions remained prosperous, there seemed no reason to doubt that the policies they had adopted could lead only to further and greater success.

61 Mackenzie loaned Pellatt considerable sums of money, some of which were still owing at the time of Mackenzie's death in 1923 and are listed in the assets of his estate as filed in the Surrogate Court, Toronto.

CHAPTER NINE

SERVING THE PRAIRIE WEST THE ANCILLARY ENTERPRISES 1903–1911

A RAILWAY IS MUCH MORE THAN TRACKS AND TRAINS. It is, in fact, an entrepreneurial empire which attracts to it a host of supporting and ancillary enterprises. Rolling stock, terminal facilities, docks, express and telegraph companies, lands, coal-mining ventures, handling and forwarding facilities, and many other undertakings became directly or indirectly associated with the Canadian Northern Railway. The railway service Mackenzie and Mann offered, and the success they enjoyed on the prairies, was often made possible by their willingness to launch a great variety of business ventures complementary to their railway.

The most important company directly associated with the Canadian Northern Railway was the private contracting partnership of Mackenzie, Mann and Company and its successor, Mackenzie, Mann and Co. Ltd. Virtually all the early construction contracts on the railway were handled by Mackenzie, Mann and Company, many of course being sublet to smaller contracting firms. Generally Mackenzie, Mann and Company also provided the funds needed to meet immediate expenditures, and were reimbursed for these when guaranteed bonds were earned and sold. Mackenzie, Mann and Co. Ltd. was incorporated as a joint stock company in 1902. In addition to the old financial and contracting services, it soon added a variety of promotional, financial, and developmental functions which the railway company could not perform under its own charter.[1]

1 *Arbitration*, 2513–15.

The charter of the Canadian Northern Railway and the general provisions of the Canadian Railway Act prevented the railway company from participation in ventures which were not directly related to its own operations. No such provisions restricted the activities of Mackenzie, Mann and Co. Ltd. It could and did acquire whatever assets seemed desirable, and organized whatever companies were needed to meet any anticipated future needs of the railway company. The result was that whenever the railway needed some new asset or facility, it was available from Mackenzie, Mann and Co. Ltd. Characteristically, such facilities had been purchased long before and were simply held for the time when they were needed by the railway. Then they were sold or transferred from Mackenzie, Mann and Co. Ltd. to the Canadian Northern Railway "at a price fixed, very often, if not altogether, at what Mackenzie, Mann and Company paid for it, plus the carrying charge."[2] The normal procedure was simply for Mackenzie, Mann and Co. Ltd. to exchange their bonds and stock holdings in the ancillary companies for Canadian Northern Railway bonds and stocks.

Two kinds of Canadian Northern Railway securities were generally used in such exchanges. Capital stock of the ancillary companies was usually, but not always, exchanged for capital stock of the Canadian Northern Railway. Put in its simplest terms, the Canadian Northern Railway might purchase the entire $1,000,000 capital stock of an ancillary company from Mackenzie, Mann and Co. Ltd. giving them in payment $1,000,000 in Canadian Northern Railway capital stock.

Special bonds were also issued in 1903, and as needed thereafter, to enable the Canadian Northern Railway to purchase bonds, and sometimes capital stock, of ancillary companies from Mackenzie, Mann and Co. Ltd. These were the 4-per-cent Perpetual Consolidated Debenture Stocks. They carried no government guarantee and ranked below the guaranteed bonds and debenture stock issued by the company prior to 1914. The amount of Perpetual Consolidated Debenture Stock was not to exceed $10,000 per mile of the company's railways constructed and in operation, plus "the cost price of securities of independent corporations from time to time deposited with the

2 *Ibid.*, 753.

trustees".[3] The first Perpetual Consolidated Debenture Stock was issued in 1903 to purchase the capital stock and the entire bond issues of five smaller companies owned by Mackenzie, Mann and Co. Ltd. Two of these, the Minnesota and Manitoba Railroad Company and the Minnesota and Ontario Bridge Company, were in fact integral parts of the Canadian Northern main line to Port Arthur. They had always been regarded as a part of that system, although their securities had been given to Mackenzie, Mann and Co. Ltd. in return for their construction services. The other three were the usual kind of ancillary companies—the Lake Superior Terminals Company Limited, the Winnipeg Land Company Limited, and the Canadian Northern Telegraph Company.[4] They were acquired by the Canadian Northern Railway in a manner that was to be repeated many times.

There were also a large number of business ventures organized by Mackenzie, Mann and Co. Ltd. that were never acquired by the Canadian Northern Railway. Only those considered vital to the operations of the railway were transferred,[5] although Mackenzie, Mann and Co. Ltd. held contracts, stock, and securities of a large number of Canadian and international enterprises. Some Mackenzie and Mann-controlled companies signed transportation contracts with the Canadian Northern Railway; others had no business dealings with the railway. Mackenzie and Mann's Canadian interests, for example, ranged from control of the whaling industry on the Pacific coast to life insurance companies, lumber, mining, meat packing, brewing, and retailing. Their international ventures, mainly in street railway and electricity projects were scattered from Cuba to South America and from England to China. Mackenzie, Mann and Co. Ltd., therefore, was not only one of Canada's largest railway contracting, financial, and promotional companies, but also a major holding company.

Suspicions were often expressed that Mackenzie and Mann tended to divert funds from one of their many accounts and interests to another in a manner likely to enrich themselves and to injure the railway company. That suspicion, of course, increased greatly when the railway company got into financial difficulties during the war years. At the

3 PAC, CNR Records, MCDXXXVII, 17–26, Meeting of Directors of the Canadian Northern Railway Company, 22 May 1903.

4 *First Annual Report, Canadian Northern Railway, 1903*, 10, 15.
5 *Arbitration*, 2513–15, 2622–3.

arbitration proceedings in 1918 Chairman William Meredith made specific reference to it and asked Donald Mann to explain what happened when the Canadian Northern and Mackenzie, Mann and Co. Ltd., "the same two in a different capacity", sat down to negotiate a transaction such as a construction contract. Donald Mann replied without hesitation, "Canadian Northern got the better of it all the time."[6] This was largely corroborated by various official inquiries into the affairs of the Canadian Northern after 1914, and perhaps most convincingly by the fact that after Mackenzie's death in 1923 his 22,500 shares in Mackenzie, Mann and Co. Ltd., with a par value of $2,250,000, were declared to have no market value whatsoever.[7] Many of Mackenzie's acquaintances, including Prime Minister Robert Borden, were convinced that money was not the real prize. Mackenzie wanted to realize great ambitions, the greatest being the completion of his transcontinental railway which could and would compete effectively with the CPR.[8]

In both the private partnership before 1902 and the later joint stock company, 50 per cent of the capital stock was owned by Donald Mann, 45 per cent by William Mackenzie, and 5 per cent by his son Roderick. All other assets and liabilities were shared in the ratio of 47.5 per cent, 47.5 per cent, and 5 per cent.[9] Since the Ontario Companies Act required five directors, Z. A. Lash and D. B. Hanna were each given the minimum number of shares needed to qualify for directorates.

The incorporation of Mackenzie, Mann and Co. Ltd. made it possible for Mackenzie and Mann to become directors and officers of the Canadian Northern Railway, and in March 1902 Mackenzie became president and Donald Mann first vice-president. Shortly thereafter D. B. Hanna was named third vice-president. The Canadian

6 *Ibid.*, 2771.
7 Ontario Surrogate Court, File No. 49474, Probate records and Passing of Accounts for the Estate of Sir William Mackenzie, particularly the 1926 Accounts.
8 CNRHQ, Janet Gordon interview; CR & MW, Jan. 1924, 31; Hanna, 229.
9 The three partners agreed that all liabilities of the company should be divided in the ratio of 47.5 per cent

for William Mackenzie, 47.5 per cent for Donald Mann, and 5 per cent for Roderick Mackenzie. A similar division was to be made for any assets, except the capital stock, which was divided as follows: 50 per cent to Donald Mann, 45 per cent to William Mackenzie, and 5 per cent to Roderick Mackenzie. PAC, CNR Records, $\overline{x}$CCXLI, Secretary's Black Book.

Northern Railway never had a second vice-president; the position was probably held for Roderick Mackenzie, William Mackenzie's eldest son, who was in charge of much of the western construction. Roderick allegedly refused the appointment, either because he could not get along with Donald Mann, or because he had serious doubts about the transcontinental extensions that his father wanted, or because of sibling rivalries within the Mackenzie family. Those closest to the partnership differed in their explanations of why Roderick never became second vice-president. The remaining official documents say very little about the personal affairs of the promoters, and circumstantial evidence indicates that any one of these three reasons, or a combination of them, could account for the Canadian Northern's lack of a second vice-president.[10]

It is not possible at this time to provide a detailed history of Mackenzie, Mann and Co. Ltd. or of the two promoters. Only the services of both to the Canadian Northern Railway are relevant here. These include contracting, financial, and promotional services, and permeate all aspects of Canadian Northern history.

An organization that would purchase and provide the rolling stock needed by the railway was one of the most important Canadian Northern ancillary companies controlled by Mackenzie, Mann and Co. Ltd. The earliest purchases of rolling stock, and of most other equipment needed by the Lake Manitoba Railway and Canal Company, were made directly by the railway. As the company grew, however, new legal and administrative arrangements were made. After the main line was completed to Port Arthur in 1902, the Imperial Rolling Stock Company was organized to buy rolling stock from manufacturers or other railways and then to lease and sell it to the Canadian Northern Railway. The usual transaction between the railway and the rolling-stock company required an immediate down payment by the railway with an agreement to repay the remainder over a twenty-year period. During this time, ownership of the rolling stock remained with the Imperial Rolling Stock Company, and the Canadian Northern Railway leased it until all payments had been made.

The Imperial Rolling Stock Company had very little capital of its

10 CNRHQ, Janet Gordon, C. D. Prosser, and Osborne Scott interviews.

own and financed all its purchases through special bond issues. The security for these bonds was the rolling stock itself, to which the Canadian Northern added its own official guarantee. The bonds of the rolling-stock company had varying dates of maturity, designed to coincide with the annual rental payments to be made by the Canadian Northern Railway. For the investor the bonds were doubly secured: first, by the mortgage on the leased rolling stock itself, and second, by the guarantee of the railway company. Yet that guarantee was really nothing more than a second formal promise to make the agreed lease-purchase payments. The usual rates of interest varied from 4.5 per cent to 6.5 per cent, but the arrangement had the advantage that it did not interfere with the regular financing or other business arrangements of the Canadian Northern Railway. Almost all the Canadian Northern rolling stock was acquired in this way while Mackenzie and Mann controlled both the Canadian Northern Railway and the Imperial Rolling Stock Company, which was never formally merged with the railway company.[11]

Rolling stock was of great importance to Mackenzie and Mann, but few issues in the early history of their railway ventures were of greater importance than the administration and sale of prairie lands. Three of the railway charters acquired by the promoters in the 1890s carried federal land-grant subsidies of 6,400 acres per mile. These were the Winnipeg Great Northern (successor of the Hudson Bay Railway), the Lake Manitoba Railway and Canal Company, and the Manitoba and South Eastern.

Under the terms of the three land-grant charters—all purchased by Mackenzie and Mann after they had been granted to others—the Canadian Northern Railway eventually earned 4,001,728 acres,[12] most of which had to be fit for settlement. The lands were earned, of course, only after the required mileage had been built. Even after

---

11 PAC, CNR Records, MCCXLVII, MCCL, MCCLI; Minute Book and Stock Certificate Books of the Imperial Rolling Stock Company. A long series of these transactions are outlined in the Minute Books of the Imperial Rolling Stock Company. A summary of the proceds of these

equipment securities is included in the statements prepared by the railway for the Commission of enquiry into Railways and Transportation, 1916, PAC, CNR Records, MMCXCIV.
12 Canada, *P.C. 1579*, 3 Aug. 1908; *Arbitration*, 2081.

construction was completed, however, there were often long delays before the railway selected and patented the lands to which they were entitled.

The main purpose of the land grant was to assist the railway in financing its construction program. Grants were certainly used in that way by the Canadian Northern Railway and its predecessors. Under the terms of the railway's first construction contract with Mackenzie and Mann it was stipulated that the contractors would receive the land grant as partial payment for their construction services. The Manitoba government had objected to this procedure and an alternative arrangement was made. Instead of receiving the land grant directly, the contractor-promoters were to be given bonds issued against the security of the lands.[13]

None of these bonds was ever issued, and in later construction contracts the lands were transferred directly to the promoters as partial payment for financial and construction services. In 1899, however, financial difficulties induced Mackenzie and Mann to surrender their entire interest in the land grant to the railway company and to take that company's fully paid capital stock instead. In an agreement signed on 17 May 1900, the contractors received $4,000,000 in Canadian Northern Railway capital stock in return for "all their right, title and interest and claims in and to all the said lands".[14] The two promoters did retain approximately 100,000 acres of land which was earned after 1900, but with that exception, the lands earned by the contractors were returned to the railway company in exchange for capital stock.

The railway company then used the lands as security for a $2,000,000 land-grant bond issue. The bond issue was actually prepared before the necessary agreement with Mackenzie, Mann and Co. Ltd. was signed, with the curious result that, on paper at least, the land transfer was dated 1900 while the bond issue was brought out in 1899. Once the transfer was made, the land-grant bonds were issued

13 PAC, CNR Records, MCCLVI, 21–5, Meeting of Directors of the Lake Manitoba Railway and Canal Company, 18 May 1896.
14 *Arbitration*, 49; PAC, CNR Records, XCCXII, Secretary's Black Book,

Agreement No. 21, Mackenzie and Mann and Co. and Canadian Northern Railway Co., Release of Land Grant Equity of Redemption by Mackenzie, Mann and Co., 17 May 1900.

and sold to the National Trust Company, which for a time also served as the Canadian Northern's land agent.[15]

The mortgaged lands could still be sold to intending settlers, but the proceeds from such sales had to go to a trustee who was charged with responsibility for safeguarding and meeting the obligations of the bondholders before any remaining funds were turned over to the railway. As early as 1907 the full $2,000,000 had been realized from land sales and was in the hands of the trustees. All further proceeds from land sales could then be credited to the Canadian Northern Railway.[16]

In addition to this land-grant bond issue, some of the lands had also become encumbered under the terms of the federal transportation contract with the Winnipeg Great Northern Railway. According to the terms of that contract the federal government agreed to pay the fixed sum of $40,000 annually for the transport of mail and other federal supplies once the railway was built half-way to the Saskatchewan River. If the actual services provided were valued at less than $40,000, the difference was to become a charge on the railway. As security for such charges, up to one-third of the land grant of the Winnipeg Great Northern could be pledged or mortgaged. The transportation contract guaranteed the railway a minimum of $40,000 per year, but it soon encumbered a large portion of the land grant. In 1903 some 533,333 acres were thus encumbered. These too could be sold, but the proceeds had to meet the obligations incurred before any remaining funds were turned over to the railway.[17]

The objective of the railway company, however, was not merely to raise money by mortgaging or otherwise encumbering the land grant. The lands had to be sold and developed by immigrants and settlers if the railways were to get the local traffic they urgently needed.

With this objective in mind, Mackenzie and Mann signed an extremely important agreement with a group of land promoters in 1903.

15 PAC, CNR Records, MCDXXXVI, 11–26, Meetings of Shareholders and Directors of the Canadian Northern Railway, 21 Feb. 1899; MCDXXXVII, 5–6, 39–40, Meeting of Directors of the Canadian Northern Railway Company, 23 Jan. 1904 and 7 July 1904.

16 *Fifth Annual Report, Canadian Northern Railway, 1907*, 9, 15; covering letter dated 16 May 1903.

17 PAC, Laurier Papers, CCLXV, 73370–1, Memo from William Mackenzie to Laurier, 1903.

By that time they had earned 2,182,400 acres, although 1,346,141 carried mortgages or other encumbrances. A land company, headed by Col. A. D. Davidson and J. D. McRae and including a number of Canadian and American land and settlement agents who had enjoyed very considerable success in handling railway lands in the United States, agreed to look after future Canadian Northern land sales.[18]

The Saskatchewan Valley and Manitoba Land Company was organized and began its unique and highly successful promotion of Canadian Northern lands in 1903. Mackenzie and Mann were not land speculators or land promoters. Their chief interest was always to get traffic-generating settlers onto the lands adjacent to their railways as quickly as possible. A firm promise from the new land company that it would do this made Mackenzie and Mann eager to sell their entire land grant immediately for what Mackenzie termed "spot cash". The sum of $12,000,000 was mentioned by the newspapers as the asking price.[19] The Saskatchewan Valley and Manitoba Land Company was unable to finance so large a purchase. Its entire capitalization was only $5,000,000. Instead, the Canadian Northern agreed to assign 911,161.42 acres to the land company. No immediate payment was required, but when lands were sold the Canadian Northern Railway was to receive $3 per acre plus one-third of any gross receipts in excess of that amount. The land company agreed that no lands would be sold for less than $5 per acre.[20] The land company thus became an agent for the Canadian Northern Railway, selling on what was in reality a commission basis.

The promotional methods used by the Saskatchewan Valley and Manitoba Land Company were unique and phenomenally successful. Group or block settlements were their specialty. They sought out large tracts of vacant land where various religious and ethnic groups could settle as a group, and without fear of major incursions by others who were religiously, culturally, linguistically, or ethnically alien. Large railway land grants usually gave the land company control of all the

18 *Manitoba Free Press*, 11 May 1903; PAC, CNR Records, MMCDLIX, Saskatchewan Valley and Manitoba Land Company Limited, Documents.
19 PAC, Sifton Papers, CXXVIII, 101060, Mackenzie to Sifton, 1 Nov. 1902; *Manitoba Free Press*, 12 May 1903.
20 PAC, CNR Records, MMCDLIX, Saskatchewan Valley and Manitoba Land Company Limited, Documents.

odd-numbered sections fit for settlement in a given area. The land company then sought to gain control of as many even-numbered sections as possible. If the lands were still vacant, the interested ethnic group might very well be told the even-numbered sections were available to them under the usual homestead provisions. If there was a danger that other settlers might apply for homestead, Saskatchewan Valley land agents often resorted to "blanketing". This simply meant that homestead claims were filed by agents and friends of the land company, although none of them ever intended to settle. These homestead claims could then be reassigned or sold to the new settlers that the company hoped to bring in.

Once a larger area was in their control, the land promoters launched aggressive and very extensive advertising campaigns, particularly in the American Midwest where younger sons of successful farmers, and often whole communities in need of more land to accommodate a new generation of farmers, were eager to take up new homesteads in the Canadian West. There was often very close co-operation between the federal government's settlement program and that of the land company. Prospective buyers were brought out at company expense and were shown the Canadian lands; most became enthusiastic and a great many bought lands for themselves and for the groups they represented. Easy financial terms with long repayment schedules were offered, and in less than two years the Saskatchewan Valley and Manitoba Land Company sold 700,360.66 acres of Canadian Northern lands at an average price well above the minimum $5 per acre.[21]

The arrangement with the Saskatchewan Valley and Manitoba Land Company was terminated on 1 July 1905. At that time, 210,800.76 acres covered under the 1903 agreement had not yet been sold, and the Saskatchewan Valley and Manitoba Land Company agreed to return these to the railway company, provided it was allowed the profit it might have made if all the remaining lands had been sold for $5.20 per acre.[22] This agreement cleared the way for a more direct Canadian Northern involvement in the sale of its lands.

---

21 *Ibid.*; *Arbitration*, 2090–1.
22 PAC, CNR Records, x̄CCXII, Secretary's Black Book, Agreement No. 58, Canadian Northern Railway and Saskatchewan Valley and Manitoba Land Company, Release of Land Grants to Canadian Northern Railway, 1 July 1905.

After 1905 Canadian Northern lands were handled in one of three ways. Davidson and McRae, the principal promoters of the Saskatchewan Valley and Manitoba Land Company, were retained as commission salesmen. They were given $20,000 per year to promote industries and immigration along the Canadian Northern lines, and a simple 20-per-cent commission on any lands they sold. They agreed not to sell below a minimum price of $6.50 per acre.[23]

The arrangement with Davidson and McRae also enabled the Canadian Northern to sell lands on its own account. Local Canadian Northern station agents became land agents and soon proved very effective in selling scattered lots in fairly well-developed regions.[24] Davidson and McRae specialized in group settlement and the local agents in the disposal of desirable but scattered lots in their regions. In addition, the Canadian Northern Railway itself could on occasion negotiate larger sales directly with other land promoters and developers.[25]

The third method of promoting Canadian Northern lands was through the agency of a new subsidiary land company. The Canadian Northern Prairie Lands Company was officially organized in 1905, shortly before the agreement with the Saskatchewan Valley and Manitoba Land Company was terminated. It had a capitalization of $1,500,000. Immediately after its organization, the Canadian Northern Railway transferred to it 500,000 acres of land and received in return the land company's entire capital stock. Thereafter, the Canadian Northern lands were sold by this company, which also negotiated an agreement whereby Davidson and McRae became its salesmen.[26]

Among the lands transferred to the Canadian Northern Prairie Lands Company were 256,000 acres, which several times became the

---

23 *Ibid.*, Agreement No. 60, Canadian Northern Railway and A. D. Davidson and J. D. McRae, Promotion of Industries and Immigration along CNR lines, 2 Oct. 1905; Agreement No. 61, Canadian Northern Railway and A. D. Davidson and J. D. McRae re Sale of Land Grants, 14 Nov. 1905.
24 *Arbitration*, 2135–6.
25 See for example PAC, CNR Records,

XCCXII, Secretary's Black Book, Agreements Nos. 63 and 64, Canadian Northern Railway and Ditlew M. Fredricksen, Chicago, re Sale of Land, 17 Jan. and 23 April 1906.
26 PAC, CNR Records, Vol. 10212, Secretary's Black Book, Agreement No. 61, Canadian Northern Railway and A. D. Davidson and J. D. McRae re Sale of Land Grants 14 Nov. 1905; *Arbitration*, 2082.

subject of major controversy. These were the lands earned for the construction of the first forty miles of the old Hudson Bay Railway. They were the subject of the "misunderstanding" between Premier Norquay and Prime Minister Macdonald in 1887. That misunderstanding had left contractors Herbert Holt and Donald Mann in possession of the provincial bonds which had been issued against the security of the lands that Macdonald refused to transfer. Nothing further was done for nearly a decade; but when Donald Mann and William Mackenzie opened negotiations with the Manitoba government for a provincial guarantee on their Lake Manitoba Railway and Canal Company bonds, the provincial government insisted that 256,000 acres of the new railway's land grant be transferred to the government as soon as they were earned. The old bonds might thus be secured and redeemed. Mackenzie and Mann agreed, thinking that they would earn the 256,000 acres if they rehabilitated the original forty miles.

In 1904 the old Hudson Bay Railway mileage was rehabilitated. Mackenzie and Mann transferred title to 256,000 acres to the provincial government and then applied to the federal government for patents to an additional 256,000 acres allegedly earned by the old Hudson Bay Railway. The federal government again refused, this time arguing that the land grant was only given because the mileage was to be part of a line to the Bay. Since that line had now been diverted elsewhere, and since Mackenzie and Mann had already earned lands on the alternate line, the federal Department of Railways and Canals ruled that the original forty miles were no longer eligible for the land grant. Mackenzie and Mann took the matter to court, where it remained until the Canadian Northern Railway was nationalized and the suit was withdrawn.[27] Mackenzie and Mann were nevertheless bound by their contract with the provincial government to transfer 256,000 acres of land. This they did, but they then immediately opened negotiations with the Manitoba government to buy back the 256,000 acres. The Manitoba government readily agreed to sell or release the lands in return for a cash payment of $400,000, that sum representing

27 Canada, Department of the Interior, File 505500-9B, Canadian Northern Railway Land Grant File re 256,000 acres of Winnipeg Great Northern land grants.

the principal and interest on the outstanding bonds. The province could thus redeem the highly controversial and troublesome bond issue without loss.[28] The transaction was, however, loudly denounced by provincial Liberals and other critics of Mackenzie and Mann. They alleged that the lands were worth far more than $400,000, or $1.56 per acre.[29]

The now-unencumbered lands were immediately transferred from Mackenzie, Mann and Co. Ltd. to the Canadian Northern Railway, which in turn transferred them to the Canadian Northern Prairie Lands Company.[30] The Canadian Northern Railway received 120,000 shares of the Canadian Northern Prairie Lands Company, valued at $5 per share, for these 256,000 acres of land. There was thus a $200,000 paper profit on the transaction.

Many of the Canadian Northern Prairie Lands Company shares that were transferred to the Canadian Northern Railway in 1904 were subsequently sold in London to small private investors. Altogether, 66,170 such shares were sold for a total of $556,606.45. It is clear that very large profits could be made from land transactions of this kind. It must be remembered, however, that the value of prairie lands rose very rapidly after 1905. Lands which had remained unsold when offered for $1.00 per acre in 1887 were purchased for $1.56 in 1904 from the Manitoba government, and some were valued as high as $15.65 in 1917.[31] It is clear that, had Mackenzie and Mann concentrated more of their energies on land speculation and land sales, they could have made much more money than they ever made on their railway.

Davidson and McRae, the Canadian Northern Railway's local station agents, and the Canadian Northern Prairie Lands Company all sought to sell acreage and get traffic-generating settlers onto the lands adjacent to the railway's lines as quickly as possible. Unsold lands, however, also became the basis for further borrowing. Land-grant bonds with a par value of $2,000,000 had been issued in 1899. In

28 *Arbitration*, 2084–5.
29 *Manitoba Free Press*, 4 June 1904, 4.
30 *Arbitration*, 2082.

31 PAC, CNR Records, MMCXCIV, Canadian Northern Railway System, Statements for Commission of Inquiry into Railways and Transportation, 30 June 1916.

1907 the Canadian Northern Railway's land claims were clarified by three orders-in-council, and a new £1,027,400 land-grant bond issue was prepared. These newly authorized bonds were quickly deposited with the Canadian Bank of Commerce as security for short-term loans. Negotiations for more stable financing on the security of these bonds were also begun with Lazard Brothers in London. There remained, however, a dispute with the federal government over additional lands to which the railway claimed it was entitled. That claim was recognized on 3 August 1908, when another order-in-council secured an additional 874,000 acres for the railway, bringing the total lands earned by the Canadian Northern Railway to 4,001,728 acres.[32]

Following the passage of the 1908 order-in-council, the 1907 land-grant bond issue was cancelled. In its place a new issue of land-grant bonds, again valued at £1,027,400, was authorized on 11 January 1909.[33] The bonds were to be redeemed as payments from land sales were received. The amount outstanding therefore varied somewhat, and was reduced each year until in 1917 only £380,700 of the 1909 land-grant bonds remained.[34]

The Canadian Northern lands became the security for a final mortgage debenture issue in 1913. By that time sufficient lands had been sold to redeem all the 1899 land-grant bonds and many of the 1909 bonds, while the value of the remaining lands had risen substantially. To raise additional money Mackenzie and Mann wanted to issue further Land Mortgage Debentures of £3,500,000, carrying a 5-per-cent rate of interest.[35] As security they were prepared to offer "their land grant subject to the prior charges, by prior issues", together with all deferred payments on lands previously sold. The London underwriters found this security inadequate and informed Mackenzie, "The Canadian Northern lands which you have left will not warrant so large a bond issue. . . . You must either reduce the amount of your bond issue

32 Canada, *P.C. 1579*, 3 Aug. 1908; *Arbitration*, 2081.

33 PAC, CNR Records, MCDXXXVIII, 3–4, Meeting of Directors and Shareholders of the Canadian Northern Railway, 11 Jan. 1909.

34 *Third Annual Systems Report, Canadian Northern Railway System, 1917*, 20.

35 PAC, CNR Records, MDLXVII, Meeting of Directors of the Canadian Northern Town Properties Company Limited. This company has apparently also been referred to at times as the Canadian Northern Townsite Company. See addenda to *Synoptical Histories*, as prepared by J. C. Andreassen.

or put in additional security."[36] Additional security was provided, but by Mackenzie, Mann and Co. Ltd., rather than by the Canadian Northern Railway.

Mackenzie, Mann and Co. Ltd. were the owners of, or held options to purchase, 516 lots of land in various cities and towns in Ontario, Manitoba, Saskatchewan, Alberta, and British Columbia.[37] They agreed to "loan" these, or make them available to the railway company so they could be pledged as additional security for the proposed land-mortgage debentures. This "loan" was effected through an inter-mediary company. A new company, the Canadian Northern Town Properties Company Limited, was incorporated on 22 October 1913 with a capitalization of $10,000,000 common stock. It issued $10,000,000 worth of 4.5-per-cent debentures. Mackenzie and Mann transferred all titles to their townsites to this new company, taking in return the entire capital stock and debenture issue of that company. These stocks and debentures were then loaned to the Canadian Northern Railway, which pledged them, together with its equity in the unsold land and the deferred payments of lands already sold, as security for the new £3,500,000 land-mortgage debentures. In the mortgage agreement the townsites were assigned a value of $2,950,834. The total value of all the collateral pledged for the new debentures was $13,450,834. Of the £3,500,000 land-mortgage debentures, $7,300,000 was successfully sold to the public in London before war-time investment restrictions in Britain made further sales impossible. The remaining $9,733,333.33 (par value) was subsequently pledged to secure short-term loans in New York during the war years.[38]

When the Canadian Northern Railway was nationalized in 1918, Mackenzie and Mann approached the railway with a view to selling their interest in the Canadian Northern Town Properties Company. An independent valuation of the townsite properties unsold in 1919

36 *Arbitration*, 2639–41.
37 PAC, CNR Records, MDLXXVI, Meeting of Directors of the Canadian Northern Town Properties Company, 30 Oct. 1913.
38 *Arbitration*, 750–1, 2639–41; Andreassen addenda to *Synoptical Histories; Report on the Canadian Northern Railway System by a special* commission composed of *Edward E. Loomis, President, Lehigh Valley Railroad Company, New York, and John W. Platten, President, United States Mortgage & Trust Company, New York,* Exhibit B, "The Canadian Northern Railway System Map Shewing Description and Distribution of Funded Debt".

placed their value at $3,342,152. The government declined a settlement on the basis of this evaluation, but in 1923 offered Mackenzie and Mann $400,000. The offer was rejected; no final settlement was negotiated until 1937, after the death of both William Mackenzie and Donald Mann. The Mackenzie and Mann claims were then settled for $275,000, many of the town lots owned by the company in 1919 having been sold in the interim.[39]

The lands certainly provided Mackenzie and Mann with considerable assistance. They provided security for a $2,000,000 bond issue in 1899 and a £1,027,400 issue in 1909, and partial security for the £3,500,000 debenture issue of 1913. Large sums of money, which were immediately used to build new railways, were thus raised. More important, however, were the railway company's receipts from land sales. The figures in this regard vary somewhat,[40] but at the arbitration proceedings in 1918, Z. A. Lash reported that the railway company had received $14,790,000 from land sales. This figure represented the net income "after payment of all expenses in connection with it". In addition, Lash reported, there were deferred payments of $4,870,000 still outstanding, and the remaining unsold lands were valued at $13,109,000. Lash therefore calculated that the land grants had been worth a total of $32,790,000 to the Canadian Northern Railway.[41] The total listed assets of the entire Canadian Northern Railway system in 1917 were given as $586,621,650.65. The land grants thus provided approximately 5.6 per cent of all the listed assets.[42]

It is difficult to evaluate the precise effect of the land grants on each of the railways that received them. The three prairie land-grant rail-

39 Andreassen addenda to *Synoptical Histories*, based on a memorandum by L. C. Groom. Copies of this memorandum and other documents relating to the Canadian Northern Town Properties Company Limited are available in PAC, CNR Records, MDLXXXVII, package of documents.
40 The main reason for the difference in the figures given in the various sources is that expenses associated with the sale of the lands are not always deducted. The figures given here represent net income from land sales.

41 *Arbitration*, 2505–6.
42 *Third Annual Systems Report, Canadian Northern Railway System, 1917*, 14. It should be pointed out, however, that many of the assets were listed at par value rather than at market value. The total figure for real Canadian Northern assets should therefore be substantially reduced to take into account the fact that the capital stock at least was not worth par. The true percentage would actually be somewhat higher.

TABLE VIII
Statement of Canadian Northern Railway
Land Sales

Year	Acres	Amount
		($)
1903	183,736	631,503
1904	64,469	313,575
1905	231,707	1,221,469
1906	204,966	1,014,351
1907	289,576	1,711,109
1908	196,946	1,746,504
1909	——	
1910	285,428	2,783,010
1911	277,414	3,336,797
1912	365,926	4,216,578
1913	182,499	2,009,642
1914	182,491	2,009,642
1915	——	——
1916	——	——
1917	17,706	298,938
1918	39,546	732,351

Source: Annual Report of the Department of the Interior for the year ending March 31, 1930, Ottawa, 1931, p. 28.

ways that became a part of the Canadian Northern system all received their grants before Mackenzie and Mann took them over. The land grants clearly did not get the railways built during the depressed period prior to 1895. It seems likely, on the other hand, that they would have been built with or without the land grant during the prosperous period after 1895. The availability of the land grant certainly increased Mackenzie and Mann's willingness to build as soon as possible, and probably hastened construction by several years. Without the land grant the Dauphin area, for example, might have waited several years longer before obtaining rail facilities.

The railway land-grant system has often been severely criticized because it allegedly retarded and dispersed settlement. "Land lock" was a frequent rural grievance. All the odd-numbered sections near the assisted railways were reserved for those railways and consequently were not available for homestead entries. To be at all useful to the railway company, the lands had to be sold. This happened, of course, only after adjacent free homestead lands were taken up; thus, the railway land grants tended to disperse early settlement. Local facilities such as schools, roads, churches, and numerous social amenities were allegedly affected if only half the lands in a given area were homesteaded. The railways were frequently accused of holding back their lands for speculative purposes. Many of the original land-grant charters were obtained by promoters whose primary interest was, indeed, land speculation.

There can be no doubt that all Canadian Northern lands were held for ultimate sale and therefore were settled somewhat later than adjacent free homestead lands of equal quality. Mackenzie and Mann's first interest, however, was their railway, and it was very much in the interest of the railway to have all lands near the railway line settled with traffic-generating settlers as quickly as possible, even if this meant lower receipts from land sales. Mackenzie and Mann were not land speculators. One of their lawyers, who had been in charge of representing the company before government committees, emphasized this point:

The chief difficulty which arose from time to time in the Private Bills Committee and in the House was whether they were just giving an opportunity for some greedy speculators to try and trade in the charters; but that difficulty never was in existence with respect to the Canadian Northern's applications or the applications of Mackenzie, Mann and Co. in connection with Canadian Northern matters. One of the things that was always said was, "These men do things, they are not speculators."[43]

This statement was largely accurate, at least in connection with Canadian Northern lands adjacent to the railway.

One of the anomalies of the railway land-grant system was that many of the lands earned might not be near the assisted railway. Wherever possible the odd-numbered sections on either side of the railway were reserved to meet the requirements of the land grant. Some of those odd-numbered sections, however, might already be

43 *Arbitration*, 2550–2.

occupied, or they might not be fit for settlement. If the railway company was unable to find sufficient suitable land within the reserved section, it could make indemnity selections elsewhere. Canadian Northern land agents were known to be extremely fastidious in their standards when selecting lands, and some of the lands were ultimately selected in areas far removed from the Canadian Northern lines. Mackenzie and Mann, of course, were much more interested in selling lands whose traffic would be tributary to their own lines, and the temptation to delay land sales and settlement in areas adjacent to other railways led to some serious abuses.[44]

The land-grant system certainly encouraged scattered early settlement to some extent. This development, however, was not entirely unfortunate. Many of the 160-acre homesteads, particularly in the south, proved too small for economic operations by the average family of four; even the most enthusiastic propaganda of the Department of the Interior could not alter the fact. But the availability of vacant railway land often allowed farmers to expand their holdings to a more economical size with a minimum of social disruption. Thus, the scattering of settlement probably wrought initial hardships, but proved unexpectedly beneficial in the long run.

Mackenzie and Mann received very few personal benefits from the Canadian Northern land grants. With the exception of 100,000 acres, which they earned under construction contracts and kept, all the lands were returned to the railway company in 1899, or remained the property of the railway if they were earned after 1899. They were used by the railway for the advantage of the railway. Nevertheless, lands were the subject of major scandals and political corruption. The Canadian Northern Railway became directly involved in at least one major scandal of this kind, although none of its own lands were directly involved.

In 1905 it became fairly well known that the Canadian Northern would ask for federal assistance to begin construction of a proposed line from Saskatoon to Calgary. Several Conservative Members of Parliament allegedly asked Mackenzie and Mann to show them detailed plans of this proposed new line. Mackenzie and Mann agreed,

44 *Ibid.*, 2505–6.

allegedly on the understanding that the Conservatives would not oppose the proposed federal bond guarantee for the line. The politicians then used information obtained from the location plans to buy up lands adjacent to the proposed railway. These lands, as it happened, were largely owned by the CPR, which was still unaware of the Canadian Northern's detailed plans. The politicians prevailed on the CPR to sell the lands to them at very favourable prices. The CPR was asking $5.00 per acre but agreed to reduce the price to $3.50 when pressed by its political friends. George Foster, a former Conservative Minister of Finance and the general manager of the Union Trust Company, provided the needed funds. He simply used trust funds of the Independent Order of Foresters which were being administered by the Union Trust Company. Once the lands were purchased, Foster and his friends quickly resold them to the Union Trust Company—but at $2 per acre more than they had paid for them. Thus, using insurance funds entrusted to the Union Trust Company, Foster and his friends netted $200,000. To the disgust of his friends, Foster apparently failed to treat even them fairly, and secretly kept 10,000 acres of the best lands for himself.[45]

The entire affair was investigated in considerable detail by a royal commission on life insurance, which was appointed in 1906 and presented its report a year later. The main concern of the Royal Commission was that life insurance funds were being invested in various unauthorized securities and other speculative ventures. The Royal Commission Report named George Foster, Rufus H. Pope, MP for Compton and later appointed to the Senate, George W. Fowler, MP for Kings County, New Brunswick, who was also later appointed to the Senate, Premier Rodmond P. Roblin of Manitoba, and Manitoba Minister of Public Works Robert Rogers in connection with the Union Trust Company affair. The name of Sir John Boyd, then Chancellor of Ontario and president of the High Court of Justice, who retired from his position with the Union Trust Company in 1905, was also

45 PAC, Minto Papers, XXIII, 121–3, Sladen to Minto, 30 Oct. 1906. Sladen also mentions R. B. Bennett of Calgary. This appears to be an error. The Royal Commission on Life Insurance refers only to a Mr. W. H. Bennett. As a result of these revelations, George Foster certainly became the target of very considerable criticism, both by the Liberals and by members of his own caucus.

mentioned, although no clear evidence was presented that he was directly involved.[46]

The official Report of the Royal Commission referred to several complex land speculations financed by trust funds of the Independent Order of Foresters, and handled and invested by the Union Trust Company. It clearly indicated a continuing practice, not an isolated incident. In this case the Union Trust Company lost nothing. It managed to sell the lands at a further and substantial profit after the railway was built. The entire transaction was really perpetrated at the expense of the CPR. It brought the Canadian Northern Conservative support—or at least silence when government-aid bills were debated—without the expenditure of a single cent, and it largely destroyed Conservative criticisms of Liberal graft and corruption, the issue on which Robert Borden intended to campaign in the next federal election. This was the kind of sharp dealing that Mackenzie and Mann enjoyed, that earned them their dubious reputation, and that brought the whole land-grant system into disrepute.

The rapidly rising values of western Canadian lands made transactions and scandals of this kind possible. Huge fortunes were made. The rise in land values, moreover, tended to accompany the arrival of the railway. There is considerable evidence that Mackenzie and Mann managed responsibly most of the lands adjacent to their railway, but they were well aware that railway locations could greatly enhance or reduce the value of other people's lands. This gave them very considerable power in an age when men who were prominent in politics were often equally prominent in land speculation. Mackenzie and

46 Canada, *7 Edw.* VII, *Sessional Papers No. 123a, Report of the Royal Commission on Life Insurance*, printed by S. E. Dawson, King's Printer, 1907. The transcripts of the hearings held by the commission are not with its other records in the Public Archives of Canada. The hearings were, however, reported in the newspapers at that time. Mackenzie and Mann came in for considerable criticism by the commission because of improper manipulation of the stock of the Manufacturers' Life Assurance Company (in which manipulation the Canadian Bank of Commerce was also associated), and because both the Manufacturers' Life Assurance Company and the Canada Life Assurance Company invested in the securities of companies controlled by Mackenzie and Mann but not approved by the Insurance Act for particular types of investments. The commissioners alleged a conflict of interest in which "the care of the insurance funds could not always have been the sole consideration."

Mann had no reluctance about using the power they had for their own purposes. Towns which proved uncooperative could be and sometimes were bypassed. Slight location changes could ruin a political enemy, and inadequate service on an existing line could lead to agitation, not only against the railway but also against the incumbent Member who was not providing his constituency with the essential services that he had generally promised in his last campaign.[47] The land-grant system itself, of course, cannot be held responsible for many of these abuses. They occurred whether the line enjoyed a land grant or not. It was one of the less attractive aspects of the great economic boom on the prairies, made possible largely by the coming of the railways, and with them the numerous settlers and homesteaders.

The land grants did not provide the only opportunity for land speculation by Mackenzie and Mann. It was easy for them to purchase lands before others were aware of the exact location plans for new railway lines. Land values tended to rise very rapidly once it became known that the lands would have access to rail service. Lots in towns that were to be developed by the Canadian Northern were particularly attractive, since the announcement that a particular location had been chosen as the divisional point on a proposed new railway sharply increased the value of all nearby lots. It was later suggested that Mackenzie and Mann might have made up in profits from acquired townsites what they lost in turning the land grant back to the railway.

It was a common practice for Mackenzie and Mann or their agents to purchase lots of land in towns and cities before announcing plans to build through these centres. Some centres, such as Dauphin, Kamsack, Kindersley, North Battleford, Warman, and numerous smaller places, owed their existence entirely to the railway, and in each case Mackenzie and Mann acquired lands there before the final plans of the railway company were known. Most of the lands and town lots

47 Numerous complaints involving all the above-mentioned activities, usually without convincing documentation, were heard by the federal Board of Railway Commissioners. Many of the complaints did not lead to any remedial action, but it is clear that the commissioners had a rather jaundiced view of the railways thus accused, and on occasion lashed out against them. See, for example, Saskatchewan, Department of Railways, Files 13 and 46, and D. A. MacGibbon, *Railway Rates and the Canadian Railway Commission*, Boston, 1917.

thus acquired by Mackenzie and Mann, however, were purchased as prospective terminal and station sites or for the development of industrial spurs and other facilities the railway might need in the new centre.[48] This practice certainly enabled the railway to obtain choice locations where excellent facilities could be developed.

Some of the lands and other assets acquired by Mackenzie and Mann were never needed by the railway and remained their property. Others were sold, sometimes at handsome profits. In the case of town lots, Mackenzie and Mann rarely retarded the development of a Canadian Northern town by withholding choice properties for speculative purposes. The rapid development and prosperity of the towns along their railway were as important to them as the quick sale and settlement of their lands. In the new towns they frequently controlled the central commercial and industrial areas, but used this control to attract traffic-producing business and development, rather than for speculative purposes. The development of the town of Dauphin set the pattern. Surveys were run and choice lands purchased for the railway station and related facilities. Attempts were then made to attract the basic business establishments—bank, store, hotel, restaurant, school, and church—all of which could obtain central lots at low cost.[49] These businesses ensured the success of the new town and facilitated the development of the surrounding countryside. By controlling the central areas, Mackenzie and Mann could ensure that the desired services were brought into the towns, often through the offer of an attractive site at a low price. Speculators inevitably arrived once the essential services were established, and residential lots were sold and resold at rapidly rising prices. But few of these residential lots were ever owned by Mackenzie and Mann. Their primary interest was the railway; to make it a success, thriving towns and prosperous settlers were needed. When asked later about land and townsite speculation, Mann claimed he was surprised, in retrospect, by the restraint he and his partner had exercised.

Station and terminal facilities in the larger centres were handled somewhat differently. Many railway promoters in the early 1900s

48 *Arbitration*, 753, 2559–60, 2599–2600, 2648.

49 Unpublished autobiography of H. W. D. Armstrong, 191–7, 230–1; CNRHQ, Gavin C. Baird interview.

believed that the most important factor in the success or failure of a railway was the access and station or terminal facilities that that railway could establish in the large urban centres. Mackenzie and Mann certainly regarded the establishment of proper grain-handling and terminal facilities in Port Arthur, Winnipeg, Saskatoon, and Edmonton, and later in Vancouver, Montreal, and Toronto, as extremely important. Their first major investment in such facilities was, understandably, in Port Arthur and Winnipeg. In these centres Mackenzie, Mann and Co. Ltd. acquired valuable properties, organized these under the specially incorporated Lake Superior Terminals Company and the Winnipeg Land Company, and in 1903 sold them to the Canadian Northern Railway.

Grain-handling facilities and some other terminal properties in Port Arthur were the primary concern of the Lake Superior Terminal Company. The properties of the company included "a tract of land 13,140 feet, the greater portion of which has a frontage on Port Arthur harbour, together with Docks, Tile Elevators of the latest improved description of 3,350,000 bushels capacity, wharves and freight shed, etc." The earnings from the elevators alone were reputed to be "of considerable magnitude and will grow proportionately as the construction of the railway increases the area of lands brought under cultivation by the steady influx of new settlers."[50] This property supplemented the terminal facilities acquired earlier by the Ontario and Rainy River Railway and the Port Arthur, Duluth and Western Railway. In fact, one of the Lake Superior Terminals Company elevators was actually built on Canadian Northern (formerly Ontario and Rainy River) lands in the city.[51]

The Port Arthur properties complemented the local and country elevators on the prairies. None of these local or country elevators alongside Canadian Northern lines became the property of the Canadian Northern Railway. Many were the property of syndicates in which Mackenzie, Mann and Co. Ltd. held substantial interests,[52]

50 *First Annual Report, Canadian Northern Railway, 1903*, 15.
51 PAC, CNR Records, MCDXXXVII, 75–8, Meeting of Directors of the Canadian Northern Railway Company, 26 Nov. 1903.

52 *Ibid.*, Legal Series, File 19–24–1, Memorandum of conclusions arrived at by Messrs. Stuart, Douglas, Piper, Mann & Lash at interview, 9 July 1902, re elevator companies and cereal company.

although these elevators were not granted special concessions by the railway. The railway company allowed other elevator companies to build alongside its lines. It also accepted grain from farmer-owned flat grain warehouses, and made cars available for direct loading by the farmers. Only the vital terminal elevators at Port Arthur became the property of the railway company.

In Winnipeg, Mackenzie and Mann were able to develop excellent station and terminal facilities. They inherited the terminal properties of the old Hudson Bay Railway and also the facilities developed by the Red River Valley Railway and its successor, the Northern Pacific and Manitoba Railway. The latter company had spent substantial sums in acquiring property and establishing both a station and a hotel in the city, although the hotel was destroyed by fire shortly before the Northern Pacific lines were turned over to the Canadian Northern Railway.[53]

In addition to these properties, Mackenzie and Mann purchased 200 acres of land in Winnipeg and St. Boniface. This land was to be used to develop railway yards and provide the location for the railway's regional offices. The land was purchased and held under a new company, the Winnipeg Land Company. That company and all its assets were sold to the Canadian Northern Railway in 1903.

This acquisition was followed, in 1907, by a further Canadian Northern purchase of Winnipeg lands. Mackenzie, Mann and Co. Ltd. held an even larger tract of land in St. Boniface under the title of another company, the St. Boniface and Western Land Company. These lands were described as "suitable for terminal and manufacturing purposes". Mackenzie and Mann sold their interests in this property, receiving Canadian Northern Common and 4-per-cent Consolidated Debenture Stock.[54]

The construction of a station, hotel, and other terminal facilities in Winnipeg prior to 1907 had in large part been financed directly by Mackenzie, Mann and Co. Ltd., who took the stock and bonds of the terminals companies or of the Canadian Northern in payment for their services. In 1906–7, however, major agreements were reached

53 MSHS, Northern Pacific Railroad Records, Pre ident's Correspondence File. Nos. 167 and 291.
54 PAC, CNR Records, MCDXXXVIII,

39–42, Meeting of Directors of the Canadian Northern Railway, 28 June 1907; *Sixth Annual Report, Canadian Northern Railway, 1908*, 9.

with the government of Manitoba, the Grand Trunk Pacific Railway,[55] and the National Transcontinental Railway. The Manitoba government agreed to guarantee additional construction bonds[56] if the Canadian Northern Railway would build a union station and other facilities to be used by all three railways. The appropriate agreements were signed without difficulty, partly because the federal Board of Railway Commissioners was strongly supporting any proposals for shared station and terminal facilities.

There was, nevertheless, an area of potential controversy. The Canadian Northern Railway, with no eastern connections of its own and a heavy eastbound grain traffic, desperately needed at least some of the westbound traffic coming into Winnipeg over the National Transcontinental Railway. That railway, however, was to be operated by the Grand Trunk Pacific Railway once construction was completed. The Grand Trunk Pacific management would certainly try to channel as much traffic as possible to its own traffic-starved prairie lines. Laurier and some other federal officials never seemed fully aware of the problems that control of the National Transcontinental Railway by the Grand Trunk Pacific Railway would create for the Canadian Northern Railway.

Mackenzie and Mann found a way to utilize their control of the Winnipeg terminal facilities to score a minor victory over the National Transcontinental, which did not have adequate terminal facilities in Winnipeg. The National Transcontinental wanted government assistance to establish terminal facilities, while the Canadian Northern was negotiating for new bond guarantees which would permit substantial enlargement of its Winnipeg facilities. The bond guarantee was granted the Canadian Northern, but only on the condition that the new station would be a union station available to the National Transcontinental. Each road would pay a portion of the station expenses, according to the amount of business done at the station by each railway.

The necessary agreement, including trackage over Canadian Northern tracks into the station, was negotiated without difficulty. Unfortunately, the National Transcontinental negotiators failed to make provision for traffic of the Grand Trunk Pacific Railway, and

55 *Ibid.*, 10 Dec. 1906, 27–30; Canada, *6–7 Edw.* VII. *Cap. 162.*

56 *Ibid.*, 15 April 1907, 17–20.

Mackenzie and Mann subsequently refused trackage for such traffic unless it was consigned to Canadian Northern trains from Winnipeg east. Without Grand Trunk Pacific traffic the National Transcontinental had very little eastbound traffic. Eventually the National Transcontinental found itself forced to build its own line track to the union station. In the process, lands owned by Mackenzie and Mann had to be crossed, and the Canadian Northern promoters demanded $2,500,000 in compensation.

This incident did not solve the Canadian Northern's basic problem, which was to get more westbound traffic at Port Arthur to offset the heavy eastbound grain shipments. The Winnipeg incident did reveal Mackenzie and Mann's penchant for sharp dealing when pressed by competitors, and a very considerable lack of business acumen on the part of the government-appointed commissioners of the National Transcontinental Railway who were in charge while the railway was under construction.[57]

The construction and use of common terminal facilities by the Canadian Northern Railway and the Grand Trunk Pacific Railway was more satisfactory in Edmonton, where the Canadian Northern Railway also built and controlled the downtown facilities. Edmonton had been a strong Canadian Northern centre from the time Mackenzie and Mann took over the Edmonton, Yukon and Pacific Railway (formerly the Edmonton District Railway) and connected it with the Calgary and Edmonton Railway. In 1901 Mackenzie, Mann and Co., the Hudson's Bay Company, and the city of Edmonton had clubbed together to purchase a large tract of land which was to be developed as a terminal and a shipping centre. This centre quickly formed the core of the business district of the city, and the $5,000 Mackenzie and Mann invested in 1901, and subsequently turned over to the Canadian Northern, was valued fifteen years later at $2,500,000. When the Grand Trunk Pacific Railway built through Edmonton, a union station on Canadian Northern property served both roads, and the Grand Trunk Pacific paid a rental or usage fee proportionate to the amount of Grand Trunk Pacific traffic handled by the station.[58]

A situation almost as advantageous as that in Edmonton developed

57 Stevens, 169–70.   58 *Arbitration*, 2681–2; Stevens, 73.

in Saskatoon. Originally Mackenzie and Mann had bypassed Saskatoon and had built their transcontinental line through the rival site of Warman, fourteen miles to the north. The business boom in Saskatoon brought on by the arrival of the Barr colonists, and the continuing business influence of the Qu'Appelle, Long Lake and Saskatchewan Railway, made it relatively easy for Saskatoon to prevail over its northern rival. When Mackenzie and Mann purchased the Qu'Appelle, Long Lake and Saskatchewan Railway they also acquired that railway's choice terminal facilities in the city. Those facilities had developed in a unique way. Saskatoon was originally founded by a Toronto-based temperance society. When the Qu'Appelle, Long Lake and Saskatchewan Railway was built in the late 1880s, the promoters feared that strict temperance regulations in the colony would hamper a prosperous business development. Consequently, they decided to avoid the east side of the South Saskatchewan River where the colony had been established. Station facilities, hopefully to be followed by the construction of a hotel and other businesses, were therefore established on the west side of the river. A bitter fight ensued, which for some time inhibited the development of the railway's facilities; but in the end the business community of the city established itself on the west side around the railway terminals. The city of Saskatoon thus grew up around the railway.[59] The establishment of the university on the east side ensured the survival of the old community but not, alas, of the temperance cause.

In Saskatoon the Grand Trunk Pacific found it inconvenient to utilize the bridge and station facilities of the Qu'Appelle, Long Lake and Saskatchewan Railway. The Grand Trunk Pacific managers also found the city itself uncooperative in making new lands available. They eventually established their station several miles farther south and constructed a new railway bridge. They then sought to promote a very unpopular taxi monopoly which would take the passengers from their station to downtown Saskatoon. Later, the CPR extended its Minnedosa line to the city and built yet another railway bridge and station. Saskatoon thus became properly known as the City of Bridges.

In Regina the Canadian Northern was able to use a union station

59 A. N. Lalonde, "Settlement in the Northwest Territories by Colonization Companies, 1881–1891", unpublished Doctorat d'Université Laval, 1971.

built by the CPR. That railway had operated the Qu'Appelle, Long Lake and Saskatchewan Railway before it was purchased by Mackenzie and Mann, and it allowed the partners continued use of the Regina facilities. At that time, the federal Board of Railway Commissioners was exerting considerable pressure on railways to avoid unnecessary and expensive duplication of station facilities.[60] In Regina this pressure produced the desired result; in Saskatoon it obviously did not.

The terminal properties acquired by Mackenzie and Mann in several other Canadian cities were held after 1907 by a single company, the Canadian Northern Systems Terminals Limited. The first property acquired by this company from Mackenzie, Mann and Co. Ltd. was a plot of land in the city of Port Arthur, which was subsequently used to build a large hotel, the Prince Arthur Hotel.

Sixteen other properties, in cities as far apart as Quebec City and Calgary, were subsequently acquired by the Systems Terminals company from Mackenzie, Mann and Co. Ltd. D. B. Hanna later explained that "a great deal of the terminal property was bought by Mackenzie, Mann, and Co. Ltd., they being in better shape financially to do so." These properties included a second hotel, the Brandon Hotel, in the city of the same name. When Mackenzie, Mann and Co. Ltd. transferred their terminal properties to Canadian Northern Systems Terminals, they received in return the entire $2,000,000 capital stock of that company.[61]

In 1912 Canadian Northern Systems Terminals mortgaged its properties for a $7,000,000 debenture issue. All of these debentures, together with the company's capital stock, were then purchased by the Canadian Northern Railway, which paid for these securities with its own 4-per-cent Perpetual Consolidated Debenture Stock.[62]

60 Canada, Board of Railway Commissioners, File 588.32. Reported in *Canadian Railway Cases*, XX, 67–72. The Board in this case ruled that even if a railway is negligent in meeting its payments, it must be given access to union-station facilities controlled or owned by another company.
61 *Synoptical Histories*, 230–1; PAC, CNR Records, MCLXXXIX, Meetings of Directors of Canadian Northern Systems Terminals Limited, Sept. 1909 and 28 May 1912; *ibid.*, MCXC, Stock Certificate Book of the Canadian Northern Systems Terminals Limited; *Arbitration*, 753.
62 PAC, CNR Records, MCLXXXIX and MCDXXXIX, Meetings of Directors of both Canadian Northern Systems Terminals Limited and Canadian Northern Railway Company, 28 May 1912.

Another and somewhat different terminal and traffic-handling facility in Port Arthur attracted Mackenzie and Mann's interest and money in 1905. At that time the Canadian Northern Railway was largely dependent on eastern sources for its supplies of coal, large amounts of which were needed to fire the locomotives and also as fuel by the settlers alongside the railway lines. Most of this coal came from the Pennsylvania mining areas. To facilitate and ensure a sufficient and reliable supply of coal Mackenzie and Mann entered into an agreement with the Pittsburgh Coal Company. Under the terms of this agreement the railway promoters and the coal company agreed to build a much needed coal-and-ore dock at Port Arthur, each company furnishing half the cost. The Canadian Northern Coal and Ore Dock was incorporated, and a $2,000,000 dock built on reclaimed lands in the Port Arthur harbour area. Mackenzie and Mann and the Pittsburgh Coal Company each took half the bonds and stock issued by the dock company. Most of the stock taken by Mackenzie and Mann was earned through construction contracts on the dock rather than by cash payments. Proceeds from the sale of bonds provided funds to pay for land and materials. Capital stock worth $1,000,000 and 5-per-cent First Mortgage Twenty Year Sinking Fund Gold Bonds in the amount of $1,750,000 were issued.[63]

It soon became clear that the interests of Mackenzie and Mann and the Pittsburgh Coal Company were not entirely harmonious, largely because the coal company wanted to sell to any interested coal purchasers, while the Canadian Northern Railway demanded preferential treatment at the dock in which Mackenzie and Mann held a 50-per-cent interest.[64] As a result, the coal company eventually agreed to sell its entire interest in the dock company to Mackenzie, Mann and Co. Ltd. in return for a fixed contract. Mackenzie, Mann and Co. Ltd. kept the stock of the dock company but sold its bonds to the Canadian Northern Railway. Payment was again in the form of Canadian Northern 4-per-cent Perpetual Consolidated Debenture Stock. Mackenzie

63 *Ibid.*, MCLVIII, Canadian Northern Coal and Ore Dock Company Limited, Agreement with Mackenzie, Mann and Co. Ltd., and the Pittsburgh Coal Co., 1 March 1915; *Arbitration*, 2570–3; *Synoptical Histories*, 179–80.

64 PAC, CNR Records, MCLVIII, 110–17, Canadian Northern Coal and Ore Dock Company Ltd., Eighth Annual Report for the year ended 30 April 1913.

and Mann, as owners of the dock company, leased it to the Canadian Northern Railway and finally sold it in 1920 after the railway was nationalized.[65]

Mackenzie and Mann hoped the dock would eventually handle not only coal but also a large volume of iron ore from the Mesabi iron range. It was for this reason that they retained control of the capital stock, since there were some doubts whether the railway company had powers to become directly involved in the ore trade and in mining ventures. In fact, the iron ore shipments through Port Arthur were never large, and the Canadian Northern Coal and Ore Dock became most valuable to the Canadian Northern Railway because of its coal business. It provided the railway with coal for its locomotives and valuable westward traffic to balance the flow of the eastbound grain trade.

Coal transported from the Pennsylvania fields was, nevertheless, expensive because of the long distance and the high freight costs. It was only natural for western railways to seek reliable coal fields closer to their main tracks in the West. Mackenzie and Mann became involved in three major and a considerable number of smaller coal developments in western Canada. They developed coal fields at Drumheller, Alberta, and on the eastern slope of the Rockies at Nordegg, Alberta, and they became heavily involved in the coal interests of the Dunsmuir family on Vancouver Island.

The Canadian Northern Railway, as distinct from Mackenzie, Mann and Co. Ltd., did not become directly involved in the ownership of the mining ventures on Vancouver Island or at Drumheller. Those mines were owned outright by Mackenzie and Mann, or by syndicates in which they held interests. The Canadian Northern purchased the coal it needed from these companies, and it also held transportation contracts. The Goose Lake line from Saskatoon to Calgary served the Drumheller mines, although the Drumheller coal turned out to be of a rather soft variety which produced sparks easily and was therefore unsuitable for extensive use on Canadian Northern locomotives.[66] When the railway did use it, there were frequent complaints about

65 *Arbitration*, 2570–88; PAC, CNR Records, MCLX, Canadian Northern Coal and Ore Dock Company Ltd., Rental Agreement with the Canadian Northern Railway Company Ltd.; *Synoptical Histories*, 180.
66 *Arbitration*, 730–41.

fires started by Canadian Northern locomotives. The coal was more useful in providing fuel for prairie settlers, and the lines to Drumheller carried most of this coal to prairie markets.

Coal from the Vancouver Island mines was suitable for and extensively used by Canadian Northern locomotives after the line was completed to the Pacific. Mackenzie, Mann and Co. Ltd. purchased control of the extensive coal-mining interests of the Dunsmuir family in 1910. Thereafter, the coal company and the railway company worked closely together but were technically independent of each other.

One coal-mining venture, however, led to the direct involvement of the Canadian Northern Railway: the development at Nordegg, Alberta. Coal deposits on the Brazeau and Big Horn rivers were discovered by Martin Nordegg, a German financier-promoter. Nordegg became convinced that the new fields held great potential but that rail facilities were needed to develop them. Nordegg initially tried to interest the Canadian Pacific or the Grand Trunk Pacific, but to no avail. As a last resort he approached Mackenzie and Mann. Their reputation for driving hard bargains and negotiating in unethical ways intimidated him. One of his friends warned, "Who sups with the devil must have a long spoon. But, of course, the coal must be sold." Nordegg's account of the ensuing negotiations is one of the few documented cases of the business methods which earned the Canadian Northern promoters their dubious reputation.

Nordegg made his first appointment with considerable trepidation. He began his appeal by discussing the prospects of his mines and the needs for markets and a railway. To his surprise Mackenzie expressed immediate interest and showed no apparent concern about the estimated $6,000,000 cost of the railway. He immediately indicated a willingness to purchase far more coal than Nordegg had expected. This immediate indication of interest in the coal, and indeed determination to get it, contrasted sharply with the bargaining techniques of the other railways which had professed lack of interest in the hope of driving the price down.

Mackenzie and Mann already had some private coal interests in the area and some plans to build the projected railway. In the negotiations with Nordegg, Mackenzie suggested an amalgamation of his coal interests with those of Nordegg's German Development Company, with each partner taking half the shares of the amalgamated company. The Canadian Northern would build the necessary railway, entering into a firm traffic agreement with the coal company.

Having discussed the general terms of the arrangement and how much each partner should contribute to the partnership, Mackenzie turned the matter over to his attorney, Z. A. Lash, who in turn assigned it to his assistant, F. H. Phippen. Phippen wrote out the terms of the proposed agreement, but when it was brought to Mackenzie he rejected it. The reason, Nordegg felt, was an attempt to force additional concessions. When Mackenzie was finally satisfied, the matter was referred to Mann, who found further fault with the arrangement and demanded further concessions. This was the kind of hard bargaining for which Mackenzie and Mann were notorious. Nordegg, by his own account, "stood by my guns as long as I could". Then he took refuge in the fact that he must refer the arrangement to his company's officials in Berlin before it could be ratified. An invitation was extended to Mackenzie to visit the president of the German company in Berlin. Mackenzie, who was about to sail to London to raise further funds, accepted.

In Berlin, with the aid of elaborate wining and dining and smooth old-world diplomacy, the Germans obtained numerous concessions from Mackenzie on important matters on which Mackenzie and Nordegg had been unable to come to an agreement. Nordegg's summary of Mackenzie and Mann's bargaining technique is enlightening.

I had many dealings with Mackenzie in the following years, and found that he invariably made a harsh deal or at least attempted it. It was his habit. But having agreed to something, he never broke his word. When he wanted to go back on his word he used his partner Mann—and appeared to stand against him, till he finally appealed to my kindness in asking me if I wanted to break his partnership with Mann. This I could not do, of course, and thus Mann was victorious.

Others who dealt with Mann found that Mackenzie served a similar function for arrangements made by Mann. Yet the nature of the partnership between the two men was such that the threat of a break-up did not appear altogether incongruous. The technique was particularly effective in dealing with politicians. The two men belonged to different political parties; each had his own political connections and friends, and used the obstinacy of his partner as an excuse when commitments were not met.

In the agreement with Nordegg there were also objections from Lash to be overcome. Again these seemed designed to improve on an agreement that Nordegg thought was already completed. Men like Nordegg were accustomed to a different kind of bargaining, and those who fell victim to Mackenzie and Mann often became very bitter. Those who understood and effectively withstood these techniques frequently found it advantageous to deal with the Canadian Northern promoters.[67]

The agreement with Nordegg for the development of the Brazeau mines proved advantageous to both companies. These mines produced a good steam coal. The required Canadian Northern line to the mine was completed in 1914 under the charter of the Canadian Northern Western Railway. Ownership of the railway was vested entirely in Mackenzie, Mann and Co. Ltd. until 1914, when the stock was transferred to the Canadian Northern Railway. The mines were owned by the syndicate in which Nordegg's German Development Company and Mackenzie, Mann and Co. Ltd., each held a 50-per-cent interest. Later, 10 per cent of the stock of the mining company was given to the London underwriters in payment for their services. Mackenzie, Mann and Co. Ltd. also found it necessary to pledge their stock as security for loans from the Canadian Bank of Commerce. During the war years and at the height of anti-German sentiment, the underwriters, Lazard Brothers, and the Bank combined to oust Nordegg from the company. Until that time, however, both the mines and the railway proved successful. In 1914, 155,322 tons of coal were taken from the Nordegg mines, and the following year the total reached 261,156 tons. All of this coal was used by Canadian Northern locomotives or by settlers and industries alongside of Canadian Northern tracks.[68]

67 Martin Nordegg, *The Possibilities of Canada Are Truly Great: Memoirs, 1906–1924*, ed. T. D. Regehr (Toronto: Macmillan of Canada, 1971), 128–35.

68 PAC, CNR Records, MCXCI and MCXCII, Minute Book and Stock Certificate Book of the Canadian Northern Western Railway Company.

Aside from land, terminal facilities, townsites, and coal companies, several other companies, notably telegraph and express companies,[69] were organized by Mackenzie, Mann and Co. Ltd. and then sold to the Canadian Northern Railway. In addition, numerous other companies were promoted by Mackenzie and Mann and provided the railway with a large volume of traffic, although many such companies retained a separate identity.

The sale of ancillary companies left Mackenzie, Mann and Co. Ltd. with all the common stock of the Canadian Northern Railway and with much of its unguaranteed 4-per-cent Perpetual Consolidated Debenture Stock. Attempts were certainly made to sell as much of the Debenture Stock as possible, but after 1903 Mackenzie, Mann and Co. Ltd. always had a great deal of it on hand. It later undermined the stability of that firm.

It is clear that Mackenzie, Mann and Co. Ltd. tried to provide for the Canadian Northern Railway whatever was needed to develop an extensive, well-balanced railway system on the prairies. By 1909 the major contours and many of the details of that prairie system were complete. The time had come when Mackenzie and Mann found it both possible and necessary to expand their operations from regional to transcontinental dimensions.

69 *Arbitration*, 2566–7; *Synoptical Histories*, 227.

CHAPTER TEN

PROGRESS IN THE EAST 1905–1911

THE CANADIAN NORTHERN RAILWAY in 1909 was a well-conceived, efficient, and profitable prairie system. Mackenzie and Mann, however, decided that it must become a transcontinental system. They believed that the Canadian Northern Railway could withstand the competition of the Canadian Pacific Railway and the Grand Trunk–Grand Trunk Pacific–National Transcontinental systems only if it also became a transcontinental system. Mackenzie stated the case succinctly in 1908 when he told Laurier, "The principal need of the Canadian Northern . . . is westbound traffic. The company must have its own lines drawing business from the ports and manufacturing centres of Eastern Canada with which to fill its cars arriving at Port Arthur grain laden."[1] When Robert Borden became Prime Minister, Mackenzie repeated the argument.

The Company was driven by the laws of self preservation to extend its line into Eastern Canada. The origin of most westbound freight, was, and is today, mainly in the hands of two railway companies, the Canadian Pacific Railway and the Grand Trunk Railway. From the former company, possessing its own western lines, naturally little or nothing was to be obtained in the shape of westbound traffic, and, when through the Grand Trunk Pacific and the National Transcontinental, the Grand Trunk invaded the western field it was to be expected that the Canadian Northern Railway Company would be entirely deprived of all sources of westbound rail traffic and limited to that freight originating on the lake and river ports during the season of navigation.[2]

---

1 PAC, Laurier Papers, DVIII, 137237, Mackenzie to Laurier, 6 March 1908.

2 PAC, Borden Papers, File OC 153, 10454, Mackenzie to Borden, 4 Jan. 1913.

To preserve its strong position on the prairies, transcontinental connections had become a necessity for the Canadian Northern Railway.

Donald Mann did not fully share his partner's convictions and was always much less enthusiastic about rapid transcontinental expansion. The Canadian Northern was a profitable prairie system which in his view should be expanded only gradually, as the available traffic justified such expansion. He and other Canadian Northern officials readily admitted the problem. "We were in the West," Mann told the Board of Arbitration, "and we were bottled up; anything we had to send there or get from the east had to go over our rival's railway. . . . I tried many times to make a satisfactory arrangement with them, but they were not friendly and could not do it."[3] At the same time he could never rid himself of the thought, voiced openly by Hanna, that "if the Canadian Northern had remained a prairie road, doing business only between the Lakes and the Mountains, it would never have been in Queer Street, but would have more than paid its operating costs, fixed charges and betterment requirements out of revenue; because it was the West's own product to meet the West's own needs."[4] Mann, with some misgivings, eventually supported expansion. Roderick Mackenzie allegedly opposed his father's new plans consistently,[5] but was overruled by the senior partners. Since the company enjoyed a reasonably strong financial position and its debentures were selling well in London, Mackenzie seemed to have the means to realize his transcontinental ambitions.

Mackenzie and Mann were certainly not strangers to eastern railway schemes. They had gained control of and were operating, rather unsuccessfully, a system of Quebec railways. Without western connections these Quebec lines were not likely to make any profits, but they might eventually become the means whereby the Canadian Northern Railway could reach the Atlantic seaboard and gain entry to the cities of Montreal and Quebec. A second eastern project, vaguely associated with some of the Quebec colonization railway schemes, had also fallen into Mackenzie and Mann's hands. This was a proposed railway running northward from Toronto via Sudbury to James Bay, where connections with the Quebec roads were to be made. The James Bay

3 *Arbitration,* 2683–6.
4 Hanna, 237.

5 CNRHQ, Janet Gordon interview.

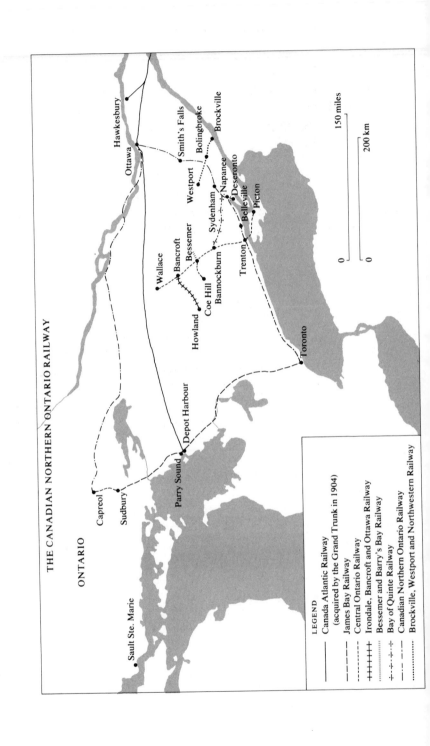

THE CANADIAN NORTHERN ONTARIO RAILWAY

ONTARIO

Sault Ste. Marie
Sudbury
Capreol
Parry Sound
Depot Harbour
Toronto
Howland
Coe Hill
Bannockburn
Wallace
Bancroft
Bessemer
Sydenham
Trenton
Belleville
Picton
Deseronto
Napanee
Westport
Bolingbroke
Smith's Falls
Brockville
Ottawa
Hawkesbury

LEGEND
——— Canada Atlantic Railway
        (acquired by the Grand Trunk in 1904)
– – – James Bay Railway
········· Central Ontario Railway
++++++ Irondale, Bancroft and Barry's Bay Railway
⋮⋮⋮⋮⋮ Bessemer and Barry's Bay Railway
÷–÷–÷ Bay of Quinte Railway
–··–··– Canadian Northern Ontario Railway
·········· Brockville, Westport and Northwestern Railway

0   150 miles
0   200 km

Railway, incorporated in 1895 by William Mackenzie, Donald Mann, and others, was sufficiently promising that its promoters had to contend with a rival group that wanted to build a parallel line from Toronto to North Bay and James Bay. The Nipissing and James Bay Railway was incorporated for this purpose, but the Mackenzie and Mann interests managed to gain control of it, and then allowed its charter to lapse.[6]

Mackenzie and Mann had first worked out tentative plans for a transcontinental railway system in 1903 and 1904. Theirs was to be an alternative to the Grand Trunk proposals and included the acquisition of the Canada Atlantic Railway, which was to be linked with Mackenzie's Toronto Street Railway by means of the James Bay Railway.[7] Failure to gain federal support for these plans in 1904 led to delays and an appeal to the provincial government for help in building the important mileage from Toronto to Sudbury. Premier Ross was sympathetic and agreed to grant a $20,000-per-mile bond guarantee for the first 268 miles of the James Bay Railway. This assistance, together with some smaller subsidies, enabled Mackenzie and Mann to complete 271.38 miles between Rosedale near Toronto and Capreol near Sudbury, and short spur lines to Key Harbour on Georgian Bay and to Parry Sound, where a connection with the Canada Atlantic Railway was effected. The line was officially opened on 2 July 1908, although much of it had been operated sporadically for several months before the official opening.[8]

The James Bay Railway gave the Canadian Northern Railway a combined rail and Great Lakes steamship route, and thus a somewhat tenuous connection with Toronto. The promoters' ambition, however, was to build an all-rail transcontinental system. To do so they needed a great deal of help from the federal government. In preparation for a major assault on the federal treasury in 1906, Mackenzie and Mann reorganized and expanded their eastern undertakings. In 1905 the

6 PAC, CNR Legal Series, Files 1056–20 and 1056–18–20.
7 PAC, Laurier Papers, DVIII, 137228–31, Andrew Thompson to Laurier, Confidential Memorandum, unofficial and for discussion only, 2 June 1904. The date assigned this memorandum by the Public Archives of Canada is 2 June 1908. It is clear from internal evidence that the correct date is 1904. For example, the writer discusses work which could be completed before the end of 1905, as well as the anticipated Canadian Northern acquisition of the Canada Atlantic Railway.
8 PAC, CNR Legal Series, File 25–20.

charter rights of the James Bay Railway were greatly enlarged when the company received authorization to build not only from Toronto northward but also from Toronto northeastward to Ottawa, and from Port Arthur to Montreal. The following year the name of the James Bay Railway was changed to one more indicative of its intended role—the Canadian Northern Ontario Railway.[9]

At the same time the anaemic Quebec lines were reorganized and revitalized. Three railways—the Great Northern Railway of Canada, the Chateauguay and Northern Railway, and the Quebec, New Brunswick and Nova Scotia Railway—were amalgamated to become the Canadian Northern Quebec Railway. Mackenzie and Mann thus completed the necessary charter arrangements for the nation's third transcontinental railway system.

Charters were relatively easy to get. Raising the required subsidies, guarantees, or loans to advance the railway beyond its paper stage was much more difficult, but the promoters began the task with enthusiasm. They followed up the eastern reorganizations with long and carefully worked-out proposals whereby the federal government should provide bond guarantees of up to $30,000 per mile to complete the necessary construction. "The Company," Mann wrote the Prime Minister, "is in the position of having three independent and disconnected railways in operation." This situation, he claimed, left the company without the means "of adequately performing its work as a great national highway in that it has not the means of forwarding and interchanging traffic between its different systems".[10] Federal guarantees were needed to loose the purse strings in London and to facilitate the desired construction.

The federal government was understandably cautious about guaranteeing bonds for a third transcontinental railway, particularly for the section north of Lake Superior. There was hardly enough transcontinental traffic for one good line. Certainly the volume of traffic had to increase very substantially before three lines could be justified. The federal government was willing to support Mackenzie and Mann's prairie lines, but there was still an unwillingness on the part of the

9 Canada, *4–5 Edw.* VII. *Cap. 110*; Canada, *P.C. 1193*, 25 June 1906.

10 PAC, Laurier Papers, CDXV, 110803–10, Mann to Laurier, 1 June 1906.

Laurier government to recognize that federal policies had made an independent eastern connection for Mackenzie and Mann a necessity. Consequently no federal action was taken in 1906. The long and expensive transcontinental link between Port Arthur and Montreal remained little more than a paper scheme for another five years.

Plans to expand and consolidate in southern Ontario with the help of provincial subsidies and guarantees also met with delay. The Liberal government of Premier Ross, which had granted generous guarantees for the first section of the James Bay Railway, was defeated in 1905. In its place a Conservative administration, led by J. P. Whitney and pledged to ending all railway subsidies and guarantees, took office. The prevailing Conservative attitude was clearly expressed by one of the new Premier's correspondents who wrote,

On every hand and upon every side the people are being bled to death by all these corporations. Millionaires are being made wonderfully fast in Canada lately by allowing them to get their hands into the public purse. . . . Mr. Mackenzie a few years ago, and his brother, were in the bush getting ties for my old friend the late engineer T. C. Bailey who built our early railways, and see what the public purse has done for the Mackenzies. The public purse should not be milked dry by a few sharpers while the masses of the people have to struggle for a bare existence.[11]

The Premier himself was equally explicit. "There can be no point in the policy initiated by us several years ago about which there can be less room for misunderstanding than that relating to the bonusing of Railways. Our declaration was and our practice is that there shall be no more grants of lands or money given to Railways."[12]

Adding further to the railway promoter's problems was the fact that the Whitney government was threatening to intervene and possibly take over privately owned hydro-electric developments in the province. Mackenzie was the president and major shareholder of the Toronto Street Railway and also had very considerable influence in the Toronto Power Company, its affiliates and subsidiaries, and the Electrical Development Company. Control or influence in these generation, trans-

11 PAO, Whitney Papers, Robert Griffith to J. P. Whitney, 18 Jan. 1906.

12 *Ibid.*, Whitney to Sir William Meredith, 5 Feb. 1906.

mission, and user companies gave Mackenzie and his associates a virtual monopoly in the Toronto area.[13] Only the Ontario Power Company, largely controlled by American interests, offered any effective competition.

Mackenzie and his associates were accused of using their strong position in the hydro-electric industry to discriminate against rival users, particularly those in the municipalities outside Toronto's city limits. Adam Beck, representing the London, Ontario, constituency, and appointed chairman of the Ontario Hydro-Electric Power Commission established by the Whitney government, led a strong movement which demanded government ownership of the generating and distributing facilities to overcome this difficulty.[14]

The private interests naturally opposed this. They wanted no government involvement in their industry. Several entrepreneurs, particularly those in the Electrical Development Company, which had just undertaken a major expansion program and was in a very vulnerable position,[15] were determined to fight the government proposals in every possible way—even if this led to the collapse of their own company, the discrediting of Canadian securities in the international money markets, and a further bitter electoral campaign. To these men the issue was "State Socialism and the interference by Municipal and Government bodies in trade and against Capital".[16]

In this situation William Mackenzie and Premier Whitney worked out a rather tentative compromise solution.[17] Mackenzie approached the problem somewhat differently than did most of his business asso-

13 H. V. Nelles, "The Politics of Development: Forests, Mines and Hydro-Electric Power in Ontario, 1890–1939" (PHD thesis, University of Toronto, 1969); Carl A. S. Hall, "Electrical Utilities in Ontario Under Private Ownership, 1890–1914" (PHD thesis, University of Toronto, 1968.
14 CAR, 1908, 298–309.
15 Ibid.; see also speech delivered by the Hon. J. P. Whitney in the Ontario Legslature, 10 March 1908, in reply to a motion by the Hon. A. G. MacKay; copy in Whitney Papers.
16 Nelles, "The Politics of Development", 441; see also PAO, Whitney

Papers, Arthur Grenfell to Whitney, 10 Aug. 1907.
17 The details of the dispute between the government and the Electrical Development Company, which at times became extremely bitter, have been given in other works. Before Mackenzie presented his plan, the government had demanded, and the Electrical Development Company had refused to provide, information about the company's operations. PAO, Whitney Papers, Frederic Nicholls to Gordon Sproule, Secretary, Hydro-Electric Power Commission, 7 March 1906.

ciates. He certainly believed in free enterprise and was as convinced as Prime Minister Laurier that governments could not operate large business ventures in an efficient manner. Unlike many of his contemporaries, however, Mackenzie did agree that if governments had a duty to assist important private enterprises they also had a right to regulate those businesses. Rate controls on both the hydro-electric and steam railway projects were acceptable to him. These controls, of course, should never be exercised in a manner likely to force private companies into unprofitable operations. Controls were acceptable, however, if they merely prevented windfall profits and other unreasonable gains. The businessman must be rewarded, and rewarded handsomely, for his endeavours and for the risks he undertook, but the government must prevent him from holding the public up for ransom.

It was consistent with this business philosophy for Mackenzie to agree that he would consolidate his holdings in the Toronto Street Railway, the Toronto Power Company, and the Electrical Development Company by buying out his more intransigent partners. He would then negotiate a new contract with the provincial government to supply the needy municipalities with power at rates to be approved by the government. Such an agreement would prevent the government from active participation in the hydro-electric industry, but would give it the necessary regulatory control to ensure reasonable and non-discriminatory rates.[18]

Premier Whitney responded enthusiastically. "As far as can be seen I think Mackenzie's getting control of the Electrical Development Company is a fine thing for us. . . . I have reason to expect and believe that he will be prepared to furnish us power at a lower rate even than our Power Commission has expected."[19]

Unfortunately the Memorandum of Understanding that Mackenzie sent to Premier Whitney, and on the basis of which he reorganized the Toronto hydro-electric interests, was not immediately translated into a binding agreement. This soon led to disagreements and misunderstandings which destroyed the amicable relations between the two men.

18 PAO, Whitney Papers, memorandum entitled "Mackenzie Plan" in Undated Memoranda.

19 PAO, Whitney Papers, Whitney to E. C. Whitney, 28 Feb. 1908; see also *ibid.*, 7 Feb. 1908.

Initial delays in signing a new contract were apparently due to unfavourable public opinion. Early in March 1908 the Premier wrote cautiously, "There will, of course, be a great outcry against it [the proposed agreement with the Electrical Development Company] and we will be accused of giving in to him [Mackenzie]. *The World* and *The Telegram* will no doubt take that line, as nothing will satisfy them but government ownership and management."[20] Mackenzie and Whitney therefore agreed that "the matter be allowed to stand until a more seasonable time,"[21] presumably until after the next provincial election. Both evidently thought the passage of time would take some of the wind out of Adam Beck's sails and thus make negotiations easier. In fact the opposite happened. The clamour for public ownership increased, and in August the Premier found it too strong to resist. Without any intimation to Mackenzie, the government let contracts for the construction of a publicly owned power transmission line which would compete with the Electrical Development Company.

This William Mackenzie had not expected. Indignantly he wrote the Premier.

The announcement that it is the intention of the government to proceed immediately with the construction of transmission lines for Niagara electric power came to me yesterday as a complete surprise. You will remember before leaving for England I had placed in your hands a memorandum as to a plan along the lines of which I thought the much vexed power question could be worked out with credit to your government and at the same time preserve the capital now invested in the industry. I assumed responsibility in connection with the Company's affairs mainly through my belief that you and I could satisfactorily adjust matters. You will remember I took several members of your government into my confidence and made no move without consulting them. I stated frankly that I was prepared to shape my policy according to your wishes, and, in the memorandum which was submitted to you, offered to leave to your Government the absolute control of the rates.[22]

The plan Mackenzie had submitted to the Premier was vague and

---

20 *Ibid.*, 18 March 1908.
21 *Ibid.*, Mackenzie to Whitney,

7 Aug. 1908.
22 *Ibid.*

without any legal standing. The ambiguity of the understanding between the two men allowed the Premier to change his policy radically when public opinion made such a change necessary. The very ambiguity of the arrangement, according to one critic, "soothed the private interests for the moment and at the same time allowed the public ownership supporters to think that the contracts would be let as matter of course."[23] In August it had become clear that the public would not be satisfied with the compromise solution of government control over rates charged by private companies.

The decision of the government to build its own transmission facilities ended the brief rapproachement between it and promoters like William Mackenzie. A year later the Premier acknowledged the rift when he wrote to Scott Griffin, an associate of Mackenzie and Mann, "The entire brigade which is attacking us both here and in England is composed of men connected—some of them closely—with the McKenzie [sic] & Mann enterprises. . . . We shall now meet these attacks in our own good time and in our own way, with—well with a full understanding where they come from, what they mean, and how they can be best met."[24]

The Premier could not immediately rescind the valuable Toronto and Niagara Falls franchises and long-term contracts held by Mackenzie unless he was prepared to launch expensive expropriation proceedings. At the same time, Mackenzie was well aware of the fact that he could not expect favourable consideration when those franchises had to be renewed. He therefore decided simply to squeeze whatever he could out of the Toronto enterprises before the inevitable government takeover. Few improvements or expansions were made and the entire arrangement led to incessant wrangling and controversy in which the citizens of Toronto became the victims of frequently inadequate services. Nevertheless, the Toronto enterprises were profitable until they were taken over by the government, despite initial losses by the Electrical Development Company which were carried by the stronger Toronto Power Company.[25]

Mackenzie's policy of seeking government support in return for

23 Nelles, "The Politics of Development", 458.
24 PAO, Whitney Papers, Whitney to Griffin, 12 July 1909.
25 Hall, "Electrical Utilities in Ontario".

specific services at government-controlled rates failed in Toronto. There was, however, a positive achievement as well. During the rather brief period when Mackenzie and Whitney were working on their compromise hydro-electric plan, Mackenzie arranged substantial provincial bond guarantees and land subsidies for his proposed Ontario steam railways.

The first request for such assistance was made almost immediately after the 1905 election. Premier Whitney, with his election campaign fresh in mind, could hardly do anything but turn down the request. One of his supporters promptly assured him, "You did well to turn down Mann & Mackenzie. That will do you a world of good in the country."[26]

The Premier became much more sympathetic a year later, after Mackenzie had indicated a willingness to be more co-operative in matters relating to the Toronto Street Railway.[27] He was personally willing to grant aid to the James Bay Railway in 1906, but the Conservative caucus rejected Mackenzie's request of that year. The Premier then wrote, rather regretfully, "We found it impossible to break through our declared policy with regard to aid to railways in order to grant the application of the James Bay people. I rather think it was not expected that we would and therefore, perhaps there was not too much disappointment."[28]

Whatever disappointments the James Bay Railway promoters suffered in 1906 were dissipated two years later when provincial assistance was voted for the Canadian Northern Ontario Railway, the successor of the James Bay Railway. During the 1908 legislative session the Ontario government agreed to a provincial guarantee on a $1,615,068 issue of 3.5-per-cent debenture stock. This aid was to assist the railway in building four smaller branch lines from its Toronto-to-Sudbury line, totalling not more than fifty miles, and to acquire various terminal and other properties in Toronto. The Premier justified this obvious departure from his campaign promises by pointing out that the government was legally responsible for the bonds already

26 PAO, Whitney Papers, James Leitch to Whitney, 20 May 1905.

27 *Ibid.*, Whitney to Scott Griffin,

16 Feb. 1906.

28 *Ibid.*, Whitney to Scott Griffin, 12 June 1906.

guaranteed by the Ross government. Those bonds might be in danger if the railway was unable to complete its terminals and traffic-producing branch lines and thus ensure profitable operations. Therefore, Whitney explained, with surprising ingenuity, "it was not a case of granting an application of a Railway for a bonus or for a guarantee, it was the case of two interested parties coming together and making mutual arrangements by which the one received increased security and in order to get it increased its responsibility to a certain extent." Precisely the same thing could, of course, be said of almost every other railway bond guarantee, including those denounced by Whitney in his 1905 campaign, but logic is rarely in abundant supply when political friends transact mutually advantageous business. In this case, however, the legislators seemed prepared to accept Whitney's assurances that "the whole thing is perfectly clear, and perfectly unobjectionable."[29]

The following year the Whitney government offered the Canadian Northern Ontario Railway a land subsidy of 4,000 acres per mile for 500 miles of track across northern Ontario between Port Arthur and Sudbury. Whitney defended this departure from his party's declared policy by stating, "It is our duty to develop the northern territory for both agricultural and mineral purposes, and the land is worthless without a railway, and is it not much better to give 2,000,000 acres subject to the above conditions than to spend $25,000,000 building the road ourselves?"[30] One can only conclude from these statements that the arguments advanced by Mackenzie and Mann for government aid and regulation, but not operation of public franchises, which appealed to most other successful Canadian political leaders of the day, also held a strong appeal for Premier Whitney. He was, however, saddled with a more "progressive" or radical following which forced him to repudiate one "understanding" with Mackenzie and to resort to devious verbal and intellectual convolutions to justify his railway aid policies.

The 1908 bond guarantee was used by Mackenzie and Mann for its intended purpose, but the 2,000,000-acre land grant did not provide sufficient assistance to justify immediate construction of the line from Port Arthur to Montreal. Attempts to obtain federal guarantees for

29 PAO, Whitney Papers, Whitney to Burnham, 21 April 1908.

30 Ibid., Whitney to E. C. Whitney, 19 March 1909.

this line in 1909 failed, as did all attempts by Mackenzie and Mann to obtain government bonuses or guarantees for a third Canadian Northern Ontario line—a line from Toronto to Ottawa. Relations between the promoters and the provincial politicians deteriorated rapidly in 1909, and federal aid for a third line along Canada's historic St. Lawrence trade route was not available. The line was nevertheless of great strategic importance to Mackenzie and Mann. Consequently, in 1909, they decided to begin construction without direct government assistance—one of only very few lines they began that way.

Both the CPR and the Grand Trunk already had direct connections between Toronto and Montreal. In addition, the route was strewn with a considerable number of local and independent lines. Many of these had already found it necessary to make arrangements with or sell out to the two larger companies before 1909, but a number were still struggling under independent management. These small independent lines were available, and Mackenzie and Mann decided to acquire any that might provide either branch-line facilities or at least some main-line mileage for their proposed line from Toronto to Ottawa. They would then simply build the needed connecting sections, much as they had done in the case of the Halifax and South Western Railway.

The basic financial arrangement for the acquisition or construction of the mileage from Toronto to Ottawa was made on 25 June 1909.[31] On that day the directors of the Canadian Northern Ontario Railway authorized the issuing of up to $30,000 per mile of unguaranteed perpetual consolidated debenture stock. This stock was to be used in very much the same way as the parent Canadian Northern's perpetual consolidated debenture stock. It would be a second charge on mileage against which guaranteed bonds had been issued and a first charge on mileage against which no guaranteed bonds were outstanding. It could be used either to purchase smaller independent local Ontario lines, or to finance construction of new mileage. Immediately £800,000 was issued and further issues were brought out as construction or acquisition proceeded. Normally, Mackenzie, Mann and Co. Ltd. bought the local lines or built the new mileage and then received Canadian Northern Ontario Railway shares or debenture stock in exchange for the

31 PAC, CNR Records, MCCLIX, Meeting of Shareholders and Directors of the Canadian Northern Ontario Railway, 25 June 1909.

acquired securities or as payment for their services.[32] Since Mackenzie, Mann and Co. Ltd. soon had considerably more perpetual consolidated debenture stock than they could dispose of in London, the
formal exchange of many of the securities of the acquired lines was
delayed until 1914 when the affairs of the various Mackenzie and
Mann railway enterprises were reorganized and consolidated.

Despite the arrangements made by the Canadian Northern Ontario
Railway directors in 1909 there was still considerable difference of
opinion among them regarding financial arrangements for the line
from Toronto to Ottawa. Mackenzie favoured the setting up of a new
and separate company.[33] He was trying to keep the market clear of
other issues directly identified with the Canadian Northern Railway
in preparation for the time when very large new issues would have to
be brought out to finance mileage from Port Arthur to Montreal and
from Edmonton to Vancouver.[34] Horne-Payne, on the other hand,
believed the securities could be more easily placed if they were clearly
identified with the Canadian Northern Railway, which enjoyed an
excellent standing in the London money markets at the time. Horne-
Payne's advice was consistent with the general policy of the Canadian
Northern Railway whereby the stronger parts of the system became
committed to the success of the weaker projects.[35] Mackenzie's in-
clinations in regard to the Toronto-Ottawa mileage did lead to the
incorporation of a separate company, the Ontario and Ottawa Railway,
but in the end Horne-Payne's advice was accepted and the line was
financed through the Canadian Northern Ontario Railway's perpetual
consolidated debenture stock.

The first local railway acquired by Mackenzie and Mann between
Ottawa and Toronto was the Central Ontario Railway. That railway,
originally incorporated as the Prince Edward County Railway, had

32 The first such transactions are
documented in the minutes of a meeting of the directors of the Canadian
Northern Ontario Railway on 16 Feb.
and 25 Aug. 1910, and are followed
by numerous similar references in the
minutes of meetings of later dates;
PAC, CNR Records, MCCLIX.
33 PAC, CNR Legal Series, File 1156–
27–20.

34 UTA, Walker Papers, H. V. F. Jones
to Walker, 7 March 1910.
35 For a lengthy discussion of the
advantages of directly identifying all
Mackenzie and Mann's railway properties with the Canadian Northern, see
series of memos and letters by
Horne-Payne and Lash in PAC, CNR
Records, I̅X̅CLXXIV, Legal Series
1014–20–3.

built a line from Picton to Trenton and from there northerly to Bancroft and finally as far as Wallace, Ontario. It financed its construction through a $20,000-per-mile 6-per-cent bond issue. This bond issue had a par value of $2,200,000 and matured in 1902, although in view of the railway's unsatisfactory operating record the market value of the bonds had depreciated sharply. Shortly before the bonds matured one of the railway's directors, T. G. Blackstock, began buying up the outstanding bonds. The directors later argued that Blackstock had been asked to do so as a trustee of the railway. Most of the bonds were brought in at very considerable discounts, but instead of turning them over to the railway at the price he had paid, Blackstock claimed he had been acting in a private capacity and demanded payment from the railway at a considerably higher price. Since the railway had not advanced any funds to Blackstock, he seemed to have a good case. The railway, however, immediately began a protracted legal battle to compel Blackstock to give up the bonds at the price he had actually paid, plus accrued interest. No settlement was reached, and when the bonds matured in 1902, the railway, being unwilling and probably unable to meet Blackstock's demands, went into receivership. George Collins was appointed receiver and general manager, but both rival factions sought to retain an influence in the affairs and policies of the troubled road. The manager complained bitterly that for several years the railway was the pawn of the two opposing groups, one representing Blackstock, the major bondholder, and the other the Ritchies of Akron, Ohio, who were the railway's major shareholders and contested Blackstock's title to the bonds. The affairs of the railway suffered accordingly, and by 1906 it was obvious to both sides that the dispute must be ended if anything was to be salvaged.

It was at this stage that Mackenzie, Mann and Co. Ltd. became involved. On 29 January 1906, despite warnings from the receiver and manager, they bought out all of Blackstock's claims and interests in the Central Ontario Railway. Negotiations were then begun with Collins and the Ritchies to resolve the long-standing and very expensive legal dispute. A rather complicated financial arrangement resulted. Mackenzie and Mann surrendered their claims to the bonds they had acquired from Blackstock. The capital stock of the railway was increased from $750,000 to $1,336,000 of preferred stock and $2,004,000 of common stock and was given to the bondholders as payment for their interest coupons on the defaulted bonds. The bonds themselves were replaced by a new $1,200,000 issue of 5-per-cent 20-year bonds. These new bonds were taken, in their entirety, by the Ritchies, who transferred all their shares, including those newly issued under the arrangement, to the Trusts & Guarantee Company Limited, in trust for Mackenzie, Mann and Co. Ltd. The net result of the transaction was that the Ritchies got $1,200,000 worth of secure 5-per-cent bonds, while Mackenzie, Mann and Co. Ltd. obtained the railway's capital stock and became responsible for the railway's various obligations.[36]

Ritchie and the other directors and former owners of the Central Ontario Railway were allowed to retain qualifying shares, and continued in their positions as directors and chief officers of the railway until 1914, when the railway formally became a part of the Canadian Northern Railway System. Control of the entire capital stock of the railway, however, passed into the hands of Mackenzie and Mann in 1906. They were happy to keep secret the fact that they owned the railway, apparently because wages on the moribund backwoods Ontario railways were considerably lower than on the larger and more prosperous lines. Mackenzie and Mann did not wish to attract union

36 The Minute Book of the Central Ontario Railway contains a great deal of correspondence and documentation on the troubled financial history of that railway. PAC, CNR Records, MCXCIII; see particularly the letter from George Collins to the shareholders as read at the shareholders' meeting on 16 May 1906 and inserted between pages 208 and 209; see also meeting of the directors on 20 Jan. 1907 and annual meeting of the shareholders on 20 May 1908, and MCXCVI, Preferred Stock Certificate Book of the Central Ontario Railway. It is clear from the Stock Certificate Books that the newly issued stock was initially transferred to the Trusts and Guarantee Co. Ltd. Transfer forms 78 to 86, moreover, were left blank, apparently pending final arrangements for the transfer of the stock in 1908 to Mackenzie, Mann and Co. Ltd. It was a fairly common practice for Mackenzie and Mann to leave transfer forms blank, sometimes for years, while they decided on the final disposition of the stock they had acquired. This practice often makes the Stock Certificate Books rather misleading. In this case the names of Mackenzie and Mann do not appear at any time in the Stock Certificate Book, although other sources make it perfectly clear that in fact they had gained control of the railway, negotiations beginning in 1906 and the final settlement being made on 5 April 1909.

TABLE IX
Operating Statistics of the Central Ontario Railway

Year	Mileage operated	Gross earnings	Operating costs	Net earnings	Net corporate profit or loss
		($)	($)	($)	($)
1904	135	225,347.17	133,796.29	91,550.88	
1905	135	207,809.35	141,485.92	66,323.43	
1906	135	242,692.93	140,510.76	102,182.17	
1907	151	283,048.25	144,510.76	138,690.27	138,690.27
1908	155	269,422.06	153,927.53	115,494.53	115,494.53
1909	166	267,437.60	145,831.36	121,606.24	97,161.80
1910	166	306,796.80	168,854.65	137,942.15	79,161.80
1911	166	314,105.85	170,521.29	143,584.56	77,939.68
1912	166	321,368.87	193,418.97	127,949.90	55,176.40
1913	166	375,048.23	243,024.59	132,023.64	70,212.09
1914	166	347,759.99	346,259.65	1,500.32	− 100,332.11

Source: The Public Archives of Canada, R.G. 46. The interest on the company's bonds was paid by Mackenzie, Mann and Co. Ltd. until 1914. Equipment rentals account for the main difference between net earnings and net corporate profit or loss.

organizers to these roads by announcing that they were now a part of a larger and more profitable system.[37]

A second Ontario line acquired by Mackenzie and Mann was the Irondale, Bancroft and Ottawa Railway in southeastern Ontario. This railway, originally incorporated as the Toronto and Nipissing Eastern Extensions Railway, was authorized to build from a point on the Toronto and Nipissing Eastern Railway's line through Victoria, Peterborough, and Hastings counties to the Ottawa River. In the 1880s and 1890s it built about forty-five miles of track in the area north of Peterborough and Belleville.[38] It ran into serious financial difficulties in the 1890s and received substantial advances from its solicitor, Z. A. Lash. These advances were initially made in order that the railway might earn its subsidy from the federal government.[39] The subsidy, however, proved inadequate to meet the railway's obligations, and in 1894 the finances of the company were reorganized. The

37 Arbitration, 796.
38 Synoptical Histories, 498; C.N.R. Tabulated History of Railway Mileage,

1836–1925, 25.
39 PAC, Laurier Papers, XXX, 9969, Z. A. Lash to Laurier, 22 Dec. 1896.

authorized capitalization was increased from $100,000 to $2,500,000, but only 535 shares valued at $100 each were issued. Four hundred and eighty-five of these came into the possession of the railway's president and chief promoter, C. J. Pusey.[40] Pusey died in 1899 and his shares were taken over by his and the railway's chief creditors, Z. A. Lash and J. H. Plummer. These men already held $450,000 of virtually unsalable first-mortgage bonds and various other short-term notes of the railway with a face value of $374,324.68.[41] A few years later Lash acquired Plummer's interest, thus becoming virtually the sole owner and creditor of the railway.

Lash retained personal control of the moribund line until 1909, when he sold his interests to Mackenzie, Mann and Co. Ltd. At the time Mackenzie still thought in terms of a separate company to build or control the Toronto-Ottawa lines, of which the Irondale, Bancroft and Ottawa Railway was to be a part. The Ontario and Ottawa Railway was incorporated for this purpose and Mackenzie and Mann sold the Irondale, Bancroft and Ottawa Railway to the new road.[42] Subsequently it was decided that all the Toronto-Ottawa mileage should be financed as part of the Canadian Northern Ontario Railway system, and the Ontario and Ottawa Railway remained little more than the old Irondale, Bancroft and Ottawa Railway, with some powers it never exercised to acquire other lines. It was formally merged with the Canadian Northern Railway System in 1914.

Mackenzie and Mann also acquired the Brockville, Westport and Northwestern Railway in 1910. This railway was originally incorporated as the Brockville and Westport Railway in 1871 and had a rather chequered history. Initial plans to build in the 1870s failed to materialize, and in 1884 the company was reorganized and renamed the Brockville, Westport and Sault Ste. Marie Railway, apparently on the time-honoured principle that lack of success in a small railway venture simply indicated the need to enlarge the undertaking greatly. With a prospectus and appropriately large bond issues promising construction

40 PAC, CNR Records, MCDXIII, 91–5, Meeting of Shareholders of the Irondale, Bancroft and Ottawa Railway, 24 April 1894.
41 *Ibid.*, 173–4, 186–8, Meetings of Shareholders of the Irondale, Bancroft and Ottawa Railway, 4 and 26 Sept. 1905.
42 *Ibid.*, 199–200, Meeting of Shareholders of the Irondale, Bancroft and Ottawa Railway, 30 Aug. 1910.

TABLE X

Operating Statistics of the Irondale, Bancroft and Ottawa Railway

Year	Mileage operated	Gross earnings	Operating costs	Net earnings	Net corporate profit or loss
		($)	($)	($)	($)
1896	45	14,767.11	7,038.31	7,728.80	
1897	45	11,283.43	9,975.80	1,307.63	
1898	48	12,905.57	10,559.90	2,345.67	
1899	48	16,834.46	15,626.04	1,208.42	
1900	48	18,731.66	20,749.06	−2,017.40	
1901	48	18,917.27	19,516.17	−598.90	
1902	48	15,483.85	16,945.16	−1,461.31	
1903	48	21,464.17	22,016.27	−552.10	
1904	48	21,702.19	25,132.07	−3,429.88	
1905	48	25,803.95	25,367.95	436.00	
1906	48	32,924.05	34,897.60	−1,973.55	
1907	49	31,685.56	31,188.44	497.12	341.31
1908	49	25,177.96	28,507.44	−1,973.55	−3,329.48
1909	49	26,958.44	32,977.80	−6,019.36	−6,019.36
1910	49	27,090.53	30,402.40	−2,411.87	−3,532.50
1911	52	26,042.29	24,762.83	1,279.46	−567.22
1912	52	26,380.46	22,853.40	3,527.06	1,287.33
1913	52	30,384.76	23,967.97	6,416.79	3,479.42
1914	52	32,332.88	36,506.28	−4,173.40	−5,110.46

Source: The Public Archives of Canada, R.G. 46. No interest was paid throughout this period on the outstanding bonds of the company. All these bonds were held by people closely associated with the Canadian Northern Railway. Equipment rentals and interest on short-term loans not directly associated with operations were deducted from net earnings to arrive at the figure for net corporate profit or loss.

from Brockville to Sault Ste. Marie, the company managed to borrow enough money to build the forty miles between Brockville and Westport that the old company had promised to build, and even to add a four-and-half-mile extension to Lyn Junction on the Grand Trunk line. Operations on this short line, however, failed to produce enough revenue to meet the railway's fixed charges.

The value of Brockville, Westport and Sault Ste. Marie Railway bonds depreciated sharply when it became clear that the railway could not meet the interest due on those bonds. A New York syndicate, allegedly with an eye on the plans of the New York Central Railroad

TABLE XI

Operating Statistics of the Brockville, Westport and
Sault Ste. Marie Railway

Year	Mileage operated	Gross earnings	Operating costs	Net earnings	Net corporate profit or loss
		($)	($)	($)	($)
1896	45	28,598.71	26,815.52	1,783.19	
1897	45	28,739.84	28,086.22	653.52	
1898	45	28,198.20	28,962.57	−764.37	
1899	45	31,797.13	30,139.41	1,657.72	
1900	45	33,106.70	28,159.52	4,947.18	
1901	45	35,115.05	32,095.87	3,019.18	
1902	45	39,232.28	33,116.47	6,115.81	
1903	45	44,502.94	29,126.94	15,376.00	
1904	45	48,431.25	30,792.66	17,638.59	
1905	45	54,045.76	30,145.74	23,900.02	
1906	45	59,318.99	29,748.85	29,570.14	
1907	47	62,023.00	27,067.37	34,955.63	7,699.95
1908	47	63,537.73	30,161.38	33,376.35	6,109.86
1909	47	57,768.52	39,305.42	18,463.19	−1,320.84
1910	47	59,863.65	37,911.49	21,952.16	1,998.07
1911	47	67,503.47	37,491.16	30,012.31	10,488.03
1912	47	75,503.81	43,252.94	32,250.87	29,488.84
1913	47	76,447.27	51,149.54	25,297.73	20,073.72
1914	47	70,742.97	84,577.82	−13,834.85	−19,415.37

Source: The Public Archives of Canada, R.G. 46. This railway was purchased by the Canadian Northern interests at a High Court sale on 14 December 1911. No further interest on bonds was paid or calculated, since a separate settlement was made with the bondholders. Mackenzie and Mann simply bought out the bondholders, taking all the railway's capital stock as well.

to expand into Canada, nevertheless began to take an interest in the line. Accordingly, the Knickerbocker Trust Company of New York was instructed to buy up the depreciated bonds of the Brockville, Westport and Sault Ste. Marie Railway.[43]

In 1903, after buying up most of the outstanding bonds, the Knickerbocker Trust Company foreclosed and obtained an order from the Master of the High Court of Justice at Brockville for the forced

43 PAC, CNR Records, CCCX; the developments leading to the reorganization of the railway are recounted in detail in the company's Minute Book.

sale of the railway. It was sold for only $150,000, and all the purchasers were men closely associated with the Knickerbocker Trust Company. The new owners renamed the railway the Brockville, Westport and Northwestern Railway and reorganized its finances through a new $450,000 First Mortgage Gold Bond Issue.[44] The railway thus had the financial backing needed to carry on in a reasonably respectable manner for several years, but on 1 December 1908 it defaulted on an important interest payment on its bonds.[45] The hopes of the owners to see it become part of an international railway had been disappointed. Hopes for the future lay with the Canadian Northern Railway, and negotiations were begun whereby Mackenzie and Mann would acquire the road. In April of 1910 these led to an offer by the New Yorkers to sell the entire $450,000 bond issue and the entire $900,000 capital stock of the railway to Mackenzie and Mann for $382,500. Two months later that offer was reduced to $362,500.[46] Mackenzie and Mann apparently did not accept the offer, but did advance funds to keep the railway going, taking a lien on its capital stock.[47] In this way they gained effective control of the railway in July of 1910, but its tangled financial affairs were ultimately settled in the courts. In 1911 the Knickerbocker Trust Company, as trustee for the railway's Gold Issue Bonds, initiated legal action against the railway for its default on interest payments on the bonds. By mutual consent of the solicitors for both the trust company and the railway, controlled since July 1910 by Mackenzie and Mann, a court order for a forced sale of the railway was sought and obtained. The railway was sold on 14 December 1911 to the Canadian Northern Railway's secretary, R. P. Ormsby, who was acting on behalf of the Canadian Northern Railway. The price was $250,000.[48] The railway remained technically in Ormsby's hands until 1914, when it became one of the constituent

---

44 *Ibid.* These bonds were valued at "one thousand dollars in gold coin of the United States", hence their name. They carried a 4-per-cent rate of interest and matured in twenty years. Meetings of shareholders and directors, and copies of mortgage agreements, 23 Nov. 1903.
45 *Ibid.* The developments leading to the sale of the railway are recounted in the minutes of a meeting of the directors on 25 Jan. 1912.
46 *Synoptical Histories*, 214; PAC, CNR Records, CCCX.
47 PAC, CNR Legal Series, File 1174–20–3.
48 PAC, CNR Records, CCCX, Meeting of Directors of the Brockville, Westport and Northwestern Railway, 13 July 1910, for complete details.

TABLE XII

Operating Statistics of the Bay of Quinte Railway
(includes operations of the Marmora Railway and Mining Co.)

Year	Mileage operated	Gross earnings	Operating costs	Net earnings	Net corporate profit or loss
		($)	($)	($)	($)
1907	123	288,087.75	170,878.02	117,209.73	68,356.91
1908	123	233,822.44	160,788.15	73,034.29	27,248.22
1909	123	153,652.92	131,688.47	21,964.45	−36,679.29
1910	123	167,735.32	132,688.45	35,046.87	−27,172.11
1911	123	216,042.89	157,860.23	58,182.66	−5,025.51
1912	123	238,833.63	186,794.60	52,039.03	−10,752.63
1913	120	257,271.58	221,051.27	36,220.31	−32,630.03
1914	120	202,734.94	206,238.43	−3,863.49	−90,737.20

Source: The Public Archives of Canada, R.G. 46.

companies of the Canadian Northern Railway System.[49]

A line in the Belleville area was also acquired in 1910. The Bay of Quinte Railway had been incorporated in 1881 and was amalgamated with the Napanee, Tamworth and Quebec Railway in 1896. In 1910 it had a total of 123 miles of track in operation, all in the Bay of Quinte area. It was owned by the Rathbun Company, from whom Mackenzie and Mann purchased it on 1 July 1910 for $500,000.[50]

A fifth and even shorter Ontario line, the Marmora Railway and Mining Company, was obtained by Mackenzie and Mann in 1909 for $100,000.[51] This line was, in effect, a short branch line of the Central Ontario Railway. Mackenzie and Mann hoped the mining developments which had led to its construction woud provide some local traffic for their system.

All these companies were operated by the Canadian Northern Ontario Railway. None was consistently profitable if full allowance is made for fixed charges which were often paid directly by Mackenzie,

49 PAC, CNR Legal Series, File 1174–20–3.
50 Synoptical Histories, 9; PAC, CNR Records, CCCII, Minute Book of the Bay of Quinte Railway, 1881–97; ibid., MCXVI, Minute Book, 1897–1926; ibid., MCXVII, Common Share Certificate Book; ibid., MCXVIII, Preference Share Certificate Book; CNR Legal Series, File 1160–29.
51 PAC, CNR Records, 1312–14, Minute Books and Capital Stock Records of the Marmora Railway and Mining Company.

Mann and Co. Ltd. rather than by the company which had issued the bonds. Formal transfer of ownership of these companies from Mackenzie, Mann and Co. Ltd. to the Canadian Northern Ontario Railway and hence to the Canadian Northern Railway System was delayed until 1914.

The railways from Sudbury to Toronto and from Toronto to Ottawa were regarded as indispensable parts of any truly national and transcontinental Canadian Northern Railway system, but they were not likely to operate profitably until the vital connection north of Lake Superior was completed. In the meantime the Ontario mileage escaped bankruptcy only because Mackenzie Mann and Co. Ltd. met all interest payments due on Canadian Northern Ontario Railway bonds and on the bonds of affiliated railways whose properties were operated by the Canadian Northern Ontario Railway.

The Ontario mileage connected with Mackenzie and Mann's Quebec system at Hawkesbury. The Quebec system itself underwent major reorganizations in 1905 and 1906. In 1905 negotiations with the bondholders of the Great Northern Railway of Canada led to a successful reorganization of that technically bankrupt company. It was agreed that new bonds were to be issued and exchanged for the old ones on which the company had been unable to pay interest since 1903. The

TABLE XIII

Operating Statistics of the Canadian Northern Ontario Railway
(includes returns for affiliated companies operated by the c.n.o.r.)

Year	Mileage operated	Gross earnings	Operating costs	Net earnings	Net corporate profit or loss
		($)	($)	($)	($)
1907	151	129,770.91	141,836.10	−12,065.19	−12,065.19
1908	151	245,601.74	245,197.82	403.92	−8,279.89
1909	360	332,553.88	378,214.19	−45,660.31	−55,105.16
1910	377	510,989.72	477,224.26	33,765.46	30,589.49
1911	377	563,390.24	541,040.21	22,350.03	24,096.14
1912	542	881,953.41	851,664.52	30,288.89	26,762.59
1913	552	1,280,524.57	1,230,213.83	50,310.74	70,185.94
1914	713	1,460,286.86	1,562,362.79	−102,075.93	−85,463.46

Source: The Public Archives of Canada, R.G. 46.

interest rate on the new bonds was to be reduced from 6 per cent to 4 per cent, and the bondholders agreed to exchange their old bonds at 75 per cent of par value.

A single important provision made it possible to exchange the old 6-per-cent bonds at 75 per cent of par value for new 4-per-cent bonds. The new bonds were to carry a Canadian Northern Railway Company guarantee. The strong and profitable prairie system pledged its support and credit to the bonds of its bankrupt Quebec affiliate. It was decided to dispose of $4,162,000 in Series A bonds, $500,000 in Series B bonds, and $173,000 in terminal and postal bonds of the Great Northern Railway in this way. The new Canadian Northern guaranteed issue was in the amount of $4,692,000, a sum sufficient to bring in all the old bonds and build some essential new mileage and facilities.[52]

The Canadian Northern guarantee of the Great Northern bonds solved the latter company's financial problems, but it raised a number of serious questions. The Canadian Northern Railway's own credit was based largely on government guarantees of its bonds. Indirectly, therefore, the guarantee by the Canadian Northern committed both federal and provincial governments to the success of the dubious Quebec scheme. The federal government was understandably reluctant to authorize the guarantee.[53] Yet Laurier wanted to see the Quebec lines reorganized and completed, and eventually agreed to the Canadian Northern proposals. The appropriate agreement whereby the Canadian Northern Railway guaranteed $4,962,000 Great Northern Railway bonds and thus committed itself to the success of that road was signed on 1 April 1905.

This guarantee was characteristic of what eventually became the transcontinental Canadian Northern Railway System. The stronger parts of the system were frequently used to support the newer and

52 PAC, CNR Records, MMMCXXXI, Indenture of Mortgage securing Guaranteed Bonds, Great Northern Railway of Canada, to the Central Trust Company of New York and the Canadian Northern Railway Company, 1 April 1905; *ibid.*, MCDXXXVII, 45–6, Meeting of Directors of the Canadian Northern Railway Company, 3 Oct. 1904; *ibid.*, MCCXXXI,

Great Northern Railway of Canada, Scheme of Arrangement; *ibid.*, MCCXXXI, Minutes of Meeting of Directors of the Great Northern Railway of Canada, 20 Dec. 1904. 53 PAC, Laurier Papers, CCCLXXVII, CCCXCV, 100364–6, 104994–6, Mann to Laurier, 4 Aug. 1905, Laurier to Mann, 9 Aug. 1905, and Mann to Laurier, 1906.

weaker sections.[54] Similarly the firm of Mackenzie, Mann and Co. Ltd. frequently gave its formal support to a weaker part of the system. Consequently the entire structure became increasingly interdependent and indivisible. In the end this conjunction contributed to the collapse of the entire system, including the strong and profitable prairie system.

A second reorganization of the Quebec railways came in 1906. On 19 July of that year the several Quebec lines controlled by Mackenzie and Mann were amalgamated to form the Canadian Northern Quebec Railway. Included in that amalgamation were the Great Northern Railway of Canada, the Chateauguay and Northern Railway, and the Quebec, New Brunswick and Nova Scotia Railway. The Montfort and Gatineau Colonization Railway Company had become the property of the Great Northern and entered the coalition as a part of that system.[55]

The Quebec, New Brunswick and Nova Scotia Railway, which was to provide a connection with the Maritimes, had been incorporated in 1903. However, the organizational meeting of the company was delayed until 21 August 1905 while Mackenzie and Mann sought government aid for the line. Very little was available, and in the end Mackenzie and Mann decided to build the first eighty miles on the strength of a Canadian Northern Railway guarantee. On 9 June 1906 first-mortgage bonds of up to $25,000 were authorized. Then, a scant fifteen minutes later on the same day, the amalgamation which created the Canadian Northern Quebec Railway was approved by the shareholders of the Quebec, New Brunswick and Nova Scotia Railway.[56]

There was considerable discussion about the name of the new amalgamated Quebec railway company. Horne-Payne, the company's London director and financial adviser, successfully urged inclusion of the name Canadian Northern to enable the new company to benefit

54 Hanna, 238–9.
55 PAC, CNR Records, MCCXXXI, Indenture of Mortgage dated 6 Oct. 1906, between the Canadian Northern Quebec Railway, the Canadian Northern Railway, the British Empire Trust Company, and the National Trust Company.
56 PAC, CNR Records, CDLX, Meeting of Provisional Directors of the Quebec, New Brunswick and Nova Scotia Railway Company, 21 Aug. 1905, and Special General Meeting of Shareholders of the Quebec, New Brunswick and Nova Scotia Railway, 9 June 1906; PAC, Laurier Papers, CCCXXXIII, CCCXCV, 89105, 104994–6, Laurier to Mackenzie, 17 Aug. 1904, Mann to Laurier, 1906.

from the strong reputation of the prairie company in British financial circles.[57]

Financing, particularly the consolidation of the actual or potential bonded indebtedness of the three amalgamating companies, was the first item of business for the new company. This indebtedness amounted to $4,962,000 in the case of the Great Northern, $2,000,000 for the Chateauguay and Northern, and a potential $2,000,000 for the Quebec, New Brunswick and Nova Scotia Railway, making a total of $8,962,000. A new Canadian Northern Quebec Railway bond issue to cover this amount, plus $20,000 per mile for any lines which might subsequently be purchased or constructed, was approved by the shareholders in October of 1906. The new issue was again guaranteed by the stronger Canadian Northern Railway Company.[58]

The 1906 reorganization did not immediately lead to extensive new construction or major operational improvements in Quebec. It did simplify the financial arrangements and it provided a much stronger argument when, in 1906, Mackenzie and Mann told Laurier that they had three railway systems in operation and asked for federal assistance to connect their prairie, Ontario, and Quebec lines.[59] This the federal government declined to do, and the Quebec mileage continued to be operated much as it had been before 1906. Interest on the new bonds was paid on schedule, and the Canadian Northern Railway was not called upon to honour its guarantee. The economic operation of railways for which D. B. Hanna had become famous in Manitoba was applied to the Quebec lines, and where revenue was insufficient to meet all fixed charges the Quebec company obtained loans to pay the bond interest.

The Canadian Northern Quebec Railway was, with some diversions and local extensions, a main-line route across the province of Quebec. While building or acquiring this main line, Mackenzie and Mann were also very much concerned with the development of local traffic in the province. It was with this end in view, together with several important

57 PAC, CNR Legal Series, File 1014–20–3, IXCLXXIV, Horne–Payne to Lash, 23 April 1906. This entire file deals with the reorganization of the Quebec and Ontario railways into the Canadian Northern Ontario Railway and the Canadian Northern Quebec Railway.

58 PAC, CNR Records, MCCXXXI, Mortgage, 6 Oct. 1906.

59 PAC, Laurier Papers, CDXV, 110803–10, Mann to Laurier, 1 June 1906.

TABLE XIV

Operating Statistics of the Canadian Northern Quebec Railway
(Great Northern Railway of Canada before 1907)

Year	Mileage operated	Gross earnings	Operating costs	Net earnings	Net corporate profit or loss
		($)	($)	($)	($)
1901	140	139,954.49	193,275.66	36,678.83	
1902	175	524,763.51	316,800.69	207,962.82	
1903	208	369,327.92	377,649.74	−8,321.82	
1904	208	338,376.63	335,984.84	2,291.69	
1905	208	421,495.78	410,193.13	11,302.65	
1906	251	483,074.34	426,911.83	56,162.51	
1907	275	658,533.09	585,267.64	73,265.45	−225,484.22
1908	294	680,201.03	709,411.11	−29,210.08	−280,453.70
1909	294	739,603.34	678,327.22	61,276.12	−309,222.48
1910	458	940,646.63	887,289.52	53,357.11	−317,404.19
1911	483	1,080,929.61	975,615.19	105,314.42	−268,962.60
1912	485	1,327,534.83	1,088,243.53	239,291.30	−124,336.63
1913	472	1,599,546.82	1,385,347.14	214,199.68	−189,136.28
1914	417	1,671,723.27	1,482,180.48	189,542.79	−453,578.32

Source: PAC, R.G. 46. These returns include operations on the Lower Laurentian Railway, the Montfort and Gatineau Colonization Railway, and the Chateauguay and Northern Railway, all of which were operated by the Canadian Northern Quebec Railway.

short-term considerations, that Mackenzie and Mann secured an interest in, and ultimately control of, another Quebec railway, the Quebec and Lake St. John Railway.

The Quebec and Lake St. John Railway was promoted as the first section of the proposed Trans-Canada Railway, and also provided the Quebec City connection for the Great Northern Railway. A suitable running-rights arrangement was easily negotiated when Mackenzie and Mann became involved with the Great Northern, but the Quebec City promoter-politicians were unwilling to surrender their control of the Quebec and Lake St. John Railway entirely. The railway had opened up farming and industrial developments at Lake St. John and was operated for several years on a profitable basis. The collapse of the Trans-Canada scheme nevertheless led to serious financial difficulties. In 1904 the Quebec and Lake St. John Railway had £1,596,800 outstanding in bonds, a $125,000 mortgage with the Quebec government, and substantial construction debts. It found itself unable to pay its contractors, Hanson Brothers, and persuaded them to accept capital stock instead of cash in payment for their services.[60] Even this expedient did not save the company from a receivership.

Hanson Brothers had very close relations with the Quebec interests, but they also had the confidence of and on occasion received financing from Mackenzie, Mann and Co. Ltd. Mackenzie and Mann were interested in the Quebec and Lake St. John Railway for several reasons. It was, first of all, the mileage over which they entered Quebec City. Its terminals and facilities in that city were excellent. As a colonization road it had good traffic potential and would serve as a good feeder or branch line for their transcontinental system; and it offered an important strategic advantage. The National Transcontinental was encountering considerable political and engineering difficulties in obtaining access into Quebec City, and early construction contracts on that railway called only for construction from La Tuque westward. If the Quebec and Lake St. John Railway, with its established terminal facilities in Quebec City, built a spur from its line to La Tuque, it could, for a time at least, serve as the eastern section of the National Transcontinental. It could expect to carry much of the construction materials required on the government road and it would gain some control over the traffic on the government-built but Grand Trunk Pacific-operated system. With the new forty-mile spur line, the railway would, at least temporarily, become profitable and at the same time provide a considerable competitive advantage.

There were, however, several political problems to overcome. The original owners and promoters of the Quebec and Lake St. John Railway were unwilling to entrust the Quebec colonization schemes to Mackenzie and Mann, Clifford Sifton's associates, who had done much to bring in foreign immigrants and thus had destroyed the balance between English and French settlers on the prairies. For a time there was a complete deadlock between the original and politically prominent promoters of the Quebec and Lake St. John Railway and Mackenzie and Mann, who were eager to acquire control of the line. Much of this dispute focused on the disposition of the railway's land grant. That matter was settled on 20 December 1906 when the original promoters, acting through the Quebec and St. Maurice Industrial Company, obtained control of the remaining acres of the railway's land grant.[61]

With the land grant sold, Hanson Brothers agreed to sell their capital stock in the Quebec and Lake St. John Railway to Mackenzie, Mann and Co. Ltd. They held $2,307,300 of the $4,524,000 (par value) capital stock issued by the railway, and agreed to sell their interest for $500,000. Mackenzie, Mann and Co. Ltd. agreed to pay this amount in seven instalments and deposited unsold Canadian Northern bonds as collateral for such payments.[62]

The transaction between Hanson Brothers and Mackenzie, Mann and Co. Ltd. aroused great hostility in the Quebec promoters. Mackenzie and Mann had obtained control of the majority of the capital stock issued, but the Quebec interests had a majority on the railway's board of directors and they immediately made preparations to issue sufficient additional capital stock to regain control. The authorized capitalization of the company was $6,000,000, of which only $4,524,000 had been issued, and of that amount Mackenzie, Mann and Co. Ltd. had acquired $2,307,300.[63] Lash was convinced that legal obstacles could be placed in the path of the Quebec interests to delay the issuing of new capital stock until the next annual meeting, at which time their majority on the board of directors would presumably be lost. He nevertheless felt that an amicable arrangement was preferable.

William Hanson of Hanson Brothers was instructed to negotiate with the Quebec promoters, and in November 1907 he arranged the purchase of the bulk of the Quebec holdings for $15 per share. When purchasing this railway, Mackenzie and Mann agreed to retain J. G. Scott, the long-time general manager of the Quebec and Lake St. John

61 PAC, CNR Records, x̄CCXXXII, Deed of Sale, the Quebec and Lake St. John Railway selling its land grant to the St. Maurice Industrial Company, 20 Dec. 1906; *ibid*., MMMCXXII, Quebec and Lake St. John Railway Company, Miscellaneous files, Agreement between the Quebec and Lake St. John Railway Company, the Quebec Bank, Mackenzie, Mann and Company Limited, Joseph Paquet, and the Quebec and St. Maurice Industrial Company, 9 May 1907.

62 *Ibid*., x̄CCXXXII, Agreement dated 12 Feb. 1907.

63 *Ibid*., Confidential memorandum for the Canadian Bank of Commerce by Lash, 9 April 1907.

Railway and promoter of the Trans-Canada scheme, as vice-president of the Canadian Northern Quebec Railway, and to entrust him with matters relating to the Quebec and Lake St. John Railway and other roads in the eastern part of Quebec. Mackenzie and Mann also agreed to facilitate the issuance of titles to the land grant and their transfer to the St. Maurice Industrial Company. Those lands had been sold to the Industrial Company late in 1906, but they had also been pledged earlier as collateral for bank loans to the railway and the contractor. Mackenzie and Mann agreed to provide funds to repay the bank and release the lands.[64]

Mackenzie and Mann thus gained control of the Quebec and Lake St. John Railway in 1907. The major stockholders of that railway, with the exception of the city of Quebec itself, agreed to sell their stock at $15 per share. Construction of the forty-mile section between La Tuque and Linton Junction was undertaken the same year. For a time this line was operated as anticipated, but the National Transcontinental built its own line to Quebec City somewhat sooner than expected. As a result, the railway again found itself in financial difficulties and a further reorganization became necessary.

This reorganization came in 1912 with the issuing of new consolidated bonds valued at $7,300,000. These new bonds were to replace the entire bonded indebtedness of the Quebec and Lake St. John Railway. Like those of the Canadian Northern Quebec Railway, they carried a guarantee by the Canadian Northern Railway. The outstanding bonds of the railway were then exchanged at 70 per cent of par value while a special issue of income bonds issued by the railway and totalling $3,000,000 was exchanged at only 13 per cent of par value.[65] In 1914 the Quebec and Lake St. John Railway, together with Mackenzie and Mann's other railway interests, formally became a part of the Canadian Northern Railway System.

The Canadian Northern systems in Quebec and Ontario were never as strong as the prairie system. There was simply too much unproductive mileage in the east, and attempts to develop major branch and

---

64 *Ibid.*, Agreement between the Quebec and Lake St. John Railway Company, Mackenzie, Mann and Company Limited and the Quebec and St. Maurice Industrial Company re La Tuque land grant.

65 *Synoptical Histories*, 677–83.

TABLE XV

Operating Statistics of the Quebec and Lake St. John Railway

Year	Mileage operated	Gross earnings	Operating costs	Net earnings
		($)	($)	($)
1903	240	431,683.38	310,581.24	121,102.14
1904	240	477,994.54	326,562.47	151,432.07
1905	244	497,205.87	360,969.62	136,236.25
1906	244	563,857.99	388,062.44	175,795.55
1907	280	601,619.68	395,715.52	205,904.16
1908	280	656,514.88	489,308.81	167,206.07
1909	326	631,389.06	553,210.15	78,178.91
1910	326	581,061.25	546,917.09	34,144.16
1911	326	630,611.30	587,091.22	43,520.08
1912	326	798,055.31	695,873.98	102,181.33
1913	328	959,380.40	836,159.75	123,220.65
1914	328	934,777.21	845,814.90	88,962.31

Source: The Public Archives of Canada, R.G. 46.

feeder lines failed to achieve satisfactory results. This failure was due in part to a much slower rate of immigration and settlement on remaining vacant eastern lands, and in part simply to the fact that those vacant lands never had the same potential for agriculture as the northern prairies. Mackenzie and Mann developed the eastern lines because they needed eastern connections. Before any of those lines would serve their intended purpose, however, one long and very expensive line still remained to be built—the line from Port Arthur to Montreal. This line would generate almost no local traffic and clearly could not be built without further massive government assistance. That assistance, however, was specifically refused by the Laurier government in 1906 and again in 1909. Mackenzie and Mann had little choice but to wait until the government changed its mind or was replaced. In the meantime they turned their attention to another major project: the building of a new railway line from Edmonton to the Pacific coast on the strength of a provincial bond guarantee of $35,000 per mile.

CHAPTER ELEVEN

THE BEST LINE
TO THE PACIFIC
1909–1911

TO MAKE THEIR RAILWAY a truly transcontinental system Mackenzie and Mann had to build from Edmonton to the Pacific coast. They controlled the Edmonton, Yukon and Pacific Railway, which had rather vaguely defined charter rights to build such a line, but an agreement to build in 1902 had been repudiated by the British Columbia government. Detailed plans for the location of the first thirty-three miles of the line were nevertheless filed with the Department of Railways and Canals in 1904.[1] At the time, Mackenzie and Mann thought of building through the Pine River Pass to a terminus in northern British Columbia, but neither the pass nor the terminus of the proposed line was shown on the 1904 plans.

Initially, both the Canadian Northern and the Grand Trunk Pacific hoped to build to a northern port. Shortly after the 1904 plans for the first thirty-three miles of the Edmonton, Yukon and Pacific Railway were filed, the Grand Trunk Pacific Railway indicated its intention to build its terminus on the Skeena River. The federal government readily approved, and it was expected that the Grand Trunk Pacific would build through one of the more northerly passes while the Canadian Northern would be compelled to build through the Yellowhead Pass to a more southerly Pacific terminus. The Pine and Peace River passes were regarded as more attractive, in part because they would help to develop the Peace River district. Lack of a second suitable northern Pacific terminus, however, forced Mackenzie and Mann to abandon such a route. On 22 October 1906 they filed new plans to

1 PAC, CNR Legal Series, File 1018–63–1.

build through the Yellowhead Pass. The intended terminus on the Pacific coast was not shown on these plans.[2]

The Grand Trunk Pacific Railway quickly recognized the mischief it could do if it decided to build through the Yellowhead Pass as well. This would almost certainly force the Canadian Northern Railway out of that pass to one of the more northerly routes. Grand Trunk Pacific occupation of the Skeena River terminus, however, would force the Canadian Northern to come south, probably to Bute Inlet or Burrard Inlet. If the Canadian Northern could be forced out of the Yellowhead Pass, its mileage to the Pacific would be very greatly increased and its competitive position weakened. The Grand Trunk Pacific Railway accordingly filed its own location plans through the Yellowhead Pass late in 1906.[3]

The charter of the Grand Trunk Pacific authorized construction "by way of either the Peace River Pass, or the Pine River Pass, or such other pass in the Rocky Mountains as is found most convenient and practicable". Hays argued that this statement provided the necessary authorization to build through the Yellowhead Pass, which Grand Trunk Pacific surveys indicated was the "shortest, most direct and most economical" route.[4] Mann was convinced that the Grand Trunk Pacific decision was designed primarily to injure the Canadian Northern and pointed out to Prime Minister Laurier the need of the Peace River country for railway connections and the logic of routing the Grand Trunk, with its northern terminus, through one of the more northerly passes.[5]

Both the Grand Trunk Pacific and the Edmonton, Yukon and Pacific Railway filed new plans to build through the Yellowhead Pass in 1906. The Department of Railways and Canals, which had to approve final location plans, looked favourably on the Grand Trunk Pacific's plans and returned the plans of the Edmonton, Yukon and Pacific Railway, asking that these be revised to show the Pacific terminus, and be drawn on the same scale as those submitted by the Grand Trunk Pacific.[6]

2 *Ibid.*
3 PAC, Laurier Papers, CDXLIV, 118716–18, Hays to Laurier, 29 Jan. 1907; *ibid.*, 118713–15, Mann to Laurier, 26 Jan. 1907.
4 *Ibid.*, 118716–18, Hays to Laurier, 29 Jan. 1907.
5 *Ibid.*, 118713–15, Mann to Laurier, 26 Jan. 1907.
6 PAC, CNR Legal Series, File 1018–63–1. For a review of the entire affair,

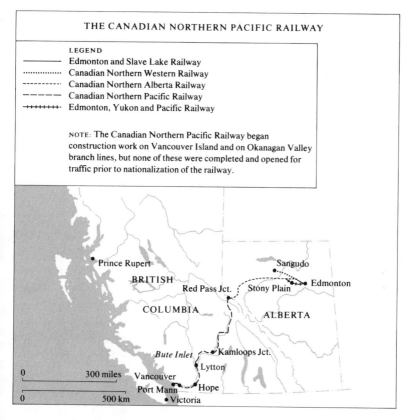

THE CANADIAN NORTHERN PACIFIC RAILWAY

LEGEND
——————— Edmonton and Slave Lake Railway
················ Canadian Northern Western Railway
---------- Canadian Northern Alberta Railway
— — — — Canadian Northern Pacific Railway
++++++++ Edmonton, Yukon and Pacific Railway

NOTE: The Canadian Northern Pacific Railway began construction work on Vancouver Island and on Okanagan Valley branch lines, but none of these were completed and opened for traffic prior to nationalization of the railway.

Canadian Northern officials thought these "very trivial objections which put the Department in a rather farcical light".[7] Meetings were held in Ottawa on 24 November and 17 December 1906, attended by departmental officials and representatives of the two railways. Since the Grand Trunk Pacific had been the first to file plans acceptable to the department it was given authority to build through the Yellowhead Pass. Mackenzie and Mann regarded the departmental decision as "a purely political one",[8] and Mann sent a very strongly worded letter of protest to Laurier. The Minister of Railways and Canals at the time was H. R. Emmerson of Moncton. Since Moncton was the eastern terminus of the Grand Trunk Pacific–National Transcontinental Railway system, and the Canadian Northern was to some extent iden-

see private memorandum prepared by D. D. Mann in reference to the approval of route plans, PAC, Laurier Papers, DLXXX, 157248–4, 23 June 1909.

7 PAC, CNR Legal Series, File 1018–63–1, Memorandum by Gerard Ruel.
8 *Ibid.*, Memoranda dated 31 Dec. 1907; PAC, Laurier Papers, 118713–5, Mann to Laurier, 26 Jan. 1907.

tified with rival Saint John interests, Emmerson was generally regarded as an opponent of Mackenzie and Mann.

Protests alone, however, would not get the Canadian Northern promoters the authorization they needed to build through the Yellowhead Pass. Once the Grand Trunk was given its authorization, Mann instructed his solicitors to make application to the Alberta government for a provincially chartered and subsidized parallel line from Edmonton west.[9] Both the Alberta and the British Columbia governments were very eager to see the Canadian Northern extended to the Pacific, and an ugly federal-provincial confrontation was in prospect if provincial legislation authorized, but federal action prevented, the construction of such a line. This threat, coupled with the resignation of the Minister of Railways and Canals on 2 April 1907 for reasons not directly related to the western dispute, led to a sharp change of attitude in the Department of Railways and Canals. George P. Graham of Brockville, a centre soon to be served by the Canadian Northern Ontario Railway, became Minister. Shortly thereafter, the department's chief engineering consultant, Collingwood Schreiber, reviewed the plans and discovered that it might be possible to crowd both railways into the Yellowhead Pass.[10] As a result, action on the provincial front was dropped. The Edmonton, Yukon and Pacific Railway submitted new plans to build through the Yellowhead Pass, changed where necessary because of existing Grand Trunk Pacific locations. These plans were approved by the Department without further difficulty.

This was followed on 6 March 1908 by a request from William Mackenzie that the federal government provide bond guarantees which would enable the Edmonton, Yukon and Pacific Railway to build westward from Edmonton to the coal fields at the headwaters of the Brazeau and McLeod rivers. He presented the line as a developmental line to the coal fields because no plans for the British Columbia section had yet been filed.[11] The federal government responded to Mackenzie's request and granted a $13,000-per-mile federal guarantee from mile 30 (the first thirty miles had already been built) to mile 80,

9 PAC, CNR Legal Series, File 1018–63–1, Memorandum by Gerard Ruel.
10 Ibid., and supporting documents.

11 PAC, Laurier Papers, DVIII, 137215–6, Mackenzie to Laurier, 6 March 1908.

and a guarantee of $25,000 per mile for the remaining 100 miles to the Brazeau coal fields. This aid was granted on condition that the Edmonton, Yukon and Pacific Railway be amalgamated with the Canadian Northern Railway, a condition that was quickly met.

Mackenzie and Mann decided in 1910 that the Brazeau coal fields could be reached more easily by building westward from Stettler and Red Deer than from Edmonton. Charter rights to build this more southerly line were obtained from the Alberta government with the incorporation of the Canadian Northern Western Railway. A provincial bond guarantee for the new line was obtained in 1911. This new guarantee, however, did not mean that Mackenzie and Mann were willing to surrender the federal guarantee already approved for the more northerly line. They approached the federal government and asked that the bond guarantee be transferred to a new company, the Canadian Northern Alberta Railway, which would take over the project. When this request was approved, the Canadian Northern Alberta Railway sought and obtained federal permission to change the line officially from a developmental line to a through line from Edmonton towards the Yellowhead Pass.[12] This change also led to the selection of a new route out of the city of Edmonton, leaving the short Edmonton, Yukon and Pacific mileage to Stoney Plain as a mere branch line. A short section of another Mackenzie and Mann-controlled railway, the Edmonton and Slave Lake Railway, was used to connect the Canadian Northern Alberta Railway with downtown Edmonton.

The Laurier government provided $13,000-per-mile bond guarantees for the first fifty miles of the Canadian Northern Alberta Railway, and $25,000 per mile for the next hundred miles. It was only after the 1911 election, however, that Mackenzie and Mann obtained from the Borden government bond guarantees of $35,000 per mile for the last 100-mile section. The Canadian Northern Alberta Railway throughout its entire length paralleled the Grand Trunk Pacific line, while the Peace River district remained without essential rail services. These two parallel lines certainly constitute some of the most foolish and useless mileage ever built in Canada.

In the meantime, the same foolish policy would have been followed

12 *Ibid.*, DCLXXXIX, 188745–7, Fielding to Laurier, 9 Aug. 1911.

on the section from the Yellowhead Pass to Vancouver if a Grand Trunk Pacific scheme had been allowed to succeed. On this section the Edmonton, Yukon and Pacific Railway filed location plans in 1908. The Grand Trunk Pacific responded with plans of its own for an almost identical line, and began a vigorous campaign to have its plans approved.[13] This time, however, the Department of Railways and Canals was in the hands of George Graham, who refused to have anything to do with the new Grand Trunk Pacific plans. He rejected the plans "to locate the Grand Trunk Pacific on the Canadian Northern Railway line to Vancouver, which is really what is asked," as "a wanton waste of money".[14] Graham suggested that all three Canadian transcontinentals use a common line, perhaps double-tracked if there were sufficient traffic, from Kamloops to Vancouver. Supercilious CPR officials immediately informed him that their track was not available for such a scheme, since they had enough traffic of their own to keep their line busy. The CPR, however, had no objection if the government wished to force its two rivals to use a common line. Grand Trunk Pacific officials grumbled that "they might just as well not go there at all" if compelled to co-operate with the Canadian Northern. Mackenzie and Mann, for their part, argued that considerations of national defence made the construction of a second transcontinental line through the Fraser Canyon a matter of vital concern. They confidently assured everyone that there was ample traffic for their proposed new line.[15]

Graham's scheme of co-operation got nowhere. He therefore decided that the Canadian Northern Railway's application, now officially filed under the name of the Canadian Northern Pacific Railway, should be approved, and he informed Laurier accordingly.

I discussed this matter with you recently after Mr. Mann's visit, and you readily agreed with me that after taking certain right of way from the CNR and giving it to the GTP, driving them from the Prince Rupert terminal, we should not now turn around and be a party to depriving them of their

13 PAC, CNR Legal Series, File 1018–63–1.
14 PAC, Graham Papers, 19445–6, Graham to Wainwright, Graham to Laurier, 20 Sept. 1909. An initialled notation by Laurier on the latter reads "I absolutely approve."
15 PAC, CNR Legal Series, File 1018–63–1.

Vancouver route. They must have a western terminal and the CNR should have the right of way to Vancouver.[16]

Laurier agreed, and the Canadian Northern's location plans were approved, while the Grand Trunk Pacific was told it must keep clear of Canadian Northern lines and locations if it wished to build into Vancouver.[17]

It was understood from the beginning that the fight over location plans was only the first phase of the struggle. Neither company had the resources to build to Vancouver without substantial government assistance. The Grand Trunk Pacific already enjoyed substantial guarantees for its line to Prince Rupert, but could not obtain similar support for a line to Vancouver. The Mackenzie and Mann negotiations with the federal government for aid to extend their system to the British Columbia border were going reasonably well, but in British Columbia much depended on the attitude and actions of Premier Richard McBride. McBride had become premier in 1902 when he opposed Premier James Dunsmuir's proposals to assist the Edmonton, Yukon and Pacific Railway in building to Bute Inlet and Vancouver Island. McBride nevertheless had much in common with the two railway promoters whose scheme he had derailed in 1902. Friendly relations were soon established. McBride, in the words of a noted British Columbia historian,

typified the spirit of the age: the optimism which verged on recklessness. Sensing that British Columbia had some distinctive quality—not quite Canadian or British or American or even a blend of all three—he dreamed of developing its vast natural resources through grandiose schemes which would make it almost an empire in itself.[18]

Substituting Canada for British Columbia, this statement might well be applied to Mackenzie and Mann.

The greatest single handicap to an aggressive development policy in British Columbia in 1902 was the fact that its treasury was de-

16 PAC, Graham Papers, 19445, Graham to Laurier, 20 Sept. 1909.
17 PAC, CNR Legal Series, File 1018–63–1.

18 Margaret A. Ormsby, *British Columbia: A History* (Toronto: Macmillan, 1958), 336.

pleted and the province dangerously close to bankruptcy. With federal assistance going to the Grand Trunk Pacific in 1904, there was no immediate need for a British Columbia-sponsored railway project, and the provincial government concentrated on setting its financial house in order. In R. G. Tatlow, Premier McBride found the finance minister he needed to transform chronic provincial deficits into respectable surpluses, thus accumulating the resources and credit necessary for more aggressive policies.

McBride's relations with the Grand Trunk Pacific were businesslike at first, but the arrogant and bullying tactics of the railway which was the special project of the federal Liberals soon cooled relations between the railway and the Conservative provincial government. At the same time, however, McBride did not feel much of the old-line Conservative loyalty to the CPR, and he was quite prepared to assist potential competitors who would help develop the resources of the province. This clearly left the door open for further negotiations with Mackenzie and Mann. According to Mann, the two promoters received a number of British Columbia invitations.[19] Late in 1908 they responded favourably, and serious negotiations for a provincial bond guarantee began. On 25 January 1909 these negotiations were sufficiently advanced to permit the Premier to announce that British Columbia would soon have another rail connection with the prairies. No further details were given, although the newspapers correctly assumed the negotiations were with Mackenzie and Mann. Meanwhile, McBride undertook a serious study and review of the Canadian Northern Railway, its various accomplishments, its potential, and its promise for his province.

In May 1909 Gerard Ruel, assistant secretary to the Canadian Northern Railway, supplied the British Columbia premier with a lengthy memorandum on the various Canadian Northern securities and guarantees and on its legislative arrangements with the federal and provincial governments.[20] The local law library was searched by McBride aides for information on the Canadian Northern.[21] Then, shortly before committing his government to a contract with Mackenzie and

19 *Arbitration*, 2684.
20 PABC, McBride Papers, Ruel to McBride, 26 May 1909.
21 *Ibid.*, C. M. Woodsworth to McBride, 14 Oct. 1909.

Mann, the British Columbia premier met with Premier Roblin of Manitoba. Railway policies dominated the discussions of the two Conservative premiers, with Roblin speaking very favourably of Mackenzie and Mann. McBride returned home resolved to link the railway policies of his province with the plans and designs of the ambitious promoters.

Manitoba Premier Roblin and Works Minister Rogers followed up their meeting with McBride with lengthy memoranda outlining the relations of their province with the Canadian Northern Railway. This information may have helped the Premier to make up his own mind, but more likely it was sent at the British Columbian's request, to be used against his critics in the province. Rogers' telegram is a succinct statement of Canadian Northern successes in Manitoba up to 1909 and of political and financial thinking at the time.

The CN contract made in February 1901 with this province, although fiercely opposed and maliciously misrepresented at first, has worked out so satisfactorily to the province that opposition thereto has ceased in view of the beneficial results to the people of this province. All the direful results predicted have proved absolutely unfounded, it has never in any sense adversely affected the financial standing or credit of the province or any of its municipalities and our credit today is better than ever. . . . The contract has resulted in manifold benefits to the province giving the people a much needed service saving millions of money with reduced freight rates, etc., and has never cost the province one dollar. So popular has it been that the demand for railway construction and extension by that railway on behalf of the people has been so great that the Canadian Northern now has a larger mileage in Manitoba than any other railway. I congratulate you upon your proposals and predict a similar satisfactory result for your province with general development and prosperity therefrom.[22]

This was high praise indeed. Premier Roblin further assured his British Columbia counterpart that the Manitoba railway policy "meets universal approval of people irrespective of political leanings".[23] These telegrams and other general assurances by various governments in other parts of the country enabled the Conservative press in British Columbia to offer a vigorous defence of Premier McBride's proposed railway policy.

Mackenzie and Mann and the Canadian Northern Railway Company come to the local government with their reputation endorsed not only by the Conservative administrations of Manitoba and Ontario, but as well by the Liberal governments of Quebec, Alberta and Saskatchewan. In addition to this it must be borne in mind that this company has been strongly entrenched by Sir Wilfrid Laurier's administration from whom it has received large subsidies. Surely the government of British Columbia could want no better evidence of the bona fides of these people than might be secured in this way.[24]

In one important respect the British Columbia premier decided to follow a policy adopted in Manitoba, but not in other provinces. He insisted that, as a condition for granting provincial aid, the provincial government must be given specific control over the rates to be charged by the new railway. The federal government had established the Board of Railway Commissioners to regulate rates, but the 1901 agreements in Manitoba had set a precedent under which provinces could enter into private agreements with railway companies for lower rates than those authorized by the federal board or its predecessors. McBride was concerned that this control be firmly vested in the province and insisted that Mackenzie and Mann agree that their railway would never apply for federal aid as a railway "in the general interests of Canada".[25] A railway thus designated and assisted was by definition subject to the federal Board. The CPR had never received aid under such conditions and was consequently exempt from many of the rulings of the federal Board, and McBride wanted the Canadian Northern to be similarly unhampered. He attached great importance to the rate reductions he expected to get from the Canadian Northern. He wrote,

Because the CPR is thus exempt and because the GTP is loaded with too much territory that will not be productive for many years, the CNR is the

24 *Victoria Colonist*, 31 Oct. 1909, in reporting on a speech by McBride in defence of his railway policy.

25 PABC, McBride Papers, McBride to Mann, 29 Oct. 1909.

only source from which we can hope to get greatly improved rates and facilities. And the effectiveness of the CNR is due largely to its being able, by reason of government bond guarantees, to get into the restricted market where money is cheap.[26]

A spirit of optimism and recklessness pervaded the country in 1909, and the suggestion that the government assist the Canadian Northern to building to the Pacific coast was in accord with this spirit. Premier McBride nevertheless knew that not all the members of his Cabinet shared his enthusiasm for such a project. R. G. Tatlow, the finance minister who had fashioned successive provincial surpluses, was firmly opposed to extensive financial commitments to the railways. F. J. Fulton, the provincial Commissioner of Lands, was also known to oppose any proposals for government aid to railways. He felt that the Canadian Northern must build to the Pacific coast if it wished to compete with established transcontinentals, and that it would do so regardless of any assistance the province might or might not grant. The province should spare itself the expense and bother. Other Conservatives, such as C. H. Tupper, held a more federal and pro-CPR outlook, and were opposed to or had grave misgivings about associating the fortunes of the province with those of an upstart regional railway lately aspiring to transcontinental ambitions.[27]

McBride had learned from the misfortunes of his predecessors of the dangers of internecine quarrels. He decided on a subtle strategy. He delayed any detailed announcements regarding the Canadian Northern project until after the dissolution of the provincial legislature on 18 October 1909. Only on the following day did the Premier announce that a contract had in fact been signed with Mackenzie and Mann, providing for substantial provincial assistance in the construction of a third railway to the Pacific. Tatlow and Fulton resigned as a result of this announcement, but in the face of an immediate provincial election there was relatively little overt criticism from disgruntled Conservatives who disliked the new policy. The party remained publicly

26 *Ibid.*, Memo re CNPR agreements, undated but almost certainly 1909.
27 P. Roy, "Railways, Politicians and the Development of Vancouver as a

Metropolitan Centre, 1886–1929" (MA thesis, University of Toronto, 1963), 150–1.

united in support of the Premier and his new and still only vaguely defined railway policy.

This strategy not only maintained Conservative unity; it also left the Liberal Opposition in a very poor strategic position. Without detailed location plans and the exact financial terms of the proposed agreement, it was difficult to offer effective criticism. Requests by the Opposition leader for more information were firmly rejected by the Premier.[28] In the election every little settlement seemed to hope for the magic touch of the new railway, and feared possible adverse effects if an Opposition member were returned. Meanwhile, the local Conservative press loudly proclaimed the advantages and benefits that Mackenzie and Mann had already brought to other parts of Canada and would now bring to British Columbia. One of the few terms of the agreement which was revealed and given wide publicity was that the provincial government would control the rates to be charged on the new railway. The Manitoba example was being followed, and the press approved.[29]

The best the provincial Liberals could do was to denounce the government for its secretiveness and to argue, rather lamely, that they would get even more railways built in the province because they would work in close co-operation with the federal government. They argued that some federal assistance would still be needed for the local project, and that the federal government might refuse to grant it if urged by a troublesome Conservative provincial administration. Indeed, the British Columbia Liberal leader was urging Laurier to be as unco-operative as possible in this regard.[30] The entire McBride project, the Liberals argued, would collapse after the election. They pointed to the earlier Mackenzie and Mann schemes in the province which had never materialized. Liberal leader John Oliver suggested that perhaps the Premier was more interested in embarrassing Ottawa than in building railways.[31] These arguments, however, did not constitute an

28 PABC, McBride Papers, John Oliver to McBride, 21 Oct. 1909, and reply of same date.

29 *Ibid.*, Memo regarding Canadian Northern Pacific Railway Agreements, undated but almost certainly 1909; *Victoria Colonist*, 22 and 31 Oct. 1909.

30 PAC, Laurier Papers, DCXLVIII, 176141–6, John Oliver to William Templeman, 17 Oct. 1910, forwarded by Mr. Templeman to George Graham, who in turn forwarded the letter to Laurier.

31 *Victoria Daily Times*, 20 Oct. 1909.

attractive alternative Liberal railway policy, and the British Columbia voters were not impressed.

The election returns demonstrated widespread popular support for McBride's proposals. The Conservatives carried all but four seats in the new legislature, with the Liberals managing victories in only two. The promise of a Mackenzie and Mann road to the Pacific had helped the British Columbia premier to an unprecedented mandate in his province; this despite the fact that few of the details of the new railway and of the promised government assistance to it had been made public.

Immediately after the provincial election a formal agreement between Mackenzie and Mann, the Canadian Northern Railway, and the British Columbia government was negotiated. It was signed on 17 January 1910 and replaced the preliminary agreement negotiated in October 1909. It provided for the incorporation of a new company, the Canadian Northern Pacific Railway, with authority to construct and operate a railway from the eastern boundary of the province near the Yellowhead Pass through the city of New Westminster to Vancouver and English Bluff. A suitable ferry and ocean-shipping facility was to be provided at Vancouver and further lines were to be built on Vancouver Island to bring the new railway to Victoria. The province agreed to guarantee the construction bonds of the railway, up to $35,000 per mile. In return, control over rates was to rest with the provincial government. Construction of the new line was to begin not later than July 1910 and the entire line was to be completed by 1 July 1914. The government agreed to give free right of way over any crown lands as required by the railway as well as land for station grounds and divisional townsites; and it permitted the railway to take timber from crown lands free of charge as required. The railway and its properties were to be exempt from provincial taxation until 1924, ten years after the completion of construction. Legislation incorporating the Canadian Northern Pacific Railway and approving the agreement with the provincial government was passed in March 1910. The weak and demoralized Opposition in the Legislative Assembly offered little more than token resistance.

One aspect of the agreement could not be included in the formal contract. That was a specific provision that the Canadian Northern Pacific Railway would use no Asiatic labour during the construction of the new railway. Incorporation of such a discriminatory clause in the legislation would have met with federal disallowance. The politicians and promoters nevertheless had an understanding on this matter, and later a separate agreement between the provincial government and the railway company was signed. The railway company agreed simply "not to employ or permit the employment of Asiatic labour to construction work on the aided lines".[32]

Mackenzie and Mann lost no time once the appropriate legislation was passed in British Columbia. The bills confirming their agreement and the incorporation of the Canadian Northern Pacific Railway were introduced in the provincial legislature on 1 March 1910. They were rushed through the required three readings without serious opposition and received royal assent on 21 March. Provisional directors of the Canadian Northern Pacific met the following day, immediately subscribing $100,000 of the capital stock. Within fifteen minutes a shareholders' meeting was held, at which the agreement with the government was approved and the directors were elected and authorized to issue government-guaranteed securities of the railway, up to the $35,000-per-mile maximum. The five directors, William Mackenzie, Donald Mann, Roderick J. Mackenzie, D. B. Hanna, and A. D. Davidson, met immediately after the shareholders' meeting and approved the terms and details of the huge bond guarantee. In less than an hour the company was organized and the issue of $21,000,000 worth of guaranteed bonds were approved.[33] Action could obviously be taken with great speed since Mackenzie and Mann owned or controlled all the capital stock. Directors and shareholders confirmed without discussion all arrangements made by Mackenzie and Mann. Governments who wanted to get things done quickly could hardly have asked for more—at least not as long as the money was readily available.

Construction of the line from Vancouver to the Yellowhead Pass was begun as soon as the company was organized. Mackenzie and Mann advanced all funds required until the guaranteed bonds could be sold. The first major construction contract was signed on 23 June

---

32 PABC, McBride Papers, Mackenzie to McBride, 17 Jan. 1910.
33 PAC, CNR Records, MCLXVIII, Meetings of the Provisional Directors,

the Shareholders, and the Directors of the Canadian Northern Pacific Railway Company, all held on 22 March 1910.

1910, with the Northern Construction Company, a subsidiary of Foley, Welch and Stewart in which Donald Mann's brother was a partner and Mackenzie and Mann held an interest. This contract called for construction of the section from Hope to Port Mann. Contracts for construction of the remaining mileage were let in 1911.[34]

Announcement of the final terms of the agreement, particularly of the route chosen, were inevitably a disappointment to some. The railway would not transform every town of interior British Columbia into a thriving metropolis, nor would it serve every economic interest in the province. There was consequently some erosion of public support. The most important single area of discontent was Kamloops, the home of F. J. Fulton, who resigned his Cabinet position in protest against the new provincial railway policy. Fulton opposed the contract on principle, but became very bitter when it appeared that Kamloops might be bypassed by the new railway. Early Canadian Northern Pacific plans indicated a crossing of the North Thompson River some five miles above Kamloops, arousing fears that the new railway would establish a divisional or terminal point across the river from Kamloops. The rival site of Fruitlands successfully offered the railway choice townsites in return for an undertaking that Fruitlands would indeed become a divisional point on the new railway. The railway's charter stated simply that the railway should run to a point at or near the city of Kamloops. Fulton and the Kamloops Board of Trade made strong representations to the Premier that this wording should be changed to read "to a point within the City". The Premier expressed general support for this change, but made no definite promises. Here, as in the case of Battleford, the railway referred to construction economies and the cost of acquiring suitable land for divisional facilities in Kamloops as the reason for not putting the main line through the city.

The agitation in Kamloops did prompt the railway to build a loop line through that centre. It retained the Fruitlands sites and established many of its divisional facilities there, although the Kamloops loop line proved more important than the Fruitlands officials thought justified under their agreement with the railway. As a result the municipality launched a rather bitter lawsuit against the railway, which was still

34 Stevens, 90–1.

before the courts when the line was nationalized in 1918.[35] Since Kamloops was already the divisional point on the CPR main line, it never faced the same bleak prospects as other centres bypassed by a new railway.

Work on the new railway was begun on schedule in July 1910 and proceeded satisfactorily until the end of 1911, although it quickly became evident that the Canadian Northern Pacific Railway would be a very different system than its parent system on the prairies. On the prairies early construction had been relatively cheap, with local traffic resources dictating the standard and quality of construction. Lines were carefully located, moreover, to serve only areas of relatively high potential. Not so in British Columbia. High construction standards, and with them extremely high costs, prevailed from the beginning. The railway's locating engineer wrote McBride as early as 27 February 1910, "I beg to point out that they [construction standards] are and will be much higher and as a matter of policy and true economy and not because the standards were forced upon us."[36] Eighty-pound rails were to be used, where the CPR twenty-five years earlier, and the Canadian Northern only ten years earlier, had been using fifty-six- or sixty-pound rails on their main lines. There was to be much more excavation and rock-filling and less temporary trestle-work, and, above all, the Canadian Northern Pacific would be built with the best grades and curvature of any transcontinental railway in North America. Construction of an inexpensive line, to be improved later, was regarded as an expensive and impractical procedure in 1910. Mann explained to McBride that such a policy would necessitate abandonment of much of the initial tunnel, bridges, and excavation work when the line was improved, since in many cases improvements would involve reversions. It was, he argued, a measure of economy to build to high standards from the start.[37] Engineers assured Mann, apparently with great pride, that "the Canadian Northern were building for their own use and for all time to come and were determined at almost any cost to have a

35 There is a good deal of correspondence, complete with a number of petitions, on the Kamloops-Fruitlands dispute in the McBride Papers, PAC, CNR Legal Series, File 1161–8–1; *Arbitration*, 2683–4.

36 PABC, McBride Papers, Wickstead to McBride, 27 Feb. 1910.
37 *Ibid.*, Wickstead to Mann, 27 Dec. 1913, and Mann to McBride, 18 Dec. 1913.

line a little better than that of anyone else."[38] Where the Canadian Pacific had regarded 2.2-per-cent grades as acceptable and had to contend with 4.5-per-cent grades near Field, British Columbia, for many years, the Canadian Northern Pacific standard was .5 per cent, or a maximum rise of twenty-six feet in every mile, and this compensated for curvature.

Mackenzie and Mann abandoned the old balance between construction costs and potential traffic, although Mann constantly assured the British Columbia premier that the system would generate some local traffic and receive sufficient through traffic from the prairies to provide the required volume of traffic.[39] In fact, the local traffic available in British Columbia was much lighter than on the prairies, but construction costs were very much higher. Mann himself admitted that 5,000 miles of good mileage on the prairies were needed to justify the British Columbia main line.[40] In 1909 the Canadian Northern had only 3,500 miles in operation on the prairies, although government assistance for the required additional mileage was voted the same year. No doubt the construction standards would have been much lower in British Columbia if the money had not been available, but the provincial guarantee of $35,000 per mile was more than four times as large as that available to Mackenzie and Mann when they began railway construction in Manitoba.

Moreover, fewer branch lines and feeder lines were available in British Columbia than elsewhere in Canada. The CPR virtually controlled the southern part of the province. Mackenzie and Mann and Premier McBride hoped that the Canadian Northern Pacific would be able to tap the rich traffic of the Okanagan Valley by a system of branch lines, but in fact none of these was put into operation while Mackenzie and Mann controlled the system. The development of local traffic resources was certainly very much a part of Mackenzie and Mann's British Columbia plans. With this objective in mind they became involved in several subsidiary and complementary enterprises. The largest of these was the Canadian Western Lumber Company, a company operating in the Fraser Valley with an annual production

---

38 *Ibid.*, Wickstead to Mann, 27 Dec. 1913; *Arbitration*, 118–23.

39 *Ibid.*, Mann to McBride, 18 Dec. 1913 and 12 Jan. 1914.

40 *Arbitration*, 2683–4.

capacity of 250,000,000 board feet of lumber. Other lumbering, mining, fishing, and even whaling enterprises received attention from Mackenzie and Mann. Few of these ventures, however, became as profitable or produced as much traffic as the promoters had expected. This was no doubt partly due to the serious financial problems of the war years, but these alone do not account for the differences between the Canadian Northern Pacific Railway and its parent system. Even the most optimistic reckoning clearly indicated that in British Columbia there would be a much less favourable ratio between construction costs —and therefore fixed charges—and the volume of traffic carried than there was on the prairies. If the British Columbia mileage was to cover operating and fixed charges, it would have to be fed a very substantial volume of traffic originating on the prairies. But optimism and confidence in the future of Canada abounded. Even when asked in 1918 whether there was enough traffic in British Columbia to justify three expensive railways, D. B. Hanna replied, "I should say there is very little for the Grand Trunk Pacific away up at Prince Rupert. There is plenty of business for two lines, originating in the Vancouver district."[41] He then referred specifically to the traffic originating with the Canadian Western Lumber Company and to other ventures in which Mackenzie and Mann held interests. He insisted that "in two years from now, with the growth we can show, the CNR on that line would be able not only to pay its operating expenses but to meet its fixed charges."[42]

Optimism reigned supreme in 1909 and 1910 as Mackenzie and Mann committed themselves to the construction of the best transcontinental railway through the Rocky Mountains. Mackenzie enthusiastically informed his directors that the British Columbia arrangements "will prove of tremendous traffic advantage to the Canadian Northern Railway system as a whole".[43] D. B. Hanna later reflected on the enthusiasm of the time and said, "The outlook up to 1912 was all that could be desired. There was no cloud in the sky; everything was beautifully blue; western development was going ahead, immigration was entirely satisfactory and there was plenty of money."[44]

41 *Ibid.*, 754–5.
42 *Ibid.*, 459.

43 *Eighth Annual Report, Canadian Northern Railway, 1910,* 9.
44 *Arbitration,* 2934.

CHAPTER TWELVE

NOT A CLOUD IN THE SKY 1911-1912

THE YEAR 1911 marked the high point in the fortunes of Mackenzie and Mann and their Canadian Northern Railway. Legislative authorization and government bond guarantees had been obtained in 1909 and 1910 for the completion of an extensive network of prairie branch lines and of the through line to the Pacific coast. Financing these enormous undertakings presented no immediate problems. In fact, bankers and financiers quarrelled with one another for a larger share in the handling and underwriting of Canadian Northern Railway securities. Construction could therefore proceed at a rapid rate on more than a dozen major projects.

Even the political disturbances and excitement of the year, centring on the controversial reciprocity proposals of the Laurier government, were not a serious threat to the Canadian Northern Railway. Appropriate arrangements had been made and construction was nearing completion on a Canadian Northern line to Duluth, providing the needed American connections if there was in fact a serious shift in traffic routes and patterns. The nationalistic clamour of the Opposition, however, made it possible for Donald Mann to persuade the government that it must officially recognize and acknowledge the Canadian Northern Railway as the country's third great national highway. With that recognition came a huge federal bond guarantee for the long and expensive line from Port Arthur to Montreal. The Canadian Northern Railway therefore became one of the principal beneficiaries of the Laurier government's attempts to demonstrate that its policies and proposals would promote freer trade without seriously disrupting existing or proposed all-Canadian transcontinental trade routes. Yet, the personal opposition of William Mackenzie and Z. A. Lash to the reciprocity proposals provided valuable contacts with the new Conservative government. It was a recommendation from the new Prime Minister, Robert Borden, which allowed the two promoters to end the year in unusually boisterous fashion. There was a spontaneous and wildly enthusiastic torchlight parade in Toronto and all-night celebrations by friends and employees of Mackenzie and Mann when it was announced that the two promoters had been named Knights of the Realm in the King's New Year's List of Honours. It was, as D. B. Hanna stated, "all that could be desired".

Finance was of the utmost importance in the affairs of the Canadian Northern Railway as it pursued its aggressive construction program. A number of different kinds of Canadian Northern securities were offered to the public in the years after 1909. There were, first of all, new land-grant bonds issued in 1909. To these were added bonds guaranteed by the province of Manitoba to assist in the construction of a station and other terminal facilities in Winnipeg, and provincially guaranteed bonds to build branch lines almost anywhere and everywhere in Manitoba, Saskatchewan, and Alberta. Several of the prairie lines also qualified as main lines or had in some other manner obtained federal guarantees that were issued separately, and in 1910 the new British Columbia guaranteed securities were brought out. A year later the federal government added its guarantee for the line from Port Arthur to Montreal.

All these government-guaranteed bonds provided the basis of Canadian Northern financing. Until 1912 all the guaranteed bonds were readily saleable in London and brought the railway anywhere from 95 per cent to 98 per cent of par value. This was in sharp contrast to earlier efforts by William Mackenzie and Horne-Payne to place their securities at favourable prices. On a number of occasions prior to 1908 the response of the market had been such that Mackenzie thought it best to negotiate short-term loans, pledging his securities as collateral. Large loans had been raised in this way in 1904 and again in 1907 and 1908, the banks refusing to advance large funds unless Mackenzie added his personal guarantee to the pledged collateral.[1]

The earliest and very encouraging indication of a changed mood in the market could be seen in the sale of the 1909 land-grant bonds. These bonds were simply a reissuing of the 1907 bonds. The old bonds

1 PAC, CNR Legal Series, Files 27–1, 27–2, 27–5, and 1014–20–1.

had been offered for sale in 1908 but Mackenzie and Horne-Payne were unable to obtain what they thought was a suitable price. Instead, they negotiated a loan from Lazard Brothers, the 1907 land-grant bonds being pledged as collateral at 80 per cent of par. The government support received by the Canadian Northern Railway in 1909, increases in land sales, better land prices, and a favourable rate of immigration made the bonds more attractive in 1909. Lazard Brothers agreed to purchase the entire £1,027,400 issue at over 95 per cent of par value.[2]

The more important issues of government-guaranteed bonds which were sold in 1909, 1910, and 1911 included $3,000,000 of Manitoba guaranteed terminal bonds sold to the Bank of Commerce, which was acting on behalf of a syndicate in which the Dominion Securities Corporation was prominent, at 96¢ on the dollar.[3] This sale was followed by the public sale, underwritten by Lazard Brothers, of £600,000 Alberta-guaranteed and £600,000 Saskatchewan-guaranteed debenture stock at over 97 per cent. Additional amounts of similar debenture stock were authorized, issued, and sold, usually in smaller amounts and directly by Horne-Payne, after 1909.[4] The Alberta-guaranteed bonds for the Canadian Northern Western Railway, which was to build a line to the Brazeau coal fields in the eastern Rockies, were also purchased by Lazard Brothers, who in this instance were associated with the Deutsche Bank of Berlin and O. C. Wassermann et Cie of Paris and Brussels. These bonds had a par value of $4,000,000.[5]

A large new issue of federally guaranteed debenture stock with a par value of £1,626,781 was brought out in 1908 and given to Mackenzie, Mann and Co. Ltd. in payment for construction work and expenses. Mackenzie and Mann used £1,263,698 of these debentures to purchase the Dunsmuir coal-mining interests on Vancouver Island. They sold smaller amounts to the Canadian Bank of Commerce Pen-

2 *Ibid.*, File 6–29. The entire Legal Series 6 relates to various Canadian Northern bond issues and short-term notes. The various loans advanced by different trust companies, banks, and other financiers are all outlined in considerable detail in the files and documents kept by the secretary of the Canadian Northern Railway in PAC, CNR Records, X̄CCXIV and X̄CCLXXXVIII,

Secretary's Black Books.
3 *Ibid.*, File 6–34.
4 *Ibid.*, File 6–35. Such sales were periodically authorized by the Board of Directors of the Canadian Northern Railway and its various affiliated companies.
5 PAC, CNR Legal Series, Files 1150–4–1 and 1150–6–1. *Ibid.*, X̄CCLXXIX, item 6, Secretary's Black Book.

sion Fund and the Mutual Life Assurance Company of Canada, Waterloo.[6]

The railway's unguaranteed 4-per-cent Perpetual Consolidated Debenture Stock, which was a first charge on acquired ancillary properties and a second charge on assisted lines, also sold very well. The railway disposed of most of this Perpetual Consolidated Debenture Stock by giving it to Mackenzie and Mann in payment for securities of ancillary companies acquired by them, and in payment for construction expenses and services.[7] In 1910, £1,000,000 of the Perpetual Consolidated Debenture Stock, underwritten by Sperling and Company, and by the railway's three banks, was offered for public sale at 95 per cent. It was quickly sold, and William Mackenzie and Horne-Payne were encouraged to bring out a new and much more speculative security.

Horne-Payne suggested and Mackenzie eventually agreed, despite serious reservations by some Canadian Northern legal advisers, to bring out up to $15,000,000 in 5-per-cent Income Charge Convertible Debenture Stock. These debentures had two unique features. The 5-per-cent interest was a charge against the net income of the company. It was only payable if the net earnings of the company, after the payment of all operating expenses and fixed charges, permitted this. The holder could, however, exchange these debentures at par, after three years, for common shares in the Canadian Northern Railway.[8]

None of the common shares of the Canadian Northern Railway had ever been offered for public sale, but to facilitate the sale of its Income Charge Convertible Debenture Stock the Canadian Northern Railway applied to the Toronto Stock Exchange for a quotation on its common shares. The Exchange responded with a quotation of 96.5, reflecting the high regard the financial community had for the Mac-

6 *Ibid.*, File 6–32.

7 The minutes of the meetings of the Board of Directors indicate that most issues of Perpetual Consolidated Debenture stock were made to Mackenzie, Mann and Co. Ltd. The stock was sold by Mackenzie and Mann on the market in much the same way as were other Canadian Northern securities. The $5,000,000 bond purchase by J. P. Morgan in 1904 was from Mackenzie, Mann and Co. Ltd. PAC, CNR Legal Series, File 6–3, covering entire series through File 6–22A.

8 PAC, CNR Legal Series, File 6–42; see particularly Memo from Gerard Ruel to D. C. Grant, 25 Nov. 1926, and Canadian Northern Railway Company Issue of £1,543,209 (or $7,500,000) Five Per Cent Income Charge Convertible Debenture Stock Prospectus, April 1911.

kenzie and Mann enterprise in 1910.[9]

A syndicate, with Sperling and Company acting as brokers, underwrote the Income Charge Convertible Debenture Stock, which was offered for public sale at surprisingly high prices. It was Horne-Payne's intention to issue the first $5,000,000 at 97.5. He was most enthusiastic when the securities were issued. "Convertible dealing in London starts tomorrow under best possible auspices and conditions," he wired Toronto. "Syndicate exclusively influential houses including all Colonial market jobbers and most important brokers throughout the country."[10] The Directors authorized the issuance of the new securities, in $5,000,000 allotments, on 30 June and 27 October 1910 and on 6 May 1911. [11] In London, contrary to Horne-Payne's early recommendations, the Income Charge Convertible Debenture Stock was brought out in two $7,500,000 groups. The first group was sold at the prices recommended by Horne-Payne. The prospectus advertising the sale of the final $7,500,000, however, stated that similar securities already sold were then being traded at 101 to 102. The new issue, directly underwritten by the Canadian Northern Railway, was offered for sale at 98 per cent of par value and sold with little difficulty.[12] Clearly the investors had complete confidence in the Canadian Northern Railway when they eargerly bought up its most speculative issues at or near par value.

The major problems created by the Income Charge Convertible Debenture Stock were not due to lack of public acceptance, but to legal and accounting difficulties. The key question was whether separate accounts had to be kept and income calculated separately for the profitable Canadian Northern Railway as it existed at the time the stock was issued, or whether losses on lines later amalgamated or new construction added to the Canadian Northern's 1910 mileage were in fact a legitimate prior charge on the system. The lawyers and solicitors of the railway disagreed among themselves on the matter.[13] Initially,

9 CAR, 1910, 607.
10 PAC, CNR Legal Series, File 6–42, Horne-Payne to Mackenzie, 23 June 1910.
11 PAC, CNR Records, MCDXXXVIII, 51–66, 80–2, 30–1. Meetings of the Shareholders and Directors of the Canadian Northern Railway, 30 June 1910, and of the Directors, 27 Oct. and 6 May 1910.
12 PAC, CNR Legal Series, File 6–42.
13 Ibid., Memo by Gerard Ruel for Mr. D. C. Grant, 25 Nov. 1926.

however, earnings were sufficient to pay the interest, and the first such interest payments were authorized on 7 October 1911.[14] All interest payments ceased, however, when the Canadian Northern was reorganized in 1914 and the various affiliated lines were included in the Canadian Northern's accounting before net income was determined.[15] Ultimately the Income Charge Convertible Debenture Stock was redeemed at 94.[16] Very little, if any, was ever exchanged for Canadian Northern common shares.

The success of the Income Charge Convertible Debenture Stock indicated the confidence and high regard financiers had for the Canadian Northern Railway. Other short-term securities for rolling stock or immediate requirements where there might be technical delays in the completion of the actual sale of securities created no problems. The *Canadian Annual Review* reported in 1910 on the finances of the Canadian Northern Railway: "Mr. Mackenzie had secured in Great Britain for use in developing the varied interests of the Company the immense sum of $40,700,000."[17] These immense sums of money, together with the promise of even larger issues in 1911 and 1912 for the British Columbia and Northern Ontario sections, facilitated a rapid and aggressive construction policy. The situation looked so promising that the Canadian Northern's third vice-president predicted that by the end of 1914 the company would operate a 10,000-mile transcontinental railway system. When he made the prediction, the Canadian Northern had 3,325 miles of track in operation west of Port Arthur, and approximately 700 miles in eastern Canada. There were, however, an equal number of miles of track under construction, and Hanna was confident that the system had been developed so successfully that its completion had become inevitable. At various times after 1910 Mackenzie and Mann or their subcontractors employed up to 10,000 construction workers. After 1912 there were times when the Ontario section alone had 7,000 men building new track.[18] Construction of the Ontario section, however, was possible only after a federal bond guarantee. This guarantee was extracted from a rather reluctant and

14 PAC, CNR Records, MCDXXXVIII, 57, Meeting of the Directors of the Canadian Northern Railway, 7 Oct. 1911.

15 *Ibid.*, MCDXXXIX, Meeting of the Directors of the Canadian Northern Railway, 9 Oct. 1914.

16 PAC, CNR Legal Series, File 6–42.

17 CAR, 1910, 609.

embattled federal government in 1911.

The reciprocity agreement with the United States, which the Laurier government negotiated in 1910 and presented to Parliament and finally to the voters in 1911, was of the utmost political and economic importance. Any major change in Canada's trade patterns would, of course, have a direct effect on the country's railways. It was generally assumed that the trade concessions offered by the Americans in 1911 would lead to an increased trade along continental north-south trade routes and a proportionate decrease in trade along the long and expensive all-Canadian routes north of Lake Superior. This would, of course, be directly contrary to the business interests, particularly the transportation enterprises, committed to the all-Canadian trade routes.

Many critics of the reciprocity treaty also believed that close economic relations with the United States, indeed economic dependence on the giant to the south, would greatly weaken and undermine Canadian political independence. Ever since the days when John A. Macdonald had introduced his National Policy, Canadian politicians had debated the issue. Bitter emotion-charged campaigns and battles had been fought—not once, but repeatedly. Conservatives who looked to England for their spiritual and political inspiration and regretted any increases in American influences in Canadian affairs, economic or political, were sure to oppose the reciprocity proposals of 1911, adding their voices to those of Canadian businessmen who had a vested interest in the Canadian tariff.

A number of men prominent in or associated with the Canadian Northern Railway fitted into one or both of these categories. Men like William Mackenzie and Zebulon A. Lash felt a strong emotional attachment to Britain and things British. Their concepts of patriotism compelled them to resist American encroachments and to facilitate the enlargement of British influence in Canadian affairs. Mackenzie had always been a Conservative. He had first sought a nomination under that party's banner in the 1891 campaign—the same campaign in which Macdonald had made the announcement, "A British subject I was born. A British subject I will die." "The Old Flag, the Old Man,

18 Stevens, 77; PAC, Borden Papers, File RLB 392, Quebec City Railway Terminals File, 1913–1914; PAC, Superintendent of Immigration records, File 594511, Railway labourers.

and the Old Policy" had then decisively defeated the forces of "Unrestricted Reciprocity".

Z. A. Lash had been a staunch Liberal for more than thirty years, but in some respects his views were very similar to Mackenzie's. Lash had been a protégé, and later a law partner, of one-time Liberal leader Edward Blake. Blake had shown very considerable concern about the trade and tariff policies adopted by his successor in 1887 and 1891. His famous West Durham letter documented a wide divergence of opinion between Blake and other members of the Liberal party. Lash voted Liberal in 1891 and there is no direct evidence to show how he regarded the reciprocity issue then. Twenty years later, however, he made it quite clear that his views on the tariff were very similar to those of Edward Blake.

Shortly after the terms of the agreement were announced, Lash decided that he must campaign publicly against the measure. He entered into discussions with Laurier, and on 10 February 1911 he sent the Prime Minister a lengthy letter in which he explained why he would campaign against political friends of a lifetime. "It is essential to the continued National unity and development of Canada," he wrote the Prime Minister, "that no trade relations with any country should be agreed to by Canada on any basis which check the growth and development of trade between the various parts of Canada with each other or between Canada and the various parts of the Empire." Lash believed that the proposed agreement would check the growth and development of such trade. The National Policy, he claimed, had produced "unexampled prosperity". The proposed agreement would increase Canadian dependence on the United States, undermine the economic unity and interdependence of the various sections of Canada, and "weaken the ties which bind us to the Empire". To Lash, the matter was "above any party and above any interests save those of our beloved Canada and our own beloved flag". He would therefore break lifelong political friendships to do battle for a principle which he believed went "to the very root of Canadian Nationality and unity and autonomy".[19]

19 PAC, Laurier Papers, DCLXIV, 180934–8. All direct quotes in this paragraph are taken from a lengthy letter from Lash to Laurier, 10 Feb. 1911.

Lash was not the only Liberal who opposed reciprocity in 1911. He did, however, provide much of the leadership and inspiration for a group of eighteen prominent Liberal businessmen and financiers in the Toronto area who launched an active campaign against reciprocity. It was Lash who drafted the manifesto which the eighteen signed. Many of the arguments, and even the wording, of this manifesto were very similar to those in Lash's letter to Laurier.[20] Among those who signed the manifesto there were four, including Lash, who had close business connections with the Canadian Northern Railway. They were Byron E. Walker, president of the Canadian Bank of Commerce, W. Thomas White, general manager of the National Trust Company, and E. R. Wood, general manager of the Dominion Securities Corporation, vice-president of the National Trust Company, and a former director of the Canadian Northern Railway.

Some historians have suggested that Canadian Northern interests instigated, financed, and co-ordinated the revolt of the Toronto Liberals.[21] One might ask, however, whether these men sought to defend a principle, as Lash's letter to Laurier and the manifesto suggest, or whether they were merely concerned about the profits and welfare of a particular business enterprise. Motives, of course, are hard to ascertain, and statements by the participants might well be misleading. It is important to note, however, that Donald Mann disagreed with his business associates and strongly defended the reciprocity agreement.[22] D. B. Hanna, the man most directly concerned with operations on the railway, remained silent, and his long-standing directive forbidding employees to take a direct and active part in election campaigns remained in force in 1911.[23]

A close examination of the affairs of the Canadian Northern Railway quickly reveals that the company was less likely to be injured by reciprocity than were the other transcontinentals. It alone had not yet entered binding commitments to build the expensive section north of Lake Superior which would have been most directly affected by

20 A copy of the manifesto is readily available in Paul Stevens, ed., *The 1911 General Election: A Study in Canadian Politics* (Toronto: Copp Clark, 1968), 66–7.

21 *Ibid.*, 64–70.
22 *Edmonton Bulletin*, 9 Feb. 1911, quoting from the *New York Herald*, 3 Feb. 1911.
23 CNRHQ, O. D. Prosser interview.

major changes in traffic patterns. The Canadian Northern Railway, moreover, was on the point of completing a very important new line, a through line from Winnipeg to Duluth via Fort Frances. It was therefore in an excellent position to benefit from an increase in traffic between Canada and the United States.

The line to Duluth was not built in anticipation of reciprocity. Mackenzie and Mann first became interested in the line because of their fascination with the mineral resources of the area.[24] They hoped, perhaps believed, that the iron deposits of the Mesabi Range extended northward into Ontario. At one time the promoters believed Atikokan on their main line would become the iron-ore capital of Canada. William Mackenzie even called his private railway car *The Atikokan* in anticipation of the importance of that name.[25] Mackenzie and Mann wanted their railway to become an important factor in the iron ore business and in some of the lumber business of the area. They were also well aware of other strategic advantages to be derived from a through line to Duluth. Proposals to build some kind of railway from Winnipeg to Duluth, in order to give western Canadian railways an alternative outlet and some influence in territory controlled by rival American roads, had received favourable consideration in Winnipeg for many years.[26] Premiers Greenway and Macdonald had tried to encourage construction of such a road in the 1880s and 1890s, and it was clear to Mackenzie and Mann that such a road would be of great strategic advantage if difficulties ever developed with the American competitors. There was, moreover, a considerable volume of Canadian traffic coming from or going to the American Lakehead terminals, in defiance of the Canadian tariff. Canadian Northern officials were understandably eager to carry such traffic as far as possible over their own system.

Mackenzie and Mann soon discovered and purchased the charter of the line they needed. It was the Duluth, Rainy Lake and Winnipeg Railway, incorporated in Minnesota in 1905 and owned and operated by the logging firm of Cook and O'Brien of Minnesota. Ninety-two

24 PAC, Laurier Papers, DLXIX, 154283–6, D. D. Mann to George Graham, 1 April 1909, together with a memorandum prepared by Z. A. Lash.

25 Hanna, 229.

26 PAM, Greenway Papers, Folio 10369.

miles of inexpensive track had been laid from Virginia, Minnesota, to Fort Frances, Ontario, when Mackenzie and Mann became interested in the railway. In 1905 Cook and O'Brien agreed to sell 51 per cent of the capital stock of their railway to Mackenzie and Mann, subject to an agreement that the railway would continue to serve the needs of their logging firm at agreed rates. There the matter rested until 1908, when Mackenzie and Mann decided to complete the line from Virginia to Duluth. Cook and O'Brien were not interested in this new railway construction and a complicated new arrangement was negotiated.

The first step in the reorganization was the incorporation of a new company in Minnesota—the Duluth, Winnipeg and Pacific Railway. It carried a capitalization of $6,000,000 and had authority to acquire the stock of the Duluth, Rainy Lake and Winnipeg Railway Company. Mackenzie and Mann immediately exchanged their 51-per-cent interest in the Duluth, Rainy Lake and Pacific Railway (the old company) for $4,000,000 worth of capital stock in the Duluth, Winnipeg and Pacific Railway (the new company). The new company was to bring out a large new bond issue, the proceeds to be used to bring in all outstanding bonds of the old company and to finance the construction from Virginia to Duluth. The new bonds were to carry a Canadian Northern Railway guarantee. The Canadian Northern Railway was to receive 51 per cent of the stock of the new company in return for its guarantee. A separate arrangement was also made whereby Mackenzie and Mann would buy out Cook and O'Brien's remaining 49-per-cent interest in the old company and exchange this for stock in the new company. The net result of this arrangement was that 51 per cent of the capital stock of the new company would be held by the Canadian Northern Railway while the remaining 49 per cent would be held by Mackenzie, Mann and Co. Ltd.[27]

The crucial element in the reorganization was the Canadian Northern Railway's guarantee of the bonds to be issued by the new American railway company. Under the terms of its federal charter, and because it had itself received federal and provincial bond guarantees, the Canadian Northern Railway needed federal authorization before it could complete the guarantee arrangement with the American sub-

27 *Arbitration*, 2539–41.

sidiary. The federal government was understandably sceptical about the arrangement. It feared that this was simply a scheme whereby the Canadian Northern, which had just been refused a federal guarantee for its proposed line from Port Arthur to Montreal, would divert Canadian traffic to American channels. At Duluth, American lines might well be eager to provide the Canadian Northern with eastern connections, either with the American Atlantic ports or with the Mackenzie-and-Mann-owned lines in eastern Canada, which it could not obtain from its Canadian competitors. Mackenzie and Mann assured Laurier that it was not their intention to divert traffic to the United States.[28] They needed the Duluth connection to ensure that Canadian-bound traffic from Duluth would pass into Canadian channels at that point, rather than go by American channels as far as Winnipeg and perhaps further. News that J. J. Hill was just then planning an important incursion into the Canadian prairies by either the Great Northern or the Northern Pacific railway was used to very good effect by the Canadian lobbyists,[29] although Hill's alleged Canadian plans never materialized. Canadian traffic, including that going to or coming from Duluth, should be carried on Canadian railways. When presented with these arguments, the federal government somewhat reluctantly authorized the guarantee in 1910. The bonds were immediately issued and sold in London, and construction was well advanced when the terms of the reciprocity treaty were announced.[30]

Thanks to the large volume of lumber traffic, reaching up to 200,000,000 board feet per annum, the road was profitable from the beginning. Annual iron-ore shipments of up to 2,000,000 tons were also anticipated, although this estimate was never fully realized. Mackenzie and Mann were confident that the line would become "the best asset in the way of a branch line that the Canadian Northern will have".[31] The line also placed the Canadian Northern Railway in a very much stronger position, either to bargain for the needed federal

28 PAC, Laurier Papers, DLXIX, 154283–4, 154285–6, and DLXXI, 154996–7, 154902, D. D. Mann to G. P. Graham, 1 April 1909, Memorandum by Z. A. Lash to Laurier, n.d., Lash to Laurier, 17 April 1909, and Laurier to Lash, 17 April 1909, respectively.

29 *Ibid.*, Mann to Graham, 1 April 1909.

30 CAR, 1910, 609.

31 PAC, Laurier Papers, DLXIX, 154283–4, Mann to Graham, 1 April 1909.

guarantee for the line from Port Arthur to Montreal, or, if reciprocity did indeed divert Canadian traffic to American channels, to take full advantage of such a diversion without the albatross of an expensive Canadian Northern line north of Lake Superior.

It must be emphasized that the Canadian Northern had not yet begun construction on that vital but expensive section of the all-Canadian route. Donald Mann had never been particularly enthusiastic about expensive new construction except on the prairies.[32] A Duluth terminus with independent and competitive eastern connections fitted well into his plans. It would also, and perhaps ironically, produce the very railway which Canadian Bank of Commerce officials in 1903 thought the only possible railway Mackenzie and Mann could build if they decided to compete with the federally sponsored Grand Trunk Pacific scheme.[33] It would seem, therefore, that the Canadian Northern had considerably less to fear from reciprocity than did the other transcontinentals. Mann could confidently assure reporters,

---

32 *Arbitration*, 2683–4.

33 Plummer wrote Walker as follows in 1902: "The only alternative course I can see is to give up for the present all idea of an independent transcontinental road; to put in more capital and develop the line as a central Canadian line; i.e. one collecting traffic and bringing it to Port Arthur, as the Chicago lines do under somewhat similar circumstances, & to form an alliance with such a line as the Chicago Great Western with a connecting link (about 200 miles thro a self supporting company) for an outlet in winter, a feeder from the South, and a possible assistant later on in a Pacific coast line. They would have a nice property." UTA, Walker Papers, Plummer to Walker, 4 Oct. 1902. If this course was regarded as financially sound in 1902, there is no reason to believe it would have been less feasible in 1911. Mackenzie and Mann had not yet invested in the expensive line north of Lake Superior. Their investments in Ontario, Quebec, and Nova Scotia were comparatively small. Connections with American lines at Duluth were certainly possible. The argument that Canadian Northern officials masterminded the revolt of the eighteen Toronto Liberals for their own selfish purposes needs re-examination. William Mackenzie's niece probably summed up the situation rather well when she said, "To Sir Wm. Mackenzie money was not the prize. He wanted to achieve great ambitions . . . not content until his railway would become transcontinental. His son Rod wanted him to have a railway from Port Arthur to Edmonton." CNRHQ, Janet Gordon interview. In 1902 the bankers were very worried "lest Mackenzie, in his strong desire to be the head & front of a rival to the CPR will let his ambitions & his temper sway his judgement." UTA, Walker Papers, Plummer to Walker, 4 Oct. 1902. In 1911 those same ambitions led the bankers to oppose the very policy they had advocated nine years earlier. They had been converted to Mackenzie's point of view.

I believe no harm can come to our Canadian Railways from this reciprocity agreement. It is true that more traffic will flow southward across the boundary. On the other hand the wider market opened to the products of the prairie Provinces will attract a greater number of settlers from Europe and the United States. Their presence will create more business for the Canadian railways east and west, as well as north and south.[34]

William Mackenzie and other Canadian Northern officials had no intention of abandoning their planned all-Canadian line and sending western traffic to Duluth. Canadian Northern promoters were convinced that Canada enjoyed an almost unlimited wealth of natural resources and that there were excellent prospects for continued spectacular Canadian development. The business community had embraced the National Policy and was determined to retain the benefits and profits which would accrue from Canadian development. They were quite unwilling to share these with the Americans. Lash, claiming to act only from "genuine patriotism and love for Canada", referred Laurier to "the great results of the policy which has been pursued in developing our trade and our natural resources in our own way, and to the danger of a change of this policy". These men believed that Canada must work out "her destiny as part of the British Empire, including the development of her own resources, in her own way and by her own people".[35] As in many other respects, short-term financial considerations alone do not offer an adequate explanation of the actions taken by Mackenzie and Mann and their financial backers in 1911. There can be little doubt that with reciprocity a Canadian Northern Railway system terminating at Duluth, even if it meant giving up the mileage in Ontario, Quebec, and Nova Scotia, which still amounted to less than 1,000 miles, would have been much more profitable than the system that was built.

Mackenzie and Mann believed in Canada and in their railway, which was to facilitate Canadian development. Their response to the reciprocity proposals of 1911 was to press for a firm commitment by the Laurier government to their vision of Canadian national development. Laurier, attacked for his alleged lack of patriotism, was willing

34 *Edmonton Bulletin*, 9 Feb. 1911.   180934–8, Lash to Laurier, 10 Feb.
35 PAC, Laurier Papers, DCLXIV,   1911.

to respond. The result was a rather hastily negotiated federal bond guarantee of $35,000 per mile for the proposed Canadian Northern line from Port Arthur to Montreal. There is no doubt that Mackenzie and Mann, despite the reciprocity proposals, were prepared to commit themselves to the Canadian transcontinental scheme. Laurier found it politically expedient to reaffirm dramatically his support for the Canadian trade patterns that had been developed. The carefully worded preamble to the federal bond guarantee firmly expressed the federal government's commitment to all-Canadian transportation routes.

It is in the interests of Canada as a whole that another line of railway designed to assist in the direct and economic interchange of traffic between the eastern and western portions of Canada, to open up and develop portions as yet without railway facilities, to promote the internal and foreign trade of Canada, to develop commerce through Canadian ports, and to afford the Government system of railways in Quebec, New Brunswick and Nova Scotia and Prince Edward Island an interchange of through traffic, should be constructed from the Pacific Ocean to the City of Montreal.[36]

The reference to the government system of railways was the result of a special arrangement. The Canadian Northern Quebec Railway was operating lines as far east as Quebec City and had plans to extend these to the Maritimes. It was clear, however, that another railway across the Maritimes was not needed and would almost certainly divert even more traffiic from the circuitous and financially troubled Intercolonial Railway. Both Laurier and Mackenzie saw considerable merit in making the Intercolonial Railway the eastern extension of the Canadian Northern. Laurier's views regarding government-operated railways were well known, and Mackenzie and Mann offered to relieve the government of its unprofitable Maritime railways. Laurier was evidently impressed and gave Mackenzie sufficiently strong assurances that the latter declared publicly, "I have got the ICR."[37]

36 Canada, *1–2 Geo. v. Cap. 6*, Preamble.
37 These negotiations were begun as early as 1909. PAO, Whitney Papers, Whitney to E. C. Whitney, 14 Jan. 1909. See also CAR, 1911, 251–4, 639–41.

These arrangements, however, overlooked one very important factor that Laurier never fully understood. If Mackenzie and Mann gained control or exclusive running rights over the Intercolonial, the National Transcontinental Railway would be effectively dead-ended in the Moncton swamps, much as the original National Transcontinental scheme had threatened to dead-end the Canadian Northern at Port Arthur. The National Transcontinental was not yet completed, and neither the Grand Trunk nor the Grand Trunk Pacific had sent any through traffic over it and the Intercolonial to Halifax or Saint John. Direct or indirect control of the eastern end of the system by the Canadian Northern would ensure that no Grand Trunk Pacific traffic would reach the Maritime ports in the future.[38] The Intercolonial had to remain in neutral hands if the National Transcontinental was to have any chance of success. Sharing the Intercolonial with the Grand Trunk Pacific did not appeal to Mackenzie and Mann, especially if it continued to operate as it had in the past. Costs were too high, and if the Canadian Northern supplied the bulk of the new traffic it might be forced to pay most of these costs without the privilege of overhauling the management and increasing the efficiency of the government road. It might well have been cheaper for Mackenzie and Mann to build an inexpensive and direct line to the Maritimes as the CPR had done, rather than to assume responsibility for the cost of the Intercolonial in proportion to the traffic sent. New Brunswick politicians were not unwilling to provide provincial assistance, but no federal encouragement was forthcoming. In fact, the federal government made aid on the Port-Arthur-to-Montreal mileage conditional on the signing of a traffic exchange agreement between the Intercolonial and the Canadian Northern. The Intercolonial Railway thus remained a public enterprise but henceforth enjoyed traffic interchanges with the Canadian Northern.

The necessary negotiations were conducted quickly and quietly. Even in the House of Commons the agreement did not produce acrimonious debate. There seemed to be a general acceptance of the fact that this was the logical outcome of the Laurier government's railway policy. The bill was given royal assent on 19 May 1911 and con-

38 Stevens, 76.

struction was begun immediately. At the end of 1911 Mackenzie and Mann had 4,500 men at work on the Ontario mileage, and in 1912 there were 9,600.[39] Exploration surveys had been carried on since at least 1905 and construction proceeded at a rapid rate. Construction practices and standards on this line were similar to those on the Canadian Northern Pacific Railway. Again grades of 0.5 per cent were obtained, as were maximum curves of six degrees. Eighty-pound rails, wide aprons, and heavy ballasting were called for throughout, and, as in the case of the British Columbia mileage, costs soon greatly exceeded original estimates. In 1911, however, Canadian Northern officials were convinced that they would have a full transcontinental service in operation by 1914.

In anticipation of the early completion of the main lines from coast to coast, Mackenzie and Mann began to devote a larger amount of attention and money to the acquisition of urban properties and the construction of terminal facilities in the larger cities. On the prairies, urban centres had often welcomed the Canadian Northern. In Edmonton and numerous smaller centres, local officials were very eager to assist Mackenzie and Mann in the quest for suitable station facilities and land. Edmonton, in fact, developed around the properties of its first railway. In Winnipeg, the inheritance of the old Northern Pacific and Manitoba Railway, coupled with judicious real-estate purchases by Mackenzie and Mann and greatly assisted by a $1,000,000 provincial bond guarantee, which was later increased to $3,000,000, provided the Canadian Northern Railway with excellent facilities in that city.[40] In the large eastern centres and in Vancouver, however, the Canadian Northern often had to contend with strongly entrenched rivals who controlled the choice access routes and much of the real estate suitable for stations and terminal facilities.

There were certainly some eastern centres where local railways acquired by Mackenzie and Mann provided excellent urban facilities. In Quebec City, for example, the facilities of the Great Northern Railway of Canada, and later those of the Quebec and Lake St. John Railway, provided excellent riverfront locations for stations and other terminal facilities. There Mackenzie and Mann were even able to

39 *Ibid.*, 169; PAC, Borden Papers, File RLB 392.

40 PAC, CNR Legal Series, File 6–34.

block the approaches to the city and create great difficulties for the rival National Transcontinental Railway. Similarly, the Central Ontario Railway and the Bay of Quinte Railway enjoyed very favourable station and shipping locations in some of the smaller centres between Toronto and Montreal. At Ottawa, however, only a rather unsatisfactory arrangement could be made after the Grand Trunk acquired the Canada Atlantic. The Canadian Northern Ontario Railway built only as far as Hurdman Junction, then on the outskirts of Ottawa. It remained far from the business centre of the city, and both freight and passenger service suffered considerably.

Mackenzie and Mann were well aware of the need to obtain downtown facilities in the large eastern centres, but the cost of terminals and right of way, even under the rather rigid expropriation procedures approved by the Board of Railway Commissioners, was enormous. Facilities in three major centres became the particular concern of the promoters. These were Montreal, Toronto, and Vancouver, although major and enormously expensive projects were undertaken only in Montreal and Vancouver.

In Montreal the Canadian Northern obtained its earliest running rights into the city under the charter of the Chateauguay and Northern Railway. Designed as a link between downtown Montreal and the main line of the Great Northern Railway of Canada, the Chateauguay and Northern track approached the city from the east and established a station on Moreau Street in East Montreal in 1903.[41] The Moreau Street station served the small local railway reasonably well. It was, at any rate, no worse than other parts of Mackenzie and Mann's unprofitable Quebec investments. The station, however, lacked both the design and the location to serve adequately as the principal eastern terminus of a transcontinental railway system. It was too far from the downtown and Montreal harbour areas to serve the needs of passengers or shippers satisfactorily. It was also a long and circuitous way of getting traffic from the west into Montreal, and as initial construction standards had been low, major renovations were needed. A more direct approach to the harbour area from the west was needed

41 See various memoranda, agreements, and prospectuses in PAC, CNR Legal Series, File 1014–20–3, re the Great Northern Railway of Canada and the Chateauguay and Northern Railway.

or, as a minimum, an extension from Moreau Street to the business section of the city. Unfortunately there was only a narrow corridor between the St. Lawrence River and the rapidly rising land of Mount Royal. The two older and established transcontinentals occupied this approach from the west; it seemed to be the only feasible approach, but it was firmly closed to the newcomers. River frontage immediately to the west of the Moreau Street station was also controlled by the older roads, or at any rate by interests considered hostile to the Canadian Northern Railway.[42]

Mackenzie and Mann devised a daring and ambitious plan to get into downtown Montreal and resolve their station and terminal problems. They were convinced that their system must have facilities in the nation's largest city as good or better than those of their competitors. Their plan was to tunnel straight through Mount Royal, Montreal's most prominent geographical feature. Such a tunnel would bring the Canadian Northern into the very heart of the business and financial district of the city, only a mile from the principal docks and wharves and to within two blocks of the stations of their rivals. A three-mile tunnel through mixed limestone and extremely hard igneous rock would have to be built.[43] It would certainly be an expensive project but perhaps the total cost would be less than the acquisition of an overland route. The tunnel, moreover, would open large areas northwest of Mount Royal to urban residents if fast train service to the downtown area were provided. Mackenzie and Mann hoped to offset some of the huge construction expenses through land transactions on the far side of the mountain.

In August 1911, before any plans or even suggestions regarding the new project were made public, Mackenzie and Mann obtained a $1,000,000 loan from Lazard Brothers.[44] With this money they began to purchase choice commercial properties in downtown Montreal and farming areas to the northwest of Mount Royal. Then, on 20 October 1911, they took out letters patent incorporating the Canadian Northern

42 *Arbitration*, 182.
43 Many of these details are given in a forty-page booklet published by the Canadian Northern Railway in Dec. 1913, entitled *The Mount Royal Tunnel, Montreal, Quebec, Canada,* being built by Mackenzie, Mann & Company, Limited. A copy is available at CNRHQ.
44 PAC, Borden Papers, File OC 163, 11943–4, Memorandum re Mt. Royal Tunnell [*sic*] & Terminal Co. Limited.

Montreal Tunnel and Terminal Company Limited.[45] Plans were then filed and authorization obtained from the city to build a double-tracked electrically operated tunnel and railway system. An elaborate complex of station and warehouse facilities, connected with an elevated freight terminal and a viaduct to the Montreal harbour, was promised. Electricity was to be used throughout to eliminate the nuisance of smoke from steam engines, and the facilities were praised as "architecturally one of the most attractive groups of a commercial nature in Canada". Much of the space in the new buildings was to be leased and this was expected "to go far towards making the Terminal developments self-supporting".[46]

At the same time a new "model city", the town of Mount Royal, was laid out on what had until recently been a large tract of farmland. The town was entirely built around the railway and its local station, Mount Royal Heights, on the northwest side of the mountain. A special network of diagonal streets, cutting across the usual city streets, was designed to facilitate rapid access to the station from any part of the new town. Mount Royal was to become an attractive dormitory town, attracting many Montrealers who would use the trains to get to work in the city itself.[47]

The Mount Royal Tunnel, and the various subsidiary enterprises associated with it, were both daring and spectacular. Mackenzie and Mann were convinced that a sound basis for profitable operations could and would be established. Continued growth and development of the Canadian economy seemed assured in 1911. There seemed to be no reasonable doubt that the required financing could be arranged. The three-year loan of $1,000,000 from Lazard Brothers facilitated an optimistic and aggressive beginning. Mackenzie and Mann confidently predicted that the tunnel and the main station would be completed in time for the opening of a Canadian Northern transcontinental service in 1914.

45 Canada, Letters Patent, 12 Aug. 1911. The Company was first incorporated as the Canadian Northern Montreal Tunnel and Terminal Company, Limited, but the name was changed in 1914 to the Mount Royal Tunnel and Terminal Company Limited.

46 *The Mount Royal Tunnel, Montreal, Quebec, Canada, being built by Mackenzie, Mann & Company, Limited*, 8.
47 The map of the proposed town of Mount Royal in this booklet clearly indicates the central position and easy accessibility of the railway station.

Most of the plans and designs for the new tunnel were drawn by Henry K. Wickstead, an American engineer who had done considerable railway work on both the National Transcontinental and the Canadian Northern railways. Technologically the project greatly excited railway engineers and designers,[48] and if judged from the present day it is obvious that the Montreal plans were well ahead of contemporary thinking. The smoke and noise associated with steam railways was to be eliminated, as were dangerous and inconvenient level crossings and the problems of snow removal. It would be possible to travel at high speeds to the very centre of the city. The project was clearly designed to give the Canadian Northern "better terminal facilities than those possessed by any company in that city".[49] It would, however, cost immense sums of money. Mackenzie and Mann ultimately spent $12,346,791 on the project, and even when that figure was reached many features outlined in 1911 were not completed.[50] That dream was only fully realized, albeit with important modifications, many decades later when the Canadian National Railways built their headquarters and the Queen Elizabeth Hotel complex in Montreal on and near the original Canadian Northern site.

In the city the project evoked a rather mixed response. City Council willingly granted permits and rezoned some areas as required. Other people found the project too new, too expensive, or too dangerous. A tunnel under large buildings and expensive homes was viewed with very considerable alarm. Once construction and blasting began, Montrealers living nearby began to look for cracks in walls and foundations, and for other damage caused by vibrations. Some of this was allegedly encouraged by the Canadian Pacific and by McGill University, on whose Board of Governors the CPR had strong representation, and under whose properties the tunnel passed. Suits were launched against the tunnel company and its contractors, but with little success. Scientists were brought into court with seismographic tracings which demon-

48 There are, for example, numerous references to various technological aspects of the project in the *Canadian Railway and Marine World*, and similar British and American magazines.
49 *Arbitration*, 182.
50 This figure does not include the residential lands, most of which were held by the Canadian Northern Montreal Land and Development Company rather than by the Mount Royal Tunnel and Terminal Company. The Land Company never had any direct financial affiliation with the Canadian Northern Railway.

strated that movements and activities in the tunnel were less perceptible than the movement of vehicles on the streets.[51] One particular suit brought the plaintiff embarrassing notoriety and the Canadian Northern's legal department great delight. This delight was in no way diminished by the alleged association of the plaintiff with McGill University. One of the Canadian Northern lawyers later talked of the case to the Board of Arbitration.

One gentleman threatened to get an injunction, in fact, he applied for one. The papers were giving reports of how far the tunnel had progressed from day to day, and he waited until the work had progressed to a point corresponding with the location of his house. Then he applied for an injunction and swore that the vibration was intolerable and that he had experienced the worst trouble at the time that the tunnel had reached a point corresponding with his own property as reported in the papers. When the case came to trial it was found that the papers were mistaken and that at the time he said he had experienced the worst trouble, the tunnel was half a mile away from his property. So nothing came of the case.[52]

Opposition of this kind was relatively easy to deal with. As long as there was enough money, the technological, political, and competitive problems would be and were met. In 1911, financing was no problem and the visionary new project was begun with great confidence and enthusiasm.

In Toronto, where the Canadian Northern Railway had its headquarters, equally daring and ambitious projects were formulated, although very little ever came of them. Mackenzie and Mann's first Ontario steam railway, the James Bay Railway, was built only from Rosedale on the outskirts of Toronto to Sudbury. Later, when the line from Toronto to Ottawa was built, it simply connected with this Sudbury line at Todmorden in northeast Toronto. The Ontario government's 1909 bond-guarantee legislation was specifically designed to provide funds to enable the now-renamed Canadian Northern Ontario Railway to establish terminal facilities in Toronto and to build several needed spur lines on the Sudbury branch. Nothing of a very respectable nature ever came of these plans. Rather temporary and ram-

51 Stevens, 74.   52 *Arbitration*, 183.

shackle open-air freight yards were built along the Don River Valley in Leaside, while the passenger and express business was taken along a Don Valley spur line to a station on Cherry Street. Smoke, noise, and safety were all inadequately dealt with at the freight yards. The entire establishment was a source of constant complaints. Arbitration chairman William Meredith later suggested that the nuisance was so great that D. B. Hanna had found it necessary to move from Leaside where he had ben living.[53] The Cherry Street station was hardly more satisfactory. It was still some two miles from the centre of the Toronto business district and was therefore rather inconvenient, although connection with the Toronto Street Railway was made.[54]

The basic problem in Toronto centred on rival hydro-electric development schemes. Steam locomotives were not well suited to operations in large urban centres. In both Montreal and Vancouver, Mackenzie and Mann resorted to electrification. They intended to do so in Toronto as well. There, William Mackenzie already controlled the electrically operated Toronto Street Railway and a number of associated hydro-electric enterprises. He hoped to extend the Toronto system along the western end of Lake Ontario to Hamilton and ultimately to the Niagara frontier. The line was to be fully integrated with the operations of the Canadian Northern Railway; the necessary charters were acquired,[55] and much of the right of way was actually purchased. It was to accommodate hydro-electric transmission lines as well as electrical and perhaps steam-railway lines. It would have the additional advantage of providing the Canadian Northern system with a vital connection with the American lines at Buffalo.[56] It was, in fact, an early and rather larger version of the Ontario government's present commuter GO trains. Mackenzie and Mann were certainly very eager to

53 *Ibid.*, 186–7.
54 Detailed maps of Canadian Northern terminal facilities in various cities are available in CNRHQ.
55 The most important of these companies were the Niagara, St. Catharines and Toronto Railway Company, the Toronto Suburban Railway Company, the Toronto Niagara and Western Railway Company, the Toronto Eastern Railway Company, and Toronto Dwellings. Most were originally owned directly by Mackenzie and Mann. Many were subsequently acquired by the Canadian Northern Railway from the promoters. Approximately sixty miles of electric lines were actually built in the Niagara peninsula, but the essential connections between Toronto and the Niagara frontier were never made by the Canadian Northern Railway.
56 *Arbitration*, 1341–3.

build at least the main Niagara, St. Catharines and Toronto line.[57] They were confident that the Buffalo connection would provide their system with additional traffic worth at least $2,000,000 annually. Control of this vital section, they alleged, gave the Canadian Pacific and the Grand Trunk railways a very unfair competitive advantage.[58]

Plans for a Toronto station were largely dependent on the success of the larger scheme. The estrangement between Mackenzie and Mann and Premier Whitney in 1909, however, left all of Mackenzie's electrical and traction companies in jeopardy. Adam Beck, with apparent support from the Premier, was determined to have the publicly owned Hydro-electric Commission build its own electric transmission line to Niagara. The politicians, moreover, seemed determined both to prevent further expansion of the Toronto Street Railway and eventually to acquire it and operate it as a public enterprise. The basic uncertainty surrounding the Toronto Street Railway and its affiliate companies, coupled with the firm refusal of both federal and provincial governments to offer any assistance for the Niagara extension, made ambitious developments in Toronto very difficult, if not impossible.[59] Consequently, in 1914, the Canadian Northern made arrangements with the Grand Trunk Railway for the joint use of that company's new Union Station in the city.[60] The nuisance of the Leaside freight yards remained. This was certainly not the way to compete with the Grand Trunk and the Canadian Pacific. The measure of the Canadian Northern's failure to establish adequate facilities in Toronto is indicated by the fact that it managed to establish only fifteen sidings and industrial spurs in the city. The Grand Trunk had 129, while the CPR built no fewer than 187.[61]

At the western end of its transcontinental system the Canadian Northern found itself confronted with an increasingly common urban problem of ambitious North American railways. Rivals, in this case the CPR and J. J. Hill, under the authority of several local charters,

57 A determined bid for government assistance was made in 1914, but it was unsuccessful.
58 *Arbitration*, 1759.
59 *Ibid.*, 1341–3.
60 *Canadian Railway and Marine World, 1915*, 416. There are numerous references to the Toronto Union Station in subsequent issues of this magazine, and to various more-or-less-petty disputes between the two railways using the facilities.
61 *Arbitration*, 3095.

controlled the main access routes to, and choice properties in, the commercial and business centre of the city of Vancouver. To get into the city, Mackenzie and Mann had to devise another spectacularly expensive scheme. For a time they gave serious consideration to an alternative route which would avoid the city, but in 1910 the provincial government insisted that the new line be built to New Westminster, Vancouver, and English Bay on the mainland. A ferry service to Vancouver Island and rail connection with Victoria were to be established. In 1910, however, Mackenzie and Mann had no idea how they would get their line into Vancouver.

The CPR controlled an admirable access to the business district of the city, since its line was built right along the shore of Vancouver Harbour. This line, however, would be very difficult to parallel. Alternative routes could not be found easily or cheaply. Mackenzie and Mann therefore decided to buy property some distance away on the outskirts of Vancouver. Two and a half miles of undeveloped waterfront on the Fraser River, a mile east of the Westminster bridge, were purchased.[62] There a terminus of sorts was established while the promoters awaited further and, they hoped, favourable developments which would permit an entry into Vancouver.

The railway yards on the Fraser River were named Port Mann. Mackenzie and Mann announced that this would be the site of their west-coast repair shops, while permanent west-coast terminal facilities would be developed in Vancouver. Land agents and speculators nevertheless began to circulate rumours that the lack of suitable access routes into the city would compel the promoters to establish permanent station and terminal facilities at Port Mann. A good deal of real estate in the area was sold and an impressive town was laid out. Mackenzie and Mann meanwhile sought ways and means of getting into Vancouver. They found that a rival project, with which they had once been associated, left them an opening, which they quickly exploited.

During the early years when Mackenzie and Mann had had hopes of building the Crow's Nest Pass Railway as part of a trans-British Columbia scheme, they had acquired interests in the Vancouver,

62 P. Roy, "Railways, Politicians and the Development of Vancouver as a Metropolitan Centre, 1886–1929" (MA thesis, University of Toronto, 1963), 195–6.

Victoria and Eastern Railway. This was to be the western half of the scheme, and it failed when the Crow's Nest Pass contract went to the CPR. Later, when the proposals for a railway to the Yukon were under active consideration, they had also taken an interest in the Vancouver, Westminster and Yukon Railway. Neither charter seemed useful to Mackenzie and Mann after 1902 and they allowed their sometime friend and adviser, J. J. Hill, to acquire controlling interests in both companies. Hill amalgamated the two schemes in 1908, after obtaining rights from the city to build and develop a large station and freight-handling facility on False Creek. His plan was to reclaim a portion of the swampy creek bed at the eastern end of False Creek (east of Westminster Street, later renamed Main Street) and to develop it as a commercial railway depot. The city of Vancouver approved of the plan in 1907, and Hill acquired a good deal of territory in the False Creek area. The city retained rights to the creek bed itself, but rented a portion to Hill under a forty-year lease.[63]

The leasing arrangement did not prove satisfactory. A further agreement was negotiated and signed on 15 May 1910. Under the new terms the False Creek properties, including the creek bed, were to be divided between the city and Hill's railway company. The railway company was to obtain clear title to all the lands it needed to construct its facilities, the city retaining the balance of the creek bed and some adjacent properties turned over to it by the railway in exchange for unobstructed rights to portions of the creek bed. The railway company agreed to make its facilities available to other railway companies. Its station was to be a union station. The Northern Pacific, the Grand Trunk Pacific, and the Canadian Northern Pacific railways were mentioned as possible users of the new facilities.[64]

The 1910 provisions for the construction of a union station should have provided Mackenzie and Mann with adequate facilities. There were difficulties, however, in arriving at a satisfactory agreement. Mackenzie and Mann, fearing harassment and possible diversion of

63 VanA., City of Vancouver Agreements File 4676, Memorandum of Agreement of 10 Dec. 1907, between the City of Vancouver and the Vancouver, Westminster and Yukon Railway Company.

64 *Ibid.*, File 1989, Memorandum of Agreement of 15 May 1910, between the City of Vancouver and the Vancouver, Victoria and Eastern Railway and Navigation Company.

traffic, did not wish to be dependent on a competitor. Their relations with Hill were relatively good, but each party clearly recognized the other as shrewd and extremely competitive in business. The union terminal, moreover, was also deemed unsuitable for Mackenzie and Mann's proposed ferry and steamship operations to Vancouver Island. Vancouver was a big centre. Mackenzie and Mann thought they could easily raise the required capital and continued to think in terms of establishing their own terminal facilities in the city.

The lands owned by the city on False Creek Inlet provided the means to achieve this objective. Negotiations were initiated on 29 August 1912, when an ambitious Canadian Northern Pacific proposal was presented to Vancouver City Council. Colonel A. D. Davidson, a director of the Canadian Northern Pacific Railway and a man very prominently associated with the sale of Canadian Northern lands, presented his company's proposals. He suggested that the city sell its False Creek lands east of Main Street. The city should also expropriate some adjacent properties needed by the railway. All this property should then be sold to his company for not more than $600,000. The Canadian Northern Pacific Railway would then do the necessary work of reclaiming and filling in the bed of False Creek and building a sea wall to protect the reclaimed lands. Within five years elaborate freight and passenger facilities would be built, with total expenditures amounting to not less than $4,000,000.[65]

Since union stations were then fashionable, Davidson promised that the proposed new Canadian Northern Pacific Railway station would also be a union station. It too would offer its facilities to interested competitors, the new provincially assisted Pacific Great Eastern Railway being a prime candidate. This proposal had the curious effect of placing two union stations almost side by side on False Creek Inlet, but in 1912 no one seemed concerned by this apparent lack of logic. Other concessions seemed more significant. Davidson, in deference to local racist prejudices, promised that all construction work would be done by non-Asiatics, preferably by residents of British Columbia, and that current wage rates would be observed. No construction crews would be required to work on the Sabbath.

65 *Ibid.*, File 2670, A. D. Davidson to the Mayor and Aldermen of the City of Vancouver, 29 Aug. 1912.

Vancouver City Council listened sympathetically, and serious negotiations were begun at once. These culminated in a formal agreement, signed on 5 February 1913. Under the terms of this agreement the city agreed to convey its lands in the False Creek area to the Canadian Northern Pacific Railway for the sum of $1. The railway, however, was to be responsible for all costs connected with the transfer of titles and the expropriation of required additional lands.[66] In return for giving away these swamplands that were worthless until reclaimed, the city required a number of specific undertakings from the railway. Not less than $4,000,000 was to be spent in reclaiming the lands, building the sea wall, and erecting suitable station and freight-handling facilities. These facilities must become the "principal permanent western terminus for both passenger and freight of the Canadian Northern Railway system". Within eight years a large trans-Pacific steamship service was to be inaugurated. Two hotels were to be built, one on the railway property and the other, with not less than 250 rooms, within the city. The approach of the railway to the False Creek terminals was to be "through the high ground to the south and east of the railway property by means of a tunnel which shall be of sufficient size to accommodate a double track railway". The tunnel was to be electrified and subject to rather rigid smoke and noise controls. A $1,500,000 bond had to be deposited as evidence of good faith to complete all these undertakings.[67]

The agreement clearly entailed very onerous obligations. It gave Mackenzie and Mann an excellent independent entrance into the city and they were confident that they could live up to its terms. Their confidence was increased by concurrent negotiations with the provincial government whereby the latter would provide a $10,000,000 guarantee of bonds. Proceeds from the sale of these guaranteed bonds

66 Arrangement for the transfer of titles was a rather complicated procedure, since the lands were formerly used for military purposes and belonged to the federal government. The federal government, however, had transferred them to the city subject to the condition that they be used for industrial, manufacturing, and business purposes only. Under the 1901 arrangement the lands could only be leased, not sold. Several orders-in-council were needed before the matter was resolved. *Ibid.*, File 4704.
67 *Ibid.*, File 2647, Articles of Agreement dated 5 Feb. 1913, between the City of Vancouver and the Canadian Northern Pacific Railway Company and the Canadian Northern Railway Company.

were to provide the funds to complete station and freight-handling facilities in Vancouver, Victoria, Steveston, and Union Bay.

The building of Vancouver terminals was the last major project to which Mackenzie and Mann committed themselves. It was a product of the time when they had plenty of money and even better credit arrangements. That happy state of affairs, however, was rapidly coming to an end. It was an ominous portent of things to come that Mackenzie and Mann had to ask the British Columbia government to increase the interest rate on the terminals bonds to 4.5 per cent.[68] Bonds guaranteed by federal and provincial governments at 3, 3.5, and 4 per cent could only be sold in London at heavy discounts. Many bonds of this kind, however, still had to be earned and sold by the Canadian Northern before it would become the transcontinental system to which Mackenzie and Mann had committed themselves in the years of plenty.

68 PABC, McBride Papers, W. H. Moore to McBride, 13 Feb. 1913.

CHAPTER THIRTEEN

A PERIOD OF FINANCIAL STRINGENCY 1912-1913

MACKENZIE AND MANN made enormous commitments between 1909 and 1912. These included the construction of at least 2,000 miles of prairie branch lines, over 700 miles of very expensive main lines in British Columbia, 1,000 miles of difficult track north of Lake Superior, and expensive new terminal facilities in Winnipeg, Montreal, and Vancouver. In addition they hoped to build a number of branch lines in British Columbia and entertained ambitions of connecting their system with the American lines at Buffalo. All the new lines would need rolling stock and a great deal of other equipment and facilities. Even by very conservative estimates the total expenditure for Mackenzie and Mann's major undertakings would exceed $150,000,000. Government guarantees of $13,000 per mile for the prairie branches, $35,000 per mile on the Lake Superior and British Columbia mileage, and $10,000,000 and $3,000,000 for the British Columbia and Winnipeg terminal facilities respectively were expected to provide approximately $100,000,000. The remainder was to be raised through the sale of Canadian Northern Perpetual Consolidated Debenture Stock and junior securities.

Government guarantees and the enviable reputation of the Canadian Northern Railway in London seemed to assure a ready market for the very large bond issues that the company intended to bring out. Indeed, until the end of 1911 all the securities offered by the Canadian Northern and its affiliates, including both guaranteed and unguaranteed debentures, sold very well. The year 1911 ended on a highly encouraging note when William Mackenzie was able to sell the entire $35,000,000 issue of federally guaranteed debentures for the line from

Port Arthur to Ottawa. The debentures were purchased outright by Lazard Brothers at a discount of approximately 9 per cent.

Mackenzie was so pleased with this large sale that he somewhat prematurely assured the Montreal press that "all the financing has been done for the completion of the Canadian Northern railway from Montreal to the Pacific Coast. The proceeds of the $35,000,000 guaranteed by the Government to build the section from Montreal to Port Arthur are in the Bank and 7,000 men are at work hurrying forward this stretch to completion."[1]

Within a year, however, the market for Canadian securities became glutted. Government-guaranteed debentures could be sold only at very substantial discounts, while the market for unguaranteed securities collapsed altogether. This made it impossible for Mackenzie and Mann to finance their undertakings in the way they had planned. Unguaranteed Perpetual Consolidated Debenture Stock became virtually unsaleable, and in order to avoid putting government-guaranteed securities on the market at big discounts, Mackenzie sought loans and issued short-term securities for which the government-guaranteed securities were pledged as collateral. This short-term financing, however, failed to provide all the required funds, and appeals had to be made for additional government help.

The financial problems of 1912–13 were the result of many domestic and international factors. In part, world-wide economic and financial conditions and fluctuations were to blame. The cyclical vicissitudes of international investment have been noted by numerous economic historians. In 1912 a prosperous, optimistic, and highly expansionist era was coming to a close, and many feared that they were witnessing the beginnings of an international long-term depression. That depression never fully materialized, thanks to the outbreak of war in 1914. War, however, further aggravated the financial situation for promoters of non-military projects.

Some of the problems of those years were, nevertheless, the result of actions by Canadian promoters such as Mackenzie and Mann. The Canadian Northern Railway was only one of a great many Canadian development projects that made large demands on the London money

1 CAR, 1912, 640.

markets. The freewheeling optimism of the years after 1909, aided and abetted by Canadian governments at all levels, had spawned numerous ambitious schemes whose promoters all descended on the London money market at much the same time. When Mackenzie sold the federally guaranteed debentures for the Canadian Northern Ontario line in December of 1911 he was reprimanded by the *Financial News* for glutting the market. "Sir William Mackenzie's issue of a loan of such magnitude, at such a time, is destined to react very unfavourably upon Canadian financial interests in London. . . . Sir William Mackenzie has quite inadvertently, we feel sure, done Canadian interests a distinctly bad turn." Mackenzie was urged to "adopt more circumspect methods in his future arrangements, and to bear in mind that in matters of this kind the loyal Canadian puts Canada first and the other interests, whatever they may be, in the second place."[2]

In view of Mackenzie's very large commitments, such advice was hardly very practical. It was certainly disregarded, and in 1912 Mackenzie managed to raise an additional £32,000,000 in London. That same year the rival Grand Trunk Pacific floated bonds and debentures worth a total of £98,800,000 while the Canadian Pacific, busy with major improvements on its main line and an ambitious branch-line construction program, borrowed £91,000,000 in London.[3] Rumours were beginning to circulate that the Canadians, and particularly Canadian railway promoters, were borrowing too much.

Canadian municipal governments were the first to feel the pinch of a tightening London money market in 1912.[4] Even a Bank of Montreal official, eager to boost confidence in Canadian investments, was forced to admit, "It is doubtless the case that public borrowing in London on the part of small Canadian municipalities has attracted much attention, aroused some unfavourable comment, and probably been responsible—or at least partially responsible—for the views openly expressed that the Dominion has been borrowing too freely."[5] Confidence is the cornerstone of international finance and investments,

2 PAC, White Papers, File 40, 6193, Newspaper clipping from the *Financial News* sent to Sir Thomas White by Lord Strathcona, 9 Jan. 1912.
3 CAR, 1912, 153.

4 For details on the serious problems encountered by the municipal governments in marketing their securities, see PABC, McBride Papers, W. H. Moore to McBride, 13 Feb. 1913.
5 CAR, 1912, 153.

and in 1912 confidence in Canadian securities declined.

Other factors aggravated the situation. Canada was not the only rapidly developing country. Others, notably Brazil and Argentina, were also attracting major British investments, thus reducing the amounts available for investment in Canada. European nations were at the same time becoming increasingly apprehensive about international tensions and wars, particularly in the Balkans. They urgently needed large amounts of capital for defence and military purposes and were willing to pay high rates of interest to get the required funds. Canadian municipalities followed a similar strategy and increased the interest rates on their securities. The demand for funds in 1912 and 1913 simply exceeded the supply.[6] Where government-backed bonds carrying a 3-per-cent rate of interest had been saleable in 1903 and 1904, there was very little demand after 1912 for securities carrying less than 4.5-per-cent interest or a substantial discount. The government-guaranteed securities to be marketed by the Canadian Northern and its affiliates carried a maximum 4-per-cent rate of interest, as did their unguaranteed Perpetual Consolidated Debenture Stock.

Equally unsettling was the realization that construction costs on the new mileage greatly exceeded original estimates. In their determination to build the best possible road, and to avoid expensive improvements and reversions at a later date, Canadian Northern engineers frequently exceeded the already onerous minimum specifications. No one could fault them for not building extremely well in British Columbia and Northern Ontario, but their high standards cost a lot of money. These costs were further increased by the fact that both labour and material costs began to rise rapidly. The same factors that led to excessive demands on the London money markets also led to increased demands, and consequently higher prices and wages, for materials and labour. The inflationary consequences of excessive optimism and rapidly increasing international tensions combined to drive up prices on almost everything needed to build a railway. Thus the amount needed to complete the railway increased. In one way or another the promoters had to find new funds and, perhaps, reduce expenditures.

Premier McBride was one of the first to become worried that the

6 PABC, McBride Papers, W. H. Moore to McBride, 13 Feb. 1913.

funds might be exhausted before the British Columbia project was completed. The original estimate for the cost of the main line from Westminster Bridge to the Yellowhead Pass was $25,297,847.24, or $50,394.11 per mile. This was revised upward to $59,662.00 per mile in 1912 and then further increased two years later to $33,029,260.11, or $66,191.00 per mile.[7] The provincial guarantee provided for only $35,000.00 per mile, less commissions, underwriting fees, and other financial charges. Prospects of raising the remaining funds through the sale of unguaranteed securities were not very good in 1912 and 1913. The proceeds from the guaranteed bonds on the main line might well be spent before the line was completed. On 6 May 1913 Premier McBride wrote Donald Mann a rather worried note.

I find from a perusal of the last estimates covering Canadian Northern Pacific construction in British Columbia that there are but three millions of dollars remaining on the mileage underway guaranteed by the government. Since it is quite obvious that it will take several millions in addition to this sum to complete the work I am anxious to secure from you some specific assurance that your company will be in a position to provide the funds necessary as the project advanced.[8]

No satisfactory assurance could be given. There was no longer a market for the Canadian Northern Pacific's 4-per-cent Perpetual Consolidated Debenture Stock.

While worrying about restricted money markets and escalating construction costs, Mackenzie and Mann had yet another problem to contend with. In 1912 the Regina Board of Trade lodged an official complaint with the Board of Railway Commissioners for Canada. It claimed that the Canadian Northern Railway and its competitors were charging discriminatory and unfair rates on Saskatchewan and Alberta traffic.

The Canadian Northern Railway had long been the leader in making prairie freight-rate reductions. In 1901 it had agreed to reduce its rate on Manitoba traffic to 10¢ per hundredweight on wheat. On

7 PABC, McBride Papers, Statement of estimates for main line, 8 Feb. 1914.

8 Ibid., McBride to T. G. Holt, 6 May 1913.

other commodities the rates were reduced to approximately 15 per cent below the then-prevailing Crow's Nest Pass rates. These Manitoba reductions had not been followed immediately by commensurate reductions in the Territories. Mackenzie and Mann agreed to reduce rates in the Territories in 1903 when they obtained federal guarantees for the main line from Grandview to Edmonton. They did not, however, agree to any specific reductions.[9] It was agreed that the rates in the Territories should be set either by order-in-council or by order of the then-proposed Board of Railway Commissioners. Mackenzie and Mann argued that the rates in the Territories could not be reduced to the Manitoba levels until the districts served by the railway were at least partially settled and built up. The Board of Railway Commissioners accepted the argument, and Canadian Northern rates in Saskatchewan and Alberta were ultimately set at 92.5 per cent of the Crow's Nest Pass Agreement rates.

The optimism and apparent wealth and prosperity of the railways in 1911 persuaded the Regina Board of Trade that the time had come to extend the full benefits of the 1901 Manitoba agreement westward. Saskatchewan was now as developed as Manitoba had been in 1901, but was still paying higher rates. The Manitoba agreement was not, of course, directly applicable to Saskatchewan. The Board of Railway Commissioners was specifically charged, however, with the responsibility of ensuring that railways did not discriminate unfairly against any region, industry, or commodity. The Regina Board of Trade complained that such discrimination was, in fact, being practised.

Canadian Northern representatives pointed out to the Board of Railway Commissioners that their company still had a very large proportion of its mileage in underdeveloped areas and that a unilateral reduction on all traffic in Saskatchewan and Alberta would be disastrous. The prairie section of the Canadian Northern had admittedly made profits from the beginning, but in 1912 and 1913 the company was building many new branch lines in the province and, more significantly, adding new main-line mileage in Ontario and British Columbia,

9 Western MPs wanted specific rates written into the agreement and Mann apparently agreed to do so, but was overruled by Mackenzie who considered immediate lowering of rates in the Territories to the Manitoba levels "perfectly absurd", PAC, CNR Legal Series, File 6–22A.

which would generate little traffic at first. The more profitable prairie lines were expected to "carry" the newer mileage until more local traffic was developed. Canadian Northern officials therefore felt their company could not sustain a 7.5-per-cent freight-rate reduction on the Saskatchewan and Alberta traffic.

Unfortunately for Mackenzie and Mann, their principal prairie competitor, the CPR, was enjoying exceedingly prosperous times. The CPR certainly could afford to reduce its prairie rates, and there could be no doubt that, in comparison with the Manitoba rates, those charged by the railways in Saskatchewan were indeed discriminatory. Canadian Northern arguments before the Board therefore seemed ineffective. Mackenzie tried to persuade the Prime Minister to intervene and prevent the Board from granting the Regina application.[10] He assured Borden that with his company's large new commitments a rate reduction would be disastrous, but Borden allowed the Board to proceed. It looked more carefully at CPR and Canadian Northern profits on their prairie business than at Canadian Northern lamentations about early deficits on newly built mileage, and ordered the rate reductions.[11] The reductions certainly did not not render operations on the established Canadian Northern mileage unprofitable. They did, however, greatly reduce the railway's ability to sustain initial operational deficits on the new mileage the company was building in British Columbia and Ontario.

Canadian Northern fortunes clearly and seriously declined in 1912. Mackenzie and his financial advisers were convinced that the Canadian Northern Railway must raise large sums through the sale of unguaranteed junior securities if all construction requirements were to be met and a fund established to cover "a period of possible lean earnings when the net surplus has been affected by the new road laid down".[12] Few financiers were interested in these junior unguaranteed securities when government-issued or government-guaranteed securities at higher rates of interest were offered. This inability to sell the unguaranteed

10 PAC, Borden Diary, 7 Oct. 1912, 8 Oct. 1912.
11 An extensive summary of the entire Regina Toll Case is given by Angus MacMurchy and Shirley Denison in *Canadian Railway Cases*, XIII

(Toronto: Canada Law Book Co., 1913), 203–16.
12 UTA, Walker Papers, H. V. F. Jones to Walker, 7 March 1910; *Arbitration*, 197.

junior securities was the crux of the Canadian Northern's financial problem in 1912 and 1913.

Even the Canadian Northern Railway's government-guaranteed securities suffered, because they carried a comparatively low rate of interest. When Canadian municipal and civic governments and the governments of apprehensive European countries raised the interest rates on their offerings to 5 and 6 per cent, the Canadian Northern Railway's guaranteed, 3-, 3.5-, and 4-per-cent debentures were no longer competitive. They remained saleable until the outbreak of the First World War, but only at substantial discounts.

Mackenzie's financial advisers in London urged him to resort to short-term financing rather than offer his government-guaranteed securities for sale at large discounts. The stringency was expected to pass. When it did, the guaranteed securities would be saleable at better prices. In the meantime, the London bankers and financiers agreed to make short-term loans at interest rates 0.5 per cent above the current bank rate if Mackenzie pledged Canadian Northern government-guaranteed debentures as collateral, usually at 80 per cent of par value. Lazard Brothers, Lloyd's Bank, the National Bank of Scotland, the Canadian Bank of Commerce, the British Empire Trust Company, and the Dominion Securities Corporation advanced funds on this basis, the individual loans ranging from £100,000 to £1,100,000.[13]

These short-term loans were similar to loans Mackenzie had negotiated with many of the same bankers in earlier years whenever the market seemed temporarily unresponsive to Canadian Northern offerings. The difference was from 1912 through 1914 there were more of them, and for larger amounts. If and when the market improved, the debentures would be sold and the loans repaid.

The financial stringency in 1912–13, however, proved to be much more serious and prolonged than earlier difficulties had been. By mid-1913 there was increasing evidence that the malaise in the London market might continue for some time. Short-term demand notes,

---

13 A detailed list of all these loans, together with lists of the securities pledged to secure each of them, is available in PAC, CNR *Records*, XCCLXXXVIII, Secretary's Black Book. Copies of many of the agreements are contained in CNR Records, XCCXIV, Secretary's Black Book. Much of the legal correspondence relating to these loans is in the CNR Records, Legal Files, Series 6.

usually for between three months and a year, were hardly a satisfactory way of proceeding. Consequently, special Canadian Northern 6-per-cent short-term Gold Notes repayable in one year were prepared. Government-guaranteed debentures were pledged as security for these notes, whose total value was not to exceed $3,500,000. The notes were issued in July of 1913 and immediately sold in their entirety to William A. Read and Company of New York at 97.25¢ on the dollar. Mackenzie and Mann thus obtained urgently needed funds and re-established connections in New York which had lapsed since the 1905 sale of guaranteed debentures to J. P. Morgan.[14]

The issuing and sale of the 6-per-cent one-year notes was followed the next month by the preparation of a £2,000,000 issue of 5-per-cent secured notes, repayable in five years. The object of both issues was simply "to avoid putting out at a big discount 4-per-cent securities during the present period of financial stringency".[15] Provincially guaranteed debentures were pledged as security for these notes, although some unguaranteed 4-per-cent Perpetual Consolidated Debenture Stock was also included. On 8 August 1913, £1,500,000 of the £2,000,000 issue of 5-per-cent notes was purchased by Messrs. Hoare, Miller and Company of London for a net price of £1,469,000.[16] The remainder were to be disposed of in smaller parcels. Hoare, Miller and Company, like the other underwriters who purchased Canadian Northern securities, prepared a prospectus and tried to sell the notes to the public. They were unable to sell all of them, in fact, but this was of no concern to Mackenzie and Mann, who had sold them outright to the underwriters.

To raise more funds, Mackenzie and Mann also brought out a new issue of Land Mortgage Debentures valued at £3,500,000 in 1913. As security for these debentures they pledged not only the company's remaining interest in its land grant, but also a large number of town lots owned privately by Mackenzie, Mann and Co. Ltd. Of the Land Mortgage Debentures, £1,500,000 was also sold to Messrs. Hoare, Miller and Company in 1913.[17]

14 See above sources, also Meetings of Directors of the Canadian Northern Railway Company, 12 and 18 July 1913, CNR Records, MCDXL.

15 PAC, CNR Records, Legal Series, File 6–50.

16 *Ibid.*, CNR Directors' Meetings, 8 Aug. and 4 Sept. 1913; PAC, CNR Records, MCDXL.

17 See Chapter IX above for details.

These were rather expensive short-term expedients. The Canadian Northern Railway's strongest securities, their government-guaranteed debentures, were pledged as collateral for short-term loans. Sufficient money was thus raised to keep the construction crews at work in 1912. These measures did not, however, provide a long-term solution. Only a general improvement in the money markets of the world, which would make it possible to sell both guaranteed and unguaranteed Canadian Northern securities at reasonable prices, would meet the railway's financial requirements. When such an improvement failed to materialize, Mackenzie was forced to appeal to Canadian federal and provincial governments for more help.

Mackenzie and Mann looked particularly to Premier McBride of British Columbia and to Prime Minister Borden. The three prairie provinces had already voted substantial guarantees for almost every conceivable local railway. More guarantees were hardly practical, especially since the incentive to build more development lines had been seriously undermined by the Regina rates cases. The best that could be done on the prairies was to try to build as quickly and cheaply as possible and earn the provincial guarantees. In Ontario the strained relations between Premier Whitney and William Mackenzie virtually precluded any thought of further aid, while Quebec had already granted substantial aid and had seen the main lines in that province completed. Much of this aid had admittedly been granted before Mackenzie and Mann took over the Quebec lines, but additional aid for completed lines was politically impractical.

Mackenzie made his first appeal for help to the Borden government early in 1912. It was a fairly simple request. Railways declared to be in the general interest of Canada were entitled to cash subsidies of between $3,200 and $6,400 per mile. Some expensive lines had received even larger federal cash subsidies. The Canadian Northern Pacific Railway, however, had never received such a subsidy, although it was clearly designed to serve national interests. The problem until 1912 had been that the rate structure of railways receiving such federal cash subsidies was subject to review and control by the federal Board of Railway Commissioners. Premier McBride had insisted that rates on the provincially assisted Canadian Northern Pacific Railway must be under the exclusive control of his government. He stipulated that the railway must not be declared in the general interest of Canada, thus qualifying for the subsidy but also becoming subject to federal rate control. In 1912 Mackenzie asked the Prime Minister to provide the federal cash subsidy for the Canadian Northern Pacific Railway, but without disrupting provincial control over rates.

Premier McBride and Prime Minister Borden were political allies and friends. Both were willing to provide assistance to the Canadian Northern Pacific Railway, especially since the request could be met by only slightly varying existing subsidy policies. There was never any doubt that the rates would be regulated. British Columbia simply hoped to reduce them even further than the federal Board might. Borden therefore agreed to provide the federal cash subsidy without requiring the declaration that would have placed Canadian Northern Pacific rates under federal jurisdiction. A federal cash subsidy of $10,000 per mile for the 535 miles of the main line from the Yellowhead Pass to the mouth of the Fraser River was accordingly provided. As in other similar cases, the subsidies would be earned by the railway and paid by the government as various sections of the assisted line were completed.

In Parliament there was no serious criticism by the Liberals about the subsidy itself. The Liberals, after all, had been granting similar subsidies for fifteen years while they were in power. The amount was admittedly larger than that provided for by the established policy, but construction of the mileage in the mountains would also cost a great deal more. The only serious Liberal criticism was that the British Columbia rates were not placed under the jurisdiction of the Board of Railway Commissioners. The Board was a Liberal creation. It was designed to establish and enforce a fair and equitable national rate structure. Regional rate regulations and inequitable reductions in a single area might jeopardize the stability of that national rate structure. The fears were precisely the same ones expressed by federal Liberals in 1901 when Manitoba made its precedent-setting rate agreement with the Canadian Northern Railway. The criticisms in 1912 again went no further than the Liberals thought necessary to ensure that they would not be blamed if the British Columbia rate situation later caused trouble. The Canadian Northern Pacific Railway got its $5,350,000 cash subsidy from the federal government in 1912 without serious difficulty.

This federal subsidy, together with the funds Mackenzie was able to raise in London, provided for the company's immediate needs. They did not provide the means to complete construction of the British Columbia and Northern Ontario mileage and of the terminal facilities in the large cities. The financial situation in London showed no signs of improvement and early in 1913 Mackenzie began a new assault on the federal treasury. He called on the Prime Minister on 7 January 1913 "with proposal to send his Co. 30 Millions and give them subsidy on 1,200 additional miles of railway".[18] Mackenzie wanted "cash subsidies of the usual amount per mile" for several important Canadian Northern lines in Ontario which had not yet received the usual variable federal subsidies. He asked for such subsidies on 1,229 miles, these being the lines from Port Arthur to Ottawa, from Ottawa to Toronto, and from Toronto to the Niagara frontier. He wanted the money immediately, not when the mileage was completed. He suggested, therefore, that the government provide the company with a $30,000,000 cash loan. This loan would bear a 4-per-cent interest rate and be repaid as the cash subsidies were earned. The government would simply retain the subsidies in partial repayment for the large loan. Any balance remaining would become payable in ten years.[19]

The application for government assistance was accompanied by financial statements which indicated that it would cost a total of $106,664,873 to complete the main line. An amount of $61,663,963 had already been raised by the sale of securities, leaving a balance of $45,000,910. None of these figures included required expenditures to complete the terminal facilities at Victoria, Vancouver, Port Mann, Ottawa, and Montreal. These facilities, it was estimated, would cost an additional $28,996,500 to complete. It was clear from the beginning, therefore, that even the $30,000,000 federal loan would not meet all requirements. Mackenzie was confident, however, that many of the

18 PAC, Borden Diary, 7 Jan. 1913.
19 PAC, Borden Papers, File oc 153, 10452–8, A Private Memorandum prepared for the Hon. R. L. Borden, Premier of Canada and His Ministers by Wm. Mackenzie, President of Canadian Northern Rly Co., 4 Jan. 1913.

still unsold government-guaranteed bonds would soon be sold or be pledged as collateral for additional loans to complete the undertaking. He also hoped that at least some of the unguaranteed securities could still be sold.

The basic argument in support of the Canadian Northern request was simple. "It is respectfully submitted, that, in view of the great national good which is to be accomplished by the completion of the company's undertaking, and the comparatively small public assistance hitherto received, that the company is entitled to substantial aid from the Parliament of Canada."[20] Both Liberals and Conservatives, federally and provincially, had in the past voted large bond guarantees and thus indicated that construction of the Canadian Northern was in the national interest. The "enormous cost of terminals in large cities, the expensive right of way through both rural and urban communities, and the high cost of labour and materials", coupled with the financial stringency in the international money markets, made it absolutely necessary that the government assist the road. The assistance requested, moreover, was no more than the rival transcontinentals had already received at an earlier date from the federal government. The Canadian Northern had received mainly guarantees, which had cost the government nothing. Mackenzie specifically pointed out to Borden that "the Government of the day gave enormous assistance to one railway to invade the Western field, and neglected to give corresponding assistance to the company which by the Government's action was forced to build in the Eastern field, although the latter enterprise was as much in the public interest."[21]

Borden was well aware of the weaknesses and shortcomings of the Liberal railway policy. He largely agreed with Mackenzie, who went on to prepare a detailed memorandum outlining the government assistance received by the three transcontinentals. The CPR had received a $25,000,000 cash subsidy and government-built mileage valued at $35,000,000 for a total cash cost to the federal government of $60,000,000. In addition it had received a 25,000,000-acre land grant. The Grand Trunk Pacific–National Transcontinental Railway scheme, according to Mackenzie's calculations, had already cost the federal

20 *Ibid.*, 10457.   21 *Ibid.*, 10454.

government a total of $243,488,000. This figure included the cost of building the National Transcontinental, the government's agreement to pay all interest charges for seven years on the National Transcontinental and on the Grand Trunk Pacific's mountain section, direct cash subsidies, a $10,000,000 loan negotiated in 1909, and government payments of $10,100,000 to buy Grand Trunk Pacific government-guaranteed debentures at par under a disputed legal provision of that company's contract with the government. The figures did not include any of the remaining obligations the federal government had undertaken by guaranteeing Grand Trunk Pacific debentures.[22]

The Canadian Northern Railway, by comparison, had received very little direct assistance from the federal government—a mere $8,358,000 had been voted, and of that amount only $4,763,000 had actually been earned and received by the company. The remainder would presumably be received when the required construction, mostly in British Columbia, was completed. Mackenzie did not think that the government's guarantees should be taken into consideration when calculating direct government assistance. Neither the politicians nor the promoters thought the government would be called upon to honour these guarantees. The Canadian Northern, despite the crisis in financing new construction, was still considered strong enough to take care of all its fixed charges comfortably. Mackenzie's comparisons led him to an obvious conclusion. "It is submitted that in all fairness the Government would be fully justified in granting to the Canadian Northern the subsidy applied for, as it is plain from the comparisons made the assistance already received is very small compared with the generous aid given to the other two transcontinentals."[23]

Borden was impressed by Mackenzie's figures. He noted in his diary "McKenzie [sic] continues to press his application, part of which seems well founded."[24] He was even more impressed a few days later when Mackenzie presented figures to show how much money he had been able to raise without the benefit of government guarantees.

22 Ibid., 10462–6, Private Memorandum submitted to the Right Hon. R. L. Borden in support of application for subsidies to aid Canadian Northern to complete its main line, submitted by William Mackenzie, President, 21 Feb. 1913.
23 Ibid., 10466.
24 PAC, Borden Diary, 21 Feb. 1913.

According to figures later tabled in the House of Commons, the Canadian Northern Railway and all its affiliated lines had issued government-guaranteed securities valued at $120,120,461. This compared with $145,379,151 worth of unguaranteed securities issued by the same companies, for a total issue of $265,499,612.[25] Detailed statements of construction contracts with Mackenzie, Mann and Co. Ltd. were not given.[26]

Borden rarely acted on impulse, even when urged to do so by promoters and colleagues who seemed to be able to make out a good case for a particular course of action. Mackenzie's request for assistance sounded reasonable, but the Prime Minister sought the counsel and advice of others before committing his government to any further assistance. The most serious obstacle in the way of granting further assistance to the Canadian Northern was the widespread belief that Mackenzie and Mann had made large profits from their Canadian Northern construction contracts and were enormously wealthy, but refused to put their own money into the railway. "The general idea," according to E. B. Osler, a bank president and CPR director, "is that the Company is rich and that Mackenzie and Mann are enormously wealthy."[27] Osler considered Mackenzie one of the richest men in Canada, worth between $15,000,000 and $100,000,000. Many Canadians could not understand why the government should provide assistance, even for a meritorious project, when its promoters already enjoyed such wealth.

Borden also tended to think of Mackenzie as a very wealthy man. Mackenzie assured him that all funds realized from the sale of guaranteed bonds had in fact been spent properly, but that international monetary conditions made further financing in the normal way impossible. Even very wealthy men cannot finance large new undertakings in an unfavourable market.

25 CAR, 1913, 691. These figures relate only to the "funded debt", not to the total liabilities.
26 Both Thomas Shaughnessy and E. B. Osler stated categorically in their letters to Borden that Mackenzie and Mann had made large construction profits, but they presented no evidence. None was required by the government in 1913, although in 1914 detailed statements had to be filed before the government granted further assistance. These showed that Mackenzie and Mann had not made any contractors' profits.
27 PAC, Borden Papers, File OC 153, 10494–1, E. Osler to Borden, 2 March 1913.

Borden carefully discussed the matter with Cabinet colleagues and with several influential business leaders, notably CPR president Thomas Shaughnessy, E. B. Osler, and railway and land promoter Senator McInnis, who had had business dealings with Mackenzie and Mann. Since Shaughnessy and Osler were both identified with the CPR, it is clear that Borden sought the opinions of those who might well be critical of Mackenzie's request.

Shaughnessy provided the Prime Minister with a detailed analysis of Canadian Northern financing. Since Shaughnessy's figures related only to the parent Canadian Northern Railway Company and to the main-line sections in Ontario and British Columbia, they are not directly comparable to the figures presented by Mackenzie and later tabled in the House of Commons. These included the liabilities of the affiliated companies as well. Shaughnessy himself admitted the need for a government accountant who could provide more authoritative figures. According to his calculations, however, the Canadian Northern had sold $98,358,614 government-guaranteed securities and $72,693,000 unguaranteed securities. The latter total, however, did not include the land-grant bonds or rolling-stock obligations of the Canadian Northern.[28]

Shaughnessy's concerns and recommendations were undoubtedly more important in this case than his financial research. He was naturally reluctant to see the government advance new funds to the Canadian Northern, which would then compete transcontinentally with his own road. To Borden he expressed grave concern regarding the honesty and reliability of promoters Mackenzie and Mann, and wondered whether the line offered adequate security for a government loan of the magnitude requested. In order fully to protect the public interest, Shaughnessy thought it advisable for the government to take 51 per cent of the common stock of the Canadian Northern Railway as security until the loan was fully repaid. He carefully explained the reasoning which led him to this rather startling recommendation.

Assuming the Government be satisfied on all these points [financial honesty of promoters] and that there be an inclination to assist the Canadian

28 *Ibid.*, 10496–500, Shaughnessy to Borden, 5 March 1913.

Northern to complete its main line by guarantees of the principal and interest of a further issue of securities, there is no reason why the Government should bear all the burden and a couple of individuals reap all the prospective advantages. The promoters and contractors of the enterprises should take their share of the risk and therefore the government should insist upon the deposit of 51 per cent of the Common Stock of the Company, to be held for the benefit of the country until such time as Government has been relieved of all its responsibilities.[29]

Shaughnessy simply could not think of Mackenzie and Mann as anything except contractors on the make. He was worried because "there would appear to be no limit to the capital stock possibilities of this enterprise" and recommended that a government accountant be appointed "to go through the contracts for the lines already constructed and those now in process of construction to ascertain the relations between the contractors or the construction companies and the various railway companies".[30] He could not put his finger on any specific instances of wrongdoing, but the suspicion remained that schemers like Mackenzie and Mann would eventually sacrifice national to private interests.

The same suspicion was more forcefully expressed by Shaughnessy's fellow director, E. B. Osler. In order to prevent improper profiteering by the contractors, Osler believed it absolutely essential that the government should "first take control until the loan is repaid". Osler was also very much concerned about the likely effect of such a large loan on the future credit of the Canadian Northern and on any future bond sales it might wish to negotiate in London. He was convinced that a large government loan would seriously undermine the company's credit and make further sales, particularly of unguaranteed securities, virtually impossible. If that was indeed the result, the government would find itself in a very awkward situation. The $30,000,000, as everyone knew, was insufficient to complete the Canadian Northern's undertaking. If additional securities found no buyers in London, the government would find itself compelled to complete the enterprise of which it had become the principal creditor. This Osler considered "an

29 *Ibid.*, 10500.   30 *Ibid.*

unknown liability for enormous sums".[31] The government, he believed, must be careful not to damage the railway's credit unless it was prepared to provide sufficient means to complete construction.

This concern, first voiced by Osler, led Borden and his colleagues to reject the idea of a federal loan to the Canadian Northern. A subsidy, even a large one, still entailed only a limited government commitment and would leave the railway's credit in London unimpaired. As long as there were reasonable hopes that further Canadian Northern securities could be sold in London, this seemed a reasonable position. It also gave the government more freedom to act in the future as it might see fit. If the railway could not be completed with the assistance provided, the finances of the company might be reorganized in the normal way. A receivership and the resulting reorganization, however, would be much more difficult if the government itself became the railway's principal creditor. In 1913 the government declined to do this.

Members of Borden's Cabinet did not agree on the policy to be followed.[32] Some continued to feel that Mackenzie and Mann should exhaust their allegedly enormous private fortunes before government aid was provided. Finance Minister White disliked the cash-subsidy proposals. They threatened to create a very large increase in government spending and would therefore make it more difficult for the government to meet other large financial obligations. Some federal loans were maturing, and White also anticipated the passage of the government's naval bills under which the Canadian treasury would provide $35,000,000 to build dreadnoughts for the British Navy. He was also very well aware of the fact that all the aid proposals under consideration in 1913 fell considerably short of providing the funds needed to complete the main line and essential terminal facilities of the railway.

It had been made clear to Mackenzie and Mann by 1 May 1913 that they would not get the $30,000,000 loan. They now began to concentrate on a drive to obtain a larger $12,000-per-mile cash sub-

31 *Ibid.*, 10494–1, Osler to Borden, 2 March 1913.
32 The subject was discussed repeatedly in Council or by Borden with senior Cabinet ministers. PAC, Borden Diary, particularly entries for late April, all of May, and early June 1913.

sidy for the line between Edmonton and the Yellowhead Pass, the line from Port Arthur to Montreal, and the mileage between Toronto and Ottawa, and Toronto and the Niagara frontier. The first two lines had already received large federal bond guarantees, but none of these lines had yet received the usual variable federal cash subsidy available for lines declared in the general interest of Canada. On 16 May Mackenzie made a strong but unsuccessful bid to obtain cash subsidies of $12,000 per mile on all these lines, for a total of $22,000,000. Borden told him "it was too large an order". Then the Prime Minister added a rather sympathetic note in his diary. "He [Mackenzie] looks rather tired and careworn and has aged greatly in two years."[33]

The Cabinet nevertheless decided to grant the Canadian Northern some cash subsidies. The proposal to do so caused at least one "great disturbance"[34] in the Conservative caucus, where members could not understand why wealthy men should be given more subsidies. Resolutions were introduced in the House of Commons on 28 May, shortly after the defeat of the naval bills in the Senate. These provided for new cash subsidies, but not in the amounts requested by Mackenzie and Mann. The Port-Arthur-to-Ottawa line was given $12,000 per mile, as was the line from Edmonton to Yellowhead Pass, but the Toronto-to-Ottawa section got only $6,400 per mile. No subsidy was provided for the proposed line from Toronto to the Niagara frontier.[35]

The total value of the subsidies thus granted was $15,640,000. In return for this assistance, the Canadian Northern was required to issue additional capital stock to the value of $7,000,000 and to transfer this, as fully paid, to the government.[36] This gave the government a 10-per-cent share in the company, $70,000,000 of common stock having been issued previously and held almost in its entirety by Mackenzie and Mann. The government thereby gained the means to obtain any and all information it needed regarding the contracts and financial obligations of the Canadian Northern Railway.

The 1913 subsidy was only an interim solution. To complete their railway Mackenzie and Mann still had to sell substantial issues of both guaranteed and unguaranteed bonds in London. The subsidy certainly

33 *Ibid.*, 16 May 1913.
34 *Ibid.*, 2 June 1913.

35 Canada, *3–4 Geo.* v. *Cap. 10, Sec. 8.*
36 CAR, 1913, 259–61.

did not weaken their credit, but they could sell nothing unless the market improved very substantially. The Liberals were well aware of this fact and stressed it repeatedly in the debates. Few objected that the government was assisting an important national enterprise at a time of financial stringency. They did object noisily to the fact that the assistance would not be sufficient and that it was in the worst form. A subsidy was in fact an outright gift to the company when a loan, albeit larger, would have got the company through its financing crisis. One Liberal spokesman professed that he did not believe "that $15,000,000 is worth a sheet of paper to them now. I think that $30,000,000 or $35,000,000 might be of some advantage to them, and if they come and ask $35,000,000 of the people of Canada and give security, I believe that the people would be willing to let them have it for the purpose of maintaining a great transcontinental road such as this."[37]

The former Liberal railways minister summed up his party's objections to the government's proposals. "I am a friend of the enterprise; I believe Canada must see it through, but I believe aid ought to be given by way of a loan, even if the amount be twice as large, and I think we should not give this money to the Canadian Northern until they place their entire line under the control of the Board of Railway Commissioners."[38] Borden explained that a loan of this magnitude would have undermined the railway's credit and future borrowing power and thereby committed the government to supplying all the funds required to complete the project.[39]

Other critics, both in the House and outside, complained that the assistance had not been made conditional on further rate reductions, particularly in western Canada. Rates had always been a rather sensitive issue in the West. The drastic rate reductions made by the Canadian Northern in 1901 had certainly gained it considerable popularity at the time. Even the 1901 agreements, however, had not reduced the western rates to the same levels as those charged by the railways in eastern Canada. There competition from American carriers and from water and canal transportation determined the rate levels. In western Canada the railways had no such competition and rates had

37 *Ibid.*, 260–1.
38 *Ibid.*, 260.

39 Canada, *House of Commons Debates, 1912–13*, 11755–7.

always been determined by calculating costs, including the costs of operating the unprofitable Lake Superior section, and then determining the requirements of the railways. During the prosperous years of the Laurier administration, comparatively few farmers had been prepared to launch a serious agitation against this discriminatory rate structure. The economic recession of 1913 made many of them much more aware of the burden of freight rates and increased the agitation for rate parity between eastern and western Canada. The railways were still regarded as wealthy corporations, and Borden received several angry letters and petitions from individuals and Boards of Trade complaining that rate parity had not been made a condition of further aid to the Canadian Northern Railway.[40] The issue ultimately went to the Board of Railway Commissioners, which held very lengthy hearings on all matters related to western rates. In the end it decided that the differential between eastern and western rates should be, and in fact was being, narrowed, but that some differences were justifiable.[41] The issue did not seriously influence the government's policies toward the Canadian Northern in 1913.

Mackenzie looked after most of the negotiations with the Borden government. Mann occasionally served as an emissary between Liberals and Conservatives, particularly during the naval debate. He also looked after the negotiations when Mackenzie was in London in search of more money, and he was in charge of most of the negotiations with Premier McBride in Victoria. The British Columbia premier had a direct interest in the completion of the line to the Pacific and could be expected to provide further assistance if this became necessary. In 1912 he had provided important new provincial guarantees of $10,000,000 for terminal facilities and $35,000 per mile for over 300 miles of proposed Canadian Northern Pacific branch lines in the Okanagan. The terminals debentures were immediately issued and eventually sold for a net income of $8,614,000.[42] Very little was ever

40 PAC, Borden Papers, File OC 153, 10501, Resolution of the Winnipeg Board of Trade, 13 May 1913; *ibid.*, 10408, Norbert O'Leary to Borden, 22 May 1913.
41 PAC, Board of Railway Commissioners, Western Tolls Case, File 18755, *Canadian Railway Cases*, XVII, 123–230.
42 *Loomis and Platten Report*, Exhibit B, "The Canadian Northern Railway System showing description and distribution of funded debt".

done to finance or construct the Okanagan branch lines.

Late in 1913, with the financial situation deteriorating, Mann approached the British Columbia premier for additional assistance. At first Canadian Northern officials thought an increase in the interest rate offered on the British Columbia guaranteed securities might well make these more attractive to investors. The suggestion was made,[43] but the Premier did not respond favourably, and Mann prepared a more conventional request. The case he presented to the Premier was a fairly simple one. The main line, not to mention the Okanagan branch lines or the Vancouver Island mileage, could not be completed without further provincial aid. Failure to complete the main line would lead to huge interest charges with virtually no revenues. The British Columbia government would then be compelled to honour its guarantee and pay all interest on provincially guaranteed bonds. This would be politically disastrous for the Premier, who had always maintained that the guarantees would not cost the provincial treasury a cent.

There was also a more positive aspect that Mann did not fail to stress. The railway originally contemplated under the 1910 contract, he claimed, was not the same one that was actually being built. A railway with much higher standards and specifications, and therefore worth much more, was actually under construction. Expenditures had greatly exceeded early estimates, but the result was a better railway. It could therefore carry a greater debt burden. The easy grades of the new line, to be achieved through the construction of sixteen bridges and forty-four tunnels, received particular emphasis. By Mann's calculations the railway was worth far more than $35,000 per mile for which the government had guaranteed bonds. He therefore asked that the government provide an additional guarantee of $10,000 per mile on the main line and $5,000 per mile on the Okanagan branch lines and on the Vancouver Island mileage.[44]

Mann carefully prepared his request in December 1913 in the relative quiet of his Toronto office. Then he ventured out to the "land of the setting sun" to present his petition. He found Premier McBride rather sceptical, particularly about the proposal to provide additional

43 PABC, McBride Papers, W. H.
Moore to McBride, 13 Feb. 1913.

44 *Ibid.*, Mann to McBride, 18 Dec.
1913.

guarantees on mileage, some of which had already been built. McBride suggested that the additional guarantees apply only to the unfinished mileage between Hope and the Yellowhead Pass. Mann meanwhile met with his officials to review the situation. What he found nearly led him to despair. "I was dumbfounded," he wrote the Premier, "at the increased cost of the road in British Columbia." He emphatically rejected the Premier's proffered aid for the unfinished mileage only and told him frankly,

the case is much more desperate than I thought it was when talking to you in Victoria. . . . The Government had the first mortgage on the Road and it is almost impossible to raise any further loans without a Government guarantee. In other countries the practice is for the Government to guarantee Second Mortgage securities, thus enabling the Company to issue First securities without a guarantee; this is the plan which Sir George Paish said we should have adopted, and I entirely agree with him.[45]

It was rather late in the day to regret earlier agreements, but the project clearly needed help. Premier McBride was almost as heavily committed to its success as Mann himself.

Having put his hand to the plough, the Premier could not now look back. A bill providing for guarantees of a further $10,000 per mile on the Canadian Northern Pacific Railway's main line was drafted and was passed rather easily by a troubled, but still co-operative, majority, in the legislature. The new bonds were to be interchangeable with those issued and guaranteed earlier. Therefore, all of them carried the 4-per-cent interest rate and could be sold in London in 1913 and 1914 only at substantial discounts. Most were simply pledged as collateral for short-term loans.[46] This helped the company, but the basic problems remained.

The 1913 subsidies granted by the federal government, the additional British Columbia bond guarantees, and the short-term loans, land-mortgage debentures, and other securities Mackenzie had been

45 *Ibid.*, Mann to McBride, 12 Jan. 1914.
46 For a complete listing of loans and short-term securities issued by the Canadian Northern Railway, from 1912 to 1918, see PAC, CNR Records, x̄CCLXXXVIII, Secretary's Black Book.

able to sell in London did provide the means to continue the construction program to the end of 1913. Mackenzie and Mann were still confident that the line could be completed from coast to coast the following year. To keep construction crews at work, however, would require new financing. A much improved financial market or substantial new government assistance would be needed.

CHAPTER FOURTEEN

GOVERNMENT HELP
AT A HIGH PRICE
IN 1914

THERE WAS NO SUBSTANTIAL IMPROVEMENT in the international monetary situation early in 1914. The discounts at which guaranteed Canadian Northern securities could be sold were somewhat smaller, but still too large to make the sale of large issues practical. Some unguaranteed debentures had been brought out in 1913 at 50 per cent of par value,[1] but large new issues of this class of securities would serve only to further weaken the market. Sir Thomas Shaughnessy analysed the situation quite correctly when he wrote that the Canadian Northern Railway "has pretty well drained the channels through which it might expect to secure any further important loans from the public".[2]

The situation became absolutely desperate after the outbreak of war in August 1914. London financiers became entirely preoccupied with the war and could not accommodate the Canadian Northern Railway's need for more money to complete construction. Yet the railway could not be operated as a transcontinental system until at least the main line and the terminals were built, although interest had to be paid on all money already spent on the transcontinental mileage. Furthermore, operating costs rapidly increased, but the Canadian Northern, under its subsidy and guarantee agreements, had to carry most of the government's wartime traffic free or at fixed low rates. Thus the effect of the war was to restrict further the amount of money Mackenzie and Mann could borrow. It also increased costs and

1 *Arbitration*, 2655. A copy of the official prospectus for the 1913 issue is available in the PAC, White Papers, File 40, 6363–7.

2 PAC, Borden Papers, File RLB 2986, 140420–6, Shaughnessy to Borden, 27 Feb. 1914.

the volume of traffic, but it did not significantly increase net revenues for the still-incomplete transcontinental system.

The response of Mackenzie and Mann to the worsening crises was threefold. In London maturing bonds were renegotiated, new short-term notes were brought out to replace those issued the previous year, and some new funds were raised through new loans. In Canada a determined attempt was made to reduce expenditures. Branch-line construction on the prairies was sharply curtailed, a mere token force was left in charge of the Vancouver Island work which Premier McBride had always considered of great importance, construction of the expensive terminal facilities in Vancouver was allowed to fall seriously behind schedule, and the expensive but strategically important Niagara connection was abandoned. All efforts came to be concentrated on the early completion of the main line. At the same time an urgent new appeal for government help was sent to the Prime Minister.

Lazard Brothers in London had become Mackenzie and Mann's principal underwriters in 1912. They were prepared to buy virtually all guaranteed securities Mackenzie and Mann had for sale, but only at the prevailing market price.[3] The prices were still too low in the early months of 1914 to make an advantageous sale. Mackenzie's financial advisers continued to urge short-term loans that would meet immediate requirements but permit the sale of the securities to be deferred to a more opportune time.[4] Mackenzie accepted this advice, and during the first six months of 1914 Lazards renewed old loans or advanced new ones which, in the aggregate, exceeded £2,000,000. Lloyd's Bank advanced £821,917, while the British Empire Trust Company provided a little more than £150,000.[5] Almost all these loans were secured by pledging unsold securities of the Canadian Northern Railway or its affiliates. In addition, the $3,500,000 issue of 6-per-cent one-year Gold Notes, purchased by William A. Read and Company of New York, were replaced with a new £735,000 issue of 6-per-cent notes. These new notes were then taken by the American financiers in exchange for the 1913 notes.[6] Substantial credits were

3 *Ibid.*, File oc 153, A. W. Wright to Borden, 3 June 1913.
4 *Arbitration*, 2655–6.
5 For details see PAC, CNR Records, XCCXIV, Secretary's Black Book;

ibid., MCDXXXVIII, Canadian Northern Minute Book, 1913, and several related files in the CNR Legal Series 6.
6 PAC, CNR Legal Series, File 6–58.

also advanced to the contracting firm of Mackenzie, Mann and Co. Ltd. by the Canadian Bank of Commerce. These credits would become payable when the Canadian Northern Railway paid Mackenzie and Mann for their construction work. In fact, in 1914 Mackenzie, Mann and Co. Ltd. assigned its construction accounts with the Canadian Northern Railway directly to the Bank of Commerce as continuing collateral.[7] From that date on, most of the credit advanced by the Bank was given to the contractors, not directly to the railway company.

The money that could be raised in this manner was insufficient, and the company was rapidly running out of guaranteed securities to pledge as collateral for further loans. Mackenzie and Mann had to assess their construction priorities and delay completion of the less urgent projects until more funds were available. Delays anywhere certainly had serious political repercussions, but there was never any doubt that completion of the transcontinental main line must be given top priority. Immense sums had already been spent in Ontario and British Columbia. Interest had to be paid, but there could be no earnings until the main line was completed.[8] All other construction projects were of lesser importance. As the financial situation deteriorated, these projects were either stopped or sharply curtailed. The first projects to feel the pinch were the branch lines.

In the four western provinces the Canadian Northern Railway had a large number of branch-line projects. Many were very urgently needed by settlers still far removed from the railway. Bond guarantees had been voted by the provincial governments, which considered the railway's acceptance of these guarantees a firm obligation to complete construction within the specified period of time.[9] Much local hardship resulted when branch-line construction projects fell seriously behind schedule. As early as 1913 the little town of Mervin in northwestern Saskatchewan took a complaint to the Board of Railway Commissioners. The complainants stated that a number of settlers had gone into the area and had broken tracts of land in anticipation of the

7 PAC, CNR Records, x̄CCXIV, Assignment of Accounts to Canadian Bank of Commerce as a continuing collateral, Nov. 1914.

8 *Arbitration*, 2656–7.

9 PAS, Scott Papers, 54380–2, Scott to O. O. Winter, 12 June 1913.

promised railway, but because the railway had not been built, many farmers simply could not continue to farm in the area. The Board of Railway Commissioners agreed with the Mervin farmers. "There is no question at all," they reported, "but that the line is most urgently needed; that many of the farmers who appeared before the Board at Edam, would probably be better off if they had broken no land and attempted to market no wheat under the adverse conditions which they are now suffering from."[10] The Railway Commissioners decided they had no power to compel the Canadian Northern to build new lines anywhere, but they sent the evidence of the hearings to the provincial government in the hope that something could be done at Regina.

The government was certainly as eager as the Commissioners, but it too lacked the power to compel the railway to build when there was no money. The bond guarantees had been voted. If the company failed to build within the specified time period, the government could refuse to grant an extension of the time limit and thus deprive the company of the guarantee. Such a procedure, however, would not get the railway any closer to the Mervin farmers. All the government could do was write increasingly angry letters of exhortation—and vote time extensions in the hope that the guarantees might yet entice the companies. The 1912 rate reductions, moreover, were sufficiently large that most of these local lines incurred deficits in the early years of operation. The enthusiasm of the railway companies for new branch-line construction was accordingly diminished.

Premier Scott of Saskatchewan had long been a strong supporter of the Canadian Northern Railway. The company's decision to abandon many of the branch-line projects in order to complete the main line in Ontario and British Columbia seriously strained relations between Scott and Mackenzie and made the Canadian Northern increasingly unpopular. Prairie interests, it appeared, were again being sacrificed to the interests of the richer and politically stronger regions of Canada. Thus, when a shipment of rails for forty miles of the Canadian Northern Pacific Railway was lost in a shipwreck near Cape Horn, rails intended for prairie branch lines were used on the British Columbia

10 Mervin, Board of Trade v. Canadian Northern Railway Co., Board of Railway Commissioners File 11929.

15, *Canadian Railway Cases*, XIV, 363–5.

main line.[11] The Canadian Northern Railway had become a national transcontinental system and was behaving as badly as its rivals, to whom it had once taught much-applauded lessons in western regional interests. The Premier of Saskatchewan was understandably irritated. To one correspondent who complained about inadequate local rail service he wrote,

> You and the people in your neighbourhood have every reason to be incensed in the matter of the failure of the Canadian Northern Railway Company to do what the Government believes no less strongly than you the Company should have done a long time ago. . . . I shall be delighted if you can put me on to any scheme or show me that the Province or the Government possess any power enabling it to exercise compulsion upon the Company so as to bring about the result which you so urgently need and desire.[12]

These were the unfortunate consequences that had to be faced when priorities were set. The problem was most acute in Saskatchewan, where the Canadian Northern had more branch lines under construction than in Manitoba or Alberta. Manitoba was already well supplied with local railways, while in Alberta the major Canadian Northern branch-line projects to be abandoned were in the south, where the CPR already offered reasonable service and the prime objective was competition rather than the opening up of entirely new territories. In British Columbia the delay and virtual abandonment of the Okanagan branch lines was considered regrettable but not disastrous. There, too, competition with the CPR and the desire of the Canadian Northern to develop local feeder lines were the main motivation for branch-line construction. Failure to complete these lines certainly deprived the railway of some much-needed local traffic. Premier W. J. Bowser, who succeeded Premier McBride in 1916, summarized the situation when he wrote to a constituent,

> I am leaving no stone unturned to secure some action with regard to the commencement of work upon the projected branch of the CNP Railway

11 PABC, McBride Papers, Mann to McBride, 18 Sept. 1914.

12 PAS, Scott Papers, 54380–2, Scott to O. O. Winter, 12 June 1913.

between Kamloops and Kelowna. The railway officials recognize the value of this proposed stretch of road and the only reason for their failure to proceed is the question of finance. I hope that this may be surmounted in the near future and this very necessary addition be added, in order that they may tap the rich Okanagan Valley.[13]

The necessity to close down construction work on Vancouver Island was a much more serious blow to the provincial government. Premier McBride was keenly aware of the long-standing rivalry and bitterness which existed between the Island and the mainland. He had carefully devised his government's railway policy to ensure that both could participate fully in the anticipated benefits which the new railways would bring. The western termini of the Canadian Northern Pacific Railway had always been Vancouver and Victoria. Construction was carried forward on both the Island and the mainland, but it was clear that completion of the main line to Vancouver had to take priority. Mackenzie and Mann continued the work on the Island as long as they possibly could, but on 7 August 1914 the Island work was shut down and the men were paid off.[14] The Premier could do little more than send an urgent cable to Mann: "Would be very disastrous to me if Island work shut down. Must insist imperative lay some steel and carry on so at least keep up appearances."[15]

The expensive terminal undertakings in British Columbia, particularly the ambitious Vancouver plans, also suffered serious delays on account of the financial stringency. The difficulties in Vancouver began almost immediately after the agreement with the city and the related provincial guarantee of terminal bonds were signed. Despite their attractive 4.5-per-cent interest rate, many of these guaranteed bonds could be sold only at substantial discounts or after discouraging delays. It quickly became apparent that the required work would not be completed within the stipulated time period unless additional funds were found, but in 1914 and 1915 all available funds were funnelled into the main line. This delay led inevitably to impatience on the part

13 PABC, Premiers' Papers, Official Correspondence, Bowser to A. W. Hamilton, 13 March 1916.

14 PABC, McBride Papers, Mann to McBride, 7 Aug. 1914.
15 Ibid., McBride to Mann, 7 Aug. 1914.

of Vancouver City Council. The city engineer began to send in reports as early as 18 February 1914 showing work actually completed and the work required under the terms of the agreement.[16] A year later, with the project very badly behind schedule, the city solicitor was asked to report on possible legal proceedings against the company for non-compliance with the terms of the agreement. There was serious talk of confiscating the $1,500,000 performance bond deposited by Mackenzie and Mann, but eventually City Council came to the conclusion that the most expeditious way of dealing with the company was through the federal Board of Railway Commissioners.[17] This move was prompted partly by political partisanship. Premier McBride was doing all he could to keep the Canadian Northern Pacific Railway beyond the jurisdiction of the federal Board, while his opponents on Vancouver City Council, particularly Alderman Gale, were prepared to bring the Board into the matter. The federal Board, on somewhat dubious grounds, agreed to hear the Vancouver complaint.[18] After the hearings it ordered the railway company to "submit plans within six months from the above date [the order was dated 22 June 1915] the whole work to be completed by June 1, 1917; the filling in for the prosposed work to be commenced and carried to completion forthwith."[19]

Early in 1915 the only work completed at Vancouver was "the filling in of the portion of the Creek conveyed to them by the City and the construction of the Freight Sheds and Terminals".[20] By that

16 VanA, City of Vancouver Correspondence File 144D, F. L. Fellowes, Supervising City Engineer, to the Chairman and Members of the Bridges and Railway Committee of the City of Vancouver, 18 Feb. 1914.
17 See several letters written by Alderman Gale in 1915 and 1916, *ibid.*, File 144D.
18 Under federal legislation passed in 1914 the federal government, with Premier McBride's reluctant consent, obtained power to declare the railway a work for the general advantage of Canada. It had not formally done so, however, when the City of Vancouver hearing was held. PAC, Borden

Papers, File RLB 2896, 140460, undated telegram from McBride to Borden; *ibid.*, File OC 163, McBride to Borden, 16 March 1914; PAC, Borden Diary, 26 March 1914; VanA., City of Vancouver Correspondence File 144D, E. F. Jones to Alderman Gale, 22 Oct. 1916.
19 VanA., City of Vancouver Correspondence File 144D, F. L. Fellowes to E. F. Jones, 19 Jan. 1916.
20 *Ibid.*, 144E, Statement of the City of Vancouver as to its position and claims under its agreement with the Canadian Northern Pacific Railway Company and a complete history of all transactions in reference to the said

time the financial situation was so bad that construction of the proposed tunnels was abandoned. Instead, the Canadian Northern Pacific sought and obtained running rights over the trackage of the Vancouver, Victoria and Eastern Railway, a Great Northern Railroad subsidiary.[21] Premier McBride, well aware of the financial problems, exerted considerable pressure on the Great Northern interests to grant the Canadian railway a reasonable running agreement which would enable it to serve the Vancouver area without the expensive tunnels.[22]

The promised Vancouver hotels never materialized. Very little was done to fulfil the promise of suitable shipping services from Vancouver to the Island, and the Canadian Northern never established a promised trans-Pacific shipping service. A Canadian Northern Steamship Company was incorporated in 1909. In time it placed three vessels on the Atlantic and was also expected to develop the British Columbia and trans-Pacific shipping business. Some lands, docks, and wharves were acquired in British Columbia, and a contract was let to the Davie Shipbuilding and Repairing Company of Quebec for the construction of a double-screw steel car ferry which was to be placed in service between Vancouver and Patricia Bay. Financial problems, however, led to the cancellation of this contract.[23] In fact, the Canadian Northern Steamship Company accomplished next to nothing on the Pacific coast, and in 1916 it withdrew from the steamship business while the parent Canadian Northern Railway entered a working alliance with the Cunard Steamship Company.[24]

The decision to concentrate all their resources in British Columbia on the completion of the main line enabled Mackenzie and Mann eventually to finish that important mileage, but it left the freight-

---

agreement from the fifth day of February 1913, when agreement was entered into by the City, Statement dated 1917; City of Vancouver Agreements File 2670, Summary of obligations to be carried out and not yet completed within the specified time, by F. L. Fellowes, City Engineer, 22 July 1920.
21 PAC, CNR Records, MCLXVIII, Meeting of the Directors of the

Canadian Northern Pacific Railway, 13 Jan. 1916.
22 PABC, McBride Papers, McBride to L. W. Hill, President of the Great Northern Railway, 1 Nov. 1915, together with related correspondence.
23 PAC, CNR Records, MCLXXXII, Meeting of Directors of the Canadian Northern Steamship Company, 21 Aug. 1916.
24 *Synoptical Histories*, 229; *Arbitration*, 99.

handling and transshipment facilities at the coast in an incompleted, and consequently a very inefficient, state. This situation seriously hampered operations, and the British Columbia mileage was unable to earn all fixed charges on its huge debt until those facilities were improved.

In Montreal the company faced somewhat different problems. Certainly some of the ambitious plans for first-class station facilities and office buildings were abandoned or seriously revised. The tunnel, however, had to be built if the railway was to gain its entrance into the city. Drilling and blasting were carried forward steadily throughout 1912 and 1913. Late in 1913 the headings of the tunnel met. Too much had already been spent and the Montreal connection was too important to be abandoned in 1914. All this work had been financed by a £1,000,000 loan from Lazard Brothers. Early in 1914 the Mount Royal Tunnel and Terminal Company brought out a £2,400,000 issue of 5-per-cent First Mortgage Notes. The proceeds from the sale of these notes were to repay the outstanding loans and provide funds to complete the undertaking. Lazard Brothers agreed to take £2,000,000, but they were unable to complete the transaction in August 1914, because of the outbreak of the First World War.[25] Consequently, construction had to be stopped. Appeals were made to the government for loans. Some money was provided, but construction on the Montreal project was slow and repeatedly interrupted because of lack of funds.[26] Mackenzie and Mann never did complete the Montreal project, although Mackenzie was well aware that without it and some of the other abandoned eastern projects "neither a satisfactory transcontinental business nor an entirely successful Eastern passenger and fast freight business can be possible."[27]

The line from Toronto to the Niagara Peninsula suffered a similar fate. The strategic importance of that line was stressed repeatedly, but lack of funds made construction impossible. Mackenzie quoted approvingly the opinion of outside examiners who found

25 PAC, Borden Papers, File OC 163, 11943–4, Memorandum re Mt. Royal Tunnell [sic] & Terminal Co. Limited.
26 Arbitration, 182–4.

27 Second Annual Systems Report, Canadian Northern Railway System, Toronto, 1916, 8.

the existing transportation service via the frontier lines is detrimental to Canada. The Niagara line is therefore greatly needed for the further development of the Dominion facilities as a whole, as well as to connect the Canadian Northern main line with the City of Hamilton, with its St. Catharines line, with the United States railroads, and with the intermediate manufacturing districts.[28]

No one disputed the usefulness of the Niagara line, or of the other projects of the Canadian Northern that had to be delayed or abandoned in 1914. The financial crisis, however, forced the promoters to determine what was "the lowest amount that it is possible to get on with".[29] Detailed calculations were made in 1914 to determine exactly what this amount was. To complete the main lines, a few branch lines already under construction, and the Montreal Tunnel, and to provide the required rolling stock would, according to the 1914 estimates, cost an additional $100,379,099. At the time the company had available for sale government-guarantee securities valued at $58,473,982. This left a balance of $41,905,117 "to be provided".[30] The 1914 estimates of additional requirements were almost the same as the ones for the previous year. The 1913 subsidy had enabled the company to continue its work, but rapidly increasing cost estimates had left the company with almost exactly the same requirements for additional government aid.

Earlier plans to raise this amount through the sale of unguaranteed securities had become impracticable. Thus, even if all the guaranteed securities were sold, the company needed urgent and massive financial assistance to complete the most essential of its undertakings. Early in 1914 William Mackenzie became a persistent and often troublesome petitioner and lobbyist as he tried to persuade the government to provide the required $42,000,000.

On 22 January 1914 Mackenzie made his expected but unwelcome visit to the Prime Minister's office,[31] urging that the government provide his company with a loan or bond guarantee. The visit can hardly

28 *Third Annual System Report, Canadian Northern Railway System,* Toronto, 1917, 12.
29 *Arbitration,* 2656.
30 PAC, White Papers, File 42, 6756,

Official Application for Government Assistance to the Canadian Northern Railway, Table 6, "Amount, if any, required to complete".
31 PAC, Borden Diary, 22 Jan. 1914.

have been a surprise, since the 1913 subsidy was known to be insufficient to complete the main lines, the market for Canadian Northern securities had not improved, and estimated costs had increased sharply. Borden nevertheless informed the promoters that he could hold out no hope for additional government assistance. The government had refused to grant the loan requested in 1913, partly because it might have then been committed to seeing the project through to completion. When that subsidy proved inadequate, Borden and several of his colleagues were prepared, on first thought, to allow the Canadian Northern to undergo a basic financial reorganization, if necessary by way of a receivership. That, after all, was the normal procedure for companies that were unable to meet their financial commitments.

Borden quickly learned that normal business reorganization and refinancing arrangements were not likely to meet the requirements of the Canadian Northern Railway situation. A large portion of the company's debentures were guaranteed by governments. A company default on these securities seemed the first step in any reorganization, unless sufficient funds were found to complete the main line. Only if the entire mileage were operated did the prospect of earning all fixed charges seem possible. Unfortunately, several of the provincial governments which had guaranteed railway debentures were in no position to pay the interest if the railway company defaulted. Saskatchewan, for example, was so heavily committed that annual interest payments on all the provincially guaranteed bonds were equal to more than half of the province's annual budget.[32] The provinces were finding it increasingly difficult to meet their normal financial commitments; yet for the sake of Canadian credit, no government-guaranteed securities could be defaulted without disastrous results. There was no doubt that if the Canadian Northern defaulted, the federal government would have to either lend the necessary money to the provinces or pay the interest on the provincially guaranteed securities itself.[33] The Minister of Trade and Commerce expressed the government's irritation in this predicament: "It is too bad that individuals go so far that they wrap

32 PAC, Borden Papers, RLB 2986, 140444–5, Hugh Clark to Borden, 12 March 1914.

33 *Ibid.*, File OC 103g, 4269–71, F. Williams Taylor to White, 7 March 1914; *ibid.*, File RLB 2986, 140420–6, Shaughnessy to Borden, 27 Feb. 1914.

themselves around national interests to an extent that means widespread damage or national help."[34]

While Borden offered the promoters no hope, the discussions continued. Borden sought a wide range of views and opinions. It quickly became clear that there were several points on which all or most of his advisers agreed. The first of these was that the Canadian Northern's transcontinental main lines must be completed. This would minimize future losses and provide services that were urgently needed.[35]

Borden's advisers also agreed that the government-guaranteed bonds could not be allowed to go into default. Therefore, if the government refused to help Mackenzie and Mann, they might well find themselves advancing very large loans to embarrassed provincial governments. Government advances to pay interest on Canadian Northern bonds would not, however, provide the means to complete the main line and would almost certainly make further financial support for that purpose more complicated. Negotiations would then have to be made with the holders of the unguaranteed debentures, who were scattered across all parts of the empire, before a suitable arrangement could be made.

Another point on which there was almost unanimous agreement was that there must be a full and complete disclosure of all aspects of Canadian Northern financing and of the railway company's relations with its contractors. If there had indeed been large contractors'

34 PAC, Foster Papers, Diary, 28 March 1914.
35 The more important memos and letters containing suggestions and proposals submitted for Borden's consideration include the following: PAC, Borden Papers, File RLB 2986, 140420–6, Shaughnessy to Borden, 27 Feb. 1914; *ibid.*, 140437–8, Memorandum re Canadian Northern Railway, 2 March 1914 by Shaughnessy; *ibid.*, Shaughnessy to White, 4 March 1914; *ibid.*, 140443–4, Memorandum re Canadian Northern situation, n.d., by Shaughnessy; *ibid.*, File OC 163, 11650, Shaughnessy to Borden, 24 April 1914; *ibid.*, File RLB 2986, 140434–44, Memo by Mr. Sifton, Respecting Canadian Northern Railway, 1914; *ibid.*, 140444–5, Hugh Clark to Borden, 12 March 1914; *ibid.*, 140437–8,

140448–50, Memoranda re Railway situation from Frederick Williams Taylor, one dated 2 March 1914 and the second n.d.; *ibid.*, File OC 103g, 4269–71, Frederick Williams Taylor to White, 7 March 1914; *ibid.*, File RLB 2986, 140464–6, J. D. Reid to Borden, 31 March 1914; *ibid.*, 140469–71, Charles Hibbert Tupper, 22 March 1914; *ibid.*, File OC 163, 11562–6, R. McBride to Borden, 25 March 1914; *ibid.*, File 2986, 140496–9, Private and Confidential Memo [apparently from Arthur Meighen] in connection with meeting last evening between Mr. Lash and Mr. Lewis; *ibid.*, 140500, White to Borden; *ibid.*, 140501–3, Calder to Borden, 17 April 1914; *ibid.*, File OC 163, 11676–7, Cahan to Borden, 30 April 1914.

profits, as was widely believed at the time, the two promoters should receive no further help until they had pledged their profits and other resources to the success of the enterprise.[36] The government must also have strong assurances that any further funds provided would be used only for the purposes intended by Parliament and not for contractors' profits. The public, according to Shaughnessy, "should learn to think of the Canadian Northern as a great railway company and not as the pocket corporation of two individuals."[37] There must also be assurances that the requested aid would indeed see the project through to completion. It would also be essential, if the Canadian Northern Railway were to operate as a transcontinental system, that the relations between the parent company and the various subordinate and affiliate companies be clearly defined. There was some concern that Mackenzie and Mann might withhold some vital section under their own name, and then use that control to demand outrageous concessions from the parent system.[38]

There were other aspects of the proposed government policy about which there was considerable disagreement. Finance Minister Thomas White in the Cabinet, and CPR President Thomas Shaughnessy outside of it, still urged some form of receivership in 1914. Shaughnessy outlined his ideas in several lengthy letters and memoranda to the Prime Minister.[39] He believed the government should ensure that all outstanding government bond guarantees be honoured but, if the company was unable to meet fixed charges on its second-mortgage unguaranteed debentures, a default on these securities should be permitted. The situation would then fall into the control of the holders of the defaulted bonds. These bondholders, Shaughnessy believed, should be allowed to take up to 90 per cent of the company's common stock, form a Canadian Northern Securities Corporation, and seek new financial help through normal channels. Shaughnessy would have preferred to

36 *Ibid.*, File RLB 2986, 140469–71, Charles Hibbert Tupper to Borden, 22 March 1914.
37 *Ibid.*, 140420–6, Shaughnessy to Borden, 27 Feb. 1914.
38 *Ibid.*, 140464–6, J. D. Reid to Borden, 31 March 1914.
39 *Ibid.*, 140420–6, Shaughnessy to Borden, 27 Feb. 1914; *ibid.*, 140437–8,

Memorandum re Canadian Northern Railway, 2 March 1914; *ibid.*, Shaughnessy to White, 4 March 1914; *ibid.*, 140443–4, Memorandum re Canadian Northern situation, n.d., by Shaughnessy; *ibid.*, File oc 163, Shaughnessy to Borden, 24 April 1914.

see Mackenzie and Mann entirely eliminated from the enterprise, but thought it might be reasonable to leave them 10 per cent of the common stock as compensation for their efforts. He thought they had been guilty of "inexcusable recklessness" and therefore were "entitled to no consideration whatever".[40]

The problem with the scheme suggested by Shaughnessy was that no one really knew what effect such a reorganization would have in London. Confidence in all Canadian securities might be very seriously undermined by the initial default. It was also doubtful whether the proposed securities corporation would be able to raise additional funds where Mackenzie and Mann had failed. The government might still find it necessary to provide assistance in order to complete the main lines. There was also considerable fear that the system might be fragmented under this procedure if individual parts went into default while Mackenzie and Mann met the financial obligations of the more prosperous parts and therefore kept control of these.[41]

After several interviews with Borden, Shaughnessy admitted that there were problems with his scheme. As an alternative he suggested that the government might provide further assistance, but that it do so only on condition that the entire system be brought under a single corporate entity and that, temporarily, all the common stock of this new company be transferred to the government. The promoters should get the common stock back only after all obligations undertaken by the government were fully satisfied. In the interim period, which Shaughnessy thought might last for six years, the government should have a voice in the construction and management of the company. This policy would diminish the influence of Mackenzie and Mann and their methods, and therefore, in Shaughnessy's opinion, would increase public confidence in the company. Why the president of the CPR should think public management would be more efficient than private management was never clearly indicated. Shaughnessy apparently still regarded Mackenzie and Mann as nothing more than contractor-promoters out for a fast dollar.

Thomas White, who also favoured a form of receivership, never explicitly outlined a detailed plan in writing. Several factors influenced

40 *Ibid.*, File RLB 2986, 140420–6, Shaughnessy to Borden, 27 Feb. 1914.

41 *Ibid.*, 140464–6, J. D. Reid to Borden, 31 March 1914.

his thinking. On the one hand, he was opposed to massive government aid, for the simple and very valid reason that the federal government did not have the money and might find it very difficult to raise the large sums required. For this reason a cash loan was considered entirely impractical. Even federally guaranteed debentures brought out by the railway company were likely to have an adverse effect on the availability of credit in London and perhaps in New York. Yet the money had to be raised if the railway's main line was to be completed. It was doubtful whether a bondholders' committee or corporation could act more successfully than Mackenzie and Mann had. Normal business procedure, none the less, provided for a receivership if a company could not meet its obligations.

White was also concerned about the Canadian Northern's, or Mackenzie and Mann's, relations with Canadian financial institutions, notably the Canadian Bank of Commerce and the National Trust Company. The Bank had advanced large sums to the contractors, larger than some of its directors thought proper when the over-all risks of the venture were taken into consideration. President B. E. Walker of the Bank and William Mackenzie of the railway company were partners in the same reckless policy. Both had immense confidence in the future of Canada and in the Canadian Northern's role in that future. It seemed clear to them that the company's financial embarrassments after 1912 were due to the unsettled and depressed state of the money markets rather than to any basic defect in the company itself. Once completed and fully operational, the railway would, they believed, certainly be a splendid success.[42] White and others worried that the Bank would go too far in advancing credit to the persuasive promoters. A default and subsequent reorganization might well bring the Bank to its senses. Such a reorganization must come, however, before Mackenzie, Mann and Co. Ltd. poured all their own resources into the enterprise. The resources of the contracting firm were the Bank's only security for its large loans. White certainly did not like the developments which were taking place,

42 For a general expression of B. E. Walker's attitude, see UTA, Walker Papers, Walker to Woodhouse, 15 April and 4 Oct. 1913, and Walker to H. Cooper, 19 Dec. 1923; G. P. de T. Glazebrook, *Sir Edmund Walker* (Toronto: Oxford University Press, 1933).

but he found it almost impossible to formulate an alternative policy. Borden described him as "excited", "nervous", and "up in the air". The Prime Minister's diary gives the general impression that his Finance Minister was greatly troubled but unable to enunciate a clear policy in the Canadian Northern matter.[43] In 1914 White apparently still thought a thorough financial reorganization would reduce the risk of a great crash later, a crash that might involve the Bank if more bank loans were made and more of Mackenzie, Mann and Co. Ltd. resources were poured into the venture.

F. Williams Taylor, a senior official of the Bank of Montreal, made somewhat different suggestions. He discovered that almost all the unguaranteed second-mortgage securities were issued by the parent Canadian Northern Railway, not by the unprofitable subsidiaries. If the system were dismembered and the government accepted responsibility, as it inevitably must, for the guaranteed interest on the British Columbia, Ontario, Quebec, and Nova Scotia mileage, the Canadian Northern Railway might well be able to look after all the other obligations. Certainly it should be able to do so "comfortably" within a few years. This solution, admittedly, would leave the government with an ill-assorted *mélange* of unintegrated and unprofitable lines, but paying fixed charges on these, perhaps integrating them with the National Transcontinental system, might well be much less expensive than the government aid needed to complete and equip a third transcontinental system. Taylor also thought that the CPR might be persuaded to purchase some of the British Columbia and Ontario lines. These lines, if integrated with the CPR system, might still become profitable.[44]

All these and other suggestions were carefully considered by Borden. The available alternatives seemed to be government assistance to Mackenzie and Mann under stringent conditions, a receivership of some form allowing the holders of the unguaranteed bonds to take over the system, or government acquisition of a part or the whole of the Canadian Northern system. After prolonged discussions the Cabinet

43 PAC, Borden Diary, 29 Jan., 25 March, 20 May 1914, and 11 Jan. 1915.

44 PAC, Borden Papers, File OC 103g, F. Williams Taylor to White, 7 March 1914; copies to Borden also available in File RLB 2986.

rather reluctantly came to the conclusion that government aid under stringent conditions might well be the best policy. Certainly it was likely to be the least disruptive. Several factors influenced the Cabinet. It was discovered that under various construction contracts between the Canadian Northern and Mackenzie and Mann there still remained more than $20,000,000 which the contractors had spent but for which they had not received payment from the railway company. This claim would undoubtedly prove very awkward if the railway company were reorganized in such a way as to eliminate Mackenzie and Mann. In addition, the contractor-promoters, not the railway company, still owned several strategic local lines. If they lost control of the common stock of the parent company they might well make their control over the local lines a means of harassing the company.[45]

Railways Minister J. D. Reid suggested that for these reasons it might be best to advance the required government assistance. This should be done, however, only if the $20,000,000 debt of the Canadian Northern Railway to the contractors was cancelled. The various lines must also be reorganized into a single integrated system. In addition, the government should take a substantial part of the common stock in order to influence, and perhaps control, future construction and operating policies of the railway.[46] If this were done, and any further problems developed, the government would be in a very much stronger position to take over the entire system, or to see it reorganized in other ways, without the danger of further harassment from Mackenzie and Mann. There was, admittedly, no indication that Mackenzie and Mann had any intention of harassing the system. All they wanted was government help to get the railway built. Reid would have preferred the establishment of an independent commission to complete and run the system. He was convinced, however, that Mackenzie and Mann could not simply be eliminated before the relationships between the various companies, and between these companies and the contractors, were fully clarified. In any event, a detailed financial statement of the Canadian Northern's financial affairs and requirements was needed before a firm policy could be established.

45 *Ibid.*, File RLB 2986, 140464–6, 31 March 1914; UTA, Walker Papers, Walker to Lyman Jones, 6 June 1914.

46 PAC, Borden Papers, File RLB 2986, J. D. Reid to Borden, 31 March 1914.

When Mackenzie and Mann first approached Borden, his response was discouraging; he did, however, ask for a full financial disclosure. Canadian Northern officials were eager to provide it. Many of the criticisms levelled against their company were not founded in fact. One of the first matters the Canadian Northern promoters wanted clarified was that they had not made any profits, either as contractors or as promoters, from their association with the Canadian Northern Railway. Z. A. Lash was charged with the preparation of the required documents to prove that in fact there had been no exploitation of the railway company by its promoter-contractors. Lash prepared a memorandum which addressed itself directly to that point.

The general impression has been that the aid which has been given to the Canadian Northern Railway System by the various governments has been greater than the interests of the country called for, and that the Contractors have made large fortunes out of the System and out of the cash and other subsidies which the Government have granted, and that any further aid is not necessary and would only add to the private fortunes of the contractors. That this impression is entirely wrong is proven by the following statements of the facts.[47]

Lash then went on to outline the development of the Canadian Northern Railway system and its various parts. He stressed that all construction costs had initially been financed by these contractors. They were repaid only when the lines were completed, the subsidies earned, or the guaranteed securities sold. Lash pointed out how and where the contractors could have legally gained large profits, had they wished to do so, but indicated that their first objective had been to build a successful railway system. They had returned land grants earned under early construction contracts to the company at prices well below real values, taking common shares of the railway instead. At no time did they retain for themselves profits other than those which might accrue from the common stock of the company.

Lash later said his statement that Mackenzie and Mann had not

47 PAC, White Papers, File 40, 6316–35, Private Memorandum, Canadian Northern Railway, undated and un-signed but, according to other evidence, clearly from Lash.

made profits from their Canadian Northern construction contracts "was rather surprising to those to whom it was made".[48] It was presented to Borden on 17 February 1914,[49] together with an invitation to the government to send its own auditors to Toronto, there to verify the statements by a full and detailed investigation of the company's books. The government eventually did send its auditors to Toronto. They reported back that all subsidies received and the proceeds from all guaranteed debentures had indeed gone into the Canadian Northern Railway, and that no profits had been taken by Mackenzie, Mann and Co. Ltd. This finding, according to Lash, "changed the whole aspect and attitude towards the application, and the Government introduced the Bill".[50]

Lash next set his hand to dispelling another Canadian Northern rumour that had wide currency at the time and, regrettably, is still perpetuated in Canadian history books despite Lash's clear and forceful statements. This was that Mackenzie and Mann had never invested any of their own resources in the Canadian Northern Railway and had therefore obtained its $70,000,000 of common stock "free". Lash pointed out that during the early years the contractors had taken the company's land grant, its federal transportation contract, and its bonds in payment for what they had spent on construction, but that they had returned or invested the lands and the transportation contract in the company's common stock. In addition, the contractors had spent substantial sums in organizing a number of companies and financing any requirements of these companies that were not met from the proceeds of bond sales. The Lake Superior Terminals Company, the Winnipeg Land Company, the Canadian Northern Telegraph Company, the Canadian Northern Express Company, the Qu'Appelle, Long Lake and Saskatchewan Railway and Navigation Company, the Duluth, Winnipeg and Pacific Railway Company, the Port Arthur, Duluth and Western Railway, and the St. Boniface and Western Land Company, all at one time or another had required substantial sums of money, which had been provided by Mackenzie and Mann. In return they had taken the capital stock of those companies and exchanged it for common shares of the Canadian Northern Railway. The value of

48 *Arbitration*, 2517–8.
49 PAC, Borden Diary, 17 Feb. 1914.
50 *Arbitration*, 2517–8.

the lands and of the Mackenzie and Mann investment in these companies was computed by Lash to be $44,610,000. In addition, they had made their town lots available for a Canadian Northern Land Debenture issue and were entitled to at least a 5-per-cent contractor's commission on the $300,000,000 construction services, since they had carried all the financial charges on construction until the railway had earned its subsidies or sold its securities. Therefore, the assets and services provided by Mackenzie and Mann, in Lash's view, exceeded $70,000,000.[51]

Lash's figures were never successfully challenged. Later investigators and accountants confirmed their general reliability. In fact, they added another large figure to those listed by Lash. Beginning in 1912, Mackenzie, Mann and Co. Ltd., as contractors, had expended considerably larger sums on construction than the railway company had been able to raise through the sale of its securities. They were entitled to an additional $21,262,527.26 from the railway company for money they had already spent for construction, and which the proceeds of the railway's securities had not met. After 1912, Mackenzie, Mann and Co. Ltd. simply kept a single account with the Canadian Northern Railway against which they credited all contractors' expenditures and charged all receipts from the railway company. This was either their own money or money they had borrowed.[52]

The net result of these financial investigations was quite simple. Mackenzie and Mann had not "bled" the railway company for the sake of contractors' profits.[53] They had, on the contrary, put a considerable amount of their own resources into the project and looked only to the value of the company's common stock for their reward. A great deal of what was freely written in the newspapers and said in the parliamentary debates simply could not be substantiated by a detailed financial examination of the company's affairs. All aid granted in the past had been used as the governments voting it had intended, and the promoters were quite prepared to accept conditions designed to ensure that any aid granted in the future would be similarly applied.

---

51 PAC, White Papers, File 42, 6691–8, Memo for Hon. W. T. White, Private and Confidential, by Z. A. Lash, 23 Feb. 1914.

52 *Arbitration*, 2518–20.
53 PAC, Borden Papers, File RLB 2986, J. D. Reid to Borden, 31 March 1914.

The financial details available to the government in February 1914 were still incomplete. The government auditors reported only on 31 March. Lash's memoranda, however, did persuade the government that additional aid could be justified. Within a week the references in Borden's diary changed substantially. On 18 February he "gave him [Mackenzie] no encouragement".[54] On 25 February the Cabinet discussions on the Canadian Northern application led to general agreement "that we can do nothing without the fullest information".[55] An independent and detailed examination of the company's affairs might, of course, take weeks, and perhaps months. In the meantime Borden decided to ask Mackenzie for two things. He wanted detailed figures that would give the government an accurate idea of the company's financial situation. These would have to be checked further by government officials but they would give the government a clear idea of what was needed. In addition, Borden wanted Mackenzie's "own personal guarantee to protect the government".[56] Mackenzie felt he could not give this, since it would injure his credit arrangements with the Bank, where the contracting company had large debts. Borden regarded Mackenzie's refusal to give his personal guarantee as "stupidly unreasonable",[57] but he nevertheless asked him specific financial questions which the government wanted answered.

Mackenzie returned to Ottawa on 4 March and the next day presented his application for a government guarantee of securities to the extent of $45,000,000.[58] With the discounts and other financing expenditures, he expected that the net receipts would come to slightly less than $42,000,000. Together with his application, Mackenzie presented a series of more detailed statements showing the charter, length, location, capitalization, indebtedness, earnings, and prospective earnings of the various lines which comprised the Canadian Northern Railway system and the immediate financial requirements to complete them. These statements showed the total indebtedness and annual fixed charges on the various lines, but they did not provide specific details about individual loans or securities, the dates and amounts of interest

---

54 PAC, Borden Diary, 18 Feb. 1914.
55 *Ibid.*, 25 Feb. 1914.
56 *Ibid.*
57 PAC, Borden Diary, 26 Feb. 1914.

58 PAC, White Papers, File 42, 6745–89, Mackenzie to Borden, 5 March 1914.

payments, or any other financial obligations of the company which must be met in the immediate future. For this reason, Borden considered the statements presented by Mackenzie as inadequate, noting in his diary, "McK [*sic*] brought his application respecting the CNR and it proved very unsatisfactory. Told him it would not go either in Council or in caucus."[59]

Mackenzie and his overworked Toronto head-office staff had to provide additional, more detailed financial statements. At the same time the government-appointed auditors were checking the books to verify any company statements made and to provide additional financial details. Mackenzie supplied the details requested by the government before a specially constituted railway committee of the Cabinet on 11 March, almost three weeks before the government auditors presented their report.[60] Mackenzie's statements were sufficiently explicit that Borden at least "got a clear understanding of their financial position".[61] The auditors' statements confirmed the company's figures and persuaded the Cabinet railway committee that the guarantee which would provide funds to complete the main lines should be granted. Many members of the government caucus, however, were still labouring under the old misapprehensions that Mackenzie and Mann were wealthy promoters who had mercilessly exploited the railway company for their own private gain. They were, in Borden's phrase, "much excited as to CNR application".[62]

The basic decision by the government to grant the Canadian Northern Railway guarantee was probably made on 12 March. It was, of course, subject to a satisfactory report from the auditors and to further hard bargaining over specific details of the agreement. It was clear that the various affiliated and allied companies must be brought together to form a single transcontinental railway system. It was also understood from the beginning that Mackenzie, Mann and Co. Ltd. must relinquish their outstanding claims against the Canadian Northern Railway for the amount still owing on the construction account. The amount of $21,262,527.26 actually spent by Mackenzie and Mann on construction was thus lost in its entirety.[63] The government also de-

---

59 PAC, Borden Diary, 5 March 1914.
60 *Ibid.*, 11 March 1914.
61 *Ibid.*, 12 March 1914.

62 *Ibid.*
63 *Arbitration*, 2518–20.

manded that, in return for its guarantee, the Canadian Northern Railway transfer to it, as fully paid up, a very large portion of the company's common stock. This, in the end, was the point on which the most determined and bitter negotiations centred.

The government and the railway promoters agreed that all the liability and equity stocks of the various affiliated companies would be brought together under a single corporate entity, the Canadian Northern Railway System. The liability capital, mainly in the form of unguaranteed bonds and debenture stock of the subsidiary companies, had generally been acquired by Mackenzie, Mann and Co. Ltd. Arrangements had then been made, but not always completed, whereby Mackenzie, Mann and Co. Ltd. exchanged these acquired securities for Canadian Northern Perpetual Consolidated Debenture Stock. All proposed arrangements of this kind were to be completed in 1914. The agreement with the government, then, provided that all the securities acquired in this way were to be pledged as a second charge for the security of the new federally guaranteed debenture stock, the first charge remaining the Trust Deed securing the Canadian Northern Perpetual Consolidated Debenture Stock.

The authorized equity capital of the sixteen companies that were to be amalgamated under this arrangement was $215,440,000. Of this amount, $145,778,500 had actually been issued, almost all of it to Mackenzie, Mann and Co. Ltd.[64] It was agreed that this should be reduced to a total capitalization of $100,000,000 for the new Canadian Northern Railway System.[65] The government then wanted half of this common stock in return for its guarantee. The proposal seemed entirely unreasonable to Mackenzie and to Lash, who tried very hard to persuade the government to reduce its demands.[66] The government was, after all, providing only a guarantee, not a subsidy or a cash payment of $45,000,000. Mackenzie and Mann were asked to forgive a very large debt, write stock valued at $145,778,500 down to $100,000,000, and transfer $43,000,000 of that to the government ($7,000,000 had already been transferred to the government as a result of the 1913 subsidy agreement) for a $45,000,000 guarantee.

64 PAC, White Papers, File 42, 6745–55, Statement No. 4, accompanying letter of William Mackenzie to Borden, 5 March 1914.
65 Arbitration, 2522–4.
66 PAC, Borden Diary, 24 March 1914.

The terms were harsh, and Borden noted in his diary, "Mackenzie looks very haggard and worn and has aged 20 years in the last 2."[67] The Canadian Northern promoters, however, were not in a strong bargaining position. It was, as Hanna said later, a case of Hobson's choice.[68] If they rejected the government offer, a receivership in which they could lose everything seemed likely. In the end the negotiations became little more than rather quarrelsome bartering sessions. Mackenzie and Mann thought it would be entirely sufficient if the government got $30,000,000 of the stock. On 28 March the government agreed to reduce its demands from $50,000,000 to $45,000,000, and in the end the figure of $40,000,000 was accepted by both sides.[69] This arrangement, according to Borden, left "all ministers greatly pleased with result and many members came and warmly congratulated me".[70] The next day Borden was even more satisfied. "Publication of CNR proposals," he wrote, "elicited warm approval. Wonder is expressed that we made so good a bargain."[71]

The government's decision to provide the large guarantee was greatly facilitated by the strong support of all the premiers whose provincial governments had provided guarantees. Liberal Premiers Sifton, Scott, and Murray, of Alberta, Saskatchewan, and Nova Scotia respectively, and Conservatives McBride and Roblin of British Columbia and Manitoba gave full support to the scheme. McBride was perhaps the least pleased because the entire Canadian Northern Railway System was to come under the jurisdiction of the federal Board of Railway Commissioners. His dream of provincial control of Canadian Northern Pacific Railway rates was doomed, since that company was to lose its separate identity in the larger system. Borden found it hard to persuade McBride, a close political friend, that this development was necessary.[72] McBride suggested that, if this was indeed the case, the federal government should also take full responsibility for the British Columbia guarantees. Rate control had been a central part of the agreements. If the federal government destroyed the

67 *Ibid.*, 14 March 1914.
68 *Arbitration*, 653.
69 PAC, Borden Diary, 28 March 1914.
70 *Ibid.*, 28 April 1914.
71 *Ibid.*, 29 April 1914.

72 PAC, Borden Papers, File OC 163, Borden to McBride, 9 May and 16 May 1914; see also PAC, Borden Diary, 25 March 1914.

separate identity of the Canadian Northern Pacific Railway, and with it the provincial control over local freight rates, it should assume responsibility for the guarantees.[73] The government declined to assume such responsibility, although in the other provinces most of the Canadian Northern main-line mileage carried federal, not provincial, guarantees.

With the support of the Liberal premiers assured, Liberal opposition to the measure in Parliament was somewhat reduced. The most outspoken critics of the agreement in Parliament were, in fact, two Conservatives, R. B. Bennett and W. F. Nickle. Bennett, a corporation lawyer with strong CPR connections, was apparently irritated because he was not brought into the negotiations and the drafting of the agreement. Much of the detailed legal work had been done by Solicitor General Arthur Meighen, and Bennett regarded it as very defective. Meighen was also a rival of Bennett as Conservative spokesman for western Canada. At one point Bennett even threatened to cross the floor of the House of Commons and sit with the Liberals. He referred to Meighen as "the gramophone of Mackenzie and Mann".[74]

Most of the Opposition charges and criticisms of the 1914 Canadian Northern guarantee centred on the alleged unreliability of the financial statements submitted by the Canadian Northern and by the government auditors, which were tabled in the House. The public image of Mackenzie and Mann as profiteering contractors and promoters was too deeply ingrained to be dispelled by a few financial statements, no matter what government officials verified them. The mere fact that the promoters were in trouble clearly indicated they had done something wrong. The government unfortunately had failed to discover what. Consequently, the debate was much more vindictive than enlightening. Opponents suggested that the shrewd promoters had simply duped the government into providing new funds for further profits. The lack of proof never seemed to disturb these opponents. To them it simply suggested that the government had not been sufficiently diligent in finding proof of the contractors' profits.

The Liberals also flirted with suggestions that the government take

---

73 *Ibid.*, McBride to Borden 14 May and 18 May 1914.

74 W. R. Graham, *Arthur Meighen, A Biography*, Vol. 2 (Toronto: Clarke, Irwin, 1963).

over the railway. This suggestion had long been the standard response by federal and provincial Opposition parties when governments voted large-scale bond guarantees or subsidies. If the government underwrites the risks, oppositionists argued, it should also reap at least some of the benefits by controlling some or all of the assisted company's capital stock. Borden had attacked the Laurier proposals of 1903 and 1904 on precisely these grounds, and in 1914 some of the federal Liberals began to edge towards the same argument. Where their provincial brethren had formed the Opposition, such arguments had already been advanced. The federal Liberals never actually came out firmly in favour of government ownership. William Pugsley moved an amendment in the debate whereby the common stock should be reduced to $30,000,000 and held in trust by the government for five years. Then the government should have an option to purchase at a price determined by arbitration.[75] Pugsley was casting a rather wide net, hoping to catch a variety of discontented political fish. Laurier followed with a similar approach. He was opposed to government ownership, but argued, "if the choice we have is between pouring more money into the coffers of the Canadian Northern Railway Company and the Government getting control of the road, I would rather get control of the road for the benefit of the people of Canada."[76] The remainder of his speech, however, suggested that the choice was not between these two alternatives.

In 1914, neither party was fully prepared to adopt a policy of outright government ownership. Both, however, detected some increase in public support for that suggestion. They made preliminary arrangements for the day when either continuing financial problems of the railways or increased public support for public ownership would make a policy change necessary. The Conservatives did so by taking 40 per cent of the Canadian Northern Railway's common stock; the Liberals by their ambiguous resolutions and by a suggestion by Pugsley that the matter might be debated in the next federal election.

Public opinion and the newspapers tended to support or oppose the agreement according to their political leanings and the reliability they attributed to the Canadian Northern's financial statements submitted

75 Canada, *House of Commons Debates*, 28 May 1914, 4391–6.

76 *Ibid.*, 2 June 1914, 4633–4.

to Parliament. Members of the business community supported the measure, or at least seemed prepared to accept it. Even Thomas Shaughnessy regarded aid in 1914 as almost inevitable, and was prepared to accept the government measure, albeit somewhat grumpily.[77]

William Mackenzie began negotiations with the underwriters for the placement of the new guaranteed securities long before the measure was approved in Parliament or the last legal details of the company's mortgage for the bonds was finalized. Finance Minister White made it very clear that the entire issue must not be brought on the market at the same time.[78] That would jeopardize all other Canadian financing. There was also considerable talk that the new securities should be placed in New York rather than in the overburdened London market.[79]

Most of William Mackenzie's financial connections were with Lazard Brothers and some of the other financial houses associated with them in London. He had also, however, placed $3,500,000 short-term notes with William A. Read and Company in New York in 1913. These had to be renewed somewhat later in 1914, and Mackenzie gave serious consideration to placing at least some of the securities guaranteed by the government in 1914 with the American firm. Negotiations with William Read and Lazards, however, indicated that Lazards were prepared to offer a slightly better price and also to subscribe directly or arrange placement for the entire $45,000,000 issue. Mackenzie decided therefore to place the first of his newly guaranteed securities with Lazards. An agreement for the immediate sale of £3,000,000 was negotiated with that firm in July 1914. The agreement could not be finalized immediately, however, because some of the legal details relating to the mortgage had not yet been settled. Solicitor General Arthur Meighen was in charge of these, but he was preoccupied with the Manitoba provincial election campaign. The resulting delays would not have been particularly serious under normal circumstances. Mackenzie, however, found his contracting company very hard pressed by a number of subcontractors. They had completed projects and were entitled to payment from Mackenzie, Mann and Co.

77 PAC, Borden Diary, 18 May 1914; PAC, Borden Papers, File OC 163, Shaughnessy to Borden, 24 April 1914.
78 PAC, White Papers, File 44,
7298–9, White to A. J. Mitchell, 30 June 1914.
79 Ibid., 7300–3, Wood to White, 3 July 1914.

Ltd., but there was no money. Mackenzie, Mann and Co. Ltd. could not collect amounts owed them by the Canadian Northern Railway. Desperate attempts were made to placate and fend off these claimants. Strong political support was enlisted, particularly in British Columbia from Premier McBride, to persuade the contractors not to launch lawsuits. On 20 June the Premier wired Mann, "Have been using all judgement and tact possible to keep things going and contractors at work."[80] Funds were juggled and most urgent accounts were paid, while other creditors were mollified with promises of payment as soon as the $45,000,000 mortgage was completed.[81] On 24 June Mann informed Premier McBride that he expected the mortgage to be completed that week, but on 4 July he wired that because of Meighen's absence in Manitoba it would be another ten days or two weeks before any money could be raised.[82] Mackenzie, meanwhile, was sending frantic telegrams to Borden.[83]

The problem of dissatisfied and impatient creditors was further aggravated by the unstable international situation. Europe was teetering on the brink of war. If war did break out, financing in London might very well become impossible. In fact, on 14 July, Lazard Brothers withdrew from their proposed agreement for the purchase of £3,000,000 because of the international uncertainty.[84] A week later, however, they did sign a formal agreement, although the purchase price of 91.5 was several points lower than that anticipated several weeks earlier.[85] This sale of 22 July 1914 provided the cash so desperately needed by the railway company and its main contractors.

Within two weeks of the signing of the agreement with Lazards for the sale of £3,000,000 of guaranteed bonds, war broke out. It was a disastrous blow to Mackenzie and Mann. Doubts were immediately raised as to whether Lazards would be permitted by the British government to send such large sums out of the country in wartime, and

80 PABC, McBride Papers, McBride to Mann, 20 June 1914.
81 *Ibid.*, Mann to McBride, 24 June 1914.
82 *Ibid.*, Mann to McBride, 4 July 1914.
83 PAC, Borden Papers, File OC 163, Mackenzie to Borden, 3 July 1914.

84 *Ibid.*, File OC 167, Borden to Perley, 14 July 1914.
85 PAC, CNR Records, x̄CCXIV, Agreement between Canadian Northern Railway Company and Lazard Brothers re sale of £3,000,000 of 4-per-cent Dominion guaranteed securities, 22 July 1914.

the sale of the remaining guaranteed securities seemed entirely fanciful. William Mackenzie, with an abundance of new government-guaranteed securities, found no one who had the slightest interest in his wares. In the London financial houses, amidst the most frantic scenes in the memory of those present, a forlorn William Mackenzie found that, as far as he and his securities were concerned, the place was absolutely dead.[86] Donald Mann immediately issued orders to prepare for the shut-down of all construction projects as soon as possible.

Premier McBride was still confident that at least the £3,000,000 already sold to Lazard Bros. would become available. In a tantalizing exchange of telegrams he urged Mann to "Hang on as long as possible. Winston will make good,"[87] while Mann wired cautiously, "Hope your friend Winston is as well prepared as we think he is."[88] No further evidence on the pressures exerted in London seems available in Canadian sources. It is clear, however, that Lazards, while permitted to pay for the securities they had purchased, were not permitted to bring them out on the British market in 1914. Thus, the underwriters were stuck with the unmarketable Canadian Northern securities. They paid the agreed purchase price and "carried out their underwriting in the most honourable way. They never squealed."[89]

With the $15,000,000, construction on the main lines could be continued for the time being. Completion of the lines, however, depended on further sales of guaranteed securities. The British market was closed, leaving only New York, where Mackenzie and Mann, together with a host of other promoters, went in August 1914. They had cancelled a large debt, reorganized their companies, and given the government 40 per cent of the common stock, only to find that the outbreak of the war made the guaranteed securities at least temporarily unsaleable.

---

86 *Arbitration*, 592–5, 2655–6.
87 PABC, McBride Papers, McBride to Mann, 6 Aug. 1914.
88 *Ibid.*, Mann to McBride, 5 Aug. 1914.
89 *Arbitration*, 2655–6.

CHAPTER FIFTEEN

WARTIME PROBLEMS

THE OUTBREAK OF WAR did not prevent the completion of the Canadian Northern Railway's main lines. Mackenzie and Mann had successfully raised approximately $400,000,000 in their drive to build a transcontinental railway system. In September 1914 the tracks were joined north of Lake Superior, and four months later the British Columbia section was completed.[1] Some of this new mileage, however, was not fully operational and required substantial improvements after 1915. The need for additional capital for construction work therefore remained.

In addition to this need for capital to complete construction work, large sums were required to meet heavy operational deficits after 1914. A variety of factors led to these deficits, which eventually necessitated a major reorganization of the railway's finances. Short-term financing and emergency government aid got the main lines built and kept the railway solvent in 1914 and 1915, but the poor operating results after 1914 eventually ruined the Canadian Northern Railway and its promoters.

Mackenzie and Mann's first impulse after the outbreak of war was to shut down all construction until the financial position could be clarified.[2] They needed slightly more than $100,000,000[3] to complete and properly equip the main lines, and they had hoped to raise this sum through the sale of the $45,000,000 debenture stock, guaranteed by the federal government in 1914, and of approximately $58,000,000 debenture stock which had received earlier federal or provincial guar-

1 CAR, 1915, 753.
2 PABC, McBride Papers, Mann to McBride, 5 and 7 Aug. 1914, and McBride to Mann, 6 and 7 Aug. 1914.
3 PAC, Borden Papers, File OC 153, 10451, application by Wm. Mackenzie

on behalf of the CNR for government aid, 4 Jan. 1913; PAC, White Papers, File 42, 6756, application for government assistance to the Canadian Northern Railway, 5 March 1914.

antees but which had not yet been sold. There was also a lingering hope that at least some of the company's other securities, mainly the unguaranteed 4-per-cent Perpetual Consolidated Debenture Stock,[4] might still be sold. The outbreak of war, however, made even the federal guarantees, obtained at a high cost in 1914, completely useless, at least where the London market was concerned. Money was no longer available to pay the construction crews.

Stopping all construction work, however, presented as many problems as it solved. Operations on the incomplete system were unprofitable and could not be properly integrated until the main lines were completed. Yet, fixed charges on all the completed and partially built mileage had to be paid. All the short-term loans also had to be serviced, and this would certainly be much more difficult if construction were halted. Consequently, when Lazard Brothers completed their purchase of the first $15,000,000 guaranteed debenture stock, which had been tied up in London for a time after the outbreak of the war,[5] the promoters decided to continue work on the main lines. It was clear, however, that the $15,000,000 alone would not complete the lines. Additional or alternative assistance was essential.

The work in British Columbia was in particular jeopardy because many of the Canadian Northern Pacific Railway's guaranteed debentures had not been sold. In contrast, the entire $35,000,000 issue of Canadian Northern Ontario debentures had been successfully placed before the financial stringency of 1912.

Fortunately, there was very little doubt in the minds of the Canadian Northern's political supporters about completion of the main lines. They must be completed as quickly as possible. As early as 13 August 1914 the federal Cabinet was discussing proposals under which the government would provide wartime assistance to the Canadian Northern and Grand Trunk Pacific railways.[6] Several weeks later Borden

---

4 The assets which were pledged as first mortgage collateral for the Perpetual Consolidated Debenture Stock also became a second mortgage security for the $45,000,000 federally guaranteed debenture stock. The government therefore had a considerable interest in both the guaranteed debenture stock and the unguaranteed perpetual consolidated debenture stock. In order to protect that interest the government later provided assistance to pay the interest on both.
5 *Arbitration*, 592–5.
6 PAC, Borden Diary, 12 Aug. 1914.

contacted the presidents of both companies and asked them to prepare applications for government assistance. He personally drafted part of Mackenzie's application.[7]

The Canadian Northern application for further aid was submitted the day after Borden asked for it. In it William Mackenzie outlined his company's large indebtedness to the banks and subcontractors, the operational problems that would arise if the through lines were not completed, and the economic disruptions if all construction crews were suddenly laid off and all contracts for supplies and materials cancelled. He regarded it as his duty to "lay the whole situation before the government for its consideration and to request that co-operation and assistance of the government may be given in such a manner and by such means as to the government may seem best."[8]

The manner or method by which the government would provide assistance was deliberately left vague. Prior discussions between Mackenzie and Lash of the Canadian Northern Railway, B. E. Walker of the Canadian Bank of Commerce, Finance Minister White, and Prime Minister Borden had revealed a wide divergence of views on the matter. Railway and Bank officials felt the government could best assist the railway if it issued Dominion notes directly to the company. The company would pledge its guaranteed but now unsaleable debentures as collateral for these Dominion notes.[9] The notes should be large enough to accomplish all the objectives set out in the 1914 guarantee legislation. The president of the Canadian Car and Foundry Company of Montreal, to whom the Canadian Northern owed substantial sums for rolling stock, succinctly outlined the arguments in favour of such direct government assistance. "Unless it is done," he wrote the Prime Minister, "all the work and worry of the government and Parliament for months to make it possible for these roads to be completed will have been in vain, and now that the matter has gone so far, I think it is the bounden duty of the government to see it through."[10]

The federal government understood the need for sufficient assistance

7 *Ibid.*, 28 Aug. 1914.
8 PAC, White Papers, File 45, 7362–3, Mackenzie to Borden, 18 Aug. 1914.
9 *Ibid.*, 7345–6, White to Lash, 16 Aug. 1914; UTA, Walker Papers, Perry to Walker, 13 Oct. 1914.

10 PAC, Borden Papers, File OC 143, 8950, N. Curry to White, 24 Aug. 1914; PAC, White Papers, File 45, 7349–50, N. Curry to George Foster, 20 Aug. 1914.

to complete and equip the new main lines. There were, however, serious political problems with the method of assistance suggested. The railway companies were by no means the only supplicants for direct federal assistance when the London money markets closed during the first weeks of August. The pre-war expansion of the Canadian economy had spawned a large number of developmental projects, many of which ran into serious financial troubles in 1914. Among those hardest hit were provincial and, particularly, municipal and civic governments in Canada. Their ambitions had often greatly exceeded a rather weak tax base, and in 1914 federal aid seemed the only possible remedy. Finance Minister White was convinced that the federal government could not possibly assist all the worthy projects which found themselves in difficulty. He explained the problem to Lash, who was a director of both the Canadian Northern Railway and the Canadian Bank of Commerce: "To make advances to all would lead to most serious inflation and it seems difficult to refuse a province and grant the request of a railway company."[11]

The government decided to adopt a rather unsatisfactory expedient whereby it escaped responsibility for setting priorities for government financial assistance to the numerous promoters of worthy projects. It was decided that all loans of this nature should be made by the chartered banks, but that the federal government would issue Dominion notes and advance these to the banks to facilitate such loans. The promoters were expected to pledge their temporarily unsaleable securities as collateral for these Dominion notes.

Bank officials were not happy with this arrangement. The Dominion notes were given for a fixed term, after which the banks had to redeem them. The bank loans to promoters, however, had to be made without any firm assurance that those promoters would be able to repay them when the Dominion notes fell due. Attempts to obtain specific guarantees that the Dominion notes would be automatically renewed if the banks could not collect from the promoters met with no success. As a result the bankers adopted a very cautious credit policy. This policy was certainly anti-inflationary, and Finance Minister White soon found it necessary to urge the bankers to relax their

11 *Ibid.*, 7345–6, White to Lash, 16 Aug. 1914.

stringent credit policies.[12] Since the attitudes of the bankers were based directly on federal financial policies, White's exhortations achieved little. The federal policy provided the government with an excuse when promoters approached it for direct assistance, but it left the credit arrangements of corporations such as the Canadian Northern Railway in a permanently unstable condition. The brave policy adopted in 1914 to provide all the funds needed to complete the new lines had given way to unstable *ad hoc* arrangements.

The scheme nevertheless provided the Canadian Northern Railway with sufficient new funds to complete its main lines at least to the point where steel could be laid from coast to coast. On 5 September 1914 the railway obtained an advance of $2,500,000 from the Canadian Bank of Commerce. As security for the loan the Bank obtained Dominion treasury notes of the same value. Guaranteed debenture stock with a par value of $3,125,000 was pledged by the Canadian Northern Railway as collateral for these Dominion notes.[13] Eventually $10,000,000 was advanced to the Canadian Northern in loans of this nature.

As soon as these funds became available, Mackenzie and Mann, strongly urged and exhorted by Premier McBride, devoted their resources and energies to the speedy completion of the British Columbia main line. Premier McBride had solemnly promised his legislature at its 1914 sitting that the provincial assistance then voted would ensure completion of the Canadian Northern Pacific main line before the legislature met again. He had good reason to fear serious political problems if this promise was not met. Agitated letters and telegrams emanated from the Premier's office in August when delays and possibly complete cessation of construction work seemed inevitable.[14] Urgent appeals for federal assistance were sent to Prime Minister Borden, in which McBride stressed the national importance of the new line, "especially in event of accident to CPR in mountains" during wartime.[15] Delays, the Premier warned, would lead to "extra-heavy expenses in

12 UTA, Walker Papers, White to Walker, 15 Aug. 1915.
13 PAC, White Papers, File 45, 7366, Minister of Finance to Deputy Minister of Finance, 11 Sept. 1914.

14 PABC, McBride Papers, McBride to Mann, 6 and 7 Aug. 1914.
15 *Ibid.*, McBride to Borden, 27 Aug. 1914.

reorganizing construction staff apart altogether from fact that system would lose so many months on its earning capacity."[16]

More than $2,000,000 of the loan obtained from the Canadian Bank of Commerce in September was used in British Columbia.[17] McBride was determined to have the main line completed before the winter freeze-up. He urged Canadian Northern officials to consider "working double shifts in the canyons especially where trestles and similar structures are likely to hold you back."[18] Lighting plants, he suggested, should be installed in the canyons so that the work could be carried on day and night.

Canadian Northern officials did what they could to accommodate the Premier. Chief Engineer White issued instructions to "leave nothing undone that will hasten the tracklaying to a connection regardless of cost and at the expense of thoroughness, which means the carrying of track over temporary structures wherever proper construction would cause delay and working night and day wherever that will ensure faster progress."[19] These rather desperate expedients made it possible to join the main line trackage at Basque, British Columbia, on 23 January 1915. William Mackenzie was on hand to drive the last spike. The Canadian Northern Railway thus achieved transcontinental status. Steel had been joined, but in a number of places the track could not meet government standards for normal operations, even if inspectors agreed to rather loose interpretations of their standards and instructions.[20]

Preparations were nevertheless made for a ceremonial driving of the last spike in February.[21] The ceremony was designed, in part at least, to demonstrate the success of the British Columbia premier's policies. All members of the provincial legislature were invited to witness the successful completion of the visionary project about which many had become rather uneasy.

Unfortunately the inadequacies of the new road, due to the desperate

---

16 *Ibid.*, McBride to Borden, 28 Aug. 1914.
17 *Ibid.*, Walker to McBride, undated but apparently Aug. 1914.
18 *Ibid.*, McBride to T. H. White, Chief Engineer, Canadian Northern Pacific Railway, 16 Sept. 1914.
19 *Ibid.*, T. H. White to McBride,

7 Dec. 1914.
20 *Arbitration*, 592–5.
21 Sir William Mackenzie had already driven the last spike at Basque, British Columbia, on 23 Jan. 1915, but a special ceremony, complete with speeches and a banquet, was to take place in February.

haste in the final stages of the construction program, took their toll even before the planned ceremony took place. On 4 February 1915 a large tunnel at mile 186 on the main line caved in. Donald Mann immediately wired Premier McBride saying the celebration had to be postponed until May at least. The tunnel cave-in made it impossible for Canadian Northern officials to get to the Pacific coast over their own line. Mann, in a classic understatement, informed the Premier that "the fact of our having to go over another line to drive the last spike would have had a bad effect."[22] British Columbia's legislators had to satisfy themselves with an escorted inspection trip as far as Cisco, and the assurances of the Premier that the track was indeed completed and would soon be open for traffic.

The financial stringency and the hurried construction work in the Fraser Canyon had an additional, and controversial, development. While blasting the roadbed in the narrow canyon, Canadian Northern Pacific contractors did not exercise due caution to prevent major rock and mud slides. The local Department of Marine and Fisheries agent reported as early as 29 September 1913: "In a number of places they have literally shot the whole side of the mountain into the river, filling up numerous bays where the fish used to rest and as at Skuzzi new points projecting far out into the stream have been formed so congesting the waterway as to make it next to impossible for the fish to get through."[23] There was particular concern about serious damage to the salmon run and the Canadian Northern Pacific Railway was first asked, then ordered, to remove the obstructions.

The Canadian Northern Pacific Railway argued that it was not responsible for the damages. They were the result of activities by the contractors and subcontractors. Specifically, the Northern Construction Company, which held the contract in the Hell's Gate area, was blamed. Eventually the government decided that if the Canadian Northern Railway Company or its contractors did not remove the obstructions within a designated time period, tenders would be called by the government for an independent company to remove the obstructions at Canadian Northern expense. This expedient eventually became neces-

22 PABC, McBride Papers, Mann to McBride, 5 Feb. 1915.
23 PAC, Department of Marine and

Fisheries File 4572, A. W. R. Wilby to Agent, Marine and Fisheries, 29 Sept. 1913.

sary and the Pacific Dredging Company was given the contract. An order-in-council was passed authorizing the Minister of Marine and Fisheries to spend up to $60,000 and that "the cost of such portion of it as should be performed by the Canadian Northern Railway, be collected from the Company."

The final cost came to over $90,000 and eventually the Deputy Minister of Marine and Fisheries asked the Department of Railways and Canals to withhold payment of Canadian Northern subsidies to that amount. The Canadian Northern in turn deducted a substantial portion of that figure from the final payments due the Northern Construction Company for its construction work.

One of the curious aspects of the case was the difficulty in determining whether the Canadian Northern Railway, the Canadian Northern Pacific Railway, or the Northern Construction Company was really responsible. Yet Mackenzie, Mann and Co. Ltd. owned outright or held substantial interests in all three. They were also interested in the fisheries threatened by the obstruction. The apparent omnipresence of Mackenzie, Mann and Co. Ltd. could be very confusing to anyone trying to collect damages or bills, as the Deputy Minister of Marine and Fisheries quickly discovered. The worst of the obstructions at Hell's Gate in the Fraser Canyon were removed, however, although the construction of the railway did some long-term damage to the salmon run.[24]

In the Fraser Canyon and elsewhere in British Columbia and Northern Ontario, construction crews remained for most of 1915. Before the main line could pass federal inspection three temporary bridges on the North Thompson River alone had to be "renewed" with steel structures and thus made "permanent". Local stations and other facilities had to be built and the roadbed improved and ballasted in many places. Finally, in August 1915, all seemed ready for the first official through train from Toronto to Vancouver.[25] Mackenzie was to be on this first train, and Premier McBride vigorously, perhaps even desperately, struck the gong of local boosterism once more. "Except

24 The entire sordid affair, complete with photographs of the various obstructions, is outlined in detail in PAC, Department of Marine and Fisheries File 4572.

25 PABC, McBride Papers, Gamble to McBride, 19 July 1915, and Mackenzie to McBride, 25 Aug. 1915.

for present war cloud," he stated in a telegram, "this would be gala day for British Columbia."[26] When Mackenzie arrived without mishap at Port Mann on 27 August, completing the trip from Toronto in ninety-one running hours, McBride warmly congratulated him "upon overcoming all financial obstacles in attaining your goal".[27]

The final inspections by the federal Board of Railway Commissioners were made in September of 1915. The official opening of the line for regular traffic was set for October 1915. Canadian Northern officials invited a large party of parliamentarians, prominent businessmen, and newspaper reporters for an excursion to the Pacific coast to mark the occasion. At the same time it was arranged that Premier McBride, his entire Cabinet, and a number of friends and associates, would leave Vancouver in order to meet the parliamentary party at the British Columbia–Alberta boundary and then accompany it to Vancouver and Victoria.[28] Seventy-eight Members of Parliament and Senators and thirty-four journalists accepted the invitation. All arrangements for the excursion were made with great care and skill by Canadian Northern officials long experienced in the fine arts of political lobbying.[29] The mood and spirit of the entire affair were sufficiently sober and restrained to meet the sensibilities of a country at war; yet they also had a quiet confidence and exuberance appropriate for the opening of one of the best transcontinental railway systems on the continent.

The excursion was an enormous success. The journalists gave it extensive and enthusiastic coverage in papers across the country. Glowing tributes were paid to the promoters, and to the politicians who had helped them. Typical of many of these reports was one that appeared in the *Toronto Daily News*.

The tour to the Coast and back has opened the eyes and removed the doubts of probably every parliamentarian who took the trip. Rival interests and hasty politicians have described the Canadian Northern Railway as two streaks of rust, a jerry-built line, and a tramway across the plains. . . .

26 *Ibid.*, McBride to Mackenzie, 27 Aug. 1915.
27 *Ibid.*; *Canadian Railway and Marine World*, 1915, 351.
28 PABC, McBride Papers, Moore to McBride, 4–5 Oct. 1915, and McBride to Mackenzie, 5 Oct. 1915.
29 *Third Annual System Report, Canadian Northern Railway System*, 1915, 8; CAR, 1915, 754.

Besides possessing the best grades of any line on the continent, it is so well constructed as to permit passenger trains to travel 45 to 50 miles an hour for long stretches.[30]

The parliamentarians sent their own tributes and congratulations. The politicians representing both major political parties said in a special address to the railway's executives,

We had not conceived it possible that a railway, possessing the standard of alignment and gradient of your road could have been constructed across Canada within so short a period. The evenness of the road bed and the facility with which one locomotive has hauled across the continent a train nearly one-quarter of a mile in length (consisting of fifteen heavy coaches) fully demonstrates the high standard of construction obtained throughout the line of travel.[31]

This was high praise indeed. Despite the reckless haste displayed in the final stages, the railway was basically very well laid out and constructed. Comparisons with the steeper grades on the CPR were made repeatedly, and Canadian Northern officials maintained that their line would be far more efficient than that of their main rivals because of the easier grades and curves.[32] The ever-alert "Billy" Moore, now William Mackenzie's special assistant, compiled an impressive scrapbook of the various reports and comments on the parliamentary excursion.[33] Together with the Canadian Northern Railway's seven-volume *Encyclopedia*, this scrapbook became an ever-present aid to the company's lobbyists in Ottawa.

The opening of the Canadian Northern main line certainly evoked considerable enthusiasm, particularly in Victoria and Ottawa. Premier McBride, however, was expressing a fervent hope rather than an accomplished fact when he congratulated William Mackenzie on overcoming all financial obstacles and achieving his goal.[34] The Canadian

30 As quoted in CAR, 1915, 754.
31 *Third Annual System Report, Canadian Northern Railway System,* 1915, 8. This report related to the fiscal year ending 30 June 1915, but it was not presented to the directors or published until early in 1916. This

is the reason it contains references to events that occurred late in 1915.
32 *Arbitration,* 118.
33 This scrapbook is now in the custody of the Historical Section of the Canadian National Railways Headquarters Library in Montreal.

Northern Railway System was, in fact, on the verge of bankruptcy. Since 1912 the company had relied on loans and short-term notes to finance its construction, hoping to avoid large discounts in the sale of its long-term securities. In order to service these loans and obtain new funds after August 1914, contacts were renewed or established in New York with the firms of William A. Read and Company, Kuhn, Loeb and Company, the Central Trust Company, the Equitable Trust Company, and the Guarantee Trust Company.[35] These American companies all indicated considerable confidence and interest in Canadian Northern securities. The low rate of interest offered on these securities, however, made large discounts almost inevitable. Mackenzie therefore sought both short-term loans and the sale of at least some long-term securities in New York in order to service maturing short-term notes and to finance necessary "improvements" and equip his main line.

The Americans believed that under "normal" conditions the Canadian Northern was a sound enterprise, but since the government was a major shareholder and guarantor they were reluctant to invest their money until they received some indication of probable government action. It was well known that several Canadian railways were in serious financial difficulty and that individual members of the government were beginning to consider nationalization and consolidation of the various troubled lines as the most practical solution of the problem. The Americans therefore sought a meeting with, and specific assurances from, the government that any investment they might make would be reasonably secure. Prime Minister Borden agreed to send his Minister of Public Works, Robert Rogers, to New York in March of 1915 to discuss various aspects of the government's railway policy.[36]

The government still had not decided on a long-term railway policy. It was willing to offer reasonable assistance, taking into account the wartime financial disruptions, in the hope that the promoters would survive the crisis. Prime Minister Borden was also willing to assure any prospective investors, including American interests, that the government would indeed honour its guarantees on railway securities if that should ever become necessary. A default by the company, and

---

34 PABC, McBride Papers, McBride to Mackenzie, 27 Aug. 1915.
35 *Arbitration*, 598–9.

36 PAC, Borden Papers, File OC 163, Borden to Rogers, 18 March 1915.

even nationalization, could not undermine this commitment, and therefore the security of the guaranteed debentures.[37]

On the basis of this information the New Yorkers, in April 1915, purchased some of the government-guaranteed Canadian Northern debenture stock at a discount of approximately 9 per cent,[38] and granted very substantial short-term loans for which similar securities were pledged as collateral. As the capital needs of the railway mounted in 1915, more and more loans were obtained in New York, and the amount of securities pledged rose accordingly. On 19 May 1915 the Canadian Northern had pledged a total of $76,411,500 worth of securities for loans and short-dated notes in London and New York or with the federal government.[39] On that date Mackenzie still had on hand $21,821,062 in land, construction, and equipment securities which could be pledged as collateral for further borrowing. Within six months these too were pledged, and William Mackenzie informed Prime Minister Borden that his company had obtained a grand total of $86,532,830 in loans and short-dated notes and had pledged securities with a par value of $111,267,385 as collateral for these loans. Included were federally guaranteed bonds and debentures valued at $32,943,334, a total of $16,296,525 guaranteed by provincial governments, and $62,027,526 worth of equipment and terminal securities, land-mortgage debentures, and Perpetual Consolidated Debenture Stock which carried no government guarantee.[40] The company's supply of unsold securities which could be pledged as collateral was virtually exhausted in October 1915, at almost exactly the same time that the parliamentarians made their successful excursion on the new line. Thereafter, every maturing loan and every major capital expenditure created very serious financial difficulties.

In November 1915 William Mackenzie worked out a new plan to stabilize the company's capital accounts. He suggested that a new series of government-guaranteed securities, carrying a competitive 5-

37 PAC, Borden Diary, 14 March 1915.
38 PAC, Borden Papers, File OC 167, Memorandum respecting amounts received by Canadian Northern Railway under the $45,000,000 Guarantee Act, 1914, 28 June 1915.

39 Ibid., File OC 163, 11980, Canadian Northern Railway System, Securities Available for Requirements of Company, 19 May 1915.
40 Ibid., 11994–12003, Mackenzie to Borden, 23 Nov. 1915.

per-cent rate of interest, be brought out. The new issue should be equal to and replace all the unsold securities pledged for short-term obligations. Thus, a new underlying and saleable issue of government-guaranteed securities was to replace the $111,267,385 which had been pledged as collateral for the various loans negotiated since 1912. Mackenzie was convinced that government-guaranteed securities with a higher rate of interest would be marketable in New York and that the proceeds would be sufficient to meet all the company's maturing obligations and its new capital requirements. He emphasized that this arrangement would not increase the railway's total bonded indebtedness.[41]

Borden and his Cabinet colleagues knew that there would be very considerable opposition in their own caucus and in the House of Commons to any new Canadian Northern guarantee. Mackenzie's proposal was considered politically impractical, although it simply sought to accomplish in wartime the very thing the government had agreed to do when it passed the 1914 guarantee legislation.[42] The demands of war made a higher rate of interest necessary.

The Prime Minister also had to consider another factor. Stabilizing the company's capital accounts was no longer sufficient. In December 1914, for the first time in its history, the Canadian Northern Railway suffered a deficit on its operations. The railway still earned enough to meet all working expenses, but it failed to earn enough to pay the interest on all its bonds. Yet, the plan suggested by Mackenzie in November of 1915 would do nothing to meet mounting operational deficits.

Mackenzie was convinced that the 1914–15 deficit was due to the unusually large amount of new mileage added to the system that year. He believed that completion of the main line would lead to a great increase in traffic, thus allowing the company to avoid further deficits. In fact, while operating returns improved in 1915, the entire Canadian Northern Railway System never again operated profitably.

There were a number of reasons for the operating deficits after 1914. The main one was that the extensive newly opened transcontinental mileage in British Columbia and Ontario generated very little

41 *Ibid.*, 12001.   42 *Ibid.*, 12002.

local traffic. The well-developed prairie section provided substantial through traffic, but more local traffic elsewhere was needed. The prairie section continued to operate profitably, but it did not generate sufficient through traffic or operational surpluses to offset the heavy deficits elsewhere.

The problem on the new lines was in part due to a lack of adequate terminal facilities in Vancouver, Montreal, and Toronto.[43] Mackenzie repeatedly referred to the terminals problem, but the war was nearly over before proper handling facilities at Vancouver and Montreal were available, while the Toronto situation remained very unsatisfactory. Without adequate terminals, operations remained inefficient.

In addition to the terminals problem, the railway also found it impossible to obtain all the rolling stock needed to operate the new lines. Large orders for new rolling stock had been placed with several manufacturers, but after the outbreak of war these manufacturers had to give priority to military orders.[44] In the meantime, the Canadian Northern found itself compelled to turn over much of its prairie traffic to the better-equipped CPR and the traffic-starved Grand Trunk Pacific Railway. D. B. Hanna, the man who had so carefully nurtured and developed the Canadian Northern's early traffic, found himself forced to turn over hundreds of cars of grain at Edmonton during harvest seasons, simply because his company lacked the necessary motive power to take it to the Lakehead.[45] The new railway, with its under-developed transcontinental connections, simply could not afford such diversions of traffic originating along its own lines. Unfortunately, the lack of sufficient rolling stock left the managers no alternative.

Rapidly increasing costs created further major difficulties. Even when manufacturers found men, materials, and facilities to complete orders for rolling stock, the problems continued. Wartime demand very rapidly drove up the prices for all manufactured commodities. Before the war, for example, the Canadian Northern paid approximately $25,000 for a new locomotive. D. B. Hanna graphically described the changed situation of 1917: "We required additional power, we got tenders from one of the companies, but when he came into the office,

43 *Second Annual System Report, Canadian Northern Railway System,* 1916, 7–8.

44 *Arbitration,* 1789.

45 *Ibid.,* 1669, 2734.

he said, 'I hesitate to give you a figure; I am afraid you will throw me out.' and I said, 'Don't be afraid; what is it?' 'Well, if you take the power now I think we could get you them for around $54,000, but if you hang off it will probably cost you $60,000, if you can get anything at all.'"[46] Freight cars that cost $1,000 before the war had a price tag of between $2,300 and $2,600 in 1917. The need to equip new and underdeveloped lines under such circumstances was nothing short of disastrous.

Operations were further hampered by commitments made by the Canadian Northern Railway to carry government supplies, including military shipments. Under the terms of the company's transportation and subsidy agreements with the federal government the railway had agreed to perform annually, without pay, services for the government worth up to 3 per cent of their subsidy. This meant that the Canadian Northern and the Grand Trunk Pacific railways had to carry a great deal of government traffic without charge during the difficult war years. Yet, military shipments had to be given priority over other traffic. As a result much of the paying traffic had to be turned over to the CPR, which also received full rates for all government traffic, since its earlier subsidy arrangements did not include any free transportation clauses. Canadian Northern officials later complained, "It is amazing, the intelligence of government officials, how they select those lines of the Canadian Northern where subsidies were received to move the munitions and other requirements for the Army so that they won't have to pay the road any revenue."[47]

Most of the military traffic, moreover, was carried on the Canadian Northern only for short and therefore relatively expensive hauls. Before the United States entered the war, the Canadian Northern's Minnesota section of the main line made it impossible for that company to carry military traffic from Winnipeg to the Lakehead. That difficulty was eventually resolved, but for several years the Canadian Northern had to carry expensive short-haul traffic west of Winnipeg and east of Port Arthur without pay from the government.[48]

Rapid increases in operating costs of all kinds seriously aggravated

46 *Ibid.*, 562–3. 48 *Ibid.*, 1687.
47 *Ibid.*, 540.

the company's problems even further. Fuel costs rose by over 30 per cent between 1914 and 1917. Labour, when it was available at all, showed a similar increase. Hanna carefully explained the disastrous results.

If the wages paid in 1915 had been maintained in 1916 the saving on that score would have been $1,193,385, and in 1917 the saving would have been $1,313,972. If the price of fuel had not advanced over 1915 prices the saving in 1916 would have been $260,299 and in 1917 the saving would have been $1,456,164. The total saving therefore, of wages and fuel alone, without regard to the one hundred and one things otherwise that enter into railroad operation . . . would have amounted to $4,224,322. . . . So that instead of there being a deficit for the two years operation there would actually have been a surplus of $1,514,058.[49]

Fuel and labour costs on a full trainload from Winnipeg to Rainy River were $76.77 in 1915 but $101.00 in 1917.[50]

The Canadian Northern was a development road which could absorb these increased operating costs only if new immigrants and settlers along its newer lines generated a greatly increased volume of traffic. All the new mileage had been built with the expectation that the massive immigration of the pre-war years would continue in the foreseeable future. With the outbreak of war, however, the flow of immigration diminished rather abruptly. In 1913 a record number of 400,870 immigrants sought homes in Canada, very many near newly built Canadian Northern lines. Two years later only 36,665 immigrants—less than 10 per cent of the 1913 figure—came to Canada. The figure did not again reach 100,000 until 1919.[51]

Canadian Northern officials believed that their railway, and the development of the territory tributary to it, were about ten years behind the CPR and would achieve a similar success under comparable conditions. Immigration after 1914, however, was certainly not comparable to that of the previous two decades. The company's anticipated

49 *Ibid.*, 543–4.
50 *Ibid.*, 562.
51 M. C. Urquhart and K. A. H. Buckley, *Historical Statistics of*

Canada, Series A254: "Immigrant Arrivals in Canada, 1852–1960" (Toronto: Macmillan, 1971), 23.

revenues, therefore, were not realized, while its operating costs rapidly increased.

The normal response of a company to an increase in costs is to raise the price for its goods and services. The Canadian Northern Railway, however, had agreed to specific maximum rates when the famous Manitoba agreements of 1901 were signed. It had been compelled as recently as 1912 to extend the full benefits of those agreements to the provinces of Saskatchewan and Alberta. Mackenzie and Mann had always expected provincial governments to be understanding and co-operative, permitting required rate increases if operating costs rose sharply.[52] That was the only way those governments could ensure that their guarantees would never cost the provincial treasuries a cent. After 1914, however, the prairie governments showed no such co-operation or understanding and determinedly refused to sanction any rate increases.

The provincial governments refused to permit rate increases for a number of reasons. In fact, several were more willing to pay interest on guaranteed railway bonds than to impose higher rates. Higher rates were simply not politically acceptable, partly because there had never been a clear understanding of the economics of railway operations among the politicians. The 10¢ rate was what the farmers thought they could afford to pay, not what the government, after careful consideration, thought the railways needed. Unless farm income rose sharply, few farmers or their elected representatives could see any justification for rate increases. Long-standing suspicions about sharp accounting procedures and widely held notions of enormous construction profits by Mackenzie and Mann inured westerners to the company's lamentations. Westerners had little interest in or understanding of the operating ratios and accounting procedures of the railways, but they had a very keen understanding of what a rate increase would cost them.

A second widely held western opinion presented even more difficulties. It was generally acknowledged that the prairie system of the Canadian Northern Railway, despite the increased costs, was still

---

52 Mackenzie and Mann were reportedly very confident that "the government will naturally never reduce the rates to a point where the net result will force it to contribute towards interest deficiency," PAC, Hays Papers, I, 109–11.

earning substantial profits. The deficits and problems were due to the unprofitable mileage in British Columbia and eastern Canada. They were therefore a national problem which certainly should not be solved at the expense of the prairie farmers. The Canadian Northern had been built and had enjoyed great success as a western Canadian railway responsive to regional needs. Unfortunately it had gone national after 1909 and had gotten into serious trouble. Most of the arguments for increased rates after 1914 were the same "national" arguments that westerners had heard *ad nauseam* from the CPR in the 1880s. A rate increase would enable the Canadian Northern to earn larger profits on its prairie system, the region still paying substantially higher rates than other parts of the country, in order to meet deficits elsewhere. Substantial increases in eastern rates were, of course, impossible because of American railway and Great Lakes–St. Lawrence shipping competition. If it could be shown that the prairie business was unprofitable under the abnormal wartime conditions, western provincial governments were prepared to meet some of the interest payments, but they adamantly opposed permanent rate increases. The fact that the CPR was still earning large profits after 1914, although admittedly less than that company's pre-war returns, further complicated the situation and increased western determination to retain the Manitoba rates.[53]

There were suggestions that if the western rates were raised, excess profits earned by the CPR might be heavily taxed. Such suggestions, however, were entirely unacceptable to prairie politicians, since the higher western rates would be paid by prairie farmers and shippers, while the excess-profits taxes would be collected by the federal government. There was, as far as western farmers and politicians were concerned, only one fair way to deal with the rate question, and that was to equalize eastern and western rates by reducing the latter to the levels determined in the east by competition. If the railways could not carry on under such an arrangement, many westerners were prepared to see the federal government subsidize or take over and operate the railways in the national interest.

53 See particularly the summary of evidence presented and the judgment rendered in the Western Tolls Case of 1914, *Canadian Railway Cases*, XVII, 123–230.

The several rate inquiries conducted by the Board of Railway Commissioners after 1912 clearly demonstrated the divergent interests and views of the railway companies on the one hand and the western politicians on the other. It has been suggested that in 1911 western farmers were urgently seeking ways and means of reducing their capital and operating costs. They looked mainly for tariff reductions in 1910 and 1911, but the defeat of reciprocity in the 1911 election threw them back on the freight-rates issue.[54] The federal election was scarcely over when the city of Regina initiated proceedings which led to the first of a series of major rate inquiries.[55]

The successful outcome of the Regina Tolls Case encouraged western politicians and farmers to challenge the remaining differentials between eastern and western rates, and the even higher rates on the Rocky Mountain sections of the transcontinental railways. Neither the railways, the shippers, nor the commissioners had any doubt that, in comparison with eastern rates, those in the West were discriminatory.

The hearings in the Western Tolls Case were held in 1913 and 1914, at a time when both the Canadian Northern and the Grand Trunk Pacific railways were encountering serious problems but the Canadian Pacific Railway was still earning substantial profits. The Board of Railway Commissioners quickly came to two conclusions. The first was that while there was clearly discrimination, nothing should be done unless that discrimination was shown to be unjust. Great Lakes shipping and American railroad competition were considered by the Board as sufficient justification for the existing rate differentials between eastern and western rates.

A second conclusion of the Board was that rates must be high enough to attract investment, render railway securities marketable, and give a fair return to the railway company. But what was a fair return? Rates which would provide the Grand Trunk Pacific, the weakest of the prairie roads, with an adequate return would provide huge profits for the CPR. Canadian Northern officials argued that their road should be accepted as a standard western road for purposes of rate-making. Federal representatives, on the other hand, argued that the

54 A. W. Currie, "Freight Rates on Grain in Western Canada," *Canadian Historical Review*, XXI (March 1940), 40–55.

55 CRC, XIII, 203–16, Regina Tolls Case.

Board should total the investment of the three companies, as well as all projected returns, and then simply authorize equitable "average" rates. This would admittedly leave the CPR with substantial profits, the Canadian Northern hard pressed to make ends meet, and the Grand Trunk Pacific with permanent deficits.

The Board, in its judgement dated 6 April 1914, provided elaborate arguments why none of the roads, individually or collectively, could be taken as a standard for purposes of rate-making. It then established its own rather vaguely defined standard. The total investments on the three prairie roads were calculated. From this cumulative figure the Board deducted the cost of lines it described as uneconomic parallel main lines or developmental branch lines. It then set rates which would permit adequate returns on the remaining "economic" prairie lines.[56]

The Board readily admitted the existence of duplicate main lines and a great and continuing need for more developmental lines on the prairies. In another concurrent case, the commissioners indicated they would compel the construction of more developmental lines if they had the power to do so. Yet the rate structure was set without any allowance for the higher costs on parallel main lines and developmental branch lines.

The conclusions of the Board were, nevertheless, a victory for the railways. No further western rate reductions were authorized. The five existing western standard tariffs were consolidated into three, but the prairie standard remained consistent with the Canadian Northern's 1901 Manitoba agreements. Thus, in 1914, the railways avoided the rate reductions sought by western farmers. After 1914 rapidly rising costs forced the railways to apply to the Board for substantial rate increases.

Early in 1915 the Canadian Northern, joined by a number of other railways, made a request that the Board of Railway Commissioners again review the rate structure and grant rate increases commensurate with increased operating costs. The Board agreed to review the eastern rates, but felt that no new review of the western situation was justified.

In the Eastern Tolls Case the figures and returns of the Grand Trunk Railway were accepted as a suitable standard for rate-making

56 *Ibid.*, XVII, 123–230, Western Tolls Case.

purposes. Eastern rates, the Board held, should be sufficient to ensure a 6-per-cent return on investment in the Grand Trunk Railway, but this calculation was not to include losses suffered on the subsidiary Grand Trunk Pacific Railway or the Grand Trunk Western Railway to Chicago.

It was clear that Grand Trunk returns had fallen well below the acceptable level, while rates in competitive eastern transportation systems had increased. The Board therefore reported that "In general a case for increases of tolls in Eastern Canada had been made out and that increases should be made where the different industries could fairly bear such increases."[57] The details of specific rate increases were left to be implemented after the ability of various industries to absorb additional transportation costs had been determined. Consequently, there was no uniform rate increase, but the average increase on eastern rates as a result of the Board's ruling came to approximately 15 per cent.

There was never any doubt that the increases authorized in the Eastern Tolls Case would not be sufficient to make the Canadian Northern Railway's eastern lines profitable. "The Canadian Northern System," according to the commissioners, "has only emerged from the construction stage, and its figures need not be considered. Its position is shortly stated by the Company to be that they need every cent of revenue that they can obtain. There is little reason to doubt the Canadian Northern Railway Company is operating in eastern Canada at a loss."[58]

Increased costs, inadequate terminal facilities and rolling stock, a large number of new and developmental lines, and the inability to obtain increased rates, led to serious operational deficits on the Canadian Northern Railway System. Revenues were simply not sufficient to meet all working expenses and fixed charges on the amalgamated lines after 1914. This was not altogether unexpected. As early as 1909, Mackenzie had begun to discuss with his bankers and financiers ways and means of "taking care of the enterprise during the few years when rates of earnings might be disturbed by the quantity of new road built".[59]

57 *Ibid.*, XXII, 4–49, Eastern Tolls Case, 1916.
58 *Ibid.*

59 UTA, Walker Papers, H. V. F. Jones to Walker, 7 March 1910.

It was generally agreed that the necessary financing to meet such deficits should be through the sale of junior securities of the company. When the matter was first discussed in 1909, the London underwriters indicated a willingness to carry the company through this period. Unfortunately, there was no market for the railway's junior securities after 1912, and after 1914 the London financiers were prevented by order-in-council from granting any of the funds suggested in 1909.

All the Canadian Northern Railway's federally and provincially guaranteed debentures, moreover, had to be applied only to construction, and could not be used to meet operational deficits. Consequently, the Canadian Northern had no funds it could use to pay fixed charges when earnings were insufficient. The promoters, Mackenzie, Mann and Co. Ltd., had to find the funds themselves if a default was to be avoided, but as contractors they found themselves very hard pressed to pay off demanding subcontractors after 1912. By 1914 they had actually paid out for construction $22,000,000 more than they had been able to collect from the Canadian Northern Railway. This had virtually exhausted their private resources and their credit with the Canadian Bank of Commerce.

The first major crisis involving interest payments came in December 1914. Bond interest of $2,000,000 was due on the last day of the year, as were several short-term loans. There was no money in the company treasury and the banks refused further credit to either the railway company or the contracting firm of Mackenzie, Mann and Co. Ltd. A default seemed unavoidable. It would force both federal and provincial governments to pay interest on bonds they had guaranteed. It would also lead to a possible receivership or government-sponsored reorganization of the company.

Mackenzie and Lash urged the federal government to provide Dominion notes so that the necessary loan could be obtained from the Bank. They were willing to pledge unsold and unpledged but government-guaranteed construction bonds as collateral. The government, however, believed it would be improper to use construction bonds in this way. Those bonds could be, and were, pledged and repledged as security for construction loans. They could not, in the government's view, be used to secure loans needed to pay interest.[60]

60 PAC, Borden Papers, File OC 163, Borden to White, 30 Dec. 1914.

On Christmas Day, 1914, Borden and his ministers decided that the Canadian Northern should go into receivership if Mackenzie and Mann could not raise the funds from their own resources to pay the interest. Premier McBride was warned that the federal government would not grant further assistance, and that British Columbia should make preparations to pay interest charges on provincially guaranteed Canadian Northern Pacific securities.[61] The federal government would do the same on federally guaranteed Canadian Northern securities.

Premier McBride wired back an urgent appeal for further federal consideration.[62] Discussions between the government, the railway promoters, and their bankers continued. The government steadfastly refused to advance any Dominion notes, or to allow any securities issued for construction purposes to be pledged as collateral for loans to meet the interest payments. Instead, Borden tried very hard to persuade the Canadian Bank of Commerce to advance the needed loan without any additional security other than the general credit and standing of the railway itself.

The Bank was reluctant to make such advances. It had not yet advanced large sums to the railway, but it did have a very large account with the promotional and contracting firm of Mackenzie, Mann and Co. Ltd., whose principal asset was the common stock of the Canadian Northern Railway. The bank could not, therefore, be indifferent to the fate of the railway. A default would greatly increase the difficulties Mackenzie, Mann and Co. might encounter in repaying their large loans. Yet the bankers did not wish to advance more funds to either the railway or the contractors unless the federal government specifically agreed to protect them against possible loss in connection with these loans. Only at the very last minute in 1914, after considerable pressure from both promoters and politicians, did the bankers agree to advance the needed funds and thus keep the endangered enterprise afloat for the time being.[63]

The government adopted a somewhat unusual policy on 25 January

61 PABC, McBride Papers, Borden to McBride, 25 Dec. 1914.
62 *Ibid.*, McBride to Borden, Dec. 1914.
63 Later rumours had it that General Manager John Aird of the Bank of Commerce actually kept a pistol in his desk, determined to commit suicide if the details of the bank loans to the Canadian Northern Railway became public knowledge, CNRHQ, O. D. Prosser interview.

1915. On that date the Prime Minister privately and confidentially informed the president of the Canadian Bank of Commerce that the federal government would protect the Bank against possible loss if the Bank would advance funds as required by the railway company to meet interest payments or maturing short-term loans which could not be immediately accommodated or renegotiated in New York.[64] In a letter dated 27 May 1915, the sum of $4,000,000 was set as the maximum assistance to be thus provided.[65] In June an additional $2,000,000 was needed and the Prime Minister gave the Bank a further private letter assuring government support for the additional amount.[66] The Prime Minister thus provided, without any parliamentary authorization, an informal guarantee for the loans made to meet interest payments. The president and general manager of the Bank advanced these large loans, allegedly without obtaining the consent of the full Board of Directors, as required under the Bank's by-laws.

The legal validity of these private letters from the Prime Minister to the president and general manager of the Canadian Bank of Commerce was rather dubious. The bankers certainly worried a great deal about the status of these loans to the Canadian Northern Railway and how they might affect their loans to Mackenzie, Mann and Co. Ltd. The loans to the railway had no real security other than the general credit of a railway operating at a deficit, and a private letter from a Prime Minister who must face an election soon. Neither the Canadian Bank of Commerce nor the Canadian Northern Railway were particularly popular with the Opposition at the time, and an election upset might leave the Bank very vulnerable. Yet refusal to advance additional funds needed by the railway would clearly undermine the ability of Mackenzie, Mann and Co. Ltd. to repay their large loans. The only solution seemed to be to persuade the government to make more adequate and satisfactory provisions.

As the Bank advances to the Canadian Northern Railway mounted, the pressure on the government increased.[67] Borden's diary clearly

64 PAC, Borden Diary, 25 Jan. 1915.
65 PAC, Borden Papers, File OC 167, Borden to Walker, 27 May 1915.
66 Ibid., Borden to Walker, 24 June 1915.

67 Ibid., John Aird to Borden, 27 May 1916; see also File OC 163, Borden to Aird, 29 Nov. 1915, two letters of the same date.

indicates repeated visits and appeals by a desperate Sir William Mackenzie, while the minute-book of the Canadian Northern Railway
became a record of frantic rearranging of obligations, of the pledging
and repledging of securities to meet maturing construction loans, and
of an all-out search for new bank loans to meet operational deficits.[68]

Borden and his Cabinet colleagues found the railway situation both
baffling and frustrating. There was, according to Borden, "not much
agreement except that situation is difficult and almost impossible."
He wrote despairingly that he "wd. personally prefer to resign & let
the grits clean up their own mess."[69] He nevertheless had to find some
way of meeting the railway problem and ending the unwelcome visits
of Sir William Mackenzie. Once, in frustration, the Prime Minister
noted in his diary that Mackenzie had again "pestered me for more
help for his infernal railway".[70]

All the government aid given during the first year of the war was
based on the hope that the railways would be able to look after their
own needs if given essential interim assistance. The desperate state of
affairs on both the Canadian Northern Railway and the Grand Trunk
Pacific Railway late in 1915 clearly indicated that more drastic measures were needed. *Ad hoc* measures would not meet the requirements
of the situation and see the new transcontinentals safely through the
war. Politicians, promoters, and financiers consequently began to
search for long-term solutions to the nation's railway problems.

---

68 PAC, CNR Records, MCDXL and
MCDXLI.

69 PAC, Borden Diary, 6 April 1916.
70 *Ibid.*, 9 June 1916.

CHAPTER SIXTEEN

THE SEARCH FOR LONG-TERM SOLUTIONS

THREE LONG-TERM SOLUTIONS to the Canadian Northern Railway's financial problems were considered in 1916 and 1917. One was a refinancing arrangement in New York, which would have allowed Mackenzie and Mann to retain control. The second was a scheme whereby the Canadian Pacific Railway would purchase the common shares from Mackenzie and Mann and amalgamate the Canadian Northern with its own system. The third involved the acquisition and operation of the Canadian Northern Railway, together with several other lines, by the government. Promoters and financiers devised the first two solutions, while politicians, bureaucrats, and royal commissioners devised the third. The modalities of these proposed solutions were left vague for many months, but gradually the divergent interests and objectives of the promoters and the government became quite clear.

Until 1915 both the federal government and the promoters had resorted to short-term *ad hoc* financial arrangements to meet the disruptions of the capital markets. Late in 1915 the necessity of more drastic and far-reaching measures had become obvious. Consequently, Mackenzie presented his politically impractical refinancing scheme, which called for a very large new issue of government-guaranteed bonds at an attractive interest rate. The old government-guaranteed bonds were to be brought in and exchanged for these new bonds which would be more readily marketable. The scheme made no provision for future operational deficits and was based on Mackenzie's belief that the operational prospects for 1915 were "as bright as the results of 1914 were depressing."[1]

1 PAC, Borden Papers, File OC 163, 11994–12013, Mackenzie to Borden, 23 Nov. 1915. The detailed traffic calculations on which Mackenzie based his optimistic predictions were forwarded to the government a few

Neither the government nor the bankers who had jointly arranged for the payment of the fixed charges in the early months of 1915 were as sanguine about the future.[2] The Bank showed its lack of confidence by insisting that Mackenzie, Mann and Co. Ltd. pledge all their common shares in the Canadian Northern Railway System as additional security for their loans. Previously the contracting firm had pledged various bonds and debenture stock which they had received in partial payment for specific construction expenditures. The dismal results of operations and the low rate of interest on these bonds and debentures had greatly decreased their market value. Hence the Bank's demand for additional collateral.[3]

Mackenzie was very reluctant to pledge the stock. He even appealed to the Prime Minister to use his influence with the bankers,[4] but in December 1915 the bankers insisted on taking a lien on the common shares. It was a serious blow for Mackenzie and Mann, who had always regarded the Canadian Northern shares as their most valuable property and their only reward for promoting the transcontinental railway.

The Canadian Bank of Commerce apparently had little alternative but to take the stock. It held very large blocks of Canadian Northern securities, mainly as security for the loans to Mackenzie, Mann and Co. Ltd., and the value of these securities had fallen. Borden feared the bankers would be compelled to write the value of these securities "down to an amount which would make a very alarming statement necessary at the end of the financial year".[5] He feared for the stability and reputation of the Canadian Bank of Commerce. By taking the capital stock of the Canadian Northern Railway as additional collateral, the position of the Bank was considerably relieved.

While the Bank was putting pressure on Mackenzie and Mann to pledge their common shares, the federal government devised measures of its own to relieve the financial crisis. It did not accept the plan

---

months later. PAC, White Papers, File 47, 7577–7608, Memo on the earning power of the Canadian Northern Railway System as prepared by L. C. Fritch and Canadian Northern Railway Traffic Notes, April 1916; QUA, Flavelle Papers, 3011, J. W. Flavelle to Rundle, 22 Aug. 1917.

2 PAC, Borden Papers, File OC 167, White to Borden, 27 Nov. 1915.
3 *Ibid.*, File RLB 2984, Borden to Perley, 27 Nov. 1915.
4 PAC, Borden Diary, 11 Dec. 1915.
5 PAC, Borden Papers, File RLB 2984, Borden to Perley, 27 Nov. 1915.

devised by Mackenzie. Instead it produced another short-term measure, but this time with a firm commitment to seek a more comprehensive and permanent solution.

Borden, wakeful at an early hour on 26 November 1915, "got the idea that [the] CNR nightmare might be dissipated by merely putting in an estimate to protect underlying securities."[6] Specifically, he wanted to include in the government's Supplementary Estimates a sufficient amount to repay the loans made by the Bank to meet interest payments in 1915, to provide additional funds for interest payments in 1916, and to buy up enough of the railway's securities to stabilize their market value. The money was to be advanced in the form of a loan to the railway company and the provisions were to apply both to the guaranteed debenture stock and to the 4-per-cent Perpetual Consolidated Debenture Stock which was pledged, as a second charge, for the bonds guaranteed in 1914.

This scheme was designed to provide substantial relief for both the railway company and the Bank, and it was politically appealing to the Prime Minister because parliamentary procedure did not permit substantive Opposition amendments on proposals or allocations under Supplementary Estimates.[7] Arthur Meighen, the government's parliamentary strategist, who had already distinguished himself by devising the first effective closure motion in the Canadian Parliament, was very enthusiastic and described the plan as "diabolically clever".[8]

The Cabinet worked at the details of the scheme for several months, but on 29 November 1915 Borden informed John Aird of the Canadian Bank of Commerce of the government's intentions and asked that the Bank continue to support the Canadian Northern Railway until the legislation could be brought forward.[9] While reasonably confident that they could introduce the legislation, Borden and his Cabinet colleagues found it very difficult to persuade their own caucus members of its merits. The caucus was opposed to further loans to the railways and Borden allegedy declared that "if he were to remain Premier the measure must receive the approval of his followers".[10] Shaughnessy of

6 PAC, Borden Diary, 26 Nov. 1915.
7 PAC, Borden Papers, File RLB 2984, Borden to Perley, 27 Nov. 1915.
8 PAC, Borden Diary, 26 Nov. 1915.

9 PAC, Borden Papers, File OC 163, Borden to Aird, 29 Nov. 1915.
10 PAC, Shaughnessy Letterbook, No. 110, 877, Shaughnessy to Osler, 7 May 1916.

the CPR believed that "some commitment was made either through Lazard Frères, or one of our Canadian Banking Institutions, that compelled the Premier to do what would appear to be an act of political madness."[11]

One of the key provisions of the new measure was that it would buy time during which the government could formulate a permanent policy. It was designed simply to hold the situation for the time being. "The Canadian railway situation," according to Finance Minister White, "is so grave as to require that it should be dealt with not in a hap-hazard manner but comprehensively. This can only be done after we have received a report from the ablest experts that can be obtained and this, of course, will require time."[12]

The government was, in fact, already very seriously considering nationalization of the two newer transcontinentals as the only possible solution. This idea had a great deal of support in the caucus, but the Cabinet decided in 1916 that a further detailed royal commission inquiry should be completed. White, when suggesting the inquiry, said the experts "might conceivably recommend the amalgamation of the Canadian Northern, the Grand Trunk and the Grand Trunk Pacific into a system in which the Government might be interested to a certain extent."[13] Borden had already warned Mackenzie that "We wd. probably have to take over the CNR,"[14] while Thomas Shaughnessy of the CPR began to urge that the CPR be included in a plan of national ownership but private management of Canadian railways. Shaughnessy admitted that "Management by the Canadian Pacific [of a government-owned national railway system] would be obnoxious to the politicians, but, beyond question, the organization and *esprit de corps* of our Company would contribute in a marked way to the success of the undertaking."[15] White's speech in defence of the government's actions was described by Borden as "a full and cogent statement setting forth the necessities and foreshadowing nationalization of all Canadian railways".[16]

The official terms of reference for the Royal Commission were very broad. The commissioners were to "enquire into Railways and

---

11 *Ibid.*
12 PAC, Borden Papers, File OC 143, 9220–3, White to Borden, 6 Jan. 1916.
13 *Ibid.*
14 PAC, Borden Diary, 12 April 1916.

15 PAC, Shaughnessy Letterbook, No. 110, 887, Shaughnessy to Osler, 11 May 1916.
16 PAC, Borden Diary, 8 May 1916.

Transportation, including territories served by the three great systems of Canada, physical conditions, operative methods, branch lines, connections in the United States, steamship connections and financial conditions, together with problems of re-organization and state acquisitions."[17] It was clearly the intention of the government that the proposed inquiry consider all possible means whereby the country's railway problems might be resolved. It was fairly clear that the government would give serious consideration to any recommendations the commissioners might make.

Borden and his colleagues were convinced that the men appointed to the commission must be widely acceptable and respected. In order to reassure voters, business executives, and investors alike, it was thought highly desirable to appoint to the commission acknowledged experts in various aspects of railway work from Canada, the United States, and Great Britain.

The Canadian chosen for this purpose was Henry L. Drayton, chairman of the Board of Railway Commissioners and a widely acknowledged expert on Canadian railways. It was under Drayton's chairmanship that the Board had heard the major railway rate cases since 1912, and there was widespread support in the business community for the moderate position the Board had taken in those cases. Businessmen thought Drayton's views that railways should earn enough to pay reasonable dividends but never charge more than the affected industries could reasonably afford to pay an eminently fair one.[18] Drayton was so obviously the Canadian expert for the commission that the government never seriously considered any other Canadian for the position. There were, in fact, very few Canadian railway experts who had not, at one time or another, been employed by the railways now to be investigated and who might therefore have unacceptable prejudices. Drayton, on the other hand, had been active in Ontario municipal politics when the nationalization of the hydro-electric interests was the dominant political issue. He might therefore be less than friendly to William Mackenzie, who had been active in that dispute.

To reassure the Americans, and particularly prospective new in-

17 Canada, PC 1680, 13 July 1916.

18 PAC, Borden Papers, File OC 294,

G. M. Murray to Borden, 17 March 1916.

vestors who might be willing to participate in any reorganization of one or more of Canada's railways, an American with practical railway experience was needed. Borden, always impressed by successful businessmen, was most eager to resolve the Canadian railway problem in an efficient and businesslike manner, and believed the American businessman on the Royal Commission would be of great importance. Borden therefore personally travelled to New York to consult with American railroad officials and financiers.

Borden's first choice for the American to serve on the Royal Commission was F. D. Underwood, president of the Erie Railroad and formerly associated with the CPR's Soo line. Thomas Shaughnessy had strongly recommended Underwood for this assignment.[19] Underwood, however, declined due to pressure of work at home.[20]

Borden then, in consultation with S. R. Bertron of Bertron, Griscom and Company, who were giving serious consideration to a Canadian Northern refinancing plan,[21] approached W. W. Atterbury, vice-president of the Pennsylvania Railroad. Atterbury impressed Borden "very favourably" and he was eager to accept the Canadian appointment.[22] The president of the Pennsylvania Railroad, however, decided he could not spare Atterbury for the Canadian assignment, and the vice-president was compelled to decline Borden's invitation.

With both Underwood and Atterbury unavailable, Borden turned to a third man, who had already indicated considerable interest. When meeting with A. H. Smith, president of the New York Central Railroad, to discuss the personnel of his commission, Borden noted: "Smith . . . seems inclined to make me realize that his own services are available."[23] Thus, on the day after Atterbury refused the appointment, Smith was asked to come to Ottawa for further discussions. These quickly led to Smith's appointment. Borden considered him the most important and influential member of the commission, and in recognition of the fact asked him to serve as chairman.[24] He believed that Smith had agreed to undertake the task in a spirit of public service, although in this

19 PAC, Borden Diary, 1 Nov. 1915.
20 *Ibid.*, 26 June 1916.
21 *Ibid.*, also 19 and 27 June 1916.
22 *Ibid.*, 29 June 1916.
23 *Ibid.*

24 PAC, Borden Papers, File OC 295, 32758, A. H. Smith to Borden, 10 July 1916. Also Canada, PC 1680, 13 July 1916.

respect he was disillusioned when, after the government had rejected Smith's proposals, the commissioner sent in a bill for $100,000 for his services.[25]

The third member of the commission was to be a British financial expert, presumably to reassure British financiers and investors who already had large investments in Canadian railways. The appointment was first offered to Sir George Paish, editor of the *London Statist*. Paish readily accepted, and the order-in-council appointing A. H. Smith, Sir Henry Drayton, and Sir George Paish as members of the Royal Commission to Inquire into Railways and Transportation in Canada was passed on 13 July 1916.[26] Within two weeks of his appointment, however, Paish suffered a nervous collapse and was obliged to withdraw from the commission. The Cabinet immediately considered the appointment of a replacement. Finance Minister White suggested that no replacement was needed, because "the financial situation of our transcontinentals is quite simple and well known."[27] Other Cabinet ministers did not agree, arguing that the report of the commission would carry more weight if a recognized financial expert were appointed. As a result, there were hurried consultations with members of the staff of the Canadian High Commission in London.

The man ultimately appointed was W. H. Acworth, a one-time schoolmaster, a lecturer in railway economics at the London School of Economics, and a long-time railway statistician. Consultations in London produced a rather cautious endorsation of Acworth. The secretary of the British Railway Department did not regard Acworth as "in the top flight". He had, however, been connected with railway matters all his life, and it was for that reason that he was considered "the best man we could get in this country for the purposes you require".[28] Businessmen regarded Acworth as being too theoretical and not sufficiently familiar with practical railway operations. The Canadian government was evidently somewhat uncertain about the appointment, perhaps in part because Acworth had written several favourable

25 PAC, White Papers, File 57, 9429–30, A. H. Smith to Borden, 29 May 1917. See also Borden Papers, OCA 191, 80964–81004. This entire file deals with the bill sent by A. H. Smith. Smith eventually received $50,000.

26 Canada, PC 1680, 13 July 1916.
27 PAC, Borden Papers, File OC 293, White to Borden, 18 Aug. 1916.
28 *Ibid.*, Griffith to Borden, 25 Aug. 1916.

articles about railway nationalization already. It wasn't until 21 October 1916—more than three months after Paish's illness and more than two months after the first direct inquiries were made about Acworth—that he was formally appointed to the commission.[29] He arrived in New York less than three weeks later, having crossed the Atlantic in the illustrious company of Lord Shaughnessy, Sir Joseph Flavelle, and Sir Thomas White. Railway affairs were frequently discussed during that crossing, and at least one Canadian Cabinet minister was convinced that Acworth had developed a prejudice against the newer transcontinentals before he even arrived in North America.[30]

The appointment, by the federal government, of acknowledged experts to examine the railway problem coincided with a second major inquiry. This was sponsored by the Canadian Northern Railway and by interested financiers in New York City. William Mackenzie had certainly not abandoned hope of arranging a major refinancing scheme, despite the rather cool reception given his proposals of November 1915. He spent much time in late 1915 and early 1916 in New York trying to persuade his American financiers to undertake a major refinancing scheme. The Americans were certainly interested and, on inquiry, received some encouragement from Prime Minister Borden.[31]

Before investing their money, the Americans suggested "a comprehensive and thorough study of the situation". They specifically wanted to know how much capital was still required to fully equip the Canadian Northern Railway and to meet all its short-term obligations, and whether, under normal operating conditions, a fully equipped and properly financed system would prove profitable. They suggested the appointment of a special commission to study the matter, assuring Mackenzie that they "would be glad to consider making a proposition towards financing if the report was satisfactory."[32]

The negotiations led to the signing of a formal agreement between Mackenzie, Mann and Co. Ltd., the Canadian Northern Railway System, and Kuhn, Loeb and Company, William A. Read and Company,

---

29 Canada, PC 2567, 21 Oct. 1916.
30 PAC, Borden Papers, File OC 447, Meighen to Borden, 20 Feb. 1917, with memorandum.

31 PAC, Borden Diary, 19 June 1916. The fact that some of the financiers were of German origin created some difficulties.
32 *Arbitration*, 1047.

and the Central Trust Company, on 25 August 1916.[33] Under the terms of this agreement an independent commission named by, or at least acceptable to, the Americans was to inspect and report fully on the Canadian Northern Railway. All expenses connected with the investigation were to be paid by the Canadian Northern Railway.

Two respected American businessmen were appointed to serve on the special commission. They were Edward E. Loomis, president of the Lehigh Valley Railroad Company, and John Platten, president of the United States Mortgage and Trust Company. They in turn engaged the services of Coverdale and Colpitts, a New York firm of consulting engineers. Colpitts, however, was a former employee of the CPR, and was very highly thought of by Shaughnessy. These men were to examine all aspects of the Canadian Northern's financial and operational structure and methods. The investigators were also instructed to formulate several alternative refinancing proposals.

The resulting investigations were both thorough and far-ranging. Engineers travelled the length and breadth of the Canadian Northern system, and accountants scrutinized the company's accounts, while traffic experts sought to ascertain its future traffic resources and earning capacity.[34] It was expected that these findings would be crucial in the refinancing scheme, which would involve immense sums of money.

Loomis and Platten completed their work and presented their report in March 1917, before the federally appointed Royal Commission had completed its work. The American report was all that Mackenzie and Mann could have desired. The investigators declared flatly, "We are unanimously of the opinion, after many months consideration of the subject, that the undertaking as a whole is sound, and that its soundness can be demonstrated at this time."[35] More specifically, the investigators reported that "about 5,911 miles of prairie lines are already so far developed as to warrant the prediction that they will carry the whole system in the comparatively near future. The Pacific, Northern Ontario, and Eastern lines may develop more

33 PAC, CNR Records, X̄CCLXXXVIII, Item 16, Agreement between Kuhn, Loeb and Company, William A. Read and Company, Central Trust Company, the Canadian Northern Railway System, and Mackenzie, Mann and Co. Ltd. to formulate a plan for more permanent and comprehensive financing of the Canadian Northern Railway (approved 25 Aug. 1916).
34 *Arbitration*, 1238–9, 1064.
35 *Loomis and Platten Report*, 1, copy of this report in PAC, White Papers, File 50, 8116–60.

slowly, but can be made self-sustaining and profitable under a proper program."[36] All these statements, however, were based on the assumption that the Canadian economy would continue to grow at approximately the same rate as during the pre-war years, and that equitable rates would prevail. The war had temporarily disrupted Canadian affairs and prevented the expected development along the lines of the Canadian Northern Railway System, but the railway's long-term prospects were declared sound.

In order to meet the railway's immediate financial requirements and to equip it properly and complete essential facilities, Loomis and Platten devised two plans. They estimated that an additional $67,000,000 would be needed under a three-year plan of reorganization, and $101,000,000 if a five-year plan were adopted.[37] These sums were expected to take care of the railway's short-term debts, its new capital requirements, and its operational deficits during the first years after the reorganization. Loomis and Platten estimated that the system would earn a net profit of $329,000 during the first year following completion of a proposed three-year plan, and $4,615,000 during the first year following completion of the five-year program.[38]

The Loomis and Platten report clearly provided a basis for successful financial negotiations in New York. S. R. Bertron, whose firm had a close association with the financial companies that initiated the study, said,

We were entirely satisfied with the report. In fact it was even more favourable in some respects than we had anticipated. . . . The favourable features were that here was a property that ran through very attractive growing territory. It was well built, with small grades that could be operated economically, a small bonded indebtedness, which indebtedness has been placed on a very low interest return basis, which made it very attractive with us; with us, we are accustomed to have obligations bearing a higher rate of interest. These features made the situation very attractive for us.[39]

The same financial group had, in fact, just completed a successful reorganization of the Union Pacific Railroad along very similar lines.

36 *Ibid.*, 2.
37 *Ibid.*, 29.
38 *Ibid.*, 41.
39 *Arbitration*, 1408, 1415–16.

The Loomis and Platten report became the basis for a Canadian Northern refinancing plan which the New Yorkers submitted to Mackenzie and Mann and to the Canadian government on 31 July 1917. The plan called for the issuing of new First and Refunding Mortgage Securities, with the federal government guaranteeing at least the refunding securities. They were to carry a higher rate of interest, and would be used to take care of the Canadian Northern's short-term obligations and new capital requirements. In addition, $100,000,000 of Preferred Stock was to be issued and exchanged for the various unguaranteed Canadian Northern securities. The common stock would remain with Mackenzie and Mann or be held in any other way to be determined "by agreement between the Dominion Government and the present holders". The Americans were not interested in acquiring the company. Theirs was simply a refinancing plan, relying on a government guarantee for at least some of the First and Refunding Mortgage Securities.[40] The Americans offered to participate in a refinancing plan even if the government decided to acquire the capital stock, provided the required federal guarantees were approved.

Several factors made this plan impractical. By the time it was submitted, the imminent entry of the United States into the war made the American financiers cautious.[41] In Canada, moreover, the Royal Commission had completed its work and the commissioners made very different recommendations. The Royal Commissioners and Loomis and Platten had worked at the same time and on the same basic figures, but their basic procedures as well as their recommendations were very different. Loomis and Platten were mainly concerned with the future traffic and earning potential of the Canadian Northern Railway. The Royal Commission resorted to a physical valuation of the several troubled Canadian railways. The cost of physically reproducing the

40 PAC, White Papers, File 51, 8336, 8529–36, Plan for the Readjustment of the Capitalization of the Canadian Northern Railway, as submitted to Sir Robert Borden and Sir William Mackenzie by J. W. Wallace, on behalf of Kuhn, Loeb and Company, and William A. Read and Company, and Central Trust Company, 31 July 1917. Wallace specifically indicated a willingness to participate in a refinancing plan even if the government nationalized the railway by taking over its common stock. See also PAC, White Papers, File 51, 8337–96, Kuhn, Loeb and Company to White and other Cabinet ministers; ibid., 8397, Kuhn, Loeb and Company, William A. Read and Company, and Central Trust Company, to Borden, 7 Aug. 1917.
41 Arbitration, 1410.

railways at pre-1914 prices was to be compared with the railways' liabilities. The net equity was calculated as the difference between physical reproduction costs and liabilities. A Harvard scientist, Professor G. F. Swain, was commissioned to make the detailed physical valuation of both the Canadian Northern and the Grand Trunk Pacific systems.

The three members of the Royal Commission did not agree among themselves about this proposed method of valuation. Smith, the practical railway man, was far more interested in potential earnings than in detailed calculations of reproduction costs and liabilities. Various items to be included or excluded in the detailed calculations also produced differences of opinion, and in the end Smith and his assistants made one set of calculations while Drayton and Acworth made another. This, in turn, resulted in two reports, with Drayton and Acworth submitting a majority report and Smith, somewhat later, his minority report.

The Drayton and Acworth calculations were similar to those used by the Board of Railway Commissioners when it reviewed freight rates after 1912. The Board had specifically ruled that 6 per cent was a fair return on capital judiciously invested in railways, although this rate of return was not extended to capital invested in unnecessary trunk lines or developmental branch lines. Calculations of this sort were probably a sound basis for rate-making, but hardly for purposes of financial reorganization. Investors and financiers are interested in operating-results and profits rather than in balance sheets, especially when these are calculated according to unrealistic pre-1914 figures. Drayton and Acworth nevertheless calculated the physical cost of reproducing the Canadian Northern and Grand Trunk Pacific at those prices. Then they deducted all liabilities and came to the conclusion that both railways had incurred liabilities which exceeded the cost of physically reproducing the line. Therefore, the commissioners reported, "The shareholders of the company have no equity either on the ground of cash put in, or on the ground of physical reproduction cost, or on the ground of the saleable value of their property as a going concern."[42]

Drayton and Acworth recommended that the Canadian government

42 *Drayton–Acworth Report*, xliv, published as Canada, *Sessional Paper No. 20*, 1917.

nationalize and consolidate the Canadian Northern, the Grand Trunk Pacific, and the Grand Trunk Railway, combining these with the railways already owned by the government to establish a single efficient transcontinental railway system. The Grand Trunk was admittedly still solvent, thanks to the eastern rate increases, but if held to its unfortunate commitments to the highly unprofitable Grand Trunk Pacific, its future was as dismal as that of the other lines. To ensure that shareholders were dealt with in an equitable manner, the two commissioners suggested the appointment of boards of arbitration to determine just procedures and prices whereby the roads could be taken over by the government.

The commissioners spent considerable time discussing the specific organizational structures the government should adopt to ensure that the new national system would not suffer from political management and patronage. They suggested an independent self-perpetuating board of directors to which the government would appoint the original directors for a seven-year term, and thereafter board members would reappoint themselves or appoint their own successors. The government-appointed directors would therefore act both as directors and as exclusive shareholders, although they would not, of course, benefit or suffer directly in proportion to the railway's operating results.[43]

The two commissioners also devoted considerable space to the CPR, giving reasons why it should neither be included in the nationalized system nor be allowed to acquire the Canadian Northern Railway. During wartime, they argued, it would be irresponsible for the Canadian government to spend huge amounts in the acquisition of a major and profitable railway system. Yet the CPR must be prevented from regaining an effective monopoly in western Canada. This would certainly happen if it acquired any significant part of the Canadian Northern's prairie lines. Thus, nationalization of the newer transcontinentals but not of the CPR was recommended.

A. H. Smith strongly disagreed. With some necessary rationalization, Smith believed the new transcontinentals could be made profitable. He devised a plan whereby the railways could be left under private ownership and management. This plan was as close to the railway

43 *Ibid.*, lii–liii.

policy formulated by Robert Borden in 1903 as the changed circumstances of 1916 would permit. Smith recommended that the Grand Trunk take over and operate the Canadian Northern's eastern lines, while the Canadian Northern should take over and operate the Grand Trunk Pacific Railway. Both were to be operated under a lease arrangement. This would make possible all the advantages of consolidation in both regions. The Canadian Northern Railway would become an exclusively western company, while the Grand Trunk would operate only in eastern Canada.[44] The two systems would complement one another, each being relieved of its most unprofitable lines, and should arrange mutually advantageous traffic exchanges. The scheme, with some variations, had commanded the one-time support of people as different as Mackenzie and Mann, Clifford Sifton, Thomas Shaughnessy, Sir Robert Borden, and Sir Charles Rivers-Wilson.

The circumstances of 1916, however, were not those of 1903. A third transcontinental line had been built north of Lake Superior. It was clear that under the Smith plan the government would be stuck with the expensive National Transcontinental Railway, which would have virtually no traffic if the Grand Trunk Railway and the Canadian Northern did indeed exchange their traffic as envisaged. This in turn would mean that very little of the new system's traffic would get to Quebec City or to the Maritime ports. Traffic would be routed along the traditional Grand Trunk route to Portland, Maine, while both the National Transcontinental and the Intercolonial railways would remain as expensive but completely useless appendages of an international railway system.

The Smith plan also raised problems regarding some of the urgent financial requirements of the Canadian Northern and the Grand Trunk Pacific. The funds needed to properly equip the eastern Canadian Northern lines and essential Grand Trunk Pacific mileage might be substantially reduced through rationalization, but large sums would still be needed if these lines were to be equipped and operated efficiently. These financial requirements could certainly not be met by the parent companies unless additional federal guarantees were provided. The government thought such guarantees politically impractical, although

44 *Smith Report*, published as Canada, *Sessional Paper No. 20*, 1917.

Smith was convinced that his plan was feasible. It would cost the federal government far less than complete nationalization, and would permit profitable operations on both sections in the near future. The Smith plan, however, received very little serious attention in 1917.

The government responded cautiously but favourably to the recommendations of the Drayton-Acworth report, while Canadian Northern officials were both shocked and dismayed. The main recommendations of the report were not altogether unexpected, but the financial facts and figures on which those recommendations were based contained very serious errors—errors which had disastrous effects on the Canadian Northern but which were so obvious that some officials suspected they were deliberate.[45] Drayton and Acworth, it seemed, had presented a false picture of Canadian Northern finances in order to make a strong case for nationalization.

The most notorious error in the Drayton-Acworth report related to the company's land-grant bonds and the trust funds set aside to retire those bonds. The bonds were calculated by Drayton and Acworth as liabilities, but the trust funds in the bank were not included among the assets. Cash in the bank designated for construction purposes was also omitted, as were the amounts still receivable for Canadian Northern land sold on instalment. The entire 2,000,000-acre Ontario land grant was also omitted from the list of the company's assets.[46]

These errors arose in a peculiar way. Professor Swain had been asked to prepare a valuation of the physical assets of the railway, based on the cost of reproduction at pre-war prices. Swain did just that, not including in his report any of the railway's cash or other assets which were not a physical part of the railway.[47] Drayton and Acworth apparently took Swain's figures as the total of all the company's assets and forgot to add the other assets, although all the loans and bonds, including those secured by the omitted assets, were calculated as liabilities.

The commissioners did not, however, accept all of Swain's figures. They arbitrarily decided to write down Swain's figures by 10 per cent, or $40,000,000, to account for depreciation. The problem in this case

45 *Arbitration*, 604–5.
46 PAC, Borden Papers, File OC 293, 32864–71, government-appointed directors of the Canadian Northern
Railway System to Borden, 21 May 1917.
47 *Arbitration*, 26.

arose mainly because of differences in accounting procedures in England and North America. Acworth was appalled that North American railways did not keep a separate depreciation account. The North American view was that a properly maintained railway was worth what it had cost. Professor Swain himself emphasized this.

If that road cost 397 million new and has been properly maintained as an operating concern, and I want to buy it, it is worth 397 million dollars to me although there may be accrued depreciation of 30 or 40 million dollars figured in the usual way by taking the elapsed life of the various parts into consideration. . . . . The railway as a whole has an indefinite life and is not depreciated as a whole if it is in good operating condition.[48]

Swain maintained that only items properly referred to as deferred maintenance be calculated as depreciation. The commissioners nevertheless insisted that Swain make at least an estimate of the total life of the various parts and components of the railway and of the time elapsed since construction.

Professor Swain was personally very much impressed by the Canadian Northern Railway. "We were surprised," he said later, "to find it in such good condition. . . . We had some impression that it was not as good as we expected to find it, but we found it in very good condition. . . . I was very favourably impressed by the road and its possibilities; its low grades and generally economical construction."[49] As a result, Swain allowed only 10 per cent for the depreciation of the various parts of the railway. The commissioners deducted the full 10 per cent from the physical valuation made by Swain, although the Harvard professor thought it quite improper for them to do so.

The commissioners made another rather serious error when they reported on the public support given to the Canadian Northern Railway and compared it with the assistance given to the CPR. The land grants earned by the railway were calculated, although none of these had been granted to Mackenzie and Mann or the Canadian Northern while they controlled it. All had been obtained when Mackenzie and Mann purchased charters held by others to whom the grants had been made. More serious, however, was the fact that the commissioners

48 *Ibid.*, 235.   49 *Ibid.*, 299, 327.

seriously confused subsidies and government guarantees. Subsidies were an outright gift, guarantees remained a first charge on the railway. Pessimists like Shaughnessy insisted that, in the end, the railways would be unable to redeem their debentures and the guarantees would be paid by the government. The two types of assistance were nevertheless very different, and by adding the two together the commissioners, in Hanna's words "added dollars to doughnuts". It was incomprehensible to the Canadian Northern vice-president how a man like Drayton, the chairman of the Board of Railway Commissioners, could make elementary errors of this kind.[50] The calculations suggested that the Canadian Northern had received more government aid than the CPR and was therefore not entitled to further sympathetic consideration. In terms of real value, the assistance given the CPR was, of course, much greater.

Several things might be said by way of explaining the Drayton-Acworth calculations. Drayton had presided over the Board of Railway Commissioners' major freight-rate investigations. The rulings of the Board in those cases had not solved the problems of the newer transcontinentals because the Board felt rates should not be raised to meet costs of duplicate main lines or developmental branch lines. The evidence presented by the railways during the rate inquiries had been compiled mainly to demonstrate the need to sustain or increase existing freight rates. In general, the railways had presented a very poor picture of their operations in the hope of getting higher rates. Drayton was therefore very well acquainted with the problems and difficulties of the railways. It is not surprising that he thought the newer railways were, or would soon be, insolvent.

Another factor must be considered. As chairman of the Board of Railway Commissioners, Drayton had generally relied on his own staff or on the submissions by the railways for detailed financial and operational information. He was not accustomed to do much of the detailed calculation himself. He was, in any case, far too busy, since he was continuing in his post with the Board while doing the work on the

50 *Ibid.*, 131–3. The testimony of Canadian Northern officials, particularly Phippen and Hanna, clearly indicates their anger and indignation whenever they spoke of the financial calculations made by Drayton and Acworth. They regarded them as inexcusably stupid or, perhaps, deliberately misleading.

Royal Commission, and in 1917 he became involved in another major rate inquiry. Drayton's conclusions, therefore, were likely to be influenced by the detailed financial information fed him by others, and by the largely pessimistic operational records that the railways had presented to him in the rates cases. He later admitted that his own calculations had been hurried and incomplete.

Acworth was the acknowledged financial expert who did much of the detailed work. He was a competent statistician, but had little understanding of railway operations. He was unwilling or unable to see beyond the figures on a balance sheet. Acworth had become wary, however, of the Canadian Northern accounting practices, perhaps because of warnings from Shaughnessy. He soon demonstrated considerable suspicion about Canadian Northern and Grand Trunk Pacific figures and officials. The depreciation matter as well as several other oddities of Canadian railway accounting offended and apparently confused Acworth's orderly statistical mind. He decided at an early date that the various figures presented to him could not be taken at their face value, and that he must recalculate all the returns. The colonials, it seemed to Acworth, were in urgent need of instruction in sound accounting procedures, and D. B. Hanna, the Canadian Northern manager and vice-president, often found himself the subject of instruction in accounting rather than the target for questions about the meaning and significance of the figures he was presenting to the commission.

The situation was aggravated by the fact that both Acworth and Drayton refused to consult with other Canadian experts. Almost all Canadians who knew anything about railways, Drayton argued, had at one time or another been employed by the Canadian railways under investigation. They might therefore be biased. "The valuation of a given property may show startlingly different results," Drayton told Canadian engineers dissatisfied with the commission's reliance on foreign experts, "arrived at by engineers whose experience and work and resultant convictions and prejudices—never mind how honest they may be—have differed one from the other."[51] This refusal to accept the railway's figures or to ask the advice of engineers familiar with Canadian railways meant that Drayton and Acworth, with limited

51 Drayton to Borden, 19 Sept. 1916, as quoted in *Sessional Paper No. 78*, 1917.

American advice, which they accepted or rejected as they saw fit, superimposed their own accounting and statistical concepts on the financial statements of the Canadian railways. In the process Acworth at least got thoroughly confused. Later, when challenged about the omission of the company's cash, he maintained that it was "earmarked for future construction . . . and therefore no more a liquid asset of the CN than money given by you to a messenger to carry into the Bank is a liquid asset of the messenger."[52] Yet the securities that had been sold to raise that cash were calculated as liabilities. Perhaps the money should not be considered a liquid asset, but it certainly was an asset. The fact that Acworth failed to see his rather elementary error, even when it was pointed out, reflects very seriously on his competence.

In the case of the unsold lands and of the amounts receivable for lands sold on instalment, the Drayton-Acworth report made specific reference to the value Canadian Northern officials placed on these items, but they were not included in the commissioners' calculations. No reason was given for the omission and it is difficult to avoid Hanna's bitter charge that "They had the data before them, and that data appeared in their own printed report, but they did not use it in making the statement which has gone abroad from them, that the common stock of this company has a non-existent value."[53] It was, moreover, that statement which became the basis of further government action.

Borden was in Europe when Drayton and Acworth submitted their report. When its main proposals were telegraphed to him the Prime Minister considered the report "not bad".[54] After he had had a chance to read the entire report and had discussed it with several colleagues and confidants, Borden was pleased to note in his diary that Clifford Sifton "is greatly impressed by it. He thinks proposals shd perhaps be modified in some details."[55] There was widespread agreement that some policy must be devised whereby the Canadian Northern, the Grand Trunk, the Grand Trunk Pacific, the National Transcontinental, and the Intercolonial railways could be operated as a large rational-

52 PAC, Flavelle Papers, Vol. 60, Acworth to Flavelle, 23 July 1917.
53 *Arbitration*, 604–5.
54 PAC, Borden Diary, 6 April 1917.
55 *Ibid.*, 2 May 1917.

ized and integrated railway network. The basic difference of opinion in 1917 centred on the question of whether such a system was best administered by public or by private enterprise. Mackenzie and Mann, together with many Canadian businessmen, were firmly convinced that they could run a railway much more efficiently than any government agency.[56] Private management, however, would require much additional government assistance and make no satisfactory arrangement for the National Transcontinental. Mackenzie, recognizing the latter problem, indicated on several occasions that with sufficient assistance he would be willing and eager to arrange for the refinancing and operation of all the troubled railways. When Mackenzie first suggested such a Canadian-Northern-sponsored and government-assisted reorganization in April, 1916, Borden noted, "He certainly possesses exp. nerve & tenacity."[57] In February 1917 he dismissed the proposal as "utterly chimerical".[58] The consolidation, if it became necessary, could not be financed by private interests on the basis of further government guarantees. The Drayton-Acworth report recommended that the government undertake what Mackenzie wanted to promote with government backing.

Canadian Northern officials were understandably chagrined when they read the Drayton-Acworth report. The adverse findings endangered their negotiations in New York and might well lead to government action based on erroneous information. Their first concern, therefore, was clearly to correct the errors and omissions of the Drayton-Acworth report and thus refute the allegations that the common stock was worthless. It fell to three of the railway's directors, who had been appointed by the government after it obtained 40 per cent of the common stock in 1914, to draw the errors to the attention of the Prime Minister and the Minister of Finance. These directors showed in considerable detail the assets omitted in the Drayton-Acworth report and claimed that inclusion of the omitted assets would show the company had a net value of approximately $80,000,000.[59]

William Mackenzie and W. H. Moore also made personal represen-

---

56 For an elaborate statement of these opinions, see Memorandum on the Railway Situation, prepared by W. H. Moore, 24 May 1917, PAC, White Papers, File 50, 8209–33.

57 PAC, Borden Diary, 12 April 1916.
58 *Ibid.*, 9 Feb. 1917.
59 PAC, Borden Papers, File OC 293, 32864–71, government-appointed directors to Borden, 21 May 1917.

tations when the Prime Minister returned from Europe, but Borden had already made up his mind that the recommendations of the Drayton-Acworth report should form the basis of his government's policy. He was rather irritated that a squabble about accounting should have broken out, and when Mackenzie came to talk about Acworth's errors, Borden informed him instead that the government would nationalize the Canadian Northern Railway. Mackenzie had come to Ottawa from Toronto on the overnight train, leaving the bedside of his dying wife. He was clearly distraught, and the Prime Minister's apparent willingness to accept the Drayton-Acworth proposals despite the glaring financial errors was too much for him. He broke down "in audible sobs" which the Prime Minister found most distressing and reminiscent of Mackenzie's near collapse nearly twenty years earlier when the Yukon Railway bill was defeated. Borden tried to comfort the distraught man and, more significantly, agreed to review the financial statements. Because of the illness of Mrs. Mackenzie it fell to W. H. Moore to make many of the specific presentations.[60]

Moore was particularly concerned to show that statements by the company's auditors, whose appointment had the approval of the government-appointed directors, were seriously at variance with the statements prepared by the royal commissioners. The auditors, Messrs. Webb, Reid, Hegen, Callingham and Company, were persuaded to write a detailed critique of the Drayton-Acworth calculations. According to these auditors, $65,762,182 worth of current assets had been "inadvertently omitted". Of these current assets there was over $27,000,000 of cash on deposit, and its omission in the accountants' opinion, "is clearly an oversight as the securities which produced the cash on deposit and other liquid assets are included by the Commission in their statement of outstanding liabilities."[61] The auditors

60 Borden Diary, numerous references in May and June 1917, particularly entry for 14 June 1917.
61 The audited Balance Sheet of the Canadian Northern Railway System for the year ending 30 June 1916 became available on 22 Nov. 1916 and was subsequently published in the Second Annual Systems Report. A detailed critique of the Drayton–Acworth Report, listing the various

assets omitted and other errors in the report, was subsequently prepared by Webb, Read, Hegen, Callingham and Co. A copy is in PAC, White Papers, File 51, 8297–309. It was submitted to White on 22 June 1917, eight days after Borden had informed Mackenzie that the government had definitely decided to take over the Canadian Northern Railway System.

discussed various aspects of the Drayton-Acworth report, and concluded that the railway's assets exceeded its liabilities by $80,596,156. The statement in the majority report of the royal commission that the common shares of the Canadian Northern Railway were worthless was specifically refuted: "This is evidently owing to the fact that the Current Assets of the Company have been overlooked in their calculations."[62]

This detailed and specific listing of errors in the Drayton-Acworth report forced the government to review the entire situation. Finance Minister White decided to refer the matter to his colleague, the Minister of Railways and Canals. It seemed to White that "the question raised by the directors might be readily disposed of, as the actual facts should be ascertainable without much difficulty."[63] The railway department, however, decided to ask another accounting firm to audit the Canadian Northern records. The firm of Marwick, Mitchell, Peat and Company were assigned this task. They were not asked to do a complete valuation of the company's assets and properties, but simply to ascertain if the complaints of the directors were founded in fact.

After a month of work, during which the Canadian Northern records were again subjected to close scrutiny, Marwick, Mitchell, Peat and Company confirmed that the Drayton-Acworth report had indeed omitted valuable assets. They also found that the Income Convertible Debenture Stock had not been calculated as a liability.[64] Officially, at least, the company, its government-appointed directors, and its auditors were vindicated. Cochrane, the railways minister, sent a copy of the Marwick, Mitchell, Peat and Company statement to Drayton asking him to explain how he and Acworth had arrived at different figures. Drayton virtually acknowledged that the Drayton-Acworth report was in error: "The firm are very competent accountants. I, personally, have no doubt that the figures they have submitted are correct. They have had a large staff of men working for something over a month; and it would be impertinence on my part to attempt to check the report and answer it in a day, or attempt to check the report in any respect."

62 *Ibid.*, Note 2, 8299.
63 *Ibid.*, File 50, 8208, White to Cochrane, 24 May 1917.
64 *Ibid.*, 8026–63, Marwick, Mitchell, Peat and Company, Chartered Accountants, Report on Canadian Northern Railway System, Investigation of Accounts as at 30 June 1916, presented to the Minister of Railways and Canals, 26 July 1917.

Drayton then went on to say that he had intended to say something in the report which a careful reading of that report simply would not support. "In my view and as I intended to express it by the report, there is no realizable equity in the property at the present time. . . . It is manifest that on paper a large surplus can be shown."[65] Yet the official report specifically and directly denied that there was such a surplus.

Canadian Northern officials also criticized the Drayton-Acworth report because it specifically refuted some of their own rather optimistic predictions of future growth and development. These had been the basis of their negotiations in New York, and the royal commissioners made a point of emphasizing that the predictions were unrealistic. Canadian Northern officials pointed out that Drayton and Acworth had not checked any of the company's operating records, or, indeed, made application for any information from the traffic department.[66] Thus, the report's comments about traffic development represented little more than the private opinions of the two commissioners.

Despite its errors, however, the Drayton-Acworth report formed the basis of government action. The recommendation to nationalize and consolidate the newer transcontinentals seemed sensible, although some of Drayton and Acworth's suggestions about management must have seemed peculiar even at that time. The errors of the report, moreover, were not fully documented until after the basic government decisions were made. Drayton, in fact, did not admit its errors until eight days after the government had set the maximum price it would pay for the common stock held by Mackenzie, Mann and Co. Ltd. An official of the Department of Railways and Canals subsequently informed the finance minister that "in the findings of the majority report of the Royal Commission appointed to investigate the Railway situation, that the statement, based on Prof. Swain's valuation of the physical property of the Canadian Northern Railway System showing there was no equity, was in error."[67]

65 *Ibid.*, File 51, 8332–3, H. L. Drayton to G. A. Bell, 28 July 1917.
66 *Ibid.*, File 50, 8300–8, Memorandum regarding that part of the Report of the Commission dealing with the equity in the Canadian Northern Railway System represented by its $100,000,000 of capital stock, sent to the Minister of Finance 22 June 1917.
67 *Ibid.*, File 50, 8332–3, H. L. Drayton to G. A. Bell, 18 July 1917; PAC, Borden Diary, 10 July 1917; PAC, White Papers, File 51, 8448–9, G. A. Bell to White, 15 Aug. 1917.

While pursuing refinancing negotiations in New York and trying to correct the errors of the Drayton-Acworth report, Mackenzie and Mann also began negotiations with the CPR. That company was very well acquainted with Mackenzie and Mann's property, and particularly with the strength of their prairie system. Sir Thomas Shaughnessy greatly feared nationalization that did not in some way include the CPR. He regarded competition between a nationalized system and a privately owned company as a monstrosity.[68] Acquisition of the Canadian Northern Railway, or preferably only of its western lines, was a means to strengthen the CPR and either prevent nationalization or so weaken the new nationalized system in western Canada that it would not be a serious threat.

Prime Minister Borden apparently encouraged Shaughnessy to open negotiations with Canadian Northern officials.[69] Borden's idea was apparently to consider the possibility of parcelling out the Canadian Northern to the CPR and the Grand Trunk Pacific. Preliminary discussions persuaded Shaughnessy that this was not a feasible plan. He nevertheless continued negotiations with a view to acquiring the entire Canadian Northern system.

Mackenzie and Mann, negotiating through Z. A. Lash, wanted $30,000,000 or 50 per cent of par value for the $60,000,000 of privately held common stock in 1917.[70] This figure, Shaughnessy wrote to Lash, "was very far in excess of anything that I had in mind," but added that he believed it was "only suggested to start negotiations on that feature of the transaction."[71] Mann later admitted that he and Mackenzie were in fact prepared to accept $20,000,000.[72]

The major obstacle to a negotiated sale lay with the $40,000,000 owned by the federal government. Shaughnessy and Mackenzie and Mann wanted the government to surrender that stock "for what it had cost". The government had received the stock in return for bond guarantees. If the CPR took over the venture, the government would

68 PAC, Borden Diary, 9 June 1917; PAC, Shaughnessy Letterbook, No. 73, 343–7, Shaughnessy to J. J. Hill, 9 Jan. 1901; *ibid.*, No. 108, 870, Shaughnessy to Borden, 11 May 1915.
69 PAC, Shaughnessy Letterbook, No. 112, 143, Shaughnessy to Borden, 28 June 1917.

70 *Arbitration*, 2713–14, 634–7, 1415–16, and PAC, Borden Diary, 9 July 1917.
71 PAC, Shaughnessy Letterbook, No. 112, 62, Shaughnessy to Lash, 4 June 1917.
72 *Arbitration*, 2713–14.

be relieved of its guarantee obligations, since the CPR's credit was strong enough even without government guarantees. The government should therefore surrender that stock without any further consideration than the cancellation of its guarantees of Canadian Northern debentures.[73]

The negotiations between the two railway companies coincided with the political upheaval that led to the formation of the union government, and the businessmen were asked to defer further discussion until the larger political issues were resolved.[74] Mackenzie and Mann played a part in the negotiations leading up to the formation of the union government. Sir Donald Mann discussed several important aspects of the proposed union with Sir Wilfrid Laurier, serving as a mediator and emissary between Borden and Laurier, although in general his role was not central to the negotiations.

The objective in proposing a union government was to permit formation of a strong and effective government which could deal decisively and effectively with serious wartime problems, the most serious and potentially divisive being military manpower and conscription policies. Both Mackenzie and Mann very strongly supported the war effort, and from the outbreak of war had involved themselves in various patriotic endeavours. Both were honorary officers in the militia and always regarded their railway as a very important part of the Canadian war effort. The formation of a strong union government was a possible first step in aggressive railway policies which might yet save the Canadian Northern Railway. Mackenzie and Mann believed they were building and operating their railway better than anyone else could, and they hoped a strong union government would recognize this fact. Laurier was certainly not considered particularly friendly towards the Canadian Northern in 1917, but his known opposition to government ownership might certainly have been useful had he seen fit to join the union government. Mackenzie and Mann certainly hoped

73 QUA, Flavelle Papers, 3045–51, Flavelle to Shaughnessy, 17 May 1917, Shaughnessy to Flavelle, 18 May 1917, Flavelle to Shaughnessy, 22 May 1917, and Shaughnessy to Flavelle, 15 June 1917; PAC, Shaughnessy Letterbook, No. 112, 62, 102, 143, Shaughnessy to Lash, 4 June 1917, Shaughnessy Memorandum for George Bury, 16 June 1917, Shaughnessy to Borden, 29 June 1917.
74 PAC, Shaughnessy Letterbook, No. 112, 62, Shaughnessy to Lash, 4 June 1917.

for a decisive and favourable railway policy, but there is no reliable evidence to suggest that they had any assurances that a union government which included Laurier would give them special consideration. Their support of a union government and their limited activity to facilitate its formation arose from a belief that such a government would conduct the nation's war effort more effectively.

The formation of a union government without Laurier certainly did not help the Canadian Northern Railway. Western representation in the Cabinet was considerably increased. Many of the western politicians tended to favour the Drayton-Acworth proposals and were adamantly opposed to a sale or other arrangement whereby the CPR might take over the Canadian Northern. The re-establishment of a CPR monopoly in western Canada was politically impossible, and the government refused to divest itself of its Canadian Northern common shares or to give its approval when a sale to the CPR was proposed. Before the formation of the union government Borden had encouraged negotiations, but later, according to Mann, the government "had forty per cent of the road and would not sell. How could we sell? The purchasers that wanted to buy it from us wanted all the stock. . . . Our partner is too rich, that is the trouble. . . . Our partner, the Dominion Government had 40 per cent and would not sell. We had an opportunity to sell if they would sell, but they would not, and that spoilt our opportunity."[75]

Mackenzie and Mann were convinced that the CPR would be willing to pay at least $20,000,000. If one takes into consideration that this would have established a virtual CPR monopoly in the West, and given the generally favourable reports on the Canadian Northern by all official inquiries except the Drayton-Acworth report, one cannot help coming to the conclusion that such a purchase would have been a great bargain for the CPR. Yet the company's president, now Lord Shaughnessy, was the embodiment of caution and conservatism. It is difficult to find a single instance, throughout his long tenure as the company's chief executive, in which Shaughnessy authorized any expenditure that could possibly have been considered really speculative. Acquisition of the Canadian Northern might have seemed a serious

75 *Arbitration*, 2708, 2713–14.

risk to him. It is nevertheless clear that, with government approval, he was willing to negotiate for the common stock of the Canadian Northern Railway.[76]

In the midst of these negotiations with the federal government and the CPR, the Canadian Northern, along with the nation's other railway companies, found it necessary to apply once more for a freight-rate increase. It was clear that the company's financial situation would deteriorate very rapidly if there was another year of serious operational deficits. Rapidly rising costs could be cited as justification for the requested increases, and the Eastern Rates Case of 1916 had barely been concluded when the Board of Railway Commissioners was again called upon to examine the situation. This time the railways asked the Board arbitrarily to increase their rates under the authority of the War Measures Act. This the Board declined to do, but it again reviewed the entire situation.[77] It was obvious to the Board that substantial rate increases were essential if escalating costs were to be met. The major obstacles to such increases, however, were the Canadian Pacific Railway's 1897 Crow's Nest Pass Agreement with the federal government and the Canadian Northern Railway's 1901 rate agreement with the Manitoba government.

The commissioners came to the conclusion that they had no authority to grant increases that violated specific acts of Parliament such as the Crow's Nest Pass Agreement. They therefore declined to authorize any rate increase beyond the levels set in that agreement. The Canadian Northern Railway's agreements with the Manitoba government, however, were considered an entirely different matter. The Board of Railway Commissioners, a federal regulatory agency, regarded provincial regulation of rates on interprovincial traffic, or on railways declared to be in the general interest of Canada, as illegal and *ultra vires*. This matter had been debated in a rather inconclusive manner in 1901, but in 1917 the Board argued that the Manitoba agreements did not and could not affect or limit federal jurisdiction under the

76 QUA, Flavelle Papers, 3045–51, Shaughnessy to Flavelle, 15 June 1917; Shaughnessy Letterbook, No. 112, 62, Shaughnessy to Lash, 4 June 1917; *ibid.*, 102, Shaughnessy to Bury,

16 June 1917.
77 CRC, Vol. 22, 49–84, Increase in Passenger and Freight Tolls, Judgment of 26 Dec. 1917.

Railway Act in regard to tolls. The commissioners therefore authorized western rate increases up to the levels set in the Crow's Nest Pass Agreement, thus effectively eliminating the 15-per-cent rate reductions western shippers and farmers had obtained as a result of the Canadian Northern Agreements. Rate increases of approximately 15 per cent, including the increases granted in the 1916 Eastern Rates Case, were at the same time authorized on eastern Canadian traffic.[78]

The final ruling of the Board did not come out until December of 1917, well after the government had made the decision and set all the terms for nationalizing the Canadian Northern Railway. The arguments of that railway's officials before the Board of Railway Commissioners, however, antagonized many in western Canada who had formerly been the Canadian Northern's strongest supporters. The ruling was unsuccessfully appealed by the Manitoba government, and a year later the War Measures Act was used to set aside the provisions of the Crow's Nest Pass Agreement as well. The Canadian Northern Railway had ceased some time before to build new prairie branch lines. With the rate increases, all the immediate benefits it had brought to the West were apparently lost. Henceforth, there was no one in government willing to support the railway. The railway was, however, entirely dependent upon the government and had to accept whatever terms the government dictated.

78 For the political and economic implications of this ruling, see correspondence, memoranda, and legal arguments in Borden Papers, File RLB 1710, 125391–506.

CHAPTER SEVENTEEN

ARBITRATION AND NATIONALIZATION

BOTH MACKENZIE AND MANN'S attempts to refinance their railway obligations in New York and the negotiations to sell the common stock of the Canadian Northern Railway to the CPR failed. The government refused to grant further guarantees or to divest itself of the $40,000,000 (par value) common stock it held after 1914. It began instead to consider ways and means of acquiring the remaining $60,000,000 (par value) common stock.

The recommendations of the Drayton-Acworth report provided the government with a blueprint for action. Public opinion, at least in Ontario and in western Canada, favoured railway nationalization. Even Donald Mann later conceded that the public wanted the government to nationalize the Canadian Northern.[1] Influential businessmen and ardent supporters of free enterprise recognized the need to rationalize and co-ordinate the country's railway systems. Unless this was done, drastic rate increases were inevitable. Most businessmen, faced with a choice between higher rates and the threat of government ownership of railways, opted for government ownership. Only the Montreal business community offered any sustained opposition to nationalization, and this may have reflected a concern about the influence of Toronto business interests in the Borden government as well as a basic concern about public ownership.[2] It is clear that in 1917 railway nationalization did command widespread support.

In 1917, however, the policy of nationalization was adopted only

1 *Arbitration*, 2708, 2714.
2 PAC, Meighen Papers, Series 2, File 30, 9833–41, Memo refuting statements made in the Montreal *Gazette* criticizing government policy to take over the Canadian Northern Railway.

For a detailed analysis of the Montreal opposition see John A. Eagle, "Sir Robert Borden and the Railway Problem in Canadian Politics, 1911–1920" (PHD thesis, University of Toronto, 1972), Chap. 8.

in regard to the Canadian Northern Railway. There was little doubt that any attempts to build a balanced public railway system must include the Grand Trunk and Grand Trunk Pacific railways. The government was not ready, however, to move against the still-solvent Grand Trunk. That company's relations with the Grand Trunk Pacific still needed some clarification, and the process of bringing in the very widely dispersed capital stock also presented major difficulties. The government therefore advanced yet another loan to the Grand Trunk Pacific, but passed legislation to acquire the Canadian Northern Railway's common stock.[3]

Negotiations between Mackenzie and Mann, the Canadian Bank of Commerce, and the government were begun very shortly after the Drayton-Acworth report was published. In these negotiations Mackenzie and Mann found themselves in an extremely poor bargaining position. Drayton and Acworth had declared their stock worthless. At the same time the promoters found themselves very hard pressed to meet fixed charges and maturing short-term loans. Only a continuing and ever-increasing line of credit from the Canadian Bank of Commerce could keep the enterprise afloat. The Bank, however, was becoming increasingly skittish.

The amounts placed in the Supplementary Estimates to pay interest on endangered bonds in 1915 and 1916 had temporarily relieved the Bank. The funds voted in this way, however, were exhausted well before the end of 1916. The promoters and the government again began to exert pressure on the Bank to advance sufficient funds to avoid insolvency, although the bankers were once again very reluctant to rely on private letters from the Prime Minister. Finance Minister White said they feared "dissolution before action can be taken to repay them as prominent Liberal members are predicting elections."[4] Yet the collapse of the Canadian Northern would destroy the value of the common stock which the Bank held as partial security for the loans it had advanced to Mackenzie, Mann and Co. Ltd. The government, moreover, was at last moving towards a definite long-term policy, and the Bank was eventually persuaded to provide further loans.

3 Canada, *7–8 Geo.* v. *Cap. 24*; oc 3225, 15 Nov. 1917; and oc 3240, 19 Nov. 1917.

4 PAC, Borden Papers, File oc 167, White to Borden, Telegram, 30 March 1917.

Prime Minister Borden was not very sympathetic to the bankers, to whom he had given private letters assuring government protection. "Am surprised," he wired White from Europe, "that bank should be so greatly influenced by caterwauling of Grit orators. If there was a direct engagement on our part there was at least an implied undertaking on theirs to carry out arrangement until after my return. They are so easily frightened and their conduct is so unworthy that we should have as little as possible to do with them."[5] In a crisis Borden was prepared to use the War Measures Act to provide sufficient funds to keep the railways solvent until a definite government policy was adopted.

Haunted by the adverse findings of Drayton and Acworth, and with the threat of a default and receivership hanging constantly over their heads, Mackenzie and Mann were in no position to drive a hard bargain when the government decided to nationalize their railway. The common stock, which they believed was worth between 60 and 80 per cent of par value, would be lost to them if the road went into receivership, and they could no longer arrange the financing necessary to avoid a collapse. Thus they were prepared to take $20,000,000, or one-third of par value, from the CPR. The government could not offer even that. Thanks to the Drayton-Acworth report, most Canadians believed the stock was worthless. There was still the erroneous impression that the promoters had made enormous construction profits and had never invested any of their own resources in the venture, and many Canadians would have been satisfied to see the railway nationalized without any compensation paid for the common stock. Ten years later a business historian summed up this popular opinion when he wrote,

By devious means this happy pair [Mackenzie and Mann] had contrived to build the endless miles of their Canadian Northern here, there and everywhere, wherever a barren spot of country could be found in which a line of subsidized railway tracks could be laid to rust itself into oblivion. . . . [They] had done very well for their partnership while their railway established itself as the two front feet of our national white elephant,

5 Ibid., Borden to White, 30 March 1917.

and served to add another steam-charged money leech to our peculiar transportation problem.[6]

The Borden government was not that harsh. Borden was well aware of the personal investments Mackenzie and Mann had made in their railway, and of the alleged errors that had led Drayton and Acworth to declare the stock worthless. He was also aware of the fact that this common stock was pledged to the Canadian Bank of Commerce in return for advances to the contractors. If the railways were nationalized, the government would, of course, become responsible for the debts of the railway itself, but not for the debts of the contractors. Mackenzie and Mann had exhausted their personal resources and their credit trying to keep the Canadian Northern afloat. There was little prospect that they would be able to repay their indebtedness to the bank if they got nothing for their common stock. For this reason, Borden and others in the Cabinet expressed concern for the stability of the Canadian Bank of Commerce.[7] To some extent, concern for the welfare of the Bank may have prompted the government to provide an opportunity for compensation of some sort.

The Canadian Bank of Commerce had extended large credits to Mackenzie, Mann and Co. Ltd., to the Canadian Northern Railway, and on major grain and munitions and supplies accounts. The enthusiasm, particularly of President B. E. Walker, for both the Canadian Northern Railway and the Canadian war effort had placed the Canadian Bank of Commerce in a rather tight position, and by 1917 it was almost certainly overextended. If the entire Mackenzie, Mann and Co. Ltd. account, almost certainly in the vicinity of $10,000,000, had been lost, and there had been a panic, the Bank might have found it very difficult, perhaps impossible, to meet all its obligations. Only an examination of the Bank's records is likely to reveal whether the situation was indeed desperate, but available evidence suggests that, short of a panic, the Bank could have survived the loss of the Mackenzie, Mann and Co. Ltd. account. The Canadian Northern account

6 Leslie Roberts, *These Be Your Gods* (Toronto: Musson, 1929), 178.
7 PAC, Borden Papers, File RLB 2984, Borden to Perley, 27 Nov. 1915;
ibid., File OC 167, Blount to Borden, White to Borden and Borden to White, 30 March 1917, and White to Aird, 2 April 1917.

was covered by Borden's private guarantees and was, therefore, much safer. Perhaps some temporary government concessions would have been necessary if the entire Mackenzie, Mann and Co. Ltd. account had been lost, and there would almost certainly have been nasty litigation over alleged irregularities, notably the failure to obtain approval from the full Board of Directors, in connection with the Bank's loans to the railway and its contractors. The government might also have been worried about a sudden contraction of credit, the calling in of various short-term loans, or, indeed, the cashing of government savings bonds held by the Bank.

Borden, however, was not motivated only by practical considerations. He was equally concerned that justice and equitable treatment be meted out. True, Mackenzie and Mann could no longer defend their investment, but most informed investigators and accountants were convinced that there remained a substantial equity in the common stock. Drayton and Acworth had specifically recommended the appointment of a board of arbitration to set the final value of the common stock. This method of determining the value of Mackenzie and Mann's equity, especially after the challenge to the Drayton-Acworth calculations, seemed a fair one, and the Prime Minister wanted to implement it.

The Drayton-Acworth report nevertheless seriously interfered with an unbiased and equitable valuation. The public had been told the stock was worthless, and very few politicians were prepared to accept a new and open valuation which, if the accountants' statements were accepted, might find the stock to be worth 50 to 75 per cent of par value and thus leave Mackenzie and Mann multimillionaires. It was politically impractical for any government to establish an arbitration board which might force the government to pay such a high price. The government felt it was absolutely necessary to establish a maximum amount beyond which it would not be required to go,[8] regardless of the valuation finally agreed upon by the arbitrators. This decision, understandably, seemed unfair to Mackenzie and Mann, but there was nothing they could do about it. They and the Bank of Commerce nevertheless argued that if any maximum should be set, it would be equally equitable also to set a minimum.[9] This clearly would provide

8 *Ibid.*, File oc 163, D. B. Detweiler to W. G. Weichel, 12 Sept. 1917.

9 PAC, Borden Diary, 26 July 1917.

considerable protection for the Bank.

The government regarded the establishment of any minimum price, irrespective of the findings of the arbitrators, as "politically impossible", and the most serious negotiations centred on the amount to be set as a maximum price. The government wanted to set $10,000,000 as the maximum. There was considerable feeling that if Mackenzie and Mann got out of the Canadian Northern with neither a major loss nor a substantial profit, the arbitration would be fair. Mackenzie and Mann actually owned $51,000,000 of the common stock, the remaining $9,000,000 having been issued to Lazard Brothers as underwriting fees, and some given to senior employees of the company.[10] The $10,000,000 maximum for the $60,000,000 (par value) common stock in private hands therefore set an $8,500,000 maximum as the amount Mackenzie and Mann would receive. This sum, apparently, would allow them to pay off their major debts but leave them very little for their own efforts.[11]

Mackenzie and Mann, of course, wanted a substantially higher maximum figure. The maximum would, after all, be paid only if the arbitrators found the stock to be actually worth more. It would clearly not be a gift of the government to the promoters. Mackenzie, Lash, and Moore all made determined attempts to persuade the government to accept a $15,000,000 maximum, but in the end they had to accept the government's figure.[12] They simply could not refuse the government offer which still left them the possibility of getting out without heavy indebtedness. Thus, on 1 October 1917, the Canadian government, Mackenzie, Mann and Co. Ltd., and the Canadian Bank of Commerce signed an agreement whereby the government would acquire the privately held Canadian Northern common stock for a price to be

---

10 A complete list of Canadian Northern shareholders is given in PAC, Department of Finance records series E–2C, File 133–5–7; PAC, CNR Records, MCDXLIX, Canadian Northern Railway Company Stock Certificate Book, 1902–8; PAC, White Papers, File 52, beginning 8462, lists of minority shareholders in companies comprising the Canadian Northern Railway System.

11 PAC, Borden Diary, 14 June 1917, Records of the Surrogate Court of the County of York, Ontario, File 49474, relating to the Estate of Sir William Mackenzie. The record of accounts passed, 1926, indicates that the 22,500 shares in the firm of Mackenzie, Mann and Co. Ltd. were declared to have no market value.

12 PAC, Borden Diary, 23 June, 24 Oct., 1, 8, and 9 Nov. 1917.

determined by arbitration, but not to exceed $10,000,000.[13] Lazard Brothers and the few other shareholders were not a party to the agreement, and not bound by the findings of the arbitrators.

The terms of reference of the proposed board of arbitration were left very vague. It was simply specified that the arbitrators must determine the value of the privately held common stock. The method by which this valuation was to be made was not specified. Yet there were at least three very distinct methods whereby the property could be evaluated. There was, first of all, the simple calculation of the likely market value of the stock in 1917. Canadian Northern stock had never been sold on the public exchanges, but it required little calculation to show that it would not bring large returns in the difficult circumstances of 1917. The fact that the government refused further guarantees and held 40 per cent of the stock, and that the system had suffered deficits for three years in a row, combined with the finding of the Drayton-Acworth Commission, would certainly discourage investors. According to this method of calculation, the stock would almost certainly be found worthless. Later government lawyers and the chairman of the Board of Arbitration called attention to this fact, but did not insist that this be the only basis of valuation.

The second method of valuation was the one adopted earlier by the Drayton-Acworth Commission. Under this method the replacement cost of the railway at pre-1914 prices was to be the basis of calculation. All liabilities should then be deducted from the replacement cost, the remaining sum being the value of the common stock. This method of calculation, of course, re-opened all the arguments about a proper calculation for depreciation and about the various items concerning which the auditors and accountants disagreed with the Drayton-Acworth report. If the accountants' figures were accepted, the valuation might go very high.

The third method, supported by Mackenzie and Mann, and earlier by Loomis and Platten and by A. H. Smith, was a calculation of the railway's potential earnings and profits. The railway, Canadian Northern officials insisted, served territory which, when fully developed, would produce as much traffic as the area served by the CPR, and perhaps more. In ten years' time, these officials claimed, the Canadian Northern would be as profitable as the CPR.[14] Mann insisted that "there is nothing on the continent of America which has better value than that road [the Canadian Northern Railway]."[15]

There is no evidence that the arbitrators agreed among themselves about the method of valuation to be adopted. They certainly never indicated how they arrived at their final conclusions, and the evidence presented in the hearings seemed designed to make the best possible case no matter what method of valuation was adopted.

The three members of the arbitration board were appointed in the usual manner. The government and the shareholders, in this case Mackenzie, Mann and Co. Ltd. and the Canadian Bank of Commerce together, each appointed one member, while the third member was named only after both sides agreed to his appointment.

Mackenzie, Mann and Co. Ltd. and the Canadian Bank of Commerce named Wallace Nesbitt, a Toronto corporation lawyer, as their nominee to the arbitration board.[16] Nesbitt was generally inclined to see the value of the stock in the way it is normally calculated on the "street"—according to the ability or inability of the company to operate profitably under "normal" conditions. Nesbitt himself made few comments and asked few questions, but he made sure that lawyers Frank H. Phippen, representing the Canadian Northern Railway, Pierce Butler, counsel for Mackenzie, Mann and Co. Ltd., and I. F. Hellmuth, the lawyer retained by the Canadian Bank of Commerce, had the opportunity to present witnesses and evidence to support the company's claims. W. N. Tilley and Gerard Ruel acted on behalf of the government.[17]

The government nominee for the Board of Arbitration was Sir William Meredith, Chief Justice of Ontario and Chancellor of the University of Toronto. Meredith was a former leader of the Ontario

14 *Arbitration*, 1809–10.
15 *Ibid.*, 2703.
16 W. D. Wallace, ed., *The Macmillan Dictionary of Canadian Biography* (Toronto: Macmillan, 1963), 548;

Arbitration, 1–2.
17 The members of the Board of Arbitration and the various lawyers who appeared before it are all listed in *Arbitration*, 1–2.

Conservative party.[18] His brother, Sir Vincent Meredith, was president of the Bank of Montreal and a director of numerous companies, among them the CPR. Meredith, who was named chairman of the Board of Arbitration, became irritated at times with the evidence relating to railway's traffic prospects and made it clear on several occasions that he was not sympathetic to the case the company's officers and lawyers were trying to build.[19]

The third member of the Board of Arbitration was appointed only after considerable consultation and negotiation. William Mackenzie, and others who were associated with him, wanted James Marwick of the accounting firm of Marwick, Mitchell, Peat and Company.[20] Marwick's firm, however, had already completed a favourable audit of the Canadian Northern books, refuting the findings of Drayton and Acworth; the firm also audited the books of the Canadian Bank of Commerce. Meredith, the government nominee, objected to Marwick because of these associations.[21]

Prime Minister Borden suggested that Robert Harris, a personal friend and a judge of the Nova Scotia Supreme Court, be appointed as the third member. Harris had considerable experience in big business and Borden believed he had "ability and industry and his character is of the highest".[22] Mackenzie was very reluctant about Harris's appointment. He realized that many businessmen were very critical of the degree of government regulation and control he had accepted in order to get government guarantees for Canadian Northern debentures. The entire Canadian Northern Railway System, moreover, was built on speculation in the hope that future growth and development would ensure profitable operations. That hope was at least deferred in 1917, and the appointment of a man with extensive business experience was

---

18 Wallace, *Dictionary*, 508–9.
19 When, for instance, one witness stated that Canadian Northern lines had not fallen away or sagged seriously in the North, Meredith quipped, "The Lord seems to be on the side of the Canadian Northern." To this the Bank of Commerce lawyer promptly responded, "I am afraid he appears to be the only one," while the Canadian Northern lawyer hoped

Sir William Meredith "will be on the side of the Lord". *Arbitration*, 1880. See also Meredith's interjections when Sir Donald Mann was testifying. *Ibid.*, 2703, 2708, 2791–2, 2807, 2814–15.
20 PAC, Borden Diary, 26 Nov. and 1, 13, and 14 Dec. 1917.
21 *Ibid.*, 2 Dec. 1917.
22 PAC, Borden Papers, File OCA 96, Borden to W. N. Tilley, 22 Dec. 1917.

certainly no assurance of a sympathetic hearing. In the end, however, Mackenzie and those associated with him reluctantly agreed to Harris's appointment.

It did not take Mackenzie long to realize that he had no friend in Robert Harris. He soon complained bitterly about the "animus of Harris against him".[23] At one point Mackenzie even tried to persuade Borden to exert some pressure on Harris, but there is no evidence that the Prime Minister intervened in any way.[24] Once the appointment was made there was little Mackenzie and Mann could do except hope that their evidence was sufficiently convincing to overcome the apparent animosity of Meredith and Harris.

In the arbitration proceedings Canadian Northern officials sought to establish several important points. In order to do so they called Professor Swain, who had made the valuations used by Drayton and Acworth; D. B. Hanna, the railway's chief operating officer; Donald Mann and Z. A. Lash, both of whom gave evidence about the relationship between the contractor-promoters and the railway company; M. H. McLeod, the chief engineer and later general manager; S. R. Bertron, the New York financier who had been prominent in the unsuccessful attempt to arrange a financial reorganization; and several other operating men who could give evidence on specific aspects of the railway's history and operation.

These witnesses, ably questioned by lawyer and former judge F. H. Phippen, were determined to establish clearly several important points. The first was to discredit the highly damaging conclusions of the Drayton-Acworth Commission. Professor Swain and D. B. Hanna were questioned closely regarding the details on which Drayton and Acworth had based their conclusions, and quickly demonstrated the errors which had been made.[25] The government lawyers made no attempt to defend the calculations of the Royal Commission.

A second and far more important point related to the claim that the Canadian Northern Railway System really had excellent prospects

23 PAC, Borden Diary, 29 April 1918.
24 The reference in the diary for 29 April 1918 clearly indicates that Borden discussed Mackenzie's complaint with some of his Cabinet colleagues but was opposed to having any pressure exerted on Harris.
25 *Arbitration*, 26, 239–40, 266, 604–5.

and would enjoy a great and profitable future if the wartime financial problems could be overcome. The losses of the war years were blamed on the great difficulties encountered in completing and operating the new transcontinental railway. These in turn were due to the unexpected financial disruptions and difficulties resulting from the war, and should not have been used to measure the road's real earning power. Very extensive tables, maps, and statistical calculations about traffic and potential earning power were presented.[26] The road, according to its officials, was very well located, well constructed, and efficiently managed. It had simply run into a disastrous financial problem because of the abnormal restrictions in the capital markets and the unusually rapid cost increases. Both had come at a particularly critical time in the company's history.

Hanna, Lash, Mann, Phippen, and Bertron all reviewed important aspects of the company's history and development. They agreed that in view of the company's wartime problems, the common stock was probably worth only 50 per cent of par value, but that within five to ten years it would be worth par. The success of the railway, according to its officers, was inextricably bound to the future growth and development of the country itself. The railway, in the long run, was as sound as the country it served and should not be judged on the basis of its wartime embarrassments. Mann was particularly emphatic: "What the soil will yield; what the mines will produce; the timber and the fisheries; all these things go to make up the commercial value of any railway; you cannot get away from that."[27] This was exactly the same sentiment as that which led Laurier to proclaim that the twentieth century belonged to Canada,[28] and Sir B. E. Walker of the Bank of Commerce to say,

The psychological moment has come and we are on the eve of a great boom. The prospects of the North-West are unlimited. We need not be afraid of over production. If the settlement increases in the same proportion as it has in the past, I believe in 4 or 5 years every railroad through that

26 PAC, CNR Records, MMCXCVII–MMCCIII.
27 Arbitration, 2703.
28 Canada, House of Commons Debates, 1905, 1422. Laurier also used this expression on several other occasions. R. M. Hamilton, ed. Canadian Quotations and Phrases, Literary and Historical (Toronto: McClelland and Stewart, 1965), 228.

country will have to double its track lines in order to handle the traffic.[29]

Company officers also emphasized repeatedly that Mackenzie, Mann and Co. Ltd. had not taken any improper contracting or promotional profits. They had invested not only their time and talents, but also their resources, in the venture. They had never received salaries or dividends or other benefits from the railway, other than the common stock. The evidence in this regard was consistent with the information which the railway's promoters had first presented to Sir Robert Borden in 1914, and which had later been confirmed by auditors' reports. It was, however, sharply at variance with the view widely held by the public that Mackenzie and Mann had received immense personal benefits from their association with the Canadian Northern Railway. Lash and Mann, who emphasized this point particularly, both agreed that when Mackenzie, Mann and Co. Ltd. and the Canadian Northern Railway negotiated an agreement or construction contract, it was the railway company that always got the best of the transaction.[30]

The allegedly excessive railway construction in Canada also received considerable attention. The railway's officers made it very clear that all the mileage built and operated by the Canadian Northern Railway had been demanded, and very often underwritten, by federal and provincial governments. Indeed, governments had often been—and some still were in 1917—impatient with the slow progress on many of the branch lines. Certainly the extensive prairie branch lines, while initially unprofitable, were absolutely essential if the objective of prairie settlement, repeatedly emphasized in Canadian national policies, was to be achieved.[31]

The main lines, some of which were admittedly unnecessary from a national economic point of view, were nevertheless the direct result of the federal government's railway policy. The policy adopted in 1904 had forced the Canadian Northern to seek its own transcontinental connections. If the railway policy was a mistake, the fault lay with the government, not with the Canadian Northern Railway. No one at

29 G. P. de T. Glazebrook, *Sir Edmund Walker* (Toronto: Oxford University Press, 1933).
30 *Arbitration*, 2551–2, 2771.

31 CRC, XIV, 363–5, Mervin, Board of Trade *v.* Canadian Northern Railway, Board of Railway Commissioners, judgment of 25 Jan. 1913.

the arbitration hearings would admit that the railway policy had been mistaken. The country was still expected to grow and soon make full use of the available railway mileage.[32] Yet, if a villain must be found, the proper place to look was in the legislatures of Ottawa and the provincial capitals, not in the Toronto boardrooms.

This evidence given before the Board of Arbitration, particularly that presented by Hanna, Lash, Mann, and Phippen, provides an interesting and instructive insight into the general business methods and philosophy of those associated with the Canadian Northern Railway. Sir William Mackenzie unfortunately refused to testify, although he attended the hearings and made corrections if he thought a witness was in error. He was apparently in agreement with the general approach taken by the others.

The Board of Arbitration presented its official report on 25 May 1918. The arbitrators agreed unanimously that the outstanding $60,000,000 (par value) Canadian Northern common stock was worth $10,800,000. The report itself was only two pages long and did not indicate how the arbitrators had arrived at the $10,800,000 figure. They did point out the errors of the Drayton-Acworth report, and calculated that the railway's assets exceeded its liabilities by at least $25,000,000. This figure was a net figure after a full $40,000,000 had been deducted for depreciation. The report, however, also spoke of the company's potential earning power as "perhaps more important than any other element". The arbitrators did not explain how they arrived at the figure of $10,800,000[33] as the value of the privately held common stock of the Canadian Northern Railway.

The unanimous report of the Board of Arbitration committed all parties to the agreement. The government insisted, however, that before any funds were paid to Mackenzie and Mann they must resign from the railway's board of directors.[34] Public opinion, in the government's view, demanded the complete removal of the two promoters from the affairs of the nationalized railway. Mackenzie and Mann, however, were still very reluctant to resign, apparently hoping they would be asked by the government to continue to manage the railway.

32 CAR, 1918, 533; *Arbitration*, 1589.
33 *Arbitration*, 532–3.
34 PAC, Borden Diary, 5 Oct. 1917, 9 May 1918, 4 Sept. 1918, 7 Sept. 1918.

They certainly believed they could run the nationalized system better than any new government-appointed directors. The Canadian Northern Railway was their life's work. They took great pride in it and were convinced that with proper management it would yet prove a great success, but they feared that it might be ruined by government patronage and inefficiency. There was, in fact, great jostling among members of the Borden Cabinet regarding the appointment of the new president, and several ministers were most eager to secure this plum.[35]

The fears of Mackenzie and Mann were somewhat allayed when the government decided not to appoint a politician as the railway's first president. Instead, D. B. Hanna, the third vice-president of the Canadian Northern Railway and a man fully imbued with the Mackenzie and Mann vision, was appointed to the presidency. The company's organizational structure was left intact, for the time being, although the management was asked to accept responsibility for the other government-owned railways, notably the National Transcontinental and the Intercolonial railways.

With these arrangements completed, Prime Minister Borden sent his railways minister, J. D. Reid, to Toronto. Reid, apparently with some assistance or pressure from the Canadian Bank of Commerce, obtained the resignations of William Mackenzie and Donald Mann as officers and directors of the Canadian Northern Railway System. The date was 6 September 1918. An exciting, spectacular, and highly controversial chapter in the transportation history of Canada had come to an end.

---

35 Borden made repeated references to several candidates for the presidency of the nationalized Canadian Northern Railway in his diary. Francis Cochrane, the Minister of Railways and Canals until 1917, was particularly eager to gain the appointment.

CONCLUSION

WITH MACKENZIE AND MANN'S resignations in hand, Prime Minister Robert Borden authorized payment for the $51,000,000-par-value Canadian Northern Railway System common stock held by Mackenzie, Mann and Co. Ltd. and pledged to the Canadian Bank of Commerce.[1] The amount was not sufficient to meet all the obligations of the contracting and promotional firm, but the Bank of Commerce agreed to carry a reduced account with the two men who had become its most important clients. Certainly both Mackenzie and Mann remained active in business until their deaths, Mann in various mining ventures and Mackenzie with real estate and Latin-American power and traction companies.[2]

Of the three partners in Mackenzie, Mann and Co. Ltd., Roderick Mackenzie, the son of Sir William Mackenzie, died first. The former western construction boss of the Canadian Northern Railway died in Los Angeles, California, in 1923. He owned only 5 per cent of the stock in the contracting firm, and after 1917 became heavily involved in real-estate and racetrack promotions in California and in oil developments in Oklahoma. He died intestate, but the Surrogate Court of Ontario established the value of his estate at $811,467.47.[3] The estate was responsible, however, for debts of nearly four times that amount outside of the province.[4]

Roderick's father, Sir William Mackenzie, died several months later,

1 Canada, PC 2211, 7 Sept. 1918.
2 CR & MW, Jan. 1924, 31–2, and Dec. 1934, 523.
3 Surrogate Court of the County of York, File 48898, Estate of Roderick J. Mackenzie.
4 As told to the author by R. F. B. Barr, the Toronto lawyer who handled many of the details relating to the winding up of Mackenzie, Mann and Co. Ltd. The Surrogate Court records in Toronto do not give a complete listing of all of Roderick Mackenzie's assets and liabilities. Many of them were in the United States and in Manitoba, where Roderick Mackenzie maintained a permanent residence. He died intestate.

in November 1923. His estate proved to be one of the most complex handled in the Surrogate Court of Ontario and had not yet been closed out in the late 1960s.[5] Mackenzie's last will and testament were made during the prosperous years before the First World War, when, on paper at least, he was a multimillionaire and was widely regarded as one of the richest men in Canada. To this will Mackenzie added five codicils shortly before his death. These dealt with special gifts that had at various times been promised to one or another of his children. The last, however, is perhaps the most pathetic. In it Sir William disinherited his son-in-law, the Viscount de Lesseps.

The first returns filed by the executor of the estate showed assets of $1,775,577.90 and liabilities of $1,000,000.00. These amounts, however, were incomplete, showing only the amounts "so far as was then ascertainable".[6] They did not include Mackenzie's major liability —the amount he still owed, directly or through the firm of Mackenzie, Mann and Co. Ltd., to the Canadian Bank of Commerce—or the securities pledged as collateral for that liability.

In the Passing of Accounts the following year, the executor showed an additional $2,000,000 indebtedness to the Canadian Bank of Commerce and listed five long pages of securities which he had released to the Bank to satisfy that indebtedness. An agreement had been made with the Bank whereby these securities were accepted as a final settlement of the account of Mackenzie, Mann and Co. Ltd. The executor produced receipts to show that he had adjusted or discharged liabilities totalling $3,924,781.10, that an additional $291,407.14 was outstanding, and that $420,055.42 was still disputed and to be adjusted.

In order to satisfy these obligations, Mackenzie's beautiful Toronto estate of Benvenuto had to be sold, as did his attractive lakeshore properties and his elaborate summer home at Kirkfield. Even the new Packard car was sold, and only $76,000 worth of furniture from

5 Surrogate Court of the County of York, File 49474, Estate of Sir William Mackenzie, including the Will, Probate Records, lists of assets and liabilities, and accounts subsequently filed by the executors and passed or approved by the Court. All materials are filed according to the original file number, but the Passing of Accounts files are kept in chronological order. It is therefore necessary to check the Passing of Accounts of each year if all the records of the Mackenzie estate are to be examined.

6 *Ibid*. This statement is also on the original File 49474.

Benvenuto was immediately distributed to his eight heirs, or to their heirs. The entire block of $10,000,000 (par value) shares in Mackenzie, Mann and Co. Ltd. was surrendered to the Bank, but noted as being of no value.[7]

Once the major liabilities were settled, the administrator and executor held only a number of speculative securities which were not readily marketable in 1923. Over the years some of these became valuable and were sold, and each of the eight heirs received approximately $100,000 from such sales over a period of forty years.[8] A grandson of William Mackenzie has informed the author that much of Mackenzie's estate "came back" after the depressed market conditions of 1923.[9] The Bank of Commerce, it would seem, settled its account with the estate by taking virtually everything that had any immediate market value in 1923. R. F. B. Barr, the lawyer who later handled some of the Mackenzie, Mann and Co. Ltd. affairs, is convinced that the company and its promoters were really insolvent, but that in matters of this kind the banks do not always insist on their full pound of flesh.[10] There can certainly be no doubt whatsoever that Mackenzie lived out his remaining days after 1918 in relative comfort, but neither he nor his heirs became wealthy as a result of his association with the Canadian Northern Railway. An examination of the Surrogate Court records clearly indicates that the firm of Mackenzie, Mann and Co. Ltd. did not pile up huge construction and promotional profits at the expense of the other companies with which Mackenzie and Mann were associated. Mackenzie and Mann argued before the Board of Arbitration, and verified accountants' reports largely confirm, that in the case of the Canadian Northern Railway the welfare of the railway actually took precedence over financial gains through promotional and contracting profits.

Donald Mann outlived his partner by nearly eleven years. He was never as heavily involved in promotional enterprises as Mackenzie, although he retained a lifelong interest in frontier developments. He

---

7 *Ibid.*, Passing of Accounts, 1926, File 49474, Estate of Sir William Mackenzie.
8 *Ibid.*, Passing of Accounts, various years but initially at six-month intervals and later at two-year intervals.
9 Interview by the author with Mr. A. G. S. Griffin of Toronto, grandson of Sir William Mackenzie.
10 Interview by the author with Mr. R. F. B. Barr of Toronto, lawyer for Mackenzie, Mann and Co. Ltd.

was particularly interested in mining developments and remained active in the promotion of several such ventures until his death. In his old age Mann became a spiritualist. When William Mackenzie died, Mann urged all his friends to pray for the soul of the departed promoter. Both men, according to Mann, had always believed in the power of prayer.[11]

In his business affairs, Z. A. Lash, and later his son Herbert, kept a very close watch on all that Mann did, and allegedly prevented several serious misfortunes.[12] Mann made several world trips. He visited China, the site of some of his early railway contracting, and died in Toronto in comfortable but not really affluent circumstances.[13] His estate was valued in 1934 at $110,755, with $76,000 of this amount in cash in the bank and $6,000 in real estate.[14] These figures make it clear that no immense fortunes were made from the promotion of the Canadian Northern Railway. They also indicate that all or most of the money received by Mackenzie, Mann and Co. Ltd. for their $51,000,000 (par value) common stock of the Canadian Northern Railway went to their creditors.

A complete assessment of the work of Mackenzie and Mann and their Canadian Northern Railway must, of course, include more than a review of the evidence presented to the Board of Arbitration and a statement of how much money they made or failed to make. Mackenzie and Mann were, above all, promoters of the Canadian frontier. They ardently believed in Canada, particularly western Canada, and its future development, and were willing to invest their time, talents, and resources to participate in and benefit from that development. The Canadian Northern Railway was very much a frontier railway, built to serve the needs of the Canadian prairie frontier. Although eastern Canadian and international investors provided much of the money behind it, the Canadian Northern was never a mere extension of metropolitan or imperialist influences of Toronto, Montreal, or London. Mackenzie and Mann, as enthusiastic exponents of prairie

11 CR & MW, Jan. 1924, 31–2.
12 Interviews by the author with Mr. R. F. B. Barr of Toronto, lawyer for Mackenzie, Mann and Co. Ltd., and Col. G. R. Stevens, historian of the Canadian National Railways.
13 CR & MW, Dec. 1934, 523.
14 Surrogate Court of the County of York, File 76027, Estate of Sir Donald Mann.

development, had to coax and persuade men like B. E. Walker, J. M. Horne-Payne, Robert Kindersley, and others, that money could be advantageously invested in prairie railways. The CPR and the Grand Trunk Pacific can properly be described as instruments of economic or metropolitan imperialism, but the Canadian Northern cannot. It was a railway which responded to the needs of the frontier, and was developed along lines which would best serve those needs. Even when the enormously expensive terminal facilities in Vancouver and Montreal were built, the emphasis always remained on western traffic and how the terminals would facilitate its movement to overseas markets. The inspiration for most of the important developments on the Canadian Northern came from the frontier, not from the head office in Toronto or from Donald Mann's hotel room in Montreal. The Canadian Northern was very much the West's own product, designed to serve the needs of the West.[15]

Mackenzie and Mann were men who had a dream. It was their vision which made possible the development of the northern prairies at a time when most other Canadian businessmen still lacked confidence in the future of the region. Almost every opportunity that came to Mackenzie and Mann was first offered to other and better-established companies—among them usually the CPR. But that company, under the conservative management of President Thomas Shaughnessy, simply lacked the vision to grasp the opportunities. Great projects were eventually undertaken by Shaughnessy and his fellow directors, but prospective profits on new ventures, or direct thefts by business rivals, had to hit Shaughnessy on the head before he would act. Even the best presentation in support of new prairie branch lines or reduced developmental rates got nowhere until Mackenzie and Mann proved conclusively that such ventures could earn substantial profits. The CPR, in Hanna's blunt words, "did not have vision".[16] Prairie farmers and western politicians simply could not afford to wait until Shaughnessy was ready to accommodate them, and they turned to Mackenzie

15 Hanna, 237.
16 *Arbitration*, 450–1; PAC, Shaughnessy Letterbooks, No. 64, 415, Shaughnessy to W. R. Baker, 19 Dec. 1898; *ibid.*, No. 66, 749, Shaughnessy to White, 15 April 1899; *ibid.*, No. 67, 816–17, Shaughnessy to White, 13 June 1899; *ibid.*, No. 73, 133–40, Shaughnessy to W. R. Baker, 26 Dec. 1900.

and Mann, who had vision, enthusiasm, and the promotional skills needed to get rail services to the frontier regions.

Shaughnessy and many other Canadian businessmen, politicians, and later, historians, never fully understood the Canadian Northern Railway and its promoters. Conditioned by years of depression to view the Canadian world in dark and sombre colours, such people could not understand the enormous optimism of men like Mackenzie and Mann. There was, in fact, a widespread belief that no one, not even Mackenzie and Mann, could seriously believe that a new developmental railway could be successful. The promoters, it was alleged, were merely money-grubbing contractors looking for easy promotional and contracting profits. Thomas Shaughnessy expressed the opinion of many when he wrote in 1900: "Contractors can be found who will enter into almost any sort of an agreement about rates, provided that they can get sufficient assistance from the Provincial Government to enable them to make a profit out of the construction of the line."[17] It was for this reason that the CPR president denounced all forms of government aid to the newer railways as "rotten to the core".[18] The CPR itself had, of course, received a great deal of government aid, but Shaughnessy believed a distinction had to be made between the CPR subsidies and the government assistance to the newer lines. The CPR syndicate had committed itself not only to build its railway, but also to operate it. Shaughnessy did not think the promoters of the newer transcontinentals had made the same commitment. In the case of Mackenzie and Mann and the Canadian Northern Railway, Shaughnessy was clearly wrong, and politicians and historians who repeated his allegations simply were not properly informed about the subject before they ventured to make judgements. Mackenzie and Mann looked almost entirely to the common stock of the Canadian Northern Railway for their profits. That stock could have no long-term value unless the railway itself was profitably operated.

Mackenzie and Mann were always developmental, but not narrowly regional, in their outlook. They were certainly willing and eager to apply their policies to a wide range of new projects in various parts

17 PAC, Shaughnessy Letterbook, No. 73, 133–40, Shaughnessy to W. R. Baker, 26 Dec. 1900.

18 *Ibid.*, 397, Shaughnessy to Wilson Southam, 26 Feb. 1901.

of Canada and the world. The northern prairies, however, responded most readily to their promotional skills, and it was there that the two had their greatest impact. Prairie freight-rate policies and branch-line construction programs were unashamedly developmental. Only continuing rapid growth and economic development, aided by good transportation facilities at reasonable cost, could make the railway a success. Very few Mackenzie and Mann lines were really expected to be profitable from the beginning, but all were expected to facilitate economic development, which would lead to very profitable operations. This was precisely the kind of railway policy western Canada wanted and needed, and that region came closer to realizing its economic and transportation objectives in the first decade of the twentieth century, when the Canadian Northern Railway was only a prairie road, than at any other time. It was the 1901 agreement with the Canadian Northern Railway that prompted Premier Roblin of Manitoba to assert that, henceforth, one of the most serious of prairie grievances—freight rates—would no longer be a problem or an issue of political and economic controversy.[19]

The statistics documenting the growth of the prairie grain economy after 1896 are well known. Homestead entries rose from 1,849 in 1895 to over 40,000 per year in 1910. While it is difficult to calculate accurately how many of these homesteaders located near Canadian Northern lines, it is known that the Canadian Northern Railway was directly responsible for the establishment of more than 550 prairie cities, towns, and villages which had been nonexistent before the coming of the railway. Obviously many of the new settlers occupied homesteads, towns, and villages opened by the Canadian Northern.[20]

The wheat exported from the prairies rose from less than 20,000,000 bushels to more than 130,000,000 bushels during Sir Wilfrid Laurier's administration. During the 1915–16 crop year the Canadian Northern, despite serious difficulties in securing rolling stock and labour, and with only makeshift terminals and a single-track line to the Lakehead, carried 31.1 per cent of the prairie grain destined for the Lakehead. The CPR still had 56.3 per cent of the grain traffic, but Canadian

19 Manitoba, *Annual Report of the Commissioner of Railways for the year ended December 31, 1901.*

20 Urquhart and Buckley, *Historical Statistics of Canada* (Toronto: Macmillan, 1971).

Northern officials were confident that their road would overtake the CPR in the grain trade when all their branch lines came into full service. The Canadian Northern had already surpassed the Canadian Pacific Railway as the nation's largest lumber carrier, and was dividing the prairie traffic in many other commodities almost evenly with the older and much richer CPR.[21] The impact of the Canadian Northern Railway, while probably not as great as that of the CPR, was obviously very great in the prairie region and, to a lesser extent, in the entire country.

This development took place as a result of a distinctly Canadian partnership between governments and entrepreneurs. Mackenzie and Mann, like most of their contemporaries in business and politics, believed that free enterprise would develop and build up the country in the most efficient way possible. They had nothing but contempt for the business acumen of governments and of most politicians. Patronage and inefficiency allegedly characterized the operations of governments and of any businesses controlled by governments. The example most frequently referred to was the Intercolonial Railway. Governments seemed to have a peculiar tendency to attract the dead-wood in the labour market, and possessed no adequate mechanism to remove incompetents from their posts. Governments, in short, should not become involved in business if private enterprise was willing and able to do the job.

Mackenzie and Mann, again like most of their contemporaries, nevertheless believed that governments did have a necessary and useful role to play in developing the Canadian economy. Governments could and should strive to create a climate favourable to enterprise by offering incentives and assistance for deserving private ventures, particularly those which were clearly in the national interest but lacked essential resources or credit or might prove initially unprofitable. Mackenzie and Mann believed their developmental projects deserved government assistance. They believed in a partnership in which governments provided concessions or charters and much of the required capital or credit, while private entrepreneurs used their available funds, insights, and skills to invest that capital to the best advantage and to manage

21 Hanna, 232–3.

and operate the undertaking in an efficient manner. The rewards of such a partnership would also be shared. Economic growth and development would be of immense benefit to all Canadians, would enlarge the governments' tax base, meet political objectives of national growth and development, and provide innumerable jobs, homesteads, and other opportunities for work and profit for Canadians. The entrepreneurs, if they invested and managed the entrusted funds wisely, would receive the benefit of the increased value of the capital stock.

The very nature of this alliance between government and business provided considerable opportunity for corruption. This had been obvious from the time when John A. Macdonald introduced his famous National Policy in 1878, tariff concessions being as subject to corruption as subsidies or guarantees. The scope for chicanery has been very great in Canadian political and business life since that time, and few businessmen have been as frequently or as bitterly accused of political manipulation and corruption as William Mackenzie and Donald Mann.

In part, these charges certainly stemmed from the character and manners of William Mackenzie. He was a rather humourless, domineering character with almost unbounded energy, tenacity, and enthusiasm. He loved to intimidate people, and attempted to do it whenever he could.[22] Often he was not particularly careful about the means he adopted to achieve his objectives, and those who felt aggrieved by his actions were not likely to take the matter lightly.[23] To those he crossed, William Mackenzie had few redeeming graces. Yet, it would be wrong to suggest that corruption and venality account for the assistance federal and provincial governments of both Liberal and Conservative persuasions gave to the Canadian Northern Railway. That railway offered a service much desired by Canadians, for which governments were prepared to pay or guarantee substantial sums. Each of the major transactions between governments and the railway could

22 Martin Nordegg, *The Possibilities of Canada Are Truly Great: Memoirs, 1906–1924*, ed., T. D. Regehr (Toronto: Macmillan, 1971), 136.
23 The hatred of those who felt they had suffered at Mackenzie's hands sometimes became very intense. It apparently drove at least one person, David Russell, to the verge of insanity. *Arbitration*, 2552. PAC, Borden Papers, File OC 163, David Russell to Borden, 29 Jan. 1918; PAC, White Papers, File 52, 8453, David Russell to Sir William Meredith, 19 Aug. 1917.

be examined and, in the terms of that day, justified on its own merits. Governments certainly preferred to deal with businessmen who had stronger financial resources than Mackenzie and Mann had in the 1890s, but few well-established businessmen were willing to accept the conditions and undertake the risks involved in Canadian frontier railways. Clifford Sifton's attempt to get branch lines for his constituency, and Premier Greenway's search for capitalists willing to build to Duluth, reflect the basic pessimism among businessmen of that time towards western development.

The records of the Canadian Northern Railway provide very little evidence of direct political graft and corruption. Companies, however, rarely enter such things in their minute-books or their legal files. When wrong-doing was discovered, as for example by the Cowper Commission in British Columbia, the arrangements and the monies involved were the personal funds of one of the promoters, not those of the railway company. Even in that case, however, the wrong-doing centred on the British Columbia Attorney General, who had allegedly received $25,000 from Roderick Mackenzie but used it, among other things, to buy himself a new car, rather than for the intended political purposes.[24]

Mackenzie and Mann certainly helped their political friends. It is doubtful whether adequate evidence will ever be found to determine to just what extent, but it is clear that the two promoters never really ingratiated themselves with either of the major political parties. Certainly the greatest benefit Mackenzie and Mann could bestow on a friendly politician was to build a new branch line in his constituency. This is what prairie farmers and politicians wanted above all else from the promoters, and political careers frequently prospered or waned according to the state of railway construction in many remote constituencies. Campaign funds were, of course, also useful to the politicians. Considerable amounts were advanced by Mackenzie and Mann personally, but there were also numerous complaints suggesting the Canadian Northern promoters were less generous in this regard than either the CPR or the Grand Trunk. Political patronage, at best, played only

24 PABC, Premiers' Papers, Transcript of Proceedings under the Public Inquiries Act re charges made by John Sedgewick Cowper. The hearings began 2 May 1917.

a small part in the affairs of the Canadian Northern Railway. Appointments, at least at the senior levels, were made on merit rather than as political rewards. A review of the top ten or twelve men in the service of the company does not produce a single individual whose appointment could be considered political.

All government assistance granted to the Canadian Northern Railway had to be publicly justified on its own merits, and every successful government seemed eager to deal with the railway that provided a service they regarded as worthy of substantial government support. The developmental prairie branch lines and rate reductions offered by the Canadian Northern Railway were far more important in explaining the reasons for government assistance than were their private campaign contributions. Lobbyists could readily explain this to political leaders, but the Canadian Northern never had a public relations department that adequately explained it to those people not living near a Canadian Northern line.

In one important way Mackenzie and Man did deal differently with governments than did most of their contemporaries. Unlike many Canadian businessmen, Mackenzie and Mann were prepared to acknowledge not only the right or duty of governments to assist worthy ventures, but also their duty to ensure that those ventures were operated in a responsible and acceptable manner. One of the great problems in western Canada in the 1880s and 1890s had been that while the federal government provided very generous subsidies for the construction of the CPR, it failed to ensure that the company would be operated at rates which would make it really useful to western farmers. Government control over rates, and if necessary further assistance to permit desirable but economically unprofitable rates, were entirely unacceptable to most Canadian businessmen at the turn of the century. Mackenzie and Mann, on the other hand, saw this kind of control as a logical extension or consequence of government assistance. Unlike the CPR, which built its main line, and then set rates which would permit profitable operations, Mackenzie and Mann consulted with the Manitoba politicians to determine what rates were politically acceptable. They knew very well that high rates would greatly inhibit settlement and make their railway useless to many potential shippers, and they explained to the politicians what kind of assistance was needed and what levels of service could be provided at designated rates. They believed that they could invest in, construct, and manage railways better than any politician or political appointee, but they acknowledged the right of government to control rates, provided those rates allowed a reasonable return on well-invested and efficiently managed capital.[25] The government guarantee, they thought, would ensure that reasonable rates would be allowed, if only to prevent calls on the provincial treasury to pay interest and principal on the guaranteed bonds.[26] They did not realize that this argument could not be used in western Canada if the requests for higher rates were necessitated by deficits on eastern lines.

In 1901 the most serious fear among businessmen discussing the Canadian Northern guarantees was that the control given the Manitoba government could and would be used to prevent excessive profits. The Canadian Northern had surrendered its right to charge rates that would generate "unreasonable" returns. Men like Charles Hays of the Grand Trunk regarded this as the Canadian Northern's most serious blemish.[27] To Shaughnessy it was evidence that Mackenzie and Mann were interested only in construction profits and not in the welfare of the railway itself.[28] To Mackenzie and Mann, on the other hand, it indicated a government commitment to the over-all success of the railway, since failure of the railway would lead to heavy demands on the provincial treasury. They were satisfied to take their reward in the form of capital stock in a railway whose success was guaranteed by government, but whose rates and operating profits would never be allowed to become "excessive".

It was a belief in the future development of Canada, and the government guarantee for Canadian Northern bonds—thus indirectly guaranteeing the success of the railway itself—which impressed many investors. The British underwriters, who had been stung frequently by nineteenth-century Canadian railway projects, were understandably

25 CAR, 1904, 628–9.
26 Mackenzie's attitude toward rate reductions is very clearly expressed in PAC, CNR Legal Series, File 6–22A; see particularly Mackenzie to Lash, 12 June 1903.

27 PAC, Hays Papers, 91–2, Hays to Wilson, 21 Feb. 1903.
28 PAC, Shaughnessy Letterbook, No. 73, 133–40, Shaughnessy to W. R. Baker, 26 Dec. 1900; No. 74, 357–62, Shaughnessy to E. B. Osler, 5 June 1901.

shy. The government guarantees, however, removed much of the risk normally associated with Canadian railway securities, and Mackenzie's energy, enthusiasm, and tenacity when peddling Canadian Northern Railway securities in London became famous.[29] He knew his railway and the country it served extremely well, and he fervently believed both were assured of a very prosperous future. The opportunity to help develop a part of the British Empire, and that without serious risk, greatly appealed to the investors. In men like Mackenzie and Mann, R. M. Horne-Payne, B. E. Walker, and R. Kindersley, the British underwriters and investors detected shades of the old African and Indian empire-builders. These were men who were accomplishing great things in the colonies, and the British invested accordingly.

Mackenzie and Mann, moreover, were remarkably successful in imparting their vision of future Canadian greatness not only to politicians, bankers, and investors, but also to their associates and employees. The permanent staff of the Canadian Northern Railway often demonstrated a remarkable dedication and *esprit de corps*. Early employees identified themselves with the company and took great pride in every additional item of traffic they helped bring to the railway and in every construction or operating economy they could devise. The challenge that the aggressive new road made to the claims and position of the CPR involved not only the promoters but their entire staff.[30]

In general, Mackenzie and Mann had very little trouble with their employees. The wages and bonuses paid on the Canadian Northern were among the best in the country.[31] They were certainly much higher than the prevailing rates in eastern Canada, and in western Canada anything the CPR could pay was also paid by the Canadian Northern. The managers did make sure, however, that every employee really

29 Nordegg, *The Possibilities of Canada Are Truly Great*, 128–30; PAC, Dunn Papers, Vol. 249, 62–3, Dunn to Schuster, 19 July 1906.
30 Hanna was very proud to refer to himself as Exhibit A of the Canadian Northern Railway, and his descriptions of how he, Lash, Macleod, Moore, and others joined and served the company reflect the strong sense of purpose and pride felt by Canadian Northern officials.
31 PAC, Department of Labour, Strikes and Lockouts Files. It is significant that the Canadian Northern had far fewer serious labour disturbances than either the Canadian Pacific or the Grand Trunk Pacific railways. The major exception is the 1902–3 strike, where collective bargaining and recognition of the union was the issue.

earned his wage. Otherwise he could expect instant dismissal.

Certainly Mackenzie and Mann had no sympathy with the adversary or class-conflict theories propounded by the leaders of the labour unions. Their concepts of employer-employee relations were much more authoritarian and paternalistic. A good man deserved a good salary, but he must work not only for the dollar but also for the success and welfare of the entire venture. He must come to identify himself with that company, not with a union bent on class warfare with management.[32]

Mackenzie and Mann had to face only one really serious strike on the Canadian Northern. That came in 1902 when employees, allegedly incited by American labour leaders and organizers, demanded the right to bargain collectively. This was entirely contrary to management's view of proper employer-employee relations and the demand was categorically rejected. A bitter strike with considerable violence resulted, but management remained adamant. D. B. Hanna, as general manager, was very willing to discuss any and all grievances with workers' committees or delegations, but every employee's first loyalty must be to the company and its success. This, in Hanna's opinion, was not possible if employees committed themselves to collective action dictated by international or even national union leaders who might know little or nothing about the policies and problems of the company. There was no way he would grant collective bargaining, and the employees had to content themselves with workers' committees as long as the Canadian Northern Railway was under private management. The workers could belong to unions, and the railway paid prevailing union rates, but bargaining was done by the workers' committees.[33]

In the generally prosperous years after 1901 the relations between management and labour were fairly amicable—certainly very much better than on the troubled Grand Trunk Pacific or even on the CPR. A good worker on the Canadian Northern had job security and got top wages, but he had to earn both, and senior Canadian Northern officials as well as junior employees often developed great loyalty to their com-

---

32 *Manitoba Free Press*, 1 July 1902.
33 *Ibid.*, 3, 4, 7, 11, and 15 July 1902 for details of the strike and 27 Jan. 1903 for details of its settlement. Nordegg also has interesting comments regarding management attitudes toward labour in Nordegg, *The Possibilities of Canada Are Truly Great*, 210–11.

pany. It was an arrangement that had obvious advantages for good employees, and when the Canadian government decided to nationalize the railway, the employees sent a petition to the Prime Minister opposing nationalization and endorsing the old management. They feared government patronage and preferred the old system, where the lazy, the incompetent, and the dishonest were dispatched without further ado, but where good employees were valued and rewarded. The chairman of four Canadian Northern employee groups asserted categorically "that the relations between the employees and the Company have always been most harmonious and it is our desire that conditions remain as nearly as possible as they are."[34]

The most serious exploitation of workers often occurred in the construction camps, and usually involved immigrant workers.[35] In the case of the Canadian Northern, however, these instances were often the responsibility of subcontractors. On occasion things certainly did get difficult for construction crews of Mackenzie, Mann and Co. Ltd., and of subcontractors, particularly during the difficult war years and on some of the very early contracts. On the early contracts, facilities for sleeping and eating were often inadequate and there were some delays in paying the men. During the war years, lack of money sometimes led to serious delays in meeting payroll obligations and this led to sporadic protests. A number of those recalling these protests, however, also expressed the firm opinion that, as long as it was within their power, Mackenzie and Mann treated their construction workers as well as any, and better than most contractors. It is significant that a man like Roderick Mackenzie could allegedly get almost anything out of his men and remain well liked all the while,[36] and long-term employees continued to think of William Mackenzie and Donald Mann as being one with them—opposed to the big business interests in general and to the CPR and the Grand Trunk in particular—long after the two promoters became big businessmen themselves. The dream or

34 PAC, Borden Papers, File OC 294, 33120–3, Chairmen of Canadian Northern employee groups to Borden, 18 May 1917.
35 PAC, Records of the Superintendent of Immigration, Vols. 230–1, File 594511, Railway Labourers. Donald

Avery, "Canadian Immigration Policy and the 'Foreign Navvy', 1896–1914". Paper read at the 1972 Annual Meeting of the Canadian Historical Association.
36 CNRHQ, Osborne Scott interview.

vision of building a big, new, and important project affected not only the promoters, politicians, and investors, but also the employees and construction workers.

Construction workers, moreover, were often on the job for only a short time. A good strong settler generating traffic for the new railway was worth far more than a cheap labourer, and Mackenzie and Mann frequently encouraged workers to take up homesteads. They also tried to give work to local homesteaders who were often in desperate need of some hard cash to buy necessary tools, but there was always the fear that this practice might interfere with the settler's farming activities. Local settlers who were used as construction workers had to be kept reasonably satisfied if they were to become good traffic prospects for the railway. The desire to get cheap labour was therefore secondary to the policy of developing as much traffic as possible.[37]

Mackenzie and Mann's relations with their subcontractors were similar to those they had with their employees. It was expected that contractors would make a reasonable profit, and several became moderately wealthy working for the Canadian Northern. To earn that profit, however, all the terms of the contract had to be fulfilled, and Mackenzie and Mann were expert at detecting shortcomings. If, for reasons beyond his control, a subcontractor found he could not meet his commitments, Mackenzie and Mann, recalling their own experience with the CPR in the state of Maine, would pay sufficient additional amounts to allow the embarrassed contractor to break even on the operation.[38] Mackenzie and Mann were proud to say that no honest and competent contractor had ever lost money on a Canadian Northern contract. Conversely, no dishonest or incompetent contractor ever made any large or windfall profits. A peculiar puritan kind of ethic prevailed in which good and honest work for the great project had its rewards, but the lazy, the shiftless, and the improvident also— and with disturbingly few exceptions—received their just deserts.

Donald Mann had made about $100,000 from his contracts with

37 The federal government tried hard, particularly in the early years, to persuade railway contractors to provide employment for settlers in need of funds with which to start farming. PAC, Department of the Interior, Superintendent of Immigration File 594511, Railway Labourers; File 39501, Crow's Nest Pass Railway; File 34214, Galician Immigrants. 38 CR & MW, Dec. 1934, 523; *Arbitration*, 2663–8.

the CPR. When he and Mackenzie left that company in 1890 they asked Thomas Shaughnessy to write letters of recommendation. The letters they received express their ideas of good contracting. "I take pleasure in saying to you that the very large amount of work which you performed under contracts with this Company was in every instance completed to the satisfaction of the Company and without quibbling when the time came for final settlement."[39] Nothing less was expected of the subcontractors who built the Canadian Northern Railway.

None of this, of course, could save the railway in 1917. It was built with the expectation that the rapid growth and development of the prairies during the pre-war period not only would continue, but would extend to the British Columbia interior and the clay belt of Northern Ontario and Quebec. Unfortunately, the sources of capital dried up, immigration fell off sharply, and operating costs rose with no commensurate rate increases after 1913. Thus the promoters who had acted on a dream failed, while their rivals who "lacked vision" continued to pile up profits from their safer investments.[40] Yet the CPR, in its time, had been as much a dream of promoters and politicians as the Canadian Northern was twenty years later. Certainly the rate and pattern of Canadian economic growth and development would have been very different and much slower if initially unprofitable transportation facilities had not been made available by promoters and governments guided by a dream or vision of what Canada might be, rather than by hard calculations of immediate profits on every new extension.

Canadian Northern officials always insisted that it was the war and the accompanying financial stringency which ruined their railway.[41] There is a good deal of truth in that claim, but it is not the whole truth. The Canadian Northern Railway certainly would have survived much longer if the war had not disrupted its financing. Long-term success, however, depended not only on financing the construction of

39 PAC, Shaughnessy Letterbook, No. 21, 343, Shaughnessy to Mann, 20 March 1890; ibid., 243, Shaughnessy to Mackenzie, 22 March 1890.
40 Arbitration, 450–1; PAC, Shaughnessy Letterbook, No. 73,

601, Shaughnessy to Roche, 16 Feb. 1901.
41 Hanna, Lash and Mann particularly emphasized this before the Board of Arbitration.

the system. The entire system depended on continuing economic growth and development. The prairies had responded to the railway as Mackenzie and Mann believed they would, and by 1917 there were indications that British Columbia might follow. Certainly the Canadian Northern Pacific's important role in the western lumber traffic augured well for the future of the Pacific section, although a very large traffic would be needed to meet high operating costs and the fixed charges on that enormously expensive mileage through the mountains.

There were no similar and encouraging prospects in the areas adjacent to many of the Canadian Northern lines in Ontario and Quebec. Many of the local lines of the Canadian Northern in those provinces were, in fact, abandoned soon after nationalization. The Ontario and Quebec system, however, could not be operated profitably if it remained merely a transit for western traffic. While Canadian Northern officials always expressed optimism about future Ontario and Quebec local traffic, it seems clear today that most of their local lines were not situated in a way that would permit the company to benefit from such developments. The hard fact was that in Ontario and Quebec Canada had very seriously overbuilt its railway system, and it would be many years before there would be enough traffic to justify all that construction. In the meantime the Canadian Northern, as the weakest and most junior eastern road with the fewest connections, had to face intense competition from the older systems for the available traffic. There was, moreover, a great deal of unnecessary duplicate railway mileage, particularly north of Lake Superior, which would never generate much local traffic. That mileage had been built for political and strategic reasons and has been a heavy burden ever since.

It is impossible to determine whether the Canadian Northern Railway could have overcome the problems of its Ontario and Quebec lines in normal times to create a profitable transcontinental railway service. In 1923 the railway was amalgamated with the Intercolonial Railway, the National Transcontinental Railway, the Grand Trunk and Grand Trunk Pacific railways, and many smaller lines to form the Canadian National Railways. All the old debts of these various companies—many of them bankrupt—were carried over to the new company, which has never been able to earn the interest and to repay all those old debts. As a result, Parliament is called upon to vote new

Canadian National Railways refinancing bills every year.[42] The advent of the internal combustion engine and government construction of roads and highways have further reduced the railway's prospects of profitable operations, rendering many previously essential prairie branch lines unprofitable and, perhaps, unnecessary.

Despite any paper losses incurred by the Canadian National Railways and its predecessors, however, this railway has offered an indispensable service to Canadians. The Canadian National Railways certainly suffers from the fact that it was never really planned as a national system. In Canada, where we are confronted with immense distances, transportation is of the utmost importance. At the turn of the century, railways were the only economically feasible means of transporting bulky freight to and from any region that did not have access to water transportation. Western Canada in particular simply could not have been settled and developed without rail service, and there, despite the mistakes that were made, the Canadian Northern Railway performed a necessary and valuable service.

Promoters and governments alike tried to build a greater and better Canada. Both devised policies to realize the objective of economic growth and development, but always in ways which would also advance their own political or financial interests. The results have been mixed. Private enterprise, aided and encouraged by government, has provided Canada with the means of transportation that were a prerequisite to successful settlement and growth. There were risks involved in this developmental policy, but D. B. Hanna expressed the philosophy of his company and of an entire era when he wrote in 1919,

The importance of impressing upon the people of Canada the true value from a national standpoint and the almost unlimited potentialities of the national road cannot be overstated. Canada must acquire a new angle of vision; the measure of our future depends on it. . . . Great things can be accomplished if the Dominion of Canada is disposed to regard railroading in the same light as the private railroaders have done in the past; as a risk that must be taken to assure a big future.[43]

42 A fairly typical recent expression of public attitudes regarding the continuing financing problems of the Canadian National Railways is given by Maurice Weston in a syndicated column entitled "One of our quainter rituals". It appeared in the *Saskatoon Star Phoenix* on 29 March 1972.

43 CR & MW, Oct. 1919, 528.

APPENDIXES

APPENDIX I

Operating Statistics:
Lake Manitoba Railway and Canal Company (1897–1899)
Canadian Northern Railway (1899–1914)
Canadian Northern Railway System (1915–1917)

Year ending	Mileage operated	Gross earnings ($)	Operating costs ($)	Net earnings ($)	Fixed charges ($)	Surplus or deficit ($)
31/12/1897	101	70,119.28	39,059.30	31,060.98	26,500.00	5,560.98
31/12/1898	161	106,698.72	54,594.40	52,104.32	40,000.00	12,104.32
31/12/1899	290	161,534.63	81,870.06	79,664.57	67,034.83	12,629.74
30/6/1900	367	132,632.81	70,060.76	62,572.05	50,341.32	12,230.37
30/6/1901	512	339,360.41	189,412.90	149,947.51	136,446.33	13,501.18
30/6/1902	1,243	1,400,960.43	839,774.11	561,196.32	481,203.50	79,992.82
30/6/1903	1,276	2,449,579.33	1,589,293.47	860,285.86	637,364.50	222,921.36
30/6/1904	1,349	3,242,702.69	2,120,772.43	1,121,930.26	805,528.55	316,401.71
30/6/1905	1,876	4,190,211.96	2,644,729.64	1,545,482.32	1,128,779.38	416,702.94
30/6/1906	2,482	5,903,755.61	3,674,732.85	2,229,022.76	1,509,448.33	719,574.43
30/6/1907	2,639	8,350,198.08	5,424,163.63	2,926,034.43	1,882,489.14	1,043,545.29
30/6/1908	2,894	9,709,462.71	6,676,775.82	3,032,686.89	2,353,757.48	678,929.41
30/6/1909	3,140	10,581,767.93	7,015,405.76	3,566,362.17	2,919,617.13	646,745.04

30/6/1910	3,325	13,833,061.63	9,488,671.60	4,344,390.03	3,313,632.58	1,030,759.45
30/6/1911	3,731	16,360,712.39	11,370,365.57	4,990,346.82	3,982,651.02	694,823.80
30/6/1912	4,316	20,860,093.63	14,979,048.52	5,881,045.11	4,630,844.12	575,396.99
30/6/1913	4,553	24,527,478.47	17,503,610.57	7,023,867.90	5,190,924.12	884,729.78
30/6/1914	4,965	23,781,328.84	16,450,763.09	7,330,565.75	5,776,060.34	304,505.41
30/6/1915	7,269	25,912,106.30	19,288,814.42	6,623,291.88	8,263,574.99	−1,640,283.11
30/6/1916	9,296	35,476,275.06	26,102,744.52	9,373,530.54	9,621,657.70	−248,127.16
30/6/1917	9,433	43,495,076.56	31,349,408.18	12,145,668.38	14,607,805.35	−2,462,136.97

Sources: Figures for the period prior to 1903 are taken from the evidence given by D. B. Hanna before the Canadian Northern Board of Arbitration. All other figures are taken from the published Annual Reports of the Canadian Northern. These figures vary somewhat from those filed by the company with the Department of Railways and Canals, mainly because of different accounting procedures for items related to the hire of equipment, taxes, and interest on floating indebtedness. The figures are, nevertheless, very similar.

None of these figures show any allowances for depreciation (other than deferred maintenance) or for the amortization of discounts on securities sold. Calculations including these items would have shown the Canadian Northern operating at a small deficit from 1903 and at substantial deficits after 1914. Such calculations were made from the Canadian Northern Board of Arbitration and were filed as Exhibit 174.

The fixed charges for 1911 through 1914 include interest paid on the Income Convertible Debenture Stock.

APPENDIX II

Canadian Northern Railway System—Government Bond Guarantees

DOMINION GUARANTEES

CNR 3% Debenture Stock	1903	$ 9,359,996.72	
CNR 3½% Debenture Stock	1908	7,896,590.00	
CNAR 3½% Debenture Stock	1911	3,149,998.73	
CNOR 3½% Debenture Stock	1911	35,770,000.00	
CNAR 3½% Debenture Stock	1912	3,569,996.86	
CNR 4% Debenture Stock	1914	44,866,667.33	
Total Dominion guarantees		————	$104,613,249.64

MANITOBA GUARANTEES

CNR 4% Ontario Division Bonds	1901	$ 5,745,586.66	
CNR 4% Consol. Deb. Stock*	1904	12,435,279.98	
CNR 4% Winnipeg Terminal Bonds	1909	3,000,000.00	
CNR 4% Debenture Stock	1910	4,319,998.87	
Total Manitoba guarantees		————	$25,500,865.51

BRITISH COLUMBIA GUARANTEES

CNPR 4% Debenture Stock	1910	$20,999,997.59	
CNPR 4½% Terminals Deb. Stock	1913	8,614,000.00	
CNPR 4½% Branch Lines Deb. Stock	1914	5,339,127.53	
CNPR 4½% Second Charge Deb. Stock	1914	4,999,998.73	
Total British Columbia guarantees		————	$39,953,123.85

ALBERTA GUARANTEES

CNR 4% Debenture Stock*	1909	$ 9,726,364.26	
CNWR 4½% Debenture Stock	1912	6,424,000.00	
CNWR 4½% Debenture Stock	1914	2,800,000.00	
Total Alberta guarantees		————	$18,950,364.26

SASKATCHEWAN GUARANTEES

CNR 4% Debenture Stock*	1909	$13,587,733.33	
CNR 4½% Debenture Stock	1914	1,174,813.33	
Total Saskatchewan guarantees		————	$14,762,546.66

ONTARIO GUARANTEES

CNOR 3½% Debenture Stock*	1908	$ 7,859,997.59	$ 7,859,997.59

Total government guarantees	$211,640,147.51

*Includes and supersedes earlier bond guarantees made by these governments within their respective provinces, often to separate locally chartered companies. The Ontario Division Bonds guaranteed by Manitoba were not included in the Consolidated Debenture Stock.

Source: "The Canadian Northern Railway System Description and Distribution of Funded Debt", prepared by Coverdale and Colpitts, Consulting Engineers, and published as Exhibit B of Edward E. Loomis and John W. Platten, *Report on the Canadian Northern Railway System*. PAC, White Papers, File 50, pp. 8116–60. Other sources give slightly different figures, the variations apparently being due in part to the calculations used in converting sterling to dollar values. The Coverdale and Colpitts calculations are dated 26 March 1917.

APPENDIX III
Statement of Cash Subsidies and Bonuses Received

Dominion Government		
Canadian Northern Railway	$2,000,332.00	
Canadian Northern Quebec Railway	707,568.03	
Canadian Northern Ontario Railway (James Bay)	1,872,960.00	
Canadian Northern Ontario Railway (Toronto–Ottawa)	1,363,122.39	
Canadian Northern Ontario Railway (Hawkesbury–Port Arthur)	10,424,627.71	
Canadian Northern Alberta Railway	3,094,104.00	
Canadian Northern Pacific Railway	5,648,626.37	
Halifax and South Western Railway	1,364,210.00	
Total Dominion subsidies		$26,843,422.50
Ontario Government		
Canadian Northern Ontario Railway		$ 1,072,800.00
Municipal Governments		
City of Port Arthur	$ 50,000.00	
Town of Parry Sound	20,000.00	
Town of Trenton	14,000.00	
Total municipal subsidies		$ 84,000.00
Total		$28,000,222.50

Source: CNR Records, Vol. 2194. Written reply, 30 June 1916, by Canadian Northern officials to series of questions from the Royal Commission on Railways and Transportation. The amounts shown were the subsidies actually collected up to 30 June 1916 by the several railways during the time that they were controlled by Mackenzie and Mann. All subsidies, as well as bond guarantees, had to be earned through the construction of specified lines. There is, consequently, a great difference between the amounts authorized by legislation and the amounts actually earned by the companies and paid by the governments. The above figures show only the amounts earned. They do not, however, include subsidies earned by any predecessor companies before they were taken over by Mackenzie and Mann.

APPENDIX IV

Canadian Northern Railway System Construction Data*

Year	Nova Scotia	Quebec	Ontario	Manitoba	Saskatchewan	Alberta	British Columbia	Minnesota	Total
1896				84.8					84.8
1897				126.0					126.0
1898				161.0					161.0
1899				290.0					290.0
1900				345.0	22.2				367.2
1901			55.4	491.7	22.2			43.7	613.0
1902			353.7	823.9	22.2			43.7	1243.5
1903			353.7	856.8	22.2			43.7	1276.4
1904			353.7	930.0	22.2			43.7	1349.6
1905			353.7	1180.5	298.5			43.7	1876.4
1906			353.7	1312.4	602.6	169.8		43.7	2482.2
1907			353.7	1427.2	600.6	214.2		43.7	2639.4
1908			353.7	1427.2	856.1	214.2		43.7	2894.9
1909			353.7	1522.1	1006.4	214.2		43.7	3140.1
1910			353.7	1530.9	1182.5	214.2		43.7	3325.0
1911			356.6	1752.3	1312.9	221.4		44.5	3687.7
1912			356.6	1758.3	1718.8	394.8		43.7	4272.2

Year									
1913			356.6	1833.8	1851.6	467.2		43.7	4552.9
1914	380.8		342.1	1836.7	2052.2	691.2		43.7	4965.9
1915	369.9	626.8	1480.7	1983.5	2111.9	962.2		215.4	7761.3
1916	369.9	626.8	2219.1	1989.1	2178.1	1181.2	516.4	215.4	9296.0
1917	370.5	636.6	2253.3	1984.4	2194.3	1244.6	531.9	217.8	9433.4

* Note: Figures used are given by D. B. Hanna in the arbitration proceedings, and in the Canadian Northern Railway's annual reports after 1903. They vary somewhat in different sources, the main reason being a dispute about the date when new mileage should be officially added to the list. These figures relate to mileage actually operated on the date annual records were closed each year. Some of this mileage may not have been officially approved by the Department of Railways and Canals until the following year. Where reductions in mileage occur, these are usually due to local improvements which eliminate curves and thus reduce mileage somewhat. There is also some difference in calculating sidings into these figures. Thus, while there may be minor variations, the above figures are those used officially in Canadian Northern reports. For a more detailed and, in some minor respects, differing statement see Canadian National Railways Tabulated History of Railway Mileage, 1836 to 1925.

It should also be kept in mind that all the above figures relate to official Canadian Northern System mileage. Some of the above mileages were built earlier than indicated, but were not formally a part of the Canadian Northern Railway System. The most notable examples of this are the lines in the east, many of which were controlled for several years by Mackenzie and Mann but were not properly a part of the Canadian Northern Railway.

APPENDIX V

Canadian Northern Railway System
Condensed General Balance Sheet
At 30th June, 1917.

Assets

PROPERTY INVESTMENT — Railway and equipment at cost to the system, including discount on Securities of constituent and subsidiary companies and acquired securities per statement on pages nos. 18 and 19		$506,960,975.01
OTHER INVESTMENTS (at cost)		2,753,780.19
NATIONAL TRUST COMPANY CERTIFICATES		
Re land grant bonds, Issue 1899. These securities held as collateral to loans		1,657,500.00
TERMINAL AND OTHER PROPERTIES		6,102,379.67
LAND ASSETS		
Deferred payments and accrued interest on sales	$ 6,728,160.49	
Cash with National Trust Company account of land sales	2,320,274.39	
Lands unsold	19,914,060.00	
		28,962,494.88
CURRENT ASSETS		
Cash held on account of—		
Dominion Government	2,470.049.27	
Province of Manitoba	45,920.63	
Province of Saskatchewan	1,202,825.24	
Province of Alberta	2,691,130.52	
Province of Ontario	419,803.94	
Province of British Columbia	4,404,501.23	
Central Trust Company of New York	141,308.13	
National Trust Company	489,333.42	
British Empire Trust Company, Trustees Account	1,696,152.09	
Sinking Fund	76,765.07	
	13,637,789.54	

Value of material and supplies on hand (book figures)	3,694,856.81	
Due from agents, station balances, etc.	2,008,428.00	
Miscellaneous accounts receivable	7,090,284.44	
British Admiralty	664,070.84	
Cash on hand	2,990,294.46	
		30,085,724.09
INSURANCE paid in advance		415,121.19
ADVANCES by the Canadian Northern Railway Company to affiliated companies		9,320,714.15
DEFERRED CHARGES — UNADJUSTED DEBITS — BALANCE		362,961.47
		$586,621,650.65

Liabilities

CAPITAL STOCK—Common		$100,000,000.00
CAPITAL STOCK—Affiliated Companies	$75,429,500.00	
Less: Held in Treasury	69,482,400.00	
		5,947,100.00
FIVE PER CENT INCOME CHARGE CONVERTIBLE DEBENTURE STOCK		25,000,000.00
FUNDED DEBT Canadian Northern Railway Schedule "A"	162,366,542.20	
Affiliated companies Schedule "B"	125,228,878.41	
		287,595,420.61
EQUIPMENT TRUST OBLIGATIONS		14,846,500.00
DEMAND AND SHORT-TERM LOANS SECURED BY COLLATERAL		56,829,769.51
DUE TO OTHER COMPANIES ON CONSTRUCTION ACCOUNT (Secured)		24,341,882.25
CURRENT LIABILITIES Pay rolls	1,996,062.19	
Audited vouchers and other floating liabilities	13,786,946.12	
		15,783,008.31

COUPON AND DIVIDEND WARRANTS DUE ON 1ST JULY (Since paid)	2,275,855.87	
ACCRUED INTEREST ON BONDS, LOANS AND EQUIPMENT SECURITIES		
Operating $2,396,839.80		
Construction 407,024.09	2,803,863.89	
		5,079,719.76
RESERVES		
Steamship replacement fund	2,050,033.20	
Equipment replacement fund	1,416,756.51	
Insurance account	638,800.27	
Taxes accrued	450,000.00	
		4,555,589.98
		9,320,714.15
AFFILIATED COMPANIES—Advances Account Surplus		
Land account	37,195,355.42	
Railway account	126,590.66	
		37,321,946.08
		$586,621,650.65

D. B. Hanna,
Third Vice-President

Auditor's Certificate.
We have examined the books and records of the Canadian Northern Railway System for the year ending 30th June, 1917, and we certify that, in our opinion, the above Balance Sheet is properly drawn up so as to exhibit a true and correct view of the affairs of the System at that date, as shown by the books and in accordance with the explanations and information given us.

WEBB, READ, HEGAN, CALLINGHAM & CO.,
Toronto, December 7th, 1917 Chartered Accountants

Source: Third Annual Report of the Board of Directors of The Canadian Northern Railway System for the Year ended 30th June, 1917.

Canadian Northern Railway System:
Acquired Securities as of 30th June, 1917

THE MINNESOTA & ONTARIO BRIDGE
    COMPANY
    4½% 1st mortgage debenture bonds $ 180,000.00
    Capital stock   100,000.00
THE MINNESOTA & MANITOBA R.R.
    5% General mortgage bonds   250,000.00
    Capital stock   400,000.00
THE LAKE SUPERIOR TERMINALS
    COMPANY, LIMITED
    5% Mortgage gold bonds   2,000,000.00
    Capital stock   500,000.00
THE CANADIAN NORTHERN TELEGRAPH
    COMPANY
    5% General mortgage bonds   2,000,000.00
    Capital stock   500,000.00
THE WINNIPEG LAND COMPANY,
    LIMITED
    5% First mortgage gold bonds   300,000.00
    Capital stock   100,000.00
THE ST. BONIFACE & WESTERN LAND
    COMPANY
    5% First mortgage bonds   750,000.00
    Capital stock   250,000.00
THE EDMONTON & SLAVE LAKE
    RAILWAY COMPANY
    5% First mortgage bonds   420,000.00
THE CANADIAN NORTHERN RAILWAY
    EXPRESS COMPANY, LIMITED
    4% First mortgage gold bonds,
      £616,438   3,000,000.00
    Capital stock   1,000,000.00
THE CANADIAN NORTHERN STEAMSHIPS,
    LIMITED
    5% First mortgage debenture stock,
      Sterling £600,000   2,920,000.00
    Capital stock   2,000,000.00
THE CANADIAN NORTHERN SYSTEM
    TERMINALS, LIMITED
    5% First mortgage debenture stock
      and bonds   7,000,000.00
    Capital stock   2,000,000.00
THE BAY OF QUINTE RAILWAY COMPANY
    Capital stock   1,395,000.00

THE CENTRAL ONTARIO RAILWAY
    COMPANY
  Capital stock   3,329,000.00
THE BROCKVILLE WESTPORT & NORTH
    WESTERN RAILWAY COMPANY
THE IRONDALE, BANCROFT & OTTAWA
    RAILWAY COMPANY
  5% First mortgage bonds   450,000.00
  Capital stock   53,000.00
THE MARMORA RAILWAY & MINING
    COMPANY
  Bonds   100,000.00
  Capital stock   100,000.00
THE QU'APPELLE, LONG LAKE & SASK. RY.
    & STEAMBOAT COMPANY
  Capital stock   201,000.00
THE NIAGARA, ST. CATHARINES &
    TORONTO RAILWAY COMPANY
  Capital stock   922,000.00
THE NIAGARA, ST. CATHARINES & TORONTO
    NAVIGATION COMPANY
  First mortgage bonds   200,000.00
THE QUEBEC & LAKE ST. JOHN RAILWAY
    COMPANY
  Capital stock   4,002,800.00
THE CANADIAN NORTHERN PACIFIC
    RAILWAY COMPANY
  Capital stock   25,000,000.00
THE CANADIAN NORTHERN ALBERTA
    RAILWAY COMPANY
  Capital stock   3,000,000.00
THE CANADIAN NORTHERN WESTERN
    RAILWAY COMPANY
  Capital stock   2,000,000.00
THE CANADIAN NORTHERN SASKATCHEWAN
    RAILWAY COMPANY
  Capital stock   1,000,000.00
THE CANADIAN NORTHERN MANITOBA
    RAILWAY COMPANY
  Capital stock   250,000.00
THE CANADIAN NORTHERN ONTARIO
    RAILWAY COMPANY
  Capital stock   10,000,000.00
THE DULUTH, WINNIPEG & PACIFIC
    RAILWAY COMPANY
  Capital stock   3,060,000.00

THE MOUNT ROYAL TUNNEL & TERMINAL
    COMPANY, LIMITED
    Capital stock   5,000,000.00

THE NORTHERN CONSOLIDATED HOLDING
    COMPANY, LIMITED
    Capital stock   4,446,700.00
        Represented by Canadian North-
            ern Quebec Railway Com-
            pany capital stock amount-
            ing to $5,144,600.00

THE CANADIAN NORTHERN QUEBEC
    RAILWAY COMPANY
    Capital stock   2,000,000.00

THE HALIFAX & SOUTH WESTERN
    RAILWAY COMPANY
    Capital stock   925,000.00

THE BESSEMER & BARRY'S BAY
    RAILWAY COMPANY
    Capital stock   125,000.00
                                      $93,229,500.00
Cost to the railway company $46,372,891.71

All these figures give the par value of the securities listed, not their market value.

Source: Third Annual Report of the Board of Directors of The Canadian Northern Railway System for the Year ended 30th June, 1917.

BIBLIOGRAPHY

Note: All the primary sources used in this study are merely listed here. A more detailed description of each collection and its relevance to this study is available at the University of Saskatchewan Archives, together with an early and much more extensively footnoted draft of the manuscript.

CANADIAN NATIONAL RAILWAYS RECORDS

1. Canadian Northern Railway Company Records, together with records of affiliated companies (PAC, RG 30)
2. Records of the Canadian Northern Board of Arbitration (PAC, RG 30, Vols. 2187, 2194–2203; RG 33, No. 74; and *Sessional Paper No. 195, 9–10 Geo. V*)
3. Tabulated and Synoptical Histories of Canadian National Railways (PAC, RG 30)
4. Tabulated History of Railway Mileage, 1836–1925 (PAC, RG 30; CNRHQ)
5. The Canadian Northern Railway Encyclopedia (PAC and CNRHQ)
6. Annual Reports of the Canadian Northern Railway and the Canadian Northern Railway System (PAC, CNRHQ, DOT)
7. Research notes and transcripts of interviews, compiled by Col. G. R. Stevens and his staff (CNRHQ)

OFFICIAL RECORDS & MANUSCRIPT MATERIALS FROM OTHER RAILWAYS

1. Northern Pacific Railroad Records (MHS)
2. Henry Villard Papers (Baker Library, Harvard Business School)
3. Van Horne Letterbooks (PAC)
4. Shaughnessy Letterbooks (PAC)

FEDERAL GOVERNMENT RECORDS

1. Records of Parliament, Senate and House of Commons (PAC, RG 14)
2. Privy Council Records (PAC, RG 2)
3. Records of the Board of Railway Commissioners (PAC, RG 46)
4. Records of the Department of Railways and Canals (PAC, RG 43)

5. Records of the Department of the Interior, Dominion Lands Branch (PAC, RG 15)
6. Records of the Department of the Interior, Superintendent of Immigration (PAC, RG 76)
7. Records of the Department of the Interior, Superintendent of Indian Affairs (PAC, RG 10)
8. Records of the Royal Canadian Mounted Police (PAC, RG 18)
9. Records of the Department of Labour (PAC, RG 27)
10. Records of the Department of Finance (PAC, RG 19)
11. Records of the Department of Fisheries and Marine (PAC, RG 23)
12. Records of federal Royal Commissions (PAC, RG 33)

    RG 33, 3,   Royal Commission on Transportation of Canadian Products through Canadian Ports, 1903–5

    RG 33, 4,   Royal Commission on Life Insurance, 1906–7

    RG 33, 5,   Royal Grain Commission, 1906–8

    RG 33, 12, Royal Commission on Railways and Transportation, 1916–17

    RG 33, 16, Royal Commission on Transportation, 1931–2

    RG 33, 23, Royal Commission on Dominion–Provincial Relations, 1937–9

    RG 33, 27, Royal Commission on Transportation, 1948–51

    RG 33, 49, Royal Commission on Transportation, 1959–62

PROVINCIAL GOVERNMENT RECORDS

Seven of the nine provincial governments successfully negotiated contracts and agreements with the Canadian Northern Railway or with Mackenzie and Mann. The archival resources in the seven provincial capitals vary considerably, but in each case the provincial orders-in-council, together with supporting documents, were very informative. In most cases these orders-in-council were still in the custody of the provincial executive council but I was generally given access to these records or provided with copies of relevant orders-in-council.

The provincial departments responsible for railways or transportation and provincial finance departments usually had extensive and relevant records, and in several cases the records of the premier's office had much useful information.

PRIVATE PAPERS

Prime Ministers

1. Bennett Papers (PAC, MG 26 K)
2. Borden Papers (PAC, MG 26 H)
3. Laurier Papers (PAC, MG 26 G)
4. Macdonald Papers (PAC, MG 26 A)
5. Meighen Papers (PAC, MG 26 I)

Provincial premiers

1. Fielding Papers (PANS)
2. Gouin Papers (PAC, MG 27, III, B-4)
3. Greenway Papers (PAM)
4. McBride Papers (PABC)
5. Ross Papers (PAO)
6. Rutherford Papers (UAA)
7. Scott Papers (PAS)
8. Taschereau Papers (PAQ)
9. Whitney Papers (PAO)

Cabinet ministers and other politicians

1. Brewin Papers (PAC, MG 27, II, H-1)
2. Choquette Papers (PAC, MG 27, II, E-3A)
3. Dafoe Papers (PAC, MG 30, D-17)
4. Fitzpatrick Papers (PAC, MG 27, II, E-1)
5. Foster Papers (PAC, MG 27, II, D-7)
6. George Graham Papers (PAC, MG 27, II, D-8)
7. Grey of Howick Papers (PAC, MG 27, II, B-2)
8. Minto Papers (PAC, MG 27, II, B-1)
9. Motherwell Papers (PAS)
10. Schultz Papers (PAM)
11. Sifton Papers (PAC, MG 27, II, D-15)
12. H. H. Smith Papers (PAC, MG 27, I, 1–19)
13. White Papers (PAC, MG 27, II, D-18)

Businessmen

1. Armstrong Memoirs (PAC, MG 30, A-1)
2. Dunn Papers (PAC, MG 30)
3. Flavelle Papers (PAC, MG 30, B-4, and QUA)

4. Hays Papers (PAC, MG 30, A-4)
5. W. L. Mackenzie Diary (PAC, MG 30)
6. Morgan Papers (PAC, MG 29, G-27)
7. Nordegg Papers (PAC, MG 30, B-10)
8. Pearce Manuscript (APC)
9. Porteous Papers (PAC, MG 29, B-24)
10. Marcus Smith Papers (PAC, MG 29, A-19)
11. Stephen Papers (PAC, MG 29, A-20)
12. Walker Papers (UTA)

NEWSPAPERS

1. *Edmonton Daily Bulletin*
2. *Financial Post*
3. *Kamloops Sentinel*
4. *Manitoba Free Press*
5. Montreal *Gazette*
6. *Montreal Star*
7. Toronto *Globe*
8. *Vancouver Daily Province*
9. Victoria *Daily Colonist*
10. *Winnipeg Telegram*
11. *Winnipeg Tribune*

RAILWAY PUBLICATIONS

1. *Canadian National Railways Magazine* (Montreal); also appeared as *Canadian Government Railways Employees Magazine* (1915–19), and *Canadian National Railways Employees Magazine* (1919–21)
2. *Canadian Rail* (Montreal)
3. *Canadian Railway and Marine World* (Toronto); also appeared as *Railway and Shipping World* (1898–1905), *Railway and Marine World* (1906–12), and *Canadian Transportation* (1937–68)
4. *Poor's Manual of Railroads* (New York)
5. *Railroad Gazette* (Chicago); amalgamated with *Railway Age* and appearing under several titles
6. *Railway Age* (New York); amalgamated with the *Railroad Ga-*

zette and appearing also under the title of *Railway Age Gazette,* and *Railroad Gazette*
7. *Railway and Locomotive Historical Society Bulletin* (Boston)
8. *Railway Gazette* (London)
9. *Railway Times* (London)

INTERVIEWS AND CORRESPONDENCE

1. R. F. B. Barr, Toronto lawyer who handled business of Mackenzie, Mann and Co. Ltd.
2. Anthony Griffin, Toronto financier and grandson of Sir William Mackenzie
3. Norman Robertson, Under-Secretary of State for External Affairs and acquaintance of the family of Sir Donald Mann
4. Col. G. R. Stevens, historian of Canadian National Railways

UNPUBLISHED THESES

Archer, J. H. "History of Saskatoon." MA thesis, University of Saskatchewan, 1948

Bocking, D. H. "Premier Walter Scott: A Study of His Rise to Political Power." MA thesis, University of Saskatchewan, 1959

Christenson, R. A. "The Calgary and Edmonton Railway and the *Edmonton Bulletin*." MA thesis, University of Alberta, 1967

Eagle, J. A. "Sir Robert Borden and the Railway Problem in Canadian Politics, 1911–1920." PHD thesis, University of Toronto, 1972

Ellis, Robert J. "Relationships of Mackenzie and Mann with the Laurier Government." MA thesis, University of Western Ontario, 1965

Finch, Martin H. J. "W. W. Rostow's Theory of Economic Growth: A Canadian Case-Study." MA thesis, McMaster University, 1965

Hall, Carl A. S. "Electrical Utilities in Ontario under Private Ownership, 1890–1914." PHD thesis, University of Toronto, 1968

Hampton, Peter. "Foreign Investment and the Theory of Economic Growth Examined Within the Framework of Economic Development." PHD thesis, University of Ottawa, 1963

Holmes, J. L. "Factors Affecting Politics in Manitoba: A Study of the Provincial Elections, 1870–1899." MA thesis, University of Manitoba, 1939

Humphries, Charles W. "The Political Career of Sir James P. Whitney." PHD thesis, University of Toronto, 1966

Hunt, Peter R. "The Political Career of Sir Richard McBride." MA thesis, University of British Columbia, 1939

Jackson, J. A. "Disallowance of Manitoba Railway Legislation in the 1880's: Railway Policy as a Factor in the Relations of Manitoba with the Dominion." MA thesis, University of Manitoba, 1945

Lai, Hermia Kwak-Yu. "Evolution of the Railway Network of Edmonton and Its Land Use Effects." MA thesis, University of Alberta, 1967

Lalonde, André. "Settlement in the North-West Territories by Colonization Companies, 1881–1891." PHD thesis, Laval University, 1971

Lower, J. A. "The Grand Trunk Pacific and British Columbia." MA thesis, University of British Columbia, 1939

MacBeth, M. E. "Life and Work of the Honourable John Norquay." MA thesis, University of Manitoba, 1925

Nelles, H. V. "The Politics of Development: Forests, Mines and Hydro-Electric Power in Ontario, 1890–1939." PHD thesis, University of Toronto, 1969

Otter, Andy den. "A Social History of the Alberta Coal Branch." MA thesis, University of Alberta, 1967

Owen, Leonard Anderson. "Sir Adam Beck and the Hydro-Electric Radial Railway." MA thesis, University of Western Ontario, 1967

Regehr, T. D. "The National Policy and Manitoba Railway Legislation, 1879–1888." MA thesis, Carleton University, 1963

———. "The Canadian Northern Railway: Agent of National Growth, 1896–1911." PHD thesis, University of Alberta, 1967

Roy, Patricia. "Railways, Politicians, and the Development of Vancouver as a Metropolitan Centre, 1886–1929." MA thesis, University of Toronto, 1963

———. "The British Columbia Electric Company, 1897–1961." PHD thesis, University of British Columbia, 1970

Smith, Brian R. D. "Sir Richard McBride: A Study in the Conservative Party of British Columbia, 1903–1916." MA thesis, University of British Columbia, 1959

Stevens, P. D. "Laurier and the Liberal Party in Ontario, 1887–1911." PHD thesis, University of Toronto, 1966

Tennyson, Brian Douglas. "The Political Career of Sir William H. Hearst." MA thesis, University of Toronto, 1963

Turner, Allan R. "W. R. Motherwell and Agricultural Development in Saskatchewan, 1905–1918." MA thesis, University of Saskatchewan, 1958

PAMPHLETS

Wherever possible the PAC catalogue number, as prepared by Magdalen Casey, is given. Many of these pamphlets are also available at CNRHQ. The pamphlets not available in the PAC pamphlet collection are listed first, in chronological order, followed by the PAC pamphlets, also in chronological order.

The Manitoba and North West Farmers Union. *Resolutions adopted at the farmers' convention held in the City of Winnipeg, 19th and 20th December 1883.* Published in Winnipeg in 1883. Macdonald Papers

Canada. *Report of the Railway Rates Commission, 7 May 1895.* Published as Sessional Paper No. 39, 1895. Copy at PAC

Great Northern Railway. *Prospectus of the Great Northern Railway of Canada, 1896.* Quebec: *Morning Chronicle,* 1896. Copy in CNR Legal Series

Shaughnessy, T. G. *Memorandum. Railway Policy of Manitoba.* Printed privately. Copy at PAC

Canadian Northern Railway, A Builder of Canada. London, 1908. Copy at CNRHQ

George A. Touche and Company. *Quebec and Lake St. John Railway. Report to the Bondholders Protection Committee, 26 April 1910.* Printed privately. Copy in CNR Legal Series

Adams, Joseph. *Ten thousand miles through Canada; the natural resources, commercial industries, fish and game, sports and pastimes of the great Dominion.* London: Methuen, 1912. Copy at CNRHQ

The Mount Royal Tunnel, Montreal, Quebec, Canada, being built by Mackenzie, Mann and Company Limited. Printed privately, December 1913. Copy at CNRHQ

The relations of the Canadian Northern Railway to the economic progress of Canada and Government assistance. n.p. March 1914. Copy at CNRHQ

Canadian Liberal Party. *Railway Question in Canada.* Ottawa, 1915. Copy at CNRHQ

Dullin, Frank T. *The Royal Road to Fortune as viewed from the Canadian Northern System.* University of Western Ontario pamphlet

Glossary of Canadian and American Statutory Laws affecting the Canadian Northern Railway Company including companies absorbed in or controlled by the Canadian Northern Railway Company. Typescript, 1916. Copy at CNRHQ

Royal Commission to Inquire into Railways and Transportation in Canada, 1917. *Proceedings at the Grand Trunk Railway Offices, Montreal, February 23 and 24 1917 before H. L. Drayton and W. M. Acworth.* Typescript copy at CNRHQ

Tait, Sir Thomas. *A Solution of the Canadian Railway Problem, 1917.* n.p. Copy at CNRHQ

Willison, Sir John. *The Railway Question in Canada; a speech delivered before the Canadian Club of Montreal, 31 January 1921.* n.p. Copy at CNRHQ

Canadian National Railways. *Canada's National Railways—their part in the war.* Toronto: CNR, 1921. Copy at CNRHQ

Scott, James Guthrie. *The origin and growth of the Railway system of the Province of Quebec. An address delivered to the Kiwanis Club of Quebec at the Château Frontenac on 17 December 1926.* n.p. Copy at CNRHQ

Gibbon, J. *Some Thoughts on our railway problem. An address by J. J. Gibbon delivered at the annual convention of the Canadian Chamber of Commerce, Vancouver, September 9, 1937.* Vancouver, 1937. Copy at CNRHQ

Dillabough, J. *Transportation in Manitoba.* Winnipeg: Manitoba Economic Board, 1938. Copy at CNRHQ

Companies comprising the Canadian Northern Railway System, portion of capital stock owned, description of property, date of incorporation and date acquired. Montreal, n.d. Copy at CNRHQ

Brown, Revelle Wilson. *Rails and Ideals—in U.S.A. and Canada; the railways of North America—their contribution to national economies. Newcommen Address at Toronto, October 6, 1949.* Copy at CNRHQ

Scott, W. G. *Mining and the Railways—Industrial Partners; an ad-*

dress to the 1956 annual general meeting, Canadian Institute of Mining and Metallurgy. Quebec, April 1956. Copy at CNRHQ

Coleman, J. T. *The History of Canadian National Railways in British Columbia.* Vancouver, 1957. Copy at CNRHQ

Charles, J. L. *Railways in Relation to the Development of Canada's Northlands.* Winnipeg: CNR, 1957. Copy at CNRHQ

Canadian National Railways. *A Brief History of the Canadian National Railways with a Selected Bibliography on Railways, Railway Economics and Railway People.* Montreal: CNR, 1959. Copy at CNRHQ

Canadian National Railways. *Digests of Royal Commissions dealing on Transportation since 1888 excepting Turgeon Commission 1950-1.* Montreal: CNR Public Relations Department, 1959

Mills, John M. *History of the Niagara, St. Catharines and Toronto Railway.* Toronto, 1967. Copy at CNRHQ

Canadian National Railways. *Brief History of the Canadian National Railways in B.C.* Vancouver: CNR Public Relations Department, 1968

Harvey, R. D. *A History of Saanich Peninsula Railways.* Victoria: Queen's Printer, 1960. Copy at CNRHQ

Clegg, Anthony. *The Mount Royal Tunnel, Canada's First Subway.* Montreal: Trains and Trolleys Book Club, 1963. Copy at CNRHQ

Harrison, Frederick G. *Cinders and Timber; a bird's eye view of logging railroads in Northeastern Minnesota Yesterday and Today.* n.p., 1967. Copy at CNRHQ

Corley, R. F. *The Edmonton, Yukon and Pacific Railway; a researched history.* Peterborough, 1971. Typescript copy at CNRHQ

Salmon, James J. *Rails from the Junction; the story of the Toronto Suburban Railway.* n.p. Lyons Productions, n.d. Copy at CNRHQ

592. Province of Manitoba. *Its Position in Confederation. Speech on Budget Debate, by Mr. Greenway, M.P.P., Leader of the Opposition in the Local Legislature, on April 23rd, 1884*

639. *Open Letter on the Agitation in Manitoba from Chas. R. Tuttle, Esq., to Joseph Mulholland, Esq., of Winnipeg.* 1884

902. The Canadian Pacific Railway. *Manitoba, the Canadian North-West. What the Actual Settlers Say.* 1886

1058. *Circular Letter to the Directors of the Canadian Pacific Rail-*

way Company from the Vice-President W. C. Van Horne. 6 September 1887

1059. *Circular Letter to the Shareholders of the Canadian Pacific Railway Company from the President George Stephen.* 1 September 1887.

1060. *An Open Letter to the Shareholders of the Canadian Pacific Railway Co. Being an answer to the circular letter of Sir George Stephen, President of the Company, addressed to the Shareholders, on the subject of the Disallowance, by the Dominion Government, of Railway Charters granted by the Legislature of Manitoba.* 1 October 1887. Issued by the authority of the Winnipeg Board of Trade and the Brandon Board of Trade

1068. *Railway Monopoly: Letters addressed to the "Toronto Mail", by F. Beverley Robinson, and The Effects of Monopoly, from the "Manitoba Sun", now published by the Conservative Anti-Disallowance Association.* Winnipeg: Manitoba Sun Printing and Publishing Company, 1887

1075. *Plain Facts Regarding the Disallowance of Manitoba Railway Charters*

1076. *Disallowance of Manitoba Railway Charters by Canadian Manufacturers.* 1887

1077. *Manitoba Anti-Disallowance Association.* Winnipeg, 24 September 1887

1194. *Report of an Argument before the Supreme Court submitted by the Railway Committee of the Privy Council arising on an Application of the Hon. Joseph Martin, Railway Commissioner of Manitoba. Reported by Holland Brothers, Senate Reporters, Ottawa.* Ottawa: Printed by A. D. Woodburn, Elgin St., 1888

1822. *For Canada Transportation The Problem. By A Grain Dealer.* Montreal: W. Foster Brown & Co., 1893

1977. *Report of the Railway Rates Commission, 7th May 1895. Printed by Order of Parliament.* Ottawa: Printed by S. E. Dawson, Printer to the Queen's Most Excellent Majesty, 1895

2112. *Prospectus of the Great Northern Railway (of Canada).* Quebec: Printed at the *Morning Chronicle* Office, 1896

2268. *The Railway Question in Canada with an examination of the*

Railway Law in Iowa, by J. S. Willison. Toronto: Warwick Bros. & Rutter, 1897

2645. *Hon. John Taggart on Transportation.* 18 April 1901

2648. *Railway Policy of Manitoba. T. G. Shaughnessy, President.* 1901

2728. *The Trans-Canada Ry.* 1902

2750. *Reports Upon Railway Commissions, Railway Rate Grievances and Regulative Legislation by Professor S. J. McLean,* PH.D., M.A. Ottawa: Printed by S. E. Dawson, Printer to the King's Most Excellent Majesty, 1902

2852. *The New Canadian Trans-Continental Railway. Views of Sir Sandford Fleming, formerly Engineer in Chief of the Intercolonial and the Canadian Pacific Railways, submitted to the Council of the Quebec Board of Trade, October 6th, 1903*

2853. [A. E. Doucet, Chief Engineer] *Trans-Canada Railway. Engineer's Report of the Physical Features of the Line and of the Resources of the Territory tributary to the Railway*

2854. *Paper on the Trans-Canada Railway read before the Literary and Historical Society of Quebec by Mr. J. G. Scott, General Manager of the Quebec and Lake St. John Railway and of the Great Northern Railway of Canada, Tuesday, 13th January, 1903. Together with Extracts from some remarks made by Mr. Henry O'Sullivan,* C.E., *Fellow of the Royal Geographical Society of London, on the same occasion.* Quebec: Chronicle Printing Co., 1903

2855. *National Transcontinental Railway. Resources of the Country between Quebec and Winnipeg, along the line of the Grand Trunk Pacific Railway (with map), compiled from authentic sources by H. M. Ami, of the Geological Survey Department, Ottawa. Printed by Order of Parliament.* Ottawa: Printed by S. E. Dawson, Printer to the King's Most Excellent Majesty, 1903

2856. *Railway Reconnaissance. By Wm. B. Mackenzie, Chief Engineer Intercolonial Railway.* 1903

2857. *Transcontinental Railway. House of Commons Debates. Speech of Right Hon. Sir Wilfrid Laurier,* P.C., G.C.M.G., *on the Transcontinental Railway. A Link uniting the Provinces on Canadian*

Soil Transportation to the markets of the world. Thursday, July 30, 1903. Ottawa: Government Printing Bureau, 1903

2858. *Transcontinental Railway. House of Commons Debates. Speech of S. E. Gourley,* K.C., M.P., *on the Transcontinental Railway and the Trade Routes of Canada, Tuesday, September 1st, 1903.* Ottawa: Free Press Print, 1903

2859. *Hon. A. G. Blair, Minister of Railways and Canals Resigns and Condemns the Government's Railway Policy.* 1903

2860. *The Grand Trunk Pacific, Canada's New Transcontinental Railway*

2945. *Address by B. E. Walker, Esq., to the Canadian Club, Ottawa, February 4th, 1904*

2955. *The Railway Question. Government Ownership and Operation. Mr. Borden's Policy Considered*

2966. *The National Transcontinental Railway Project. Speeches delivered by Mr. R. L. Borden,* K.C., M.P., *in 1903 and 1904. With Introduction. Shall We Have "A Government Owned Railway, or, a Railway Owned Government?" "If the People Undertake Nine-tenths of the Obligations, Why Not the Whole, and Own the Railway?"*

3084. Lawrence J. Burpee. *How Canada is Solving Her Transportation Problem.* Ottawa, Canada. Reprinted from *The Popular Science Monthly*, September 1905

3105. *Niagara's Power, Past, Present, Prospective. Address to the Members of the Empire Club, 19th January, 1905, given by Mr. Frederic Nicholls*

3327. *Canadian Credit and Enterprise. Address of B. E. Walker, President, The Canadian Bank of Commerce, delivered on 6th March, 1908, before the Canadian Club of Halifax, N.S.*

3371. *Insurance Investigation. Hon. A. B. Aylesworth, Minister of Justice, in Reviewing Ex-Minister Foster's Defence, brings out several points in the Insurance Investigation Report* (from Hansard, 10 April 1907). 1908

3427. *A Mile A Day For Eleven Years. Canadian Northern. How a country within a country has been opened up by a railway that has grown from nothing in 1896, to be the second system in Canada. The Canadian Northern. To the business-like public of the*

United Kingdom, at the Franco-British Exhibition in the Summer of 1908. The London Offices: Bond Court, Walbrook, E.C.

3428. *The National Transcontinental Railway. Statement of "Cost to Canada" as presented by Opposition Leader reviewed by Mr. Fielding. Canada will have the best Transcontinental road ever built in America. Cheap transportation secured by a well constructed road. What is the real burden on the people of Canada? Cost to the people small in comparison with what was paid for the Canadian Pacific. Speech of Hon. W. S. Fielding, Minister of Finance, in the House of Commons, Ottawa, July 11th, 1908*

3731. *The Burden of Railway Rates. Freight and express charges levied upon the people of Western Canada unjustifiably higher than those in Eastern Canada and in the adjoining States.* Pamphlet No. 2. Compiled from articles published in the *Manitoba Free Press*, Winnipeg, July–November, 1911

3740. *The Burden of Railway Rates. Freight and express charges levied upon the people of Western Canada unjustifiably higher than those in Eastern Canada and in the adjoining States.* Pamphlet No. 1. Compiled from articles published in the *Manitoba Free Press*, Winnipeg, April–June, 1911

3768. *Address of Sir Edmund Walker, C.V.O., President of the Canadian Bank of Commerce, delivered at the Annual Dinner of the Canadian Manufacturers' Association, in Montreal on the 19th January, 1911*

3912. *Address of Sir Edmund Walker, C.V.O., President of the Canadian Bank of Commerce. Delivered at the Eighth Annual Banquet of the Canadian Club of New York, on the 12th November, 1912*

3933. F. B. McCurdy, MP, Shelburne-Queens. *The National Transcontinental Railway's Prospective Atlantic Ports.* 1912

3937. *Premier McBride's Speech on the Government's Railway Policy.* 1912

4033. *Ocean Freight Rates. Report by H. L. Drayton, K.C., Chief Commissioner, The Board of Railway Commissioners for Canada.* Ottawa: Government Printing Bureau, 1913

4410. Clarus Ager. *The Farmer and the Interests. A Study in Economic Parasitism.* Toronto: Macmillan of Canada, 1916

4496. *A Solution of the Canadian Railway Problem. Suggested by Sir Thomas Tait.* Montreal, April 1917

4516. *Canada's Railway Problem and its Solution by W. F. Tye, M. Can. Soc. C.E. Read at a Monthly Meeting of the Society, January 18th, 1917.* The Canadian Society of Civil Engineers Press

4584. *Government Ownership v. Private Ownership of Railways in Canada.* Reprinted for private circulation from the *Journal of Political Economy*, vol. 25, no. 2 (February 1917)

5056. *The Canadian National Railway System. Letter addressed to the Rt. Hon. Arthur Meighen, Prime Minister of Canada, by Sir Joseph Flavelle, Bart. August 12, 1921*

5080. *Dominion Elections, 1921.* The National Liberal and Conservative Party Publicity Pamphlets.

No. 29 *Transcontinentals without Cost*

No. 34 *Laurier's Admiration for Mackenzie and Mann*

No. 35 *The Government and the Railways*

5081. *Election Pamplets*

No. 23 *The Railway Situation of 1921* (issued October 1921)

BOOKS

Acworth, W. H. *The Elements of Railway Economics.* Oxford: Clarendon, 1905

————. *The Railways of England.* London: John Murray, 1889

Adler, Dorothy C. *British Investment in American Railways, 1834–1898.* Charlottesville: University of Virginia Press, 1970

Bank of Nova Scotia. *The Canadian Primary Iron and Steel Industry.* Ottawa: Queen's Printer, 1956

Barr, John, and Anderson, Owen, eds. *The Unfinished Revolt: Some Views on Western Independence.* Toronto: McClelland & Stewart, 1971

Bates, Stewart. *Financial History of Canadian Governments: A Study Prepared for the Royal Commission on Dominion–Provincial Relations.* Ottawa: King's Printer, 1939

Berghaus, Erwin. *The History of Railways.* London: Barrie and Rockcliffe, 1964

Berton, Pierre. *The Last Spike: The Great Railway, 1881–1885.* Toronto: McClelland & Stewart, 1971

————. *The National Dream: The Great Railway, 1871–1881.* Toronto: McClelland & Stewart, 1969

Biggar, E. B. *The Canadian Railway Problem.* Toronto: Macmillan, 1917

————. *Hydro-electric Development in Ontario.* Toronto: Ryerson, 1920

Boam, Henry J., comp. *Twentieth Century Impressions of Canada: Its History, People, Commerce, Industries, and Resources.* London: Sells Ltd., 1914

Bone, P. Turner. *When the Steel Went Through: Reminiscences of a Railroad Pioneer.* Toronto: Macmillan, 1947

Borden, Robert Laird. *Robert Laird Borden: His Memoirs.* Toronto: Macmillan, 1938. Republished as Carleton Library Series Nos. 46 and 47. Toronto: McClelland & Stewart, 1969

Bowman, Isaiah. *The Pioneer Fringe.* New York: American Geographical Society, 1931

Bradwin, Edmund. *The Bunkhouse Man.* Toronto: University of Toronto Press, 1972

Brewis, T. N. *Growth and the Canadian Economy.* Carleton Library Series No. 39. Toronto: McClelland & Stewart, 1968

Britnell, G. E. *The Wheat Economy.* Toronto: University of Toronto Press, 1939

Brown, R. C., and Prang, M. E. *Confederation to 1949.* Toronto: Prentice-Hall, 1966

Burley, Kevin, ed. *The Development of Canada's Staples.* Toronto: McClelland & Stewart, 1971

Burpee, Lawrence. *Sandford Fleming: Empire Builder.* Toronto: Oxford, 1915

Canada. Department of Transport. *The Canadian National and Canadian Railway Systems: Origin and Growth with Statutory Authorities.* Ottawa: Queen's Printer, 1948

————. *Report of the Royal Commission on Life Insurance.* Ottawa: King's Printer, 1907

Carrigan, Owen. *Canadian Party Platforms, 1867–1968.* Toronto: Copp Clark, 1968

Caves, R. E., and Holton, R. H. *The Canadian Economy.* Cambridge, Mass.: Harvard University Press, 1959

Chandler, Alfred D., comp. *The Railroads, the Nation's First Big Business: Sources and Readings.* New York: Harcourt, Brace & World, 1965

Cleveland, F. A., and Powell, F. W. *Railroad Promotion and Capitalization in the United States.* New York: Longmans, Green & Co., 1909

——. *Railroad Finance.* New York: Appleton, 1912

Cochran, Thomas C. *Railroad Leaders, 1845–1890: The Business Mind in Action.* Cambridge, Mass.: Harvard University Press, 1953

Cook, Ramsay. *The Politics of John W. Dafoe and the Free Press.* Toronto: University of Toronto Press, 1963

Copeland, John M. *The Trail of the Swinging Lanterns: A Racy Railroading Review of Transportation Matters, Methods and Men.* Toronto: Addison and Mainprice, 1918

Creighton, D. G. *John A. Macdonald: The Old Chieftain.* Toronto: Macmillan, 1955

Currie, A. W. *Economics of Canadian Transportation.* Toronto: University of Toronto Press, 1959

——. *The Grand Trunk Railway of Canada.* Toronto: University of Toronto Press, 1957

Dafoe, J. W. *Clifford Sifton in Relation to His Times.* Toronto: Macmillan, 1931

——. *Laurier: A Study in Canadian Politics.* Toronto: T. Allen, 1922

Dales, J. H. *Hydroelectricity and Industrial Development, Quebec 1898–1940.* Cambridge: Harvard University Press, 1957

——. *The Protective Tariff in Canada's Development.* Toronto: University of Toronto Press, 1966

Daniells, Lorna M., comp. *Studies in Enterprise: A Selected Bibliography of American and Canadian Company Histories and Biographies of Businessmen.* Boston: Harvard University Press, 1957

Dawson, C. A. *Group Settlement: Ethnic Communities in Western Canada.* Toronto: Macmillan, 1936

——. *Pioneering in the Prairie Provinces: The Social Side of the Settlement Process.* Toronto: Macmillan, 1940

Denison, Merrill. *The People's Power*. Toronto: McClelland & Stewart, 1960

Donald, W. J. A. *The Canadian Iron and Steel Industry*. Boston: Houghton Mifflin, 1915

Donnelly, M. S. *Dafoe of the Free Press*. Toronto: Macmillan, 1968

——. *The Government of Manitoba*. Toronto: University of Toronto Press, 1963

Easterbrook, W. T., and Aitken, Hugh G. *Canadian Economic History*. Toronto: Macmillan, 1956

Easterbrook, W. T., and Watkins, M. H., eds. *Approaches to Canadian Economic History*. Carleton Library Series No. 31. Toronto: McClelland & Stewart, 1967

England, Robert. *The Central European Immigrant in Canada*. Toronto: Macmillan, 1929

——. *The Colonization of Western Canada: A Study of Contemporary Land Settlement, 1896–1934*. London: King, 1936

Fine, S. *Laissez-faire and the General-Welfare State: A Study of Conflict in American Thought, 1865–1901*. New York: Macmillan, 1962

Fleming, H. A. *Canada's Arctic Outlet: A History of the Hudson's Bay Railway*. Berkeley and Los Angeles: University of California Press, 1957

Fogel, Robert W. *Railroads and American Economic Growth: Essays in Econometric History*. Baltimore: Johns Hopkins, 1964

Fournier, Leslie T. *Railway Nationalization in Canada: The Problem of the Canadian National Railways*. Toronto: Macmillan, 1935

Fowke, V. C. *Canadian Agricultural Policy: The Historical Pattern*. Toronto: University of Toronto Press, 1946

——. *The National Policy and the Wheat Economy*. Toronto: University of Toronto Press, 1957

Gates, Paul Wallace. *The Illinois Central Railroad and Its Colonization Work*. Cambridge, Mass.: Harvard University Press, 1934

Gibbon, J. M. *Canadian Mosaic: The Making of a Northern Nation*. Toronto: McClelland & Stewart, 1938

——. *Steel of Empire*. Toronto: McClelland & Stewart, 1935

Gilbert, Heather. *Awakening Continent: The Life of Lord Mount*

Stephen. Aberdeen: University of Aberdeen Press, 1965

Glazebrook, G. P. de T. *A History of Transportation in Canada*. Toronto: Ryerson Press, 1938

————. *Sir Edmund Walker*. London: Oxford University Press, 1933

Gluek, Alvin C. *Minnesota and the Manifest Destiny of the Canadian Northwest: A Study in Canadian–American Relations*. Toronto: University of Toronto Press, 1965

Graham, Roger. *Arthur Meighen*. Historical Booklet No. 16. Ottawa: Canadian Historical Association, 1964

————. *Arthur Meighen: A Biography*. 3 vols. Toronto: Clarke, Irwin, 1960, 1963, 1965

Grant, Rev. George M. *Ocean to Ocean. Sandford Fleming's Expedition through Canada in 1872, being a diary kept during a journey from the Atlantic to the Pacific with the expedition of the Engineer-in-Chief of the Canadian Pacific and Intercolonial Railways*. Toronto: James Campbell and Son, 1873. Republished by Coles Publishing Co., 1970

Gray, James H. *The Boy from Winnipeg*. Toronto: Macmillan, 1969

————. *Men Against the Desert*. Saskatoon: Modern Press, 1967

Grodinsky, Julius. *Transcontinental Railway Strategy, 1869–1893: A Study of Businessmen*. Philadelphia: University of Pennsylvania, 1962

Hanna, D. B. *Trains of Recollection, drawn from fifty years of railway service in Scotland and Canada*. Toronto: Macmillan, 1924.

Harris, T. H. *The Economic Aspects of the Crowsnest Pass Rates Agreement*. McGill University Economic Studies No. 13, National Problems of Canada. Toronto: Macmillan, 1930

Hedges, James B. *Building the Canadian West: The Land and Colonization Policies of the Canadian Pacific Railway*. New York: Macmillan, 1939

————. *The Federal Railway Land Subsidy Policy of Canada*. Harvard Historical Monographs III. Cambridge: Harvard University Press, 1934

————. *Henry Villard and the Railways of the Northwest*. New Haven: Yale University Press, 1930

Hill, Douglas. *The Opening of the Canadian West*. London: Heinemann, 1967

Hill, James J. *Highways of Progress.* New York: Doubleday, Page and Co., 1910

Historical Association of Saskatoon. *Narratives of Saskatoon, 1882–1912, by Men of the City.* Saskatoon: The University Bookstore, 1927

Holbrook, Stewart H. *The Golden Age of Railroads.* New York: Random House, 1960

Innis, H. A. *A History of the Canadian Pacific Railway.* Toronto: McClelland & Stewart, 1923

———. *Problems of Staple Production in Canada.* Toronto: Ryerson Press, 1933

———. *Select Documents in Canadian Economic History 1497–1783.* Toronto: University of Toronto Press, 1929

Innis, Mary Quayle. *An Economic History of Canada.* Toronto: Ryerson Press, 1935

Irwin, L. B. *Pacific Railways and Nationalism in the Canadian–American North-West, 1845–1873.* Philadelphia: L. B. Irwin, 1939

Jackman, W. T. *Economics of Transportation.* Toronto: University of Toronto Press, 1926

Joerg, W. L. G., ed. *Pioneer Settlement: Cooperative Studies by Twenty-six Authors.* New York: American Geographical Society, Special Publication No. 14, 1932

Johnson, Enid. *Rails across the Continent: The Story of the First Continental Railroad.* New York: Julian Massuer, 1965

Josephson, Matthew. *The Robber Barons: The Great American Capitalists.* New York: Harcourt, Brace, 1934

Kellett, John R. *The Impact of Railways on Victorian Cities.* Toronto: University of Toronto Press, 1969

Kilbourn, William. *The Elements Combined: A History of the Steel Company of Canada.* Toronto: Clarke, Irwin, 1960

Kolko, Gabriel. *Railroads and Regulation, 1877–1916.* Princeton, N.J.: Princeton University Press, 1965

La Forest, G. V. *Disallowance and the Reservation of Provincial Legislation.* Ottawa: Department of Justice, 1955

Lessard, J. C. *Transportation in Canada: A Study Prepared for the Royal Commission on Canada's Economic Prospects.* Ottawa: Queen's Printer, 1957

Logan, H. A. *Trade Unions in Canada, Their Development and Functioning*. Toronto: Macmillan, 1948

Longley, R. S. *Sir Francis Hincks: A Study of Canadian Politics, Railways and Finance in the 19th Century*. Toronto: University of Toronto Press, 1943

Lower, A. R. M., and Innis, H. A. *Settlement and the Forest and Mining Frontiers*. Toronto: Macmillan, 1936

MacBeth, Roderick George. *The Romance of the Canadian Pacific Railway*. Toronto: Ryerson Press, 1924

McCormick, Col. J. H. *Lloydminster, or Five Thousand Miles with the Barr Colonists*. London: Dranes, 1923

McDiarmid, O. J. *Commercial Policy in the Canadian Economy*. Cambridge, Mass.: Harvard University Press, 1946

McDougall, J. L. *Canadian Pacific: A Brief History*. Montreal: McGill, 1968

MacGibbon, D. A. *The Canadian Grain Trade, 1931–1951*. Toronto: University of Toronto Press, 1952

———. *The Grain Trade*. Toronto: Macmillan, 1932

———. *Railway Rates and the Canadian Railway Commission*. New York: Houghton Mifflin, 1917

Mackintosh, W. A. *The Economic Background of Dominion–Provincial Relations*. Ottawa: King's Printer, 1939. Republished as Carleton Library Series No. 13. Toronto: McClelland & Stewart, 1964

———. *Economic Problems of the Prairie Provinces*. Toronto: Macmillan, 1935

———. *Prairie Settlement: The Geographical Setting*. Toronto: Macmillan, 1934

Maclean, Hugh. *Man of Steel: The Story of Sir Sandford Fleming*. Toronto: Ryerson, 1969

Macmillan, David S. *Canadian Enterprise: Studies in Business History, 1497–1971*. Toronto: McClelland & Stewart, 1972

MacNaughton, John. *Lord Strathcona*. The Makers of Canada Series: Anniversary Edition, Vol. x. London and Toronto: Oxford University Press, 1925

McPherson, Logan Grant. *Railroad Freight Rates in Relation to the*

Industry and Commerce of the United States. New York: Holt, 1909

Martin, Albro. *Enterprise Denied: Origins of the Decline of American Railroads, 1897–1917.* New York: Columbia University Press, 1971

Martin, Chester. *The Natural Resources Question: The Historical Basis of Provincial Claims.* Winnipeg: King's Printer, 1920

Mavor, James. *Niagara in Politics: A Critical Account of the Ontario Hydro-Electric Commission.* New York: E. P. Dutton and Company, 1925

Meyer, John R., *et al. The Economics of Competition in the Transportation Industries.* Cambridge, Mass.: Harvard University Press, 1959

Middleton, Philip Harvey. *Railways of Thirty Nations: Government Versus Private Ownership.* New York: Prentice-Hall, 1937

Miller-Barstow, Donald H. *Beatty of the C.P.R.: A Biography.* Toronto: McClelland & Stewart, 1951

Moody, John. *The Railroad Builders: A Chronicle of the Welding of the States.* New York: U.S. Publishers Association, 1919

Moore, William H. *Railway Nationalization and the Average Citizen.* Toronto: McClelland & Stewart, 1917

———. *Railway Nationalization and the Farmer.* Toronto: McClelland, Goodchild & Stewart, 1917

Morton, A. S., and Martin, Chester. *History of Prairie Settlement and Dominion Lands Policy.* Toronto: Macmillan, 1938

Morton, W. L. *Manitoba: A History.* Toronto: University of Toronto Press, 1957

Myers, Gustavus. *History of Canadian Wealth.* Chicago: Kerr, 1914

———. *History of Great American Fortunes.* 3 vols. Chicago: Kerr, 1911–1917

Neufeld, E. P. *The Financial System of Canada, Its Growth and Development.* Toronto: Macmillan, 1972

———, ed. *Money and Banking in Canada.* Carleton Library Series No. 17. Toronto: McClelland & Stewart, 1964

Newman, Peter C. *Flame of Power.* Toronto: Longmans, Green & Co., 1960

Nordegg, Martin. *The Possibilities of Canada Are Truly Great: Memoirs, 1906–1924*. Edited by T. D. Regehr. Toronto: Macmillan, 1971

Ormsby, M. A. *British Columbia: A History*. Toronto: Macmillan, 1958

Overton, Richard C. *Burlington Route: A History of the Burlington Lines*. New York: Knopf, 1965

———. *Burlington West: A Colonization History of the Burlington Railroad*. Cambridge, Mass.: Harvard University Press, 1941

Peel, Bruce. *A Bibliography of the Prairie Provinces to 1953*. Toronto: University of Toronto Press, 1956

Phillips, R. A. J. *Canada's Railways*. Toronto: McGraw-Hill, 1962

Porter, John. *The Vertical Mosaic: An Analysis of Social Class and Power in Canada*. Toronto: University of Toronto Press, 1965

Preston, W. T. R. *The Life and Times of Lord Strathcona*. London: Nash, 1914

Pyle, J. G. *The Life of James J. Hill*. 2 vols. Toronto: McClelland & Stewart, 1917

Ramsey, Bruce. *PGE Railway to the North*. Vancouver: Mitchell, 1962

Reid, J. H. Stewart, *et al*. *A Source Book of Canadian History: Selected Documents and Personal Papers*. Toronto: Longmans, Green & Co., 1959

Riegel, Robert Edgar. *The Story of the Western Railroads*. New York: Macmillan, 1926

Ripley, William Z. *Railroads: Rates and Regulation*. New York: Longmans, Green & Co., 1912

Roberts, Leslie. *These Be Your Gods*. Toronto: Musson, 1929

Robin, Martin. *Radical Politics and Canadian Labour*. Kingston: Queen's University Press, 1968

———. *The Rush for Spoils: The Company Province, 1871–1933*. Toronto: McClelland & Stewart, 1972

Ross, Hugh R. *Thirty-five Years in the Limelight: Sir Rodmond P. Roblin and His Times*. Winnipeg: Farmers' Advocate, 1936

Ross, Victor. *A History of the Canadian Bank of Commerce*. 3 vols. Toronto: Oxford University Press, 1920–34

Rountree, George M. *The Railway Worker: A Study of the Employ-*

ment and Unemployment Problems of the Canadian Railways. Toronto: Oxford University Press, 1936

Russell, Peter, ed. *Nationalism in Canada.* Toronto: McGraw-Hill, 1966

Ryan, W. F. *The Clergy and Economic Growth in Quebec, 1896–1914.* Quebec: Laval University Press, 1966

Schull, Joseph. *Laurier: The First Canadian.* Toronto: Macmillan, 1965

Secretan, James H. E. *Canada's Great Highway from the First Stake to the Last Spike.* London: John Lane, 1924

Shepherd, George. *West of Yesterday.* Toronto: McClelland & Stewart, 1965

Skelton, O. D. *Life and Times of Alexander Tilloch Galt.* Toronto: Oxford University Press, 1920. Republished as Carleton Library Series No. 26. Toronto: McClelland & Stewart, 1966

———. *Life and Letters of Sir Wilfrid Laurier.* 2 vols. Toronto: Oxford University Press, 1921. Republished as Carleton Library Series Nos. 21 and 22. Toronto: McClelland & Stewart, 1965

———. *The Railway Builders.* Toronto: Glasgow and Brooke, 1916

Smalley, Eugene. *History of the Northern Pacific Railroad.* New York: G. P. Putnam, 1883

Stevens, G. R. *Canadian National Railways.* 2 vols. Toronto: Clarke, Irwin, 1960–62

———. *History of the Canadian National Railways.* Don Mills, Ontario: Collier-Macmillan, 1973

Stevens, Paul, ed. *The 1911 General Election: A Study in Canadian Politics.* Issues in Canadian History Series. Toronto: Copp Clark, 1970

Talbot, F. A. *The Making of a Great Canadian Railway: The Story of the Search for and Discovery of the Route, and the Construction of the Nearly Completed Grand Trunk Pacific Railway.* Toronto: Musson Book Co., 1912

Taylor, G. R. *The Transportation Revolution, 1815–1860.* New York: Harper & Row, 1951

Thomas, Lewis G. *The Liberal Party in Alberta, 1905–1921.* Toronto: University of Toronto Press, 1959

Thompson, Norman, and Edgar, J. H. *Canadian Railway Develop-*

ment from the Earliest Times. Toronto: Macmillan, 1933

Thomson, Lesslie R. *The Canadian Railway Problem: Some Economic Aspects of Canadian Transportation and a Suggested Solution for the Railway Problem.* Toronto: Macmillan, 1938

Urquhart, M. C., and Buckley, K. A. H. *Historical Statistics of Canada.* Toronto: Macmillan, 1965

Vaughan, Walter. *The Life and Work of Sir William Van Horne.* New York: The Century Company, 1920

Victor, E. A., ed. *Canada's Future, What She Offers after the War: A Symposium of Official Opinion.* Toronto: Macmillan, 1916

Waite, P. B. *Canada, 1874–1896: Arduous Destiny.* Toronto: McClelland & Stewart, 1971

Walker, Frank N. *Daylight Through the Mountains: Letters and Labours of Civil Engineers Walter and Francis Shanly.* Montreal: Engineering Institute of Canada, 1957

Wallace, W. S. *The Macmillan Dictionary of Canadian Biography.* Toronto: Macmillan, 1963

Ward, N., and Spafford, D. *Politics in Saskatchewan.* Toronto: Longmans, Green & Co., 1968

Warkentin, John, ed. *The Western Interior of Canada.* Carleton Library Series No. 15. Toronto: McClelland & Stewart, 1964

Wettenhall, R. L. *The Iron Road and the State: W. M. Acworth as Scholar, Critic and Reformer.* Hobart: University of Tasmania, 1970

White, Thomas. *The Story of Canada's War Finance.* Montreal: The Canadian Bank of Commerce, 1921

Wilgus, William J. *The Railway Interrelations of the United States and Canada.* Toronto: Ryerson, 1937

Willison, J. S. *Sir Wilfrid Laurier and the Liberal Party.* Toronto: Morang, 1903

Willison, Sir John. *Sir Wilfrid Laurier.* Makers of Canada Series: Anniversary Edition. London and Toronto: Oxford University Press, 1926

Willson, Beckles. *Life of Lord Strathcona and Mount Royal.* Boston: Houghton Mifflin, 1915

Wilson, George W., and Darby, Larry. *Transportation on the Prairies. Supporting Study No. 2 for the Saskatchewan Commission on*

Consumer Problems and Inflation. Saskatoon: Modern Press, 1968

ARTICLES

Acworth, W. H. "The American Railway Situation", *Economic Journal,* Vol. 30 (1920), pp. 177–95

———. "Government Railways in a Democratic State", *Economic Journal,* Vol. 2 (1892), pp. 629–36

———. "Railways under Government Control", *Forum* (New York), Vol. 11 (1891), pp. 79–90

———. "The Relations of Railways to the State", *Economic Journal,* Vol. 18 (1908), pp. 501–19

Aikin, J. Alex. "When the West Was Young", *Canadian National Railways Magazine,* Vol. 22, No. 2 (February 1936), pp. 5, 31

Arrington, Leonard J. "The Transcontinental Railroad and the Development of the West", *Utah Historical Quarterly,* Vol. 37 (Winter 1969), pp. 3–15

Artibise, Alan F. J. "Advertising Winnipeg: The Campaign for Immigrants and Industry, 1874–1914", *Historical and Scientific Society of Manitoba Transactions,* Series III, Vol. 27 (1970–71), pp. 75–106

Athearn, Robert G. "A Brahmin in Buffaloland", *The Western Historical Quarterly,* Vol. 1 (January 1970), pp. 21–34

———. "Contracting for the Union Pacific", *Utah Historical Quarterly,* Vol. 37 (Winter 1969), pp. 16–40

Bladen, M. L. "Construction of Railways in Canada to the Year 1885", *Contributions to Canadian Economics,* Vol. 5 (1932), pp. 43–60

Breen, D. H. "The Canadian Prairie West and the Harmonious Settlement Interpretation", *Agricultural History,* Vol. 47 (January 1973), pp. 63–75

Brook, Leslie. "They Were Tent Towns Fifty Years Ago", *Canadian National Railways Magazine,* Vol. 18, No. 10 (9 October 1932), pp. 8–9, 26

Brown, R. C. "The Nationalism of the National Policy". In *Nationalism in Canada,* edited by Peter Russell. University League for Social Reform. Toronto: McGraw-Hill, 1966

Busfield, J. C. "The Mount Royal Tunnel", *The Journal of the Engineering Institute of Canada*, Vol. 2 (April 1919), pp. 267–98

CNR. "The Pioneer Road of the North", *Canadian National Railways Magazine*, Vol. 15 (1929), p. 7

Cochran, Thomas. "Land Grants and Railroad Entrepreneurship", *Journal of Economic History*, Vol. 10 (November 1950) (Supplement), pp. 53–67

Creighton, D. G. "Economic Nationalism and Confederation", Canadian Historical Association *Report* (1942), pp. 44–51

Cuff, Robert. "The Conservative Party Machine and the Election of 1911", *Ontario History*, Vol. 57 (September 1965), pp. 149–56

———. "Organizing for War: Canada and the United States During World War I", Canadian Historical Association *Report* (1969), pp. 141–56

———. "The Toronto Eighteen and the Election of 1911", *Ontario History*, Vol. 57 (December 1965), pp. 169–80

Currie, A. W. "Freight Rates on Grain in Western Canada", *Canadian Historical Review*, Vol. 21 (March 1940), pp. 40–55

Dales, J. H. "Fuel, Power and Industrial Development in Central Canada", *American Economic Review, Papers and Proceedings*, Vol. 43 (May 1953), pp. 181–98

Davidson, J. W. "The Canadian Northern Railway", *Queen's Quarterly*, Vol. 13 (October 1906), pp. 97–108

Deutsch, J. J. "War Finance and the Canadian Economy, 1914–20", *Canadian Journal of Economics and Political Science*, Vol. 6 (November 1940), pp. 525–42

Donovan, Frank Pierre. "The Railroad in Literature: A Brief Survey of Railroad Fiction, Poetry, Songs, Biography, Essays, Travel, and Drama in the English Language, Particularly Emphasizing Its Place in American Literature", *The Railway and Locomotive Historical Society, Inc.* (1940). Entire issue

Dyos, H. J. "Transportation History in University Theses", *Journal of Transport History*, Vol. 4 (May 1960), pp. 161–73

Eadie, James A. "Edward Wilkes Ruthburn and the Napanee, Tamworth and Quebec Railway", *Ontario History*, Vol. 63 (June 1971), pp. 113–30

Easterbrook, W. T. "Recent Contributions to Economic History:

Canada", *Journal of Economic History*, Vol. 19 (March 1959), pp. 76–102

Engerman, Stanley L. "Some Economic Issues Relating to Railroad Subsidies and the Evaluation of Land Grants", *Journal of Economic History*, Vol. 32 (June 1972), pp. 443–63

Gates, Paul. "The Railroad Land Grant Legend", *Journal of Economic History*, Vol. 14 (Spring 1954), pp. 143–46

Glynn, S. "The Transport Factor in Developmental Policy: Pioneer Agricultural Railways in the Western Australian Wheat Belt, 1900–1930", *Australian Journal of Politics and History*, Vol. 15 (August 1969), pp. 60–78

Graham, Roger. "Meighen and the Montreal Tycoons: Railway Policy in the Election of 1921", Canadian Historical Association *Report* (1957), pp. 71–85

Hanna, D. B. "Canada's Great National Asset", *Canadian Railway and Marine World* (October 1919), pp. 528–9

Henry, Robert S. "The Railroad Land Grant Legend in American History Texts", *Mississippi Valley Historical Review*, Vol. 32 (September 1945), pp. 171–94

Hidy, Ralph W., and Hidy, Muriel E. "Anglo American Merchant Bankers and the Railroads of the Old Northwest, 1848–1860", *Business History Review*, Vol. 34 (Summer 1960), pp. 150–69

Humphries, Charles W. "The Sources of Ontario's 'Progressive' Conservatism, 1900–1914", Canadian Historical Association *Report* (1967), pp. 118–29

Innis, H. A. "Transportation as a Factor in Canadian Economic History", *Proceedings of the Canadian Political Science Association*, Vol. 3 (1931), pp. 166–84

Jackman, W. T. "Critical Position of Canadian Railways", *Queen's Quarterly*, Vol. 29 (January 1922)

Jenks, L. H. "Railroad as an Economic Force in American Development", *Journal of Economic History*, Vol. 4 (1944), pp. 1–20

Knox, F. A. "Canadian War Finance and the Balance of Payments, 1914–1918", *Canadian Journal of Economics and Political Science*, Vol. 6 (May 1940), pp. 226–57

Lalonde, A. M. "Colonization Companies in the 1880's", *Saskatchewan History*, Vol. 24 (Autumn 1971), pp. 101–14

Le Bourdais, D. M. "Canada's National Railway Experiment", *Current History*, Vol. 22 (April 1925), pp. 45–49

Lyon, W. H. "The Canadian Northern: A Railroad with no Stock on the Market, which may Soon Become Canada's Third Transcontinental Line", *Moody's Magazine* (March 1909), pp. 212–16

McClelland, Peter D. "Social Rates of Return on American Railroads in the Nineteenth Century", *Economic History Review*, Vol. 25 (August 1972), pp. 471–88

MacDermott, W. "The Political Ideas of Sir John A. Macdonald", *Canadian Historical Review*, Vol. 14 (September 1933), pp. 247–64

McEvoy, Dermot. "Elevators and Modern Granaries", *Canadian Magazine*, Vol. 21 (July 1903), pp. 204–9

Mackintosh, W. A. "Economic Factors in Canadian History", *Canadian Historical Review*, Vol. 4 (March 1923), pp. 12–25

Macquarrie, Heath. "The Formation of Borden's First Cabinet", *Canadian Journal of Economics and Political Science*, Vol. 23 (February 1957), pp. 90–104

———. "Robert Borden and the Election of 1911", *Canadian Journal of Economics and Political Science*, Vol. 25 (August 1959), pp. 271–86

McQueen, R. "Economic Aspects of Federalism: A Prairie View", *Canadian Journal of Economics and Political Science*, Vol. 3 (August 1935), pp. 352–67

Martin, Chester. "The Colonial Policy of the Dominion", *Transactions of the Royal Society of Canada*, Third series, Vol. 16, Section ii (1922), pp. 35–47

———. "Our Kingdom for a Horse: The Railway Land Grant System in Western Canada", Canadian Historical Association *Report* (1934), pp. 73–80

Mercer, Lloyd J. "Land Grants to American Railroads: Social Cost or Social Benefit?" *Business History Review*, Vol. 43 (Summer 1969), pp. 134–51

Moore, W. H. "A New National Highway", *Canadian Magazine*, Vol. 18 (February 1902), pp. 334–7

Murray, Walter. "Continental Europeans in Western Canada", *Queen's Quarterly*, Vol. 38 (Winter 1931), pp. 63–75

Oliver, Edmund H. "The Beginnings of White Settlement in Northern Saskatchewan", *Transactions of the Royal Society of Canada*, Third series, Vol. 19, Section ii (1925), pp. 83–129

———. "The Coming of the Barr Colonists", Canadian Historical Association *Report* (1926), pp. 65–86

———. "The Institutionalizing of the Prairies", *Transactions of the Royal Society of Canada*, Third series, Vol. 24, Section ii (1930), pp. 1–21

———. "The Settlement of Saskatchewan to 1914", *Transactions of the Royal Society of Canada*, Third series, Vol. 20, Section ii (1926), pp. 63–87

Oszmun, Bill. "When Steel Invaded the Prairies", *Canadian National Railways Magazine*, Vol. 11 (June 1925), p. 27

Regehr, T. D. "The Canadian Northern Railway: The West's Own Product", *Canadian Historical Review*, Vol. 51 (June 1970), pp. 177–86

———. "Historiography of the Canadian Plains After 1870", *A Region of the Mind: Canadian Plains Studies I*. Regina: Canadian Plains Studies Centre, 1973

———. "Serving the Canadian West: The Canadian Northern Railway", *The Western Historical Quarterly*, Vol. 3 (July 1972), pp. 283–98

Reid, Escott. "The Saskatchewan Liberal Machine Before 1929", *Canadian Journal of Economics and Political Science*, Vol. 2, No. 1 (February 1936), pp. 27–40

Shortt, Adam. "Railroad Construction and National Prosperity: An Historical Parallel", *Transactions of the Royal Society of Canada*, Third series, Vol. 8, Section ii (1914), pp. 295–308

Stephenson, G. P. "The West, The Railways and Change", *Manitoba Centre for Transportation Studies Proceedings* (1968–1969), pp. 43–60

Studness, Charles W. "Economic Opportunity and the Westward Migration of Canadians during the Late Nineteenth Century", *Canadian Journal of Economics and Political Science*, Vol. 30 (November 1964), pp. 570–84

Talman, J. J. "The Impact of the Railway on a Pioneer Community", Canadian Historical Association *Report* (1955), pp. 1–12

Thomas, L. G. "The Liberal Party in Alberta, 1905–1921", *Canadian Historical Review*, Vol. 28 (December 1947), pp. 411–27

Thompson, John Beswarick. "Sources of Railway Information in the Public Archives of Canada", *Canadian Rail* (April 1970), pp. 128–31

Wickstead, Henry K. "Spanning an Historic Range", *Canadian National Railways Magazine*, Vol. 9 (July 1923), p. 25

INDEX

Abbey Effervescent Salts Company, 146
Accidents, 56, 59, 162–3
Accounting methods of Canadian
  Northern Railway, 53*n*.
Acton, Ontario, birthplace of Donald
  Mann, 30
Acworth, W. H., Commissioner, Royal
  Commission to Inquire into Railways
  and Transportation, 416–7, 424–8. *See
  also* Royal Commission to Inquire into
  Railways and Transportation
Adelpha, Manitoba, 206, 208
Africa, 189
Aikins, J. C., 5*n*.
Aird, John, 407*n*., 412
Akron, Ohio, 268
Alaska, 106
Alberta government, votes bond guar-
  antees, 198–200, 215, 304–5, 474;
  supports Canadian Northern route
  locations, 288; opposes freight rate
  increases, 401
Alberta Great Waterways Railway, 202
Alberta Midland Railway, 198–9, 200–1,
  208
Alberta (province), 177, 476–7; branch
  lines in, 197–204, 211, 233, 294, 336–
  7, 360
Allan, Sir Hugh, promotes the Manitoba
  and North Western Railway, 33; grants
  running rights to Lake Manitoba Rail-
  way and Canal Co., 44; employs D. B.
  Hanna, 45
Alsask, Alberta, 208
Amalgamations (Canadian Northern),
  Lake Manitoba Railway and Canal Co.
  and Winnipeg Great Northern Railway,
  74–5; with Manitoba and South Eastern
  Railway, 75; with Ontario and Rainy
  River Railway, 83; with Morden and
  North Western Railway, 194; with
  Western Extension Railway, 194; with
  Northern Extension Railway, 195; with
  Winnipeg and Northern Railway,
  195; with Canadian Northern Mani-
  toba Railway, 195; with Saskatchewan

and North Western Railway, 198–9;
  with Alberta Midland Railway, 198–9;
  with Saskatchewan Midland Railway,
  199; with Canadian Northern Saskatch-
  ewan Railway, 199; with Canadian
  Northern Alberta Railway, 200; with
  Canadian Northern Western Railway,
  200, 202; with Edmonton, Yukon and
  Pacific Railway, 289; creating Canadian
  Northern Railway System, 378; creating
  Canadian National Railways, 469
Amalgamations (Canadian Northern
  Quebec Railway), 258, 278–9
Arctic, the, 188
Argentina, 335
Asiatic labour, 297, 329
Atikokan, Ontario, 105, 312
Atlantic, the, 106, 119, 120, 122, 124, 188,
  216, 255, 314
Atterbury, W. W., asked to serve on
  Royal Commission, 415
Auditors, report of statements by Z. A.
  Lash, 374, 376

Bailey, T. C., 259
Balkans, 335
Bancroft, Ontario, 268
Bank of Commerce, *see* Canadian Bank
  of Commerce
Bank of Montreal, 334, 371, 446
Bank of Nova Scotia and *La Presse*
  affair, 147–51
Bank of Scotland, grants credit to Cana-
  dian Northern, 104, 214–6
Barker, Samuel, opponent of William
  Mackenzie, 148
Barr colonists, employed as construction
  workers, 57, 170, 246
Barrington Passage, Nova Scotia, 153
Barwick, Walter, negotiates with Manitoba
  and North Western Railway, 44
Basis of Understanding, between Macken-
  zie and Mann and Melville and
  McNaught, 133–4, 138
Basque, British Columbia, last spike
  driven at, 390

plans, 101; complete construction of line to Port Arthur, 104–5; personal investment in Canadian Northern Railway, 104; transcontinental ambitions, 106–7, 152, 156, 254–5, 257, 259, 285; regarded as mere opportunists, 108; aggressive policy of Hays towards, 108–9; pressured by Canadian Bank of Commerce, 110–11; obtain new federal guarantees for Edmonton and Prince Albert lines, 112–3; accept government rate controls, 114–5; survive first Grand Trunk attack, 125; seek eastern connections, 126; attempt to purchase Canadian Atlantic Railway, 126–30; acquire interest in Great Northern Railway of Canada, 133–5; acquire Chateauguay and Northern Railway, 135–6; acquire Great Northern Railway of Canada, 137–8; Quebec interests in 1903, 139; and *La Presse* affair, 140, 142–5, 147, 149–52; acquire Nova Scotia railways, 152–6; and the struggle with the Grand Trunk, 157; construction policies on prairies, 159–61; branch-line policy, 163–4; policy re freight rates, 164; early construction of Edmonton, Yukon and Pacific Railway, 165–7; construction of Edmonton and Prince Albert main lines, 168–72; and Indian lands, 173–4; contractors for Hudson Bay Railway, 176; acquire Qu'Appelle, Long Lake and Saskatchewan Railway, 179–83; eager to build prairie branch lines, 191–3; build Manitoba branch lines, 194–7; build Saskatchewan and Alberta branch lines, 197–204; political influence on Canadian Northern, 213; encouraging financial picture, 216–7; abandon cheap construction policies, 217; acquire ancillary enterprises, 219–20; acquisition procedures, 221–2; land dealings, 225–41; and Canadian Northern Town Properties Company Limited, 233–4; western lands scandal, 237–40; townsite development, 241; terminals development, 242–8; and Canadian Northern Coal and Ore Dock Co., 248–9; coal-mining interests, 249–52; reorganized Quebec railway, 258, 278–9; British Columbia route location, 285–9; obtain federal bond guarantees in Alberta, 291; sign agreement in British Columbia, 297; Canadian Northern Pacific Railway construction, 298–9; construction standards in British Columbia, 300; British Columbia branch lines, 301–2; various British Columbia ventures, 302; career high point in 1911, 303; early relations with Borden government, 304; financial arrangements in 1910–11, 305–9; build railway to Duluth, 312–4; federal guarantees in 1911, 316–9; acquire or build eastern terminals, 319–31; commitments made 1909–12, 332; and the 1912 freight rates case, 336–8; obtain funds in New York and London, 339–40; appeal to federal and B.C. governments for help, 341–3; federal aid in 1913, 343–51; response to crisis early in 1914, 357; curtail branch-line construction, 358–61; curtail construction of Vancouver terminals, 361–3; construction of Montreal terminals, 364; and federal aid in 1914, 365–82; agree to amalgamations creating Canadian Northern Railway System, 378; transfer substantial shares to government, 379; war a disastrous blow to, 383, 385; proposed government wartime aid, 386–9; complete British Columbia main line, 389–91; and the freight rates problem, 401; default seems unavoidable, 406; propose new financial solutions, 410; and the Smith Report, 423; and land grants, 425; negotiate to sell Canadian Northern to CPR, 433–6; participate in formation of Union government, 434; failure of attempts to refinance, 438; terms and details of nationalization of Canadian Northern, 439–43; method of valuation of Canadian Northern shares, 444–5; relations with Canadian Northern Railway, 449; resign from Canadian Northern Railway, 450–2; developmental work, 455–8, 468–70; relations with governments 459–64; relations with employees, 464–6; relations with sub-contractors, 466–8

Mackenzie, Mann and Co. Ltd., incorporated to circumvent difficulties with the Railway Act, 47, 219; employment practices as contractors, 56–7; Basis of Understanding with Melville and McNaught, 134; and Indian lands on Cote's reserve, 173–4; contractors for prairie branch lines, 200; financial arrangements, 214; acquire ancillary enterprises, 220–3; acquire Canadian Northern securities, 220–1; value of shares in, 222; and Canadian Northern